Evidence Analysis

A Research Process Map

Basic Principle:

SOURCES provide **INFORMATION**
from which we select **EVIDENCE** for **ANALYSIS**.
A sound **CONCLUSION** may then be considered "**PROOF.**"

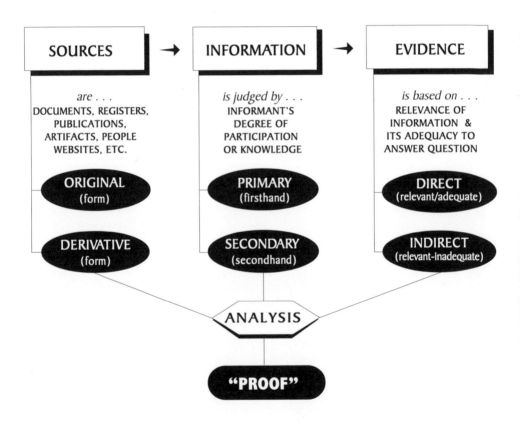

SOURCES	→	INFORMATION	→	EVIDENCE
are . . . DOCUMENTS, REGISTERS, PUBLICATIONS, ARTIFACTS, PEOPLE WEBSITES, ETC.		*is judged by . . .* INFORMANT'S DEGREE OF PARTICIPATION OR KNOWLEDGE		*is based on . . .* RELEVANCE OF INFORMATION & ITS ADEQUACY TO ANSWER QUESTION
ORIGINAL (form)		PRIMARY (firsthand)		DIRECT (relevant/adequate)
DERIVATIVE (form)		SECONDARY (secondhand)		INDIRECT (relevant-inadequate)

ANALYSIS

"PROOF"

EVIDENCE
EXPLAINED

EVIDENCE EXPLAINED

Citing History Sources
from Artifacts to Cyberspace

Elizabeth Shown Mills

2007
Genealogical Publishing Company
Baltimore, Maryland

Library of Congress Cataloging-in-Publication Data

Mills, Elizabeth Shown.
    Evidence explained : citing history sources from artifacts to cyberspace /
Elizabeth Shown Mills.
        p. cm.
    Includes bibliographical references and index.
    ISBN-13: 978-0-8063-1781-6 (alk. paper)
    1. History--Sources--Handbooks, manuals, etc. 2. History--
Research--Handbooks, manuals, etc. 3. Event history analysis--Handbooks,
manuals, etc. 4. History--Methodology--Handbooks, manuals, etc. I. Title.
    D5.M55 2007
    907.2--dc22
                                    2007019749

PUBLISHED BY
Genealogical Publishing Company, Inc.
3600 Clipper Mill Road, Suite 260
Baltimore, Maryland 21211

Made in the United States of America

In memory of
GRADY McWHINEY
Mentor & friend

Who taught me to probe the past carefully
and report it as it was, not as I wish it were

Contents

Foreword

All sources lie.
—Lawrence of Arabia

Sir Lawrence's hyperbole is understood by all who seek to reconstruct history. Sources err. Sources quibble. Sources exaggerate. Sources mis-remember. Sources are biased. Sources have egos and ideologies. Sources jostle for a toehold in the marketplace of ideas.

So why do we invest so much of our own energy into the citation of those sources? Because all sources are not created equal.

History is not a collection of raw facts we simply look up and copy down. The past is still a little-known universe that we explore with curiosity and confusion. As we probe its depths, we appreciate resources that save us time. We crave materials we can confidently trust. Yet historical truths are rarely rooted in either shortcuts or comfort.

In principle, Sir Lawrence was right. There are no historical resources we can simply *trust*. There are no records whose riddles we do not have to thoughtfully decipher. How we react to what we find determines both our success and our credibility. We mine courthouse basements and attics for crumbling files that human hands seem not to have touched since their creation. When we find a diamond among that dust, do we critically examine its setting—or do we treat the dust as a mere distraction? As we spin through microfilmed letters and ledgers, do we consider whether the words used in those ancient documents meant the same as they do today? As we Google our way through cyberspace, where mountains of data offer both gold and garbage, do we seriously ask, *How do we discern the difference?*

At the root of everything we find in history is a source. The information we pull from a source will not likely be any better than the source itself. The conclusions we reach from it can be no better than the effort we have made to identify that source, to understand its nuances, and to interpret the evidence its information provides.

Evidence Explained is a guidebook for all who explore history and seek to piece together its surviving bits and shards. As a guide, it is built on one basic thought:

> We cannot judge the reliability of any information unless we know
> - *exactly* where the information came from; and
> - the strengths and weaknesses of that source.

As students, when we were introduced to research principles, we may have been told that identifying sources is important for two reasons. First, we provide "proof" for what we write. Second, we enable others to find what we have used. Both purposes are valid, but they miss the most critical point of all:

> *We identify our sources—and their strengths and weaknesses—*
> *so we can reach the most reliable conclusions.*

As a guidebook, *Evidence Explained* has two goals. Obviously, it provides citation models for most source types of history—especially original materials not covered by classic citation guides. Beyond that, it can help us understand each type of record and identify each in such detail that we and our readers will know not only *where to go to find our source* but, equally important, the *nature* of that source so that the evidence can be better interpreted and the accuracy of our conclusions can be appraised.

Acknowledgments

Ten years have passed since the first printing of the handbook *Evidence!* Across that decade, thousands of its faithful users have offered suggestions, requests, and samples of records whose quirks have stumped them. Many have asked questions that have stumped me also, sending me in quest of materials I had not previously encountered in my own research.

No one can be an expert on everything. Any guide that ranges as broadly as this one cannot be the work of a sole person. I am indebted to many colleagues—attorneys, geneticists, genealogists, geographers, historians, and librarians—who have introduced me to new resources and helped me understand them, particularly Jane Ailes, Kenneth Aitken, Virginia Aldridge, Margaret Amundsun, Anne Scaberry Anderson, Liv Hjelkrem Anderson, Patricia Abelard Anderson, Lynne Slocovich April, Gale Williams Bamman, CindyLee Butler Banks, Mary McCampbell Bell, Ernest Blevins, Jeanne Larzalere Bloom, Helen E. Brieske, Jana Sloan Broglin, Deborah Carder Mayes, Cheri Casper, Earl F. Charvet, Margarita Choquette, Sandra McLean Clunies, John Philip Colletta, Kathleen Wardle Cortez, Natalie Cottrill, Christine Crawford-Oppenheimer, Alvie Davidson, Robert de Beradinis, Donn Devine, Wendy Elliott, Carmen Finley, Katherine E. Flynn, Kay Haviland Freilich, Amy Larner Giroux, Eric G. Grundset, Ruth Ann Hager, James L. Hansen, Marje Harris, Polly Held, Ronald Hill, Birdie Holsclaw, Debbie Horton, Annette Hulse, John Humphrey, Kay Germain Ingalls, Everett B. Ireland, Sherry Irvine, Jim Isom, Judy Jones, Thomas W. Jones, Roger D. Joslyn, Elizabeth Kelly Kerstens, Michael LeClerc, Rachal Mills Lennon, Jeane Lund, Rudena Mallory, Barbara Matthews, Kahlile Mehr, Kory L. Meyerink, Gary Mokotoff, George G. Morgan, Joseph B. Mullon III, Marya Myers, Jane Nardy, John Michael Neill, Nancy Simons Peterson, Elissa Powell, Janice Prater, Joy Reisinger, Lauren H. Richardson, Linda Anderson Roof, George Ryskamp, Frederic Z. Saunders, Rick Sayre, Beau Sharbrough, Patricia O'Brien Shawker, Thomas H. Shawker, Douglas S. Shipley, Kevin Sholder, Drew Smith, Patricia Stamm, Nick Vine Hall, Linda Vixie, Mary Linn Wernet, Barbara Zanzig, and June Riedrich Zublic.

Immense debts are due to Ann C. Fleming, Alison Hare, Rondina Muncy, and Craig Roberts Scott, who volunteered to vet the full manuscript and forfeited weeks of personal and professional time in doing so; to a legion of archivists at the National Archives and many of its state-level counterparts, who ask for no acknowledgment but deserve my gratitude; to Jackie Weston Stewart, who has plucked many nits from my works across the years; and, especially, to Marian Hoffman who has proved once more that editors are angels sent from on high to keep authors humble.

The generosity and expertise of all these friends and colleagues have made *Evidence Explained* a much stronger guide.

—ESM

Fundamentals of
EVIDENCE
ANALYSIS

1

Guidelines

Fundamentals of
EVIDENCE ANALYSIS

BASIC ISSUES

1.1 Analysis & Mindset

As history researchers, we do not speculate. We test. We critically observe and carefully record. Then we weigh the accumulated evidence, analyzing the individual parts as well as the whole, without favoring any theory. Bias, ego, ideology, patronage, prejudice, pride, or shame cannot shape our decisions as we appraise our evidence. To do so is to warp reality and deny ourselves the understanding of the past that is, after all, the reason for our labor.

The historian Barbara Tuchman has famously described evidence as a kaleidoscope.* As researchers, we can appreciate that analogy. When we gather under a lens all our bits and shards of evidence, we form a mental picture of a time, place, event, or person. Yet the next time we peer into our kaleidoscope, those same fragments may form a different picture. Tuchman's analogy, taken out of the context, could also suggest that evidence is random and that one view can be as good as another. Experienced researchers know better.

History's surviving fragments might also be likened to a chain of DNA. To the untrained eye, the endlessly twisted coils of letters appear to be a string of random repeats. They make sense only when we learn to read the string, interpreting both the parts and the whole, and then explain those interpretations to others in a meaningful way.

Every research project produces a chain of records with some obvious patterns—both repeats and mutations. As with physical DNA, those patterns identify the people we study and the circumstances in which

---

* Barbara W. Tuchman, *The Guns of August* (1962; reprint, New York: Ballantine Books, 1994), 442.

they lived. They provide answers to specific research questions and context for related issues. This chapter explains the basics of converting kaleidoscopic fragments and the twisted coils of history into a meaningful account of a past time or a past life.

As careful researchers, we cannot apply an easy, generic label—*reliable* or *unreliable*—to any document, much less any *type* of document. We cannot assign numerical values to pieces of information and add up a score to decide whether we should believe something we have found. We cannot base conclusions on the number of times a source or fact is cited; a dubious factoid repeated over and again cannot outweigh a reality correctly reported by a single, impeccable source.

Research is much more than an accumulation of data. It is a process that requires continual comparison of new information against the old. At every step of that process, we appraise the credibility of *each* detail in *each* document. We apply every conceivable test for authenticity, contemporaneousness, and credibility of informants. As we acquire historical and social perspective of a place and time—and gain experience in evaluating its material legacies—evidence analysis becomes a fascinating part of the research process.

1.2   Completeness of Research

Reliable conclusions are rarely rooted in half-tilled soil. Any relevant record that goes unexamined is a land mine waiting to explode our premature theories. The risk is great enough when, in a rare run of luck, we are blessed with documents all leaning toward the same conclusion. The risk cannot be chanced when—as more often happens—we must interpret a trail of implications marked by spotty records, instead of the gloriously explicit document we had hoped to find.

If we know that potentially relevant records exist, we should use them. If records are unknown to us but discoverable by a thorough literature search, we are expected to find them. Even so, research can never be *complete*. An intensive search in all relevant catalogs, guides, and other finding aids can still fail to turn up random records of potential value. Some materials remain hidden to the world, and others are not available for public scrutiny.

All things considered, our task as history researchers is to learn the sources, learn the methods, learn the standards, and apply them all as carefully and diligently as possible.

1.3   **Conclusions: Hypothesis, Theory & Proof**
Each and every assertion we make as history researchers must be
supported by *proof*. However, *proof* is not synonymous with *a source*.
The most reliable proof is a composite of information drawn from
multiple sources—all being quality materials, *independently created,*
and accurately representing the original circumstances.

For history researchers, there is no such thing as proof that can never
be rebutted. We were not there when history happened, and the
eyewitness accounts of those who were—if and when those accounts
exist—may not be reliable. Every conclusion we reach about circumstances, events, identities, or kinships is simply a decision we base
upon the weight of the evidence we have assembled. Our challenge is
to accumulate the best information possible and to train ourselves to
skillfully analyze and interpret what it has to say.

In this process, we typically reach conclusions of three types, each of
which carries a different weight:

Hypothesis—a proposition based upon an analysis of evidence at hand;
used to define a focus for additional research. In testing any hypothesis, we must labor to *disprove* it as diligently as we labor to prove it.
Our role is not just that of judge and jury, but also that of devil's
advocate.

Theory—a tentative conclusion reached after a hypothesis has been
extensively researched but the evidence still seems short of proof. A
theory should never be presented as a *fact*. Any theory we propose
should carry qualifiers. *Perhaps, possibly, likely,* and similar terms can
express our degree of confidence in a theory, but we are still obliged
to explain our reasoning.

Proof—a conclusion based upon the sum of the evidence that supports
a valid assertion or deduction (i.e., a conclusion drawn from aggregated clues). Proof must be backed by thorough research and documentation, by reliable information that is correctly interpreted and
carefully correlated, and by a well-reasoned and written analysis of the
problem and the evidence.

A conclusion cannot always be reached. When the accumulated
materials are appropriately appraised, the evidence may or may not
support a decision. If it does not, then the question remains open—
the fact of the situation remains unknown—until sufficient evidence
is developed. If extenuating circumstances pressure for a decision (as

with, perhaps, impending court testimony in a dispute over historical property or heirship), then the researcher is obligated to present all relevant evidence, interpreted accurately, and to appropriately qualify whatever hypothesis seems warranted. This is commonly done through the use of terms that denote *levels of confidence*. (See 1.6.)

1.4 Fact vs. Assertion or Claim

Society speaks loosely of *historical facts* as though the events of history are immutably chiseled in stone. In reality, most details we accumulate in our research will be *assertions* or *claims,* not *facts*. We may know 'for a fact' that *we* were involved in a particular event on a specific day. Beyond our personal experiences, however, we deal mostly in the realm of assertions and opinions—each of which we are obliged to test for validity.

Contrary to the old cliché, facts do not speak for themselves. Facts are chameleons whose shape and color reflect their handlers. A beginning researcher and a skilled one can read the same information in a record and draw two separate conclusions, based upon the degree of knowledge and experience each brings to bear on the subject. As history researchers, we bear the responsibility of not just collecting facts (i.e., information), but studying the principles of research methodology, document analysis, and evidence correlation in order to correctly interpret the information we find.

1.5 Family-History Standards

Modern family history (aka genealogy) draws heavily from law in its handling of evidence. However, family-history standards require a higher level of proof than does most litigation. The justice system demands that a date be set for trial, that all known and valid evidence be considered at that time, and that a decision be made then and there on the basis of that evidence. To avoid clogging the courts, the law permits decisions on civil suits to be made in the closest of cases—even when the evidence on one side barely outweighs that on the other (i.e., the legal standard of proof called *preponderance of the evidence*). Except for courtroom presentations of genealogical evidence, family history rarely has an arbitrary time by which one must decide an identity or kinship. If sufficient evidence does not exist to accept or reject a hypothesis, we can—and should—simply delay a decision until that evidence is found or accumulated.

Modern standards for family history also require more precision and rigor than commonly applied in the social sciences, where individual oversights or errors on common folk tend to cancel each other out in the broader interpretations of society. Family history's standards of proof approach those of the hard sciences, whose repeated experiments will expose errors. Genealogy, by its nature, focuses upon the individual; and every individual—great or small—is a life to be studied, genetically identified, and placed properly in the human family tree. Correct identity is the foundation upon which all else rests.

Unlike science, however, genealogy accepts no margin of error. A single error in identity or kinship will be multiplied exponentially with each generation beyond the error. Errors *will* occur. But family historians today approach their work with the mindset that erring is unacceptable.

The standard of proof set by genealogy's scholars and professionals—the Genealogical Proof Standard—poses five conditions that a valid conclusion must meet:

- thorough research;
- complete and accurate citation of sources;
- skilled analysis and correlation of data;
- resolution of any conflicts in the evidence;
- a soundly reasoned, *written* conclusion that details all the evidence, analyses, and documentation—i.e., a *proof argument*.

1.6   Levels of Confidence

Within sound historical studies, statements about dates, events, identities, places, relationships, and similar matters are frequently prefaced by qualifiers such as *apparently, likely, possibly,* or *probably.* By and large, the use of these terms adheres to no universal scheme. Rather, the terms take on whatever sense writers create with their supporting details and interpretations. The following offers one set of parameters that can be applied in a logical hierarchy:

Certainly: The author has no reasonable doubt about the assertion, based upon sound research and good evidence.

Probably: The author feels the assertion is more likely than not, based upon sound research and good evidence.

Possibly: The author feels some evidence supports the assertion, but the assertion is far from proved.

Likely: The author feels the odds weigh at least slightly in favor of the assertion.

Apparently: The author has formed an impression or presumption, typically based upon common experience, but has not tested the matter. (A presumption is not a blank check, however. In law, for example, Federal Rule 301* holds that the author of a presumption is still expected to produce evidence to meet or rebut the presumption.)

Perhaps: The author suggests that an idea is plausible, although it remains to be tested.

1.7   Objectivity

As history researchers, we are also biographers studying individual lives for a myriad of reasons. Whether our fascination with a character is born of respect or revulsion, the more we pursue our subject, the more difficult objectivity becomes. Even so, no one should be a hero or a devil to his biographer. If our reconstruction of the past is to be credible, our devotion can be only to the evidence itself, and the direction in which that evidence takes us is the one we are constrained to follow. Our role is not to defend or to prosecute. Our objective should not be to promote any certain image or any particular point—only to discover and explain.

1.8   Presentism

Presentism, the interpretation of the past by present standards, cannot coexist with objectivity and sound evidence analysis. Past societies lived by different standards, followed different laws, spoke in different terms, and defined ethnicity differently. When we evaluate and interpret records of past times and other places, we must do so in the context of *their* ideology, not ours. When we record our findings, we should not alter the language of the records. If we do, odds are, we will change the original intent and distort our portrayals.

As an example, consider the pre–1840 U.S. censuses that enumerate a class of citizens called "free people of color." That class included not only African Americans (full and part) but also Native Americans (full and part) and other ethnicities popularly viewed as something other than white. If we replace the label "free people of color" with terms common to our era—as, for example, *African American* or *Black*—we will skew statistics and alter many individual identities. Similarly, historical records such as free papers, court testimonies, and vital registrations denote color, ethnicity, mental and physical illness, or religious affiliation, using words that are considered inappropriate today. Each word, however, carries meanings particular to its era, and each is an identifier no less valuable than a personal name.

---

* *Federal Civil Judicial Procedure and Rules* (St. Paul, Minnesota: West Group, published annually).

As history researchers, we are obliged to preserve the evidence intact. Our calling requires us to *interpret*. Yet the evidence, in both our research notes and our citations, must remain unwarped. Our analyses must view that evidence through the eyes of the society that created it, not with those of our present world.

1.9 Quantity vs. Quality

Investigators in all humanistic fields are trained to seek multiple sources for any information they report—the theory being that one source can confirm another. However, *quantity* cannot trump *quality*. Multiple sources might copy the same information from an earlier source that was unreliable. Multiple sources for a particular statement confirm each other only when each is a reliable source of *independent* origin offering firsthand knowledge. For the history researcher who has no living firsthand witnesses to interview, establishing the independence of recorded assertions means that each must be traced back through its paper trail until its origin can be determined.

Conversely, we may never find a document that states directly what we need to know—the proverbial smoking gun in journalistic terms. Yet we may find multiple pieces of quality evidence that *indirectly* suggest a particular solution, with no contradictions we cannot validly resolve. If so, we might build a credible case based on that indirect or circumstantial evidence. (See Proof Arguments, 1.15.)

1.10 Technical Knowledge

Accurate evaluations of evidence require researchers to acquire sound technical knowledge of the materials they use. We cannot expect to pull a census and scan names or run statistics without thoroughly understanding the circumstances under which that record was created. The instructions given to enumerators, the conditions under which they labored, the types of schedules taken simultaneously that year, the abbreviations that differ from modern usage, and the distinctions between data recorded by the enumerators and later markings added by Census Bureau clerks—all affect our interpretations. Similarly, we cannot get full value from an incoming ship roll without knowing the processes and prior records on which that roll is based, or the reasons why some immigrants were grouped by health conditions or some other status rather than family unit, or the significance of the cryptic notations later added to rolls by immigration officials as they verified claims made on naturalization petitions. Every source type has its peculiarities that affect both the meaning and the weight of the evidence we draw from those sources.

1.11 Truth

Historian Robert Winks once wrote, *The past was real, but truth is relative.** It is also intangible and indefinable. Unlike Justice Potter Stewart's famed definition of obscenity, we cannot say, "I'll know it when I see it."† We won't. Historical truth is physically pliable. We begin every research project with a vision of that pot of truth awaiting us at the rainbow's end. When we reach that end, we have only a mound of dough—dough that will be manipulated, stretched, shaped, and flavored by our own experience, judgment, and standards.

The principles covered in the rest of this chapter—and the practices explained in the rest of this manual—are designed to help history's truthseekers leaven, knead, and bake their dough into something that, one hopes, will resemble probability.

CLASSES OF EVIDENCE

1.12 Generic Labels

For more than a century, journalists and historians have borrowed from law two terms that are used generically to weigh the merits of their evidence—*primary source* and *secondary source*—with an occasional reference to a hybrid genre called *printed primary source*. As ubiquitous as the terms are, their definitions vary from one field to another and one authority to another. In the public mind (indeed, even among those trained in the same discipline), confusion and disagreement are common. The most usual concepts are these:

PRIMARY SOURCE
• one created by someone with firsthand knowledge
• one created at or about the time an event occurred

PRINTED PRIMARY SOURCE
• a primary source that has been transcribed or abstracted and published (ostensibly by reliable editors)

SECONDARY SOURCE
• all else

Within this framework, contradictions abound between theory and practice, causing ambiguous analyses and unreliable conclusions. Consider, for example:

---

* *The Historian as Detective: Essays on Evidence* (New York: Harper Colophon Books, 1968), 39.
† *Jacobellis* v. *Ohio,* 378 U.S. 184, 197 (1964).

- A source might be created by someone with firsthand knowledge, writing *long after* the event. The first criterion of a primary source would be met, but the second would not.

- A source might be created promptly after an event occurred, but that person might have had only secondhand knowledge. In those cases, the second criterion of a primary source—timeliness—would be met, but the first would not.

- A collection of papers accumulated by a key historical figure, once transcribed, annotated, and published, would typically be called a *printed primary source*. Yet the records in these collections often represent both firsthand and secondhand information, and the editorial interpretations and annotations typically were made long after the fact. As a source, such collections contradict in multiple ways the basic definitions of *primary source*.

1.13   Legal Terminology

Other familiar legal terms are frequently used by lay researchers in an effort to add weight to their conclusions—particularly these:

BEYOND REASONABLE DOUBT
Applied in criminal cases, this legal standard requires evidence to be virtually certain—an impractical bar for history researchers under most circumstances.

CLEAR AND CONVINCING EVIDENCE
This legal standard is interchangeable with *beyond reasonable doubt* in some jurisdictions. In others, it is an intermediate standard between *beyond reasonable doubt* and *preponderance of the evidence*. The *clear and convincing* concept most closely approximates the standard history researchers apply. Still, considerable fog hovers over the issues of what represents *clear* and what it takes to be *convincing*.

PREPONDERANCE OF THE EVIDENCE
As a legal standard for civil cases, *preponderance of the evidence* is the easiest bar to pass. Evidence on one side of an argument needs to outweigh but *slightly* the evidence on the other side. History researchers of the past who used the term usually raised its bar to a level that approached *beyond reasonable doubt,* adding another layer of public confusion to the issue of proof standards.

1.14   Process Map for Evidence Analysis

Many history researchers today follow an analytical process to analyze and evaluate their resources, following the schema diagrammed on the endpapers of this manual. (See Research Process Map.) This model separates a *source* from the *information* that source offers, and it evaluates each of those by its relevant criteria.

The process is built upon two axioms:

1.

Sources give us *information* from which we select *evidence* for analysis. A sound conclusion may be considered *proof.*

2.

Historical data have three basic characteristics: (*a*) their *form*, (*b*) the *knowledge* of the informant, and (*c*) the *relevance* and *adequacy* of the evidence to answer a specific historical question. Within each characteristic, quality will vary.

The four key parts of the process model—sources, information, evidence, and proof—are handled by the following principles:

SOURCES
Sources are artifacts, books, digital files, documents, film, people, photographs, recordings, websites, etc. Sources are classified according to their *physical form:*

Original sources—material in its first oral or recorded form. Examples: the testimony of someone relating events that he or she personally experienced or witnessed; or an original document created by a party with firsthand knowledge of the information recorded.

Derivative sources—material produced by copying an original or manipulating its content; e.g., abstracts, compilations, databases, extracts, transcripts, translations, and authored works such as historical monographs or family histories.

As a rule, original sources carry more weight than derivatives, even though original sources can err by accident or design. Derivative sources also span the entire spectrum of reliability—depending upon the form they take; the circumstances of their creation; and the skill, bias, or aim of their creators. Some derivatives might be considered equivalent to originals under certain circumstances. (See Duplicate Originals, 1.25; Image Copies, 1.26; and Recorded Copies, 1.27.)

INFORMATION
Information refers to the *content* of a source—that is, its factual

statements or its raw data. Information is classed or weighed according to its origin:

Primary information—details provided by someone with firsthand knowledge of the information reported, such as a participant in an event or an eyewitness.

Secondary information—details provided by someone with secondhand or more-distant knowledge of the person, event, or situation. Hearsay, tradition, and local lore all represent secondary information.

As a rule, primary information carries more weight than secondary, although either class of informants can err, intentionally or otherwise. Moreover, any statement can represent both firsthand and secondhand knowledge. Landowners in colonial South Carolina, for example, were required to go before the council and orally memorialize their land. A new landowner of, say, 1760 might recite a chain of title back to the grantee in 1660. Reading his memorial, we can reasonably conclude that he had firsthand (primary) knowledge of his own acquisition of the property. However, the statements he made about the original grant and other sales and leases in the preceding century would logically represent only secondhand (secondary) knowledge.

Thus, each piece of information within a source has to be appraised separately. Each has to be critically examined for evidence of bias, fraud, memory or time lapses, and other factors that can affect reliability. (See Textual Criticism, 1.30 through 1.41.)

EVIDENCE

Evidence represents *our interpretation* of information we consider relevant to the research question or problem. Evidence is usually one of two basic types:

Direct evidence—relevant information that seems to answer the research question or solve the problem all by itself.

Indirect evidence—relevant information that cannot, alone, answer the question; rather, it must be combined with other information to arrive at an answer.

Direct evidence may be clearer to grasp, but indirect evidence can carry equal or even greater weight. The term *evidence* is also used in a sense that is less tangible but just as critical:

Negative evidence—an inference we can draw from the absence of information that should exist under particular circumstances.

PROOF

The term *proof* is one laymen use interchangeably with both *source* and *evidence*. None of the three are synonymous in the context of historical research. Each has a different meaning. A source may offer relevant information whose evidence we carefully consider. Yet at the end of that consideration we may decide that its evidence proves nothing.

Proof is a conclusion supported by three things: (*a*) thorough research and documentation; (*b*) reliable evidence correctly interpreted and carefully correlated; and (*c*) a well-reasoned analysis. The most reliable proof is a composite of information drawn from multiple sources— all being quality materials, independently created and accurately representing the original facts.

If proof exists in the form of direct evidence—and we eventually conclude that this direct evidence is indeed the best evidence possible—our reporting of the fact may require nothing more than simply citing its source. More often, proof involves an assimilation of indirect evidence or a resolution of contradictory evidence—situations commonly referred to as *building a case*. In those circumstances, a written proof argument is essential.

1.15 Proof Arguments

The paper or writing by which we present our case for a conclusion is called a *proof argument*. Although every proof argument is shaped by the nature of both the problem and the evidence found, a proof argument typically contains five essential parts:

- explanation of the problem;
- identification of known resources;
- presentation of evidence, supported by thorough source citations and analyses;
- explicit discussion of any conflicting evidence;
- summation of main points and a reiteration of the conclusion.

A proof argument is expected to be clearly organized, logically reasoned, and totally documented. When contradictory or conflicting evidence exists, we must address it and offer quality evidence or reasoning to rebut the contradiction or resolve the conflict.

PROBLEMATIC CONCEPTS

1.16 "Definitive Sources"

For history researchers, there exists no such thing as a *definitive* source.

Any source can err. Almost all do err to one extent or another. As with every kind of research, we should consult every relevant source, seek alternative views and materials for every issue, and carefully weigh each finding against the other.

1.17   "Direct Sources"

Casually used by some researchers to describe sources that are critical to their research, the phrase conflicts with standard classifications of both sources and evidence. Better terms for the concept would be *major sources, principal sources,* or *key sources.*

1.18   "Final Conclusions"

The case is never closed on a historical conclusion. Just as scientists revise their theories in the wake of new discoveries, so do historians. Any decision we make today could be changed tomorrow by the discovery of previously unknown information.

1.19   "Indirect Sources"

Some guides to writing and citation use this term to refer to sources that are cited by others as the source of their source. Some suggest making an "indirect source" the primary focus (or lead element) in our own citation—even though we have not actually consulted it— followed by an attribution to the source where we found the reference. For example:

> [*A full citation of the "indirect" source*], as quoted in Jones, "Historic San Saba," 369.

This manual discourages both the term "indirect source" and the practice of "borrowing sources," each for a different reason.

FOR CLARITY

The term *indirect* is already used in evidence analysis to describe *evidence*, something that is not synonymous with *source*. Thus, the phrase *indirect source* is ambiguous and can be misleading. A clearer term for the concept would be, simply, *the source of our source.*

FOR CREDIBILITY & INTEGRITY

Citations are built on the principle that we cite only what we have used. It is a sound practice to identify, in our research notes, the sources on which other authors base their assertions or conclusions. Sound practice then dictates that we *actually consult* those sources that are relevant to our works. We need to confirm the accuracy of what other writers report and glean additional perspectives those earlier sources can offer. For credibility and integrity, we should not borrow sources from other writers or present what amounts to hearsay as credible fact. (See also Citing the Source of a Source, 2.21.)

1.20 **"The Name's the Same" Rule**

A significant challenge faced by those who write historical biography or microhistory is the correct identification of *people*—particularly those who played minor roles on the stages of history. When we encounter records that bear the right name, in the right place and time, it is tempting to assume the record applies to our person of interest. The temptation is especially great when the name is not a common one, when courthouse fires and other natural disasters have destroyed many local records, or when we explore the random but seemingly endless offerings of cyberspace.

With every find we must remember: *"The name's the same" does not mean the person is.* It takes far more than a name to create an identity. Age, economic and social status, haunts and habits, land ownership (and the recorded legal description of that property), literacy, occupation, organizational affiliations, religion—and, above all, *associates*—are essential elements of each person's identity.

The only way to protect ourselves against errors of false identification is by thorough research, careful correlation of data, and the study of individuals in the context of their neighbors, associates, and kin.

1.21 **"Three Sources" Rule**

A popular maxim among some researchers contends that proof requires one to have three sources reporting the same fact. Like many adages, this one is more of a platitude than a sound premise. If three sources take their information from the same wrong source, they are all wrong. Conversely, highly skilled research may yield no single document that states a fact outright, yet a convincing case for a conclusion can be built upon numerous pieces of indirect evidence.

PROCESSED RECORDS (FORMATS)

1.22 **Abstracts vs. Extracts**

Used in the context of *records,* these two terms are not interchangeable.

ABSTRACTS
Abstracts are condensed versions of a record, preserving all important details (and, ideally, in original sequence). An abstract may contain

verbatim extracts (selected passages quoted precisely) from a record, in which case the verbatim material is placed in quotation marks. An abstract should not contain the abstractor's analyses, unless those injections are enclosed entirely within square editorial brackets. (*Caveat:* In the context of a thesis or other research paper, the term *abstract* has a different meaning. There, it refers to a brief summary or précis of principal points.)

EXTRACTS

Extracts are verbatim transcripts of selected portions of documents. Although they are more precise than abstracts, they still do not represent the compete record. (See also Transcriptions vs. Translations, 1.28.)

1.23   Databases & Indexes

Neither databases nor indexes are records *per se.* They are research tools—finding aids or summaries compiled from a larger body of materials. Many databases and indexes offer valuable assistance in historical research but, regardless of how detailed they might be, they cannot match the weight or validity of the original record set from which selected data have been extracted.

1.24   Duplicate Copies Etc.

As defined by Federal Rule 1002 (4), a duplicate original is "a coun–terpart produced by the same impression as the original, or from the same matrix, or by means of photography, including enlargements and miniatures or by mechanical or electrical rerecording, or by chemical reproduction or by other equivalent techniques which accurately reproduce the original." Under Rule 1003, in most circumstances a duplicate would be as admissible as the original. However, the presenter of a duplicate is obligated to explain why the original is not submitted.

History researchers, on the other hand, usually draw distinctions between the three record types covered by this legal definition— duplicates, images, and record copies. In a historical context, these distinctions are covered by 1.25–1.27.

1.25   Duplicate Originals (Counterparts)

Duplicate originals can be defined as matching copies of a document, created more or less simultaneously. Typical examples would be (*a*) the grantor and grantee copies of a deed drawn by an attorney; or (*b*) the federal and local copies of a particular U.S. census, both prepared by the same enumerator and, supposedly, with exactly the same information. As a rule, duplicate originals of legal records are loose documents, often found in probate packets or court-case jackets, although researchers will find some random collections that have been bound.

Historically, two-party legal documents that required counterparts (duplicate originals) were called *indentures*. To safeguard against the creation of a fraudulent counterpart by one party, the two duplicate originals would be written on the same sheet of stationery and cut apart with an irregular line. A privately held document that did not precisely fit the official counterpart (or *stub*) would fail in a legal challenge.

1.26 Image Copies

Image copies are typically defined as photographic reproductions made digitally or on film. Theoretically, they are the equivalent of an original. However, they may or may not be of equal merit. Modern history researchers rely heavily upon microform and digital images, not only for long-distance access but also to preserve the fragile originals. Yet any image copy can present problems. Imagers may have missed a page of a register or a loose document from a file. They may have had difficulty filming text in the crack of a record book. Lighting conditions might have produced inferior copies. Moreover, the black-and-white medium long used for image copies can mask content problems that are visible on the original, such as erasures in a record and alterations or additions in a different color or type. Photocopies made by other researchers also may have been altered to provide evidence for one purpose or another.

As history researchers, we are justified in treating image copies as originals so long as (*a*) the images are legible; and (*b*) their information does not conflict with other evidence. In case of conflicts or poor legibility, we should treat the image copy as a derivative and seek access to the material from which the images were made.

1.27 Record Copies (aka Clerk's Copies)

Official record copies are typically made from a duplicate original that was presented to the court for filing. Most are entered into a register. They are more likely than the originals to be microfilmed or digitized. In most locales, they will be the only surviving copy. Nonetheless, every recopying of a record can create an error, and often a significant one. Thorough researchers attempt to locate the originals—particularly probate packets and civil and criminal court files—not only as a safeguard but also because those packets routinely include documents not copied by the clerk into the official record books.

1.28   Transcriptions (Transcripts) vs. Translations

Whether in manuscript or typescript form, both transcriptions (aka transcripts) and translations are typically full copies and are expected to be faithful to the original. By most editorial standards, transcripts should attempt to render the words and punctuation just as the original scribe presented them. Translations, which convert writings into another language, are expected to be faithful to the intent of the original, choosing the most appropriate words and grammar within the new language.

History researchers work with many supposedly original materials that are actually transcriptions—although they may be the best version that survives. The record copies discussed at 1.27 are a prime example. In other situations, extant record books are early transcripts of older registers that have disintegrated—meaning they are tertiary (thirdhand) materials. Census marshals of the past often transcribed additional copies for submission to multiple offices. While these transcriptions are typically treated as duplicate originals, the true original and the transcription can have radical differences that affect our research and conclusions. (By way of example: the federal copy of a census— typically the one we consult on microfilm—may identify people by their initials only, while the local or state copy may carry their full names.) The thorough researcher will seek out all known copies of a particular record.

1.29   Transcriptions (Transcripts), Edited or Embellished

These more-or-less verbatim copies typically apply editorial conventions ranging from correction of punctuation, grammar, and spelling to augmentation of facts. Published diaries, memoirs, and presidential papers are common examples that blur the traditional lines between best evidence and second-best. The original records, themselves, could represent either primary (firsthand) or secondary (secondhand) information—or both in a single document. The edited or embellished transcripts may be more or less trustworthy, depending upon the skill of the editor and upon the degree of license the editor felt he or she was entitled to take.

TEXTUAL CRITICISM

1.30   **Authenticity & Credibility**

Textual analysis is a cornerstone of all research into matters historical. While different fields apply different terms to their methods and standards, most have a common goal and similar criteria. Reliable history researchers carefully evaluate the authenticity of every document they use, analyzing it externally and internally for clues to its origin and veracity. The rest of this chapter provides an overview of the most common criteria.

1.31   **Certifications & Certificates**

In a court of law, certification by an official creates authenticity once the court verifies the official status of the creator. In historical research, certification adds little or no weight and in some respects can seriously diminish reliability. Certified photocopies of legal records will mask distinctive characteristics of the originals—erasures, differences in ink, etc. Modern clerks who create form-type certificates of vital records from old manuscript registers frequently misread names of people, make erroneous assumptions about places where the events occurred, and omit details that could be critical to the researcher.

1.32   **Content**

Psychologists frequently point out that those who lie tend to provide more detail than those who speak the truth. That same tendency can be seen in spurious records from the past. Those who forge documents out of a need to prove the otherwise unprovable are frequently undone by the very details they add to infuse an aura of authenticity. The Horn Papers that purportedly chronicled life on the Monongahela and Upper Ohio and the Minor Collection that promised new insight into Abraham Lincoln were outed by careful studies of their *content*. *

It is tempting, when faced with more materials to explore than time to do it well, to accept statements at their face value. Research into collateral figures who have no real relevance to our project can seem pointless—or at least a luxury we can ill afford. The most reliable work, however, is done by researchers who take the time to *test contextual statements* for accuracy, to *compare assertions* against contemporary

---

* For the investigations that exposed these two historical frauds, see Arthur Pierce Middleton and Douglass Adair, "The Mystery of the Horn Papers," *William and Mary Quarterly*, 3d series, 4 (October 1947): 409–43; and Worthington Chauncey Ford, Paul M. Angle, and Oliver Rogers Barrett, *The Atlantic Monthly Hoax* (Springfield, Illinois: The Abraham Lincoln Association, 1929).

records, and to *identify others* who allegedly interacted with our subject. Named associates who cannot be found, cited events that are misdated or placed into the wrong set of circumstances, and anecdotes that are so appealing or appalling that we want them to be true are all red flags we should not ignore.

1.33   Creator's Veracity & Skill

The veracity and skill of the creator of a physical source will have shaped its content. To appraise these factors, we not only study the information inherent in a record but also acquaint ourselves with the personal habits and qualifications of both the scribe who penned the original document and any compiler or compilers who prepared derivative works. For example:

- *Local government records:* Does the court clerk's other work exhibit signs of care or carelessness? Was he an unqualified or disinterested political appointee?

- *Published records (abstracts or transcripts):* How experienced is the compiler or editor? What are his or her credentials and reputation as a researcher or producer of historical materials?

1.34   Informant's Purpose & Reliability

The purpose of a record and the motivation of its creators often affect its truthfulness. Many documents are created for self-serving purposes, and all are made by individuals with varying degrees of reliability. As researchers, we can take no record at face value. In appraising diverse types of materials, we apply such tests as these:

- *Affidavits or other sworn statements* (in legal cases, pension applications and damage or monetary claims, for example): To what extent did the complainants, defendants, and witnesses have cause for bias or gain? Records created under oath generally carry greater weight than statements made otherwise; but self-serving statements abound, notwithstanding the threat of legal penalties.

- *Diaries, family Bibles, memoirs, etc.:* To what extent would the creator have had cause to misrepresent a fact? A journal entry might exaggerate the writer's role in an event because he anticipates that his journal could be made public. A published diary might reflect a desire on the part of the transcriber or editor to present the diarist in a better light. A marriage entry in an original family Bible might have been backdated to hide the early birth of a firstborn. All these factors must be weighed before the reliability of a firsthand account can be decided.

- *Tax and militia records:* Did the law, at that place and time, set certain age brackets between which men were tithables and militia service was obligatory? Legal statutes and local regulations passed by county and city governing bodies during the period under study will establish minimum and maximum legal ages for life events. However, prior to the twentieth century, the fact that vital registrations of births were not common in most American states led many males to adjust their ages upward or downward to avoid military service, taxation, and other civic burdens. Conversely, adolescents might exaggerate their age in order to enlist.

1.35   Language Characteristics

The style and vocabulary of a document should be consistent with its place and time, as well as with other documents the writer is known to have penned. Grammar should reflect the known educational level and social milieu of the writer. While spelling was not standardized until relatively modern times, phonetic patterns within a document can help to prove or disprove authorship. Preambles to legal records can point to personal identifiers and affiliations, as with the wills of Quakers that begin with an affirmation rather than an oath. Some writers spoke with a stilted voice, others wrote with their ears clearly attuned to cadence and rhythm.

Modern computer technology can also help us analyze the composition of documents in ways that were impractical for earlier generations. They can compare, say, the ratio of two- and three-letter words to long ones, or the lengths of sentences between different pieces of writing. By defining such characteristics, we can better judge authenticity of authorship or the validity of records themselves.

1.36   Material Characteristics

The types of ink, paper, pen, and printing processes in use when a document was supposedly created are also critical elements. The various dip pens of quill, steel, and glass made distinctly different impressions upon paper—as did the reservoir pens that used solid ink or were fountain-filled. From a more personal perspective, an aging individual with an unsteady hand might cut a ragged nib on his quill, creating strokes quite different from those of someone using a cleanly cut point. Ink itself offers much silent evidence waiting to be perceived. Iron-gall ink, for example, was well suited for quill pens but became less common when writers switched to writing instruments of corrosive steel in the mid-1800s.

The size and weight of stationery, the shape of seals, the quality of sealing wax, and the layout of words on the paper—all help to authenticate and date documents, as well as identify their scribes. Photographic processes (daguerreotypes, ambrotypes, etc.), clothes, and props speak not only to the date of an image but also the culture and wealth of the individuals portrayed. The same can be said for the composition of tombstones (whether iron, marble, concrete, etc.), the wording of epitaphs, and the symbolism depicted.

1.37   Penmanship

A sound analysis of penmanship goes far beyond the ability to read a piece of writing. The manner in which letters were formed can reflect a common style of the era or a distinctive characteristic of a particular person. Some individuals used dashes in lieu of periods. Some used double-line hyphens (=) to break words at the end of lines. In periods when penmanship styles were evolving, some clung to old-style letter-forms while others adopted the newer style—as, for example, in late-eighteenth-century America when tailed versions of the *s* were giving way to the current form and the thorn (*y*) was being replaced by the modern *th*.

Records that seem relevant to a research problem should have their penmanship evaluated in several ways, depending upon whether we are working with private writings or public documents:

PRIVATE WRITINGS

For various reasons, individuals do authorize others to draft documents or sign them in their names. Yet as careful researchers, when we study literate individuals or those who made distinctive marks, we try to accumulate as many examples as possible of the manner in which they put pen to paper. Then we closely compare those instances. Aberrations among writing styles, signatures, and marks on documents that bear the same name must be logically explained, with supporting evidence, if we assert that any document was created by a specific individual.

PUBLIC RECORDS

Here, we appraise not only the document of interest but also the handwriting used elsewhere within the record book or collection. For example, a church register that appears to be an original could be an administrative copy. So we ask:

- Is the penmanship of a style common to the era in which the events occurred?

- Are all entries made in the same hand, or do we see the variances one would expect from data entered over many months or years?

- Do original signatures appear on marriage and baptismal acts, as is common with many sacramental registers of the past?

- Are the entries recorded in a form-type book for a period in which such books were not the rule? Preprinted registers discreetly carry printing dates that may reveal their creation long after the original events occurred.

1.38 Record's Custodial History

A record's custodial history can bear strongly upon its authenticity. The annals of history are rife with cases of forged documents created long after the fact by someone with questionable intent. Affidavits, Bible records, deeds, letters, marriage bonds, and wills—these and more have been fabricated by people who had an irresistible urge to prove something that just was not so.

Protecting ourselves against fraud requires us to question each document we use: Is it in proper custody? Was it out of that custody at any time in its past? A photocopied document that should be on public record but cannot be found is always suspect until proved otherwise. Reliable researchers help others find that proof by providing full citations for their source.

We also consider that even proper custody is no guarantee of authenticity or accuracy. Numerous instances exist of forged documents that have been filed legally, of spurious papers slipped into case jackets long after the fact, and of mean alterations made to registers.

Modern technology has increased both the necessity and the difficulty of analyzing every document's authenticity. Sophisticated electronic tools permit the production of fake records of remarkable semblance to time-weathered materials. Entrepreneurs "recreate" ship rolls and family records for display; the unscrupulous can digitally add to those rolls passengers who never saw the ship. Couples can be posed together in photographs who, in real life, were never joined by marriage, kinship, or even proximity. Microfilming obscures many characteristics that might, on the original document, give away fraud—such as a correction in mismatched ink or paper inappropriate for the era of whatever is penned upon it.

1.39 Record's Degree of Processing

The reliability of every derivative work is influenced by the degree of processing it has undergone. A mortgage book in the town clerk's office could be a second-generation copy made from the original documents or it could be a third-generation copy made when the first was partially damaged by fire or flood. As cautious researchers, we also examine the inside covers and the initial and closing pages of each record book for a clerical notation that the book had been recopied.

Each additional layer of processing adds to the likelihood of transcription errors. The rank, post, title, or education of each individual who transformed the data can increase or reduce the likelihood of error. It does not, however, change the fact that each mutation is likely to be less accurate than the parent copy. Thus, we diligently track the ancestry of derivative works, hoping to trace each to its original source or, at the least, to the earliest extant version.

1.40   Record's Timeliness

Timeliness can be a critical factor in weighing the accuracy of information within a document. Did months or years elapse between the event and the creation of the record that relates its details? A record that is created closer to the time of the event typically carries more weight than one created long after. Common questions we apply in this regard are these:

- *Affidavit for a court case or pension application:* Was the testimony taken promptly after the event or many years removed? If the account is significantly delayed, what was the informant's state of health at that later date? Did he create other contemporaneous records that reflect a still-active lifestyle, sound memory, and community respect?

- *Bible record:* What is the Bible's publication date? Is that date compatible with the first entry of family data, or does it appear that someone entered events from earlier years or generations? Are the ink and penmanship consistent throughout all the entries—suggesting that they were made in one sitting by someone writing from memory or copying from something else? Or are the entries penned in hands of varying style and steadiness—suggesting that they may have been recorded, as they occurred, over the life span of one person or across several life spans?

1.41   Source Description

Critical analysis of our sources and our evidence is not a personal, private act. It is not something that we do so that *we* can make a judgment that we expect our readers to accept. Nor is it a one-time effort, an on-the-spot conclusion, during which we decide whether to accept or reject a source. As researchers, we should continue to evaluate the credibility of every source against new evidence. To do that, our research notes must do more than merely name a source and cite its *location*. Our notes should also *describe* the source in sufficient detail that we, at any future point, can reconsider our evaluation. As writers, we owe our readers that same *description,* so that they can better assess the soundness of our judgment.

The citation principles and models presented in the chapters that follow are crafted around these three essentials: evaluation, identification, and description.

Fundamentals of
CITATION

2

Guidelines

Fundamentals of
CITATION

—◦—

BASIC ISSUES

2.1   Art vs. Science

Citation is an art, not a science. As budding artists, we learn the principles—from color and form to shape and texture. Once we have mastered the basics, we are free to improvise. Through that improvisation, we capture the uniqueness of each subject or setting. As historians, we use words to paint our interpretations of past societies and their surviving records. In order to portray those records, we learn certain principles of citation—principles that broadly apply to various types of historical materials. Yet records and artifacts are like all else in the universe: each can be unique in its own way. Therefore, once we have learned the principles of citation, we have both an artistic license and a researcher's responsibility to adapt those principles to fit materials that do not match any standard model.

2.2   Citation Style Choices

Researchers in different fields consult particular types of materials. Citing them efficiently calls for various formats, depending upon the needs and habits of the field. History researchers, arguably, use the widest variety of all, given their focus on documents and artifacts rather than published works. Before we enter the realm of original manuscripts, however, our literature survey of published materials involves a fairly narrow range of sources traditionally covered by several classic style manuals:*

ASSOCIATED PRESS STYLEBOOK
Associated Press Style is followed primarily by journalists working with newspapers and magazines.

---

* See Appendix B, Bibliography, for a full identification of these manuals.

THE BLUEBOOK

Bluebook Style, developed by the *Harvard Law Review* and widely used within the legal profession, focuses mainly on published laws, court cases, and congressional materials.

THE CHICAGO MANUAL OF STYLE

Chicago Style, which is followed by scholarly researchers in many fields, offers a choice between

- *Humanities Style,* which places full citations in footnotes or endnotes and gives the author freedom to add unlimited comments relevant to the source; or

- *Author-Date Style,* which is common in scientific fields. Featuring an economy of words, this style calls for parenthetically citing, amid the text, the author's surname and date of publication. Readers then match this abridged note to an appended list of the publications cited.

MLA HANDBOOK

MLA Style, developed by the Modern Language Association, is used mainly in the library and literature fields.

TURABIAN'S MANUAL

Turabian Style, a standard for college and university students since 1937, is essentially an abbreviated version of Chicago Style.

Among these options, *The Chicago Manual*'s Humanities Style has been the most effective for history researchers. *Evidence Explained* is rooted in that style. However, most *Evidence* models treat original or electronic sources not covered by the manuals above, as well as some modifications that better meet the analytical needs of history researchers.

2.3   Citations, Definition & Purpose

Citations are statements in which we identify our source or sources for a particular assertion. In history, citations are typically written in sentence and paragraph form. We may cite multiple sources in a single citation. We may create many citations for a single source—each attached to a specific statement that needs supporting evidence. The term *citation* is obviously not synonymous with the term *source,* and the two should not be used interchangeably.

Citing a source is not an end to itself. Our real goal is to rely only upon the *best possible* source. In the research stage, we record every source consulted, regardless of our immediate opinion of its value. When we recognize that a source is deficient or that a better source might exist, the better source should be sought and used. When we convert our raw notes into an interpretative account, we want our information and conclusions to be supported by evidence of the highest quality possible. Toward that end, source citations have two purposes:

- to record the specific location of each piece of data; and
- to record details that affect the use or evaluation of that data.

Most researchers intuitively recognize the first function. However, to help ourselves and our readers evaluate the reliability of our evidence, we often need to discuss issues relating to a source's *quality* and *content,* not just identity and whereabouts.

2.4   Citations, Types of

History sources are tracked in three basic ways: *source lists* (used interchangeably with *bibliographies*), *reference notes,* and *source labels.*

SOURCE LISTS

As a master list of materials we have used, a source list does not document any particular fact. During our research—where it might be called a *working source list*—its primary purpose is to keep track of the materials that have been examined and essential details about the nature of those works. In a publication, where the source list is commonly called a *bibliography* and typically omits descriptive data, its function is to provide readers with a convenient list of key materials. Chapters 3 through 14 offer explicit examples of how to construct individual entries within a working source list. Appendix B illustrates a finished bibliography.

REFERENCE NOTES

Whether presented as footnotes or endnotes, we use these in narrative writing to identify the source of *individual statements*. Reference notes should offer a *complete* citation to the specific part of a source that provided the information we are using, and they may provide other relevant details about the source. Chapters 3 through 14 also demonstrate the construction of reference notes, whose forms can differ radically from source list entries.

SOURCE LABELS

Source labels are citations we add to image copies of documents or to abstracts or transcriptions of documents.

2.5   Common-Knowledge Rule

Any statement of fact that is not common knowledge must carry its own individual statement of source. Distinguishing common knowledge from a statement that needs documentation is mostly a matter of common sense. If we record that the Battle of the Bulge began on 16 December 1944, no supporting evidence is needed to attest the validity of that statement or to help locate information about the event. Details about the battle are widely available. However, a statement that a certain obscure infantryman was killed by enemy fire in the course of that battle would require a citation to a reliable source.

2.6   Copyrights, Plagiarism & Fair Use

Even a full citation of source may not be sufficient, legally or ethically, when copying from another work. Simply crediting other authors, or citing the whereabouts of specific documents, may not be adequate protection for us if we publish. The issues of copyright, plagiarism, and fair use also come into play. Limits exist on the amount of material we can quote from another source. Most publishers require permission—as well as acknowledgment—if any graphic or more than a few words are reproduced. The following rules of thumb are reasonably safe guidelines to follow in the research phase:

- When copying a string of *three or more words* from another source, we should treat those words as a quote. The source of the quote should be clearly identified. The use of other people's words, thoughts, or material without giving them credit is *plagiarism.*

- When using *three or more short paragraphs* from another source, we obtain permission from the author and the publisher. If permission is granted, our credit line acknowledges that permission.

- When quoting from *manuscript material* owned by an individual, agency, or institution, we also seek permission. Some archives severely limit copying, quoting, or publishing from their manuscript collections.

These rules apply to material published online as well as to printed works. In applying these guidelines, we should also consider two other questions that relate to the principle of *fair use:*

- What is the proportion of our copied material in comparison to the body of information from which we took it? Court decisions rarely uphold reuse of more than a small fraction of the whole.

- Will we market our work in competition against the individual or agency whose work we have merged into our own? If our venture is not commercial, will the mere distribution of our work decrease the demand for the work we have copied? If so, our reuse would not be fair use at all.

2.7 Discursive Notes & Overlong Citations

Citations to most historical materials are lengthy. Citations to electronic publications, if they adequately identify and describe the original material, can be even longer. If we are committed to full citations, there will be little we can do to reduce the length of the essential elements. We can, however, reduce the mass of our citations by avoiding *discursive* notes—separate discussions of issues that should be woven into the text or discussions of peripheral matters that do not directly relate to our subject.

Source notes, ideally, should identify and discuss our *sources*. Matters that relate to our *subject* should be discussed in the *narrative*. Self-discipline in this matter not only trims bloated source notes but also produces clearer and cleaner writing.

2.8 Privacy

Citations that involve living people must respect privacy. In our working notes, we record the name and contact information for each person we interview and each person who supplies information that is not publicly available. When we publish or circulate our material, for authenticity the minimal identifying information should be *name, city,* and *state*. However, we should not publish or circulate personal contact information, either in print or online, without the authorization of our informants, so long as they are alive. After their deaths, the contact information becomes historical data that can be useful for research purposes.

2.9 Selectivity & Thoroughness

Thoroughness in citing sources does not mean that our final product must cite every source we used. In the research phase we will create a working source list that logs every source we consulted. If a source contains information relevant to our search, we will take notes from it in that research phase.

When our research is reasonably complete and we begin to craft a narrative, we become selective. At this point, we base our conclusions upon the most authoritative sources and those are the materials we cite. On occasion, we may choose to cite other works that gave us special insight into the subject. It may also be appropriate to cite works that err, in order to correct their errors.

2.10   Symbols & Terms

Many sources used by history researchers are available today in alternate formats—audio, digital, and visual. Throughout this manual, as individual source types are discussed, you will find the following symbols flagging alternate citations for various media:

☊   Audio citations

📢   Broadcast citations

💿   CD-ROM citations

▣   Microfiche citations

🎞   Microfilm citations

💻   Online citations

Five basic terms are used throughout this manual as instructional terms and are capitalized at each usage for quick recognition:

First Reference Note—This term refers to the first time you cite a source in a particular database, manuscript, or published work. It embraces both footnotes and endnotes. This first reference to a source should always provide a full citation of the source and, when helpful, a discussion of the source's quality or evidentiary value.

Subsequent Note—Once a source has been cited in full, all subsequent notes that refer to that source are conventionally cited in a shortened form. For each First Reference Note modeled in this manual, you will find a short form for subsequent references.

Source List—This term refers to the master list of all sources you are using for a particular research project.

Master Source—This term is used in many database management programs to refer to individual items in your Source List. Typically, a Master Source is a simplified citation. Once you choose it from your Source List to create a Reference Note, you amplify that Master Source with details that relate to the particular instance under discussion. *Evidence Explained* occasionally uses the term in this context.

Source List Entry—This term is the one routinely used herein to demonstrate the citation of specific items in a Source List.

COMMON PRACTICES

2.11 Citing Derivatives & Imaged Sources

The range of materials and media in use today defies standardization. When we examine a publication to define the elements that need recording, we should bear in mind that this material commonly has two formats in need of identification:

- most such material *originated in manuscript or book format*—whether in modern times or antiquity;
- most such material is *now being published in a new format* by a firm or an agency that is not the original creator.

Therefore, our citation should do the following:

- distinguish between image copies and other derivatives, such as abstracts, transcripts, and information extracted into databases;
- credit properly the original creator;
- credit properly the producer of the film or electronic publication;
- identify clearly the nature of the material;
- identify the film or electronic publication completely enough for others to locate it;
- cite the specific place (page, frame, etc.) on the roll, fiche, or database at which we found the relevant detail; and
- cite the date on which the microform or electronic data set was created (if that information is provided), updated, or accessed—as well as the date of the relevant record.

Some publishers of film and electronic reproductions supply a preface informing us that they obtained their data from another firm or individual. Even so, to analyze the reliability of their material we also need to know

- the identity of the *original* compiler (individual or agency) who first assembled that data set;
- the original source(s) from which the data were taken;
- whether the database represents full or partial extraction from those sources; or
- whether it was generated from materials randomly encountered by the original compiler.

Tracking the provenance (origin) of material of this type can be difficult. A currently marketed database may have been purchased from a firm no longer in existence, which may have bought its information from a book compiler, who may have assembled materials randomly published elsewhere. Such a database could be of radically different quality from one issued by, say, a learned society using skilled copyists to extract every document in a record set or an image collection created by a company that contracts with an archive to reproduce an entire record series.

If our attempts to track the origin of the material are unsuccessful, we should say so and explain the efforts we made. This will help us and others avoid unnecessary repetition of the same. When we carefully report our steps, we or a user of our work may be able later to plug some of the gaps in our research process or our findings.

2.12   Citing Indexes & Finding Aids

In the framework of history research, an index is usually a tool, rather than a record. Typically, indexes are used in three ways, each of which involves different considerations for citations and analyses.

INITIAL STEP IN THE RESEARCH PROCESS

When an index points us to a source and we proceed to consult that source, we rarely need to cite the index. An exception would be a case in which an index provides some sort of special insight.

TEMPORARY STEP IN AN ONGOING RESEARCH PROCESS

In the course of our research, we may access a microfilmed index or an electronic database to a record set, while the records themselves are not immediately available. In such cases, we take our notes from that index and we cite that index as the source of those notes. As a rule, this is a policy for our working files only. Our pursuit of reliable evidence dictates that we proceed to use the actual records rather than make judgments on the basis of index details that the compiler has presented out of context. Once we examine the actual record set, we report our findings from that search and cite the actual records.

STATISTICS OR BACKGROUND PERSPECTIVES

On occasion, to add perspective to our conclusions, we may compile statistics from an index or analyze it for patterns. In other cases, clerks who created index entries at the same time they recorded legal and sacramental acts may have amplified the index with details about the parties that do not appear in the main documents. In such cases, the index itself is a source to be cited on its own merits.

2.13   Citing National Archives Materials

The national archives of most western nations offer their own style guides for researchers, illustrating preferred treatments of their materials. The style formats recommended by the U.S. National Archives and Records Administration (NARA) are especially lengthy, prompting many researchers to seek shorter forms that are adequate to their need. NARA's own journal, *Prologue,* also has applied various minimalistic citation styles over the years. However, creating shorter forms that adequately identify the records requires a basic understanding of NARA's system of archiving and cataloging materials. The few moments you might save by stripping down the citation may well result in many lost hours or days in relocating the record.

The most problematic area of NARA's style manual is its treatment of microform, which calls for a full citation to the *original* records from which the film was made, with only a parenthetical reference to the film by publication number. Many researchers prefer to make a full citation of either the film *or* the originals—depending upon which they consulted. That practice is soundly grounded. A citation should clearly indicate *exactly* what material was consulted, and it should not imply that original record sets may have been examined when only the film was used. Quality and content often are not the same.

Chapter 11 presents specific citation formats for the national archives and other government records of several major nations.

2.14   Citing Page Numbers, Etc.

Modern citations for books, articles, and uncomplicated manuscripts typically omit the word *page* (or its abbreviation *p.*) before a page number. However, if a publication or manuscript contains other numbered elements to be cited—as with column, entry, or note numbers—we should explicitly identify each numbered part (e.g., page 2, note 3; or p. 2, n. 3).

2.15   Citing Personal Knowledge

A citation to "Personal knowledge of So-and-So" is a valid citation only if that person has primary (firsthand) knowledge of the event or circumstance. If the person is relating hearsay, local lore, or tradition, it is not a personal-knowledge situation. If colleagues provide us specifics about individuals or subjects they have studied historically, we do not have a personal-knowledge situation. Such informants should identify the source of whatever detail they provide, after which we have two choices:

- we may cite our informant and quote his or her source statement, clearly indicating that we have not personally used that source; or

- we may personally study our informant's source, cite it directly, and—if appropriate—credit our informant for pointing us to that material.

2.16 Citing Personal Names

When a source citation includes a personal name, we take particular care to cite that name exactly as it appears in the source. With publications and unpublished writings, similar titles may have been penned by similarly named authors; and the addition or deletion of even an initial could create problems in relocating the correct work. The misspelling of an author's name by just one letter could make a name 'invisible' in a database or on the Internet. In the case of documentary materials—when, say, an Indian factor's account book identifies a trader as *O. D. "Bear" Wysong* and we know the trader was Audibert Vinson—we should cite the entry exactly as it appears, not by the standardized spelling. We would then insert the correction in square editorial brackets immediately after the name given in the document—i.e., O. D. "Bear" Wysong [Audibert Vinson].

Personal names with suffixes such as *Jr.* or *III* no longer carry a comma between the name and the suffix when the name is written in common sequence—e.g., John Brown III. When given names and their surname are inverted for alphabetical listing in a Source List, a comma is inserted between the given name and its suffix—e.g., Brown, John, Jr.

2.17 Citing Personal Titles, Credentials & Degrees

Formally published citations, as a rule, do not include the titles, credentials, or degrees that authors hold. In our working notes, we will likely want to include *relevant* degrees and credentials to assist us in future evaluations of the weight of that source. For situations in which credentials would be a relevant part of a citation, see 3.44 and 4.28.

2.18 Citing Published vs. Unpublished Materials

Many citation rules involve distinctions between published and unpublished material. Authorities define publications in various ways. In history research, the distinctions are typically these:

Published material—Material that is printed, imaged on film, reduced to electronic disks, or placed online with the intent to sell or disseminate it widely.

Unpublished material—Material in the same formats as above that is created for preservation only or for very limited sharing.

To illustrate: a set of estate papers in a courthouse might exist in any and all of these varied forms:

Original loose papers .... unpublished
Original manuscript volumes .... unpublished
Microfilmed copies of the loose papers,
    supplied to a state archive without
    permission to rent or sell copies........................ unpublished
Digital images marketed on CD-ROM .... published
Digital images online, for sale or free use .... published
Microfilmed copies of the originals,
    made with the intent to rent or sell .... published

2.19 Citing Repositories

When citing manuscripts that exist in only one place, the identity of that repository is an essential part of our citation. When citing books, film, and other published materials that are widely available, the name of the repository at which we used the source is *not* included in our formal citation. (Libraries holding copies of specific *published* works are identifiable through the Online Computer Library Center's World-Cat database, and similar resources.) In our working notes, we may wish to include the repository at which we found the publication, simply as an aid in case we need to reconsult it. However, a citation to the facility most convenient to us personally would be of little value to users of our work who live elsewhere.

2.20 Citing Several Sources for a Single Fact

Thorough research often yields multiple sources for the same information. When we convert our notes into a narrative or permanent database, we select the best evidence we have found. If several sources for a fact are of equal value, we may cite all of them in the same reference note. If those sources are basic books or journal articles that involve no digital reprints or other complications, we might even cite them all in the same sentence. In that situation, we separate each source from the others with semicolons. For example:

> 1. E. A. Wrigley, ed., *Identifying People in the Past* (London: Edward Arnold, 1973), 12; Arthur Best, *Evidence: Examples & Explanations* (Gaithersburg, New York: Aspen Law & Business, 1999), 140–50; Sam Wineburg, *Historical Thinking and Other Unnatural Acts* (Philadelphia: Temple University Press, 2001), 82–83.

However, citations to original manuscripts, digital productions, and similar materials are typically complex and contain internal semicolons. For these materials, it is best to cite each source in a separate sentence within the reference note. (See also 2.74 Semicolons.)

2.21   Citing the Source of a Source

We do not cite sources we have not used. "Borrowing" sources from other writers is both unethical and risky. When we use the work of others, we cite what we actually used. When other authors identify their source for a detail that is relevant to us, we should add to our note a statement such as,

> The author cites "Register 3, page 235, St. Peter's Parish, Wilmington, Delaware."

Credit should always be given where it is due. By the same token, we would not wish to assume the blame for an error another writer made in using a record we have not seen.

If the source we consulted cites an original record, we should then examine the original to verify the accuracy of the prior writer's assertions. Having consulted the original, we are entitled to cite the original as our own reference. If the other author has given us special insight into the use or interpretation of that original, we should credit the prior author for the insight. If the original material is something we might not have found on our own, we might also credit the earlier author for pointing us to it. Conversely, if the earlier author misrepresents facts from the original, then our citation might need to note that error and add an appropriate but tactful discussion.

2.22   Citing Titles, Basic Rules

Four basic rules govern our citation of titles, regardless of the type of record or publication we are using:

PUBLISHED BOOK, JOURNAL, WEBSITE, CD, ETC.
For published works, you copy the exact title and put it in italics.

NAMED PART OF A PUBLISHED BOOK, JOURNAL, WEBSITE, CD, ETC.
For parts of a published work, such as a chapter in a book, an article in a journal, or a database at a website, you should copy the exact title and put quotation marks around it.

TITLED, BUT UNPUBLISHED MANUSCRIPT, REGISTER, ETC.
For an unpublished manuscript or typescript, you should copy the title exactly and put quotation marks around it.

UNTITLED, UNPUBLISHED MANUSCRIPT, REGISTER, ETC.
When a manuscript or record book has no title, you should create your own generic description. You do not place your words in italics, because the item is unpublished. You do not use quotation marks, because you are not quoting anything. You may want to add an explanation in square editorial brackets.

2.23 Citing Titles in Foreign Languages

When a work's title appears in a language other than our own, we have options for describing the record. We may simply copy the title of the document exactly as it appears. Or we may add, after the title, a translation in square editorial brackets. Our translation should appear in roman type, not italics, and it will not carry quotation marks because our translation is not an exact quote. For example:

> 1. Jean Milfort-Leclerc, *Mémoire, ou, Coup-d'oeil rapide sur mes différens voyages et mon séjour dans la nation Creek* [Memoir: Or, a Quick Glance at My Different Travels and My Sojourn in the Creek Nation] (Paris: Giguet et Michaud, 1802), 41.

FAMILY HISTORY LIBRARY

2.24 FHL, GSU & LDS

The world's largest library of historical document images is found in Utah—millions of reels of microfilm preserved in a granite mountain, with copies deposited at Salt Lake's Family History Library (FHL). Most of the library's film, fiche, and digital images are not publications but preservation copies made throughout the world by FHL's sister agency, the Genealogical Society of Utah (GSU). Both the FHL and the GSU are operated by The Church of Jesus Christ of Latter-day Saints (LDS). The microforms are circulated throughout the FHL system of family history centers, but neither the FHL nor the GSU consider the circulated prints to be publications. The FHL also holds copies of film created by governmental and commercial agencies.

While GSU-created films are not publications, other microforms in the FHL may be published. Consequently, it is important to determine the type of film being used. This is usually done by observing the filmer's *target* (the title board or card at the beginning of a filmed item that precedes the content and describes it). Various differences between citing filmed manuscripts and publications will be covered throughout this manual. The term *FHL film* will be used throughout for GSU-created film.

2.25 FHL Basic Rule

Because FHL films are not considered to be publications and are only circulated within its library system rather than sold or given to the public, they are not cited as a publication. For special issues involving FHL film, in addition to 2.26–2.30 below, see also 3.19.

2.26 FHL Film Numbers (Call Numbers)

Many researchers add the FHL film number (call number) to their citations. Doing so is a convenience for the future and it records the fact that we used the film version rather than the original. While the two are theoretical equivalents, differences do exist in legibility and filmers do occasionally omit pages and documents.

Citing the FHL film number for GSU-produced film in your First Reference Note is a simple matter:

First Reference Note
1. Sussex County, New Jersey, Mortgage Book B:368, Doud to Bescherer, 1798; FHL microfilm 959,863.

Note the use of the comma within the film number. FHL recommends that researchers apply this conventional use of commas when using FHL film—"for ease of reading and for keeping track of the digits"*— even though some databases omit commas in FHL film numbers.

Citing FHL film numbers in your Source List Entry calls for a case-by-case judgment. If you are citing a record series that covers numerous rolls of film, all of them consecutively numbered, it is easy to cite the run in the Source List Entry. For example:

Source List Entry
New Jersey. Sussex County. Mortgages, 1766–1868. County Clerk's Office, Newton. FHL microfilm 995,855–959,880. Family History Library, Salt Lake City, Utah.

In many cases, the FHL call numbers for a series of records will *not* be sequentially numbered, and citing the various sets of numbers would be cumbersome. In such cases, your Source List Entry might simply cite the total number of rolls involved. Your Reference Notes would then cite individual rolls.

---

* Kahlile Mehr, FHL User Guidance Manager, 10 January 2007.

Source List Entry
American Medical Association. "Deceased American Physicians, 1864–
1970, Card File." Microfilm. 237 rolls. Family History Library,
Salt Lake City, Utah.

First Reference Note
1. American Medical Association, "Deceased American Physicians, 1864–1970, Card File," data card for Richard Finley, 1843–1915,
Centerville, South Dakota; FHL microfilm 2,032,837.

When citing call numbers for FHL film, you should observe two
cautions. One, the FHL call number alone is not an adequate citation;
it is only supplemental to the citation. Two, you should not append
FHL's number to a citation without explicitly identifying it as belonging to FHL. When other libraries hold the same film, they will have
their own call numbers. (For the use of this library's full name or
initials, see 3.19 for Citing FHL in Reference Notes.)

2.27   FHL Film of Unpublished Records
Records of local, state, and federal agencies, when filmed by GSU and
consulted at FHL, are cited the same way we would cite those records
if we used them in their original depositories—after which we add the
FHL film number. To create our citation, we should copy precisely the
label from each filmed book or file. If a register or file is not labeled,
we should look for the target that the GSU imagers placed at the start
of the material.

If the target is missing or seems to be inaccurate, consult the catalog
entry and create a generic label (record type and time period) using the
descriptive note for that film. Be aware, however, that the FHL
catalog description frequently uses a generic label to describe the
contents of an entire roll. The actual title of a specific register or file
may not appear in the cataloging entry.

2.28   FHL Item Numbers
When a roll of GSU film contains multiple items, each is normally
preceded by a target that identifies its *item number* on that roll. We
record that item number immediately after the film number:

FHL microfilm 1,234,567, item 8.

2.29   Published Books Filmed by FHL
FHL preservation microfilm of books and unpublished authored
manuscripts should be cited the same way as the original book or

manuscript. Again, we would add the appropriate FHL call number.

> 1. James Morrin, ed., *Calendar of the Patent and Close Rolls of Chancery in Ireland of the Reigns of Henry VIII, Edward VI, Mary and Elizabeth* (Dublin: Alexander Thom, 1861), 17; FHL microfilm 1,696,657, item 5.
> 2. [Anonymous], "Calendar of the Patent Rolls of James 1" (MS, Armagh County Museum, Armagh, Ireland), 17; FHL microfilm 1,278,356, item 21.

2.30 Published Film Used at FHL

We are not citing FHL microfilm when we use an FHL copy of film produced and published by another agency or firm (for example, the U.S. National Archives, Scholarly Resources, etc.). For published film consulted at FHL, we should identify the film by the name its publisher assigned, along with the original publication details. We can find this information at the start of the film, in the same manner that book publications carry title pages with publishing information.

2.31 Repositories, Citing When Using Film

When using records that GSU has filmed in other repositories, you should always cite the location of the original records in your Source List Entry. You may later need to consult those originals to clarify an issue. Whether or not you need to repeat that location of the original records in your Reference Note citations should be a matter of judgment.

- If the original is maintained where one would expect it to be (e.g., court records in the county clerk's office, church records in the parish rectory), there is no need to cite that location in your reference note when you have used the film. (See, for example, the Sussex County note at 2.26). You *may* include the location in your First Reference Note, if you wish; but it is not essential.

- If the record being cited has a generic title that does not connect it to a particular government office—say, a record book titled "Court Minutes, 1850–1860" in a county that has several different courts—then your Source List Entry and First Reference Note should identify either the particular court or the office that has custody of the record.

- If the original has been removed to another repository other than the one where it is expected (e.g., parish records removed to a diocesan archive, county records removed to a library, a U.S. census record held by a state archive instead of NARA), then your

First Reference Note should include the whereabouts of the original, followed by a reference to the film you have used. For example:

> 1. Christian County (Kentucky), 1799 Tax Book, List 2; Kentucky State Historical Society, Frankfurt; FHL microfilm 7,926.

2.32   Temple Work, Etc.

When citing FHL film of temple-work submissions, ancestor charts, family group sheets, etc., our citation should fully identify the compiler of the individual record. For these materials, we should always record the FHL call number and cite FHL as the repository, because the material is unique to that facility. (See, for example, 7.32–7.35.)

ONLINE MATERIALS

2.33   Core Elements to Cite

Citations to online materials pose particular problems, given the evolving nature of this medium. Chapters 3 through 14 provide many examples for handling most types of online history sources. The guidelines at 2.34–2.37 provide an overarching framework that covers almost all types of websites. That framework is built on the following foundation:

Online sources are publications with the same core elements as print publications. Most websites are the online equivalent of a book. Thus, we cite the

- author/creator/owner of the website's content (if identifiable);
- title of the website;
- type of item (as with a book's edition data);
- publication data:
- place (URL);
- date (posted, updated, copyrighted, or accessed—specify which); and
- specific detail for that citation (page, section, paragraph, keywords, entry, etc.).

If the website offers multiple items by different creators, it is the equivalent of a book with chapters by different authors. That calls for citations of two additional items:

- title of database, article, set of abstracts, or image collection;
- name of creator of the database, etc.

Within this architecture, a website is *not* a repository. Conceptually, the repository is the Internet or the World Wide Web. The distinction matters. When a citation template within our data-management software asks us to identify a repository, we invoke a basic rule covered at 2.19: in published citations, repositories are cited only for manuscript material exclusive to the repository where we used it. Repositories are *not* cited for published sources. To enter a website's name as our *repository* would be to say that the website's name is not an essential part of the citation. Therefore, the software might automatically omit it in printing out reference notes.

Identification of authors, creators, and website titles may require careful scrutiny of not only the relevant page but also its root pages. At each site we use, we should thoughtfully consider its construction and meticulously record every piece of information that might help us or someone else relocate the material in the event of a broken link. When we cite material that is available at multiple websites, we should consider which provider is likely to be the most permanent.

2.34 Databases vs. Images vs. Essays

Web providers of historical content typically offer digital material in three forms: (*a*) images of original records; (*b*) databases that compile historical data from the original images or other sources; and (*c*) essays and other writings that interpret this material. The three types do not carry the same weight on any scale by which evidence is appraised. Thus our citations to websites should specifically state the type of digital file we are using, if the title itself does not state that information.

2.35 Multiple Offerings at One Site

Websites that offer multiple items (articles, databases, etc.) by different individuals are the online equivalent of books with chapters by different authors. Thus, our citation needs to cover not only the website and its creator and publication data but also the

- author/creator of item (when identifiable); and
- title of item.

2.36 Punctuation

Punctuation in online citations follows most rules for books and their chapters, or journals and their articles.

- Website titles (like book titles) appear in italics.
- Database titles (like article and chapter titles) appear in quotation marks.

- Publication data such as the Uniform Resource Locator (URL) and date of posting or access are the equivalent of publication data for books. Logically, they should appear in parentheses within the reference notes.

  Note: Angle brackets around URLs were recommended in the early days of the Internet. However, as electronic citations have evolved, the use of angle brackets has been discouraged because it conflicts with their use in HTML coding.

- Citations to specific details such as paragraph numbers (like page numbers in a book) appear after the parentheses that enclose the publication data.

2.37 Web Addresses (URLs)

Identification of a website's address—its URL—can be tricky. Long URLs typically represent dynamic pages created on the fly when we enter a search term. We may find a long URL reusable so long as we do not clear our computer's browser cache. However, it likely will not work for others or for us at a later time. An alternative is to cite the website's home page, along with keywords in the path that takes a browser to the proper site. That method is not more permanent, however. The reorganization of a website could eventually make our cited keywords and path unworkable. By recording the access date, we may have a reference point usable at some Internet caches to retrieve the material.

CAPITALIZATION

Many URLs are case sensitive. We should copy a URL exactly, with no corrections of capitalization or alteration of style. When a URL appears at the beginning of a sentence, immediately following a period (as in most bibliographic entries), we should not capitalize the first letter.

HYPHENS, TILDES & UNDERLINES

We should take special care in reproducing hyphens (-), tildes (~), and underlines (__). Each has a distinct coding and one cannot be substituted for the other.

LINE BREAKS & PUNCTUATION

When it is necessary to break a URL at the end of the line, we should not hyphenate the line break. If a URL contains a hyphen, we do not break the line immediately after the hyphen. A break may be made between syllables or after a colon, slash, or double slash. However, if we need to break the line near any other embedded punctuation mark, then we place the punctuation mark at the start of the next line.

In Evidence Style citations, URLs are followed by a space and a colon, then the appropriate date. This practice serves two purposes: (1) it follows the practice already used in library cataloging of books, whereby the publication place is followed by a space, then a colon, then a space before information on the publisher and date; and (2) the space between the URL and the colon creates a clear and finite break between the URL and other punctuation that might follow it in the sentence under present or future protocols.

ORGANIZATION

2.38   Reference Notes vs. Source Lists
Reference Notes and Source Lists have significant differences in the way they are formatted.

REFERENCE NOTES (FOOTNOTES OR ENDNOTES)

AUTHORS' NAMES .... Names of authors are written in ordinary sequence (e.g., Laurel Thatcher Ulrich).

INDENTATION .... The citation is written in paragraph style, with (usually) the first line indented.

SEPARATION
OF ELEMENTS .... All elements that describe the source are linked together, sentence style. A period appears at the *end* of each source's citation. No period appears in the middle of elements that describe a source (aside from an occasionally abbreviated word). Specific punctuation is used to set off certain elements. For example:

> 1. Paul Kirn, *Politische Geschichte der deutschen Grenzen* (Mannheim: Bibliographisches Institut, 1958), 32.
> 2. *Vital Records of Manchester, Massachusetts, to the End of the Year 1849* (Salem: Essex Institute, 1903), 39.

SOURCE LISTS (BIBLIOGRAPHIES)

AUTHORS' NAMES .... Names of authors (or titles of sources when no authors exist) are arranged in alphabetical order by the first word of the Source List entry (e.g., Ulrich, Laurel Thatcher). See also 2.48.

INDENTATION .... The citation is formatted with a hanging indent that makes the alphabetized element easy to spot. The first line of each entry is flush with the margin; the carryover lines are indented.

SEPARATION
OF ELEMENTS .... The major elements that describe the source are separated by periods. In the examples below, the three major elements are (*a*) author [first model only], (*b*) title of book, and (*c*) publication data.

> Kirn, Paul. *Politische Geschichte der deutschen Grenzen*. Mannheim: Bibliographisches Institut, 1958.
> *Vital Records of Manchester, Massachusetts, to the End of the Year 1849*. Salem: Essex Institute, 1903.

2.39 Reference Notes, Choices of Style

Writers typically handle reference notes in one of four ways: as endnotes, footnotes, parenthetical citations, or hypertext. The first two represent Humanities Style; the third represents Scientific-Notation Style. Hypertext, a recent innovation for electronic publishing, might follow either style. All four options are not of equal merit for history researchers.

HUMANITIES STYLE

The recommended form for historians is Humanities Style. References are cited in full as either footnotes (at the bottom of a page) or endnotes (at the end of a section, chapter, or the book itself). Historical writing—when based on original research—often involves long and complex citations that would interrupt the flow of the discussion if the notes were placed amid text. Using Humanities Style for our reference notes allows unlimited space for full identification and discussion.

SCIENTIFIC NOTATION STYLE

This style embeds abridged citations in the text, within parentheses (e.g., "Jones, 1963"). To fully identify the source, readers consult an appended reference list that fully cites the 1963 item by Jones. The style is effective for scholarly fields such as scientific disciplines, where virtually all citations are to published materials. The style is not favored by history researchers whose sources are more often original manuscripts requiring complex citations, as well as descriptions or discussions of the source.

ENDNOTES OR FOOTNOTES

The choice here is a matter of personal preference or editorial style sheet. However, footnotes have two advantages. First, readers prefer them because footnotes do not require one to continually flip from text page to endnote page. Second, when footnotes are used, photocopies of any page will automatically include the source notes that support the text.

HYPERTEXT

Hypertext is a shortcut used in electronic publications that involves highlighting specific spots in a narrative. A mouse click on the highlighting will then jump the viewer to the source note, author's comment, relevant figure, appendix, or even a digital copy of the original source. When digital files containing hypertext are downloaded and printed, however, the hypertext links (hence, the documentation) may be lost. When citing sources for digital publication, we should ensure that the digital formatting will not sacrifice our reference notes.

2.40 Reference Notes, Full Citations vs. Short Citations

Reference notes have two basic forms: *full citations* and *short citations*. Our choice depends upon the kind of work we are producing:

NARRATIVES

When we write a narrative based on our research, the first time we cite a source, we give full details for that source. For subsequent citations of the same source, we may use a short form that our readers can easily recognize and associate with the first full citation.

RESEARCH NOTES (TRANSCRIPTS, ABSTRACTS, PHOTOCOPIES & SCANS)

When we transcribe, abstract, photocopy, or scan records, the use of short citations is risky. If we take multiple excerpts from a book, collection, or file, we should *affix a full citation to each sheet* of our research notes and *add a source label on each photocopy or digital scan*. That way, if our pages later become separated or shuffled, we will not be left wondering about the exact source of the information on any particular page.

2.41 Reference Notes, Numbering of

Source notes that are keyed to narrative text should be numbered consecutively. The corresponding numbers should appear in correct sequence within the text.

2.42   Reference Numbers, Placement of

In classic expository writing, note numbers within the text are typically placed at the end of sentences, outside the closing punctuation mark. However, some history researchers apply more precision in various situations. For example:

DISTINGUISHING BETWEEN ASSERTIONS FROM DIFFERENT SOURCES

If a single sentence contains information from first one source, then another, genealogical standards call for identifying *precisely* what detail came from which source. To do this, the writer places a reference number at each point where details from each source end. The practice is illustrated by this excerpt from a journal essay:*

> Sally was not merely "at Monticello" during Jefferson's return; she had the run of his private quarters. It was her "duty ... to take care of his chamber and his wardrobe"[128]—that "chamber" being a bedroom and study which Jefferson's grandson later described as a "sanctum sanctorum even his own daughters never sat in."[129]

> ———

> [128]Madison Hemings' 1873 interview. [PREVIOUSLY CITED IN THE ESSAY].
> [129]Brodie, "The Great Jefferson Taboo," 56. [PREVIOUSLY CITED IN THE ESSAY].

Given the maxim *All sources are not created equal,* the author's separation of the two pieces of information within her one sentence enables her readers to make a more informed decision about the veracity of the different assertions.

DISTINGUISHING SOURCED INFORMATION FROM PERSONAL OPINIONS

If a sentence contains not only information from a source but also our own interpretation or observations, it is best to place the reference number at the point where the information from the source actually ends and our own thoughts begin, as illustrated by another passage in this same work:†

> A family of the surname *Woodson,* rooted in distant Greenbrier County, claims [Sally's] first child as its forebear;[33] and some past scholars have accepted the claim without an intense scrutiny.

> ———

> [33]The most detailed case by the family is laid out in Byron W. Woodson Sr., *A President in the Family: Thomas Jefferson, Sally Hemings, and Thomas Woodson* (Westport, Connecticut: Praeger, 2001).

---

* Helen F. M. Leary, "Sally Hemings's Children: A Genealogical Analysis of the Evidence," *Jefferson–Hemings: A Special Issue of the "National Genealogical Society Quarterly"* 89 (September 2001): 183.
† Ibid., 170.

When a reference number appears in the middle of a sentence, as in the previous example, the superscript number should appear immediately after any punctuation mark (except the dash) that divides the two parts of the sentence.

DISTINGUISHING REFERENCE NUMBERS FROM GENERATION NUMBERS
When assembling a family genealogically—regardless of the numbering system that you use—a *reference* number should not appear directly after a given name unless there is intervening punctuation. In all the standard genealogical numbering systems, the superscript position immediately after a given name is the place reserved for an individual's generation number. In the following example, note that the two sets of numbers are further distinguished by another typographic distinction: the generation numbers are in both superscript and italics, while the reference number is only superscripted:*

> **Jane**[2] **Williams** (John[1]) born about 1820 in Washington, D.C.;[72] died 2 August 1872, in Boston, Suffolk County, Massachusetts.[73]

_____

[72] *Philadelphia Public Ledger,* Philadelphia, Pennsylvania, 31 August 1855, p. 1.
[73] Jane Harris entry, Boston Death Records, Book 1872, no. 4511.

2.43   Short Citations, Creating

After our reference notes have cited a source in full, we use a briefer citation for subsequent references to that source. Typically, the short form is created by repeating the author's surname and the first few words of the title. That short form should be one that is easily matched to the full citation that preceded it.

First Reference Note
1. Peter Linebaugh and Marcus Rediker, *The Many-Headed Hydra: Sailors, Slaves, Commoners, and the Hidden History of the Revolutionary Atlantic* (Boston: Beacon Press, 2000), 56.

Subsequent Note
11. Linebaugh and Rediker, *The Many-Headed Hydra,* 56.

As a rule for a local-records volume, when we have cited a title once in full, our short forms should use the opening words of the title and thereafter extract from it any words relating to *place, type of record,* and *time period.* For example:

_____

* Kathryn E. Flynn, "Jane Johnson Found: But Is She 'Hannah Crafts'?" in Henry Louis Gates Jr. and Hollis Robbins, eds., *In Search of Hannah Crafts: Critical Essays on "The Bondwoman's Narrative"* (New York: Basic Books, 2004), 398, 405.

First Reference Note
    1. Goldene Fillers Burgner, *Greene County, Tennessee, Minutes of the Court of Common Pleas, 1783–1795* (Easley, South Carolina: Southern Historical Press, 1982), 35.

Subsequent Note
    11. Burgner, *Greene County, Tennessee ... Common Pleas, 1783–1795*, 35.

When we omit words from the middle of the title, as with Burgner, we should replace the words with an ellipsis (three dots preceded and followed by a space). When we use only the first few words and omit the remainder, as with Linebaugh and Rediker, no ellipsis points are needed.

2.44   Short Citations, "Hereinafter Cited As"

When we craft a short citation well, our first full citation to a source does not need to add the wordy phrase *hereinafter cited as ...* followed by the exact text of the planned short citation. Typically, *hereinafter cited as* is used when the writer chooses an initialism or a very short form that readers might not recognize. Because clarity is a prime concern, creating self-explanatory short citations is the best course. If the *hereinafter* phrase is necessary, we should not shorten that word to *hereafter*. We cannot decree that everyone hereafter must use our chosen short form. We can say only that here*in*after (that is, in whatever we are writing), we will use this short form.

2.45   Short Citations, Precautions When Using

If source citations are to be effective, they should be easy to grasp, easy to remember, and easy to match to the full reference. With this goal in mind, good writers avoid the following:

CITING A SOURCE SO BRIEFLY IT CANNOT BE CORRECTLY IDENTIFIED

For example, a short citation frequently seen in publications on the Gulf borderlands is "Mills, *Natchitoches,* [page number]." However, five volumes with "Natchitoches" in the title have been published by three different individuals named Mills. A slight expansion to *Natchitoches Colonials* or *Natchitoches, 1800–1825: Translated Abstracts* would eliminate the identification problem.

REDUCING MANY SOURCE CITATIONS TO ACRONYMS & INITIALISMS

This practice saves space but creates confusion. Few readers can—or care to—retain a mental directory of KVR, QVRPX, LCTV, BWPC, LSNI, PMXE, and a dozen other mixtures of alphabet soup. Both *acronyms* (initial letters that are written and pronounced as a word) and *initialisms* (initial letters that are written as a quasiword but are individually pronounced) are best restricted to those so widely used in the field that a key is hardly needed. (Examples: NARA, the acronym for the U.S. National Archives and Records Administration; FHL, the initialism for the Family History Library at Salt Lake City; and LAC, the initialism for Library and Archives Canada.) Each abbreviated form should be fully identified the first time it appears. This is typically done by first writing the name completely, followed by the abbreviation placed in parentheses. For example:

First Reference Note
1. Claim of Samuel Goodman Levey , no. 61, Mixed Commission of British and American Claims, Case Files; Records of Boundary and Claims Commissions and Arbitrations, Record Group (RG) 76; National Archives and Records Administration (NARA), Washington, D.C.

Subsequent Note
11. Claim of Samuel Goodman Levey, no. 61, Mixed Commission of British and American Claims, Case Files, RG 76, NARA.

If you feel that numerous initialisms are necessary, you should add a key to the front of the manuscript or publication.

REFERRING READERS TO ANOTHER NOTE FOR THE ACTUAL REFERENCE
Example: when note 72 states, "See note 49." Source notes are, by nature, a distraction. Readers of the text must break their train of thought to search for the note. Being sent to yet another location, simply because the writer did not want to repeat the source, is an annoyance that encourages many readers to ignore citations.

Worse, the diligent reader who does follow the chain of citations to another note often finds that it does not match the text that launched the search, because of one danger inherent in this kind of citation: writers revise their early drafts. They add, delete, or rearrange information—sometimes forgetting to correct the corresponding notes. Modern word-processing programs adjust footnote or endnote numbers automatically. But when a reference internally states, "See note 49" and note 49 is renumbered to become 51, the embedded mention of note 49 will not be automatically corrected.

2.46 Source Labels
Full citations should appear on every photocopied or scanned document and on every page of a research report. To avoid altering the face

of a photocopy, some researchers place the source label on the blank back side. As that photocopy goes into circulation, however, the inevitable happens: someone in the circulation chain fails to copy the reverse of the record. Thereafter, others have a document with no identification.

Similarly, some researchers use the cryptic digital-file label of the scan to substitute for a source label. Aside from the insufficient identification of the source, another problem ensues. As the file is distributed electronically, others in the chain are likely to change the file label to suit their own filing system, thereby eliminating all clues to the source.

The modern practice is to pen or type the citation into the *margin* of the photocopy's face. If an adequate margin does not exist, we can use the photocopier's reduction feature to allow enough margin for a source citation. When we scan a document, we usually find a size-adjustment feature in our image-editing software, along with a tool that allows us to type a source label into the margin of the scan.

Other problems occur when researchers type their handwritten research notes or reformat those entered on-site into a portable computer. To save time, they may identify the repository on just the first page of the report or—when an abstract runs onto a second page—identify the abstract only at its beginning. Once the notes are reduced to hard copy, those sheets of paper will inevitably become shuffled and individual sheets will stray into other files. Even if the data remain in electronic form, any reorganization will likely separate one note from another, creating mystery objects out of some valuable notes.

2.47   Source List Arrangements

Source lists can become a quagmire if we simply collect citations without an overall scheme for organizing them. The most effective system for history researchers is one that divides sources into broad categories, such as

- author and title (for published and authored sources);
- collections (for manuscript sources);
- geographic locales;
- repositories;
- source types.

Appendix B, Bibliography, illustrates these schemes. Sections 2.48 through 2.54 discuss the particulars.

2.48 Source List Arrangements: By Author-Title

For published materials and other authored works (articles, books, manuscripts, maps, newspapers, theses, typescripts, etc.—whatever the media) the custom is to itemize works alphabetically, following these procedures:

- List authored sources in alphabetical order by author's surname.

- List anonymously authored works alphabetically by the title's first word. As an alternative, we may use the word *Anonymous* in the author's field, placing it in square editorial brackets, although this practice has fallen out of favor.

- If an author produced some works alone and some with other writers, we first group all those produced alone, citing the author's name first and then arranging the works alphabetically by their titles. Under that cluster we create a second grouping for that author's jointly written works; again, the principal author is cited first, with the joint works arranged alphabetically by the names of the second authors, etc. For example:

> *Source List Entries:*
>
> McWhiney, Grady. *Braxton Bragg and Confederate Defeat.* New York: Columbia University Press, 1969.
>
> ———. *Reconstruction and the Freedmen.* Chicago: Rand McNally, 1963.
>
> McWhiney, Grady, and Forrest McDonald. "The South from Self-Sufficiency to Peonage: An Interpretation," *American Historical Review* 85 (December 1980): 1095–1108.
>
> ———. "The Antebellum Southern Herdsman: A Reinterpretation," *Journal of Southern History* 41 (May 1975): 147–66.
>
> McWhiney, Grady, and Sue McWhiney, eds. *To Mexico with Taylor and Scott, 1845–1847.* Waltham, Massachusetts: Blaisdell Publishing Co., 1969.

See also 2.65 for an explanation of the 3-em dash used in source lists to indicate (*a*) the sole author cited in the preceding entry or (*b*) all the authors cited in the preceding entry.

2.49 Source List Arrangements: By Collection

When citing manuscript materials, we frequently find multiple documents of value in each collection we examine. Efficiency then suggests that our source list should cite items only at the collection level, rather than list every document. Entries cited at the collection level would be similar to these:

> Chief Justice's Law Clerks' Correspondence, 1927–38. Records of the Supreme Court, Record Group 267. National Archives, Washington, D.C.
>
> Personnel and Payroll Records, 1844–1906. Records of the Coast and Geodetic Survey, Record Group 23. National Archives, College Park, Maryland.

2.50 Source List Arrangements: By Geographic Locale

Manuscript materials often have a natural geographic base. Censuses, church and cemetery records, and courthouse registers and files are prime examples. Many researchers prefer to arrange these types of sources by geographic area in their source lists.

For materials that are geographically based, the convention is to begin an entry with the largest unit of the location (country or state) and work down to the local jurisdiction. That largest unit can be positioned as a header, as in the manner below, or it can be repeated as the first word of each entry. Whichever method you choose, you should be consistent.

New Mexico:
Sandoval County. Naturalization Records, 1910–1926. Thirteenth Judicial District Court of New Mexico, Bernalilo.
Socorro County. Homestead Records, 1882–1906. Probate Clerk's Office, Socorro.
———. Mining & Milling Claims, 1884–1906. County Recorder's Office, Socorro.

New York:
Orange County. Surrogate Court Records, 1787–1850. Surrogate Office, Goshen.
Rensselaer County. Deed Records, 1791–1900. County Clerk's Office, Troy.
———. Van Rensselaer Manor Papers, ca. 1650–1880. Secretary of State's Office, Albany.

Oklahoma:
Canadian County. Tax Records, 1930–1950. Tax Assessor's Office, El Reno.
———. Permit Records, 1890–98. Oklahoma Historical Society, Oklahoma City.
Kingfisher County. Civil Appearance Dockets, 1901–1929. County Clerk's Office, Kingfisher.

USE OF 3-EM DASH
For the 3-em dash used in lieu of the author's name, see 2.65.

2.51 Source List Arrangements: By Repository

When we have numerous citations to an archive with wide-ranging collections—such as a national, state, or university archive—we might choose to arrange the manuscript portion of our source list by repositories. Typically, we would begin our entry with the largest geographic location of the archive (country and/or state), followed by the name and city of the archive and the specific agency whose records are used. For example:

> France. Archives Nationales, Paris.
> ———. Section ancienne. Mélanges, Série M.
> ———. Section moderne. Comité des colonies, Série D XXV.

> United States. National Archives, Washington, D.C.
> ———. Office of the Quartermaster General, Record Group 94.
> ———. Southern Claims Commission, Record Group 56.
> ———. Treasurer of the United States, Record Group 50.
> ———. Wage Adjustment Board, 1941–1947, Record Group 236.

2.52 Source List Arrangements: By Source Type

In a working source list or a published bibliography, we may wish to subdivide our sources by type or quality. The most common division is between *Manuscripts* and *Published Sources*. Academic bibliographies often add a category such as *Theses, Dissertations, and Unpublished Papers*. Unless our editor or publisher specifies a certain format, we are free to choose the arrangement that best fits our sources.

2.53 Source Lists, Alphabetizing of

When your Source List Entry begins with an article (in English: *a, an,* or *the*), you have two choices:

- alphabetize the entry under the second word, or
- invert the name.

A source list that cites The Church of Jesus Christ of Latter-day Saints as the author of a publication might state the name exactly in that order but alphabetize it under the Cs in the following sequence:

> Cameron, Allen ...
> The Church of Jesus Christ of Latter-day Saints ...
> Clark, Jonathan ...

Or, your source list might carry the entry under the Cs as

> Cameron, Allen ...
> Church of Jesus Christ of Latter-day Saints, The ...
> Clark, Jonathan ...

2.54   Source Lists, Numbering of

Individual entries in a source list are rarely numbered. An exception is made for lecture handouts or syllabus material used in instructional settings where we refer our audiences to bibliographic items. In those situations, bibliographic items are usually numbered for quick reference during the presentation. We do not have to list those numbered items alphabetically if our instruction might progress more smoothly by numbering the sources in the sequence in which we reference them in class.

STYLISTIC MATTERS

2.55   Abbreviations

Because abbreviations rarely save a significant amount of space, the thoughtful writer avoids all but the truly obvious ones. The following summarizes standard conventions in historical writing:

COLUMN, NOTE, PAGE, SERIES, VOLUME, ETC.
In reference notes, we may abbreviate common words that refer to parts of a publication, such as *col.* for *column, n.* for *note, p.* for *page, ser.* for *series,* and *vol.* for *volume.* Page numbers need not be preceded by *p.* when citing books and articles. When citing censuses, newspapers, or other records that involve references to several types of numbers (e.g., p. 3, col. 2), the inclusion of *p.* before the page number and *col.* before the column number is needed for clarity.

CREDENTIALS, DEGREES & HONORIFICS
Traditionally, the abbreviations for credentials, degrees, and honorifics have been punctuated with periods. However, most are commonly written today as initialisms without punctuation, sometimes in a mix of upper- and lower-case letters. For example:

CG	Certified Genealogist
JD	Doctor of Jurisprudence
MLS	Master of Library Science
PhD	Doctor of Philosophy

PERSONAL NAMES
We abbreviate personal names only if they are abbreviated in our source. An author who writes under the name *William Randolph Meriwether* should not be cited as "Wm. Meriwether" or "W. R. Meriwether." Similarly, an author who is known historically by his or her initials should be identified that way (e.g., O. Henry, H. G. Wells).

PLACE NAMES

The canons of narrative writing (outside of newspapers) frown on abbreviations of place names amid text. In reference notes, we may use standard abbreviations (see 2.56), within reason.

POSTAL CODES

After the adoption of postal codes by various nations, style guides typically limited the use of these codes to postal addresses and encouraged the continued use of standard abbreviations. That distinction is no longer required by most guides, although narrative writers are still governed by the proscription against abbreviating the names of states and provinces within narrative text.

TEXT

Abbreviations are used sparingly in narrative writing. The most common usage is for standard titles that precede a name (e.g., Mrs. John Wentworth, or Gen. Oliver Spoonsypher).

TITLES OF WORKS

Words that are spelled out in full in the original title should not be abbreviated when citing that title. If we are creating a title or label of our own, we do not abbreviate. If we are citing a title that includes an abbreviation, we must copy that abbreviation exactly. (Example: If *Indiana* appears in a title as *Ind.*, we do not change that to the modern postal code *IN*.)

2.56 Abbreviations, Standard

adv.	=	*adversus*	no.	=	*number*
aka	=	*also known as*	n.p.	=	*no page number shown*
assn.	=	*association*		=	*no publication place*
bk.	=	*book*		=	*no publisher shown*
c./ca.	=	*circa*	NS	=	*new series, new style*
cf.	=	*compare*	OS	=	*old series, old style*
Chap.	=	*chapter*	p. (pp.)	=	*page(s)*
Co.	=	*County, Company*	par.	=	*paragraph*
col.	=	*column*	p.p.	=	*privately printed*
comp.	=	*compiler*	pt.	=	*part*
dept.	=	*department*	q.v.	=	*which see (cross reference)*
ed.	=	*edition, editor*	rev. ed.	=	*revised edition*
eds.	=	*editors*	RG	=	*record group*
e.g.	=	*for example*	sect.	=	*section*
et al.	=	*and others*	ser.	=	*series*
fo.	=	*folio*	supp.	=	*supplement*
ff.	=	*and following*	transcr.	=	*transcriber*
ibid.	=	*ibidem*	transl.	=	*translator*
i.e.	=	*that is to say*	v./vs.	=	*versus*
MS (MSS)	=	*manuscript(s)*	vers.	=	*version*

n. (nn.)	=	*note(s)*	viz.	=	*namely*
n.d.	=	*no date of publication*	vol.	=	*volume*

2.57 Acronyms & Initialisms

Acronyms for resources and repositories should be kept to a minimum. When we make a decision to use one throughout our work, the following guidelines apply:

TEXT

The first mention of that entity should state the name in full, followed by the acronym in parentheses. Example:

> Library and Archives Canada (LAC)

CITATIONS

Our Source List Entries should write the name in full and may include the acronym if we wish. In any piece of writing or database, the First Reference Note in which you mention the item should follow the same practice we follow in writing text. We do not have to add the common but wordy phrase *hereinafter cited as*. Thereafter, we may simply use the acronym. For example:

Source List Entry

Pennsylvania. Bedford County. Assessment Books, 1841–1844. Board of County Commissioners Office, Bedford. Microfilm. Family History Library (FHL), Salt Lake City, Utah.

Virginia. Buckingham County. Land Tax Roll, 1804. Library of Virginia, Richmond. FHL microfilm 29,290. Family History Library, Salt Lake City, Utah.

First Reference Note

1. Bedford County (Pennsylvania), Assessment Book, 1842: Dublin Township, p. 8, William Henesy; microfilm 1,449,113, Family History Library (FHL), Salt Lake City, Utah.

2. Buckingham County (Virginia), 1804 Land Tax Roll, District 1, unpaginated but alphabetized entry for John Smith Anderson; FHL microfilm 29,290.

2.58 Braces & Brackets

BRACES { }

Also known as *curly brackets*, braces are a device common to mathematical and technical fields. Given their specific applications in computer programming, it is best to avoid them in narrative writing and citations.

73

ANGLE BRACKETS < >
In the past, angle brackets were frequently used to set off electronic addresses. The practice is now discouraged because HTML computer language uses angle brackets in a different sense.

SQUARE (EDITORIAL) BRACKETS [ ]
Square brackets, also called editorial brackets, have two common uses:

- *To signify that we have added words not found in the original source.* Parentheses should not be substituted, because authors regularly use parentheses in their writing. If we use parentheses for editorial additions, our readers will have no way of knowing that the parenthetical material is not that of the original writer.

- *To create "parentheses within parentheses"*—e.g.,

> In 1829, Randolph disposed of Evergreen Plantation (some researchers allege that it was seized to satisfy a court judgment [Riddell, *The Randolphs,* 239] or a tax lien [Mason, *Randolphs and Lewises,* 39] although neither offer evidence); he then migrated ...

When you quote material containing editorial brackets (as when quoting from edited papers and translated works) you should quote that material exactly, followed by your own note of explanation in parentheses. To illustrate, you might write the following passage:

> Census takers of the 1800s were often political appointees, unfamiliar with the cultures they canvassed. The edited diary of one enumerator vents his frustration this way: "Of all the trials I've faced, the Spaniards back in the hills take the prize. From the house of Adow Tobasco [Adout Basco] down to Honkey E. Barb [José y Barbo], not a one could speak decent English." (Brackets added by the diary's editor.)

2.59 Capitalization, General Usage

Within narrative writing, by American practice, capitalization should be limited to proper nouns—names of people, names of places, official names of organizations and agencies, official titles, etc. We do not capitalize names of parts such as *volume, book, roll,* and *census* unless they are part of a formal title that we place in quotation marks or italics.

2.60 Capitalization, Publication Titles

BASIC RULE
INITIAL CAPS .... English titles typically follow Headline Style, capitalizing all words except articles (*a, an, the*),

coordinating conjunctions (*and, but, nor, or*), and prepositions. However, all of these are capitalized when used as the first word of a title or subtitle. The casual practice of capitalizing long words and lower-casing small words is incorrect.

Foreign languages follow other conventions. French titles capitalize only the first word and proper nouns. German titles capitalize only nouns. For other languages, consult a style guide for that language. Using sentence-style capitalization, in which you capitalize only the first word and proper nouns, is a practical alternative.

Note: American library catalogers also capitalize only the first word of a title. However, that practice has not been accepted by most style manuals for writing and publishing.

OTHER CONVENTIONS

ALL CAPS .... Setting a title entirely in capital letters is frowned upon as an offense to typography. It crowds the lines of type and visually overwhelms. Instead, book titles should be italicized, or underlined if italics are not available.

ASCII FILES .... When creating messages for listserves or databases that require the use of ASCII, the limitations of that computer language create an exception to the All Caps rule above. Capitalization of titles (but not other words in the text) is an acceptable substitute for italics whenever italics cannot be generated by the electronic system in use. As an alternative, you may insert an asterisk or an underscore immediately before and after the title to indicate italics.

CORRECTIONS .... If a publication's title page uses incorrect capitalization, we should correct the usage in our citations. (Capitalization in original documents or register titles should be left "as is.") If the title of a book or article ignores punctuation conventions or omits diacritical marks, we should correct the problem. Otherwise, our readers will assume *we* committed the offense. (See also 2.76 for titles to unpublished works.)

75

> This correction is an exception to the rule that we do not alter titles. While we cannot change the *words* of the title, we can and should properly capitalize and punctuate the title.

2.61 Capitalization, Small Caps

Small caps are uppercase letters reduced to *x-height*—i.e., the height of the lowercase *x* in the font we are using. Many word-processing programs have a small-caps option to automatically create a proper size and weight. Small caps are conventionally used for postnominals after a name and sometimes for acronyms and initialisms, particularly long ones that visually overwhelm text lines when letters are set in all caps. Examples:

ACRONYMS & INITIALISMS

> UNICEF *rather than* UNICEF

CREDENTIALS & DEGREES

> Donald Lines Jacobus, FASG
> James Meredith, PhD

2.62 Capitalization, Untitled Items

When citing documents or manuscripts that have no formal title, we have to create a label that answers the basic questions *who, what, when,* and *where.* For those labels, we may choose to follow the Initial Caps Rule given at 2.60 for publication titles, or we may capitalize only the first letter of the first word. For example:

- Defaulters' Tax List of 1799, Natchitoches Post, Louisiana
- Defaulters' tax list of 1799, Natchitoches Post, Louisiana

2.63 Colons

Following conventional citations for the most part, Evidence Style citations use colons in four ways.

PERIODICALS

A colon, followed by a space, appears before the page number(s) in citations to articles in journals and magazines.

PUBLICATION DATA

A colon, followed by a space, separates the place of publication from the publisher and date of publication (or, in website citations, the URL from the date of publication).

URL CITATIONS

A colon—preceded by a space and followed by a space—separates the URL (the website publication address) from the date of publication (or date of access). The extra space is inserted between the URL and the colon so that the punctuation mark will not be perceived as part of the URL itself.

VOLUME: PAGE

When a volume is cited by its number or letter, rather than its name, a colon separates the volume number or letter from the page number. We may insert a space after the colon or use none (e.g., 2: 33 or 2:33). Whichever manner we choose, we should be consistent.

2.64   Commas

Historical writing and citing call for care in the use of commas in two particular ways:

SEPARATION OF CITATION ELEMENTS

Citations to manuscript materials typically identify a number of elements, each of which may have internal parts. Semicolons are used to mark the major divisions (see 2.74). Within each of those units, commas separate the smaller parts. For example:

> 1. Compiled service card for David Kiepler, Pvt., Co. C, 131st New York Infantry; Carded Records, Volunteer Organizations, Civil War; Records of the Adjutant General's Office, 1780s–1917, Record Group 94; National Archives, Washington, D.C.

In this example, the major parts (the soldier's identification and the names of the collection, the record group, and the archive) are each separated by semicolons. Commas are then used internally when a major element has multiple parts.

SEPARATION OF DATES AND LOCALES

Places and dates often include a string of elements that, for clarity, are separated by commas. For example:

> On April 16, 1746, at Culloden ...
> Boise, Idaho, was settled in 1863 ...

In each case, the element with the comma before and after it modifies the one immediately preceding it. The year *1746* modifies *April 16.* *Idaho* modifies *Boise.* In grammatical terms (the Appositive Rule), 1746 and Idaho are *appositives,* and should be both preceded *and followed* by commas. The closing comma should not be overlooked, any more than we would omit closing a set of parentheses.

2.65 Dashes vs. Hyphens

Historical writing and sourcing commonly use four types of dashes, in addition to hyphens. Most word-processing programs and operating systems have shortcuts, macros, or codes that can be used to create the special em dash and en dash characters. Most style guides suggest that dashes, like the hyphen, should carry no space before or after them. The differences in these characters are as follows:

HYPHEN (-)

The hyphen, an extremely short raised line, is used to *connect* compound words or to join parts of a word that is broken at the end of a line of text. It is also used to connect the segments of long numbers such as those used for Social Security and telephone numbers.

EM DASH (—)

This raised line, which is the width of the letter *m* in most fonts, is used to strongly *separate* items—as in this sentence, where it sets one thought off from another related thought. If a thought is set off by an em dash in the *middle* of a sentence, an em dash should both precede and follow the thought. (Example: the first sentence at 2.37.)

EN DASH (–)

This raised line, which is the width of the letter *n* in most fonts, is used for several functions—almost always to *connect* items.

To connect a range of dates or numbers, as in

pages 35–67
the 1942–45 internment of Japanese Americans

The en dash represents the thought *from ... to.* The frequently seen usage "from pages 35–67" is redundant and incorrect.

To connect compound adjectives, when one of the adjectives is itself a compound, as in

the post–Civil War period

To indicate that a date or number sequence is open-ended, as in

Boston: Atlas Press, 2000–
Michael Mucklefuss (1950–)

2-EM DASH (——)

This raised line, formed by typing two consecutive em dashes, is used to show that part of a word is missing. We occasionally find it used in historical documents when the writer expressed an expletive by using the first letter of the word followed by a dash.

3-EM DASH (————)

This raised line, formed by typing three consecutive em dashes, is commonly used in bibliographic entries for authors who have produced multiple works. In those cases, the author's name is given fully in the first instance. For each additional source by that author, the author's name is replaced by the 3-em dash. For example:

> Debo, Angie. *And Still the Waters Run*. New York: Gordian Press, 1966.
> ————. *Rise and Fall of the Choctaw Republic*. 2d ed. Norman: Oklahoma
>   University Press, 1961.

SUBSTITUTIONS

A single hyphen should never be substituted for an em dash, given that the hyphen's purpose is to *connect,* while the em dash's purpose is to *separate.* Traditionally, the rules have been these:

- A hyphen may be substituted for an *en* dash.
- Two consecutive hyphens can substitute for an *em* dash.

The proper use of an em dash or two hyphens can be thwarted by substitutions built into some popular software programs that automatically convert double hyphens and em dashes into single hyphens. Doing so unfortunately *connects* what we intend to *separate.* One work-around with some software is to substitute three hyphens for the em dash.

2.66   Dates

The popular convention for citing dates in the United States differs from the more-common international convention. History researchers whose work crosses national bounds, however, favor the international convention. For example:

AMERICAN USAGE .... On April 16, 1746, at the Battle of Culloden ...
INTERNATIONAL USAGE ..... On 16 April 1746 at the Battle of Culloden ...

The common American usage follows the Appositives Rule cited at 2.64, using a comma for clarity to separate the *day* (expressed as a number) from the *year* (expressed as a number). The international convention for dates is an exception to the Appositives Rule, because no comma is needed for clarity.

The American military convention, which places a zero before one-digit dates (04 July rather than 4 July) is often followed in historical databases but not in historical narratives.

See also 2.75, Slashes (Virgules).

2.67 Ellipses

When copying text or titles exactly, if you choose to omit words, you should mark the omission with ellipsis points—i.e., three dots, preceded and followed by a space. Some style manuals recommend also putting a space between each dot. Most word-processing programs, however, add spaces only before and after the series and may automatically 'correct' us when we use the extra spaces.

When considering whether to use ellipses to shorten very long titles, two guidelines apply. First, use them cautiously; you do not want to omit critical words of the title or subtitle. Second, use them only if you are omitting words in the *middle* of a title. If you simply drop the final words of a long subtitle, you do not place ellipsis points at the end of your short form. By way of example, consider this publication:

FULL TITLE

    1. H. F. O'Beirne, *Leaders and Leading Men of the Indian Territory, with Interesting Biographical Sketches: Choctaws and Chickasaws, with a Brief History of Each Tribe, Its Laws, Customs, Superstitions and Religious Beliefs, Profusely Illustrated with over Two Hundred Portraits and Full-Page Engravings* (Chicago: American Publishers Association, 1891).

SHORTER TITLE, USING AN ELLIPSIS

    1. H. F. O'Beirne, *Leaders and Leading Men of the Indian Territory ... Choctaws and Chickasaws* (Chicago: American Publishers Association, 1891).

2.68 Italics (or Underscoring)

Italics are used for emphasis. The five common circumstances that require italics are these:

FOREIGN WORDS

The first time you use a foreign word in a piece of writing, you should italicize it. Thereafter, you may set the word in roman type.

LEGAL CASE LABELS

Legal-style citation guides suggest various practices, depending upon the jurisdiction, the court, and the style manual they follow. For Humanities Style writing, simpler rules apply.

- Case labels of *published* criminal and civil suits—those officially published in court reporters (see 13.5, 13.18, and 13.20)—typically italicize the plaintiff and defendant names. The Latin adverbs that link the two *(versus* and *adversus)* are rendered in roman type:

    Hansford v. *George*
    George adv. *Hansford*

- Case labels of *unpublished* criminal and civil suits—i.e., those *not* officially published in court reporters—should not be placed in italics because italics signify that the case has been published. Unpublished cases can be written simply as

    Hansford v. George
    George adv. Hansford

When using roman type for an unpublished case label, as above, we may italicize the Latin adverbs that link the plaintiff and defendant names, if we wish. Note, however, that legal citations use *v.* to abbreviate *versus,* rather than *vs.* which prevails in nonlegal usage.

PUBLICATION TITLES
When italics are used for the title of a work, they tell readers that the work has been *published.* Readers who need to locate the work will then seek that title in catalogs for books, periodicals, or published film and digital recordings.

Italics should not be used for the titles of unpublished manuscripts or preservation microfilm.

Individual parts of a publication are *not* italicized—for example: chapters within a book, articles within a journal, or databases on a CD. (Titles to these parts are placed in quotation marks. See 2.72.)

SHIP NAMES
The names of ships should be italicized. When the name is preceded by an initialism that describes the type of vessel, the initialism is not italicized. Example:

    MV *Cape Washington*
    SS *Humboldt*
    USS *Asheville*

WORDS AS A TERM
When we need to refer to a word, as a word, we italicize it or place it in quotation marks. Examples:

> The word *infant* is legally defined as ...
> The term "son-in-law" once meant ...

Either usage is acceptable and one or the other may be preferable, depending upon the context of what you are writing.

2.69 Latinisms

Latin terms were once commonly used as a means of shortening citations. *Op. cit.* (previously cited), *supra* (above), and *vide infra* (see below) are now obsolete.

Two other Latinisms remain in everyday use: *sic* (meaning "There's an error here that I'm copying exactly, but I'm also pointing it out so you won't think the error is mine") and *ibid.* Several particulars need to be borne in mind when using the latter:

- *Ibid.* is presented in regular (roman) type amid text and notes without italics. *Sic* always carries italics.
- *Ibid.* means "in the same source as above."
- *Ibid.* is not used if the prior note cites multiple sources.
- *Ibid.* is not used if the prior note includes a discussion as well as a citation of the source.
- *Ibid.* is not used until the final manuscript is prepared. When used in preliminary drafts, a rearrangement of text or notes can separate an *ibid.* from the preceding note to which it belongs. Thereafter, the citation represented by that *ibid.* will be incorrect.

Ibid., when used in place of citation elements, is not italicized.

2.70 Parentheses

Parentheses are used by writers to add details that modify or amplify something they have just cited. The most common usages are these:

MODIFIERS

In text or in a citation, parentheses are often used to add descriptors or identifiers—e.g.,

> 1. Montgomery County, Alabama, Conveyance Book R (Old Series), 631; Office of the Probate Judge, Montgomery.

NAMES, MAIDEN

The discipline of genealogy uses parentheses to distinguish the *maiden* names of married females. In the case of females who have a succession of husbands, the parentheses should not be placed around the other surnames she acquired by marriage—e.g.,

> Hannah (Baskel) Phelps Phelps Hill
>
> *not*
> Hannah (Baskel) (Phelps) (Phelps) Hill

When you are uncertain whether a woman's surname represents her maiden name, you should not use parentheses. Many females from the late-eighteenth century forward have carried family surnames as their second given name—e.g., Ann Smith Anderson.

If you assumed that Smith must be her maiden name and added parentheses around that name, you would mislead yourself and others.

PUBLICATION DATA

Parentheses are typically used in Humanities Style citations to set off the publication data for books and journals. By extension, they should also be used to set off website publication data. For example:

> 1. Yaakov Kleiman, *DNA and Tradition* (New York: Devora Publishing, 2004), 23.
> 2. Ira Berlin, "Southern Free People of Color in the Age of William Johnson," *The Southern Quarterly* 43 (Winter 2006): 9–17.
> 3. Cornell University Library, *Making of America* (http://cdl .library.cornell.edu/moa/ : 16 July 2006), search term: *Browse*.

Because parentheses modify the word or term before them, a common punctuation rule applies: Parentheses may be *followed* by another punctuation mark, but they are never *preceded* by one—except when enumerating. To illustrate:

PERMISSIBLE USE OF COLONS & SEMICOLONS BEFORE PARENTHESES

Land Entry files created by the General Land Office consist of 4 types: (1) credit files, 1800–30 June 1820; (2) cash files, 30 June 1820–30 June 1908; (3) donation files, 1842–1903; and (4) homestead files, 1863–30 June 1908.

IMPROPER USE OF PUNCTUATION BEFORE PARENTHESES

> 4. Howard H. Wehmann and Benjamin L. DeWhitt, *A Guide to Pre-Federal Records in the National Archives,* (Washington: National Archives and Records Administration, 1989).

Commas and colons, in Humanities Style citations, serve another function that distinguishes a book citation from a journal citation. As illustrated by note 1 above, a *comma* is placed after the closing parenthesis that contains book-publication data. As shown in note 2 above, a *colon* is placed after the closing parenthesis for a periodical's publication date. The distinction is minor, but expected.

2.71 Placement of Punctuation

When two separate punctuation marks appear in sequence, rules usually govern their placement. The following represent the most common of them.

COMMAS &

QUOTATION MARKS ...... Commas go *inside* double quotation marks and usually appear *outside* single quotation marks.

PARENTHESES .... A comma never appears *before* an opening parenthesis, except when enumerating items. One may go *after* a closing parenthesis.

QUOTATION MARKS

DOUBLE .... The closing double quotation mark is placed *inside* a semicolon. It is placed *outside* a comma or a period. If the quoted matter is itself a question, then the question mark also goes *inside* the closing quotation mark.

SINGLE .... If single quotation marks are used around a word or phrase in the *so-called* sense, then the closing quotation mark is placed *before* a colon, comma, period, question mark, or semicolon. If single quotation marks are used for a quotation inside of other quoted matter, then the closing mark usually belongs *before* all other punctuation marks. If the quoted matter itself is a question, then the question mark also goes *before* the single closing quotation mark.

REFERENCE NOTE NUMBERS

When a reference note number appears adjacent to another punctuation mark, it is placed *after* that other mark.

2.72 Quotation Marks

Quotation marks can be the most important punctuation devices in the tool kit of researchers and writers. They are the tools we use to guard against errors, avoid plagiarism, and prevent unintentional violations of copyright. As prompters on the stage of history, they silently shout an aside in almost every scene: "When you see me, it means that my words are copied exactly from another source!"

Quotation marks have two forms: *double-quote* marks and *single-quote* marks. The most common usage for single quotes is for words that are quoted within a larger quote.

Quotation marks also have a secondary usage as a literary device that can create ambiguity in historical writing. In a literary sense, they are sometimes placed around a word—often in a pejorative or derogatory context, or to denote irony—to give that word the sense of *so-called*. Because precision and accuracy are paramount to historical research, there may be times when you will want to use single quotation marks for this *so-called* sense.

In historical writing and sourcing, double quotation marks are typically used in three ways:

EXACT QUOTES
Whenever a string of *three or more words* are copied from another source, those words should be placed in double-quote marks.

When we quote *two or more paragraphs* from a document, the preferred convention is to indent and block the quotation, in which case no quotation marks are needed. If, however, our indented and blocked material represents an extract from a document, in which we copy some words and phrases exactly and paraphrase or summarize other passages, we should place quotation marks around the words that are copied exactly.

Less preferable for long quotations, but sometimes necessary, is to weave the quotation into the text. When we do so, the convention is to put quotation marks in three places—(*a*) the start of the quotation, (*b*) the start of each new paragraph of that quotation, and (*c*) the end of quotation. In other words: every paragraph has an opening quotation mark at its beginning, but only the final paragraph has a closing quotation mark at its end.

MANUSCRIPT TITLES
Whenever a manuscript carries a formal title, you should copy that title exactly and place double-quote marks around it. Whenever you create a label for an untitled manuscript, you *do not* place those words in quotation marks. You are not quoting anything; you are creating a new string of words.

NICKNAMES
The genealogical convention for writing nicknames is to place them in quotation marks immediately after the formal name for which they substitute—e.g., Margaret "Peg" Monroe.

PUBLISHED TITLES
When you cite a titled *part* of a publication—e.g., a chapter of a book,

an article in a journal, or a database at a website that has many offerings—you should copy the title exactly and place quotation marks around it.

2.73 Roman Numerals

Roman numerals have a long history in publishing. Most of their uses, however, have gone the way of other Latinisms. Of the three situations in which roman numerals have been traditionally cited, only one (page numbers) remains essential. The prevailing practices are as follows:

PAGE NUMBERS

Traditionally, a book's prefatory material has been numbered with small roman numerals, while the main body of the book is numbered in arabic. This practice is changing to the use of a single sequence of arabic numbers. However, when we cite pages that bear roman numerals, our citation must use those roman numerals.

PUBLICATION DATES

When a publication uses roman numerals for its date, the modern practice is to convert these to arabic numbers.

VOLUME NUMBERS

When a publication uses roman numerals for its volume numbers or part numbers, the modern practice is to convert these to arabic.

2.74 Semicolons

As a grammatical device, semicolons separate major elements in a sentence. In *narratives,* they commonly appear in two situations:

COMPOUND SENTENCES

When we construct a compound sentence—one containing two or more complete subject-verb constructions—we place a semicolon between the two parts of the sentence.

SIMPLE SENTENCES

When a simple sentence—a sentence with just one complete subject-verb construction—refers to several items in a series and when one or more of those items have internal commas, we use semicolons to separate the items.

In *citations,* semicolons are used for the same separation purposes. The five most common situations in which we employ them in citations are these:

SEPARATING MAJOR ELEMENTS IN A COMPLEX CITATION

A manuscript typically exists in a collection that is part of a series that is in turn part of record group, etc. To fully identify the manuscript, we have to cite all these levels in the archival hierarchy. Often, the description we use at each level will have internal commas. Therefore, we use semicolons to separate the major levels. For example:

> 1. Moses Daniell claim, June 1838, "Original Record of Spoilations, No. 2," pp. 262–63; Decisions on Spoilation Claims, 1838; Records of the First Board of Cherokee Commissioners; Cherokee Removal Records, 1817–1884; Records of the Bureau of Indian Affairs, Record Group 75; National Archives, Washington, D.C.

SEPARATING A SOURCE FROM A DISCUSSION OF THAT SOURCE

In our working files, when we cite a source we should describe the nature of that source. Doing so ensures that we and others can, now and later, appraise more accurately the reliability of the information that source provides. When we publish our own work and cite a source, we may want to include a comment about the nature and validity of the source. If the comment is short, we can include that comment in the same sentence that identifies the source. For example:

> 1. Ron Tyler and Lawrence R. Murphy, eds., *The Slave Narratives of Texas* (Austin: State House Press, 1997), 83; this work offers snippets from each slave's reminiscence, rearranging the snippets by subject.

SEPARATING THE ORIGINAL SOURCE FROM ITS DERIVATIVE FORM

Citations to published, filmed, or digitized historical materials often involve two levels of citation—one for the source, the other for the derivative format in which we used it. Typically, a semicolon separates the two. For example:

> 1. Ontario Registrar General, "Death Registrations, 1869–1933," Nicholas B. Gustin registration no. 2668 (1869); microfilm 1,846,464, Family History Library, Salt Lake City, Utah.

SEPARATING MULTIPLE SOURCES CITED IN SAME REFERENCE NOTE

Historians often synthesize findings from a number of sources—combining their views into a paragraph or so. At the close of that paragraph, they may insert a single reference number keyed to a note that cites all the published sources they have just synthesized. In this practice, the citations of all those publications will be linked into a single sentence, typically with semicolons separating each source from the other.

Evidence Style encourages a greater level of precision in the identification of sources, for two reasons.

- Chapter 1 set forth a principle already followed in some disciplines: every statement of fact should carry its *own individual citation of source*. Following that principle guarantees that we and our readers will always know the exact source of every piece of information, so that we can better appraise the reliability of each and every statement.

- Users of *Evidence* are typically heavy users of manuscript materials that require complex citations. Those citations normally contain internal semicolons—as with the National Archives citations at 2.45, at the beginning of this present section (2.74) and much more fully in Chapter 11. If we use semicolons to link multiple sources that each contain internal semicolons, we make it difficult to discern where one source stops and the next source starts.

SEPARATING THE SOURCE FROM ITS SOURCE

When we use a published source that cites its own source, our citation will focus upon the derivative that we actually used. However, it is good practice to record also where our source obtained his or her information. Depending upon the complexity of the situation, we may need to separate the two with a semicolon, as in example 1, or we may separate them more simply with a comma, as in example 2.

> 1. David Hackett Fischer, *Albion's Seed: Four British Folkways in America* (New York: Oxford University Press, 1989), 372; Fischer states in n. 8 that he computed fertility cycles from data first published by Carville Earle, *The Evolution of a Tidewater Settlement System* (Chicago: University of Chicago Press, 1975), 159.
>
> 2. Marylynn Salmon, *Women and the Law of Property in Early America* (Chapel Hill: University of North Carolina Press, 1986), 31, citing "Hening, *Laws of Virginia*, 4:397–401."

For clarity and precision, *Evidence* recommends that *periods—not semicolons*—be used to separate sources when it is necessary to cite multiple sources in a single citation. In the example below, the periods on lines three and seven make clear divisions between three sources that have complex descriptions.

> 1. Recensement général de habituoux et habitans de la Louisianne ... premier Janvier 1726; Archives Colonies G^1 464; Archives d'Outre-Mer, Aix-en-Provence, France. De la Chaise to Directors of the Company, 6 and 10 September 1723, translated in Dunbar Rowland and

Albert Godfrey Sanders, *Mississippi Provincial Archives, 1701–1729: French Dominion*, vol. 2 (Jackson: Mississippi Department of Archives and History, 1929), 315.   Rex vs. Cesario, Francisco, et al., labeled "Año de 1777 ... Criminales: Quiere sigue de oficio contra los Negros Cezario, Fran^{co} Christoval, Noel, y la Negra Margarita," folder 3671, doc. no. 1777-03-13-01, Judicial Records of the Spanish Cabildo, Louisiana Historical Center, New Orleans; 58 unnumbered pages.

2.75   Slashes (Virgules)

Slashes, also known as virgules, are conventionally used to express *alternatives*. As such, historical writers typically use them in three contexts:

CITING DATES

During the long transition from the Julian Calendar to the modern Gregorian Calendar, many English and American documents used a system of double-dating. The Julian Calendar began its year on 25 March. The Gregorian Calendar begins on 1 January. Most European countries made the conversion between 1582 and 1587. England and its colonies did not convert until 2 September 1752. By the 1700s, many scribes were double-dating events that occurred between 1 January and 25 March. In this practice, the date

> 1 February 1732/3

would be 1732 under the Julian Calendar and 1733 under the Gregorian Calendar. Note that, in double-dating, only the *last* digit is replaced—not the last two digits, except at the turn of a decade:

> *For double-dating due to a calendar change:*
> 1 March 1732/3
> 1 March 1749/50

Some writers and software programs substitute slashes for en dashes to indicate a *range* of dates, as in

> The transatlantic voyage occurred about 1676/77 ....

Using slashes for this purpose creates ambiguity. While the writer would intend, above, to say that the voyage occurred *sometime during those two years*, the statement could be interpreted to mean that it occurred during January–March of the year called 1676 by the Julian Calendar or 1677 by the Gregorian Calendar.

As discussed at 2.65, date ranges are conventionally expressed with en dashes (1676–77).

NARRATIVE WRITING

In *narrative writing*, slashes typically indicate alternatives, as in

She/he *or* Abram/Abraham

TRANSCRIBING

When *transcribing* a document, some researchers prefer to use a slash to mark the ends of lines or page breaks.

Slashes should be used sparingly. Long strings of words joined by slashes are disconcerting, if not confusing. Particularly egregious to most readers is a string placed in all capital letters, such as

Robert ROBICHAUX/ROBICHAU/ROBICHO/ROBISHO/ROBISHOW.

Variant spellings such as these are more effectively handled with parentheses and commas, as in

Robert Robichaux (var. Robichau, Robicho, Robisho, Robishow).

2.76 Titles

The punctuation of titles is variously handled, depending upon whether you are citing a manuscript or a published work. For manuscripts whose titles are copied exactly and placed within quotation marks, capitalization should conform to the original and any punctuation you add should be placed in square editorial brackets. On the other hand (as discussed at 2.60), titles of published works such as books or CDs are often *typographically designed* titles that break up the title across several lines and omit punctuation marks at the ends of those lines. When we convert those titles to a sentence-style citation, we are expected to add the proper punctuation for clarity. Principally, this involves:

- adding a colon between the title and subtitle; and

- ensuring that appositives have a comma after them as well as before them (see 2.64).

ARCHIVES & ARTIFACTS

3

QuickCheck Models

Guidelines & Examples (beginning page 116)

QuickCheck Model
ARCHIVED MATERIAL: ARTIFACT
Creator as lead element in Source List

Source List Entry

CREATOR	ARTIFACT TITLE (QUOTED EXACTLY)	ITEM TYPE

Horst, "Aunt Ella," et al. "Amish Friendship Sampler Album." Quilt.

CREATION DATE	COLLECTION	REPOSITORY ...

ca. 1876–1900. Michigan Quilt Project. Michigan State University

...	REPOSITORY LOCATION

Museum, East Lansing.

First (Full) Reference Note

CREATOR	ARTIFACT TITLE	ITEM TYPE

1. "Aunt Ella" Horst et al., "Amish Friendship Sampler Album," quilt,

CREATION DATE	ITEM NO.	COLLECTION	REPOSITORY ...

ca. 1876–1900; item 01.0011, Michigan Quilt Project; Michigan State

...	REPOSITORY LOCATION	DESCRIPTIVE DETAIL ...

University Museum, East Lansing, Michigan. The archival description

... RELEVANT TO THE RESEARCH PROJECT

identifies the quilt makers collectively as "Friends of Annie Risser Horst."

Subsequent (Short) Note

CREATOR	ARTIFACT TITLE	COLLECTION ...

11. Horst et al., "Amish Friendship Sampler Album," Michigan Quilt

...

Project.

93

QuickCheck Model
ARCHIVED MATERIAL: DIGITAL ARCHIVES
Collection (database) as lead element in Source List

Source List Entry

COLLECTION   ITEM TYPE or...

"Southeastern Native American Documents, 1730–1842." Images and

... FORMAT   WEBSITE CREATOR-OWNER   WEBSITE TITLE

transcriptions. University System of Georgia. *Digital Library of Georgia.*

URL (DIGITAL LOCATION)   YEAR

http://dlg.galileo.usg.edu : 2006.

First (Full) Reference Note

COLLECTION   ...

1. "Southeastern Native American Documents, 1730–1842," Uni-

... WEBSITE OWNER / CREATOR   WEBSITE TITLE   URL (DIGITAL LOCATION) ...

versity System of Georgia, *Digital Library of Georgia* (http://dlg.galileo.usg

...   DATE   ITEM TYPE or FORMAT   DOCUMENT TITLE ...

.edu : accessed 22 August 2006), transcription, "Cherokee Council Minutes,

... (QUOTED EXACTLY)   PAGE   CREDIT LINE ...

1818 May 20 [to] 27, Cherokee Agency," p. 9; crediting "State Library

... (SOURCE OF THE SOURCE)

Cherokee Collection, Tennessee State Library and Archives, Nashville."

Subsequent (Short) Note

COLLECTION   ...

11. "Southeastern Native American Documents, 1730–1842," *Digital*

... WEBSITE TITLE   DOCUMENT TITLE (SHORTENED)   PAGE

Library of Georgia, "Cherokee Council Minutes, 1818," 9.

QuickCheck Model
ARCHIVED MATERIAL: MANUSCRIPT RECORDS
Collection as lead element in Source List

Source List Entry

<u>COLLECTION ...</u>

Vaudreuil Papers (Papers of Pierre de Rigaud, Marquis de Vaudreuil), 1740–

...   <u>REPOSITORY</u>   ...

1753. Loudoun Collection. Huntington Library and Art Gallery, San

... REPOSITORY LOCATION

Marino, California.

First (Full) Reference Note

<u>RECORD TITLE (QUOTED EXACTLY) ...</u>

1. "État De La Force Actuel De La Comp^e De La Mazillier destaché Au

...   <u>RECORD DATE</u>   <u>ITEM or PIECE</u>   <u>ITEM or PIECE NUMBER</u>   <u>COLLECTION ...</u>

Illinois," 2 September 1752; Letterbook, MS LO 377; Vaudreuil Papers

...

(Papers of Pierre de Rigaud, Marquis de Vaudreuil), 1740–1753; Loudoun

...   <u>REPOSITORY</u>   <u>REPOSITORY LOCATION</u>

Collection; Huntington Library and Art Gallery, San Marino, California.

<u>EVALUATION</u>

[ADD DESCRIPTIVE DETAILS THAT AFFECT YOUR ANALYSIS OF THE DOCUMENT.]

Subsequent (Short) Note

<u>RECORD TITLE & DATE (SHORTENED)</u>   <u>COLLECTION</u>   <u>ITEM or PIECE NUMBER</u>

11. "État De La Force ... Illinois," 1752, Vaudreuil Papers, MS LO 377.

QuickCheck Model
ARCHIVED MATERIAL: MANUSCRIPT RECORDS
Document as lead element in Source List

Source List Entry

<u>TITLE OF DOCUMENT (QUOTED EXACTLY) ...</u>

"Muster Roll of Captain [Joseph] Martin's Company of Pittsylvania Militia

<u>...</u>   <u>SERIES NO. & NAME</u>   <u>COLLECTION</u>   <u>...</u>

in 1774." Series XX, Tennessee Papers, Draper Manuscripts. Wisconsin

<u>... REPOSITORY</u>   <u>REPOSITORY LOCATION</u>

Historical Society, Madison.

First (Full) Reference Note

<u>DOCUMENT TITLE (QUOTED EXACTLY) ...</u>

1. "Muster Roll of Captain [Joseph] Martin's Company of Pittsylvania

<u>...</u>   <u>SERIES NO. & NAME</u>   <u>LOCATION WITHIN SERIES</u>   <u>...</u>

Militia in 1774," Series XX, Tennessee Papers, vol. 1, p. 6; Draper

<u>... COLLECTION</u>   <u>REPOSITORY</u>   <u>REPOSITORY LOCATION</u>

Manuscripts, Wisconsin Historical Society, Madison.

Subsequent (Short) Note

<u>DOCUMENT TITLE & DATE (SHORTENED)</u>   <u>SERIES</u>

11. "Muster Roll of Captain Martin's Company ... 1774," Series XX,

<u>VOL./ PAGE</u>   <u>COLLECTION</u>

1: 6; Draper Manuscripts.

QuickCheck Model
ARCHIVED MATERIAL: MANUSCRIPT RECORDS
Series as lead element in Source List

Source List Entry

SERIES	COLLECTION ...

Cape Girardeau County Records, 1794–1842. Western Historical Manu-

...	REPOSITORY	REPOSITORY LOCATION

script Collection. University of Missouri, Columbia.

First (Full) Reference Note

AUTHOR (GRANTOR)	RECIPIENT	RECORD ID (GENERIC)

1. Alexander Baillie to Samuel Randol, bill of sale for slave Suzanne,

RECORD DATE	FILE NO.	FILE NAME	...

18 June 1805; folder f.8, Miscellaneous Documents, 1800–1836; Cape

... SERIES	COLLECTION ...

Girardeau County Records, 1794–1842 (C3676); Western Historical Manu-

...	REPOSITORY	REPOSITORY LOCATION

script Collection, University of Missouri, Columbia.

Subsequent (Short) Note

AUTHOR &RECIPIENT (SHORTENED)	RECORD I.D. (SHORTENED)	SERIES

11. Baillie to Randol, bill of sale, 1805, Cape Girardeau County Records,

COLLECTION

Western Historical Manuscript Collection.

QuickCheck Model
ARCHIVED MATERIAL: PERSONAL BIBLE
Original owner as lead element in Source List

Source List Entry

BIBLE ID (ORIGINAL OWNER & INCLUSIVE DATES)   BIBLE ...

Jefferson, John G. Family Bible, 1800–1931. *The Holy Bible, Containing*

... TITLE   PUBLICATION PLACE   PUBLISHER

the Old and New Testaments. Cooperstown, New York: H. & E. Phinney,

YEAR PUB'D   COLLECTION   REPOSITORY   REPOSITORY LOCATION

1827. Bible Records Collection. Library of Virginia, Richmond.

First (Full) Reference Note

BIBLE I.D. (ORIGINAL OWNER & INCLUSIVE DATES)   BIBLE ...

1. John G. Jefferson Family Bible, 1800–1931; *The Holy Bible, Contain-*

... TITLE   PUBLICATION PLACE   ...

ing the Old and New Testaments (Cooperstown, New York: H. & E.

PUBLISHER   YEAR PUB'D   MANUSCRIPT NO.   COLLECTION   REPOSITORY

Phinney, 1827); accession no. 26698, Bible Records Collection; Library of

...   REPOSITORY LOCATION   DESCRIPTIVE DETAIL ...

Virginia, Richmond. [ADD PROVENANCE; FOR "FAMILY RECORD" PAGES, ADD

...

ANALYSIS OF HANDWRITING, PENMANSHIP, AND TIMELINESS OF THE ENTRIES.]

Subsequent (Short) Note

BIBLE ID   SPECIFIC DATA

11. John G. Jefferson Family Bible, Family Record p. 2.

QuickCheck Model
ARCHIVED MATERIAL: PORTRAIT
Subject as lead element in Source List

Source List Entry

SUBJECT	CREATION DATE	COLLECTION

Metoyer, Agnes (Poissot). Portrait. ca. 1835. Pat Henry Jr. Collection.

REPOSITORY

Cammie G. Henry Research Center. Northwestern State University,

REPOSITORY LOCATION

Natchitoches, Louisiana.

First (Full) Reference Note

SUBJECT	CREATION DATE	COLLECTION

1. Agnes (Poissot) Metoyer Portrait, ca. 1835; Pat Henry Jr. Collection,

REPOSITORY

Cammie G. Henry Research Center; Northwestern State University,

REPOSITORY LOCATION	ARCHIVAL DESCRIPTION

Natchitoches, Louisiana. A full-color oil, 30" x 36" (framed), signed "Feuille."

Subsequent (Short) Note

SUBJECT	CREATION DATE	COLLECTION

11. Agnes (Poissot) Metoyer Portrait, ca. 1835, Pat Henry Jr. Collection.

QuickCheck Model
ARCHIVED MATERIAL: RESEARCH REPORT
Author as lead element in Source List

Source List Entry

AUTHOR &
PROFESSIONAL CREDENTIALS   REPORT TITLE or SUBJECT ...

Mills, Gary B., PhD (Hist.). "Cultural Reconnaissance of the Mallard–Fox

...   ITEM TYPE   RECIPIENT   REPORT DATE ...

Creek Property." Report to Tennessee Valley Authority. 18 September

...   COLLECTION   REPOSITORY

1983. Alabama Collection, Hoole Library, University of Alabama,

REPOSITORY
LOCATION

Tuscaloosa.

First (Full) Reference Note

AUTHOR &
PROFESSIONAL CREDENTIALS   REPORT TITLE or SUBJECT...

1. Gary B. Mills, PhD (Hist.), "Cultural Reconnaissance of the

...   PAGE   ITEM TYPE   RECIPIENT

Mallard–Fox Creek Property," p. 12; report to Tennessee Valley Authority,

REPORT DATE   COLLECTION   REPOSITORY ...

18 September 1983; Alabama Collection, Hoole Library, University of

...   REPOSITORY LOCATION

Alabama, Tuscaloosa.

Subsequent (Short) Note

AUTHOR   REPORT TITLE

11. Mills, "Cultural Reconnaissance of the Mallard–Fox Creek Property,"

PAGE

12.

QuickCheck Model
ARCHIVED MATERIAL: UNPUBLISHED NARRATIVE
Author as lead element in Source List

Source List Entry

AUTHOR	MANUSCRIPT ...

Rennell, James, Major. "Journal of a Voyage to the Sooloo Islands and

... TITLE	MANUSCRIPT NO.

the North West Coast of Borneo [1762–1763]." MS. Add. 19299.

REPOSITORY	REPOSITORY LOCATION

The British Library, London.

First (Full) Reference Note

AUTHOR	MANUSCRIPT ...

1. Major James Rennell, "Journal of a Voyage to the Sooloo Islands and

... TITLE	PAGE	MANUSCRIPT NO.

the North West Coast of Borneo [1762–1763]," p. 12; MS. Add. 19299,

REPOSITORY	REPOSITORY LOCATION

The British Library, London.

Subsequent (Short) Note

AUTHOR	MANUSCRIPT TITLE (SHORTENED)	PAGE

11. Rennell, "Journal of a Voyage to the Sooloo Islands," 12.

QuickCheck Model
ARCHIVED MATERIAL: VERTICAL FILE
Author as lead element in Source List

Source List Entry

AUTHOR	ITEM TITLE ...

Oklahoma Heritage Association. "Oklahoma Ghost Town Mining Camps and

...	ITEM DATE	FOLDER LABEL ...

Boomtowns Map." 1990. Folder: "Oklahoma: Maps—Historical & Spe-

...	COLLECTION	REPOSITORY ...

cial Interest." Vertical files. OSU–OC Library, Oklahoma State Uni-

...	REPOSITORY LOCATION

versity, Oklahoma City.

First (Full) Reference Note

AUTHOR	ITEM TITLE ...

1. Oklahoma Heritage Association, "Oklahoma Ghost Town Mining

...	ITEM DATE	FOLDER ...

Camps and Boomtowns Map" (1990); folder: "Oklahoma: Maps—His-

... LABEL	COLLECTION	REPOSITORY ...

torical & Special Interest," vertical files; OSU–OC Library, Oklahoma

...	REPOSITORY LOCATION

State University, Oklahoma City.

Subsequent (Short) Note

AUTHOR	ITEM TITLE ...

11. Oklahoma Heritage Association, "Oklahoma Ghost Town

...

Mining Camps and Boomtowns Map."

QuickCheck Model
PRESERVATION FILM: FHL-GSU FILM
Compiler as lead element in Source List

Source List Entry

	COMPILERS		MANUSCRIPT SERIES ...

Barbour, Lucius Barnes, and Lucius A. Barbour. "Barbour Collection of Con-

... TITLE	NO. OF VOLS.	ITEM TYPE or FORMAT	CREATION DATE

necticut Vital Records prior to 1850." 50 vols. Bound transcripts. 1874–

...	OWNER REPOSITORY	OWNER LOCATION	FILM ID	NO. OF ROLLS

1934. Connecticut State Library, Hartford. FHL microfilm, 98 rolls.

FILM REPOSITORY	FILM LOCATION

Family History Library, Salt Lake City, Utah.

First (Full) Reference Note

COMPILERS	MANUSCRIPT SERIES ...

1. Lucius Barnes Barbour and Lucius A. Barbour, "Barbour Collection of

... TITLE	NO. OF VOLS.	ITEM TYPE	CREATION DATE

Connecticut Vital Records prior to 1850," 50 vols. (bound transcripts, 1874–

...	OWNER REPOSITORY	OWNER LOCATION	VOL. USED	SECTION	ITEM ...

1934, Connecticut State Library, Hartford), vol. 14, Town of Goshen: Abigail

... OF INTEREST	FILM ID

Cook, born 25 January 1761; FHL microfilm 2,970.

Subsequent (Short) Note

COMPILERS	TITLE OF MANUSCRIPT SERIES ...

11. Barbour and Barbour, "Barbour Collection of Connecticut Vital

...	VOL. USED	SECTION & ITEM

Records," vol. 14, Goshen: Abigail Cook, 1761.

QuickCheck Model
PRESERVATION FILM: IN-HOUSE FILM
Collection as lead element in Source List

Source List Entry

COLLECTION	FILM ID	...

Cane River Collection. THNOC microfilm MSS 182, 5 rolls. The Historic

... REPOSITORY	REPOSITORY LOCATION

New Orleans Collection, New Orleans, Louisiana.

First (Full) Reference Note

RECORD TITLE (QUOTED EXACTLY)

1. "Marie Louise Margarite Lecomte to Jean Baptiste Siriac, Manumission,"

RECORD DATE	FILE	COLLECTION	FILM ID & ...

7 August 1829; folder 281, Cane River Collection; THNOC microfilm MSS

... ROLL NO.	REPOSITORY	LOCATION

182, roll 1; The Historic New Orleans Collection, New Orleans, Louisiana.

Subsequent (Short) Note

RECORD TITLE ...

11. "Marie Louise Margarite Lecomte to Jean Baptiste Siriac, Manumis-

...	YEAR	FILE	COLLECTION

sion," 1829, folder 281, Cane River Collection.

QuickCheck Model
PRIVATE HOLDINGS: ARTIFACT
Compiler as lead element in Source List

Source List Entry

COMPILER	ARTIFACT ID	CREATION DATE	CURRENT or LAST KNOWN ...

Stabler, Zella (Lovell). Scrapbook. ca. 1930–80. Privately held by Mrs.

... OWNER	OWNER'S LOCATION	YEAR OWNED

Stabler, [ADDRESS FOR PRIVATE USE,] Williamsport, Pennsylvania. 2007.

First (Full) Reference Note

ITEM ID (GENERIC)

1. G. B. Wuster obituary, undated clipping from unidentified newspaper,

ARTIFACT ID	CREATION DATE	CURRENT or LAST KNOWN ...

in Zella (Lovell) Stabler Scrapbook, ca. 1930–80; privately held by Mrs.

... OWNER	OWNER'S LOCATION	YEAR OWNED	...

Stabler, [ADDRESS FOR PRIVATE USE,] Williamsport, Pennsylvania, 2007. [ADD

... DESCRIPTIVE DETAIL

DESCRIPTION & PROVENANCE OF SCRAPBOOK.]

Subsequent (Short) Note

ITEM I D (SHORTENED)	ARTIFACT ID

11. G. B. Wuster obituary, Zella (Lovell) Stabler Scrapbook.

QuickCheck Model
PRIVATE HOLDINGS: DIARY or JOURNAL
Author as lead element in Source List

Source List Entry

	MANUSCRIPT TITLE	RECORD TYPE	
AUTHOR			PLACE ...

Brown, Sarah Jane (Hickman). "Journal." MS. Fernwood Station,

... CREATED	RECORD DATES	CURRENT or LAST KNOWN OWNER	...

Mississippi, 1896–1902. Privately held by Anne S. Anderson, [ADDRESS

... OWNER'S LOCATION	YEAR OWNED

FOR PRIVATE USE,] Gulfport, Mississippi. 2005.

First (Full) Reference Note

AUTHOR	TITLE OF MANUSCRIPT	PAGE	RECORD TYPE	RECORD DATES

1. Sarah Jane (Hickman) Brown, "Journal," p. 123; MS, 1896–1902

PLACE CREATED	CURRENT or LAST KNOWN OWNER	...

(Fernwood Station, Mississippi; privately held by Anne S. Anderson, [AD-

... OWNER'S LOCATION	YEAR OWNED	DESCRIPTIVE ...

DRESS FOR PRIVATE USE,] Gulfport, Mississippi, 2005. [ADD PROVENANCE, DESCRIP-

... DETAIL

TION, ETC.]

Subsequent (Short) Note

AUTHOR	TITLE	PAGE

11. Brown, "Journal," 123.

QuickCheck Model

PRIVATE HOLDINGS: FAMILY BIBLE RECORDS

Original owner as lead element in Source List

Source List Entry

BIBLE ID (ORIGINAL OWNER & INCLUSIVE DATES)   TITLE OF BIBLE ...

Greene, John Lynde, Sr., Family Bible Records, 1807–1944. *The Holy*

... PLACE OF PUBLICATION   PUBLISHER   YEAR PUB'D   CURRENT or LAST ...

Bible. Philadelphia: Matthew Carey, 1811. Privately held by John

... KNOWN OWNER   OWNER'S LOCATION

Lynde Green IV, [ADDRESS FOR PRIVATE USE,] Germantown, Maryland.

YEAR OWNED

2001.

First (Full) Reference Note

BIBLE ID (ORIGINAL OWNER & INCLUSIVE DATES)   TITLE OF ...

1. John Lynde Greene Sr. Family Bible Records, 1807–1944, *The Holy*

... BIBLE   PUB'N PLACE   PUBLISHER   YEAR PUB'D   PAGE or SECTION   CURRENT ...

Bible (Philadelphia: Matthew Carey, 1811), "Marriages"; privately held

... or LAST KNOWN OWNER   OWNER'S LOCATION

by John Lynde Greene IV, [ADDRESS FOR PRIVATE USE,] Germantown, Mary-

... YEAR OWNED   DESCRIPTIVE DETAIL ...

land, 2001. [ADD PROVENANCE AND ANALYSIS OF HANDWRITING, PENMANSHIP,

...

AND TIMELINESS OF THE ENTRIES.]

Subsequent (Short) Note

BIBLE ID   PAGE or SECTION

11. John Lynde Greene Sr., Family Bible Records, "Marriages."

QuickCheck Model
PRIVATE HOLDINGS: FAMILY CHART or GROUP SHEET
Compiler as lead element in Source List

Source List Entry

<u>COMPILER</u>   <u>COLLECTION</u>

Ollsen, Jerg. Ollsen Family Charts and Group Sheets, 1548–1948.

<u>OWNER or SUPPLIER</u>   <u>OWNER'S or SUPPLIER'S LOCATION ...</u>

Privately held by Ollsen, [ADDRESS FOR PRIVATE USE,] Vestero, Laeso,

     <u>YEAR</u>
<u>...</u>   <u>SUPPLIED</u>

Denmark. 1989.

First (Full) Reference Note

<u>COMPILER</u>   <u>ITEM (GENERIC ID)</u>   <u>...</u>

1. Jerg Ollsen, Erik Ollsen–Anna Hansen Family Group Sheet, Ollsen

<u>... COLLECTION</u>   <u>SUPPLIER</u>   <u>...</u>

Family Charts and Group Sheets, 1548–1948; supplied by Ollsen, [ADDRESS

     <u>YEAR</u>
<u>... SUPPLIER/COMPILER'S LOCATION</u>   <u>SUPPLIED</u>   <u>DESCRIPTION & ...</u>

FOR PRIVATE USE,] Vestero, Laeso, Denmark, 1989. This sheet offers only a generic

<u>... EVALUATION BY RESEARCHER</u>

list of materials used, with no specific documentation for any piece of data.

Subsequent (Short) Note

<u>COMPILER</u>   <u>ITEM (GENERIC ID)</u>   <u>...</u>

11. Ollsen, Erik Ollsen–Anna Hansen Family Group Sheet, previ-

<u>REFERRAL TO PRIOR EVALUATION</u>

ously evaluated at note 1.

QuickCheck Model
PRIVATE HOLDINGS: HISTORIC LETTER
Writer as lead element in Source List

Source List Entry

WRITER	WRITER'S LOCATION	RECIPIENT ...

Charleville, F. A. (Fiddletown, California) to "Dear Sister" [Athanaise Charleville

...	ITEM TYPE	RECORD DATE	CURRENT or LAST KNOWN OWNER

Faris]. Letter. 15 November 1867. Privately held by Clayton Mills,

	OWNER'S LOCATION	YEAR OWNED

[ADDRESS FOR PRIVATE USE,] Nashville, Tennessee. 2007.

First (Full) Reference Note

WRITER	WRITER'S LOCATION	RECIPIENT ...

1. F. A. Charleville (Fiddletown, California) to "Dear Sister" [Athanaise

...(IDENTITY ADDED)	ITEM TYPE	RECORD DATE	CURRENT or LAST KNOWN ...

Charleville Faris], letter, 15 November 1867; privately held by Clayton

... OWNER	OWNER'S LOCATION	YEAR OWNED	DESCRIPTIVE ...

Mills, [ADDRESS FOR PRIVATE USE,] Nashville, Tennessee, 2007. [ADD EXPLANA-

... DETAIL or OTHER RELEVANT DISCUSSION

TION OF HOW THE RECIPIENT HAS BEEN IDENTIFIED.]

Subsequent (Short) Note

WRITER	RECIPIENT	RECORD DATE

11. F. A. Charleville to "Dear Sister," 15 November 1867.

QuickCheck Model
PRIVATE HOLDINGS: INTERVIEW
TAPE & TRANSCRIPT

Informant as lead element in Source List

Source List Entry

PERSON INTERVIEWED · LOCATION · ITEM TYPE · NAME ...

Cortez, Camila (Sanchez). Tehachapi, California. Interview by Kathleen

... OF INTERVIEWER · RECORD DATE · ITEM FORMAT · CURRENT ...

Wardle Cortez, 29 November 2002. Video and transcript. Privately

... or LAST KNOWN OWNER · OWNER'S LOCATION

held by interviewer, [ADDRESS FOR PRIVATE USE,]Woodacre, California.

YEAR OWNED

2007.

First (Full) Reference Note

PERSON INTERVIEWED · ...

1. Camila (Sanchez) Cortez, wife of Melcio Cortez ([ADDRESS,]

... LOCATION · ITEM TYPE · INTERVIEWER · ...

Tehachapi, California), interview by Kathleen Wardle Cortez, 29

RECORD DATE · ITEM FORMAT · CURRENT or LAST KNOWN OWNER

November 2002; video and transcript privately held by interviewer,

OWNER'S LOCATION · YEAR OWNED

[ADDRESS,] Woodacre, California, 2007.

Subsequent (Short) Note

PERSON INTERVIEWED · ITEM TYPE · RECORD DATE

11. Camila (Sanchez) Cortez, interview, 29 November 2002.

QuickCheck Model
PRIVATE HOLDINGS: LEGAL DOCUMENT
UNRECORDED FAMILY COPY
Collection as lead element in Source List

Source List Entry

COLLECTION	CURRENT or LAST KNOWN OWNER

Bertrand-Lennon Family Archives. Privately held by Rachal M.Lennon,

OWNER'S LOCATION	YEAR OWNED

[ADDRESS FOR PRIVATE USE,] Cottontown, Tennessee. 2007.

First (Full) Reference Note

GRANTOR (AUTHOR)	RECIPIENT

1.   Pierre Bertrand Jr., master surgeon, to town of Verdun, France,

RECORD ID (GENERIC)	RECORD DATE	ITEM FORMAT	COLLECTION ...

donation of property, 24 April 1760; original, family copy, Bertrand-Lennon

...	CURRENT or LAST KNOWN OWNER	OWNER'S LOCATION ...

Family Archives; privately held by Rachal M. Lennon, [ADDRESS FOR PRIVATE USE,]

...	YEAR OWNED	EVALUATION, DESCRIPTION, ETC.

Cottontown, Tennessee, 2007. [ADD PROVENANCE AND/OR DESCRIPTIVE DETAILS.]

Subsequent (Short) Note

GRANTOR & RECIPIENT (SHORTENED)	GENERIC ID/DATE (SHORTENED)

11.   Pierre Bertrand Jr. to town of Verdun, donation, 1760.

QuickCheck Model
PRIVATE HOLDINGS: PERSONAL CORRESPONDENCE
Collection as lead element in Source List

Source List Entry

COLLECTION	RESEARCHER'S ID	CONTACT ...

April Research Files. Privately held by Lynne Slocovich April, [ADDRESS FOR

... INFORMATION

PRIVATE USE,] Northport, Alabama.

First (Full) Reference Note

WRITER	WRITER'S AFFILIATION (IF RELEVANT) ...

1. Ruth Gómez Schirmacher, International Reference Section, Family

...	WRITER'S LOCATION	RECIPIENT	ITEM TYPE ...

History Library, Salt Lake City, Utah, to Lynne Slocovich April, letter, 20

... RECORD DATE	SUBJECT or NATURE OF DATA PROVIDED

November 1996, translating the baptismal record of Margherita Zaballi;

FOLDER	SERIES or RESEARCH PROJECT	COLLECTION

Personal Correspondence, 1996; Zaballi Family, April Research Files;

RESEARCHER & CONTACT INFORMATION

privately held by April, [ADDRESS FOR PRIVATE USE,] Northport, Alabama.

Subsequent (Short) Note

WRITER & RECIPIENT	RECORD DATE

11. Schirmacher to April, 20 November 1996.

QuickCheck Model
PRIVATE HOLDINGS: PERSONAL E-MAIL
Collection as lead element in Source List

Source List Entry

COLLECTION	RESEARCHER'S ID	CONTACT ...

Flynn Research Files. Privately held by Katherine E. Flynn, [(E-ADDRESS) &

... INFORMATION

STREET ADDRESS FOR PRIVATE USE,] Loveland, Ohio.

First (Full) Reference Note

WRITER	WRITER'S LOCATION	WRITER'S CONTACT INFORMATION

1. J. Fernando Peña, New York City [(E-ADDRESS FOR PRIVATE USE),] to

RECIPIENT	ITEM TYPE	RECORD DATE	SUBJECT ...

Katherine E. Flynn , e-mail, 27 January 2003, "Catalogs of Emily Driscoll,

... LINE	FILE	RESEARCH SERIES	...

Antiquarian Bookseller," Emily Driscoll File, Hannah Crafts Project, Flynn

... COLLECTION	RESEARCHER & CONTACT INFORMATION ...

Research Files; privately held by Flynn, [(E-ADDRESS) & STREET ADDRESS FOR

...

PRIVATE USE,] Loveland, Ohio.

Subsequent (Short) Note

WRITER & RECIPIENT	ITEM TYPE	RECORD DATE

11. Peña to Flynn, e-mail, 27 January 2003.

QuickCheck Model
PRIVATE HOLDINGS: RESEARCH REPORT
Author as lead element in Source List

Source List Entry

AUTHOR &
PROFESSIONAL CREDENTIALS / REPORT TITLE (QUOTED …

Bamman, Gale Williams, CG. "William Ball of Giles County, Tennessee:

… EXACTLY) / ITEM TYPE / RECIPIENT / RECIPIENT'S LOCATION …

Project No. 2." Report to R. C. Ball [ADDRESS FOR PRIVATE USE,]

… / REPORT DATE / ITEM FORMAT / OWNER & CONTACT INFORMATION

Houston, Texas, 17 March 1990. Photocopy held by [NAME, ADDRESS].

First (Full) Reference Note

AUTHOR &
PROFESSIONAL CREDENTIALS / REPORT TITLE …

1. Gale Williams Bamman, CG, "William Ball of Giles County,

… (QUOTED EXACTLY) / PAGE / ITEM TYPE / RECIPIENT / RECIPIENT'S LOCATION …

Tennessee: Project No. 2," p. 5; report to R. C. Ball, [ADDRESS FOR PRIVATE

… / REPORT DATE / ITEM FORMAT / OWNER & CONTACT INFORMATION

USE,] Houston, Texas, 17 March 1990; photocopy held by [NAME, ADDRESS].

Subsequent (Short) Note

AUTHOR / REPORT TITLE

11. Bamman, "William Ball of Giles County, Tennessee: Project No. 2,"

PAGE

p. 5.

QuickCheck Model
PRIVATE HOLDINGS: TRADITION, RECORDED
Collection as lead element in Source List

Source List Entry

COLLECTION	COMPILER	RECORD TYPE	CREATION DATE

Sherman Family Traditions. Ruth Randall, compiler. MSS notes, ca. 1980–

...	CURRENT or LAST KNOWN OWNER	OWNER'S LOCATION ...

1985. Privately held by Randall, [ADDRESS FOR PRIVATE USE,] Albuquerque,

...

New Mexico.

First (Full) Reference Note

COLLECTION	COMPILER	RECORD TYPE	...

1. Sherman Family Traditions, Ruth Randall, compiler (MSS notes, ca.

CREATION DATE	CURRENT or LAST KNOWN OWNER	OWNER'S LOCATION

1980–85; privately held by Randall, [ADDRESS FOR PRIVATE USE,] Albuquerque,

...	SUBJECT	SOURCE OF INFORMATION

New Mexico); parentage of Henry Sherman (born ca. 1843), reported by

...	SOURCE'S RELATIONSHIP TO SUBJECT, ETC.	ITEM DATE	...

Lena Sherman, Henry's daughter and Randall's aunt, ca. 1980. [ADD

PROVENANCE & EVALUATION OF TRADITION

RELEVANT DETAILS.]

Subsequent (Short) Note

GENERIC LABEL (SHORTENED)

11. Sherman Family Traditions about Henry Sherman (born ca. 1843),

REFERENCE TO PRIOR DISCUSSION

previously evaluated in note 1.

GUIDELINES
& Examples

———◆———

BASIC ISSUES

3.1 Archival Arrangements

Major archives typically organize their materials in a multilevel fashion. Each level represents a part of the citation we create when we use their records. The usual levels (from largest to smallest) are these:

RECORD GROUPS .... Commonly, a record group deals with an agency, commission, department, or other bureaucratic division. In some archives, the record group carries only a number; in some, only a name. In others, it carries both. Your citation should follow the practice of the archive whose material you are using. While there, ask for a citation guide. If visiting the repository's website, you may find citation suggestions there.

COLLECTIONS,
SERIES, ETC. .... Large record groups are typically broken down into subgroups—often called *collections, series, classes,* or some similar term. In some archives, these will represent two or more separate levels. They may carry either a title, a number, or both. Some archives prefer that their collections be cited by title only, because their call numbers may change over time. Other archives prefer that the collection numbers be used.

The term *collection* is also used occasionally as part of the name of an archive that has a highly specialized focus. Examples in this chapter include two well-known archives, the Western

Historical Manuscript Collection and the Historic New Orleans Collection—both illustrated within the QuickCheck Models for ARCHIVED MATERIAL: MANUSCRIPT (Series) and PRESERVATION FILM: IN-HOUSE FILM.

FILES .... The term *file* is typically used for a cluster of material contained in one bundle, folder, jacket, or wrapper. A file's label may identify it by name, number, or both. Occasionally, you will have used an entire file and will want to cite the whole. More commonly, your Reference Note will need to cite a specific item within the file.

ITEM OR PIECE .... The *item* or the *piece* is usually the smallest element of the citation. It will be the specific document, letter, etc., in which you found the information you are referencing. The manner in which you cite an item will depend upon the nature of the record. It may be

- *titled,* as in the muster-roll example below—in which case you will copy that title precisely and place quotation marks around it—or

- *untitled,* in which case you will create a generic label that answers such questions as *who, what, when,* and *where.* The bill of sale cited in the QuickCheck Model for ARCHIVED MATERIAL: MANUSCRIPT (Series) illustrates this type of item.

Other archives may subdivide holdings into fewer levels. Consider the Draper Manuscripts, a collection of American frontier materials held by the Wisconsin Historical Society. More than five hundred volumes are divided into fifty-six series. Traditional citations to items within this collection typically follow the pattern shown below:

Source List Entry
Draper Manuscripts. Wisconsin Historical Society. Madison, Wisconsin.

First Reference Note
1. "Muster Roll of Captain [Joseph] Martin's Company of Pittsylvania Militia in 1774," Series XX, Tennessee Papers, vol. 1, p. 6; Draper Manuscripts, Wisconsin Historical Society, Madison.

Subsequent Note
> 11. "Muster Roll of Captain [Joseph] Martin's Company of Pittsyl-vania Militia in 1774," Series XX, 1:6, Draper Manuscripts.

Two particular points should be considered in this basic example:

- The Source List Entry cites to the collection level, while each Reference Note cites the specific document. (See also 3.4.)

- The First Reference Note cites both the series number and the name (i.e., Series XX, Tennessee Papers), while the short form uses only the number. You could, if you preferred, cite the series name instead of the series number in the short form. You do not have to repeat both.

After a manuscript has been fully cited, some archives recommend that subsequent citations be even more abbreviated than the short form used above. Typically, the more-abbreviated form will follow the style used within the legal profession. As demonstrated by the models in chapter 13, Legal Style citations (*Bluebook* and otherwise) bear little resemblance to those cited in Humanities Style. In addition to being far more cryptic, they reverse the order of the elements within footnotes and cite them from largest to smallest. The society that owns the Draper Manuscripts is a repository that recommends Legal Style for short-form references to Draper. Following its style guide, the Subsequent Note for the muster roll would be simply

> 11. Draper Manuscripts 1 XX 6.

> *That is:* COLLECTION NAME • VOL. NO. • SERIES NO. • PAGE NO.

For citing a microfilm edition of this manuscript collection, see 3.18.

3.2 Archival Style Guides

Because each archive has its own preferences for citing its materials, you should ask each facility whether it has a citation guide it would like you to follow. If you choose to use each facility's recommended style, you can expect to have considerable inconsistencies within your citations. If you prefer to use a consistent style, you will still benefit by studying the format recommended by the archive whose material you have used. From it, you will learn which pieces of information the archive needs you to cite in order to relocate the material.

3.3 International Differences

Different nations have not only different records but also varying customs for citing sources—particularly loose manuscripts. Traditionally, citations in the United States have used a dual system that calls for one arrangement in reference notes and another in the Source List. As a generalized overview:

UNITED STATES .... Reference Note citations start with the smallest element in the citation and work up to the largest (the archive and its location).

INTERNATIONALLY .... Typically, Reference Note citations start with the largest and work down to the smallest.

Obviously, U.S. researchers who attempt to cite international sources using software templates designed primarily for the U.S. market face a dilemma. So do international researchers using U.S. sources or software. For consistency, *Evidence* follows U.S. conventions. If you prefer an international format for manuscript materials, you should feel free to modify the U.S. models appropriately. In either event, the international examples within this manual will assist you in identifying the essential elements to cite.

3.4   Source List Entries vs. Reference Notes

When citing unpublished documents in traditional U.S. style, your Source List Entry will be different from your Reference Notes in several ways.

SOURCE LIST ENTRY: Bibliographic entries rarely cite individual documents or individual record volumes within an archive. The smallest level is usually a collection or series. You may, in fact, create your own generic description, such as

Draper Manuscripts. Pre-1830. Wisconsin Historical Society, Madison.

A generic description such as this is designed to reflect the material or the time period you actually studied, even though the collection may not subdivide its material into any such category.

FIRST NOTE: Your First Reference Note for a source should cite that source in full. Almost always, *that will be a fuller citation than the entry in your Source List*. The First Reference Note in which you identify a particular source is also the place in which you alert your readers to special issues involving that source—discussions of legibility problems, recopied or damaged records, bias on the part of an informant, etc.

3.5 Unpublished Writings

Unpublished compilations and narratives typically have limited access. Locating them requires the use of catalogs and databases different from those in which you locate books. Therefore, unpublished writings are cited differently from published ones. The main differences are these:

- The exact title of a manuscript appears in quotation marks.

- That exact title is set in roman (regular) type, rather than the italics used for publications.

- In lieu of the publication data that would appear in parentheses for published works, you will

  (*a*) state that it is a manuscript, typescript, thesis, dissertation, etc.;

  (*b*) cite the year (or time frame) of compilation; and

  (*c*) identify the archive, library, or other place at which you found the copy—or, for theses and dissertations, the institution at which the degree was granted. (By comparison, if the manuscript had been published as a book, you would cite the publisher and its place of publication, but you would not normally cite the repository because published books can be found in many other repositories.)

SPECIAL ISSUES

3.6 Archives as Lead Element in Source Lists

Most archives house many records in many collections. Your Source List will need to specifically identify the material you have used. Therefore, you will rarely name an archive as the lead element in your Source List Entry.

3.7 Author, Creator, Compiler, Etc., as Lead Element in Source List

If you use a record with a named author—especially if it is the only document you access from the collection—you may want your Source List to place the entry alphabetically under that author's name. (For more on the MSS number in the example below, see 3.10.)

Source List Entry
Ball, John, to Thomas Massie. Letter, 14 April 1792. Massie Papers,
     MSS 1M3855c. Virginia Historical Society, Richmond.

First Reference Note
     1. John Ball to Thomas Massie, letter, 14 April 1792; Massie
Papers, MSS 1M3855c; Virginia Historical Society, Richmond.

Subsequent Note
     11. John Ball to Thomas Massie, letter, 14 April 1792.

3.8   Collection as Lead Element in Source List

If you use multiple items from one archival collection, you may prefer
to emphasize the collection by making it the lead element of your
Source List Entry. In that case, the specific document and/or its writer
will still be the lead element(s) in the First Reference Note. (See also
3.10 for "MSS vs. MS.")

Source List Entry
Massie Papers, MSS 1M3855c. Virginia Historical Society. Richmond.

First Reference Note
     1. John Ball to Thomas Massie, letter, 14 April 1792; Massie
Papers, MSS 1M3855c; Virginia Historical Society, Richmond.

Subsequent Note
     11. John Ball to Thomas Massie, 14 April 1792, Massie Papers.

3.9   Document as Lead Element in Source List

See QuickCheck Model *for* ARCHIVED MATERIAL: MANUSCRIPT (Document)

If you use only one item from one archival collection and it has no
named author, you may prefer to emphasize the document in your
Source List by making it the lead element of your Source List Entry.
For example, the military roll from the Draper Manuscripts treated at
3.1 might be handled as follows:

Source List Entry
"Muster Roll of Captain [Joseph] Martin's Company of Pittsylvania
     Militia in 1774." Series XX, Tennessee Papers. Draper Manuscripts.
     Wisconsin Historical Society, Madison.

First Reference Note
     1. "Muster Roll of Captain [Joseph] Martin's Company of Pittsyl-
vania Militia in 1774," Series XX, Tennessee Papers, vol. 1, p. 6; Draper
Manuscripts; Wisconsin Historical Society, Madison.

Subsequent Note
> 11. "Muster Roll of Captain [Joseph] Martin's Company of Pittsylvania Militia in 1774," Draper Manuscripts, Series XX, 1:6

In note 1, the page number is positioned immediately after the volume number; it is not appended to the identification of the document. The page number's position signifies that the muster roll appears on page 6 of volume 1. Conversely, if the page number were to immediately follow the reference to the document itself, that would signify that you were citing the sixth page of a long document.

3.10 Document No. vs. Collection No.

See QuickCheck Model *for* ARCHIVED MATERIAL: MANUSCRIPT (Collection)

Some archives assign file numbers to their manuscript collections, some to their documents, and some to both. As a careful notetaker, you want to indicate whether any cited archival number applies to the document or to the collection, or perhaps to a subseries that stands between the document and the major collection.

In the Ball-to-Massie letter used in 3.7–3.8, the citation indicates in two ways that the number "MSS 1M3855c" applies to the collection rather than the document:

MSS VS. MS
- The "MSS" that precedes the number is the abbreviation for manuscripts *plural.*
- The MSS number follows the name of the *collection.* In the sequence of elements, it does not appear next to the *document.*

However, in the Vaudreuil example on the following page:
- The archival number is preceded by "MS," meaning "manuscript" *singular.*
- The archival number falls immediately after the name and date of the *document,* signifying that this number applies to the document—not to the whole collection.

PUNCTUATION
Properly used, punctuation also clarifies whether an archival number belongs to the document, a subseries, or the whole collection. Within Reference Note citations to archival records:
- A comma separates elements that are on the same level.
- A semicolon separates elements on one level from elements on a higher level.

In the Vaudreuil example, the placement of the semicolon in the Reference Note also tells us that the MS number applies to the item, not the collection. There, the semicolon acts as a divider between details that describe the document and details that describe the collection. Also note that the MS number does not appear in the Source List Entry, because that Source List Entry cites to the collection, not to the individual manuscript.

Source List Entry
Vaudreuil Papers (Papers of Pierre de Rigaud, Marquis de Vaudreuil), 1740–1753. Loudoun Collection. Huntington Library and Art Gallery. San Marino, California.

First Reference Note
1. "État De La Force Actuel De La Comp^e De La Mazillier destaché Au Illinois," September 1752, MS LO 377, Letterbook; Vaudreuil Papers (Papers of Pierre de Rigaud, Marquis de Vaudreuil), 1740–1753; Loudoun Collection; Huntington Library and Art Gallery, San Marino, California. [ADD DESCRIPTIVE DETAILS THAT AFFECT YOUR ANALYSIS OF THE DOCUMENT.]

Subsequent Note
11. "État De La Force ... Illinois," September 1752, Vaudreuil Papers.

3.11   Exact Title vs. Generic ID
When citing a document that has a formal title, as with the French roll above, use quotation marks around that exact title. When citing an untitled document, as with the Ball-to-Massie letter at 3.7–3.8, do not add quotation marks around the words you use to identify it; you are not quoting anything. In neither case do you place the title in italics, because italics are used for the titles of *publications,* not manuscripts.

3.12   Foreign-Language Titles & Generic Labels
See QuickCheck Models *for*
- ARCHIVED MATERIAL: MANUSCRIPT (Collection)
- ARCHIVED MATERIAL: MANUSCRIPT (Series)

When the title of a document appears in a language other than the one in which you are writing, you have options for handling the record. You may simply copy the title of the document exactly as it appears; that option is illustrated at 3.10. Or, as illustrated below, you may add a translation in square editorial brackets placed immediately after the title. Your translation should appear in roman type, not italics; and it should not carry quotation marks, because your translation is not a quote. Only the first word and proper nouns should be capitalized within your translation.

First Reference Note

1. "État De La Force Actuel De La Comp^e De La Mazillier destaché Au Illinois" [Statement of the actual strength of the De La Mazillier's Company detached at Illinois], September 1752, MS LO 377; Vaudreuil Papers ...

In other cases, you may need to create a generic label for the document. In the example below, the actual label on the document is a mix of both French and English, because the document was created in a bilingual society. For simplicity, the document is cited here in English, generically (descriptively), as a deed might normally be:

Source List Entry

Baillie, Alexander, to Samuel Randol. Bill of sale for slave Suzanne. Cape Girardeau County Records, 1794–1842. Western Historical Manuscript Collection. University of Missouri, Columbia.

First Reference Note

1. Alexander Baillie to Samuel Randol, bill of sale for slave Suzanne, 18 June 1805; folder f.8, Miscellaneous Documents, 1800–1836; Cape Girardeau County Records, 1794–1842 (C3676); Western Historical Manuscript Collection, University of Missouri, Columbia.

Subsequent Note

11. Baillie to Randol, bill of sale, 1805, Cape Girardeau County Records, Western Historical Manuscript Collection.

ARCHIVED MATERIALS: BY TYPE

3.13 Basic Format: Artifacts

See QuickCheck Model *for* ARCHIVED MATERIAL: ARTIFACT

Historical artifacts vary widely in nature, but the basic citation format is fairly standard. You will include most of the elements that you cite for manuscripts. Additionally, you will add descriptive material that conveys a graphic sense of the item and/or explains the item's connection to the subject you are researching.

Source List Entry

(*Creator as lead element in Source List*)

Horst, "Aunt Ella," et al. "Amish Friendship Sampler Album." Quilt. ca. 1876–1900. Michigan Quilt Project. Michigan State University Museum, East Lansing, Michigan.

First Reference Note
1. "Aunt Ella" Horst et al., "Amish Friendship Sampler Album," quilt, ca. 1876–1900; item 01.0011, Michigan Quilt Project; Michigan State University Museum, East Lansing. The archival description identifies the quilt makers collectively as "Friends of Annie Risser Horst."

Subsequent Note
11. Horst et al., "Amish Friendship Sampler Album," Michigan Quilt Project.

ET AL. ("AND OTHERS")
The creator of this artifact is a group of twenty-three women identified in the museum's catalog as friends of Annie Risser Horst—one of whom is called "Aunt Ella" Horst. When multiple creators (authors, etc.) exist, the convention is to identify at least one individual (but rarely more than three), then use *et al.* (the abbreviation for *et alii,* meaning "and others") to indicate that additional creators are involved.

3.14 Basic Format: Documents
The basic model below gives you two choices for your Source List Entry, following the principles introduced at 3.7–3.8. The first option alphabetizes the entry under the name of the author—a method you might choose if you have many letters by this author. The second places the entry under the name of the collection.

Source List Entry
(Author as lead element in Source List)
James, Lucy, to John DeWolf, Esq. Letter, 17 March 1820. DeWolf Papers. Bristol Historical and Preservation Society, Bristol, Rhode Island.

(Collection as lead element in Source List)
DeWolf Papers. Bristol Historical and Preservation Society, Bristol, Rhode Island.

First Reference Note
1. Lucy James to John DeWolf, Esq., letter, 17 March 1820; file A-20, DeWolf Papers; Bristol Historical and Preservation Society, Bristol, Rhode Island.

Subsequent Note
11. James to DeWolf, 17 March 1820, DeWolf Papers.

3.15 Bibles & Bible Records: Archived
See also QuickCheck Model *for* ARCHIVED MATERIAL: PERSONAL BIBLE

Most archives have a recommended format for citing materials from their collections. Typically, it is similar to the Basic Format at 3.14. However, the critical analyses that historical researchers apply to family Bible records require more details about a record than the basic archival format usually recommends.

Citing a family Bible record from a digital archive involves other considerations discussed at 2.33. The following example applies those considerations, using the document title assigned by the owner-archives, but adds a given name for a more precise identification. This record involves one other element that also needs to be covered: the form of the record—i.e., whether the archive holds the original item or some type of facsimile (photocopy, digital image, microform, etc.).

Bible Pages, Transcribed Online 💻

Source List Entry
Jefferson [Thomas] Family Bible Record, 1707–1882. *The Book of Common Prayer ... Together with the Psalter or Psalms of David.* Oxford: Thomas Baskett, 1752. Facsimile by Meriden Gravure Co., 1952. Online images of family pages. *The Library of Virginia.* http://lvaimage.lib.va.us/Bible/28314/index.html : 2007.

First Reference Note
1.   [Thomas] Jefferson Family Bible Record, 1707–1882, *The Book of Common Prayer ... Together with the Psalter or Psalms of David* (Oxford: Thomas Baskett, 1752; facsimile, n.p.: Meriden Gravure Co., 1952), images of family pages, *The Library of Virginia* (http://lvaimage.lib.va.us/Bible/28314/index.html : 25 January 2007); citing call no. 28314.

Subsequent Note
11.   [Thomas] Jefferson Family Bible Record, family pages only.

3.16   Digital Archive Records

See QuickCheck Model *for* ARCHIVED MATERIAL: DIGITAL ARCHIVES

Many traditional repositories are developing virtual archives that bring together documents selected from many of their collections. Some, such as the Georgia archive in the example below, also offer documents held by other facilities that relate to a chosen theme. Researchers who use them have several citation levels to consider:

- identification of the original document and its creator;
- identification of the electronic format and the digital archive by owner, archive (website) name, digital location (URL), and date;
- identification of the location of the original document.

Citations to online databases and the images attached to them are simpler if you follow the principle that online material is *published* material. In that format, the following equivalents apply:

- website titles are equivalent to book titles;
- database/collection titles are equivalent to chapter titles within a book;
- URL (digital location) and date of access or copyright are equivalent to a book's publication place and date; and
- websites with multiple databases created by different parties are equivalent to a book that has different chapter authors—therefore, creators at both levels need to be cited, if both are identified.

The following examples illustrate citing varied material from different institutions. In note 1, the website offers only one database; therefore the citation does not include a database title in addition to a website title. In notes 2 and 3, the website offers a number of databases; the collection or database that is cited ("Southeastern Native American Documents, 1730–1842") has no creator identified.

Online Digital Documents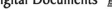

Source List Entry

(Author as lead element in Source List)

Everett, Lucia Eugenia Lamb. Journal, 1862. Database and images. Utah Academic Library Consortium. *Trails of Hope: Overland Diaries and Letters, 1846–1869.* http://overlandtrails.lib.byu.edu : 2007.

"Southeastern Native American Documents, 1730–1842." Transcriptions and images. University Systems of Georgia. *Digital Library of Georgia.* http://dlg.galileo.usg.edu : 2007.

First Reference Note

(Author as lead element)

1. Lucia Eugenia Lamb Everett Journal, 1862, online images, Utah Academic Library Consortium, *Trails of Hope: Overland Diaries and Letters, 1846–1869* (http://overlandtrails.lib.byu.edu : 25 January 2007), p. 7; citing MSS 583, Marriott Library, University of Utah, Salt Lake City.

(Database/collection as lead element, citing an image)

2. "Southeastern Native American Documents, 1730–1842," University Systems of Georgia, *Digital Library of Georgia* (http://dlg.galileo.usg.edu : accessed 25 January 2007), image copy, "Cherokee Council Minutes, 1818 May 20 [to] 27, Cherokee Agency," p. 9;

crediting "State Library Cherokee Collection," Tennessee State Library and Archives, Nashville.

(Database/collection as lead element, citing a transcription)
    3. "Southeastern Native American Documents, 1730–1842," University Systems of Georgia, *Digital Library of Georgia* (http://dlg.galileo.usg.edu : accessed 25 January 2007), transcription, Return Jonathan Meigs, "Answers to Enquiries Relating to the Cherokees, 1817 Aug., Cherokee Agency."

Subsequent Note
    11. Lucia Everett Journal, 7, *Trails of Hope*.
    12. "Southeastern Native American Documents, 1730–1842,"*Digital Library of Georgia*, "Cherokee Council Minutes, 1818," 9.
    13. "Southeastern Native American Documents, 1730–1842,"*Digital Library of Georgia*, Meigs, "Answers to Enquiries ... 1817."

INCLUSION OF PAGE NUMBER
Whether or not you cite a specific page number for an archived record depends upon whether you are referencing specific material or the document in general. Notes 1 and 2 single out a particular page of a document. Note 3 refers to the whole document.

3.17   Filmed or Fiched Manuscripts, Preservation Film vs. Publications

To protect fragile originals, as well as to make material more widely available, many manuscripts are now accessed via film or fiche. Citations to these have a triple need:

- to identify the original document with identification of its owner;
- to identify the film itself (not only to give credit to the filmer but also because some materials are offered on film by multiple agencies, with significant differences in quality or content); and
- to describe both the document and the film fully enough to permit their evaluation and relocation.

In many libraries and archives, you are likely to encounter two types of microfilmed or microfiched records: (1) film made for preservation purposes only; and (2) film made for distribution and/or sale and treated as a publication. Some significant differences exist in citations between the two. You can usually determine the type you are using by studying the first few frames of the roll. If the film is published, you will typically find publication facts at the start of the roll. If the film yields no clue to its creator, you might ask the repository's staff whether the film is that repository's own creation and, if so, whether they classify it as a publication or as a preservation film.

3.18   Filmed or Fiched Manuscripts, Commercial Publications
Many materials from academic and state archives are being commercially filmed for widespread distribution. Typically, they are cited as a publication. Within data-management software, they will usually fit the QuickCheck Model for BOOK: BASIC FORMAT (chapter 12).

The first example below treats a film edition of manuscripts from a single archive, the Draper Manuscripts previously discussed at 3.1. The film edition follows the same organization used for the original collection. The second example uses a film edition of manuscripts assembled from many different archives.

Commercially Published Microfilm

Source List Entry

The Draper Manuscripts. Microfilm edition, 123 rolls. Teaneck, New Jersey: Chadwyck-Healey, n.d.

Southern Women and Their Families in the 19th Century: Papers and Diaries; Part 6, *Virginia.* Anne Firor Scott, editor. Microfilm publication, 30 rolls. Bethesda, Maryland: University Publications of America, 1992. Roll 1.

First Reference Note

1.   "Muster Roll of Captain [Joseph] Martin's Company of Pittsylvania Militia in 1774," *The Draper Manuscripts*, microfilm edition, 123 rolls (Teaneck, New Jersey: Chadwyck-Healey, n.d.), roll 42, Series XX, Tennessee Papers, vol. 1, p. 6.

2.   *Southern Women and Their Families in the 19th Century: Papers and Diaries;* Part 6, *Virginia,* Anne Firor Scott, ed., microfilm publication, 30 rolls (Bethesda, Maryland: University Publications of America, 1992), roll 1, frame 123, document 2.

Subsequent Note

11.   "Muster Roll of Captain [Joseph] Martin's Company of Pittsylvania Militia in 1774," *Draper Manuscripts,* roll 42.

12.   *Southern Women ... 19th Century: Papers and Diaries ... Virginia,* roll 1, frame 123, document 2.

CITING EDITION VS. PUBLICATION

These terms carry different meanings. With the Draper Manuscripts, the microfilm offers a new version of an already-existing entity—it is a microfilm *edition* of a collection of manuscripts housed at the Wisconsin Historical Society. The Southern Women microfilm, however, is not just a new edition of an entity that already existed. It is a totally new entity, a *publication* created by the publishers from records scattered across many locales—material not previously assembled.

CITING ROLL NUMBER IN THE SOURCE LIST

If you use material from multiple rolls of a microfilmed collection, you may wish to cite the whole collection in your Source List Entry, as with the Draper Manuscripts above. If only one roll of a large collection is relevant to your research, you may prefer to cite that specific roll in the Source List, so that you will have fewer details to add into your Citation Detail Field every time you cite that source again in your data-management program.

3.19 Filmed or Fiched Manuscripts, Preservation Copies

Many manuscript materials are microfilmed or microfiched for preservation purposes only. They are not sold to the public and are not considered publications. Copies typically exist only at the library or archives that created the film.

As noted at 2.24, film created by the Genealogical Society of Utah and deposited at its sister agency, the Family History Library in Salt Lake City, are not considered publications. Many university and state archives, as well as local record offices, also produce preservation film. Many hold copies of FHL film made within their facility, received as a gift from GSU after they granted permission to film those holdings.

When citing preservation microfilm, you have no publisher to cite. Instead, you identify

- the archive or library that owns the original material; and
- the agency that created the film (which may be the owner).

For film created by the repository where you used it, you will cite

- whatever label appears on the film; and
- whatever cataloging numbers the archive assigns.

If the preservation film is formally titled, you do not italicize its title because it is not a publication.

Archival Microfilm

See QuickCheck Model *for* PRESERVATION FILM: IN-HOUSE FILM

Source List Entry
(*Collection as lead element in Source List*)
Cane River Collection. THNOC microfilm MSS 182, 5 rolls. The Historic New Orleans Collection, New Orleans, Louisiana.

First Reference Note
1. "Marie Louise Margarite Lecomte to Jean Baptiste Siriac, Manu-

mission," 7 August 1829; folder 281, Cane River Collection; THNOC microfilm MSS 182, roll 1; The Historic New Orleans Collection, New Orleans, Louisiana.

Subsequent Note
11. "Marie Louise Margarite Lecomte to Jean Baptiste Siriac, Manumission," 1829, folder 281, Cane River Collection.

FHL-GSU Microfilm

See also QuickCheck Models *for* PRESERVATION FILM: FHL-GSU FILM

When you use film at the Family History Library or one of its worldwide Family History Centers, you will be citing one of three types of film:

- commercial film (or fiche) published by other agencies (see 3.18);

- preservation copies of records originally created by The Church of Jesus Christ of Latter-day Saints (LDS), for which FHL is the official repository of the preservation copy;

- preservation copies of non-LDS records, filmed by GSU, for which originals are held in record offices and archives elsewhere.

Regardless of the type of film, your citation should emphasize the original document. Then you add the appropriate reference to the FHL microfilm. Authored manuscripts that have been filmed will usually fit within the QuickCheck Model for UNPUBLISHED NARRATIVE. You simply add a note with the FHL film and item numbers. (See also 2.24–2.32.)

The following example illustrates a common case in which the FHL film contains a number of unrelated items on the same roll. In such cases, you need to cite both the roll number and the item number—in addition to the original manuscript.

Source List Entry
Croom, Emily Anne. "A Chronicle of Tennessee Crooms." Typescript [no place], 1970. FHL microfilm 897,288, item 3. Family History Library, Salt Lake City, Utah.

First Reference Note
1. Emily Anne Croom, "A Chronicle of Tennessee Crooms" (typescript, n.p., 1970), p. 39; FHL microfilm 897,288, item 3.

Subsequent Note
11. Croom, "Chronicle of Tennessee Crooms," 39.

CITING FHL IN REFERENCE NOTES

Your First Reference Note for preservation microfilm should, as a rule, cite in full the creator of the film. That rule is followed above for the film The Historic New Orleans Collection created from its own holdings. However, the breadth of the Family History Library's microfilming program means that historical researchers typically accumulate hundreds or thousands of citations to FHL film. Repeating FHL's identity in each case would be excessive. *Evidence* recommends citing FHL in full in the Source List Entry. For published papers, it recommends that the First Reference Note to an FHL film identify FHL in full. Past that point, all FHL film can be cited in the short form shown above in note 1 for the Croom manuscript.

CITING FHL FILM OR FICHE NUMBERS IN SOURCE LIST

The above example for citing FHL film differs in two significant regards from the QuickCheck Model for PRESERVATION FILM: FHL-GSU FILM.

- The Croom manuscript is unpublished and is not deposited in any library, so far as you can tell from the preservation microfilm; therefore, it is appropriate to cite FHL as a repository.

- The Croom manuscript is small and confined to just one roll of film. Thus, the film number can be cited in the Source List Entry.

- Because this manuscript appears on the same roll of film as several other unrelated items, you will want to note the item number as well as the roll.

3.20   Photographs, Portraits & Sketches

See QuickCheck Model *for* ARCHIVED MATERIAL: PORTRAIT

A citation to photographs, drawings, and other artwork usually contains three parts and sometimes four:

- basic information on the identity of the subject;
- whereabouts of the artifact;
- a brief physical description;

and sometimes
- the artist or photographer, if that person's identity is known.

In the examples that follow, the first cites the artifact by the name of the creator (the artist, photographer, etc.). The second cites the artifact by the name of the subject (the person being painted, photographed, or sketched). Whether you choose one option or the other will likely depend upon which person is more important to your research. When the emphasis is upon the painter, the art is typically treated as a titled work, with its title in quotation marks.

Source List Entry

(Creator as lead element in Source List)
Sargent, John Singer. "Portrait of Madame X." 1884. Arthur H. Hearn
　　Fund no. 1653. Metropolitan Museum of Art, New York.

(Subject as lead element in Source List)
Metoyer, Agnes (Poissot). Portrait. ca. 1835. Pat Henry Jr. Collection.
　　Cammie G. Henry Research Center. Northwestern State Univer-
　　sity, Natchitoches, Louisiana.

First Reference Note

　　1.　John Singer Sargent, "Portrait of Madame X," 1884; Arthur H.
Hearn Fund, no. 1653; Metropolitan Museum of Art, New York. Oil on
canvas, 82½" high by 43¼" wide, signed and dated "John S. Sargent,
1884."
　　2.　Agnes (Poissot) Metoyer Portrait, ca. 1835; Pat Henry Jr.
Collection, Cammie G. Henry Research Center; Northwestern State
University, Natchitoches, Louisiana. A full-color oil, 30" x 36" (framed),
signed "Feuille."

Subsequent Note

　　11.　Sargent, "Portrait of Madame X," 1884, Metropolitan Museum
of Art.
　　12.　Agnes (Poissot) Metoyer Portrait, ca. 1835, Pat Henry Jr. Collection.

CITING MAIDEN NAMES

The name *Poissot* appears in parentheses above because conventions
for precise identity in the genealogical field place maiden names in
parentheses when identifying a woman by her married name. See
2.70.

3.21　Research Reports

See QuickCheck Model *for* ARCHIVED MATERIAL: RESEARCH REPORT

A historical or genealogical research report that is found amid an
archival collection in a public repository follows the basic form for an
archived manuscript but adds two pieces of data. The *identity of the
report's recipient* is included because that detail can point to a potential
source of additional records. The *author's relevant credentials* are
added, because that information can affect the weight you would
assign to the evidence you draw from that report.

Source List Entry
(Author as lead element in Source List)

Brown, Sharon Sholars, CG. "James Ball in Fannin, Grayson, and Red River Counties, Texas." Report to R. C. Ball. 17 February 1991. Ball Family Research Collection. Clayton Library. Houston, Texas.

Mills, Gary B., PhD (Hist.). "Cultural Reconnaissance of the Mallard–Fox Creek Property." Report to Tennessee Valley Authority. 18 September 1983. Alabama Collection, Hoole Library. University of Alabama, Tuscaloosa.

(Collection as lead element in Source List)

King Papers (George Harrison Sanford King, 1914–1985). MSS 1K5823a. Virginia Historical Society. Richmond.

First Reference Note

1. Sharon Sholars Brown, CG, "James Ball in Fannin, Grayson, and Red River Counties, Texas," p. 25; report to R. C. Ball, 17 February 1991; vol. 13, Ball Family Research Collection; Clayton Library, Houston, Texas.

2. Gary B. Mills, PhD (Hist.), "Cultural Reconnaissance of the Mallard–Fox Creek Property," p. 12; report to Tennessee Valley Authority, 18 September 1983; Alabama Collection, Hoole Library; University of Alabama, Tuscaloosa.

3. George Harrison Sanford King, "The Madison Family of Virginia," p. 3; report to [unidentified], 18 November 1974, Madison Family Folder; King Papers, MSS 1K5823a; Virginia Historical Society, Richmond.

Subsequent Note

11. Brown, "James Ball in Fannin, Grayson, and Red River Counties Texas," 25.

12. Mills, "Cultural Reconnaissance of the Mallard–Fox Creek Property," 12.

13. King, "The Madison Family of Virginia," 3.

3.22   Unpublished Manuscripts

See also QuickCheck Model *for* ARCHIVED MATERIAL: UNPUBLISHED NARRATIVE

A citation for unpublished manuscripts, when an author or compiler is known, uses the same structure as one for an authored book, with minor but important differences:

AUTHORED BOOKS	AUTHORED MANUSCRIPTS
• Author's name	• Author's name
• *Title of Book*	• "Title of Manuscript"
	• Type of compilation & perhaps place (or) academic program/affiliation

- Publication place, publisher
- Year of publication
- Repository, repository place
- Year(s) of compilation, if known

The examples below illustrate the handling of two types of material:

- a card file, with cards or slips arranged in alphabetical sequence;
- a bound manuscript that is not paginated.

Source List Entry

Barbour, Lucius Barnes, and Lucius A. Barbour. "Barbour Collection of Connecticut Vital Records prior to 1850." Card file. N.d. Connecticut State Library, Hartford.

Barbour, Lucius Barnes, and Lucius A. Barbour. "Barbour Collection of Connecticut Vital Records prior to 1850." 50 vols. Bound transcripts. 1874–1934. Connecticut State Library, Hartford.

First Reference Note

1. Lucius Barnes Barbour and Lucius A. Barbour, "Barbour Collection of Connecticut Vital Records prior to 1850" (card file, n.d., Connecticut State Library, Hartford), alphabetical entry for Abigail Cook, born at Goshen, 25 January 1761.

2. Lucius Barnes Barbour and Lucius A. Barbour, "Barbour Collection of Connecticut Vital Records prior to 1850," 50 vols. (bound transcripts, 1874–1934, Connecticut State Library, Hartford), vol. 14, Town of Goshen: Abigail Cook, born 25 January 1761.

Subsequent Note

11. Barbour and Barbour, "Barbour Collection," card file, alphabetical entry for Abigail Cook, Goshen, 1761.

12. Barbour and Barbour, "Barbour Collection," vol. 14, Goshen: Abigail Cook, born 1761.

CITING REPOSITORY IN PARENTHESES

When citing bound manuscripts that compose a large series, the organization often affects the manner in which you punctuate the elements of the Reference Note. In the Draper Manuscripts example at 3.1, the nature of the elements lent itself to a basic smallest-element-to-largest-element arrangement—i.e.,

DOCUMENT < SERIES < COLLECTION < REPOSITORY, LOCATION.

A semicolon separates each major element. In contrast, the more complex arrangement of the material within the Barbour Collection—particularly the fifty-volume set treated in note 2—requires a different handling. Its elements are more akin to those of a multivolume book that is unpublished: i.e.,

AUTHOR, TITLE, NUMBER OF VOLUMES, AVAILABILITY DATA (IN PARENTHESES), SPECIFIC VOLUME, SECTION, SPECIFIC ITEM OF INTEREST.

CITING ENTRY & SECTION, IN LIEU OF PAGE NUMBER

Some compilations, such as the Barbour Collection, are not consecutively paginated and entries are not numbered. In citing unnumbered card files, you would identify the entry by person and date; you would also note how the cards are arranged. In citing Barbour's bound volumes, you would identify the volume, the town (i.e., the section within the volume), and the specific entry (person, event, and date).

The original cards and manuscript volumes that compose this Barbour Collection have also been filmed for preservation purposes by the Family History Library. Users of the film need to make only a small modification, adding a film notation to the Source List Entry and the First Reference Note, as follows:

FHL-GSU Preservation Microfilm

See QuickCheck Model *for* PRESERVATION FILM: FHL–GSU FILM

Source List Entry

(To cite the full collection)

Barbour, Lucius Barnes, and Lucius A. Barbour. "Barbour Collection of Connecticut Vital Records prior to 1850." 50 vols. Bound transcripts. Connecticut State Library, Hartford. FHL microfilm, 98 rolls. Family History Library, Salt Lake City, Utah.

(To cite a single roll from the collection)

Barbour, Lucius Barnes, and Lucius A. Barbour. "Barbour Collection of Connecticut Vital Records prior to 1850." 50 vols. Bound transcripts. Connecticut State Library, Hartford. FHL microfilm 2,970 (Vital Records, towns of Fairfield–Griswold only). Family History Library, Salt Lake City, Utah.

First Reference Note

1. Lucius Barnes Barbour and Lucius A. Barbour, "Barbour Collection of Connecticut Vital Records prior to 1850," 50 vols. (bound transcripts, 1874–1934, Connecticut State Library, Hartford), vol. 14, Town of Goshen: Abigail Cook, born 25 January 1761; FHL microfilm 2,970.

Subsequent Note

11. Barbour and Barbour, "Barbour Collection of Connecticut Vital Records prior to 1850," vol. 14, Goshen: Abigail Cook, born 1761.

CITING FHL FILM NUMBERS IN SOURCE LIST

If the filmed collection covers many rolls of microfilm, as with the Barbour example above, it is not practical to cite all the rolls of film in the Source List. On occasion, you might wish to include that information, using inclusive numbers for all the rolls. However, items that are part of a large series at FHL often do not have consecutive film numbers, in which case it would be impractical to cite several sets of starting and ending numbers. The common approach for multi-roll film sets is for the Source List to simply cite the total number of film rolls in that set, while individual reference notes will identify the specific roll for each piece of material being cited.

As an alternative, if you use only one roll of film from the collection, you may wish to identify that one roll of film in your Source List Entry. In that case, you will need to make it clear that the entire collection does not appear on just that one roll. As an example, notice the handling of the single-roll citation in the Source list Entry above. The roll is cited by number. Then in parentheses immediately following the number, readers are told that the roll covers "Vital Records [for] towns of Fairfield–Griswold only."

3.23   Vertical Files

See QuickCheck Model *for* ARCHIVED MATERIAL: VERTICAL FILE

Many archives and libraries maintain *vertical files,* wherein loose textual material and photographs on related subjects are collected in folders within file cabinets. In some local societies and museums, they are variously known as *family files.* When you cite these, your emphasis may be on the author or the subject:

Source List Entry
Oklahoma Heritage Association. "Oklahoma Ghost Town Mining Camps and Boomtowns Map." 1990. Folder: "Oklahoma: Maps— Historical & Special Interest." Vertical files. OSU–OC Library, Oklahoma State University, Oklahoma City.

Morris-Reese Research Notes. Neely Family folder. Vertical files. Elizabeth M. MacDonell Library. Allen County Historical Society. Lima, Ohio.

First Reference Note
1. Oklahoma Heritage Association, "Oklahoma Ghost Town Mining Camps and Boomtowns Map" (1990); folder: "Oklahoma: Maps— Historical & Special Interest," vertical files; OSU–OC Library, Oklahoma State University, Oklahoma City.

2. [Anonymous], "Information sent by Rosa Peltier from the Bible," p. 4; Morris-Reese Research Notes, Neely Family folder, vertical files; Elizabeth M. MacDonell Library, Allen County Historical Society, Lima, Ohio.

Subsequent Note

11. Oklahoma Heritage Association, "Oklahoma Ghost Town Mining Camps and Boomtowns Map."
12. "Information sent by Rosa Peltier from the Bible," 4.

PRIVATELY HELD MATERIALS

3.24   Basic Elements

Citations to papers, mementos, correspondence, and other items that are privately preserved usually cover four essentials:

- identification of the item according to type;
- current or last-known whereabouts of the item;
- description of the item;
- a statement of provenance—that is, the chain of title by which it passed from its original owner to the present. As a researcher, you will inquire about this when you consult with the owners. However, their information on provenance may be incomplete, in which case you will record whatever is known or discoverable.

3.25   Basic Format, Family Artifacts

See. QuickCheck Model *for* PRIVATE HOLDINGS: ARTIFACT

The basic format illustrated below can be adapted to a wide variety of artifacts in private possession, such as

- artwork and craft products
- baby books
- business and calling cards (at-home cards)
- certificates of membership, ownership, etc.
- funeral announcements and programs or mass cards
- medals and awards
- military discharges and other military papers
- photographs, photograph albums, scrapbooks
- quilts, samplers, etc.
- school records
- scout badges, pins, and other scouting records
- social invitations
- tax receipts
- war-ration coupon books
- wedding books

Source List Entry

Block Family Collection. Privately held by Wilma Washington, [AD-
DRESS FOR PRIVATE USE,] Whitehorse, Yukon, Canada. 2000.

Mills Family Papers, 1681—. Privately held by Elizabeth Shown Mills,
[ADDRESS FOR PRIVATE USE,] Tuscaloosa, Alabama.

First Reference Note

1. Betty Block tea towel, Block Family Collection; privately held by
Wilma Washington, [ADDRESS FOR PRIVATE USE,] Whitehorse, Yukon,
Canada, 2000. Embroidered with the birth date *1 May 1800*, the towel
is cross-stitched in rose and gray on yellowed linen; it measures 18" x 24"
and is frayed at one corner. It passed through six generations of the
Block-Washington family to Wilma Washington, who inherited it in
2000.

2. James T. Hanson funeral notice, Marthaville, Louisiana, citing
services on 9 December 1888; Mills Family Papers, 1681—, privately
held by Elizabeth Shown Mills, [ADDRESS FOR PRIVATE USE,] Tuscaloosa,
Alabama. This printed, black-bordered announcement, 5" x 7", was
passed from Hanson's aunt Mary Hanson Morse (1821–1902) to her
grandson Hugh E. Mills (1880–1961) to his grandson Gary B. Mills
(1944–2002), from whom the current owner inherited it in 2002.

Subsequent Note

11. Betty Block tea towel, Block Family Collection.
12. James T. Hanson funeral notice, 1888, Mills Family Papers.

CITING YEAR OF CREATION

In the Block example, the creation date of the towel is unknown;
therefore, a date does not appear in the Subsequent Note. In the
Hanson example, the item's creation date is internally identified
and the year can be carried forward to the subsequent note to
maintain a clearer context for the source.

CITING YEAR OF OWNERSHIP

If you are citing material you consulted in someone else's personal
possession, as with the Block example, you will need to cite the
year or date that you consulted it. If you are citing material you
now hold in your possession—as with the present author's Mills
Family Papers above—you do not have to cite the year of
possession because that would require continuous update to the
Source Entry.

3.26 Bible Pages, Loose, from Unidentified Bible

Researchers frequently encounter family records on pages that were
clearly torn from a Bible, although nothing is known about that Bible
or the creator of the data. The citation to these family pages follows

the same format as in 3.25, with a change of wording to specify the kind of artifact. Although the basic citation is short, you will also want to add an explanatory note that discusses two key issues:

- whatever provenance is known for the material;
- any characteristics (ink, penmanship, damage, etc.) that affect your analysis or interpretation of the data within this source.

The following examples illustrate both photocopied and digitized records, as well as the types of details commonly explained.

Source List Entry
Hulse Bible Records, 1850–1914. Family pages only. Digital images made by Annette Hulse, [ADDRESS FOR PRIVATE USE,] Los Altos, California. 2002.

Waddle Bible Records, 1812–1938. Family pages only. Photocopy held by Jane Ailes, [ADDRESS FOR PRIVATE USE,] White Post, Virginia. 2004.

First Reference Note
1. Hulse Bible Records, 1850–1914, loose "Family Record" pages from unknown Bible; digital images made by Annette Hulse, [ADDRESS FOR PRIVATE USE,] Los Altos, California, 2002. The Bible apparently originated with William F. Hulse, whose birth is the earliest entry; comparisons of ink and penmanship suggest most entries were recorded 1900–1910. The Bible or its pages passed to William's granddaughter Gertrude (Hulse) Gooch, and then to her son, the Reverend John Gooch of Liberty, Missouri, who still owns the original torn-out leaves.

2. Waddle Bible Records, 1812–1938, family pages; photocopies held by Jane Ailes, [ADDRESS FOR PRIVATE USE,] White Post, Virginia, 2004. Entries suggest that the earliest owners were Julius Caesar Waddle (1812–86) and wife Mary Jane Mullin (1816–89), who married in 1837. Photocopies of the pages were supplied years ago to Mrs. Ailes' mother, apparently by William and Mary Jane's granddaughter Catherine.

Subsequent Note
11. Hulse Bible Records, 1850–1914, family pages only.
12. Waddle Bible Records, 1812–1938, family pages only.

Bible Pages, Transcribed Online

Source List Entry
Stroud, F. E., Bible Records. Family pages only. Photocopy held by Frederic Z. Saunders, [ADDRESS FOR PRIVATE USE,] Salt Lake City, Utah. Online transcription by Saunders. http://www.rootsweb.com/~tnwcogs/biblerec/stroud01.html : 2007.

First Reference Note

1. F. E. Stroud Bible Records, family pages only; photocopy held by Frederic Z. Saunders, [ADDRESS FOR PRIVATE USE,] Salt Lake City, Utah, 2007; online transcription by Saunders, *Stroud Family Bible* (http://www.rootsweb.com/~tnwcogs/biblerec/stroud01.html : accessed 31 January 2007). The original Bible was last in possession of Stroud's daughter Mildred (Stroud) Blair of Sun City, Arizona, now deceased. The first entries appear to have been made at the 1858 marriage of O. B. Stroud to M. E. Moody, with earlier records added at that time.

Subsequent Note

11. F. E. Stroud Bible, family pages only, online transcription.

3.27   Bibles with Family Data

See QuickCheck Models *for*

- ARCHIVED MATERIAL: PERSONAL BIBLE
- PRIVATE HOLDINGS: FAMILY BIBLE RECORD

When citing family data pages for surviving Bibles, a full citation covers two separate elements:

- the actual Bible, cited in Basic Format: Books (12.3). The details from the title page are important to record, so that you and others can compare the Bible's age with the time span of the entries. Family data may have been entered contemporaneously or later— a difference that can affect the reliability of the information that Bible offers.

- the identity of the original owner and the Bible's provenance, as well as the identity and location of the current owner.

Source List Entry

Greene, John Lynde Sr., Family Bible Records, 1807–1944. *The Holy Bible*. Philadelphia: Matthew Carey, 1811. Privately held by John Lynde Greene IV, [ADDRESS FOR PRIVATE USE,] Germantown, Maryland. 2001.

First Reference Note

1. John Lynde Greene Sr. Family Bible Records, 1807–1944, *The Holy Bible* (Philadelphia: Matthew Carey, 1811), "Marriages"; privately held by John Lynde Greene IV, [ADDRESS FOR PRIVATE USE,] Germantown, Maryland, 2001. [ADD PROVENANCE AND ANALYSES OF HANDWRITING, PENMANSHIP, AND TIMELINESS OF THE ENTRIES.]

Subsequent Note

11. John Lynde Greene Sr. Family Bible Records, "Marriages."

3.28 Charts & Family Group Sheets

See also QuickCheck Model *for* PRIVATE HOLDINGS: FAMILY CHART ...

Ancestral charts and family group sheets of modern compilation, supplied by others, are cited as authored works. Because they are modern manuscripts, rather than publications, you should add contact information on the compiler. Careful researchers also comment upon the apparent reliability of the data. Citations that do not provide an appraisal imply that researchers have uncritically accepted the work as reliable.

Source List Entry

(Collection as lead element in Source List)

Ollsen Family Charts and Group Sheets, 1548–1948. Privately held by Jerg Ollsen, [ADDRESS FOR PRIVATE USE,] Vestero, Laeso, Denmark. 1989.

(Compiler as lead element in Source List)

Orveld, Johann. "Pedigree Chart for Leopold Orlicek." Supplied by compiler, [ADDRESS FOR PRIVATE USE,] Vienna, Austria. 1995.

First Reference Note

1. Jerg Ollsen, Erik Ollsen–Anna Hansen Family Group Sheet, Ollsen Family Charts and Group Sheets, 1548–1948; supplied by Ollsen, [ADDRESS FOR PRIVATE USE,] Vestero, Laeso, Denmark, 1989. This sheet offers only a generic list of materials used, with no specific documentation for any piece of data.

2. Johann Orveld, "Pedigree Chart for Leopold Orlicek," supplied 1995 by Orveld, [ADDRESS FOR PRIVATE USE,] Vienna, Austria; thoroughly documented with quality sources.

Subsequent Note

11. Ollsen, "Erik Ollsen–Anna Hansen Family Group Sheet," previously evaluated at note 1.

12. Orveld, "Pedigree Chart for Leopold Orlicek," thoroughly documented with quality sources.

CITING "SUPPLIED BY" VS. "PRIVATELY HELD"

When you cite photocopied material in your own possession but the originals are held by someone who supplied those copies to you, you should credit the supplier of the material—i.e., it was "supplied by." If you cite material owned by someone else who allowed you to consult it but did not supply you with a copy, then you would use the phrase "privately held by." If you cite material that you created yourself, you would also use the "privately held" phrasing, identifying yourself as the owner.

3.29   Diaries, Journals & Authored Manuscripts

See QuickCheck Model *for* PRIVATE HOLDINGS: DIARY or JOURNAL

Unpublished diaries and journals are frequently consulted in two forms: originals and typescripts. When citing a typescript and the transcriber is known—as in the second option below—that person should be identified. Whether your Source List carries the transcribed diary under the name of the diarist or the transcriber is a call you will make according to which element is more important to you.

Source List Entry

(To cite the original manuscript)

Brown, Sarah Jane (Hickman). "Journal." MS. Fernwood Station, Mississippi, 1896–1902. Privately held by Anne S. Anderson, [ADDRESS FOR PRIVATE USE,] Gulfport, Mississippi. 2005.

(To cite the typescript by original author)

Brown, Sarah Jane (Hickman). "Journal of Sarah Jane (Hickman) Brown, Fernwood Station, Mississippi, 1896–1902." Typescript by Bettye Collier Smith, CGRS, ca. 1990. Copy privately held by Anne S. Anderson, [ADDRESS FOR PRIVATE USE,] Gulfport, Mississippi. 2005.

(To cite the typescript by transcriber)

Smith, Bettye Collier, CGRS, transcriber. "Journal of Sarah Jane (Hickman) Brown, Fernwood Station, Mississippi, 1896–1902." MS. ca. 1990. Copy privately held by Anne S. Anderson, [ADDRESS FOR PRIVATE USE,] Gulfport, Mississippi. 2005.

First Reference Note

(To cite the original manuscript)

　　1. Sarah Jane (Hickman) Brown, "Journal" (MS, Fernwood Station, Mississippi, 1896–1902), p. 123; privately held by Anne S. Anderson, [ADDRESS FOR PRIVATE USE,] Gulfport, Mississippi, 2005. Ms. Anderson is the great-granddaughter of the journal's author.

(To cite the typescript)

　　2. Bettye Collier Smith, CGRS, transcriber, "Journal of Sarah Jane (Hickman) Brown, 1896–1902, Fernwood Station, Mississippi" (typescript, ca. 1990), p. 87; copy in possession of Anne S. Anderson, [ADDRESS FOR PRIVATE USE,] Gulfport, Mississippi, 2005.

Subsequent Note

　　11. Sarah Jane (Hickman) Brown, "Journal [1896–1902]," 123.
　　12. Smith, "Journal of Sarah Jane Hickman," 87.

CREATING THE SHORT TITLE

If the short form at note 11 had followed the usual format of citing the author's last name and manuscript title (i.e., Brown, "Journal"), the commonness of the surname and the generic nature of the title would convey very little information. Therefore, in note 11, the short form includes the full name of the author to help readers better identify the source and evaluate the reliability of the assertion this citation supports.

3.30   Family Records (Non-Bible)

In many families, the handed-down record is simply a sheet or sheaf of papers that have no connection to a Bible. Most are compiled long after the events occurred. In other cases, the artifact may be a bound manuscript volume of one or another type. Most of these will follow the basic model for family artifacts, 3.25. However, individual citations will differ slightly, based upon the nature of the material.

Source List Entry

Ball Plantation Book. MS. ca. mid-1800s. Photocopy privately held by
   R. C. Ball, [ADDRESS FOR PRIVATE USE,] Houston, Texas. 1990.
Gordon Family Record. MS. Privately held by Wright Bomford Jr.,
   [ADDRESS FOR PRIVATE USE,] Houston, Texas. 1998.

First Reference Note

1.   Ball Plantation Book (MS, ca. mid-1800s), p. 23; photocopy privately held by R. C. Ball, [ADDRESS FOR PRIVATE USE,] Houston, Texas, 1990. A photocopy of this record book was supplied to R. C. Ball in 1984 by Mrs. Evelyn Hight of Houston. The book's creator appears to have been Elizabeth Jane (Ball) Allen Mounger, born 1814 at Milledgeville, Georgia, daughter of one William Ball.

2.   Gordon Family Record (MS, no date), privately held by Wright Bomford Jr., [ADDRESS FOR PRIVATE USE,] Houston, Texas, 1998. Untitled, these handwritten notes by Emily Bomford Gordon cover four generations; a photocopy is in possession of Nancy Simons Peterson, [ADDRESS FOR PRIVATE USE,] Vaughn, Washington, 1998.

Subsequent Note

11.   Ball Plantation Book, 23.
12.   Gordon Family Record, previously discussed.

"PREVIOUSLY DISCUSSED"

The phrase *previously discussed* (or its arcane precursor, *op. cit.*) is not mandatory. It is not used in note 11 above, where the source is cited by book and page. In note 12, where the information is less specific and there is no collection to cite, the use of "previously discussed" will alert readers to the fact that a fuller explanation of the record's whereabouts and origin has already been supplied.

3.31   Frakturs

German *frakturs*—illuminated certificates of births, baptisms, and marriages—were originally commissioned by families to commemorate events and were prized as both art and family record. When using an original fraktur, your citation should include the name of the artist, if known, along with the other basic data.

In later years, certificates were mass-produced, in which case the printer's name and publication facts might be noted. As with citing a family Bible, the proximity of the printing date to the date of the event affects one's evaluation of the information within the record.

In the following example, the Source List Entry cites a preprinted fraktur under the family name. Even there, you have an option, depending upon whether you have one sole document to cite or whether you have multiple frakturs for the family.

Source List Entry

(If only one fraktur is cited)
Haberling, Georg Samuel. Fraktur (certificate). Birth and baptism, 1829. Printed Allentown, Pennsylvania: H. Ebner & Co., n.d. Owned by John Humphrey, [ADDRESS FOR PRIVATE USE,] Washington, D.C. 2004.

(If citing multiple frakturs for the same family)
Haberling Family Frakturs. Owned by John Humphrey, [ADDRESS FOR PRIVATE USE,] Washington, D.C. 2004.

First Reference Note

1. Georg Samuel Haberling Fraktur (certificate), birth and baptism, 1829 (Allentown, Pennsylvania: H. Ebner & Co., printer, n.d.); owned 2004 by John Humphrey, [ADDRESS FOR PRIVATE USE,] Washington, D.C., who purchased the item at an antiques market.

Subsequent Note

11. George Samuel Haberling Fraktur, birth and baptism, 1829.

Frakturs (Online Images)

Source List Entry

(If only one fraktur is cited)
Grotz, Georg. Taufschein (certificate of baptism). 1779. Image copy by John Bieber, *Pennsylvania Dutch Fraktur Gallery*. http://home .att.net/~fraktur/ : 2007.

(*To cite an online collection*)
Bieber, John, *Pennsylvania Dutch Fraktur Gallery*. http://home.att.net/
~fraktur/ : 2007.

First Reference Note
  1. Georg Grotz Taufschein [certificate of baptism], 1779; image
copy by John Bieber, *Pennsylvania Dutch Fraktur Gallery* (http://home
.att.net/~fraktur/ : accessed 31 January 2007).
  2. John Bieber, *Pennsylvania Dutch Fraktur Gallery* (http://
home.att.net/~fraktur/ : 31 January 2007), for Georg Grotz Taufschein
(certificate of baptism), 1779.

Subsequent Note
  11. Georg Grotz Taufschein, 1779.
  12. Bieber, *Pennsylvania Dutch Fraktur Gallery*, for Georg Grotz
Taufschein, 1779.

FOREIGN LANGUAGE TITLES, TRANSLATION OF
See 2.23 *and* 3.12

3.32   Interview Tapes & Transcripts
See also QuickCheck Model *for* PRIVATE HOLDINGS: INTERVIEW

Citations to interviews need to include

  • the identity of both the informant and the interviewer;
  • contact information for the informant;
  • the date and place conducted;
  • the format of the material produced;
  • present whereabouts of the notes or tapes; and
  • any relationship between the interviewer and the interviewee.

The address of the informant is information needed for your working
files, but you should not publish it (in print, online, or in any other
media) without the authorization of the informant, so long as he or
she is alive. If the notes or tapes are in the private possession of
someone other than yourself, you would extend that person the same
privacy rights. After their deaths, the residency information becomes
historical data useful for research purposes. In the examples that
follow, the informants are all deceased.

Whether you include the date of the interview in your Source List
Entry will depend upon whether you have just one interview with this
person or multiple interviews. For more than one interview, you
would cite a time frame, rather than a specific date.

Source List Entry

(If citing a single interview with the informant)
Graham, Ardell. Tuscola, Illinois. Interview by Helen E. Brieske. 14 April 1993. Transcript. Privately held by Brieske, [ADDRESS FOR PRIVATE USE,] Salida, Colorado. 2006.

(If citing multiple interviews with the informant)
Graham, Ardell. Tuscola, Illinois. Interviews by Helen E. Brieske. 1992–93. Transcripts. Privately held by Brieske, [ADDRESS FOR PRIVATE USE,] Salida, Colorado. 2006.

First Reference Note

1. Ardell Graham (212 East Sale, Tuscola, IL 61953), interview by Helen E. Brieske, 14 April 1993; transcript privately held by Brieske, [ADDRESS FOR PRIVATE USE,] Salida, Colorado, 2006. Ardell, a son of Tillie, spoke from personal knowledge when he related her death.

Subsequent Note

11. Ardell Graham, interview, 14 April 1993.

Audiotaped Interview

Source List Entry

(If citing a collection of interviews, privately held)
Cane River Oral History Collection. Interviews by Elizabeth Shown Mills and Gary B. Mills. 1972–1976. Audiotapes and transcripts. Privately held by E. S. Mills, [ADDRESS FOR PRIVATE USE,] Tuscaloosa, Alabama. 2007.

(If citing a single interview with one informant)
Larner, John William, Jr. Altamonte Springs, Florida. Interview by Nathan J. Giroux. 2 September 2001. Audiotape and transcript. Privately held by Amy Larner Giroux, [ADDRESS FOR PRIVATE USE,] Orlando, Florida. 2007.

First Reference Note

1. Lee Etta Vaccarini Coutii (Isle Brevelle, Louisiana), recorded interview by Elizabeth Shown Mills and Gary B. Mills, 30 August 1972; Cane River Oral History Collection; audiotapes and transcripts privately held by E. S. Mills, [ADDRESS FOR PRIVATE USE,] Tuscaloosa, Alabama, 2007.

2. John William Larner Jr. (445 Citadel Drive, Altamonte Springs, FL 32714), interview by Nathan J. Giroux, 2 September 2001; audiotape and transcript privately held by Amy Larner Giroux, [ADDRESS FOR PRIVATE USE,] Orlando, Florida, 2007. Larner, now deceased, was the father of Amy and the grandfather of Nathan.

Subsequent Note
11. Lee Etta Vaccarini Coutii, interview, 30 August 1972.
12. John William Larner Jr., interview, 2 September 2001.

3.33 Jewelry, Medals & *Objets d'Art*

Most privately held mementos can be cited using Basic Format: Family Artifacts, 3.25. The following examples illustrate three types of items frequently found in private possession. Whether you cite to a family collection (as with the Hyams-Charleville and Morgan examples) or to an individual (as with Prout) will depend upon the origin and extent of the material you are holding.

Source List Entry

Hyams-Charleville Artifacts. Privately held by Adele Sperier, [ADDRESS FOR PRIVATE USE,] Woodlawn, Texas. 1991.

Morgan Family Collection. Owned by George G. Morgan, [ADDRESS FOR PRIVATE USE,] Odessa, Florida. 2007.

Prout, Rigaude Placide LaTrobe DeMontalt Mementos. Owned by Andrea Butler-Ramsey, [ADDRESS FOR PRIVATE USE,] The Bronx, New York. 1999.

First Reference Note

1. Eleazar Hyams–Aurora Charleville wedding silver, engraved "1859," in Hyams-Charleville Artifacts; privately held by Adele Sperier, [ADDRESS FOR PRIVATE USE,] Woodlawn, Texas. Sperier's mother was niece and heir to the Widow Hyams of Natchitoches Parish, Louisiana.

2. Laura Augusta "Minnie" (Wilson) Morgan, wedding ring, 1902, Morgan Family Collection, owned by George G. Morgan, [ADDRESS FOR PRIVATE USE,] Odessa, Florida, 2007. The band is inscribed *Ego Amo Te*.

3. Rigaude Placide LaTrobe DeMontalt Prout (Santa Lucia, Barbados, and New York City), Croix de Guerre, World War I; owned by granddaughter Andrea Butler-Ramsey, [ADDRESS FOR PRIVATE USE,] The Bronx, New York, 1999.

Subsequent Note

11. Eleazar Hyams–Aurora Charleville wedding silver, 1859, Hyams-Charleville Artifacts.

12. Laura Augusta "Minnie" (Wilson) Morgan, wedding ring, 1902, Morgan Family Collection.

13. Rigaude Placide LaTrobe DeMontalt Prout, Croix de Guerre, World War I.

3.34 Legal Documents, Unrecorded Family Copies

Unrecorded legal records preserved in private possession call for essentially the same basic elements as other privately held materials and can be cited in Basic Format: Family Artifacts, 3.25, as demonstrated by the following deed.

Source List Entry
Bertrand-Lennon Family Archives. Privately held by Rachal M. Lennon, [ADDRESS FOR PRIVATE USE,] Cottontown, Tennessee. 2007.

First Reference Note
1. Pierre Bertrand, master surgeon, to town of Verdun, donation, 24 April 1760; original family copy, Bertrand-Lennon Family Archives; privately held by Rachal M. Lennon, [ADDRESS FOR PRIVATE USE,] Cottontown, Tennessee, 2007. [ADD PROVENANCE.]

Subsequent Note
11. Bertrand donation to town of Verdun, 1760, Bertrand-Lennon Family Archives.

3.35   Letters, Historic
See QuickCheck Model *for* PRIVATE HOLDINGS: HISTORIC LETTER

When citing historic letters in private possession, you have three principal parties to cite: the creator (author), the person to whom the letter is addressed (the recipient), and the current owner of the document. If the recipient is not specifically named but is otherwise known, as in the example below, the identity should be inserted in square editorial brackets. You would then add to the citation an explanation of how you know that identity.

Source List Entry
(*Collection as lead element of Source List*)
Mills Family Papers, 1850–. Privately held by Clayton Mills, [ADDRESS FOR PRIVATE USE,] Nashville, Tennessee. 2007.

(*Writer as lead element of Source List*)
Charleville, F. A. (Fiddletown, California) to "Dear Sister" [Athanaise Charleville Faris]. Letter. 15 November 1867. Privately held by Clayton Mills, [ADDRESS FOR PRIVATE USE,] Nashville, Tennessee. 2007.

First Reference Note
1. F. A. Charleville (Fiddletown, California) to "Dear Sister" [Athanaise Charleville Faris], letter, 15 November 1867; Mills Family Papers, 1850–, privately held by Clayton Mills, [ADDRESS FOR PRIVATE USE,] Nashville, Tennessee, 2007. A descendant of Athanaise gave the inherited letter to F. A. Charleville's great-grandson Charles King, Oakland, California, who passed it to Mills' mother in 1972.

Subsequent Note
11. F. A. Charleville to "Dear Sister," 15 November 1867, Mills Family Papers.

POSITION OF PLACE DATA
As a rule, when your citation involves multiple people and you are identifying a place for one of them, that place should appear immediately after the name of the person to whom it applies. In the example above, if you were to cite "F. A. Charleville to 'Dear Sister,' Fiddletown, California, letter, ... " you would imply that Charleville's sister was the person in Fiddletown.

3.36 Newspaper Clippings
News clippings in private collections often do not identify the newspaper or the date the item was published. When this occurs, you should note the absence of that information and add the provenance of the item. That provenance will typically include the identity of the current owner and how that owner came to acquire it. You would adapt Basic Format: Family Artifacts, 3.25, to fit the situation.

Source List Entry

(If listed by subject's name)
Hensel, F. J., Sr. "F. J. Hensel, Sr., Is Dead at 80." Undated clipping. ca. mid-1950s, from unidentified newspaper. Privately held by Patricia (Walls) Stamm, [ADDRESS FOR PRIVATE USE,] St. Louis, Missouri. 2007.

(If cited as part of a family collection)
Walls Family Papers. Privately held by Patricia Walls Stamm, [ADDRESS FOR PRIVATE USE,] St. Louis, Missouri. 2007.

First Reference Note
1. "F. J. Hensel, Sr., Is Dead at 80," undated clipping, ca. mid-1950s, from unidentified newspaper; Walls Family Papers, privately held by Patricia (Walls) Stamm, [ADDRESS FOR PRIVATE USE,] St. Louis, Missouri, 2007. Inherited in 1992 by Mrs. Stamm from her mother Stella (Paddock) Walls, wife of John M. Walls of Wilmington, Delaware.

Subsequent Note
11. "F. J. Hensel, Sr., Is Dead at 80," Walls Family Papers.

3.37 Photographs, Portraits & Sketches
A photograph that is held by the family also takes Basic Format: Family Artifacts, 3.25. The following example demonstrates the citing of a scanned image.

Source List Entry

Peebley, Frances "Fanny" (Austin). Photograph. ca. 1840. Digital image. Privately held by Douglas S. Shipley, [ADDRESS FOR PRIVATE USE,] El Paso, Texas. 2002.

First Reference Note

1. Frances "Fanny" (Austin) Peebley photograph, ca. 1840; digital image ca. 1997, privately held by Douglas S. Shipley, [ADDRESS FOR PRIVATE USE,] El Paso, Texas, 2002. Fanny gave the original to her daughter-in-law, Almadie, (Mrs. Jube) Austin. About 1983, Jube and Almadie's granddaughter, Jackie Lugrand, supplied a copy to her cousin Jack Frey, who allowed Shipley to scan it. The location, condition, and characteristics of the original are not known.

Subsequent Note

11. Frances "Fanny" (Austin) Peebley photograph, Peebley-Austin Family Collection.

3.38 Samplers

Citations for samplers are essentially the same as those for other family artifacts (3.25). In the example below, the current location of the original is unknown. The citation is only to a photograph of the sampler; it credits the photographer for both his work and the details he provides about the last-known whereabouts of the original artifact.

Source List Entry

(If listed by family name)

Larzelere, Elisabeth. Sampler dated 1812. Photograph of the original. *ca.* 1980s. By Robert Leland Larzalere. Privately held by Larzalere, [ADDRESS FOR PRIVATE USE,] Fort Collins, Colorado. 2006.

(If listed by title of sampler)

"Elisabeth Larzelere her sampler wrought in the 13th year of her age 1812." Photograph of the original, ca. 1980s. By Robert Leland Larzalere. Held by Larzalere, [ADDRESS FOR PRIVATE USE,] Fort Collins, Colorado. 2006.

First Reference Note

1. "Elisabeth Larzelere her sampler wrought in the 13th year of her age 1812," photograph of the original taken ca. 1980s by Robert Leland Larzalere, [ADDRESS FOR PRIVATE USE,] Fort Collins, Colorado (of no known kinship to the creator), who discovered the sampler by a chance encounter. The present location of the original is unknown.

Subsequent Note

11. "Elisabeth Larzelere her sampler wrought in the 13th year of her age 1812," photograph taken ca. 1980s.

3.39   School Records, Heirloom Copies

Citations to original school records handed down in a family may be cited by Basic Format: Family Artifacts, 3.25. Your treatment will vary, depending upon whether the items are

- original *administrative* records in private possession, as in the Union Grade School example, below; or

- original *student* records passed through the generations, as with the Sholder-Stabler example.

For current transcripts provided by a school board, see the QuickCheck Model for SCHOOL RECORDS: STUDENT TRANSCRIPT, chapter 4.

Source List Entry

(Administrative records—school's name as lead element in Source List)
Union Grade School, Bear Creek Township, Hancock County, Illinois. "School Register, 1898–1911." Privately held by Connie Neill, [ADDRESS FOR PRIVATE USE,] Carthage, Illinois. 2007.

(Student record—student's name as lead element in Source List)
Stabler, Frederic. Common School Diploma. 1919. Privately held by Kevin Sholder, [ADDRESS FOR PRIVATE USE,] Centerville, Ohio. 2007.

(Student record—collection as lead element in Source List)
Sholder Family Papers. Privately held by Kevin Sholder, [ADDRESS FOR PRIVATE USE,] Centerville, Ohio. 2007.

First Reference Note

1. "School Register, 1898–1911," p. 3; Union Grade School, Bear Creek Township, Hancock County, Illinois; privately held, 2007, by Connie Neill, [ADDRESS FOR PRIVATE USE,] Carthage, Illinois, who found the register in the effects of her great-grandmother Trientje "Tena" Ufkes of Carthage.

2. Frederic Stabler, Common School Diploma, 1919, Lycoming, Pennsylvania; original certificate given by Mr. Stabler to his grandson Kevin Sholder, [ADDRESS FOR PRIVATE USE,] Centerville, Ohio, 2000; privately held by Sholder, 2007.

Subsequent Note

11. "School Register, 1898–1911," Union Grade School.
12. Frederic Stabler, Common School Diploma, 1921.

CITING NICKNAMES

As discussed in 2.72 and demonstrated above in note 1, nicknames are conventionally placed in double quotation marks, immediately after the given name. They should not be placed in parentheses, because that convention is used for the maiden surname of females, as discussed at 3.20 and illustrated further at 3.37 and 3.40.

3.40 Scrapbooks & Albums

See QuickCheck Model *for* PRIVATE HOLDINGS: ARTIFACT

When you cite a photograph album or a scrapbook, your Source List Entry may emphasize the creator or it may focus on the collection in which the scrapbook is held. Either approach fits within the Basic Format: Family Artifacts, 3.25. For citing newspaper clippings that are not in scrapbooks, see 3.36.

Source List Entry

(*Creator as lead element in Source List*)
Stabler, Zella (Lovell). Scrapbook. ca. 1930–80. Privately held by Mrs. Stabler, [ADDRESS FOR PRIVATE USE,] Williamsport, Pennsylvania. 2007.

(*Collection as lead element in Source List*)
Stabler-Lovell Family Archives. Scrapbook of Zella (Lovell) Stabler. ca. 1930–80. Privately held by Mrs. Stabler, [ADDRESS FOR PRIVATE USE,] Williamsport, Pennsylvania. 2007.

First Reference Note

1. G. B. Wuster obituary, undated clipping from unidentified newspaper, in Zella (Lovell) Stabler Scrapbook, ca. 1930–80, unpaginated; privately held by Mrs. Stabler, [ADDRESS FOR PRIVATE USE,] Williamsport, Pennsylvania, 2007.

Subsequent Note

11. G. B. Wuster obituary, Zella (Lovell) Stabler Scrapbook.

PERSONAL FILES & KNOWLEDGE

3.41 Correspondence

See also QuickCheck Model *for* PRIVATE HOLDINGS: PERSONAL CORRESPONDENCE

When you cite a letter you have received from a contemporary to support historical information, your citation needs to do two things:

- identify the letter by writer, recipient, date, and location for each of you; and
- state why the letter deserves to be considered an authority for the historical information it provides.

Source List Entry

(Collection as lead element in Source List)

Ingalls Correspondence Files. Privately held by Kay Germain Ingalls, [RESEARCHER'S CONTACT INFORMATION]. 2007.

(Writer as lead element in Source List)

Pitcher, Flossie (Shimmin). Letter. 26 January 1981 to Kay Germain Ingalls. 26 January 1981. Privately held by Ingalls, [RESEARCHER'S CONTACT INFORMATION]. 2007.

First Reference Note

1. Flossie (Shimmin) Pitcher (111 Humniston Street; Pontiac, IL 61764) to Kay Germain Ingalls, letter, 26 January 1981; privately held by Ingalls, [RESEARCHER'S CONTACT INFORMATION,] 2007. The late Mrs. Pitcher, wife of Albert W. Pitcher, was the granddaughter of the Illinois state legislator William H. Dunn, whose 1912 campaign literature she provided with this letter.

Subsequent Note

11. Pitcher to Ingalls, 26 January 1981.

3.42 E-Mail

See also QuickCheck Model *for* PRIVATE HOLDINGS: PERSONAL E-MAIL

E-mail addresses should be treated with the same privacy guidelines as residential addresses. You should record them in your personal notes but should not publish them in any format without permission.

When it is necessary to break an e-mail address at the end of a line, the ideal break is immediately after the @ symbol; otherwise, you should follow the same rules given for URL breaks at 2.37.

Digital Files

See also QuickCheck Model *for* PRIVATE HOLDINGS: PERSONAL E-MAIL

Source List Entry

(Collection as lead element in Source List)

Fleming Research Files. Privately held by Ann Carter Fleming [(E-ADDRESS), & STREET ADDRESS FOR PRIVATE USE], Chesterfield, Missouri. 2007.

(Writer as lead element in Source List)

Gomez, Raymundo. "Ortodoxia, simbología, leyes y tradición en Mexico." E-mail from [(E-ADDRESS FOR PRIVATE USE),] to Paul Martin. 13 January 2001. Privately held by Martin. [(E-ADDRESS), & ADDRESS FOR PRIVATE USE], Hamilton, Bermuda Islands. 2004.

First Reference Note

1. Kay Haviland Freilich, Wayne, Pennsylvania [(E-ADDRESS FOR PRIVATE USE),] to Ann Carter Fleming, e-mail, 14 November 2003, "Elusive 1870 census entry," Personal Correspondence Folder, Fleming Research Files; privately held by Fleming, [(E-ADDRESS), & STREET ADDRESS FOR PRIVATE USE], Chesterfield, Missouri, 2007.

2. Raymundo Gomez, Mexico City, Mexico [(E-ADDRESS FOR PRIVATE USE),] to Paul Martin, e-mail, 13 January 2001, "Ortodoxia, simbología, leyes y tradición en Mexico"; privately held by Martin [(E-ADDRESS), & STREET ADDRESS FOR PRIVATE USE], Hamilton, Bermuda Islands, 2004.

Subsequent Note

11. Freilich to Fleming, e-mail, 14 November 2003.
12. Gomez to Martin, e-mail, 13 January 2001.

3.43   Personal Knowledge

Personal knowledge is a source that historical researchers rarely have occasion to cite. It is justified only when you discuss circumstances in which you are a firsthand witness or participant. When you record information given to you by others, you record that as an interview, a letter, a tradition, or whatever means may be the case.

Given the limited use of personal knowledge as a source, you would not need to list it in a *published* Source List. For data-entry purposes, your *working* Source List will likely carry the generic citation "Personal knowledge of the author." However, you should personalize that with the addition of your name and address, to preserve your identity as the source when and if your file is later merged with the research of others.

Each time that you select this source, you will want to add specific details to explain why you are qualified to be a source for that event or fact (i.e., the nature of your firsthand participation in that event).

Source List Entry

Richardson, Lauren H. Personal knowledge. [RESEARCHER'S CONTACT INFORMATION.]

First Reference Note

1. Personal knowledge of the author, Lauren H. Richardson, [RESEARCHER'S CONTACT INFORMATION]. Richardson, the daughter of Shirley U. Hubbard, attended Mrs. Hubbard's burial on 27 April 1966.

Subsequent Note

11. Personal knowledge of the author, Lauren H. Richardson.

3.44   Research Files & Reports, Personal File Copy

See QuickCheck Models *for*
• ARCHIVED MATERIAL: RESEARCH REPORT
• PRIVATE HOLDINGS: RESEARCH REPORT
and Business & Institutional Records, Chapter 4

In the course of research, you may exchange notes and files with others who are working on the same topics. The examples below illustrate a paginated, professional research report that is now privately held, as well as two ways of handling a GEDCOM (database) file created by a private researcher.

Source List Entry

Bamman, Gale Williams, CG. "William Ball of Giles County, Tennessee: Project No. 2." Report to R. C. Ball, [ADDRESS FOR PRIVATE USE], Houston, Texas, 17 March 1990. Photocopy held by [NAME, ADDRESS].

"Kincaid GEDCOM File." Compiled by TexAnna Kincaid [(E-ADDRESS), & MAILING ADDRESS], Boise, Idaho. Supplied by Kincaid, 23 August 2006. Copy held by [RESEARCHER & CONTACT INFORMATION].

First Reference Note

1. Gale Williams Bamman, CG, "William Ball of Giles County, Tennessee: Project No. 2," p. 5; prepared for R. C. Ball, [ADDRESS FOR PRIVATE USE,] Houston, Texas, 17 March 1990; photocopy held by [NAME, ADDRESS].

2. Biographical sketch of Lois Kincaid, no. 1234, "Kincaid GEDCOM File," compiled by TexAnna Kincaid [(E-ADDRESS), & MAILING ADDRESS], Boise, Idaho; supplied by Kincaid, 23 August 2006, with no citation of source; copy held by [RESEARCHER & CONTACT INFORMATION].

(For a different sketch in the same source)
3. Biographical sketch of John Kincaid, no. 321, "Kincaid GEDCOM File," by TexAnna Kincaid, citing "Resignations of militia officers, November 1832–January 1833 General Assembly Session, North Carolina State Archives."

Subsequent Note

11. Bamman, "William Ball of Giles County, Tennessee: Project No. 2," p. 5.

12. Biographical sketch of Lois Kincaid, no. 1234, "Kincaid GEDCOM File."

13. Biographical sketch of John Kincaid, no. 321, "Kincaid GEDCOM file."

CITING CONTACT INFORMATION FOR THE COMPILER

When citing a report by a credentialed professional researcher, contact information is not necessary in the citation—although you may record it if you wish. Currently credentialed professionals are easily located through online and published directories of the credentialing agency. On the other hand, when you cite reports and GEDCOM files prepared by private researchers, contact information is essential.

CITING FILE VS. AUTHOR IN SOURCE LIST ENTRY

Example 1 above cites the report under the name of its author. Examples 2 and 3 cite the file under the file name, with the compiler's name relegated to second place. The difference lies in the fact that contact information needs to be supplied for the compiler of the GEDCOM file. If her name was the lead element in the citation, then her e-mail address and mailing address would be awkwardly placed in the citation *before* the name of the file.

CITING GEDCOM FILES

The **GE**nealogy **D**ata **COM**munications file format was developed by The Church of Jesus Christ of Latter-day Saints as a means of exchanging genealogical databases compiled by researchers using a wide range of data-management software. As a rule, a citation to any GEDCOM file would be only a temporary citation. A GEDCOM file that purports to be reliable will cite its sources, in which case you will examine those other sources and cite whatever you examined. If you cite a GEDCOM file temporarily while waiting access to other materials, then you add a notation quoting the cited source or else note that the asserted fact is undocumented.

3.45   Traditions

See QuickCheck Model *for* PRIVATE HOLDINGS: TRADITION, RECORDED

Oral history is a resource that is at once important yet questionable. Its credibility greatly rests upon the reliability of the channel through which the information has been conveyed and the veracity of the original source. Identifying that channel is the first step in the process toward potential verification, correction, or disproof. The channel, like provenance of an artifact, should be explained in the first reference note, along with any factors that might weigh for or against the credibility of the source.

Source List Entry

Sherman Family Traditions. Ruth Randall, compiler. MSS notes, ca. 1980–85. Privately held by Randall, [ADDRESS FOR PRIVATE USE,] Albuquerque, New Mexico.

First Reference Note

1. Sherman family traditions regarding parentage of Henry Sherman (born ca. 1843), Ruth Randall, compiler (MSS notes, ca. 1980–85; privately held by Randall, [ADDRESS FOR PRIVATE USE,] Albuquerque, New Mexico), as reported by Lena Sherman, Henry's daughter and Randall's aunt, 1980. [ADD EVALUATION.]

Subsequent Note

11. Sherman family traditions about Henry Sherman (born ca. 1843), previously evaluated in note 1.

●

BUSINESS & INSTITUTIONAL RECORDS

4

QuickCheck Models

Guidelines & Examples (beginning page 176)

QuickCheck Model
CORPORATE RECORDS
BOUND VOLUME
Corporate collection as lead element in Source List

Source List Entry

NAME OF COLLECTION		SERIES ...

Duveen Brothers Records, 1876–1981. General Business Records, 1907–

...	REPOSITORY	REPOSITORY LOCATION

1964. Getty Research Institute, Los Angeles, California.

First (Full) Reference Note

RECORD BOOK TITLE (QUOTED EXACTLY)	PAGE	...

1. "Clients Property Book #1, ca. 1907–1919," p. 129; General

... SERIES	FILE LOCATION	CORPORATE COLLECTION ...

Business Records, 1907–1964; Box 119, Duveen Brothers Records, 1876–

...	REPOSITORY	REPOSITORY LOCATION

1981; Getty Research Institute, Los Angeles, California.

Subsequent (Short) Note

RECORD BOOK TITLE	PAGE	COLLECTION ...

11. "Clients Property Book #1, ca. 1907–1919," 129, Duveen Brothers

...

Records.

QuickCheck Model
CORPORATE RECORDS
DOCUMENT (LOOSE RECORD)

Corporate collection as lead element in Source List

Source List Entry

CORPORATE COLLECTION	SERIES
Ford Motor Company Records.	A. K. Mills Record Series, 1950–1954.

RECORD GROUP and/or SUBGROUP	REPOSITORY ...
Administrative Files Subgroup.	Benson Ford Research Center at The

... REPOSITORY LOCATION
Henry Ford, Detroit, Michigan.

First (Full) Reference Note

ITEM	ITEM TYPE	RECORD DATE	FILE LOCATION
1. Allan Nevins to A. K. Mills,	letter,	11 July 1951;	Accession 506, Box 1;

SERIES	RECORD GROUP and/or SUBGROUP
A. K. Mills Records Series, 1950–1954;	Administrative Files Subgroup,

CORPORATE COLLECTION	REPOSITORY
Ford Motor Company Records;	Benson Ford Research Center at The Henry

... REPOSITORY LOCATION
Ford, Detroit, Michigan.

Subsequent (Short) Note

ITEM	RECORD DATE	SERIES	CORPORATE ...
11. Nevins to Mills,	11 July 1951,	A. K. Mills Record Series,	Ford Motor

... COLLECTION
Company Records.

QuickCheck Model
CORPORATE RECORDS
EXTRACT SUPPLIED BY STAFF
Corporate writer as lead element in Source List

Source List Entry

CORPORATE WRITER	WRITER'S LOCATION	RECIPIENT	ITEM TYPE	...

Nichols Funeral Homes (Haleyville, Alabama) to Jane Nardy. Letter. 2

RECORD DATE	RECORD OWNER	OWNER'S ...

December 2004. Privately held by Nardy, [ADDRESS FOR PRIVATE USE,]

... LOCATION	DATE OWNED

Atlanta, Georgia. 2007.

First (Full) Reference Note

CORPORATE WRITER	WRITER'S LOCATION	RECIPIENT	ITEM TYPE

1. Nichols Funeral Homes (Haleyville, Alabama) to Jane Nardy, letter,

RECORD DATE	SUBJECT or NATURE OF DATA PROVIDED

2 December 2004, extracting data for E. L. Kelley, buried 6 January 2002;

RECORD OWNER	OWNER'S CONTACT INFO	YEAR OWNED

privately held by Nardy, [ADDRESS FOR PRIVATE USE,] Atlanta, Georgia, 2007.

Subsequent (Short) Note

CORPORATE WRITER	RECIPIENT	RECORD DATE

11. Nichols Funeral Homes to Nardy, 2 December 2004.

QuickCheck Model
CORPORATE RECORDS
MICROFILM

Corporate collection as lead element in Source List

Source List Entry

CORPORATE COLLECTION   SERIES   ...
Hudson's Bay Company Archives. Post Records: Fort Victoria. Abstracts

   ... SUBSERIES   MICROFILM ID/ROLL NOS.   ...
of Servant Accounts, 1855–1869. Microfilm 1M797–1M799. Archives

... REPOSITORY   REPOSITORY LOCATION
of Manitoba, Winnipeg, Canada.

First (Full) Reference Note

RECORD TITLE   SPECIFIC ITEM OF INTEREST   ...
1. "Outstanding Balances," Cyprien Dion entry, 1859–1860; Abstracts of

... SUBSERIES   SERIES   FILE LOCATION
Servant Accounts, 1855–1869; Post Records: Fort Victoria; B.226/g/7,

CORPORATE COLLECTION   MICROFILM ID/ROLL NO.   REPOSITORY
Hudson's Bay Company Archives (microfilm 1M798), Archives of Manitoba,

REPOSITORY LOCATION
Winnipeg, Canada.

Subsequent (Short) Note

RECORD TITLE   SPECIFIC ITEM OF INTEREST   SUBSERIES ...
11. "Outstanding Balances," Cyprien Dion, 1859–1860; Abstracts of

   ...   SERIES   CORPORATE COLLECTION
Servant Accounts, Fort Victoria; Hudson's Bay Company Archives.

QuickCheck Model
CORPORATE RECORDS
ONLINE DATABASE
Database as lead element in Source List

Source List Entry

DATABASE TITLE   ITEM TYPE or FORMAT   WEBSITE ...

"The Erie Railroad Glass Plate Negative Collection." Database. Syracuse

... CREATOR   WEBSITE TITLE   ...

University Library. *Erie Railroad Company: Digital Edition.* http://

URL (DIGITAL LOCATION)   YEAR

library.syr.edu/digital/images/e/ErieRailroad : 2006.

First (Full) Reference Note

DATABASE TITLE   ITEM TYPE or FORMAT

1. "The Erie Railroad Glass Plate Negative Collection," database,

WEBSITE CREATOR / OWNER   WEBSITE TITLE   ...

Syracuse University Library, *Erie Railroad Company: Digital Edition* (http://

... URL (DIGITAL LOCATION)   DATE

library.syr.edu/digital/images/e/ErieRailroad : updated 19 September 2006),

DIGITAL PATH (WHEN NECESSARY)   ITEM OF INTEREST

keyword "Collection Inventory," entry for M. L. Goshen, Image A-107.

Subsequent (Short) Note

DATABASE TITLE   WEBSITE ...

11. "The Erie Railroad Glass Plate Negative Collection," *Erie Railroad*

... TITLE   ITEM OF INTEREST

Company: Digital Edition, entry for M. L. Goshen, Image A-107.

QuickCheck Model
CORPORATE RECORDS
ONLINE IMAGES
Collection as lead element in Source List

Source List Entry

<table>
<tr><td align="center">COLLECTION</td><td align="center">ITEM TYPE
or FORMAT</td></tr>
</table>

"New York Emigrant Savings Bank Records, 1850–1883." Digital images.

<table>
<tr><td align="center">WEBSITE TITLE</td><td align="center">URL (DIGITAL LOCATION)</td><td align="center">YEAR</td><td align="center">CREDIT LINE ...</td></tr>
</table>

Ancestry.com. http://www.ancestry.com : 2006. From NYPL microfilm

<table>
<tr><td align="center">... (SOURCE OF THE SOURCE)</td></tr>
</table>

*R-USLHG *Z1-815. New York Public Library, New York City.

First (Full) Reference Note

<table>
<tr><td align="center">COLLECTION</td><td align="center">ITEM ...</td></tr>
</table>

1. "New York Emigrant Savings Bank Records, 1850–1883," digital

<table>
<tr><td align="center">... TYPE</td><td align="center">WEBSITE TITLE</td><td align="center">URL (DIGITAL LOCATION)</td><td align="center">DATE</td></tr>
</table>

images, *Ancestry.com* (http://www.ancestry.com : accessed 1 August 2006),

<table>
<tr><td align="center">ITEM OF INTEREST</td><td align="center">...</td></tr>
</table>

image for Eleanor and Catherine Sullivan, account no. 28 (1850); citing

<table>
<tr><td align="center">... CREDIT LINE</td></tr>
</table>

"Depositor Account Ledgers, NYPL microfilm *R-USLHG *Z1-815, roll

<table>
<tr><td align="center">... (SOURCE OF THE SOURCE)</td></tr>
</table>

15, New York Public Library, New York City."

Subsequent (Short) Note

<table>
<tr><td align="center">COLLECTION</td><td align="center">WEBSITE TITLE</td></tr>
</table>

11. "New York Emigrant Savings Bank Records, 1850–1883," *Ancestry.com,*

<table>
<tr><td align="center">ITEM OF INTEREST</td></tr>
</table>

Eleanor and Catherine Sullivan, account no. 28 (1850).

QuickCheck Model
LINEAGE-SOCIETY RECORDS
APPLICATION FILE
Organization as lead element in Source List

Source List Entry

ORGANIZATION   COLLECTION   REPOSITORY ...

Mayflower Descendants, General Society of. Application files. Office of the

...   REPOSITORY LOCATION

Historian General, Plymouth, Massachusetts.

First (Full) Reference Note

FILE   ...

1. Membership application, Elizabeth Abercrombie Crichton, no.

MEMBERSHIP
NO.   ORGANIZATION   REPOSITORY ...

48558, General Society of Mayflower Descendants, Office of the Histo-

...   REPOSITORY LOCATION

rian General, Plymouth, Massachusetts.

Subsequent (Short) Note

FILE   ...

11. Membership application, Elizabeth Abercrombie Crichton, no.

NO.   ORGANIZATION

48558, Mayflower Descendants.

QuickCheck Model
LINEAGE-SOCIETY RECORDS
ONLINE DATABASE
Organization as lead element in Source List

Source List Entry

ORGANIZATION	WEBSITE TITLE
Colonial Dames of America, National Society.	*Ancestor Bibliography Register.*

ITEM TYPE or FORMAT	URL (DIGITAL LOCATION)	YEAR
Database.	http://www.ancestorbibliography.org :	2006.

First (Full) Reference Note

	ORGANIZATION	WEBSITE ...
1.	National Society of the Colonial Dames of America,	*Ancestor*

... TITLE	ITEM TYPE or FORMAT	URL (DIGITAL LOCATION)	...
Bibliography Register,	database	(http://www.ancestorbibliography.org : ac-	

DATE	ITEM OF INTEREST
cessed 4 September 2006),	Edmund Bacon entry.

Subsequent (Short) Note

ORGANIZATION (SHORT TITLE)	WEBSITE TITLE
11. National Society, Colonial Dames,	*Ancestor Bibliography Register,*

ITEM OF INTEREST
Edmund Bacon entry.

QuickCheck Model
ORGANIZATIONAL RECORDS
ARCHIVED IN-HOUSE
Organization as lead element in Source List

Source List Entry

ORGANIZATION   COLLECTION ...

American Association of Variable Star Observers. AAVSO Organization

...   REPOSITORY   REPOSITORY LOCATION

Collection. AAVSO Archives, Cambridge, Massachusetts.

First (Full) Reference Note

RECORD TITLE (QUOTED EXACTLY)   FILE   SERIES ...

1. "Texas Observers, Burleson, Texas, 1929"; Box 3, Campbell Era, 1915–

...   COLLECTION   REPOSITORY ...

1949, AAVSO Organization Collection; AAVSO Archives, American Asso-

... ORGANIZATION   REPOSITORY LOCATION

ciation of Variable Star Observers, Cambridge, Massachusetts.

Subsequent (Short) Note

RECORD TITLE   COLLECTION ...

11. "Texas Observers, Burleson, Texas, 1929," AAVSO Organization

...

Collection.

QuickCheck Model
ORGANIZATIONAL RECORDS
ARCHIVED OFF-SITE
Organization as lead element in Source List

Source List Entry

ORGANIZATION (CREATOR)   FILE TITLE

American Medical Association. "Deceased American Physicians, 1864–1970,

ITEM TYPE
or FORMAT   REPOSITORY ...

Card File." National Library of Medicine—History of Medicine Division.

...   REPOSITORY LOCATION

National Institutes of Health, Bethesda, Maryland.

First (Full) Reference Note

ITEM OF INTEREST

1. Richard Finley (1843–1915; Centerville, South Dakota) data card;

ITEM TYPE
FILE TITLE   or FORMAT   ORGANIZATION ...

"Deceased American Physicians, 1864–1970, Card File," American Medical

... (CREATOR)   REPOSITORY ...

Association, National Library of Medicine—History of Medicine Division,

...   REPOSITORY LOCATION

National Institutes of Health, Bethesda, Maryland.

Subsequent (Short) Note

ITEM OF INTEREST (SHORTENED)   FILE TITLE (SHORTENED) ...

11. Richard Finley (1843–1915) data card, "Deceased American

...   ORGANIZATION (CREATOR)

Physicians Card File," American Medical Association.

QuickCheck Model
PROFESSIONAL REPORTS
GENETIC TESTING
Corporate author as lead element in Source List

Source List Entry

CORPORATE AUTHOR · CORPORATE LOCATION · REPORT ...

DNA Print Genomics (Sarasota, Florida). "DNAPrint 2.5 Autosomal Report,

... TITLE · RECIPIENT · RECIPIENT'S ...

Kit TGDP 172," prepared for E. E. Watson, [ADDRESS FOR PRIVATE USE,]

... LOCATION · REPORT DATE · WHERE & WHEN HELD

West Memphis, Arkansas. 1 June 2006. Privately held by Watson, 2007.

First (Full) Reference Note

CORPORATE AUTHOR · CORPORATE LOCATION · REPORT ...

1. DNA Print Genomics (Sarasota, Florida), "DNAPrint 2.5 Autosomal

... TITLE · RECIPIENT · RECIPIENT'S ...

Report, Kit TGDP 172," prepared for E. E. Watson, [ADDRESS FOR PRIVATE

... LOCATION · REPORT DATE · WHERE & WHEN HELD

USE,] West Memphis, Arkansas, 1 June 2006; privately held by Watson,

...

2007.

Subsequent (Short) Note

CORPORATE AUTHOR · REPORT ...

11. DNA Print Genomics, "DNA Print 2.5 Autosomal Report, Kit TGDP

... TITLE · REPORT DATE

172," 1 June 2006.

QuickCheck Model
PROFESSIONAL REPORTS
HISTORICAL RESEARCH: CORPORATE
Author as lead element in Source List

Source List Entry

RESEARCHER (AUTHOR) & PROFESSIONAL CREDENTIALS	CORPORATE AFFILIATION	CORPORATE LOCATION

Stott, Clifford L., AG, CG, FASG. (Agent for ProGenealogists, Salt Lake City,

...	REPORT TITLE (QUOTED EXACTLY)	ITEM TYPE	RECIPIENT ...

Utah.) "English Origins of the Wheatley Family." Report prepared for

...	RECIPIENT'S LOCATION	REPORT DATE	...

V. Watson Pugh, [ADDRESS FOR PRIVATE USE]. 29 December 2003. Copy

... WHERE HELD	WHEN HELD

privately held by [NAME, ADDRESS FOR PRIVATE USE]. 2007.

First (Full) Reference Note

RESEARCHER (AUTHOR) & PROFESSIONAL CREDENTIALS	CORPORATE AFFILIATION	CORP. ...

1. Clifford L. Stott, AG, CG, FASG (Agent for ProGenealogists, Salt Lake

... LOCATION	REPORT TITLE (QUOTED EXACTLY)	PAGE	ITEM TYPE

City, Utah), "English Origins of the Wheatley Family," p. 6; report

RECIPIENT	RECIPIENT'S LOCATION	REPORT DATE ...

prepared for V. Watson Pugh, [ADDRESS FOR PRIVATE USE], 29 December

...	WHERE HELD	WHEN HELD

2003; copy privately held by [NAME, ADDRESS FOR PRIVATE USE], 2007.

Subsequent (Short) Note

AUTHOR	REPORT TITLE	PAGE

11. Stott, "English Origins of the Wheatley Family," 6.

QuickCheck Model
PROFESSIONAL REPORTS
HISTORICAL RESEARCH: ONLINE
Corporate author as lead element in Source List

Source List Entry

CORPORATE AUTHOR
(RESEARCHERS NOT IDENTIFIED)   CORPORATE LOCATION   REPORT TITLE ...

Heritage Research Center (Missoula, Montana). "Report on Bank of America

... (QUOTED EXACTLY)

Predecessor Institutions Research Regarding Slavery and the Slave Trade."

REPORT DATE   WEBSITE TITLE   URL (DIGITAL LOCATION) ...

4 August 2005. *Heritage Research Center.* http://www.heritageresearch

ACCESS
...   YEAR

.com/BofAReport.htm : 2006.

First (Full) Reference Note

CORPORATE AUTHOR
(RESEARCHERS NOT IDENTIFIED)   CORPORATE LOCATION   REPORT TITLE ...

1. Heritage Research Center (Missoula, Montana), "Report on Bank of

... (QUOTED EXACTLY)

America Predecessor Institutions Research Regarding Slavery and the Slave

...   REPORT DATE   WEBSITE TITLE   URL ...

Trade," report dated 4 August 2005, *Heritage Research Center* (http://www

... (DIGITAL LOCATION)   DATE   PAGE ...

.heritageresearch.com/BofAReport.htm : accessed 1 September 2006), unpagi-

... or SPECIFIC PART

nated, "Conclusion."

Subsequent (Short) Note

SPECIFIC
AUTHOR   REPORT TITLE (SHORTENED)   PART

11. Heritage Research Center, "Report on Bank of America," conclusion.

QuickCheck Model
SCHOOL RECORDS
ADMINISTRATIVE MATERIAL
Institutional author as lead element in Source List

Source List Entry

INSTITUTIONAL AUTHOR — RECORD/VOLUME TITLE — REPOSITORY ...

University of Alabama. "Minutes of the Faculty, 1842–." University Archives,

REPOSITORY ... — REPOSITORY LOCATION

Hoole Library, Tuscaloosa.

First (Full) Reference Note

INSTITUTIONAL AUTHOR — RECORD/VOLUME TITLE — PAGE

1. University of Alabama, "Minutes of the Faculty, 1842–," p. 65,

ITEM OF INTEREST — REPOSITORY ...

"Case of Discipline: J. M. Foster" (1844); University Archives, Hoole

REPOSITORY ... — REPOSITORY LOCATION

Library, Tuscaloosa.

Subsequent (Short) Note

INSTITUTIONAL AUTHOR — RECORD (VOLUME) — PAGE

11. University of Alabama, "Minutes of the Faculty, 1842–," 65.

QuickCheck Model
SCHOOL RECORDS
STUDENT TRANSCRIPT
Person as lead element in Source List

Source List Entry

STUDENT & CLASS   RECORD ID (GENERIC)   INSTITUTION ...

Kuhle, Albert Anton. Class of 1915. Academic Transcript. University of

...   LOCATION OF INSTITUTION   RECORD HOLDER

Notre Dame, Notre Dame, Indiana. Privately held by Katherine E. Flynn,

WHERE & WHEN HELD

[ADDRESS FOR PRIVATE USE,] Loveland, Ohio. 2005.

First (Full) Reference Note

STUDENT & CLASS   RECORD ID (GENERIC)   ...

1. Albert Anton Kuhle, Class of 1915, academic transcript; University

INSTITUTION   LOCATION OF INSTITUTION   RECORD DATE   ...

of Notre Dame, Notre Dame, Indiana; supplied 17 November 1992 to

RECIPIENT   WHERE ...

Kuhle's granddaughter, Katherine E. Flynn; privately held by Flynn,

... & WHEN HELD

[ADDRESS FOR PRIVATE USE,] Loveland, Ohio, 2005.

Subsequent (Short) Note

STUDENT & CLASS   RECORD ID   ...

11. Albert Anton Kuhle, Class of 1915, academic transcript, University

INSTITUTION

of Notre Dame.

GUIDELINES
& Examples

BASIC ISSUES

4.1 Private Records

Most business records are private materials, although older resources are often deposited at archives and libraries that allow on-site research. Some major firms have corporate archives that are available to serious researchers from the public sector. Random business records can be found at county courthouses and city halls. All these materials can be cited in much the same fashion as other archival collections (chapter 3) or as local civil records (chapters 9 and 10).

Other institutions have records of immense historical value but usually limit public access to their files. Funeral homes, hospitals, penal institutions, and schools are common examples. In these cases, your citations will be to communications and, perhaps, photocopies you have received from those institutions.

In citing business records particularly, researchers are plagued by corporate changes. Companies fold and merge. Historic records may be discarded. A document or file that is properly cited to a business one year may later be difficult to locate from that citation. Nonetheless, a thorough reference note will provide a starting point for future efforts to find elusive records.

When constructing your Source List, if you are the person who obtained the record from the institution, your Source List Entry should reference the institution, not yourself or your collection of papers. However, some researchers prefer to list or group these records by an individual or a family name, rather than institutional name. This chapter offers alternative models for all these approaches.

4.2 Published Records

When you use business records that have been extracted and published in print form, this chapter does not apply. You are not using an actual record or an original communication from a firm. You are using a derivative *publication* that can be simply cited by the basic QuickCheck Models for books and periodicals in chapters 12 and 14. If you are using online *images* of the original or a database of the originals, then you will find models in this chapter.

4.3 Records Cataloged as Files vs. Individual Items

Business and institutional records are an assorted lot. The same type of item may be handled differently from one site to another, depending upon the cataloging system preferred by the archive. For example, when creating a Reference Note:

LOOSE ITEMS

These are typically cited in a smallest-to-largest pattern, such as

ITEM OF INTEREST, "RECORD"; FILE, COLLECTION; ARCHIVE, LOCATION.

BOUND VOLUMES

When found in large or formal archives, bound volumes follow this same pattern more or less. In smaller archives, bound volumes may be shelved and cited like authored manuscripts (as with the Stocks Funeral Home example at 4.9). The pattern for registers held by small libraries is typically this:

"TITLE OF VOLUME," PAGE/ITEM; RECORD TYPE; LIBRARY, LOCATION.

4.4 Records Cataloged by U.S. vs. International Systems

Increasing globalization of industry means that history researchers working in business archives now encounter cataloging systems that differ from those typically used in American academic and governmental archives. International cataloging styles vs. U.S. cataloging styles has already been discussed at 3.3.

The Reference Notes to the Canadian Hudson's Bay Company records at 4.5 follow the coding system commonly seen internationally, in which (*a*) the specific item is identified, then (*b*) the file location (series, file, subseries, and item) is coded from the largest element to the smallest —i.e., D.38/6, wherein

D	=	Section (Record Group)
38	=	Series
6	=	Item number

In contrast to the international-style example at 4.5, the bank-records citation at 4.6 follows the conventional American style.

CORPORATE & INSTITUTIONAL RECORDS

4.5   Basic Formats

See QuickCheck Models *for* CORPORATE RECORDS: BOUND VOLUME [&] MICROFILM

Banks, insurance companies, manufacturers, mercantile establish-
ments and a host of other businesses have archived a wide assortment
of customer and employee records that can provide biographical and
personal data on past lives—when those companies are willing to
make them available. The following examples are from two open-
access corporate archives of considerable significance to North American history. The Emigrant Savings Bank citation is based on the
traditional U.S. format for bound volumes. The Hudson's Bay
Company example for a loose document is structured on the Canadian
series system.

Source List Entry

Emigrant Savings Bank Records, 1841–1945. New York Public Library, New York City.

Hudson's Bay Company Archives. Governor's Papers and Commissioner's
Office. Archives of Manitoba, Winnipeg.

First Reference Note

1. Eleanor and Catherine Sullivan, account no. 28 (1850); Depositor Account Ledgers, vol. 1, unpaginated; Emigrant Savings Bank
Records, 1841–1945; New York Public Library, New York City.

2. John Clark, clerk, personnel record [1873–75]; folio 9, Records
of Commissioned Officers, Clerks & Postmasters; Confidential Reports, 1873–1894; Governor's Papers and Commissioner's Office;
Document D.38/6, Hudson's Bay Company Archives, Archives of
Manitoba, Winnipeg.

Subsequent Note

11. Eleanor and Catherine Sullivan, account no. 28 (1850); Depositor Account Ledgers, vol. 1; Emigrant Savings Bank Records.

12. John Clark, clerk, personnel record, folio 9, D.38/6, Hudson's
Bay Company Archives.

4.6   Banking Records, Derivative Forms

Records of defunct corporations that you use in microform or consult
as digitized, online images are cited somewhat differently than the
originals. The next several examples use records of the nineteenth-
century, New York–based Emigrant Savings Bank, introduced above,
to follow a single item through several of the formats in which these
records are available.

Preservation Microfilm—Produced In-House

Source List Entry
Emigrant Savings Bank Records, 1841–1945. Microfilm, 59 rolls. New
    York Public Library, New York City.

First Reference Note
    1. Eleanor and Catherine Sullivan, account no. 28 (1850); De-
positor Account Ledgers, vol. 1, unpaginated; Emigrant Savings Bank
Records, 1841–1945; NYPL microfilm *R-USLHG *ZI-815, roll 15;
New York Public Library, New York City.

Subsequent Note
    11. Eleanor and Catherine Sullivan, account no. 28 (1850); De-
positor Account Ledgers, vol. 1; Emigrant Savings Bank Records.

Twenty rolls of this record set have been digitized and are available
online at a subscription-based website. The cataloging data supplied
there provide only a partial identification of the original record books.
If you access the Sullivan entry through the online source, your
citation might be as follows:

Online Images

See also QuickCheck Model *for* CORPORATE RECORDS: ONLINE IMAGE

Source List Entry
"New York Emigrant Savings Bank Records, 1850–1883." Digital
    images. *Ancestry.com.* http://www.ancestry.com : 2006. From
    NYPL microfilm *R-USLHG *Z1-815, New York Public Library,
    New York City.

First Reference Note
    1. "New York Emigrant Savings Bank Records, 1850–1883,"
digital images, *Ancestry.com* (http://www.ancestry.com : accessed 1
August 2006), image for Eleanor and Catherine Sullivan, account no. 28
(1850); citing "Depositor Account Ledgers, NYPL microfilm *R-
USLHG *Z1-815, roll 15, New York Public Library, New York City."

Subsequent Note
    11. "New York Emigrant Savings Bank Records, 1850–1883,"
Ancestry.com, Eleanor and Catherine Sullivan, account no. 28 (1850).

Aside from the expected differences in format between microfilm and
online images, one other difference exists between these two entries:

- The microfilm example cites the Depositor Account Ledgers and the specific volume, because your personal examination of that microfilm provides you with those data.

- The online image citation does *not* identify the exact volume, because the website does not provide that level of detail. From what you actually see at the website, you can cite only the series, the account, and the year.

CITING THE SOURCE OF A SOURCE

Commercial firms that provide historical content should identify their own source, to at least some extent. In such cases, you should note relevant details for both the website and the source of its data, with a semicolon dividing one source from the other. In such cases, the first part of your citation should always be to the source you actually use. The source of your source is cited secondarily, until and unless you personally consult it. (See also 2.21.)

4.7 Credit Reports

Restrictions on access to credit reports mean that history researchers typically use only three types:

- current or twentieth-century records found in family papers, cited like other family mementos covered in chapter 3.

- archived records of credit-evaluation companies, which (*a*) are usually available only to researchers with academic affiliations; and (*b*) have restricted content that cannot be used for publication without the permission of the archive that holds the collection.

- research notes from these company files, which may be found in collections deposited elsewhere.

The holder of the R. G. Dun & Co. Collection requests that research notes taken on premises be cited in the manner shown under First Reference Note below. The corresponding forms below, for Source List Entry and Subsequent Note, are extrapolated from the library's recommendation for the First Reference Note.

Source List Entry
Dun, R. G., & Co. Collection. Baker Library, Harvard Business School, Boston, Massachusetts.

First Reference Note
1. John P. Parker credit data, Ohio, vol. 17, p. 240, R. G. Dun & Co. Collection, Baker Library, Harvard Business School, Boston, Massachusetts.

Subsequent Note
> 11. Ohio, vol. 17, p. 240, R. G. Dun & Co. Collection.

When you find notes from this source in research collections elsewhere, you will produce a two-level citation:

• First, you will identify the source you have actually used.
• Second, you will identify the material cited by your source.

For example:

Source List Entry
> Sprague, Stuart S. Research Notes. John P. Parker Files. Union Township Public Library, Ripley, Ohio.

First Reference Note
> 1. John P. Parker credit data, Stuart S. Sprague Research Notes, John P. Parker Files; Union Township Public Library, Ripley, Ohio; Sprague identifies his source as "Ohio vol. 17, p. 240, R. G. Dun & Co. Collection, Baker Library, Harvard Business School, Boston, Mass."

Subsequent Note
> 11. John P. Parker credit data, Sprague Research Notes.

4.8   Funeral-Home Records, Extract Supplied by Staff
See also QuickCheck Model *for* CORPORATE RECORDS: EXTRACT SUPPLIED BY STAFF

These materials, being private, may not be available for personal examination while the company remains in business. Typically, researchers must rely upon the staff to search its records and provide needed details. The results can usually be handled in this manner:

Source List Entry
> Nichols Funeral Homes (Haleyville, Alabama) to Jane Nardy. Letter. 2 December 2004. Privately held by Nardy, [ADDRESS FOR PRIVATE USE,] Atlanta, Georgia. 2007.

First Reference Note
> 1. Nichols Funeral Homes (Haleyville, Alabama) to Jane Nardy, letter, 2 December 2004, extracting data for E. L. Kelley, buried 6 January 2002; privately held by Nardy, [ADDRESS FOR PRIVATE USE,] Atlanta, Georgia, 2007.

Subsequent Note
> 11. Nichols Funeral Homes to Nardy, 2 December 2004.

4.9   Funeral-Home Records, Personal Examination
Record books from inactive institutions are often found at local

libraries or in the custody of a descendant of the owner. The following examples illustrate citations to both situations, using a case in which a contemporary individual inherited a record book from her grand-father's funeral home, held it for a while, then donated it to a local society.

Source List Entry

(When held by a library)
Stocks Funeral Home (Morrisonville, Illinois). "Ledger, 1918–41." Christian County Genealogical Society Library, Taylorville, Illinois.

(When privately held)
Stocks Funeral Home (Morrisonviile, Illinois). "Ledger, 1918–41." Privately held by Linda Anderson Roof, [ADDRESS FOR PRIVATE USE,] Youngstown, Ohio. 2000.

First Reference Note

1. Stocks Funeral Home (Morrisonville, Illinois), "Ledger, 1918–41," p. 270, for Mary Ellen Anderson burial entry, 7 April 1925; Christian County Genealogical Society Library, Taylorville, Illinois.

2. Stocks Funeral Home (Morrisonville, Illinois), "Ledger, 1918–41," p. 270, for Mary Ellen Anderson burial entry, 7 April 1925; privately held by Linda Anderson Roof, [ADDRESS FOR PRIVATE USE,] Youngstown, Ohio, 2000. Ms. Anderson acquired the record book from her grandfather, Adam Leo Stocks of Morrisonville.

Subsequent Note

11. Stocks Funeral Home, "Ledger, 1918–41," 270.

CITING COMPANY AS AUTHOR

Section 4.3 discusses "Records cataloged as files vs. individual items." The examples above and at 4.5 demonstrate the difference. The funeral-home register cited above follows the author-book-page format. The Reference Note examples at 4.5 use the traditional smallest-to-largest pattern for files and collections, beginning each citation with the specific item, then citing the bound volume or collection in which it appears, etc.

The difference lies in the nature of the material. The collections at 4.5 are each part of large series that are formally classified in a major archive. The funeral-home register above is one sole volume less-formally shelved in a small library. Thus, the funeral home is treated as a corporate author and the book is cited in a simpler fashion.

CITING STREET ADDRESSES

In the first instance above, where the record is held by a library open to the public, you need not record its exact street address in your formal citation. In the second instance, when the record is held by an individual, an address can be essential to relocating the record.

4.10 Genetic Databases (Corporate Sponsored)

Some corporations that conduct genetic testing also sponsor online databases by which clients can share the results of their genetic tests with others who seek an ancestral match. Some cultural institutions and organizations are also sponsoring online databases. Both types can be cited by these models:

Online Database

Source List Entry

(When citing a specially named website that offers just one database)
FamilyTreeDNA. *MitoSearch.* Database. http://www.mitosearch .org : 2006.

(When citing a corporate-name website that offers multiple databases)
Relative Genetics. Online databases. *Relative Genetics.* http://www.relative genetics.com : 2005.

First Reference Note

1. FamilyTreeDNA, *MitoSearch,* database (http://www.mito search.org : 2 September 2006), results for Haplotype I Search: User ID: 6ZM82; mtDNA ancestor: Elmira [—?—] Boyd, born ca. 1823, Mississippi.

2. Relative Genetics, "Exact Y-Match" database, *Relative Genetics* (http://www.relativegenetics.com : 1 August 2005), match results for personal genetic markers entered under I1a haplotype.

Subsequent Note

12. FamilyTreeDNA, *MitoSearch,* results for Haplotype I Search: User ID: 6ZM82.

13. Relative Genetics, "Exact Y-Match" database, match results for personal genetic markers entered for I1a haplotype.

CITING WEBSITE & WEBPAGE TITLES

Because consistency is difficult to achieve when citing websites and webpages, you will often make judgment calls in deciding how to treat them. In the examples above:

• The FamilyTreeDNA site is relatively simple. It has a corporate creator (author), a distinctive title to its whole website (hence, that title appears in italics), but no special name for its database (if one existed, it would have been placed in quotation marks).

- The Relative Genetics site has no name other than that of the corporation itself, and that name appears again in the URL.

In the Source List Entry above, Relative Genetics is used as the corporate author to parallel FamilyTreeDNA, but no specific database is cited there for Relative Genetics, because its website offers several useful databases. You should identify the specific database in your First Reference Note for *each* database you use at that website.

4.11   Hospital & Physician Records

Relatively few medical-records collections are available for public scrutiny. When citing hospital or physician records, as a rule, you will not be citing a collection from an archive. Likely, you will be citing a letter from that institution, with extracts of selected details from its files (see 4.8) or a photocopied file supplied by the institution, as illustrated here.

Source List Entry

(Institution as lead element in Source List)
Western State Hospital. Tacoma, Washington. Medical File, Bluford Neiswonger, 1896.

(Personal collection as lead element in Source List)
Neiswonger Medical Files. Photocopies privately held by Linda Vixie. [ADDRESS FOR PRIVATE USE,] Colorado Springs, Colorado. 2005.

First Reference Note

1. Bluford Neiswonger medical file, 1896, no. 2528, M.F. #3036; Western State Hospital, Tacoma, Washington; photocopy supplied 10 March 2000, to Linda Vixie, [ADDRESS FOR PRIVATE USE,] Colorado Springs, Colorado. In 1896 the facility was known as Western Washington Hospital for the Insane and was based in Steilacoom, Washington.

Subsequent Note

11. Bluford Neiswonger medical file, 1896, Western State Hospital.

CHANGES IN INSTITUTIONAL OR CORPORATE IDENTITY

History researchers who use institutional and corporate records often face dilemmas in identifying the institution. An agency or a firm may have changed its name or merged into another institution. As illustrated with the hospital example above and the insurance-company example below, you will need to identify both the firm that created the record and the current firm that holds it.

4.12   Insurance-Company Records

If your research covers numerous policies issued by the same company, you will likely want to make that company name the lead element of your Source List Entry. If the company that issued the policies has merged into another, your Source List Entry may feature the records of the original company, as a corporate collection, or it may use the current company as the lead element.

If your research uncovers just one policy from that company, you may prefer to list it under the policyholder's name in your Source List. If you have a number of policies for the same family, issued by various companies, you might choose to create a "[SURNAME] Insurance Policies Collection" to serve as your Source List Entry.

Source List Entry

(Company as lead element in Source List)
Guardian Life Insurance Company. New York City.

(Corporate collection as lead element in Source List)
Germania Life Insurance Company Files. Germania Life Insurance Company, New York City.

(Policyholder as lead element in Source List)
Ring, Joseph. Insurance policy. Germania Life Insurance Company Files. Guardian Life Insurance Company, New York City. Photocopy held by John Philip Colletta, [ADDRESS FOR PRIVATE USE,] Washington, D.C. 2007.

(Personal collection as lead element in Source List)
Ring Insurance Policies. Photocopies held by John Philip Colletta, Washington, D.C. 2007.

First Reference Note

1. Joseph Ring insurance policy, no. 29541, issued 21 July 1871, Germania Life Insurance Company (currently Guardian Life Insurance Company of America), New York City; photocopy supplied by Guardian Life to John Philip Colletta, [ADDRESS FOR PRIVATE USE,] Washington, D.C., 1995.

Subsequent Note

11. Joseph Ring policy, no. 29541, issued 21 July 1871.

INCOMPLETE CITATIONS TO CORPORATE RECORDS

Corporate staffs that supply photocopied files may not provide full citations by the standards of history researchers. The above model represents the elements that are likely to appear within the material provided; but it does not include, for files and collections, the names and numbers someone might later need to find that record again.

4.13 Insurance Slave-Policy Registries

A newly emerging source for historical research is slave-policy registries or databases created by the insurance industry internationally. A typical registry, whether maintained by a corporation or a state agency, would be cited as follows.

Online Database

Source List Entry

California Department of Insurance. Database. *Slavery Era Insurance Registry.* http://www.insurance.ca.gov/SEIR/SlaveHolder.htm : 2002.

First Reference Note

1. California Department of Insurance, database, *Slavery Era Insurance Registry* (http://www.insurance.ca.gov/SEIR/SlaveHolder.htm : posted May 2002), entry for Ben Varnum, slave of W. C. Hamilton.

Subsequent Note

11. California Department of Insurance, *Slavery Era Insurance Registry,* database entry for Ben Varnum, slave of W. C. Hamilton.

Because many slaves appear under a single name, you should identify both the slave and the master in order to identify the slave properly.

4.14 Orphanage Records

History researchers typically cite orphanage records under one of two circumstances: (*a*) they find a register or files at a library to which the records have been transferred; or (*b*) they have obtained photocopied or extracted data from the institution itself. These options can be handled via the models below.

In the first example, the name of the home identifies its location. In the second, the home is part of a national organization; thus, the citation identifies that organization as the corporate author of the record and then identifies the location of the specific home in parentheses.

Source List Entry

(*To cite a collection examined at a library*)
Warrick County Orphan's Home Records. Boonville-Warrick County Public Library, Boonville, Indiana.

(*To cite records supplied by the institution*)
Salvation Army Boys' and Girls' Home (Lytton, California) to Carmen Finley. Letter. 5 June 1984. Privately held by Finley, [ADDRESS FOR PRIVATE USE,] Santa Rosa, California. 2005.

First Reference Note

(To cite a collection examined at a library)
1. Entries for Ray and Fay Williams, "W" section, 30 June 1906; "Record for Warrick Co. Orphan's Home from Jan. 1, 1910," Warrick County Orphan's Home Records; Boonville-Warrick County Public Library, Boonville, Indiana.

(To cite records supplied by the institution)
2. Salvation Army Boys' and Girls' Home (Lytton, California) to Carmen Finley, 5 June 1984, cover letter and photocopied, undated application for Ardith Bernice Bobst; privately held by Finley, [ADDRESS FOR PRIVATE USE,] Santa Rosa, California, 2005.

Subsequent Note

11. "Record for Warrick Co. Orphan's Home from Jan. 1, 1910," "W" section, entries for Ray and Fay Williams.
12. Salvation Army Boys' and Girls' Home to Carmen Finley, undated application for Ardith Bernice Bobst.

Entries for the library-held Warrick County Orphan's Home records, above, vary from the model that illustrates the library-held Stocks Funeral Home register at 4.9. Principal differences are these:

- The Stocks ledger is the only item for that firm held by the library. Thus, the ledger is explicitly named in the Source List.

- The orphan's home register cited here is just one item in a collection the library holds for the orphanage. Thus, the Source List Entry cites the collection, rather than the individual volume.

4.15 Prison Records
See also QuickCheck Model *for* CORPORATE RECORDS: EXTRACT SUPPLIED BY STAFF

Files that are accessed through a state archive or other public institution are typically cited using Basic Format: Documents, 3.14. Those that are available online in database form may be cited by the database model at 4.13. However, most prison and penitentiary records are not open for public research; so you will be citing a letter from that institution or a photocopied document supplied by the institution, as illustrated below.

Source List Entry

(Institution as lead element in Source List)
Waupun Correctional Institution, Waupun, Wisconsin. Prisoner Index Cards.

(Historic person as lead element in Source List)
Green, Robert. Prisoner Index Card, no. 579. 1860. Waupun Correctional Institution, Waupun, Wisconsin. Photocopy privately held by Lynn Hargreaves, [ADDRESS FOR PRIVATE USE,] Richfield, Minnesota. 2002.

First Reference Note
1. Robert Green Prisoner Index Card, no. 579 (1860), Waupun Correctional Institution, Waupun, Wisconsin; copy supplied by Waupun Record Office to Lynn Hargreaves, [ADDRESS FOR PRIVATE USE,] Richfield, Minnesota, February 2002.

Subsequent Note
11. Robert Green Prisoner Index Card, no. 579 (1860), Waupun Correctional Institution.

CITING CONSECUTIVE SETS OF DIGITS WITH DIFFERENT MEANINGS
The Waupun card, cited above, typically states no date other than the year of admission. In the Source List example for a single card filed under the name of the person rather than the institution, a period separates the year from the card number. The meanings of those two separated number sets are clear enough.

By comparison, the Reference Notes use sentence-style punctuation with minor items separated by commas rather than periods. There, if the card number in the Reference Note was immediately followed by a year, the year might be perceived as part of the card number. You need to differentiate the two consecutive sets of digits that have different meanings. Here, this could be done by adding the word *year* before "1860," or by placing the year in parentheses, as above.

4.16 Railroad Records
See QuickCheck Model *for* CORPORATE RECORDS: ONLINE DATABASE

Railroad company records maintained within company archives may be cited by any of the first four QuickCheck Models at the start of this chapter—depending upon the form of the record. However, the railroad records most commonly used for biographical research are those of the Railroad Retirement Board, a federal agency treated at 11.53. Researchers may also find online databases or images that extract material from archived railroad records, as illustrated below.

Online Database

Source List Entry
"The Erie Railroad Glass Plate Negative Collection." Database.

Syracuse University Library. *Erie Railroad Company: Digital Edition*. http://library.syr.edu/digital/images/e/ErieRailroad : 2006.

First Reference Note

1. "The Erie Railroad Glass Plate Negative Collection," database, Syracuse University Library, *Erie Railroad Company: Digital Edition* (http://library.syr.edu/digital/images/e/ErieRailroad : updated 19 September 2006), keyword "Collection Inventory," entry for M. L. Goshen, Image A-107.

Subsequent Note

11. "The Erie Railroad Glass Plate Negative Collection," *Erie Railroad Company: Digital Edition,* entry for M. L. Goshen, Image A-107.

4.17   School Records

See also QuickCheck Models *for*

• SCHOOL RECORDS: ADMINISTRATIVE MATERIAL
• SCHOOL RECORDS: STUDENT TRANSCRIPT

History researchers use a variety of records created by the schools their subjects attended. Typically, these include

• administrative records and minutes that are sometimes open for public research;
• student transcripts, supplied by the institution via correspondence; and
• student transcripts supplied by the institution, but subsequently passed down in the family.

The three options might be cited as follows:

Source List Entry

(Administrative records—institution as lead element in Source List)
University of Alabama. "Minutes of the Faculty, 1842–." University Archives, Hoole Library, Tuscaloosa.

(Student transcript—institutional author as lead element in Source List)
University of Notre Dame. Notre Dame, Indiana. Academic Transcripts.

(Student transcript—student as lead element in Source List)
Jeffcoat, Thulmar. Transcript of Attendance Record. Howling Wolf School, 1921. Supplied by Sunflower County Board of Education, Indianola, Mississippi. 1998. Privately held by [RESEARCHER'S NAME AND CONTACT INFORMATION].

First Reference Note

1. University of Alabama, "Minutes of the Faculty, 1842–," p. 65,

"Case of Discipline: J. M. Foster" (1844); University Archives, Hoole Library, Tuscaloosa.

    2. Albert Anton Kuhle, Class of 1915, academic transcript; University of Notre Dame, Notre Dame, Indiana; supplied 17 November 1992 to Kuhle's granddaughter, Katherine E. Flynn; privately held by Flynn, [ADDRESS FOR PERSONAL USE,] Loveland, Ohio, 2005.

    3. Thulmar Jeffcoat, Transcript of Attendance Record, Howling Wolf School, 1921; supplied by Sunflower County Board of Education, Indianola, Mississippi, 1998; privately held by [RESEARCHER'S NAME AND CONTACT INFORMATION].

Subsequent Note
    11. University of Alabama, "Minutes of the Faculty, 1842–," 65.

    12. Albert Anton Kuhle, Class of 1915, academic transcript, University of Notre Dame.

    13. Thulmar Jeffcoat, Transcript of Attendance Record, Howling Wolf School, 1921.

CITING DATES IN FULL OR BY YEAR ONLY

When the date of a document or entry is cited in a note, it may need to be written in full or it might be shortened for brevity. Two differences are illustrated above and below:

- In the University of Alabama example, above, the record book has numbered pages and the entry can be found whether or not the full date is referenced. On that basis, only the year is cited as a reference point. It is added only because the year of the event differs from that specified in the volume's title.

- With the Pumphrey store records, below at 4.18, the ledger's pages are not numbered. In order to locate a specific entry, one must have the full date as well as the creditor's name.

4.18   Store Ledgers

Merchant-account books are typically accessed in two ways:

- as part of a probate case filed in a city or county office. (For probated registers, see chapter 10.)

- as part of a manuscript collection in an academic or a public archive, as illustrated below.

Source List Entry
Pumphrey Collection. Jane C. Sween Library, Montgomery County Historical Society, Rockville, Maryland.

First Reference Note
    1. Henry Prather account, entry of 3 October 1907, "W. R.

Pumphrey & Son, Rockville, Md. [1907–1909]," undated, unpaginated ledger; envelope 9, Pumphrey Collection; Jane C. Sween Library, Montgomery County Historical Society, Rockville.

Subsequent Note
  11. Henry Prather account, 3 October 1907, "W. R. Pumphrey & Son [1907–1909]," ledger.

ADDING DATES TO TITLE OF RECORD
In the University of Alabama example at 4.17, the title of the record book (as shown on its first inside leaf) carries a date by which that record book can be distinguished from all others. In the Pumphrey case above, the ledger's title carries no dates or volume number. Thus, beginning and ending dates of the register are added in square editorial brackets within the title for an appropriate identification.

CITING ENTRY DATES VS. PAGE OR FOLIO NUMBERS
In the Pumphrey example above, the ledger carries no pagination. The date of the entry must be recorded in order to relocate the entry within the ledger. In the Edwards example below, the ledger's folios are individually numbered; so the folio is cited, not the date.

Microfilm Publication

Source List Entry
Glassford and Company (Glasgow, Scotland, and Colchester, Virginia). *Records of John Glassford and Company, 1743–1886.* Microfilm edition, 71 rolls. Library of Congress. Washington, D.C.

First Reference Note
  1. *Records of John Glassford and Company, 1743–1886*, microfilm, 71 rolls (Washington: Library of Congress, 1984), roll 59, frame 30, for James Edwards cash account, in Colchester Store, 1758–69, Liber E (1765), folio 20.

Subsequent Note
  11. *Records of John Glassford and Company*, roll 59, frame 30, James Edwards cash account.

CITING COMPANY AS AUTHOR
For the Source List Entry above, the company is cited as author/creator, in order to place the entry alphabetically in the Source List under the name of the company. In the First Reference Note, no author is cited because the creator's identity is part of the publication title. Repetition there is unnecessary.

LINEAGE-SOCIETY MATERIALS

4.19 Application Files

See also QuickCheck Model *for* LINEAGE-SOCIETY RECORDS: APPLICATION FILE

Most lineage societies have house styles for citing their materials. You should ask for a style guide from the particular organization whose records you are using. The following offers a sampling for three major societies:

Source List Entry

Colonial Dames of America, Massachusetts Society. Case files. Office of the Registrar General, Boston.

Daughters of the American Revolution, National Society. Application files. Office of the Registrar General, Washington, D.C.

Mayflower Descendants, General Society of. Application files. Office of the Historian General, Plymouth, Massachusetts.

First Reference Note

(*To cite a specific document from a file*)

1. Nancy Bates Atkinson death certificate, 2 December 1895, in final papers of Anna Elizabeth Warren Leitch (no. 2500, Oregon), microfilmed case files; Massachusetts Society of the Colonial Dames of America, Office of the Registrar General, Boston.

(*or, to cite an entire file*)

1. Final papers, Anna Elizabeth Warren Leitch, no. 2500, Oregon, microfilmed case files; Massachusetts Society of the Colonial Dames of America, Office of the Registrar General, Boston.

2. Membership application, Alys June Orr Reese, National no. 58355, on Margaret Strozier (1741–1842, Georgia), approved 18 April 1994; National Society Daughters of the American Revolution, Office of the Registrar General, Washington, D.C.

3. Supplemental application, Priscilla Anne Scabery Anderson, National no. 651950, Add vol. 674, on Captain Thomas Anderson (1755–1800, Virginia), approved 1988; National Society Daughters of the American Revolution, Office of the Registrar General, Washington, D.C.

4. Membership application, Elizabeth Abercrombie Crichton, no. 48558; General Society of Mayflower Descendants, Office of the Historian General, Plymouth, Massachusetts.

Subsequent Note

11. Final papers, Anna Elizabeth Warren Leitch, no. 2500, Oregon, Massachusetts Society, Colonial Dames of America.

(*or*)

    11. Nancy Bates Atkinson death certificate, final papers of Anna Elizabeth Warren Leitch, no. 2500, Massachusetts Society, Colonial Dames of America.

    12. Membership application, Alys June Orr Reese, National no. 58355, National Society DAR.

    13. Supplemental application, Priscilla Anne Scabery Anderson, National no. 651950, Add vol. 674, National Society DAR, on Capt. Thomas Anderson.

    14. Membership application, Elizabeth Abercrombie Crichton, no. 48558, Mayflower Descendants.

CITING DOCUMENT VS. FILE

Notes 1 and 11 demonstrate two situations faced by history researchers. On occasion you will need to cite an entire file, as in the first option under each note. More often, you will refer to a specific document within the file—the record that provides the information reported in your text, as in the second option. In some organizations, as with Colonial Dames above, the documents are part of the application case file. In other organizations, separate documentation files exist. See 4.21.

Online Database, Members-only Access

Source List Entry

Colonial Dames of America, National Society. "IDDL Search [Claimant Lineage Reports]." Members-only database. *Register of Ancestors.* http://www. nscda.org : 2006.

First Reference Note

    1. National Society of the Colonial Dames of America, "IDDL Search," members-only database, *Register of Ancestors* (http://www .nscda.org : accessed 4 September 2006), Brigham Young data, Claimant Lineage Report for Claimant ID #191A.

Subsequent Note

    11. National Society, Colonial Dames, Claimant Lineage Report for Claimant ID #191A.

Online Database, Open Access

See also QuickCheck Model *for* LINEAGE-SOCIETY RECORDS: ONLINE DATABASE

Source List Entry

Colonial Dames of America, National Society. *Ancestor Bibliography Register.* Database. http://www.ancestorbibliography.org : 2006.

First Reference Note

    1. National Society of the Colonial Dames of America, *Ancestor Bibliography Register,* database (http://www.ancestorbibliography.org : 4 September 2006), Edmund Bacon entry.

Subsequent Note

    11. National Society, Colonial Dames, *Ancestor Bibliography Register*, Edmund Bacon entry.

CITING WEBSITE & WEBPAGE TITLES

The two examples above handle the names of the databases differently because there are differences in the structure of the websites.

- In the first example, "IDDL Search" is placed in quotation marks, indicating that it is the exact title of an individual database or article that is part of a larger website publication. To access it, one must go to the website of the NSCDA (www.nscda.org). As the URL indicates, the user cannot go straight to the IDDL database.

- In the second example, the name of the database, *Ancestor Bibliography Register,* is placed in italics because it is a separate website publication of the NSCDA. As its URL indicates, it carries its own web address.

4.20   Compiled Records (GRC Reports), DAR

Members of the Daughters of the American Revolution have actively compiled local records for most of the past century. Citing them can be a particular challenge. Copies held at the local level or in state-level repositories typically carry the title assigned to them by the compiler. Copies held at the national level may have a different title, one assigned to it by the national library in an effort to standardize the whole series. The examples below present models for materials at both levels.

NATIONAL-LEVEL COPY

The national DAR Library treats each set of state records as a serial, assigning a consistent title to all the states—i.e.,

[State Name] DAR Genealogical Records Committee Report

The organization requests that the title to the series be italicized. (This is an exception to the prevailing rule that italics are reserved for titles of *published* works.) Each state series is cited as a periodical, using series numbers, volume numbers, page numbers, and years of issuance. Within this framework, each compilation is cited in the same manner in which one would cite a journal article.

Source List Entry

Simmerman, Winifred. "Marriage Records, Ohio County, 1808–1828,"
  Kentucky DAR Genealogical Records Committee Report, series 1,
  volume 129 (1948).

First Reference Note

  1. Winifred Simmerman, "Marriage Records, Ohio County, 1808–
  1828," *Kentucky DAR Genealogical Records Committee Report,* series 1,
  vol. 129 (1948): 30.

Subsequent Note

  11. Simmerman, "Marriage Records, Ohio County, 1808–1828," 30.

Style-Change Notice

Users of *Evidence! Citation & Analysis for the Family Historian,* 1st ed.
(Baltimore, 1997), will notice a difference between the citation model
recommended therein and the one shown above. In the interval, the
organization has reorganized these records and changed its citation
style.

LOCAL OR STATE COPY

A local- or state-level copy of a Genealogical Records Committee
(GRC) report treats the individual compilation in traditional fashion—that is, an unpublished, bound manuscript, using quotation
marks around the title and citing the repository as well as the
sponsoring society. For example:

Source List Entry

Mark, Clara G., compiler. "Three Old Cemeteries along Zane's Trace in
  Salt Creek Township, Pickaway County, Ohio; Tarlton Cemetery,
  Stumpf or Jerusalem Cemetery, Imler Cemetery." Typescript,
  1952–56, Washington Court House [Ohio] Society, Daughters of
  the American Revolution. Copy at Ohio State Library, Columbus.

First Reference Note

  1. Clara G. Mark, compiler, "Three Old Cemeteries along Zane's
  Trace in Salt Creek Township, Pickaway County, Ohio; Tarlton Cemetery, Stumpf or Jerusalem Cemetery, Imler Cemetery" (typescript,
  1952–56, Washington Court House [Ohio] Society, Daughters of the
  American Revolution; copy at Ohio State Library, Columbus), 16.

Subsequent Note

  11. Mark, "Three Old Cemeteries along Zane's Trace," 16.

The DAR also offers an online database to access the GRC reports. As
a rule, after the database points you to a report, you will contact or visit

the library to obtain a copy of the report. Then you will cite the report itself. As an interim measure, you will need to record the source of the database information. The following example cites the database entry that led to the Winifred Simmerman report discussed under "National-Level Copy."

Online Database

Source List Entry
Daughters of the American Revolution. "GRC National Index." Database. *DAR Library*. http://grc.dar.org/dar/darnet/grc/grc.cfm?Action=New_Search : 2007.

First Reference Note
1. Daughters of the American Revolution, "GRC National Index," database, *DAR Library* (http://grc.dar.org/dar/darnet/grc/grc.cfm?Action=New_Search : accessed 26 February 2007), Peter Shown entry, citing "Kentucky DAR GRC report; s1 v129, 30."

Subsequent Note
11. DAR, "GRC National Index," Peter Shown entry.

4.21 Documentation Files

At 4.19, notes 1 and 11, the Colonial Dames example illustrates citing a particular document from an application file that contains not only the application but also the supporting evidence. In other organizations, the documentation files are maintained separately, as with the following example for material maintained by the Daughters of the American Revolution.

Source List Entry
Daughters of the American Revolution, National Society. Documentation files. Office of the Registrar General, Washington, D.C.

First Reference Note
1. Widow's pension application, Revolutionary War (R10279, Peter Strozier, Ga. Line) in documentation file supporting Membership Application of Alys June Orr Reese (National no. 58355) on Margaret Strozier (1741–1842, Georgia), approved 18 April 1994; National Society Daughters of the American Revolution, Office of the Registrar General, Washington, D.C.

Subsequent Note
11. Widow's pension application, DAR documentation file, Alys June Orr Reese (National no. 58355).

OTHER MEMBERSHIP ORGANIZATIONS:
FRATERNAL, PROFESSIONAL & VETERAN

4.22   Documents & Registers, Archived In-House

See also QuickCheck Model *for* ORGANIZATIONAL RECORDS: ARCHIVED IN-HOUSE

When organizations maintain their own archive internally, the citation closely follows the Basic Model (4.5), as illustrated by the following roster of local volunteers affiliated with a national learned society.

Source List Entry

American Association of Variable Star Observers. AAVSO Organization Collection. AAVSO Archives, Cambridge, Massachusetts.

First Reference Note

1. "Texas Observers, Burleson, Texas, 1929," Box 3, Campbell Era, 1915–1949, AAVSO Organization Collection; AAVSO Archives, American Association of Variable Star Observers, Cambridge, Massachusetts.

Subsequent Note

11. "Texas Observers, Burleson, Texas, 1929," AAVSO Organization Collection.

4.23   Documents & Registers, Archived Off-site

See also QuickCheck Model *for* ORGANIZATIONAL RECORDS: ARCHIVED OFF-SITE

Most researchers consult historic records of this type at institutions other than the parent organization. Your citations will vary according to (*a*) whether you cite an individual volume, loose documents, or a collection of assorted materials; and (*b*) whether you enter the item in your Source List under the name of the organization, under one of its chapters or posts, or under the collection. The samples below use one veterans' organization to illustrate several variants.

Source List Entry

(Assorted materials—local post as lead element in Source List)
Eddy Post No. 231, Grand Army of the Republic. GAR Miscellaneous Records, 1884–1930. Plymouth Museum, Plymouth, Michigan.

(Individual volume—organization as lead element in Source List)
Grand Army of the Republic—Department of Michigan. "Minute Book (1911–1930), Eddy Post No. 231." Plymouth Museum, Plymouth, Michigan.

(Mixed materials—collection as lead element in Source List)
Grand Army of the Republic Collection, Ransom Post No. 131. Missouri Historical Society, St. Louis.

First Reference Note

(Individual volume)
    1. Grand Army of the Republic—Department of Michigan, "Minute Book (1911–1930), Eddy Post No. 231," p. 15; Plymouth Museum, Plymouth, Michigan.

(Loose document)
    2. Biographical Sketch of William Henry Heath, Biographical Sketch Forms ("volume" 4, A–Z); Series III–Ransom Post No. 131, St. Louis; Grand Army of the Republic Collection, Missouri Historical Society, St. Louis.

Subsequent Note

    11. Grand Army of the Republic, "Minute Book (1911–1930), Eddy Post #231," 15.
    12. Biographical Sketch of William Henry Heath, Ransom Post, Grand Army of the Republic Collection, Missouri Historical Society.

EN DASH TO SEPARATE ELEMENTS ON SAME LEVEL
In note 2 above, an en dash appears between *Series III* and *Ransom Post,* rather than a comma or semicolon, because Series III and Ransom Post are one and the same. Series III is not just one item in a Ransom Post file, and the Ransom Post material is not just one part of Series III.

CITING VOLUME NUMBER
In note 2 above, the word *volume* is placed in quotation marks because it is called a volume in the cataloging system. However, the biographical sketches are loose items that are not actually bound into volumes. Under ordinary circumstances, quotation marks would not appear around the word *volume* in a citation.

4.24 Extract Supplied by Staff
See also QuickCheck Model *for* CORPORATE RECORDS: EXTRACT SUPPLIED ...

Many membership organizations do not make their archive publicly available but will conduct searches in response to mail inquiries and provide an extract or abstract of their findings. If you have just one communication of this type from an organization, you would likely place it in your Source List as an individual letter, with the organization's formal name as the author. If you have numerous letters from the organization (typically representing different geographic areas and different historic individuals), you may want to create a "personal collection" and generically cite that collection in your Source List.

Source List Entry

(If you have only one such letter from an organization)
Grand Lodge of Mississippi, Free and Accepted Masons (Meridian, Mississippi) to Thelma J. Shown, Cleveland, Mississippi. Letter, 21 November 1973. Privately held by [RESEARCHER'S NAME AND CONTACT INFORMATION].

(If you have a collection of letters from a single organization)
Masonic Record Extracts. Grand Lodge of Mississippi, Free and Accepted Masons, Meridian, Mississippi.

First Reference Note

1. Grand Lodge of Mississippi, Free and Accepted Masons (Meridian, Mississippi), to Thelma J. Shown, Cleveland, Mississippi, letter, 21 November 1973, extracting data for H. J. Jeffcoat, Huntsville Lodge #213, 1859–1901; privately held by [RESEARCHER'S NAME & CONTACT INFORMATION], 2006.

Subsequent Note

11. Grand Lodge of Mississippi … Masons, to Thelma J. Shown, 21 November 1973.

4.25 Membership Card Files

See also QuickCheck Model *for* ORGANIZATIONAL RECORDS: ARCHIVED OFF-SITE

Citations to card files, because they are loose items, require a slightly different structure than citations to bound manuscript volumes. Typically, within card files there are multiple individuals of the same name. The data you provide in your citation should distinctly identify the individual of interest. In the example below, the membership organization cards provide the year of birth, year of death, and place of death—all items that are natural identifiers.

Source List Entry

(Organization as lead element in Source List)
American Medical Association. "Deceased American Physicians, 1864–1970, Card File." National Library of Medicine—History of Medicine Division. National Institutes of Health, Bethesda, Maryland.

First Reference Note

1. Richard Finley (1843–1915; Centerville, South Dakota) data card; "Deceased American Physicians, 1864–1970, Card File"; American Medical Association; National Library of Medicine—History of Medicine Division, National Institutes of Health, Bethesda, Maryland.

Subsequent Note
11. Richard Finley (1843–1915) data card, "Deceased American Physicians Card File," American Medical Association.

FHL-GSU Preservation Microfilm

See also QuickCheck Model *for* ORGANIZATIONAL RECORDS: ARCHIVED OFF-SITE

In citing FHL film for archival records, one typically identifies the archive that owns the record. It is also, usually, the archive that gave permission for the filming. The AMA records cited above are an exception. At the time of the filming, the original card file was in the possession of the organization itself. After filming, the card file was donated by the AMA to the National Genealogical Society. That organization subsequently donated the collection to the National Institutes of Health.

When you use FHL film, you will normally obtain your information on provenance from the FHL cataloging data. In the case of this AMA card file, that cataloging entry credits only AMA itself. Your own citation need only credit AMA, although you are certainly free to add whatever additional information you feel would benefit you or other researchers.

The basic citation for microfilmed card files would be as follows:

Source List Entry
American Medical Association. "Deceased American Physicians, 1864–1970, Card File." Microfilm, 237 rolls. Family History Library, Salt Lake City, Utah.

First Reference Note
1. American Medical Association, "Deceased American Physicians, 1864–1970, Card File," data card for Richard Finley, 1843–1915, Centerville, South Dakota; FHL microfilm 2,032,837.

Subsequent Note
11. American Medical Association, "Deceased American Physicians Card File," data card for Richard Finley, 1843–1915.

PROFESSIONAL REPORTS

4.26 Basic Guidelines

History researchers use a variety of research reports—archaeological, genealogical, genetic, historical, legal, medical, etc. Some are prepared by individuals. Some are by companies that assign projects to individual researchers, in which case the quality of the report will rest as much upon the skill of the researcher as upon the reputation of the company. Some reports are by companies such as genetic labs that never identify the individual researchers or testers. Some researchers who operate a solo business are credentialed and can be easily located through the credentialing organization or their affiliation with a trade organization. Others are little known, have no professional affiliation, and may be extremely difficult to locate at a later date. All these circumstances must be considered when creating a citation to a research report. (For *archived* professional reports, see 3.44 and the QuickCheck Models in chapter 3.)

4.27   Genetic Testing Reports

See also QuickCheck Model *for* PROFESSIONAL REPORTS: GENETIC TESTING

Genetic labs conduct several types of tests useful for historical and genealogical research. Regardless of the type of test conducted, their reports will usually fit the following models:

Source List Entry

African Ancestry (Washington, D.C.) to Del E. Jupiter, [ADDRESS FOR PRIVATE USE,] Atlanta, Georgia. Letter reporting Matriclan™ Analysis, 29 March 2006. Privately held by Jupiter. 2007.

DNA Print Genomics (Sarasota, Florida). "EURO-DNA 1.0 Results: Genotypes, #UPETGDP 172." Report. Prepared for Elizabeth Shown Mills, [ADDRESS FOR PRIVATE USE,] Tuscaloosa, Alabama, 16 March 2006. Privately held by Mills. 2007.

FamilyTreeDNA (Houston, Texas). "Certificate—mtDNA ... HVS-1 Sequencing from Sample #156." Report. Prepared for Donn Devine, [ADDRESS FOR PRIVATE USE,] Wilmington, Delaware, 25 March 2001. Privately held by Devine. 2007.

First Reference Note

1. African Ancestry (Washington, D.C.) to Del E. Jupiter, [ADDRESS,] Atlanta, Georgia; letter reporting Matriclan™ Analysis, 29 March 2006; privately held by Jupiter, 2007.

2. DNA Print Genomics (Sarasota, Florida), "EURO-DNA 1.0 Results: Genotypes, #UPETGDP 172," report prepared for Elizabeth Shown Mills, [ADDRESS FOR PRIVATE USE,] Tuscaloosa, Alabama, 16 March 2006; privately held by Mills, 2007.

3. FamilyTreeDNA (Houston, Texas), "Certificate—mtDNA ... HVS-1 Sequencing from Sample #156," report prepared for Donn Devine, [ADDRESS FOR PRIVATE USE,] Wilmington, Delaware, 25 March 2001; privately held by Devine, 2007.

Subsequent Note

    11. African Ancestry to Del E. Jupiter, letter reporting Matriclan™ Analysis, 29 March 2006.

    12. DNA Print Genomics, "EURO-DNA 1.0 Results: Genotypes, #UPETGDP 172," 16 March 2006.

    13. FamilyTreeDNA, "Certificate—mtDNA ... HVS-1 Sequencing from Sample #156," 25 March 2001.

CD-ROM Database

Some testing labs issue their reports on compact discs, rather than in printed form. When you cite these, you are citing an *unpublished* CD. Therefore, whatever label appears on that disk should not be italicized. If you quote the label exactly, you place those words in quotation marks.

Source List Entry

DNA Print Genomics (Sarasota, Florida). "AncestryByDNA: Clay Bernard, BNC52655: Ancestry [version] 2.5." 28 March 2006. CD-ROM. Genetic test report held by Bernard, [ADDRESS FOR PRIVATE USE]. 2007.

First Reference Note

    1. DNAPrint Genomics (Sarasota, Florida), "AncestryByDNA: Clay Bernard, BNC52655: Ancestry [version] 2.5," 28 March 2006, CD-ROM, genetic test report held by Bernard, [ADDRESS FOR PRIVATE USE], 2007.

Subsequent Note

    11. DNA Print Genomics, "AncestryByDNA: Clay Bernard, BNC52655: Ancestry [version] 2.5," 28 March 2006.

CITING VERSION NO. FOR CD-ROM REPORTS, DNA TESTS

The version number cited above does not refer to the software used to create the CD-ROM material (the more common context in which version numbers are cited). Here, it refers to the version of the genetic test itself. When the version number of a specific test is identified in the label of a test report, you should include it in your citation.

Online Database, Members-only Access

Some genomic projects also create webpages for participants, who may or may not have the opportunity to mask personal identities. Some projects require a password; some ask only for a kit or participant number. Any citation to online genetic data at a restricted website should be made only with the informed consent of the individual whose testing data are reported there. In such cases, the citation might be as follows:

Source List Entry

National Geographic Society. "Your Genetic Journey." Genetic Certificate: Kit no. [EXACT NUMBER]. *The Genographic Project*. https://www3.nationalgeographic.com/genographic/report.html : 2007.

First Reference Note

1. National Geographic Society, "Your Genetic Journey," Genetic Certificate: Kit no. [EXACT NUMBER], *The Genographic Project* (https://www3.nationalgeographic.com/genographic/report.html : 2 September 2007), "Certificate of Y-Chromosome Testing: [INDIVIDUAL NAME]."

First Reference Note

11. National Geographic Society, "Your Genetic Journey," Genetic Certificate: Kit no. [EXACT NUMBER], *The Genographic Project*.

4.28   Historical Research Reports, Corporate vs. Individual Consultant

See also QuickCheck Models *for* PROFESSIONAL REPORTS: HISTORICAL RESEARCH

Unpublished reports of an intellectual nature are evaluated by not only their content but also the credentials of the person who conducted the research. For that reason, *tested, professional* credentials should be included in the citation, *if they are earned in the profession that is being practiced.* Honorifics should not be part of a source citation.

The format for citing an authored research report by a credentialed consultant well known in the field and easily located is basically that of an authored but unpublished manuscript (3.22). However, for corporate reports and those by individual consultants without professional affiliations, a citation typically includes an address or other contact information.

Source List Entry

(When prepared by an independent researcher with professional affiliation)
Lennon, Rachal Mills, CGRS. "Philomene Daurat, Woman of Color (b. c1840–42, Natchitoches Parish, Louisiana)." Report prepared for Lalita Tademy, [ADDRESS FOR PRIVATE USE]. 12 May 1997. Copy held by [NAME, ADDRESS FOR PRIVATE USE]. 2007.

(When prepared by an independent researcher, recipient unknown)
Murky, Mildred (123 Any Street, Vancouver, British Columbia). "Report on John Robert and Georgia (Chilcoat) Lennon, Yukon

Territory." 1 June 1996. Report prepared for unidentified client. Copy held by [NAME, ADDRESS FOR PRIVATE USE]. 2007.

(When cited as a corporate work, available from the corporation)
Stott, Clifford L., AG, CG, FASG. "English Origins of the Wheatley Family." Report prepared for V. Watson Pugh. 29 December 2003. E-file: Pugh V Watson 031229. ProGenealogists, Salt Lake City, Utah.

(When cited as a corporate work, privately held)
Stott, Clifford L., AG, CG, FASG. (Agent for ProGenealogists, Salt Lake City, Utah.) "English Origins of the Wheatley Family." Report prepared for V. Watson Pugh, [ADDRESS FOR PRIVATE USE]. 29 December 2003. Copy privately held by [NAME, ADDRESS FOR PRIVATE USE]. 2007.

First Reference Note

1. Rachal Mills Lennon, CGRS, "Philomene Daurat, Woman of Color (b. c1840–42), Natchitoches Parish, Louisiana," p. 58; report prepared for Lalita Tademy, [ADDRESS FOR PRIVATE USE], 12 May 1997; copy privately held by [NAME, ADDRESS], 2007.

2. Mildred Murky, "Report on John Robert and Georgia (Chilcoat) Lennon, Yukon Territory," page 10; prepared by Murky, 123 Any Street, Vancouver, British Columbia, for unidentified client, 1 June 1996; copy held by [NAME, ADDRESS], 2007.

3. Clifford L. Stott, AG, CG, FASG, "English Origins of the Wheatley Family," p. 6; report prepared for V. Watson Pugh, 29 December 2003; copy held by ProGenealogists as e-file "Pugh V Watson 031229."

4. Clifford L. Stott, AG, CG, FASG (Agent for ProGenealogists, Salt Lake City, Utah), "English Origins of the Wheatley Family," p. 6 and attachment 11; report prepared for V. Watson Pugh, [ADDRESS FOR PRIVATE USE], 29 December 2003; copy privately held by [NAME, ADDRESS FOR PRIVATE USE], 2007.

Subsequent Note

11. Lennon, "Philomene Daurat, Woman of Color," 58.
12. Murky, "Report on John Robert and Georgia (Chilcoat) Lennon, Yukon Territory," 10.
13. Stott, "English Origins of the Wheatley Family," 6.
14. Ibid. and attachment 11.

EARNED CREDENTIALS VS. HONORIFICS

In the field practiced by Stott, above, postnominals that begin with *F* (indicating *Fellow of ...*) are almost always an honorific rather than a credential—that is, a postnominal bestowed by a society for contributions of one type or another. The one exception is the *FASG* carried by Stott. His *Fellow of the American Society of Genealogists* is a credential earned on the basis of the quality and quantity of peer-reviewed, published scholarship in that field. Therefore, it is relevant to the quality of the report you are citing. (See also 2.17.)

REPEAT CITATIONS IN CLOSE PROXIMITY

Notes 3 and 4, above, differ in one regard—one refers to an e-file in corporate possession, the other to a paper copy in private possession. However, the Subsequent Notes to both are exactly the same. Rather than produce the same citation for two consecutive entries in Subsequent Notes, notes 13 and 14 illustrate the *ibid.* convention. Ibid., being an abbreviation for *ibidem* (meaning "in the same place"), is used any time a citation refers to exactly the one and only source immediately above it.

Online Reports

See also QuickCheck Models *for*
• PROFESSIONAL REPORTS: HISTORICAL RESEARCH: CORPORATE
• PROFESSIONAL REPORTS: HISTORICAL RESEARCH: ONLINE

Source List Entry

(*When citing an online corporate report*)
Hefti, Paul A. "Tierney in Ireland." Report. *ProGenealogists.* http://www.progenealogists.com/tierney.htm : 2005.

(*When citing an online report by a professional in solo practice*)
Lenzen, Connie, CG. "House History of 5726 North East Cleveland Avenue, Portland, Oregon." Report. 4 March 2006. *Board for Certification of Genealogists.* http://www.bcgcertification.org : 2007.

First Reference Note

    1. Paul A. Hefti, "Tierney in Ireland," undated report, *ProGenealogists* (http://www.progenealogists.com/tierney.htm: accessed 27 September 2005), para. 10.
    2. Connie Lenzen, CG, "House History of 5726 North East Cleveland Avenue, Portland, Oregon," report dated 4 March 2006, *Board for Certification of Genealogists* (http://www.bcgcertification.org : accessed 12 February 2007), p. 7.

Subsequent Note

    11. Hefti, "Tierney in Ireland," paras. 12–13.
    12. Lenzen, "House History of 5726 North East Cleveland Avenue, Portland, Oregon," 7.

CITING PAGE NOS. VS. PARAGRAPH NOS.

The report cited in notes 1 and 11 is posted online in standard HTML form, which carries no pagination and no page breaks. Therefore, specific information is flagged by citing its paragraph number. In contrast, the report cited in notes 2 and 12 are posted online in PDF, a format that preserves the original pagination. For PDF reports, page numbers can be cited as one would do with the original report or a photocopy of the original.

4.29 Legal Research Reports, Title Abstract

Reports produced by attorneys, title companies, and similar firms that issue opinions supported by legal documents can be cited in much the same way that you cite history research reports. The key elements are the corporate author and location, title of report, recipient (if known), date of report, current whereabouts, and any specific document or detail to which you wish to call attention.

Source List Entry

Guarantee Abstract Company (Georgetown, Texas). "Abstract of Title: Supplemental, to 140 Acres, Rebecca Burleson Survey, Williamson County, Texas, in Name of O. C. Kirk." Report to Martindale Mortgage Co., San Antonio. Undated [last internal record dated 1 October 1940]. Privately held by James O. Kirk, [ADDRESS FOR PRIVATE USE]. 2006.

First Reference Note

(To cite the full report)

1. Guarantee Abstract Company (Georgetown, Texas), "Abstract of Title: Supplemental, to 140 Acres, Rebecca Burleson Survey, Williamson County, Texas, in Name of O. C. Kirk"; report to Martindale Mortgage Co., San Antonio, undated [last internal record dated 1 October 1940]; privately held by James O. Kirk, [ADDRESS FOR PRIVATE USEM] 2006.

(or to cite one document from the report)

1. Texas Title Association, Uniform Certificate, 27 July 1932; Guarantee Abstract Company (Georgetown, Texas), "Abstract of Title: Supplemental, to 140 Acres, Rebecca Burleson Survey, Williamson County, Texas, in Name of O. C. Kirk"; report to Martindale Mortgage Co., San Antonio, undated [last internal record dated 1 October 1940]; privately held by James O. Kirk, [ADDRESS FOR PRIVATE USE,] 2006.

Subsequent Note

11. Guarantee Abstract Company, "Abstract of Title: Supplemental, to 140 Acres, Rebecca Burleson Survey."

(or)

11. Texas Title Association, Uniform Certificate, 27 July 1932; Guarantee Abstract Company, "Abstract of Title: Supplemental, to 140 Acres, Rebecca Burleson Survey."

CEMETERY RECORDS

5

QuickCheck Models

Guidelines & Examples (beginning page 220)

QuickCheck Model
CEMETERY OFFICE RECORDS
PERSONALLY USED
Cemetery office as lead element in Source List

Source List Entry

CEMETERY (AUTHOR)	LOCATION	ITEM TYPE or FORMAT

Bellevue Cemetery Office (Lawrence, Massachusetts). Plat Records.

First (Full) Reference Note

CEMETERY (AUTHOR)	LOCATION	ITEM TYPE or FORMAT

1. Bellevue Cemetery Office (Lawrence, Massachusetts), undated plat,

SUBJECT OR NATURE OF DATA PROVIDED	ANALYTICAL COMMENTS ...

citing Clarissa Wardrobe, lot 99, group 10. The actual gravestone (viewed by

... BY RESEARCHER

the author, 1996) reads *Elvira L.*Wardrobe, rather than *Clarissa*.

Subsequent (Short) Note

CEMETERY	LOCATION	RECORD TYPE

11. Bellevue Cemetery Office (Lawrence, Mass.), undated plat.

QuickCheck Model
CEMETERY OFFICE RECORDS
SUPPLIED BY STAFF
Cemetery office as lead element in Source List

Source List Entry

CEMETERY (AUTHOR)   LOCATION   RECIPIENT ...

Woodlawn Cemetery Office (Everett, Massachusetts) to Katherine E.

...   ITEM TYPE   YEAR

Flynn. Letter. 2002.

First (Full) Reference Note

CEMETERY (AUTHOR)   LOCATION   RECIPIENT...

1. Woodlawn Cemetery Office (Everett, Massachusetts) to Katherine E.

...   ITEM TYPE   RECORD DATE   SUBJECT or ...

Flynn, letter, 24 May 2002, providing administrative record for Jane Harris,

... NATURE OF DATA PROVIDED

grave 74, row 2, Pilgrim's Rest, North Section.

Subsequent (Short) Note

CEMETERY   RECORD DATE   RECIPIENT   RECORD DATE

11. Woodlawn Cemetery Office (Everett, Mass.) to Flynn, 24 May 2002.

QuickCheck Model
CEMETERY OFFICE RECORDS
ONLINE IMAGES
Compiler as lead element in Source List

Source List Entry

CREATOR	WEBSITE TITLE	...

The Spring Grove Family (Cincinnati, Ohio). *Spring Grove Cemetery.* Card

... ITEM TYPE & FORMAT	URL (DIGITAL LOCATION) ...

file, database and images. http://www.springgrove.org/sg/genealogy/

...	YEAR

sg_genealogy_home.shtm : 2007.

First (Full) Reference Note

CREATOR	WEBSITE TITLE

1. The Spring Grove Family (Cincinnati, Ohio), *Spring Grove Cemetery,*

ITEM TYPE & FORMAT	URL (DIGITAL LOCATION) ...

card file, digital images (http://www.springgrove.org/sg/genealogy/sg_gene

...	DATE	ITEM OF INTEREST ...

alogy_home.shtm : accessed 22 February 2007), card for Abram Jones, no.

...	CREDIT LINE (SOURCE OF THIS SOURCE)

9180; citing section 40, lot O, space 235.

Subsequent (Short) Note

WEBSITE TITLE	ITEM TYPE & FORMAT	ITEM OF INTEREST

11. *Spring Grove Cemetery,* card file image, Abram Jones, no. 9180.

QuickCheck Model
CEMETERY OFFICE RECORDS
PRESERVATION FILM, FHL-GSU

Cemetery office as lead element in Source List; emphasis on a single register

Source List Entry

CEMETERY (AUTHOR)   LOCATION   RECORD BOOK ...

St. Louis Cemetery No. 2 (New Orleans, Louisiana). "Death Records,

...   MICROFILM ID   FILM REPOSITORY

Dec. 1864–Dec. 1867." FHL microfilm 910,850. Family History

...   REPOSITORY LOCATION

Library, Salt Lake City, Utah.

First (Full) Reference Note

CEMETERY (AUTHOR)   LOCATION   RECORD BOOK ...

1. St. Louis Cemetery No. 2 (New Orleans, Louisiana), "Death Records,

...   PAGE   ITEM   MICROFILM ...

Dec. 1864–Dec. 1867," p. 35, Valentine Avegno entry; FHL microfilm

... ID

910,850.

Subsequent (Short) Note

CEMETERY   LOCATION   RECORD BOOK ...

11. St. Louis Cemetery No. 2 (New Orleans), "Death Records, Dec.

...   PAGE

1864–Dec. 1867," 35.

QuickCheck Model
GRAVE MARKERS: RURAL
Cemetery as lead element in Source List

Source List Entry

CEMETERY	LOCATION	ACCESS DATA: ...

Brian Cemetery (Lawrence County, Illinois; 5.5 miles SW of Sumner, off

... DISTANCE, DIRECTION, GPS READING, ETC.	RECORD TYPE

Highway 1801 in Section 30, Township 3N, Range 13W). Grave markers.

First (Full) Reference Note

CEMETERY	LOCATION	ACCESS DATA: ...

1. Brian Cemetery (Lawrence County, Illinois; 5.5 miles SW of Sumner,

... DISTANCE, DIRECTION, GPS READING, ETC.	ITEM ...

off Highway 1801, in Section 30, Township 3N, Range 13W), Samuel Witter

...	DATA COLLECTION INFO	DATE READ or PHOTOGRAPHED

marker, photograph supplied by Eugene Laws, landowner, February 1974.

Subsequent (Short) Note

CEMETERY	LOCATION	ITEM

11. Brian Cemetery (Lawrence Co., Ill.), Samuel Witter marker.

QuickCheck Model
GRAVE MARKERS: URBAN
Cemetery as lead element in Source List

Source List Entry

CEMETERY	LOCATION	ITEM TYPE or FORMAT

Waldheim Cemetery (Forest Park, Cook County, Illinois). Grave markers.

First (Full) Reference Note

CEMETERY	LOCATION	ITEM ...

1. Waldheim Cemetery (Forest Park, Cook County, Illinois), Egbert

... OF INTEREST	SECTION, LOT or ROW	DATA COLLECTION INFO	DATE

Petersen marker, section 555C; personally read, 1992.

Subsequent (Short) Note

CEMETERY	LOCATION	ITEM

11. Waldheim Cemetery (Forest Park, Ill.), Egbert Petersen marker.

QuickCheck Model
GRAVE MARKERS: IMAGES ONLINE
Creator as lead element in Source List

Source List Entry

CREATOR	WEBSITE TITLE	ITEM TYPE or FORMAT	URL ...
Genealogy.com.	*Virtual Cemetery*.	Digital images.	http://www.gene

... DIGITAL LOCATION	YEAR
alogy.com/vcem–welcome.html :	2007.

First (Full) Reference Note

	CREATOR	WEBSITE TITLE	ITEM TYPE or FORMAT	URL ...
1.	Genealogy.com,	*Virtual Cemetery,*	digital images	(http://www

... DIGITAL LOCATION	DATE	...
.genealogy.com/vcem–welcome.html :	accessed 29 January 2007),	photo-

... ITEM OF INTEREST
graph, gravestone for Mary E. Gill (1862–1928), Fordyce, Arkansas.

Subsequent (Short) Note

	CREATOR	WEBSITE TITLE	ITEM OF ...
11.	Genealogy.com,	*Virtual Cemetery*,	photograph, gravestone for

... INTEREST
Mary E. Gill (1862–1928), Fordyce, Ark.

QuickCheck Model
MEMORIAL PLAQUES
Cemetery as lead element in Source List

Source List Entry

CEMETERY | LOCATION | ITEM ...

Congregation Beth Am Sanctuary (Altamonte Springs, Florida). Yahrzeit

... TYPE or FORMAT

(memorial) plaques.

First (Full) Reference Note

CEMETERY | LOCATION

1. Congregation Beth Am Sanctuary (Altamonte Springs, Florida),

ITEM | DATA COLLECTION ...

Arthur B. Friedman *yahrzeit* (memorial) plaque; photographed by Gladys

... INFO | DATE READ or PHOTOGRAPHED

Friedman Paulin, 1 October 2005.

Subsequent (Short) Note

CEMETERY | LOCATION | ...

11. Congregation Beth Am Sanctuary (Altamonte Springs, Fla.), Arthur

... ITEM

B. Friedman yahrzeit plaque.

QuickCheck Model
DERIVATIVES: CEMETERY ABSTRACTS
VERTICAL FILE

Compiler unidentified—file as lead element in Source List

Source List Entry

FILE LABEL	ITEM TYPE or FORMAT

"Monroe County [Wisconsin] Cemetery Gravestone Record." Vertical file.

CREATION DATE	REPOSITORY

No date. Monroe County Local History Museum and Research Room,

REP'Y LOCAT'N

Sparta.

First (Full) Reference Note

FILE LABEL	ITEM ...

1. "Monroe County [Wisconsin] Cemetery Gravestone Record" (vertical

TYPE	CREATION DATE	REPOSITORY

file, n.d., Monroe County Local History Museum and Research Room,

REP'Y LOCAT'N	FOLDER	ITEM ...

Sparta), Cemetery 41-27, St. Patrick's Catholic Cemetery, Sparta; entry for

... OF INTEREST

Mabel Youngman Holloway (1886–1911).

Subsequent (Short) Note

FILE LABEL	FOLDER ...

11. "Monroe County [Wisc.] Cemetery Gravestone Record," Cemetery

...	ITEM OF INTEREST

41-27, entry for Mabel Youngman Holloway.

QuickCheck Model
DERIVATIVES: CEMETERY ABSTRACTS
CARD FILE

Compiler unidentified—file as lead element in Source List

Source List Entry

	ITEM TYPE
FILE LABEL	or FORMAT ···

"Monroe County [Wisconsin] Cemetery Gravestone Index." Card file. No

CREATION	
DATE	REPOSITORY

date. Monroe County Local History Museum and Research Room,

REP'Y
LOCATION

Sparta.

First (Full) Reference Note

	ITEM TYPE
FILE LABEL	or FORMAT

1. "Monroe County [Wisconsin] Cemetery Gravestone Index" (card file,

		REP'Y
DATE	REPOSITORY	LOCATION

n.d., Monroe County Local History Museum and Research Room, Sparta),

ITEM OF ...

joint entry for "Father: Michael Reisinger (1877–1945)" and "Mother:

... INTEREST

Frances Reisinger (1883–1946)."

Subsequent (Short) Note

FILE LABEL	ITEM ...

11. "Monroe County [Wisc.] Cemetery Gravestone Index," joint entry for

...

Michael and Frances Reisinger.

QuickCheck Model
DERIVATIVES: DATABASE ONLINE
Compiler as lead element in Source List

Source List Entry

CREATOR   DATABASE TITLE ...

Madsen, Ken, compiler. "Downers Grove and Lisle Township Cemetery

ITEM TYPE or FORMAT   WEBSITE TITLE   URL ...

Index." Database. *DuPage County (IL) Genealogical Society.* http://

... DIGITAL LOCATION   YEAR

www.dcgs.org/downers/ : 2006.

First (Full) Reference Note

CREATOR   DATABASE TITLE

1. Ken Madsen, compiler, "Downers Grove and Lisle Township Cem-

ITEM TYPE or FORMAT   WEBSITE TITLE   URL ...

etery Index," database, *DuPage County (IL) Genealogical Society* (http://

... DIGITAL LOCATION   DATE   ITEM OF ...

www.dcgs.org/downers/ : accessed 1 October 2006), database entry for Harry

... INTEREST

L. Sedwick (1870–1930).

Subsequent (Short) Note

CREATOR   DATABASE TITLE

11. Madsen, "Downers Grove and Lisle Township Cemetery Index,"

ITEM OF INTEREST

database entry for Harry L. Sedwick (1870–1930).

GUIDELINES
& Examples

BASIC ISSUES

5.1 Cultural Differences & Similarities

Terminology varies from one culture to another, but the basic records in this category are essentially the same. So are the patterns we follow in citing them.

While Americans typically use the term *cemetery* to refer to all types of burial grounds, Australians often refer to them as graveyards, and British researchers typically make a distinction between a *cemetery* and a *churchyard*. Similarly, U.S. researchers tend to speak interchangeably of inscriptions from *cemeteries, grave markers, gravestones,* and *tombstones,* while in Scotland and England, the term is typically *monumental inscriptions*. You should use the appropriate term for the culture in which you are doing research.

5.2 Cemetery as "Author"

When citing cemetery records you will greatly reduce the length of your Source List if you cite the facility as the author (creator) of the records, rather than use the gravestone or the record book as the lead element in a Source List Entry.

5.3 Identification of Facility

The cemetery should be identified precisely—not generically by the name of the town in which it is located. For example:

> New Cleveland Cemetery (Cleveland, Mississippi)
> *not* Cleveland Cemetery

This principle applies even if an area had only one known burial ground during the time period you are researching. Forgotten sites continue to be discovered. Identifying the specific town is equally important because researchers frequently find multiple burial grounds of the same name within the same county or state.

5.4 Identification of Individuals

Your First Reference Note should include the name of the key person(s) in the entry if (*a*) he or she is not identified in the text to which you attach the note; or (*b*) the original record spells the name differently from the standardized spelling you use in your text.

5.5 Identification of Record Dates

If your text does not give the date of the record, you will want to include that date in your First Reference Note.

ADMINISTRATIVE RECORDS

5.6 Correspondence with Extracts

See QuickCheck Model *for* CEMETERY OFFICE RECORDS: SUPPLIED BY STAFF

When your inquiry to a cemetery office results in a letter response that contains transcribed or abstracted data, your source will be that piece of correspondence, with an added mention of the data contained in it. Even if that letter tells you the exact date, lot, name of person buried, etc., you will want to cite the details in a way that does not imply you personally visited the site and personally read the stone. The data on the stone may, in fact, be different from the data in the cemetery office files (as illustrated at 5.7). A typical citation to correspondence from a cemetery office would be handled as follows:

Source List Entry
Woodlawn Cemetery Office (Everett, Massachusetts) to Katherine E. Flynn. Letter. 2002.

First Reference Note
1. Woodlawn Cemetery Office (Everett, Massachusetts) to Katherine E. Flynn, letter, 24 May 2002, providing administrative record for Jane Harris, grave 74, row 2, Pilgrim's Rest, North Section.

Subsequent Note
11. Woodlawn Cemetery Office (Everett, Mass.) to Flynn, 24 May 2002.

FULL IDENTIFICATION OF LOCATION IN SUBSEQUENT NOTES
In the shortened citation above, the location of the cemetery is cited

by city *and state* in the short form; but in the St. Louis Cemetery microfilm example at 5.8, only the city is cited. The difference is a matter of clarity. New Orleans is a city known worldwide. Everett is not, and Woodlawn is a cemetery name in many locales.

5.7 Files, Plats, Registers & Sexton Records

See QuickCheck Model *for* CEMETERY OFFICE RECORDS: PERSONALLY USED

The office files maintained by larger cemeteries may offer ownership, financial, and other information not found on the stones, or they may cite burial information for plots where no marker now exists. Your citation should clearly indicate that the data came from the office files. Typical situations include the following.

Source List Entry

Bellevue Cemetery Office (Lawrence, Massachusetts). Plat records.

First Reference Note

1. Bellevue Cemetery Office (Lawrence, Massachusetts), undated plat, citing Clarissa Wardrobe, lot 99, group 10. The actual gravestone (viewed by the author, 1996) reads *Elvira L.* Wardrobe, rather than *Clarissa*.

Subsequent Note

11. Bellevue Cemetery Office (Lawrence, Mass.), undated plat.

CORRECTION OF ERRORS

When citing cemetery office records, if the office data are at odds with the details on the stone, you will want to note that fact, along with a statement of how you obtained the information from the stone—i.e., by a personal visit, from published abstracts, or via other means.

FHL-GSU Preservation Microfilm

See also QuickCheck Model *for* CEMETERY OFFICE RECORDS: PRESERVATION FILM

When citing cemetery office registers filmed by the Genealogical Society of Utah and deposited at the Family History Library, the key issue is whether you wish your Source List Entry to be the whole collection of office records for that cemetery or whether your Source List will individually itemize the cemetery's varied types of materials.

The following example treats the cemetery office as the author and offers options for the Source List Entry. The register's title, copied exactly, is placed in quotation marks.

Source List Entry

(*Emphasis on whole series*)
St. Louis Cemetery No. 2 (New Orleans, Louisiana). Death and Burial
    Registers. FHL microfilm, 18 rolls. Family History Library, Salt
    Lake City, Utah.

(*Emphasis on a single register*)
St. Louis Cemetery No. 2 (New Orleans, Louisiana). "Death Records,
    Dec. 1864–Dec. 1867." FHL microfilm 910,850. Family History
    Library, Salt Lake City, Utah.

First Reference Note

1. St. Louis Cemetery No. 2 (New Orleans, Louisiana), "Death
Records, Dec. 1864–Dec. 1867," p. 35, Valentine Avegno entry; FHL
microfilm 910,850.

Subsequent Note

11. St. Louis Cemetery No. 2 (New Orleans), "Death Records, Dec.
1864–Dec. 1867," 35.

Online Databases & Images

See also QuickCheck Model *for* CEMETERY OFFICE RECORDS: IMAGES ONLINE

Some cemetery offices place their card files online, offering digitized
images accompanied by databases or search engines. The following
examples demonstrate how you might combine both types of resources into a single Source List Entry. The QuickCheck Model, cross-
referenced above, demonstrates a citation only to the digital images.

Your source for these online records is the website, not the cemetery
or the marker. As noted at 5.8, cemetery office data can differ from the
data on the marker itself. Online data can differ from both. As the next
example illustrates, the database and the card data can also differ.

When either type of source identifies its graves by section, lot, and
space number, as these examples do, you may wish to include that
detail in your citation. If so, you should state that the *database* (or the
card) cites the section, lot, and space—clearly indicating in your notes
that you have not verified this location through a personal visit.

In this example, the creator of the data is "The Spring Grove Family,"
a corporation that encompasses multiple cemeteries, a funeral home,
and a heritage foundation. The cited website was created by this
corporation but the website's name indicates that it covers only one
cemetery. Neither the database nor the introductory page to the

images carries a formal name. Thus, they are generically described, with no quotation marks around the words chosen to identify them.

Source List Entry

The Spring Grove Family (Cincinnati, Ohio). *Spring Grove Cemetery.* Card-file database and images. http://www.springgrove.org/sg/ge nealogy/sg_genealogy_home.shtm : 2007.

First Reference Note

(*To cite the database entry*)

1. The Spring Grove Family (Cincinnati, Ohio), *Spring Grove Cemetery,* card-file database (http://www.springgrove.org/sg/geneal-ogy/sg_gene alogy_home.shtm : accessed 22 February 2007), entry for Abram Jones, no. 9180, citing section 40, lot O, space 235.

(*To cite a card image*)

2. The Spring Grove Family (Cincinnati, Ohio), *Spring Grove Cemetery,* card-file images (http://www.springgrove.org/sg/genealogy/ sg_genealogy_home.shtm : accessed 22 February 2007), card for Abram Jones, no. 9180, citing section 40, lot O, space 235.

Subsequent Note

11. *Spring Grove Cemetery,* database entry, Abram Jones, no. 9180.
12. *Spring Grove Cemetery,* card file image, Abram Jones, no. 9180.

PLACEMENT OF CARD FILE & DATABASE DETAIL

The Spring Grove Cemetery situation is one in which the cited website is entirely a database of card file images. Therefore, the specific detail relating to the database and the card file is placed immediately after the identification of the website—creating the sequence COMPILER, WEBSITE TITLE, RECORD TYPE/FORMAT (PUBLICATION DATA), SPECIFIC ITEM. By comparison at 5.19, the website offers multiple items, of which a separately titled cemetery database is just one. In that case, the sequence of elements is COMPILER, "DATABASE TITLE," RECORD TYPE/FORMAT, WEBSITE TITLE (PUBLICATION DATA), SPECIFIC ITEM.

5.8 Orders for Interment (Burial Permits, Transit Permits, Etc.)

The operators of modern cemeteries typically require mortuary firms to submit a formal *order for interment* that not only requests the preparation of a grave site but also supplies personal detail on the deceased. If the cemetery office merely sends you a letter extracting details from the order, then you would use 5.6, Correspondence. If you acquire these documents onsite at the cemetery office or receive a photocopy by correspondence, the basic citation would follow this pattern:

Source List Entry
Homewood Cemetery Office (Pittsburgh, Pennsylvania). Orders for
  interment.

First Reference Note
    1. Homewood Cemetery Office (Pittsburgh, Pennsylvania), order
for interment of Mildred W. Roy, submitted by E. B. Laughlin, Inc., 13
May 1983.

Subsequent Note
    11. Homewood Cemetery Office (Pittsburgh, Penn.), order for
interment of Mildred W. Roy, 13 May 1983.

5.9 Plot Ownership Certificates

These certificates are commonly found among family papers, rather
than the administrative records of the cemetery. Therefore they are
normally cited as family artifacts. *See* 3.25.

MARKERS & PLAQUES

5.10 Basic Elements

Citations to the original inscriptions should identify at least the
following:

- the cemetery;
- its location;
- the date the marker was read; and
- the data collection information—i.e., the identity of the individual who gathered the data and whether the marker was
  transcribed fully, abstracted, and/or photographed.

If the burial ground is large or if it is laid out in an orderly fashion, you
will want to cite the section, plot number, or specific row. In very large
urban cemeteries, a row might actually be a named street. Along with
these basic elements that would appear in a published citation, you
should also record in your notes information about

- the condition of the stone—a factor that affects legibility; and
- the type of material from which the stone is made—a factor that
  bears upon whether the stone is contemporary to the burial.

5.11 Cenotaphs & Memorial Plaques

See also QuickCheck Model *for* MEMORIAL PLAQUES

The markers that researchers find in burial grounds and mausoleums do not always mark a burial site. The first example below illustrates the handling of a *cenotaph* (a tomb or monument erected in honor of a person or group of persons whose remains are elsewhere). The second demonstrates a citation to a Jewish memorial plaque (*yahrzeit*) typically placed on the anniversary of a death.

Source List Entry

(Cenotaph—rural cemetery as lead element ["author"] in Source List)
Sharon Presbyterian Church Cemetery (Lee County, Iowa). Markers and memorials.

(Memorial plaque—individual as lead element in Source List)
Friedman, Arthur B. *Yahrzeit* plaque. Congregation Beth Am Sanctuary. Altamonte Springs, Florida.

First Reference Note

   1. Sharon Presbyterian Church Cemetery (Lee County, Iowa, between Donnellson and Primrose), James A. Davis cenotaph; photographed 1 June 2005 by the researcher.

   2. Congregation Beth Am Sanctuary (Altamonte Springs, Florida), Arthur B. Friedman *yahrzeit* (memorial) plaque; photographed by Gladys Friedman Paulin, 1 October 2005.

Subsequent Note

   11. Sharon Cemetery (Lee Co., Iowa), James A. Davis cenotaph.

   12. Congregation Beth Am Sanctuary (Altamonte Springs, Fla.), Arthur B. Friedman yahrzeit plaque.

5.12   Grave Markers: Churchyard (Monumental Inscriptions)

Some countries distinguish between churchyard burials and interments in public cemeteries. The basic format is the same, but when a culture uses distinctive terms for a situation, you should observe those distinctions. England and Scotland, for example, not only distinguish between churchyards and cemeteries but also prefer the term *monumental inscriptions* rather than *tombstone* or *grave marker* inscriptions.

Source List Entry

Raveningham Churchyard, St. Andrew's Church (Hales, Norfolk, England). Monumental inscriptions.

First Reference Note

   1. Raveningham Churchyard, St. Andrew's Church (Hales, County of Norfolk, England), James Bonfellow monumental inscription, read by T. Baxter, 1 May 1986.

Subsequent Note

   11. Raveningham Churchyard, St. Andrew's Church (Hales, Co. Norfolk), James Bonfellow monumental inscription.

The American custom of placing the word "county" *after* the name of a county is not followed in England. In a string of place names, the above locales would be typically written as *Hales, Norfolk, England.* That pattern is analogous to the U.S. convention of writing *City, State, U.S.A.* When it is necessary to specifically identify a place name as a county—something a researcher may need to do for readers outside the U.K.— the custom is to write the place name as *County of Norfolk* or, in short form, *Co. Norfolk.* The identification may also be handled by placing the jurisdiction label in brackets, as demonstrated with the several jurisdictions involved in the census entries at 6.51.

5.13   Grave Markers: Rural

See QuickCheck Model *for* GRAVE MARKERS: RURAL

When citing a rural cemetery you will want to include directions for locating it, unless you have already done so in your text. Typically, these directions will reference the nearest town and cite distance by way of a certain highway or road. In U.S. public-land states, which are surveyed by sections, townships, and ranges, these legal descriptions also serve as convenient locators.

Source List Entry

Brian Cemetery (Lawrence County, Illinois; 5.5 miles SW of Sumner, off Highway 1801, in Section 30, Township 3N, Range 13W). Grave markers.

First Reference Note

1. Brian Cemetery (Lawrence County, Illinois; 5.5 miles SW of Sumner, off Highway 1801 in Section 30, Township 3N, Range 13W), Samuel Witter marker; photograph supplied by Eugene Laws, landowner, February 1974.

Subsequent Note

11. Brian Cemetery (Lawrence Co. Ill.), Samuel Witter marker.

5.14   Grave Markers: Rural, Citing by GPS

You may cite a Global Positioning System location if you use a GPS tracking device. Even so, most users of your citation will want to know the access road, nearest town, and distance from that town. Most GPS systems give you a choice between citing the location by (*a*) "L-L," referring to latitude and longitude; or (*b*) UTM, referring to the Universal Transverse Mercator system favored in the historic preservation field. Note the following about each:

227

L-L SYSTEM

- Latitude and longitude may be expressed by decimals or by degrees, minutes, and seconds. Most L-L readings are decimal.

- A GPS latitude number that is expressed as a positive signifies north; expressed as a negative, it signifies south. A longitude number expressed as a positive represents east; negative is west.

- In the Allen Cemetery example below, the GPS reading *349506, 0874612* would be interpreted as latitude 34.9506 North and longitude -87.4612 West.

UTM SYSTEM

- The Universal Transverse Mercator location is expressed in terms of its global zone, its East-West position within that zone (in meters), and its North-South position within that zone (in meters).

- In the McCrury Cemetery example below, the Zone 15 289906mE 3698272mN reading means that the site's East-West location is 289906 and its North-South location is 3698272, all in UTM Grid Zone 15.

Source List Entry
Allen Cemetery (Lauderdale County, Alabama; LAT/LON 349506N, -874612W; 5 miles SW of Lexington on Highway 470). Grave markers.
McCrury Cemetery (Red River Co., Texas; Zone 15 289906mE 3698272mN; 5 miles south of Bogata on State Highway 37, then 2 miles west on Farm-Market Road 196). Grave markers.

First Reference Note
1. Allen Cemetery (Lawrence County, Alabama; LAT/LON 349506N, -874612W; 5 miles SW of Lexington on Highway 470), George Massengill marker; read by Beau Sharbrough, 20 October 2002.
2. McCrury Cemetery (Red River County, Texas; Zone 15 289906mE 3698272mN; 5 miles south of Bogata on State Highway 37, then 2 miles west on Farm-Market Road 196), James Washington Lewis marker; read 2 March 1995.

Subsequent Note
11. Allen Cemetery (Lawrence Co., Ala.), George Massengill marker.
12. McCrury Cemetery (Red River Co., Texas), James Washington Lewis marker.

5.15 Grave Markers: Urban

See QuickCheck Model *for* GRAVE MARKERS: URBAN

When citing an urban cemetery, it may be necessary to cite a street on which the cemetery is located or a street within the bounds of a large cemetery. Other urban cemeteries identify their plots by section and lot numbers. When a cemetery is located in a village that is not well known, as with the Forest Park example below, you may wish to give the county for better identification.

Source List Entry

Waldheim Cemetery (Forest Park, Cook County, Illinois). Grave markers.

First Reference Note

1. Waldheim Cemetery (Forest Park, Cook County, Illinois), Egbert Petersen marker, section 555C; personally read, 1992.

Subsequent Note

11. Waldheim Cemetery (Forest Park, Ill.), Egbert Petersen marker.

5.16 Images: Markers & Plaques

See QuickCheck Model *for* GRAVE MARKERS: IMAGES ONLINE

Photographs of isolated stones cannot replace all the evidentiary value of actually walking a cemetery and placing each person's resting place into the context of the community of people in which they are buried. Nonetheless, the virtual-cemetery concept that provides online gravestone images allows you to interpret the full content of stones as opposed to relying upon extracts and readings made by others.

Online Images

Source List Entry

Genealogy.com. *Virtual Cemetery*. Digital images. http://www.gene alogy.com/vcem_welcome.html : 2007.

First Reference Note

1. Genealogy.com, *Virtual Cemetery*, digital images (http://www .genealogy.com/vcem_welcome.html : accessed 29 January 2007), photograph, gravestone for Mary E. Gill (1862–1928), Fordyce, Arkansas.

Subsequent Note

11. Genealogy.com, *Virtual Cemetery*, photograph, gravestone for Mary E. Gill (1862–1938), Fordyce, Ark.

DERIVATIVES (COPIES & COMPILATIONS)

5.17   A Caution When Using Derivatives

Many cemetery compilations are created in a manner that can affect the reliability of their information and your evaluation of it. Transcriptions from a cemetery may alphabetize all entries. City-wide or county-wide databases often present entries in alphabetical order. In such cases, you should add an explanation of the shortcomings or limitations. For example:

> *First Reference Note*
> 1. Alton Lambert, "Fifty-Five Tuscaloosa County, Alabama, Cemeteries," 2 vols. (typescript, ca. 1970, Tuscaloosa County Public Library), 2: 37. Tombstone abstracts in this volume are arranged alphabetically and the author has added information from "personal knowledge," making it impossible to determine who is buried next to whom or exactly what information appears on the original marker.

Similarly, when a compilation is very thorough and preserves contextual information, as with the publication at 5.21, you would want to note that also in your identification of the work.

5.18   Compiled Cemetery Records: Card Files & Vertical Files

Many local libraries maintain a card file or vertical file of gravestone data abstracted from burial grounds in their area. These compiled works are cited in much the same manner as authored manuscripts, alphabetizing the Source List Entry under the name of the compiler, if known. If no compiler is known, you might choose to make the source a geographic-based entry or place it under the name of the library or the society.

When multiple cards exist for individuals of the same name and the cards themselves are not numbered, your citation should include some piece of data that distinguishes your particular card from others for people of the same name.

The following examples use one data set to demonstrate citations to three forms in which researchers typically consult this type of compilation—i.e., the original card file (alphabetized by the names of the deceased), a vertical file of transcriptions (arranged by cemetery, ideally maintaining the original gravestone order); and an FHL microform version of the card file. Note especially three points:

IDENTITY OF THE "AUTHOR"

No specific author is named because the card file is the creation of many different volunteers over a ten-year period. If one particular individual was known to have overseen the project, that person would be named.

IDENTITY OF THE CEMETERY

When citing a compilation, you may need to identify the specific cemetery. Typically, your discussion of the burial in your text will do so. Whether it is needed in the citation depends upon whether the cemetery has to be cited in order to access the record. In the Card File example below, the cemetery is not included in the citation because the card file covers all cemeteries in the county, interfiling cards alphabetically by name of the deceased. To locate an individual, one does not need to know the name of the cemetery. In the Vertical File example, the cemetery is named because one must know the name of the cemetery in order to locate data from a specific marker.

IDENTITY OF THE STATE

The official title of the gravestone index names the county but not the state. In such cases, you should clarify the title by adding the state in square editorial brackets.

CARD FILE

See QuickCheck Model *for* DERIVATIVES: CEMETERY ABSTRACTS: CARD FILE

Source List Entry

"Monroe County [Wisconsin] Cemetery Gravestone Index." Card file. No date. Monroe County Local History Museum and Research Room, Sparta.

First Reference Note

1. "Monroe County [Wisconsin] Cemetery Gravestone Index" (card file, n.d., Monroe County Local History Museum and Research Room, Sparta), joint entry for "Father: Michael Reisinger (1877–1945)" and "Mother: Frances Reisinger (1883–1946)."

Subsequent Note

11. "Monroe County [Wisc.] Cemetery Gravestone Index," joint entry for Michael and Frances Reisinger.

VERTICAL FILE

See also QuickCheck Model *for* DERIVATIVES: CEMETERY ABSTRACTS, VERTICAL FILE

Source List Entry

"Monroe County [Wisconsin] Cemetery Gravestone Record." Vertical
    file. No date. Monroe County Local History Museum and Research
    Room, Sparta.

First Reference Note

1. "Monroe County [Wisconsin] Cemetery Gravestone Record"
(vertical file, n.d., Monroe County Local History Museum and Research
Room, Sparta), Cemetery 41-27, St. Patrick's Catholic Cemetery,
Sparta; joint entry for "Father: Michael Reisinger (1877–1945)" and
"Mother: Frances Reisinger (1883–1946)."

Subsequent Note

11. "Monroe County [Wisc.] Cemetery Gravestone Record," Cemetery 41-27, joint entry for Michael and Frances Reisinger.

FHL-GSU Microfiche of Card Files

Source List Entry

"Monroe County [Wisconsin] Cemetery Gravestone Index." Card file.
    Monroe County Local History Museum and Research Room,
    Sparta. FHL microfiche 6,334,151. Family History Library, Salt
    Lake City, Utah.

First Reference Note

1. "Monroe County [Wisconsin] Cemetery Gravestone Index"
(card file, Monroe County Local History Museum and Research Room,
Sparta), joint grave marker for "Father: Michael Reisinger (1877–
1945)" and "Mother: Frances Reisinger (1883–1946)"; FHL microfiche 6,334,151.

Subsequent Note

11. "Monroe County [Wisc.] Cemetery Gravestone Index," joint
grave marker for Michael Reisinger and Frances Reisinger.

Online Transcriptions of Card Files

Source List Entry

Hendersin, Ralph. "Monroe County [Wisconsin] Cemetery Gravestone
    Index." Abstracts. *Monroe County Local History Museum and Re-
    search Room.* http://www.rootsweb.com/~wimonroe/MCLH
    MaRR/cemetery/ : 2006.

First Reference Note

1. Ralph Hendersin, abstractor, "Monroe County [Wisconsin]
Cemetery Gravestone Index," *Monroe County Local History Museum and
Research Room* (http://www.rootsweb.com/~wimonroe/MCLH MaRR

/cemetery/ : accessed 8 October 2006), Pilgrim's Rest Cemetery entry
for Christene Frohmader (1855–1878).

Subsequent Note
11. Hendersin, "Monroe County [Wisc.] Cemetery Gravestone Index," Pilgrim's Rest Cemetery entry for Christene Frohmader (1855–
1878).

5.19   Compiled Cemetery Records: Databases
See QuickCheck Model *for* DERIVATIVES: DATABASE ONLINE

Section 5.18 introduces the question whether you need to include the
identity of the cemetery in your citation. The example below illustrates
another consideration: the database itself does not identify the cemetery. From the data it makes available, you could not include the
cemetery name in your citation. You will also note that your source for
these online records is the database—not the cemetery or the marker.

Online databases

Source List Entry
Madsen, Ken, compiler. "Downers Grove and Lisle Township Cemetery
    Index." Database. *DuPage County (IL) Genealogical Society.* http://
    www.dcgs.org/downers/ : 2006.

First Reference Note
1. Ken Madsen, compiler, "Downers Grove and Lisle Township
Cemetery Index," database, *DuPage County (IL) Genealogical Society*
(http: //www.dcgs.org/downers/ : accessed 1 October 2006), database
entry for Harry L. Sedwick (1870–1930).

Subsequent Note
11. Madsen, "Downers Grove and Lisle Township Cemetery Index," database entry for Harry L. Sedwick (1870–1930).

5.20   Compiled Cemetery Records: Photographic Works
Bound compilations that offer photographs of tombstones rather than
abstracts are cited like unpublished, authored manuscripts.

Source List Entry
Tawse, Dawn; Ross Cromarty; and Magnus Cromarty. "Anna Bay
    Cemetery, New South Wales, Australia, *c.* 1877–1971." MS, ca.
    1980–81. Tomaree Regional Library. Nelson Bay, New South
    Wales, Australia.

First Reference Note
1. Dawn Tawse, Ross Cromarty, and Magnus Cromarty, "Anna

Bay Cemetery, New South Wales, Australia, *c.* 1877–1971" (MS, ca. 1980–81, Tomaree Regional Library, Nelson Bay, New South Wales, Australia), p. 13; the compilation offers photographs, rather than abstracted data, and includes a row plan and a location plan.

Subsequent Note
11. Tawse, Cromarty, and Cromarty, "Anna Bay Cemetery, New South Wales," 13.

5.21 Compiled Cemetery Records: Published Works
Published cemetery transcriptions or abstracts from are cited as publications, according to type—e.g., book, database, periodical article, etc. As an aid to your ongoing analysis of the data from this source, you will want to also note the quality of the compilation. (*See also* 5.17.)

Source List Entry
North Hills Genealogists. *Pioneer Cemeteries of Pine and Richland Townships, Allegheny County, Pennsylvania.* Pittsburgh: North Hills Genealogists, 2003.

First Reference Note
1. North Hills Genealogists, *Pioneer Cemeteries of Pine and Richland Townships, Allegheny County, Pennsylvania* (Pittsburgh: North Hills Genealogists, 2003), 205, James Beveridge obelisk, photographed by Reed Powell. This publication's format follows the physical layout of the graves in each cemetery, describes each marker, transcribes its entire content, and provides representative photographs.

Subsequent Note
11. North Hill Genealogists, *Pioneer Cemeteries of Pine and Richland Townships, Allegheny County, Pennsylvania,* 205.

5.22 Compiled Cemetery Records: Typescripts
Transcriptions that are compiled in book format but have not been published are cited like unpublished, authored manuscripts.

Source List Entry
Smith, Mavis. "Fairview Cemetery, North of Roland." Typescript. 1985. Manitoba Genealogical Society Library, Winnipeg.

First Reference Note
1. Mavis Smith, "Fairview Cemetery, North of Roland" (typescript, 1985, Manitoba Genealogical Society Library, Winnipeg), p. 10.

Subsequent Note
11. Smith, "Fairview Cemetery, North of Roland," 10.

CENSUS RECORDS

6

QuickCheck Models

Guidelines & Examples (beginning page 257)

QuickCheck Model
ORIGINAL MANUSCRIPTS
LOCAL COPY, FEDERAL CENSUS
Place & year as lead elements in Source List

Source List Entry

JURISDICTION   CENSUS I.D. (GENERIC)   SCHEDULE & COPY

Alabama. Pike County. 1860 U.S. census, population schedule. Local copy.

REPOSITORY   REPOSITORY LOCATION

Office of the Probate Judge, Troy, Alabama.

First (Full) Reference Note

CENSUS ID   JURISDICTION   SCHEDULE

1. 1860 U.S. census, Pike County, Alabama, population schedule

COPY ID   CIVIL DIVISION   PAGE   HOUSEHOLD ...

(local copy), Pea River post office, p. 324, dwelling 1034, family 1046,

PERSON OF INTEREST   REPOSITORY   REPOSITORY LOCATION

Charles C. Sammonds; Probate Judge's Office, Troy, Alabama.

Subsequent (Short) Note

CENSUS ID   JURISDICTION   SCHEDULE & COPY   CIVIL DIVISION ...

11. 1860 U.S. census, Pike Co., Ala., pop. sch. (local copy), Pea River

... PAGE   HOUSEHOLD ID   PERSON OF INTEREST

P.O., p. 324, dwell. 1034, fam. 1046, Charles C. Sammonds.

QuickCheck Model
ORIGINAL MANUSCRIPTS
NATIONAL ARCHIVES COPY

NARA Style citation for manuscript consulted on-site

Source List Entry

SERIES | SUBGROUP ...

Second Census of the United States, 1800. Manuscript Schedules of Decennial

... | RECORD GROUP (NAME & NO.) ...

Population Censuses, 1790–1870. Records of the Bureau of the Census,

... | REPOSITORY | REPOSITORY LOCATION

Record Group 29. National Archives, Washington, D.C.

First (Full) Reference Note

ITEM OF INTEREST | PAGE | NARA "FILE UNIT" (JURISDICTION: SMALLEST TO...

1. Daniel[?] Smith household, p. 192-A, Crown Point, Essex County,

... LARGEST) | NARA SERIES & VOLUME

New York; Second Census of the United States, 1800, vol. 2, New York:

... | NARA SUBGROUP ...

Clinton–Green Counties; Manuscript Schedules of Decennial Population

... | NARA RECORD GROUP (NAME & NO.) ...

Censuses, 1790–1870; Records of the Bureau of the Census, Record

... | REPOSITORY | REPOSITORY LOCATION

Group 29; National Archives, Washington, D.C.

Subsequent (Short) Note

ITEM OF INTEREST | PAGE | JURISDICTION | NARA ...

11. Daniel [?] Smith, p. 192-A, Crown Point, Essex Co., N.Y.; Second

... SERIES & SUBGROUP (SHORTENED) | RECORD GROUP | REPOSITORY

Census of U.S., 1800; Manuscript Schedules, RG 29, NA-Washington.

QuickCheck Model
DIGITAL IMAGES
CD/DVD

Place & year as lead elements in Source List

Source List Entry

JURISDICTION	CENSUS ID (GENERIC)	SCHEDULE

Puerto Rico. Dorado Township. 1910 U.S. census, population sched-

...	PUBLICATION TITLE ...

ule. *1910 Dorado Municipality, Puerto Rico, Federal Census: Dorado Town-*

...	FORMAT	PUBLICATION PLACE	PUBLISHER	YEAR

ship. CD-ROM, digital images. Green Creek, New Jersey: AllCensus, 2005.

First (Full) Reference Note

CENSUS ID	JURISDICTION	SCHEDULE ...

1. 1910 U.S. census, Dorado Township, Puerto Rico, population

...	GEOGRAPHIC DIVISION	ENUM. DIST. (FROM 1880 FORWARD)	PAGE ...

schedule, Town of Dorado, enumeration district (ED) 108, p. 5-B

... ID	HOUSEHOLD	PERSON OF INTEREST	PUBLICATION ...

(penned), dwelling 36, family 41, José Sánchez y Pérez; *1910 Dorado*

... TITLE	FORMAT ...

Municipality, Puerto Rico, Federal Census, Dorado Township, CD-ROM, digital

...	PUBLICATION PLACE	PUBLISHER	DATE	CREDIT LINE ...

images (Green Creek, New Jersey: AllCensus, 2005); citing National Archives

... (SOURCE OF THIS SOURCE)

micro-film publication T624, roll 1762.

Subsequent (Short) Note

CENSUS ID	JURISDICTION	SCHEDULE	ENUM DIST.	PAGE

11. 1910 U.S. census, Dorado, Puerto Rico, pop. sch., ED 108, p. 5-B

...	HOUSEHOLD ID	PERSON OF INTEREST

(penned), dwell. 36, fam. 41, José Sánchez y Pérez.

QuickCheck Model
DIGITAL IMAGES
ONLINE COMMERCIAL SITE

Place & year as lead elements in Source List

Source List Entry

JURISDICTION	CENSUS ID (GENERIC)	SCHEDULE	ITEM TYPE or …

Iowa. Marion County. 1850 U.S. census, population schedule. Digital

FORMAT	WEBSITE TITLE	URL (DIGITAL LOCATION)	YEAR

images. *Ancestry.com*. http://www.ancestry.com : 2007.

First (Full) Reference Note

CENSUS ID	JURISDICTION	SCHEDULE

1. 1850 U.S. census, Marion County, Iowa, population schedule,

CIVIL DIVISION	PAGE ID	HOUSEHOLD ID	PERSON(S) …

Lake Prairie, p. 290 (stamped), dwelling 151, family 156, Virgil W. and

… OF INTEREST	ITEM TYPE or FORMAT	WEBSITE TITLE	URL (DIGITAL LOCATION)	…

Wyatt B. Earp; digital image, *Ancestry.com* (http://www.ancestry.com : ac-

… DATE	CREDIT LINE (SOURCE OF THIS SOURCE)

cessed 16 January 2006); citing NARA microfilm publication M432, roll 187.

Subsequent (Short) Note

CENSUS ID	JURISDICTION	SCHEDULE	PAGE ID	…

11. 1850 U.S. census, Marion Co., Iowa, pop. sch., p. 290 (stamped), dwell.

HOUSEHOLD ID	PERSON(S) OF INTEREST

151, fam. 156, Virgil W. and Wyatt B. Earp.

QuickCheck Model
DIGITAL IMAGES
ONLINE ARCHIVES (FRANCE)
Place & year as lead elements in Source List

Source List Entry

JURISDICTION	CENSUS ID (GENERIC)	FORMAT

France. La Mayenne. Laval. Évron. 1836 census of France. Digital images.

WEBSITE CREATOR-OWNER	WEBSITE TITLE	...

Archives Départementales de la Mayenne. *Archives en ligne*. http://

... URL (DIGITAL LOCATION)	YEAR

www.lamayenne.fr?SectionId=591&PubliId=2883&Controller : 2007.

First (Full) Reference Note

CENSUS ID	JURISDICTION ...

1. 1836 census of France, canton Évron, arrondissement de Laval,

...	PAGE	HOUSEHOLD ID	PERSON OF INTEREST	FORMAT

La Mayenne, p. 12, no. 314, family 92, Émile Prudhomme; digital image,

WEBSITE CREATOR-OWNER	WEBSITE TITLE	...

Archives Départementales de la Mayenne, *Archives en ligne* (http://

... URL (DIGITAL LOCATION)	...

www.lamayenne.fr?SectionId=591&PubliId=2883&Controller : accessed

... DATE	CREDIT LINE (SOURCE OF THIS SOURCE)

24 February 2007); original manuscript not cited.

Subsequent (Short) Note

CENSUS ID	JURISDICTION	PAGE	HOUSE'D ...

11. 1836 census of France, Évron, Laval, La Mayenne, p. 12, no. 314,

... ID	PERSON OF INTEREST

fam. 92, Émile Prudhomme.

QuickCheck Model
DIGITAL IMAGES
ONLINE ARCHIVES (U.K., WALES)
Place & year as lead elements in Source List

Source List Entry

JURISDICTION	CENSUS ID (GENERIC)	ITEM TYPE or FORMAT	...

Wales. Monmouthshire. 1901 census of Wales. Digital images. *The*

... WEBSITE TITLE	URL (DIGITAL LOCATION)

National Archives. http://www.1901census.nationalarchives.gov.uk :

YEAR
2006.

First (Full) Reference Note

CENSUS ID	JURISDICTION	CIVIL DIVISIONS ...

1. 1901 census of Wales, Monmouthshire, Bedwelty, Glammorgan

...	PAGE ID	PERSON OF INTEREST	ITEM TYPE or FORMAT	...

Mountain Ash, p. 5 (stamped), Moses Frame; digital image, *The*

... WEBSITE TITLE	URL (DIGITAL LOCATION)	...

National Archives (http:// www.1901census.nationalarchives.gov.uk : accessed

DATE	CREDIT LINE (SOURCE OF THIS SOURCE)

1 September 2006); citing PRO RG13/4943.

Subsequent (Short) Note

CENSUS ID	JURISDICTION	CIVIL DIVISIONS

11. 1901 census of Wales, Monmouthshire, Bedwelty, Glammorgan

...	PAGE ID	PERSON OF INTEREST

Mountain Ash, p. 5 (stamped), Moses Frame.

QuickCheck Model
MICROFILM
NATIVE-AMERICAN TRIBAL CENSUS
Citing agency & exact publication title;
Place & year as lead elements in Source List

Source List Entry

JURISDICTION	CENSUS ID (GENERIC: YEAR & TRIBE)	AGENCY/CREATOR

Montana. Fort Belknap Agency. 1923 Groventre census. Bureau of Indian

...	PUBLICATION TITLE	FILM ID ...

Affairs. *Indian Census Rolls, 1885–1940*. NARA microfilm publication

...	PUBLICATION PLACE	PUBLISHER ...

M595, roll 129. Washington, D.C.: National Archives and Records

...	YEAR

Service, 1967.

First (Full) Reference Note

CENSUS ID	JURISDICTION	PAGE ID

1. 1923 Groventre census, Fort Belknap Agency, unpaginated,

HOUSEHOLD ID	PERSON OF INTEREST	AGENCY/CREATOR ...

entry no. 499/484, Ah ginig [aka] James Snow; Bureau of Indian

...	PUBLICATION TITLE	FILM ID

Affairs, *Indian Census Rolls, 1885–1940*, microfilm publication M595

PUBLICATION PLACE	PUBLISHER	YEAR	ROLL NO.

(Washington, D.C.: National Archives and Records Service, 1967), roll 129.

Subsequent (Short) Note

CENSUS ID	JURISDICTION	PAGE ID	H'HOLD

11. 1923 Groventre census, Fort Belknap Agency, unpaginated, entry

... ID	PERSON OF INTEREST

499/484, Ah gi nig [aka] James Snow.

QuickCheck Model
MICROFILM: "NONPOPULATION" SCHEDULES
NARA FILM

NARA film cited by number, not title;
Place & year as lead elements in Source List

Source List Entry

JURISDICTION   CENSUS ID (GENERIC)   SCHEDULE TITLE ...

Tennessee. Bedford County. 1880 U.S. census. "Defective, Dependent, and

... (CITED EXACTLY)   FILM ID

Delinquent Classes" schedule. NARA microfilm publication T1135, roll

...   PUB'N PLACE   PUBLISHER

39. Washington, D.C.: National Archives and Records Administration,

YEAR

n.d.

First (Full) Reference Note

CENSUS ID   JURISDICTION   SCHEDULE ...

1. 1880 U.S. census, Bedford County, Tennesssee, "Defective,

... TITLE   SECTION   CIVIL ...

Dependent, and Delinquent Classes," Insane Inhabitants, 25th civil

... DIVISION   ENUM. DIST. (1880 FORWARD)   PAGE   PERSON OF INTEREST

district, enumeration district (ED) 19, p. 28608-A, John M. Cable;

FILM ID

NARA microfilm publication T1135, roll 39.

Subsequent (Short) Note

CENSUS   JURISDICTION   SCHEDULE ...

11. 1880 U.S. census, Bedford Co., Tenn., "Defective, Dependent, and

...   SECTION   CIVIL DIVISION   ENUM. DISTRICT   PAGE

Delinquent Classes," Insane Inhabitants, 25th civil dist., ED 19, p. 28608-A,

PERSON

John M. Cable.

QuickCheck Model
MICROFILM: "NONPOPULATION" SCHEDULES
FHL-GSU PRESERVATION FILM
Place & year as lead elements in Source List

Source List Entry

JURISDICTION   CENSUS ID (GENERIC)   SCHEDULE (GENERIC ID)

Delaware. Sussex County. 1870 U.S. census, social statistics schedule.

OWNER REPOSITORY   REPOSITORY LOCATION   FILM ID

Hall of Records, Dover, Delaware. FHL microfilm 1,421,306, item 2.

FILM REPOSITORY   FILM LOCATION

Family History Library, Salt Lake City, Utah.

First (Full) Reference Note

CENSUS ID   JURISDICTION   SCHEDULE ...

1. 1870 U.S. census, Sussex County, Delaware, social statistics

... PAGE ID   ITEM OF INTEREST   OWNER REPOSITORY   ...

schedule, p. 1, "Newspapers and Periodicals"; Hall of Records, Dover,

... LOCATION   FILM ID

Delaware; FHL microfilm 1,421,306, item 2.

Subsequent (Short) Note

CENSUS   JURISDICTION   SCHEDULE   ...

11. 1870 U.S. census, Sussex Co., Del., social statistics sch., p. 1,

ITEM OF INTEREST

"Newspapers and Periodicals."

QuickCheck Model
MICROFILM: "NONPOPULATION" SCHEDULES
UNC MICROFILM PUBLICATION
Place & year as lead elements in Source List

Source List Entry

JURISDICTION   CENSUS ID (GENERIC)   SCHEDULE (GENERIC)

Mississippi. Newton County. 1860 U.S. census, agricultural schedule.

FILM TITLE ...

Agricultural and Manufacturing Census Records of Fifteen Southern States for

...   FILM ID ...

the Years 1850, 1860, 1870, and 1880. UNC microfilm publication MN3-

...   PUBLICATION PLACE   PUBLISHER   YEAR(S)

534, roll 179. Chapel Hill, N.C.: University of North Carolina, 1960–65.

First (Full) Reference Note

CENSUS ID   JURISDICTION   SCHEDULE ...

1. 1860 U.S. census, Newton County, Mississippi, agricultural

... PAGE   PERSON OF INTEREST   FILM TITLE ...

schedule, p. 1, Harvey Williams; *Agricultural and Manufacturing Census*

...

Records of Fifteen Southern States for the Years 1850, 1860, 1870, and 1880,

FILM ID   PUBLICATION PLACE   ...

UNC microfilm publication MN3-534 (Chapel Hill, N.C.: University

PUBLISHER   YEAR(S)   ROLL NO.

of North Carolina, 1960–65), roll 179.

Subsequent (Short) Note

CENSUS ID   JURISDICTION   SCHEDULE   PAGE   PERSON ...

11. 1860 U.S. census, Newton Co., Miss., ag. sch., p. 1, Harvey

... OF
INTEREST

Williams.

QuickCheck Model
MICROFILM: POPULATION SCHEDULES
1790–1840

NARA film cited by number, not title;
Place & year as lead elements in Source List

Source List Entry

JURISDICTION	CENSUS ID (GENERIC)	FILM ID ...

Maine. York County. 1810 U.S. census. NARA microfilm publication

...	PUBLICATION PLACE	PUBLISHER ...

M252, roll 12. Washington, D.C.: National Archives and Records

...	YEAR

Administration, n.d.

First (Full) Reference Note

CENSUS I.D.	JURISDICTION	CIVIL DIVISION	PAGE ...

1. 1810 U.S. census, York County, Maine, town of York, p. 435

... ID	PERSON OF INTEREST	FILM ID ...

(penned), line 9, Jabez Young; NARA microfilm publication M252,

...

roll 12.

Subsequent (Short) Note

CENSUS ID	JURISDICTION	CIVIL DIVISION	PAGE ID ...

11. 1810 U.S. census, York Co., Maine, town of York, p. 435 (penned),

...	PERSON OF INTEREST

line 9, Jabez Young.

QuickCheck Model
MICROFILM: POPULATION SCHEDULES
1850–1870

NARA film cited by number, not title;
Place & year as lead elements in Source List

Source List Entry

JURISDICTION   CENSUS ID (GENERIC)   SCHEDULE   FILM ...

Georgia. Wilkes County. 1870 U.S. census, population schedule. NARA

... ID   PUBLICATION PLACE   ...

microfilm publication M593, roll 184. Washington, D.C.: National

... PUBLISHER   YEAR

Archives and Records Administration, n.d.

First (Full) Reference Note

CENSUS ID   JURISDICTION   SCHEDULE

1. 1870 U.S. census, Wilkes County, Georgia, population schedule,

CIVIL DIVISION   PAGE ID   HOUSEHOLD ID ...

Washington Post Office, p. 223 (stamped), dwelling 19, families 19–

... PERSON(S) OF INTEREST   FILM ID ...

20, Cozart and Hogue; NARA microfilm publication M593, roll 184.

Subsequent (Short) Note

CENSUS ID   JURISDICTION   SCHEDULE   CIVIL DIVISION

11. 1870 U.S. census, Wilkes Co., Ga., pop. sch., Washington P.O.,

PAGE ID   HOUSEHOLD ID   PERSON(S) OF INTEREST

p. 223 (stamped), dwell. 19, fams. 19–20, Cozart and Hogue.

QuickCheck Model
MICROFILM: POPULATION SCHEDULES
1850–1860: SLAVES

NARA film cited by number, not title;
Place & year as lead elements in Source List

Source List Entry

JURISDICTION   CENSUS ID (GENERIC)   SCHEDULE   ...

Delaware. New Castle County. 1860 U.S. census, slave schedule. NARA

FILM ID   PUB'N PLACE   ...

microfilm publication M653, roll 100. Washington, D.C.: National

... PUBLISHER   YEAR

Archives and Records Administration, n.d.

First (Full) Reference Note

CENSUS ID   JURISDICTION   SCHEDULE

1. 1860 U.S. census, New Castle County, Delaware, slave schedule,

CIVIL DIVISION   PAGE ID   PERSON OF INTEREST

Appoquinimink Hundred, p. 7 (stamped), Richard Lockwood, owner or

...   FILM ID

manager; NARA microfilm publication M653, roll 100.

Subsequent (Short) Note

CENSUS ID   JURISDICTION   SCHEDULE   CIVIL ...

11. 1860 U.S. census, New Castle Co., Del., slave sch., Appoquinimink

... DIVISION   PAGE ID   PERSON OF INTEREST

Hundred, p. 7 (stamped), Richard Lockwood, owner or manager.

QuickCheck Model
MICROFILM: POPULATION SCHEDULES
1880–1930

NARA film cited by number, not title;
Place & year as lead elements in Source List

Source List Entry

JURISDICTION	CENSUS ID (GENERIC)	SCHEDULE	FILM ...

Indiana. Allen County. 1900 U.S. census, population schedule. NARA

... ID	PUBLICATION PLACE	...

microfilm publication T623, roll 359. Washington, D.C.: National

... PUBLISHER	YEAR

Archives and Records Administration, n.d.

First (Full) Reference Note

CENSUS ID	JURISDICTION	SCHEDULE

1. 1900 U.S. census, Allen County, Indiana, population schedule,

CIVIL DIVISION(S)	PAGE ID

Adams Township, Fort Wayne City, ward 8, p. 246-B (stamped),

ENUM DIST. & SHEET NO.	HOUSEHOLD ID	PERSON ...

enumeration district (ED) 45, sheet 12-B, dwelling 245, family 257, Ernest

... OF INTEREST	FILM ID

Burkhardt; NARA microfilm publication T623, roll 359 .

Subsequent (Short) Note

CENSUS ID	JURISDICTION	CIVIL DIVISIONS	ED & ...

11. 1900 U.S. census, Allen Co., Ind., Fort Wayne City, ward 8, ED 45,

... SHEET NO.	HOUSEHOLD ID	PERSON OF INTEREST

sheet 12-B, dwell. 245, fam. 257, Ernest Burkhardt.

QuickCheck Model
MICROFILM: POPULATION SCHEDULES
STATE-LEVEL COPIES, IN-HOUSE PRESERVATION FILM
Place & year as lead elements in Source List

Source List Entry

JURISDICTION	CENSUS ID (GENERIC)	SCHEDULE & ...

Mississippi. Hinds County. 1850 U.S. census, population schedule. State-

... COPY	FILM ID	OWNER/REPOSITORY ...

level copy. MDAH microfilm 2528. Mississippi Department of Archives

...	LOCATION

and History, Jackson.

First (Full) Reference Note

CENSUS ID	JURISDICTION	SCHEDULE & ...

1. 1850 U.S. census, Hinds County, Mississippi, population sched-

... COPY	CIVIL DIVISION	PAGE ID	HOUSEHOLD ...

ule (state-level copy), no township, p. 21 (penned), dwelling 156,

... ID	PERSON OF INTEREST	FILM ID ...	OWNER ...

family 156, James B. Smylie; MDAH microfilm 2528, Mississippi

... REPOSITORY	LOCATION

Department of Archives and History, Jackson.

Subsequent (Short) Note

CENSUS ID	JURISDICTION	SCHEDULE & COPY

11. 1850 U.S. census., Hinds Co., Miss., pop. sch., state-level copy,

PAGE ID	HOUSEHOLD ID	PERSON OF INTEREST

p. 21 (penned), dwell. 156, fam. 156, James B. Smylie.

QuickCheck Model
MICROFILM: STATE-SPONSORED CENSUSES
FHL-GSU PRESERVATION FILM
Place & year as lead elements in Source List

Source List Entry

JURISDICTION	CENSUS ID (GENERIC)	SCHEDULE	REPOSITORY ...

Kansas. Allen County. 1895 state census, population schedule. Kansas State

...	REPOSITORY LOCATION	FILM ID	FILM REPOSITORY ...

Historical Society, Topeka. FHL microfilm 570,221. Family History

...	FILM LOCATION

Library, Salt Lake City, Utah.

First (Full) Reference Note

CENSUS ID	JURISDICTION	SCHEDULE

1. 1895 Kansas state census, Allen County, population schedule,

CIVIL DIVISION	PAGE	HOUSEHOLD ID	PERSON(S) ...

Carlyle township, p. 5, dwelling [blank], family 27, for Fred Reese

... OF INTEREST	REPOSITORY	LOCATION

in E. E. Cain household; Kansas State Historical Society, Topeka;

FILM ID

FHL microfilm 570,221.

Subsequent (Short) Note

CENSUS ID	JURIS'N	SCHEDULE	CIVIL DIVISION	PAGE

11. 1895 Kansas state census, Allen Co., pop. sch., Carlyle twp., p. 5,

HOUSEHOLD ID	PERSON OF INTEREST

dwell. [blank], fam. 27, Fred Reese.

QuickCheck Model
DERIVATIVES: DATABASE, CD/DVD
Compiler as lead element in Source List

Source List Entry

DATABASE (PUBLICATION) TITLE   RECORD ...

1851 British Census: Devon, Norfolk, and Warwick Only.   CD-ROM

... FORMAT   PLACE OF PUBLICATION   PUBLISHER ...

database. Salt Lake City, Utah: The Church of Jesus Christ of Latter-

...   YEAR

day Saints, 2001.

First (Full) Reference Note

DATABASE (PUBLICATION) TITLE   RECORD ...

1. *1851 British Census: Devon, Norfolk, and Warwick Only*,   CD-ROM

... FORMAT   PLACE OF PUBLICATION   PUBLISHER ...

database (Salt Lake City, Utah: The Church of Jesus Christ of Latter-day

...   YEAR   ITEM OF INTEREST ...

Saints, 2001), entry for William Stumbles (age 39), Nottingham St. Mary's

... WITH IDENTIFYING DETAIL   CREDIT LINE (SOURCE OF THIS ...

Parish, Nottinghamshire, England, folio 483; citing Public Record Office

... SOURCE)

HO 107/1751.

Subsequent (Short) Note

DATABASE (PUBLICATION) TITLE   ITEM ...

11. *1851 British Census: Devon, Norfolk, and Warwick Only,* database entry

... OF INTEREST, WITH ABBREVIATED DETAIL ...

for William Stumbles (39), Nottingham St. Mary's Par., Nottinghamshire,

...

f. 483.

QuickCheck Model
DERIVATIVES: DATABASE, ONLINE
Compiler as lead element in Source List

Source List Entry

COMPILER   DATABASE TITLE

Ontario Genealogical Society. "Federal Census of 1871 (Ontario Index)."

ITEM TYPE
or FORMAT   WEBSITE CREATOR-OWNER   WEBSITE TITLE

Database. Library and Archives Canada. *Canadian Genealogy Centre.*

URL (DIGITAL LOCATION)   YEAR

http://www.collectionscanada.ca /genealogy/index-e.html : 2007.

First (Full) Reference Note

COMPILER   DATABASE TITLE

1. Ontario Genealogical Society, "Federal Census of 1871 (Ontario

ITEM TYPE
...   or FORMAT   WEBSITE CREATOR-OWNER   WEBSITE TITLE

Index)," database, Library and Archives Canada (LAC), *Canadian Genealogy*

...   URL (DIGITAL LOCATION)   ...

Centre (http://www.collectionscanada.ca/genealogy/index-e.html : ac-

DATE   ITEM OF INTEREST ...

cessed 21 February 2007), entry for Patrick Lennon (age 67), Ellice, Perth

...   CREDIT LINE (SOURCE OF THIS SOURCE)

North district; citing division 1, p. 36, LAC microfilm C-9940.

Subsequent (Short) Note

COMPILER   DATABASE TITLE

11. Ontario Genealogical Society, "Federal Census of 1871 (Ontario

...   ITEM OF INTEREST

Index," database entry for Patrick Lennon (67), Ellice, Perth North dist.

QuickCheck Model
DERIVATIVES: SOUNDEX & MIRACODE, MICROFILM

NARA film cited by number, not title;
Place & year as lead elements in Source List

Source List Entry

STATE   CENSUS ID   FILM ID

Texas. 1910 U.S. census, Soundex. NARA microfilm publication T1277, roll

...   PUBLICATION PLACE   PUBLISHER

12. Washington, D.C.: National Archives and Records Administration,

YEAR

n.d.

First (Full) Reference Note

CENSUS ID   STATE   ...   PERSON ...

1. 1910 U.S. census, Soundex, Texas, code C240, William W. Chesly

... OF INTEREST   FILM ID

(age 26), LeFlore County; NARA microfilm publication T1277, roll 12.

Subsequent (Short) Note

CENSUS ID   STATE   CODE   PERSON OF INTEREST ...

11. 1910 U.S. census—Soundex, Texas, C240, William W. Chesly (26),

...

LeFlore Co.

QuickCheck Model
DERIVATIVES: STATISTICAL DATABASE, ONLINE
USER-DEFINED REPORTS
Compiler as lead element in Source List

Source List Entry

COMPILER	DATABASE ...

University of Virginia, Geospatial & Statistical Data Center. "Historical

... TITLE	ITEM TYPE or FORMAT	WEBSITE TITLE	URL (DIGITAL ...

Census Browser." Database. *GeoStat Center*. http://fisher.lib.virginia.edu/

... LOCATION)	YEAR

collections/stats/histcensus/ : 2007.

First (Full) Reference Note

COMPILER	...

1. University of Virginia, Geospatial & Statistical Data Center, "Histori-

... DATABASE TITLE	ITEM TYPE or FORMAT	WEBSITE TITLE	URL ...

cal Census Browser," database, *GeoStat Center* (http://fisher.lib.virginia

... (DIGITAL LOCATION)	DATE	ITEM OF ...

.edu/collections/stats/histcensus/ : accessed 23 February 2007), user-defined

... INTEREST

report for "1850" and "free colored males attending school."

Subsequent (Short) Note

COMPILER	DATABASE TITLE	...

11. Univ. of Va. GeoStat Center, "Historical Census Browser," user-

... ITEM OF INTEREST

defined report for "1850" and "free colored males attending school."

GUIDELINES
& Examples

BASIC ISSUES

6.1   **"Ancient" vs. "Modern" Censuses**

Censuses are among the oldest form of recorded historical information, dating back to Biblical times. In some countries, extant censuses
exist from the 1300s and 1400s. These from antiquity are typically
random-year documents, held by archives, and are commonly cited in
the manner of other archival documents. (See Chapter 3.) Censuses
from the 1700s forward are often part of a systematic, geographically
broad enumeration effort whose citations may be more complex.

This chapter focuses on enumerations from relatively modern times
(ca. 1700 forward) and covers a range of types: civil and church,
national and regional, basic population schedules and special enumerations, from the U.S. and elsewhere.

6.2   **Arrangement of Elements in Reference Notes**

Researchers hold divided opinions as to whether the person of interest
should be identified at the beginning or the end of a census citation.
The first edition of *Evidence!* followed traditional American-style
references that begin by citing the specific item of interest. However, in many data-management programs, data entry is more stream-
lined if the identities of the individual and household are placed at the
end of the citation. This chapter (like its companion *QuickSheet:
Citing Online Historical Resources, Evidence! Style*) follows the latter
pattern.

6.3   **Arrangement of Elements in Source List (Bibliography)**

When working with censuses, historical researchers usually organize
their Source List in one of two ways:

CHRONOLOGICAL

In this arrangement, each entry cites first the year, then the locale, with the jurisdictions arranged in largest-to-smallest order. Entries are arranged chronologically, thereunder alphabetically.

For example:
    Census. 1815. Italy. Palermo. Gratteri ...
    Census. 1831. Canada, Lower. Bellechasse County ...
    Census. 1840. U.S. Ohio. Huron County ...
    Census. 1840. U.S. Tennessee. Davidson County ...
    Census. 1850. U.S. Delaware. New Castle County ...
    Census. 1850. U.S. Delaware. Sussex County ...
    Census. 1850. U.S. Indiana. Montgomery County ...
    Census. 1850. U.S. Louisiana. Bossier Parish ...
    Census. 1850. U.S. Massachusetts. Sussex County ...
    Census. 1860. U.S. Mississippi. Newton County ...
    Census. 1870. U.S. Georgia. Upton County ...
    Census. 1880. U.S. Ohio. Washington County ...
    Census. 1901. Wales. Monmouthshire ...

GEOGRAPHICAL

This arrangement cites elements from largest to smallest, as with civil and legal records. By using it, you keep together all references that relate to a specific area.

For example:
Canada, Lower. Bellechasse County. 1831 census ...
Italy. Palermo. Gratteri. 1815 census ...
U.S. Delaware. New Castle County. 1850 census ...
___. Georgia. Upton County. 1870 census ...
___. Indiana. Montgomery County. 1850 census ...
___. Louisiana. Bossier Parish. 1850 census ...
___. Mississippi. Newton County. 1860 census ...
___. Mississippi. Simpson County. 1860 census ...
___. Mississippi. Simpson County. 1870 census ...
___. Mississippi. Simpson County. 1880 census ...
___. Ohio. Huron County. 1840 census ...
___. Ohio. Washington County. 1880 census ...
___. Tennessee. Davidson County. 1840 census ...
Wales. Monmouthshire. 1901 census ...

This chapter follows the traditional geographical arrangement. If you prefer chronological arrangement, feel free to reverse the order of the elements in both the Source List and the Reference Notes. What you emphasize in your Source List is a matter of preference. What is crucial is that (*a*) you include all the needed data and (*b*) you keep together the citation elements that belong together—that is, those that modify or complement the other, such as CENSUS ID with PAGE NO. or FILM ID with FRAME NO.

Most researchers find that the Source List is *not* the place to list census entries by *household* or *personal name*. That level of detail in a Source List soon makes the list unmanageable.

6.4   Citing Dates of Enumeration

For most national censuses, the *year* of the enumeration is a standard part of the citation. However, the *visitation date* (the specific date on which a census taker visited a particular household) is part of the household data that you record in your research notes. That visitation date is not included in the citation because it is not used to locate an entry on the census. Citing to the page, rather than the visitation date, is the standard method of locating a specific household within a census. As an exception, if multiple censuses are taken of a locale in the same year, as in 6.43, you should include the specific date.

6.5   Citing Dwelling & Family Numbers

From about 1850, most censuses number households by dwelling and family. When these numbers appear, use them. Sometimes both numbers are the same for a household. Regardless, the numbers are useful not only for relocating the family but also because they enable you and your readers to better evaluate your findings, as with proximity and distance between cited households.

6.6   Citing Household Heads or Others of Interest

If, in your text, you identify a household, you do not have to repeat that detail in your citation. If the head-of-household or the person of interest appears in the census under a spelling other than the consistent form you are using, you should use in the citation *the exact spelling used by that census*. (You may, if you wish, show your preferred spelling in square editorial brackets, immediately after the version the census uses.) If you are discussing someone who is a subordinate in a household, and the household head bears a different surname, you will likely want to identify that head, as well as your individual, to assist in finding the entry again. If the household is a large boarding house, hotel, hospital, penitentiary, etc., you would want to note that the household is an institution and note the official capacity of that household head. If the institution is so large that it stretches across multiple pages, you should cite inclusive page numbers for the whole household and specify the page on which your person of interest appears.

6.7   Citing Line Numbers

If the census does not identify a household by dwelling and family number (as with the 1790–1840 U.S. decennial censuses, for example), then your citation should include the line number for the household as well as the page number. When you do cite dwelling and family numbers, adding a line number is superfluous.

Note: NARA Style citations, discussed at 6.14 and more extensively in Chapter 11, call for citing line numbers rather than family or dwelling numbers, reflecting an expectation that researchers are interested only in individuals. Census pages, however, do not always have line numbers, and history researchers appraise census data in the context of *households* and *families,* rather than isolating individuals from those with whom they lived.

6.8   Citing Page, Folio, or Sheet Numbers

Census citations should always include the specific page for the item of interest. Across time, you will find censuses paginated in many ways—often multiple ways within the same record. The most common systems are these:

FOLIO NUMBERS (RECTO & VERSO)

Typically, folio numbers appear on just one side of a sheet, usually the right side. When you record a folio number, you will need to note whether you are referring to the front or back side. You may use the classic terms *recto* (front) and *verso* (reverse side) if you choose, or you may cite "folio 32 (front)" or "folio 32 (back)." You could simply say "page 32 (front)" or "page 32 (back)," even though the page is technically a folio. Any of these methods will serve the basic purpose of clearly identifying where you found that census entry.

FOLIO/SHEET NUMBERS (A, B, C, D)

Folios originated as large sheets of paper folded to create four sides, or some other multiple of four, that might later be bound. When these folios were used for census data, all sides of the sheet usually carried the same arabic number, with an added A, B, C, or D, etc., on each individual sheet. When you encounter this situation, you should use both the number and the letter—e.g., page 349-C.

FRAME NUMBER vs. PAGE NUMBERS

If no page numbers are visible on a filmed census image, you should check the borders of the microfilm to see if frame numbers are imprinted there. If so, the frame number on the film itself will serve as a means by which the unnumbered census page can be located. Conversely, if pages carry their own numbers, you do not have to record the film's frame number. When you do cite a frame number, you should clearly identify it as a *frame* number and attach it to the part of the citation that identifies the film, not the portion that cites the original census.

PENNED NUMBERS vs. STAMPED NUMBERS

Many census pages carry more than one set of page numbers. For U.S. federal censuses, enumerators carried loose sheets on their rounds and numbered them as they used them. After they submitted copies to the Census Bureau, those copies were bound into volumes that contained the returns of several enumerators, each of whom had already numbered their pages. The Bureau then created a consecutive numbering scheme for the whole volume. Typically, the Bureau's number will be stamped, while the original number will be penned.

When a census has both penned and stamped numbers, your citation will need to state which number you are referencing. If you simply cite "p. 39" for a particular entry and that census contains more than one page 39 (particularly in large jurisdictions), your entry may take considerable time to relocate. Specifying "p. 39 (penned)" or "p. 487 (stamped)" eliminates confusion. See also 6.20, Citing Page Numbers.

SHEET NUMBERS (BY ENUMERATION DISTRICT)

Beginning in 1880, U.S. censuses divided counties and cities into enumeration districts (EDs). The census forms are typically printed, with "Page___" or "Sheet ___" appearing in a top corner, and each ED starts its numbering with page or sheet *1*. If you choose to cite the page or sheet number that corresponds to an enumeration district, rather than a stamped page number, you should (*a*) use the exact term *sheet* or *page,* whichever appears for that year, and (*b*) place that number immediately *after the ED number to which it belongs.*

WEBSITE IMAGE NUMBERS

Online providers of census images may assign an image number that is different from any of the page numbers above. Citing the image number is not advised. Those can change when a website is reorganized or more material is imaged.

6.9 Citing Roll Numbers

When you use microfilm, your Reference Notes need to cite the specific roll on which you find your data. In your Source List Entry, you will likely *not* cite the roll. Most researchers use numerous rolls for each census year and find that their Source List is much more manageable if they cite only the state (or province) and county, together with the microfilm or digital publication details. Exceptional situations exist, as when citing the relatively rare state-level copies or special schedules held by a state, as in 6.32 and 6.34–6.35.

6.10 Databases vs. Images, Indexes, Soundexes

Each of these is a different source type, even when drawn from the same original census. Each offers different information, may have many providers, and can differ in reliability. Each is cited differently from the other. You will want to ensure that your citation clearly identifies the type of source you used, as well as the provider or creator.

6.11 Databases, CD/DVD or Online

Census databases are typically electronic indexes that point you to an image copy, although some offer extracted data as well. Every database has a creator—a person, society, company, or occasionally a government agency. Your citation to a census database takes basically the same form as a citation to an online article. It bears little resemblance to a citation for an actual census in manuscript or imaged form.

6.12 Image Copies, Digital or Microfilm

Most image copies of censuses are publications—digitized online or microfilmed. Therefore you have two separate sets of material to cite:

- the original census, in ordinary fashion; *plus*
- the publication (or preservation film) where you found this census.

For each medium, the publication (production) data would include:

MICROFILM
- creator of the film (the publisher or filming agency);
- name or number of the microfilm publication (publication ID);
- roll number (comparable to a volume number for books).

ONLINE IMAGES
- the creator of the images (corporation or archive, etc.);
- the website name;
- the publication place (URL);

- the publication date (the year created or posted; if neither can be found at the website, you record the date you accessed it).

6.13   Indexes, Soundex & Miracode

Soundex, Miracode, and other indexes based on the sound of names rather than their spelling are typically consulted on microfilm and are cited as a microfilm publication. The key point to remember is that a microfilmed Soundex or Miracode index is *not* the same as the original census. It is simply a finding aid that points you to the original. Your citation must make it clear that you are citing the Soundex or Miracode cards rather than the original returns. See 6.41.

6.14   Microfilm, National Archives (NARA) Publications

Most federal censuses have been published by the U.S. National Archives and Records Administration. If you use them elsewhere, such as the Family History Library at Salt Lake City, you do not cite the roll number assigned by that library. The microfilm is a NARA publication, and it should be cited to NARA's publication number (usually prefaced by M or T) and roll number.

Like most major archives, NARA has developed its own citation style. The 1900 population schedule for Adams Township, Fort Wayne, Indiana, for example, would be cited NARA Style as

> 1. Entry for Ernest Burkhardt, sheet 12, line 33, enumeration district 45, Adams Township, Fort Wayne City, Allen County, Indiana; Census of Population (National Archives Microfilm Publication T623, roll 359); Twelfth Census of the United States, 1900; Records of the Bureau of the Census, Record Group 29; National Archives–Chicago Branch.

While *Evidence* adheres to NARA Style for *manuscripts, Evidence* Style citations follow most presses in using a simpler format for microfilmed censuses. For further discussion of the issues involved, see 2.13, 6.7, and Chapter 11. For a comparison of this entry to an *Evidence* Style citation, see QuickCheck Model *for* MICROFILM: POPULATION ... 1880–1930.

6.15   Microfilm, Enhancements & Image Copies

Most image copies of national-level censuses are created by the national archives that holds them. As such, they are considered to be the "authentic" edition and are presumed to be the best image available. Some archives and suppliers market "enhanced" images. However, other image copies and enhanced editions may not be legally considered "authentic." Users should identify the producer of the particular images they have consulted.

6.16   Shortened Citations, Essential Elements in

The first time each census is cited, you will have to cite it in full, providing two sets of details:

- the data for the original census, plus
- the data for the microfilm, website, or archive where you used a manuscript copy.

Because census references are among the most complicated citations, researchers have a great urge to shorten them. As a rule, shortened forms for use after the first full citation are created by eliminating the publication data (microfilm or website) or the identification of the archive that houses the originals you consulted. After that first full citation, it may be possible to drop some additional details. Even so, your shortened format will typically be longer than short forms for other record types. The following guidelines should help you decide when and how to shorten a census citation:

BASIC IDENTIFICATION

The year, the governmental authority (U.S., U.K., State of Iowa, etc.), and the type of schedule (population, slave, agricultural, etc.) should never be omitted for the years that multiple schedules exist.

COUNTY & STATE (OR PROVINCE)

Most censuses center upon some political jurisdiction. Frequently that was the state or province, then the county or an independent city. Those pieces of information are ones you would not want to omit.

CIVIL DIVISIONS

Within a county, province, or equivalent, the enumeration is frequently divided into smaller civil divisions (towns, villages, or post offices), then into wards or precincts. If page numbers are consecutive throughout the entire enumeration of that county or province, and if dwelling/family numbers are consecutive throughout the county, your short form might safely omit the smaller civil divisions.

SUPERVISOR'S DISTRICT & ENUMERATION DISTRICT

In the late 1800s, many censuses began to be subdivided into supervisor's districts, under which there would be several enumeration districts. The supervisor's district (SD) number on U.S. censuses is not essential to the location of data. The enumeration district (ED) number *is* essential.

U.S. CENSUSES

6.17 Background

The U.S. censuses that have been taken at ten-year intervals since 1790 have varied drastically across the years. As the population grew, the returns became more complex, and the number of questions increased. One-line returns for a whole household in 1790 evolved into multiline returns by 1850—requiring a change in the manner in which your citations identify households. As the population grew, counties and cities had to be subdivided into enumeration districts, adding yet another necessary piece of data to your citations. Additional schedules were added, a fact that will require your citations to identify *precisely* which schedule you have used.

Additionally, multiple copies were made from 1830 through 1870 (and thereafter for some schedules). Regulations variously called for one or two "fair copies" of the full originals—one to be submitted to the federal district court or the Census Bureau, a second to be deposited with the state. While the originals, in those years, were to be kept locally, the state and federal copies are deemed *duplicate originals*. Other years (1790–1820, 1880–90) required only one full copy of the population schedule, to be filed with the Census Bureau. However, abbreviated copies were to be made in 1880 for local use; and unofficial copies survive randomly for other years. Where multiple copies exist, you will cite them differently, depending upon where you found them—that is, at the federal, state, or local level.

POPULATION SCHEDULES

6.18 Original Returns: National Archives

See also QuickCheck Model *for* ORIGINAL MANUSCRIPTS: NATIONAL ARCHIVES ...

The original, federal-level schedules of the U.S. census are rarely consulted. For preservation, they have been filmed, when and where they survive, and researchers are expected to use the microfilmed images. On occasion, the filmed images are so unreadable that the National Archives will grant access to the originals. References to an original follow standard archival form for all types of textual records at the National Archives (see Chapter 11).

In the Source List example below, NARA's preferred citation style would normally begin with the phrase "First Census of the United States. ..." However, that style would cause your citation to appear under the F's in your alphabetized Source List, rather than amid your block of censuses that are arranged—say—by state, county, year, and type of census. To circumvent this, the example begins the NARA Style citation with a generic label (Maine. Cumberland County. 1790 U.S. census) consistent with other census citations in this chapter.

Source List Entry
Maine. Cumberland County. 1790 U.S. census. First Census of the United States, 1790. Manuscript Schedules of Decennial Population Censuses, 1790–1870. Records of the Bureau of the Census. Record Group 29. National Archives, Washington, D.C.

First Reference Note
1. John Starkey household, page 277, Freeport, Cumberland County, Maine; First Census of the United States, 1790, volume 2, Maine; Manuscript Schedules of Decennial Population Censuses, 1790–1870; Records of the Bureau of the Census, Record Group 29; National Archives, Washington, D.C.

Subsequent Note
11. John Starkey, p. 277, Freeport, Cumberland Co., Maine; First Census of U.S., 1790; Manuscript Schedules, RG 29, NA-Washington.

6.19   1790 U.S. Census
The 1790 census is typically consulted in one of three forms: an official printed edition, microfilm, or digital images.

Official Transcription
This first census, 1790, is the only one for which the Census Bureau published a complete transcription of surviving returns. Because this version is a derivative with all the misreadings that derivatives typically have, it is cited as a publication, not as an actual census.

Source List Entry
Bureau of the Census. *Heads of Families at the First Census of the United States Taken in the Year 1790: South Carolina.* Washington, D.C.: Government Printing Office, 1907.

First Reference Note
1. Bureau of the Census, *Heads of Families at the First Census of the United States Taken in the Year 1790: South Carolina* (Washington, D.C.: Government Printing Office, 1907), p. 11, col. 1, Mary Odam.

Subsequent Note
11. Bureau of the Census, *Heads of Families ... 1790: South Carolina,* p. 11, col. 1, Mary Odam.

CITING COLUMN NUMBERS

The preceding Mary Odam citation carries different page and column numbers from the following Mary Odam citations for microfilm and digital images. In the published version above, Odam appears in col. 1 of p. 11. On the original, below, she appears in col. 3 of p. 492. Obviously, if you use the published transcript but cite it as simply "1790 U.S. census, Beaufort District, South Carolina"—then add the page and column numbers from the publication—you would create an erroneous citation.

Microfilm (NARA Publication)

Source List Entry
South Carolina. Beaufort District. 1790 U.S census. NARA microfilm
    publication M637, roll 11. Washington, D.C.: National Archives
    and Records Administration, n.d.

First Reference Note
    1. 1790 U.S. census, Beaufort District, South Carolina, p. 492
(penned), col. 3, line 26, Mary Odam; NARA microfilm publication
M637, roll 11.

Subsequent Note
    11. 1790 U.S. census, Beaufort Dist., S.C., p. 492 (penned), col. 3,
line 26, Mary Odam.

CITING COLUMNS ON ORIGINAL RETURNS

The U.S. government did not create standardized and printed forms for enumerators until 1830. (State governments individually created their own forms in 1800–20.) Left entirely to their own devices in 1790, enumerators used many schemes. Some used small sheets with one column of names per page and subcolumns dividing the age/sex/status categories. Others used very large sheets of paper that could carry as many as 400 names—in which case they had several name-columns per page, with subcolumns for the data in each household.

You may or may not need to cite column numbers, depending upon the complexity of the page or sheet you are citing. Beaufort District's 1790 return is one of those situations in which citations benefit from the inclusion of the column number.

CITING JURISDICTIONS

Census citations should refer to jurisdictions by their proper name for that particular year. In 1790, South Carolina did not have counties. Its jurisdictions at that level were called *districts*.

Online Database (Ancestry)

Source List Entry

"1790 United States Federal Census." Database. *Ancestry.com*. http://www.ancestry.com : 2007.

First Reference Note

1. "1790 United States Federal Census," database, *Ancestry.com* (http://www.ancestry.com : accessed 2 February 2007), entry for Mary Odam, Beaufort, South Carolina.

Subsequent Note

11. "1790 United States Federal Census," *Ancestry.com,* database entry for Mary Odam, Beaufort, S.C.

SEQUENCE OF ELEMENTS

The nature of the search, when using databases and search engines for online images, calls for citing census details in a different sequence from that used for the microfilm.

Microfilm—The film example for Odam approaches the search by identifying the year, the state and the county, then the type of schedule, district, page, and finally the dwelling and family we need. Thus, your Source List Entry and your Reference Notes present the data in that order—i.e., from largest element down to smallest.

Database—In the database example for Odam, you approach the search by identifying the database, the website, and the publication information (URL and access date). Then you search for the individual. Having found her, the smallest element of your interest, you proceed to cite the essential details from that smallest element to the largest—i.e., the person, the county, and the state.

ABBREVIATIONS IN CITING DATABASES

You may choose to abbreviate counties, states, and countries in your Reference Notes, as shown above for "S.C." in note 11. However, you should not abbreviate "United States" in the database title. The title of that database writes the words in full. Your citation should not alter the words in the title.

Online Images (Ancestry)

Source List Entry

South Carolina. Beaufort District. 1790 U.S. census. Digital images. *Ancestry.com*. http://www.ancestry.com : 2007.

First Reference Note
    1. 1790 U.S. census, Beaufort District, South Carolina, p. 492 (penned), col. 3, line 26, Mary Odam; digital image, *Ancestry.com* (http://www.ancestry.com : accessed 2 February 2007); citing National Archives and Records Administration microfilm M637, roll 11.

Subsequent Note
    11. 1790 U.S. census, Beaufort Dist., S.C., p. 492, Mary Odam.

CITING SUBSCRIPTION WEBSITES
Online subscription material is usually accessed directly through the provider's own website, as with the Ancestry example above. However, some providers do not offer subscriptions directly to the public—only through libraries, as with ProQuest's handling of *Heritage-Quest Online,* cited below.

When you access a commercial database through a library, your computer screen may not identify any URL for you to cite. Using the library's personal URL to identify your source would produce a nonworking citation if the library discontinues its subscription. *Evidence* recommends merely saying that the material is available at participating libraries. Each user of your citation can then check his or her own area libraries, just as researchers already do when they encounter citations to books and periodicals.

Online Images (HeritageQuest)

Source List Entry
South Carolina. Beaufort District. 1790 U.S. census. Digital images. ProQuest, *HeritageQuest Online.* 2006.

First Reference Note
    1. 1790 U.S. census, Beaufort District, South Carolina, p. 492, col. 3, line 26, Mary Odam; digital image, ProQuest, *HeritageQuest Online* (access through participating libraries : accessed 8 December 2006); citing National Archives microfilm M637, roll 11.

Subsequent Note
    11. 1790 U.S. census, Beaufort Dist., S.C., p. 492, col. 3, line 26.

6.20   1800 U.S. Census
For 1800 and later enumerations, the Census Bureau has not issued an official printed version. Odds are, you will be citing a microfilm copy produced by the National Archives or a digital image of that

microfilm that you access through an online database. These media are handled as follows:

Microfilm (NARA Publication)

Source List Entry

New York. Westchester County. 1800 U.S. census. NARA microfilm publication M32, roll 27. Washington, D.C.: National Archives and Records Administration, n.d.

First Reference Note

1. 1800 U.S. census, Westchester County, New York, town of York, p. 741 (penned at bottom right), line 18, Underhill Strang; NARA microfilm publication M32, roll 27.

Subsequent Note

11. 1800 U.S. census, Westchester Co., N.Y., York, p. 741 (penned at bottom right), Underhill Strang.

CITING PAGE NUMBERS

Section 6.8 recommends that, when a census page carries multiple page numbers, you indicate whether the number is penned or stamped. The above census of Westchester demonstrates an additional quirk. Many of its pages carry three different penned numbers, as well as stamped numbers on some pages. Moreover, most of the numbers are filmed out of sequence. To help relocate this census entry, the page citation states not only that it is a penned notation but also tells researchers which set of penned numbers to focus upon.

CITING TOWNS IN 1800

For most U.S. censuses of 1800, you are not given a specific town to cite—only the county. When these early returns specify a town, district, hundred, etc., that civil division might not be needed to relocate the entry because the early returns were relatively short and straightforward. However, the above example for Westchester—a return on which pages carry multiple numbering schemes and are filmed out of sequence—illustrates a situation in which you should be especially careful to identify the local jurisdiction.

Online Database (HeritageQuest)

Source List Entry

"Search Census." Database. ProQuest, *HeritageQuest Online*. 2006.

First Reference Note

1. "Search Census," database by ProQuest, *HeritageQuest Online*

(access at participating libraries : 8 December 2006), entry for Underhill "Strong" [Strang], Westchester County, New York, 1800.

Subsequent Note

11. "Search Census," *HeritageQuest Online* database entry for Underhill "Strong" [Strang], Westchester Co., N.Y., 1800.

CORRECTING DATABASE ERRORS

Census database entries, as with indexes, are rife with misreadings of names (or interpretations that differ from our own). When you cite a database entry, you should cite it exactly, even if you disagree with it. You may put a correction in square editorial brackets if you choose. You may also wish to put the aberrant spelling (or reading) in quotation marks to show that you are quoting exactly what the database says, even though it is not the spelling or reading you consider correct.

Online Database (Ancestry)

Source List Entry

"1800 United States Federal Census." Database. *Ancestry.com.* http://www.ancestry.com : 2006.

First Reference Note

1. "1800 United States Federal Census," database, *Ancestry.com* (http://www.ancestry.com : accessed 8 December 2006), entry for Underhill Strang, North Salem and York, Westchester County, New York.

Subsequent Note

11. "1800 United States Federal Census," *Ancestry.com,* database entry for Underhill Strang, North Salem and York, Westchester Co., N.Y.

GENERIC SOURCE-LIST LABELS FOR DATABASE TITLES

As the examples above and below demonstrate, online census data-bases and indexes use no standard format for their titles. Some state the location first. Some state the date first. Some use other phrasing. Odds are, the database title or index title will *not* follow the standard-ized format you use for censuses within your source list. If you wish those database listings to fall within your listings of original censuses, by year and locale, then you will have to create a generic label as the lead element for the Source List Entry. In that case, you should still include the precise title of the database.

The Ancestry and Heritage Quest examples above might be adapted like this:

Source List Entry
United States. 1800 census. "1800 United States Federal Census." Database. *Ancestry.com*. http://www.ancestry.com : 2007.
United States. 1800 census. "Search Census." Database. ProQuest, *HeritageQuest Online*. 2007.

Online Images (Ancestry)

Source List Entry
1800 U.S. census. Westchester County, New York. Digital images. *Ancestry.com*. http://www.ancestry.com : 2007.

First Reference Note
1. 1800 U.S. census, Westchester County, New York, Town of York, p. 741 (penned at bottom right), line 18, Underhill Strang; digital image, *Ancestry.com* (http://www.ancestry.com : accessed 30 January 2007); citing National Archives microfilm publication M32, roll 27.

Subsequent Note
11. 1800 U.S. census, Westchester Co., N.Y., York, p. 741, Underhill Strang.

6.21   1810 U.S. Census
See also QuickCheck Model *for* MICROFILM: POPULATION SCHEDULES, 1790–1840

Microfilm (NARA Publication)

Source List Entry
Maine. York County. 1810 U.S. census. NARA microfilm publication M252, roll 12. Washington, D.C.: National Archives and Records Administration, n.d.

First Reference Note
1. 1810 U.S. census, York County, Maine, town of York, p. 435 (penned), line 9, Jabez Young; NARA microfilm publication M252, roll 12. This census rearranges households into semi-alphabetical order.
2. Ibid., town of Alfred, p. 1108 (stamped), line 1, James Ridley.

Subsequent Note
11. 1810 U.S. census, York Co., Maine, town of York, p. 435 (penned), Jabez Young.
12. Ibid., town of Alfred, p. 1108 (stamped), James Ridley.

DESCRIPTIVE COMMENTS
When you encounter unusual situations on censuses, such as the rearrangement of households in alphabetical order, you should note

them. These aberrations often affect your analyses of both data and circumstances.

IBID, USE OF, IN CENSUS CITATIONS

When you have two *consecutive* citations to the same county and state, and the first cites only that source, you may use *ibid.* in the second. To do so, state the word *ibid.*, repeat the last element that the two citations have in common (in the above entry, the commonality ends with the words "town of"), then add the additional data (name of town, page, line, household) that differs from the first citation.

Do not use ibid. during data entry. As you continue research and add data from other sources, other citations will typically be interjected between two source notes that were once consecutive. Some database management programs automatically create *ibid.* citations each time new reports are generated from the database. If your software does not do this, you should create *ibid.* references *only* at your final edit.

Online Databases & Images

Citations for this year typically follow the online formats previously given for 1790 and 1800.

6.22   1820 U.S. Census, Population Schedule

Microfilm (NARA Publication)

Source List Entry

District of Columbia. Washington County. 1820 U.S. census, population schedule. NARA microfilm publication M33, roll 12. Washington, D.C.: National Archives and Records Administration, n.d.

First Reference Note

1. 1820 U.S. census, Washington County, District of Columbia, population schedule, p. 68 (typed tag), for signed certification of census by "James Thomas, respectable citizen"; NARA microfilm publication M33, roll 12.

Subsequent Note

11. 1820 U.S. census, Washington Co., D.C., pop. sch., p. 68 (typed tag), James Thomas signature.

CITING THE SCHEDULE

The 1820 census is the first U.S. census for which any auxiliary schedules survive apart from the population schedule. Therefore, when we cite the 1820 U.S. enumeration, we should indicate which schedule we are citing—population or manufactures. For examples of citations to the several auxiliary schedules in later years, see 6.33–6.35.

NON-HOUSEHOLD DATA

Many censuses carry supplemental information of research value other than specific household data. The above example cites one type that is often found at the end of the enumeration of a district or county, the certification that enumerators were required to provide. (While the certifying party might not be of interest to you, the certification reveals the ending date of a population count that does not otherwise carry dates of visitation.)

Online Databases & Images

Citations for 1820 typically follow the online formats previously given for 1790–1800, with one difference. For 1820 we need to add an identification of the type of schedule we are citing.

6.23   1830 U.S. Census

Microfilm (NARA Publication)

Source List Entry

Tennessee. Jefferson County. 1830 U.S. census. NARA microfilm publication M29, roll 180. Washington, D.C.: National Archives and Records Administration, n.d.

First Reference Note

1. 1830 U.S. census, Jefferson County, Tennessee, p. 283 (stamped), line 150 [*sic*], "Solomon–Free" [Solomon, free man of color]; NARA microfilm publication M29, roll 180.

Subsequent Note

11. 1830 U.S. census, Jefferson Co., Tenn., p. 283 (stamped), "Solomon–Free."

LINE NUMBERS, NON-STANDARD

Some pre-1850 enumerators, as with Jefferson County above, numbered households consecutively throughout their district. This practice created unorthodox line numbers that readers of your citation (or you at a later date) might assume to be a typo. You might add *sic* in square editorial brackets after the unorthodox number, as above, or you might more precisely identify it as a "household" number.

Online Databases & Images
Citations for 1830 typically follow the online formats previously given for 1790–1800.

6.24   1840 U.S. Census, Population Schedule

Microfilm (NARA Publication)

Source List Entry

Alabama. Lowndes County. 1840 U.S. census. NARA microfilm publication M704, roll 6. Washington, D.C.: National Archives and Records Administration, n.d.

First Reference Note

1. 1840 U.S. census, Lowndes County, Alabama, no township, p. 241 (stamped), line 1, for Thomas Hamilton, pensioner in E. H. Cook household; NARA microfilm publication M704, roll 6.

Subsequent Note

11. 1840 U.S. census, Lowndes Co., Ala., p. 241 (stamped), line 1, Thomas Hamilton, in E. H. Cook household.

CITING NON-HEADS OF HOUSEHOLD

Most pre-1850 censuses officially required the name of only the head of household. The 1840 enumeration is an aberration. The second page for each household calls for adding the name of any U.S. pensioner residing with the family. If that pensioner is your person of interest, you would cite both him and the head of the household in which he is found. Other enumerators in other years occasionally named non-heads of household for other special reasons. When you encounter one of these, you would use this same format.

Online Databases & Images
Citations for 1840 typically follow the online formats previously given for 1790–1800. If your person of interest is a pensioner living in the household of someone else, then you should add that data, as illustrated above for the microfilm citation.

6.25   1850 U.S. Census, Population Schedules
Two population schedules were taken in 1850 and 1860—one for "free inhabitants" and the other for "slave inhabitants." In common parlance, they are typically called *population schedule* and *slave schedule*.

The slave schedule, however, rarely identifies an individual slave. Like the 1790–1840 censuses for all the population, most slave schedules name only the free head of the household (which is not necessarily the owner) and then tallies the slave population by age, class, color, and gender.

The slave schedule example cited at notes 2 and 12 below represents two of the less-common situations:

- a schedule that identifies slaves by name; and
- a sheet appended to the free population schedule—an 1850 and 1860 situation in some states that had few slaves to enumerate.

For a more typical citation to slave schedules, see 1860 at 6.26.

Microfilm (NARA Publication)

See also QuickCheck Model *for* DIGITAL IMAGES: ONLINE COMMERCIAL SITE

Source List Entry

Iowa. Marion County. 1850 U.S. census, population schedule. NARA microfilm publication M432, roll 187. Washington, D.C.: National Archives and Records Administration, n.d.

Utah. Utah County. 1850 U. S. census, slave schedule. NARA microfilm publication M432, roll 919. Washington, D.C.: National Archives and Records Administration, n.d.

First Reference Note

1. 1850 U.S. census, Marion County, Iowa, population schedule, Lake Prairie, p. 290 (stamped), dwelling 151, family 156, Virgil W. and Wyatt B. Earp; NARA microfilm publication M432, roll 187.

2. 1850 U.S. census, Utah County, Utah, slave schedule, Deseret, p. 147, William Crosby, owner or manager (slaves Vilate and Toby); NARA microfilm publication M432, roll 919. This enumeration actually identifies each slave by name.

Subsequent Note

11. 1850 U.S. census, Marion Co., Iowa, pop. sch., p. 290 (stamped), dwell. 151, fam. 156, Virgil W. and Wyatt B. Earp.

12. 1850 U.S. census, Utah Co., Utah, slave schedule, Deseret, p. 147, William Crosby, Vilate, and Toby.

CITING PERSONS NAMED ON SLAVE SCHEDULES

Occasionally, but not often, slaves may be named on a slave schedule; sometimes by both first and last names. More commonly, the census names the "head" of that group of slaves, in the manner that the pre-1850 census named only household heads. When we cite an individual who appears on the slave schedule, we will likely want to specify whether that person is a slave or a household head.

When naming someone in that capacity, the natural inclination is to refer to that person as, say, "William Crosby, white" or "William Crosby, owner." Odds favor both assumptions. However, not all slave owners were white and not all household "heads" named on slave schedules were owners. While census instructions asked for names of owners, many returns cite managers of farms with absentee owners.

All we can accurately say, without independent evidence, is that the individual was an "owner or manager." That phrase should also cover situations in which quasi-free slaves were allowed to live independently, renting rooms from a white or free-black person who would, theoretically, provide oversight.

Online Database (Ancestry)

Source List Entry
"1850 United States Federal Census." Database. *Ancestry.com.* http://www.ancestry.com : 2007.

First Reference Note
1. "1850 United States Federal Census," database, *Ancestry.com* (http://www.ancestry.com : accessed 16 January 2007), entry for Virgil W. Earp (age 6), Lake Prairie, Marion County, Iowa.

Subsequent Note
11. "1850 United States Federal Census," *Ancestry.com,* database entry for Virgil W. Earp, Lake Prairie, Marion Co., Iowa.

Online Images (Ancestry)

Source List Entry
Iowa. Marion County. 1850 U.S. census, population schedule. Digital images. *Ancestry.com.* http://www.ancestry.com : 2007.

First Reference Note
1. 1850 U.S. census, Marion County, Iowa, population schedule, p. 290 (stamped), dwelling 151, family 156, Virgil W. and Wyatt B. Earp; digital image, *Ancestry.com* (http://www.ancestry.com : accessed 16 January 2007); citing National Archives microfilm publication M432, roll 187.

Subsequent Note
11. 1850 U.S. census, Marion Co., Iowa, pop., sch., p. 290 (stamped), dwell. 151, fam. 156, Virgil W. and Wyatt B. Earp.

6.26   1860 U.S. Census, Population Schedule
See QuickCheck Model *for* MICROFILM: POPULATION SCHEDULES, 1850–1860: SLAVE
Two population schedules were again taken in 1860, one for the free

population and one for the enslaved population. The New Jersey example below demonstrates typical citations to slave schedules. For less-typical situations, see 6.25.

Microfilm (NARA Publication)

Source List Entry

New Jersey. Monmouth County. 1860 U.S. census, slave schedule. NARA microfilm publication M432, roll 55. Washington, D.C.: National Archives and Records Administration: n.d.

New York. Orange County. 1860 U.S. census. Population schedule. NARA microfilm publication M653, roll 833. Washington, D.C.: National Archives and Records Administration, n.d.

First Reference Note

1. 1860 U.S. census, Monmouth County, New Jersey, slave schedule, Atlantic township, p. 57, Wm. Haight, owner or manager; NARA microfilm publication M432, roll 55.

2. 1860 U.S. census, Orange County, New York, population schedule, West Point–Cornwall, p. 52 (penned), dwelling 360, "family" 360 (cadet barracks), George Custer; NARA microfilm publication M643, roll 833.

Subsequent Note

11. 1860 U.S. census, Monmouth Co., N.J., slave sch., Atlantic Twp., p. 57, Wm. Haight, owner or manager.

12. 1860 U.S. census, Orange Co., N.Y., pop. sch., West Point-Cornwall, p. 52 (penned), dwell. 360, fam. 360, George Custer.

6.27   1870 U.S. Census, Population Schedule

See QuickCheck Model *for* MICROFILM: POPULATION SCHEDULES, 1850–1870

Microfilm (NARA Publication)

Source List Entry

Georgia. Wilkes County. 1870 U.S. census, population schedule. NARA microfilm publication M593, roll 184. Washington, D.C.: National Archives and Records Administration, n.d.

First Reference Note

1. 1870 U.S. census, Wilkes County, Georgia, population schedule, Washington Post Office, p. 223 (stamped), dwelling 19, families 19–20, Cozart and Hogue; NARA microfilm publication M593, roll 184.

Subsequent Note

11. 1870 U.S. census, Wilkes Co., Ga., pop. sch., Washington P.O., p. 223, dwell. 19, fams. 19–20, Cozart and Hogue.

SHARED DWELLINGS

When the family of your interest shares a household with another family, you will likely want to note that fact and record the identity of the other family as well. If the shared dwelling is a tenement with many families, you might want to identify the dwelling as such—i.e., dwelling 123 (tenement)— rather than name all other families in the citation. In this case, your research notes for the entry would be the place to record all the fellow inhabitants, in the same manner that you record neighboring households for single-family dwellings.

6.28   1880 U.S. Census, Population Schedule

Beginning in 1880, census pages included two new bureaucratic levels at the top of each sheet: supervisor's district and enumeration district. It is essential that you note the latter (the ED), in order to ensure that the entry can be relocated by you or another person using your notes. The 1880 enumeration is also the first that specifically calls for the street address of each household. You will want to record that detail in your research notes, along with the rest of the household data, but the street address is not usually a citation element needed to relocate the family when the ED is properly cited.

Microfilm (NARA Publication)

Source List Entry

Missouri. City of St. Louis. 1880 U.S. census, population schedule. NARA microfilm publication T9, roll 717. Washington, D.C.: National Archives and Records Administration, n.d.

First Reference Note

1. 1880 U.S. census, City of St. Louis, Missouri, population schedule, enumeration district (ED) 1, p. 2 (stamped), p. 4 (penned), dwelling 16, family 17, Nick Metzen; NARA microfilm publication T9, roll 717.

Subsequent Note

11. 1880 U.S. census, City of St. Louis, Mo., pop. sch., ED 1, p. 2 (stamped), dwell. 16, fam. 17, Nick Metzen.

CITING INDEPENDENT CITIES

Some U.S. cities are independent cities—that is, they are not part of a county jurisdiction. No county name should be included in your citation for these censuses after the date on which they became independent. When the name of the independent city is also the name of a county in that state, your note should explicitly say that you are referring to the city.

CD-ROM Database (LDS)

Source List Entry

1880 United States Census and National Index. CD-ROM database. Salt Lake City, Utah: The Church of Jesus Christ of Latter-day Saints, 2001.

First Reference Note

1. *1880 United States Census and National Index,* CD-ROM database (Salt Lake City, Utah: The Church of Jesus Christ of Latter-day Saints, 2001), entry for Nick Metzen, p. 2C, St. Louis City, Missouri; citing National Archives microfilm publication T9, roll 717.

Subsequent Note

11. *1880 United States Census and National Index,* entry for Nick Metzen, p. 2C, St. Louis City, Mo.

Online Database (LDS)

Source List Entry

"1880 United States Census." Database. The Church of Jesus Christ of Latter-day Saints. *FamilySearch.* http://www.familysearch.org : 2007.

First Reference Note

1. "1880 United States Census," database, The Church of Jesus Christ of Latter-day Saints, *FamilySearch* (http://www .familysearch.org : accessed 2 February 2007), entry for Nick Metzen (age 43), p. 2C, St. Louis City, Missouri; citing "NA film no. T9-0717."

Subsequent Note

11. "1880 United States Census," *FamilySearch,* database entry for Nick Metzen (43), St. Louis City, Mo.

6.29 1890 U.S. Census, Population & Social Statistics Schedule

In 1890, the population schedule underwent a name change, as well as a reformatting that created one sheet per household. However, only one original copy was made of that schedule and most of it has been destroyed. When you cite one of the surviving fragments, you might want to add an informational note about the extensive destruction.

Microfilm (NARA Publication)

Source List Entry

New Jersey. Hudson County. 1890 U.S. census, population and social statistics schedule. NARA microfilm publication M407, roll 3. Washington, D.C.: National Archives and Records Administration, n.d.

First Reference Note
        1. 1890 U.S. census, Hudson County, New Jersey, population and social statistics schedule, Jersey City, enumeration district (ED) 38, p. 1018, James Nelson; NARA microfilm publication M407, roll 3. Only five family schedules survive for New Jersey, 1890; all are in Jersey City.

Subsequent Note
        11. 1890 U.S. census, Hudson Co., N.J., pop. sch., ED 38, p. 1018, James Nelson.

6.30   1900 U.S. Census, Population Schedule
See also QuickCheck Model *for* MICROFILM: POPULATION SCHEDULES, 1880–1930

Returns for 1900 can be cited in the same manner as the population schedule of 1880—with one special situation. An "Indian Population" form was designed for this year and sometimes used. In regions with known Native Americans, you will find both types of forms filmed together, usually with the Indian Population forms placed at the end of the county. The following examples illustrate handling both the regular population schedule and the Indian population schedule.

Microfilm (NARA Publication)

Source List Entry
North Dakota. Standing Rock Indian Reservation. 1900 U.S. census, population schedule. NARA microfilm publication T623, roll 1234. Washington, D.C.: National Archives and Records Administration, n.d.

First Reference Note
(When citing a regular population schedule)
        1. 1900 U.S. census, Standing Rock Indian Reservation, North Dakota, population schedule, enumeration district (ED) 260, p. 4-A, Joseph St. George; NARA microfilm publication T623, roll 1234.
(When citing an Indian population schedule)
        2. 1900 U.S. census, Standing Rock Indian Reservation, North Dakota, population schedule, ED 260, p. 53-A, Indian population, Frederick Dog; NARA microfilm publication T623, roll 1234.

Subsequent Note
        11. 1900 U.S. census, Standing Rock Indian Res., N.D., pop. sch., ED 260, p. 4-A, Joseph St. George.
        12. 1900 U.S. census, Standing Rock Indian Res., N.D., pop. sch., ED 260, Indian pop., p. 53-A, Frederick Dog.

COUNTY NAMES OMITTED (INDIAN RESERVATIONS)
Indian reservations frequently straddled county lines and even

state lines. If so, there will be no county or state name in your citation.

IBID., USE OF

When you edit the final draft of your manuscript, you would typically use *ibid.* in situations such as notes 2 and 12 to replace the portion of the data that is being duplicated. For example:

1. 1900 U.S. census, Standing Rock Indian Reservation, North Dakota, population schedule, ED 260, p. 4-A, Joseph St. George.
2. Ibid., ED 260, p. 53-A, Indian population, Frederick Dog.

However, you would not want to use *ibid.* while preparing your preliminary drafts or entering information into your data management software. Subsequent changes to your draft or additions of new data would likely cause the *ibid.* note to become separated from the preceding note to which it refers.

6.31   1910–1930 U.S. Census, Population Schedule

Although the censuses for each year underwent some alteration in content, your basic format for citing them is the same as in 1900.

Microfilm (NARA Publication)

Source List Entry

New York. New York County. 1910 U.S. census, population schedule. NARA microfilm publication T624, roll 999. Washington, D.C.: National Archives and Records Administration, n.d.

First Reference Note

1. 1910 U.S. census, New York County, New York, population schedule, Bronx Assembly District 33, precinct 19, p. 269 (stamped), enumeration district (ED) 38, sheet 6-A, dwelling 37, family 124, Jacob Sounheimer; NARA microfilm publication T624, roll 999.

Subsequent Note

11. 1910 U.S. census, N.Y. Co., N.Y., Bronx Dist. 33, prect. 19, p. 269 (stamped), ED 38, sheet 6-A, dwell. 37, fam. 124, Jacob Sounheimer.

CD/DVD Images

See QuickCheck Model *for* DIGITAL IMAGES: CD/DVD

Source List Entry

Puerto Rico. Dorado Township. 1910 U.S. census, population schedule. *1910 Dorado Municipality, Puerto Rico, Federal Census, Dorado*

Township. CD-ROM, digital images. Green Creek, New Jersey: AllCensus, 2005.

First Reference Note
1. 1910 U.S. census, Dorado Township, Puerto Rico, population schedule, Town of Dorado, enumeration district (ED) 108, p. 5-B (penned), dwelling 36, family 41, José Sánchez y Pérez; *1910 Dorado Municipality, Puerto Rico, Federal Census, Dorado Township,* CD-ROM digital images (Green Creek, New Jersey: AllCensus, 2005); citing National Archives microfilm publication T624, roll 1762.

Subsequent Note
11. 1910 U.S. census, Dorado, Puerto Rico, pop. sch., ED 108, p. 5-B (penned), dwell. 36, fam. 41, José Sánchez y Pérez.

6.32   Population Schedules, State & Local Copies
From 1830 through 1880, regulations required enumerators to create one or two *fair copies* (*duplicate originals*). One copy was to be forwarded to the U.S. District Court—later to the Census Bureau, after that agency was created—while the original (in 1850–1870) or an abbreviated *exhibition copy* (in 1880) was to be deposited with local officials. In years that required two additional copies, the second was to be supplied to a state office. Some of the state- and local-level duplicate originals survive. How you cite these non-federal copies depends upon where they are found. State-level copies frequently have been microfilmed. Local copies typically exist only in original form.

LOCAL COPY, U.S. CENSUS

Source List Entry
Alabama. Pike County. 1860 U.S. census, population schedule. County-level copy. Probate Judge's Office, Troy, Alabama.
Alabama. Tuscaloosa County. 1880 U.S. census. Population schedule. County-level copy. Probate Judge's Office, Tuscaloosa, Alabama.

First Reference Note
1. 1860 U.S. census, Pike County, Alabama, population schedule, Pea River post office, p. 324, dwelling 1034, family 1046, Charles C. Sammonds household; county-level copy, Probate Judge's Office, Troy.
2. 1880 U.S. census, Tuscaloosa County, Alabama, population schedule, enumeration district (ED) 157, unpaginated, alphabetized entries, vol. 2 (Smallwood's 15th District), section "E," for Willis Eatman (35); county-level copy, Probate Judge's Office, Tuscaloosa. This exhibition copy of the census alphabetizes entries within each district.

Subsequent Note
> 11. 1860 U.S. census, Pike Co., Ala., pop. sch., Pea River post office, p. 324, dwell. 1034, fam. 1046, Charles C. Sammonds; county-level copy.
> 12. 1880 U.S. census, Tuscaloosa Co., Ala., pop. sch., ED 157, vol. 2, sect. "E," Willis Eatman (35); county-level copy.

STATE-LEVEL COPY, U.S. CENSUS

Microfilm (State Archive)

Source List Entry
> Mississippi. Hinds County. 1850 U.S. census, population schedule. State-level copy. MDAH microfilm 2528. Mississippi Department of Archives and History, Jackson.

First Reference Note
> 1. 1850 U.S. census, Hinds County, Mississippi, population schedule (state-level copy), no township, p. 21 (penned), dwelling 156, family 156, James B. Smylie; MDAH microfilm 2528, Mississippi Department of Archives and History, Jackson.

Subsequent Note
> 11. 1850 U.S. census, Hinds Co., Miss., pop. sch., state-level copy, p. 21 (penned), dwell. 156, fam. 156, James B. Smylie.

"NONPOPULATION" SCHEDULES

6.33 Background

During 1810, 1820, and 1850 forward, census law called for the creation of various supplemental schedules. The Census Bureau has labeled these *nonpopulation schedules,* although all of them actually do enumerate people, with one exception. The extant "nonpopulation" schedules are as follows:

- Agricultural, 1850–80
- Defective, Dependent, and Delinquent, 1880
- Industrial (including Mining & Fisheries), 1850–70
- Manufactures, 1820, 1850–1880 (1810 was mostly destroyed during War of 1812; surviving fragments are with population schedule)
- Mortality, 1850–80
- Social Statistics, 1850–80 (does not enumerate individuals)

Many of the originals, however, are not owned by the National Archives. Prior to the creation of that agency, they were distributed to the states or to various archives or libraries willing to house them.

Nonpopulation schedules have been microfilmed principally by the National Archives, the University of North Carolina, and the Genealogical Society of Utah (for deposit at FHL). Some exist only as originals at the owner repository. How you cite them will depend upon whether you consult manuscripts or film and whether that film is a NARA publication or has been produced by another institution.

6.34   Nonpopulation Schedules, NARA Film

See QuickCheck Model *for* MICROFILM: "NONPOPULATION" SCHEDULES , NARA FILM

Microfilm (NARA Publication)

Source List Entry

Florida. Gadsden County. 1850 U.S. census, agricultural schedule. NARA microfilm publication T1168, roll 1. Washington, D.C.: National Archives and Records Administration, n.d.

Illinois. Massac County. 1850 U.S. census, mortality schedule. NARA microfilm publication T1113, roll 58. Washington, D.C.: National Archives and Records Administration, n.d.

Tennessee. Bedford County. 1880 U.S. census, "Defective, Dependent, and Delinquent Classes" schedule. NARA microfilm publication T1135, roll 39. Washington, D.C.: National Archives and Records Administration, n.d.

First Reference Note

1.   1850 U.S. census, Gadsden County, Florida, agricultural schedule, p. 79, Alexander Croom; NARA microfilm publication T1168, roll 1.

2.   1850 U.S. census, Massac County, Illinois, mortality schedule, p. 615, for commentary on crime; NARA microfilm publication T1133, roll 58.

3.   1880 U.S. census, Bedford County, Tennessee, "Defective, Dependent, and Delinquent Classes," Insane Inhabitants, 25th civil district, enumeration district (ED) 19, p. 28608-A [*sic*], John M. Cable; NARA microfilm publication T1135, roll 39.

Subsequent Note

11.   1850 U.S. census, Gadsden Co., Fla., ag. sch., p. 79, Alexander Croom.

12.   1850 U.S. census, Massac Co., Ill., mortality schedule, p. 615, commentary on crime.

13.   1880 U.S. census, Bedford Co., Tenn., "Defective, Dependent, and Delinquent Classes," Insane Inhabitants, 25th civil dist., ED 19, p. 28608-A, John M. Cable.

CITING EXACT TITLE VS. GENERIC DESCRIPTION

If you cite a special schedule by its exact title, as with the complex 1880 example above, you should put quotation marks around that exact title. If you use a generic description, as with the 1850 and 1870 examples above and below, you do not use quotation marks.

6.35 "Nonpopulation Schedules," Other Filmers

See QuickCheck Model *for* MICROFILM: "NONPOPULATION" SCHEDULES, FHL-GSU

Microfilm (FHL-GSU): "Nonpopulation" Schedules

Source List Entry

Delaware. New Castle County. 1870 U.S. census, social statistics schedule. Hall of Records, Dover, Delaware. FHL microfilm 1,421,306, item 1. Family History Library. Salt Lake City, Utah.

Maine. Penobscot County. 1870 U.S. census, mortality schedule. Division of Vital Statistics, Augusta, Maine. FHL microfilm 9,941. Family History Library. Salt Lake City, Utah.

First Reference Note

1. 1870 U. S. census, New Castle County, Delaware, social statistics schedule, p. 1, "Newspapers and Periodicals," for *Smyrna Times*; Hall of Records, Dover, Delaware; FHL microfilm 1,421,306, item 1.

2. 1870 U.S. census, Penobscot County, Maine, mortality schedule, p. 1, Town of Veazie, Ellen Sheen; Division of Vital Statistics, Augusta, Maine; FHL microfilm 9,941.

Subsequent Note

11. 1870 U.S. census, New Castle Co., Del., social statistics sch., p. 1, "Newspapers and Periodicals."

12. 1870 U.S. census, Penobscot Co., Maine, mortality sch., p. 1, Town of Veazie, Ellen Sheen.

IDENTIFYING LIBRARY CALL NUMBER

Both the FHL example above and the two examples below represent instances in which the original schedules are owned by institutions other than the federal government. However, there are some differences that need to be reflected in our citations:

- The Delaware schedules, above and below, are owned by the state but were filmed by GSU for preservation. Copies are deposited at both FHL and the Delaware Hall of Records. If we use the FHL copy, it is appropriate to cite FHL's microfilm number, because FHL represents the producer of the film. If we use the copy at the Delaware Hall of Records (illustrated below), it is appropriate to cite that agency's identification number because that agency owns the original records.

- The Mississippi schedules, below, are also owned by the state and are among those of many states that were filmed by the University of North Carolina. Because the UNC film has been widely disseminated (i.e., published), our citation does not have to identify any specific library in which we use that film. The rule cited at 2.19 still holds. When material is published, one cites the publication and the publisher, not the facility where it was used.

Other Preservation Film: "Nonpopulation" Schedules

(Preservation film used at the owner-repository)

Source List Entry

Delaware. New Castle County. 1870 U.S. census, social statistics schedule. Microfilm Dela 5-4. Hall of Records, Dover.

Missouri. Clay County. 1850 U.S. census, agricultural schedule. In-house microfilm. State Historical Society of Missouri, Columbia.

First Reference Note

1. 1870 U.S. census, New Castle County, Delaware, social statistics schedule, p. 1, "Newspapers and Periodicals," for *Smyrna Times;* U.S. Census Collection (microfilm Dela 5-4, roll 3); Delaware Hall of Records, Dover.

2. 1850 U.S. census, Clay County, Missouri, agricultural schedule, p. 679, William Tapp; in-house microfilm; State Historical Society of Missouri, Columbia.

Subsequent Note

11. 1870 U.S. census, New Castle Co., Del., social statistics sch., p. 1, "Newspapers and Periodicals."

12. 1850 U.S. census, Clay Co., Mo., ag. sch., p. 679, William Tapp.

IDENTIFYING LIBRARY FILM SERIES

Occasionally, as with the Missouri example above, you will encounter repositories that produce in-house film for preservation purposes but do not assign that film any series identity or microfilm roll numbers.

UNC Published Film Series: "Nonpopulation" Schedules

Source List Entry

Mississippi. Newton County. 1860 U.S. census, agricultural schedule. *Agricultural and Manufacturing Census Records of Fifteen Southern States for the Years 1850, 1860, 1870, and 1880.* UNC microfilm publication MN3-534, roll 179. Chapel Hill: University of North Carolina, 1960–65.

First Reference Note
    1. 1860 U. S. census, Newton County, Mississippi, agricultural schedule, p. 1, Harvey Williams; *Agricultural and Manufacturing Census Records of Fifteen Southern States for the Years 1850, 1860, 1870, and 1880*, UNC microfilm publication MN3-534 (Chapel Hill: University of North Carolina, 1960–65), roll 179.

Subsequent Note
    11. 1860 U.S. census, Newton Co., Miss., ag. sch., p. 1, Harvey Williams.

SPECIAL POPULATION SCHEDULES

6.36 1880 Native American Population Schedules
The Census Bureau conducted a separate enumeration of the Native American population in 1880. The following depicts a typical citation. (Also see 6.40 for Native American tribal censuses taken by the Indian Bureau rather than the Census Bureau.)

Microfilm (NARA Publication)

Source List Entry
California. Round Valley Agency. 1880 U.S. census, Indian schedule. NARA microfilm publication M1791, roll 5. Washington, D.C.: National Archives and Records Administration, n.d.

First Reference Note
    1. 1880 U.S. census, Round Valley Agency, California, Indian schedule, Ukie Tribe, enumerator's sheet no. 34, dwelling 27, family 34, Ol-Koi'-ye [aka] Song Breast [and] Jane Panne; NARA microfilm publication M1791, roll 5.

Subsequent Note
    11. 1880 U.S. census, Round Valley Agency, Calif., Indian schedule, Ukie Tribe, enum. sheet 34, dwell. 27, fam. 34, Ol-Koi'-ye [aka] Song Breast [and] Jane Panne.

ENUMERATOR'S SHEET NUMBER
The 1880 Indian Schedule is not paginated in the typical manner. A whole folio was filled in for each household. The first page of the folio is a cover sheet preprinted with the words "Enumerator's Sheet No. ____." The enumerator, then, was to consecutively number the folios as he visited each household.

6.37   1890 Union Veterans & Widows Schedule

The United States created a special enumeration in 1890, identifying surviving veterans of the Civil War (Union service) and their widows. Returns for states whose name begins with the letters A–K were mostly destroyed. Surviving returns for the other states and some navy and shipyard returns are commonly cited in one of two ways: either by the title given to the microfilm publication (*Schedules Enumerating Union Veterans and Widows of Union Veterans of the Civil War, 1890*) or by the actual title of the schedule, as it appears on each page of the original enumeration.

The example below uses the original title (in quotation marks, to indicate that the title is being copied exactly) and cites the return following the same format used for other Census Bureau schedules.

Microfilm (NARA Publication)

Source List Entry
Mississippi. Warren County. 1890 U.S. census, "Special Schedule: Surviving Soldiers, Sailors, and Marines, and Widows." NARA microfilm publication M123, roll 26. Washington, D.C.: National Archives and Records Administration, n.d.

First Reference Note
1. 1890 U.S. census, Warren County, Mississippi, "Special Schedule: Surviving Soldiers, Sailors, and Marines, and Widows," Vicksburg, enumeration eistrict (ED) 98, p. 1, Henry Clayton; NARA microfilm publication M123, roll 26.

Subsequent Note
11. 1890 U.S. census, Warren Co., Miss., "Special Schedule: Surviving Soldiers ... and Widows," Vicksburg, ED 98, p. 1, Henry Clayton.

6.38   1900 Indian Population Schedule

See 6.30, 1900 Population Schedule

6.39   1900 (and Later) Military Population Schedules

Beginning in 1900, separate military schedules were created for personnel on naval vessels and U.S. bases abroad—including some civilian employees and an occasional wife. If you cite your censuses by geographic location, you might have to create a different style of entry in your Source List, because the censuses conducted outside the continental U.S. are not geographic-based returns that enumerate all people in a specific locale. Rather, they record only selected people over widely scattered areas. The 1900 Source List example, below, creates a generic label "Pacific (U.S. Stations)" because that covers all three locations involved in the citations. You might choose a different label. The 1920 census more specifically cites the seaport, because (*a*) "Seaport: San Diego, Calif." is the only geographic division stated for that part of the return; and (*b*) it is the only military return being cited here for that year. Hence, the Source List example for 1920, below, can be more specific than that for 1900.

Microfilm (NARA Publication)

Source List Entry

Pacific (U.S. Stations). 1900 U.S. census, military and naval population schedule. NARA microfilm publication T623, roll 1838. Washington, D.C.: National Archives and Records Administration, n.d.

San Diego, California ("Seaport"). 1920 U.S. census, military and naval population abroad schedule. NARA microfilm publication T625, roll 2041. Washington, D.C.: National Archives and Records Administration, n.d.

First Reference Note

1. 1900 U.S. census, military and naval population schedule, China, Sucharing Pay Office, enumeration district (ED) 131, p. 1, line 2, William M. Long; NARA microfilm publication T623, roll 1838.

2. 1900 U.S. census, military and naval population schedule, Samoan Islands, U.S. Naval Station Tutuila, enumeration district (ED) 119, p. 1-B, line 54, Joe W. Jewett; NARA microfilm publication T623, roll 1838.

3. 1900 U.S. census, military and naval population schedule, USS *Brooklyn,* port: St. John, China, enumeration district (ED) 12, p. 92-A (penned), p. 59 (stamped), line 39, Soren F. Sorenson; NARA microfilm publication T623, roll 1838.

4. 1920 U.S. census, military and naval population abroad schedule, USS *Meade,* TBD [Torpedo Boat Destroyer] 274, "Seaport": San Diego, California [no ED shown], sheet 18 (stamped), 1-A (penned), Jesse T. Chadick; NARA microfilm publication T625, roll 2041.

Subsequent Note

11. 1900 U.S. census, mil. and naval pop., China, Sucharing Pay Office, ED 131, p. 1, line 2, William M. Long.

12. 1900 U.S. census, mil. and naval pop., Samoan Islands, Naval Station Tutuila, ED 119, p. 1-B, Joe W. Jewett.

13. 1900 U.S. census, mil. and naval pop., USS *Brooklyn*, port: St. John, China, p. 92-A (penned), Soren F. Sorenson.

14. 1920 U.S. census, mil. and nav. pop. abroad, USS *Meade*, port: San Diego, Calif., sheet 18 (stamped), 1-A (penned), Jesse T. Chadick.

SHIP NAMES

Italics should be used for names of naval vessels and ships. Initialisms that preface the ship's name (i.e., USS) appear in regular type.

6.40 Native-American Tribal Censuses, 1885–1940

See QuickCheck Model *for* MICROFILM: NATIVE-AMERICAN TRIBAL CENSUS

Between 1885 and 1940, U.S. Indian agents and superintendents took annual rolls of the population under their charge. Unlike all the preceding decennial censuses, these tribal enumerations were not conducted under the authority of the Census Bureau; they were administered by the Bureau of Indian Affairs (BIA). They are organized by agency, rather than state and county, and the jurisdiction of an agency could extend across county lines and state lines.

Consequently, there are major differences between citations to the regular U.S. census and these BIA tribal censuses. Most significantly: Census Bureau film is commonly cited by identifying only its publication number, together with census year and place, while the BIA film is cited like all other published NARA film. Because most readers expect U.S. censuses to be taken by the Census Bureau, for clarity your citation should identify the BIA as the author/creator of the material. The format illustrated below is also appropriate for the random Indian Bureau censuses taken of various tribes prior to 1885.

Microfilm (NARA Publication)

Source List Entry

Montana. Fort Belknap Agency. 1923 Groventre census. Bureau of Indian Affairs. *Indian Census Rolls, 1885–1940.* NARA microfilm publication M595, roll 129. Washington, D.C.: National Archives and Records Service, 1967.

First Reference Note

1. 1923 Groventre census, Fort Belknap Agency, unpaginated, entry no. 499/484, Ah gi nig [aka] James Snow; Bureau of Indian Affairs, *Indian Census Rolls, 1885–1940,* microfilm publication M595 (Washington, D.C.: National Archives and Records Service, 1967), roll 129.

Subsequent Note

11. 1923 Groventre census, Fort Belknap Agency, unpaginated, entry 499/484, Ah gi nig [aka] James Snow.

Also see 6.30 and 6.36 for Indian schedules of the decennial censuses.

MISCELLANEOUS CENSUS MATERIALS

6.41   1880–1920 Soundex & Miracode

See QuickCheck Model *for* DERIVATIVES: SOUNDEX & MIRACODE. MICROFILM

For the censuses of 1880, 1900, 1910, and 1920, the U.S. government created phonetic indexing systems called Soundex and Miracode that assign numbers to specific sounds. For each year, some details from every household were copied onto "abstract cards" that were then numerically arranged according to the coded sound of each surname.

The Soundex and Miracode cards are filmed separately from the actual census schedules. As a matter of practice, you will use the Soundex or Miracode only as a finding aid. Your final citation will then be to the original census, not the Soundex or Miracode. In other situations you will need to cite the finding aid—as when (1) you have a Soundex card but the original page is missing or illegible on the film, or (2) as an interim measure when your access to the original is delayed. In those cases, two thoughts should guide the crafting of your citation:

- Your Reference Note should clearly show you are using the Soundex or Miracode for that family, not the actual census schedule.

- Your Source List Entries for the Soundex microfilm can be grouped by state but not by county because the Soundex and Miracode do not separate counties within a state.

Microfilm (NARA Publication)

Source List Entry

Texas. 1910 U.S. census, Soundex. NARA microfilm publication
    T1277, roll 12. Washington, D.C: National Archives and Records
    Administration., n.d.

First Reference Note

    1. 1910 U.S. census, Soundex, Texas, C240, William W. Chesly (age
26), LeFlore County; NARA microfilm publication T1277, roll 12.

Subsequent Note

    11. 1910 U.S. census, Soundex, Texas, C240, William W. Chesly
(26), LeFlore Co.

6.42   Enumeration District Maps & Descriptions

The U.S. National Archives also has published on microfilm complete sets of enumeration district descriptions and enumeration district maps for some years. Both types are cited in your Source List in conventional fashion for NARA microfilm publications—i.e., by exact title, number, and publication data rather than by the number-only format commonly used for the actual census returns.

Microfilm (NARA Publication)

Source List Entry

U.S. Bureau of the Census. *Descriptions of Census Enumeration Districts, 1830–1950.* NARA microfilm publication T1224, 156 rolls. Washington, D.C.: National Archives and Records Service, 1978.

U.S. Bureau of the Census. *Enumeration District Description Maps for the Fifteenth Census of the United States, 1930.* NARA microfilm publication M1930, 36 rolls. National Archives and Records Administration: Washington, D.C., 2001.

First Reference Note

1. U.S. Bureau of the Census, *Descriptions of Census Enumeration Districts, 1830–1950,* microfilm publication T1224 (Washington: National Archives and Records Service, 1978), roll 74 , City of St. Louis, 1930 enumeration, vol. 36, enumeration district (ED) 2, pp. 2-3.

2. U.S. Bureau of the Census, *Enumeration District Description Maps for the Fifteenth Census of the United States, 1930,* microfilm publication M1930 (Washington: National Archives and Records Administration, 2001), roll 20, 1930 census, enumeration district map, City of St. Louis, ward 2; ward maps appear in numerical sequence.

Subsequent Note

11. Bureau of the Census, *Descriptions of Census Enumeration Districts,* City of St. Louis, 1930, ED 2, pp. 2–3.

12. Bureau of the Census, *Enumeration District Description Maps ... 1930,* enumeration district map, City of St. Louis, ward 2.

Some enumeration district maps are also available online at random sites. A typical citation would be this:

Online Databases & Images

Source List Entry

"1930 Census, Enumeration District Map, City of St. Louis." Digital image. *Saint Louis Public Library Showcase.* http://exhibits.slpl.org/ enumeration/data/stlouiscity.asp#CityMap : 2006.

First Reference Note

1. "1930 Census, Enumeration District Map, City of St. Louis," digital image, *Saint Louis Public Library Showcase* (http://exhibits.slpl.org/ enumeration/data/stlouiscity.asp#CityMap: accessed 27 December 2006); no source is cited for the origin of the map.

Subsequent Note
    11. "1930 Census, Enumeration District Map, City of St. Louis," digital image, *Saint Louis Public Library Showcase.*

6.43   Pre-federal Censuses

Prior to the formation of the United States, the various European governments who created colonies within North America took random censuses of their population. Some of these still survive. For uniformity in your Source List, you may wish to itemize a record of this type in the same generic PLACE, YEAR style that you use to itemize your U.S. censuses.

That identification might also be used in your Reference Notes. However, your Reference Notes should also cite the *exact title* of the document. Because these censuses are not part of a systematic enumeration scheme, they might be difficult to relocate without that precise identification. As demonstrated with the examples below, in which two separate censuses were taken of the same community in the same year by two different governments, a generic citation to just year and place could mislead.

Source List Entry

Louisiana. Natchitoches Post. 1766 French census. Miscellaneous Collection 3. Cammie G. Henry Research Center, Northwestern State University, Natchitoches, Louisiana.

Louisiana. Natchitoches Post. 1766 Spanish census. Legajo 2585, Audencia de Santo Domingo. Archivo General de Indias, Seville, Spain.

First Reference Note

(If you choose to copy the title of the census exactly without translation)
    1. 1766 French census, Natchitoches Post, Louisiana, "Récensement du poste des Natchitoches Pour l'Année Sept Cent Soixante Seis, 1766," p. 1 for "Mr. Borme, Captain"; Miscellaneous Collection 3, Cammie G. Henry Research Center; Northwestern State University, Natchitoches, Louisiana.

(If you choose to translate the title of the census)
    2. 1766 Spanish census, Natchitoches Post, Louisiana, Census and List of the Militiamen and Inhabitants of the Post of Natchitoches, 6 May 1766, p. 3, Juan Luis Borme; legajo 2585, Audencia de Santo Domingo; Archivo General de Indias, Seville, Spain.

Subsequent Note
    11. 1766 French census, Natchitoches Post, La., p. 1.
    12. 1766 Spanish census, Natchitoches Post, La., p. 3.

6.44 Religious Censuses

See Chapter 7, Church Records—specifically, QuickCheck Model, IM-AGE COPIES: MICROFILM–FHL-GSU (LDS RECORDS) and 7.13 (LDS church census); also see 7.46 (Swedish parish census).

6.45 School Censuses

Enumerations of families with school-aged children have been compiled by many states, although more randomly than systematically. Some have been abstracted into online databases. The North Dakota example, below, models a citation to the original and to online abstracts. Because the online version is not the actual census, but a modern derivative, the citation to the electronic source is to the creator and his product—not the census itself.

Original Documents

Source List Entry

North Dakota. Stutsman County. 1941 school census. County Auditor's Office, Jamestown, North Dakota.

First Reference Note

1. 1941 school census, Stutsman County, North Dakota, District 36, Valley Spring, Lillian Haas entry; County Auditor's Office, Jamestown, North Dakota.

Subsequent Note

11. 1941 school census, Stutsman Co., N.D., Valley Spring, Lillian Haas.

Online Database

Source List Entry

Barron, George L., "Indexes to the School Censuses for Stutsman County, North Dakota." Database. *NDGenWeb Archives.* http://ftp.rootsweb.com/pub/usgenweb/nd/stutsman/school/1941sch/hi.txt : 2007.

First Reference Note

1. George L. Barron, "Indexes to the School Censuses for Stutsman County, North Dakota," database, *NDGenWeb Archives* (http://ftp.rootsweb.com/pub/usgenweb/nd/stutsman/school/1941sch/hi.txt : 18 January 2007), entry for Lillian Haas, Valley Spring, District 36.

Subsequent Note

11. Barron, "Indexes to the School Censuses for Stutsman County, North Dakota," database entry, Lillian Haas, Valley Spring, Dist. 36.

6.46 State-sponsored Censuses

Many states have taken censuses at regular intervals between federal counts—often at the five-year mark. Most of these, such as the Kansas example that follows, are cited in much the same fashion as the federal ten-year censuses. Other states and territories, early in their settlement, took censuses during random years. Some of these can also be cited in standard form. However, specialized censuses are typically cited by their exact title because those titles more precisely describe their content, as with the Mississippi example below.

Differences in access to the state-authorized censuses can also create differences in citation formats. Schedules for these state-level counts are not maintained by the National Archives and are not part of NARA's M and T census series. They are also far less widely available in digital formats. Most citations will be to the preservation film held by FHL or by the archive that owns the schedules.

As with prior examples of nonstandard censuses cited by an exact title, a generic label is created and placed at the start of the entry, so the citation falls into the expected place-year sequence in the Source List.

SPECIAL COUNTY CENSUSES

Microfilm (State Archives, Preservation Film)

Source List Entry

Mississippi. Hinds County. 1824 census. "A List Containing the Number of Births, Deaths & Persons over the age of 70 years." MDAH microfilm 2528. Mississippi Department of Archives and History, Jackson.

First Reference Note

    1. 1824 census, Hinds County, Mississippi, "A List Containing the Number of Births, Deaths & Persons over the age of 70 years," p. 2, line 11, household of Hezekiah Billingsley; MDAH microfilm 2528; Mississippi Department of Archives and History, Jackson.

Subsequent Note

    11. 1824 census, Hinds Co., Miss., p. 2, line 11, Hezekiah Billingsley.

STATEWIDE CENSUSES

See QuickCheck Model *for* MICROFILM: STATE-SPONSORED CENSUSES

Microfilm (FHL-GSU)

Source List Entry

Kansas. Allen County. 1895 state census, population schedule. Kansas

State Historical Society, Topeka. FHL microfilm 570,221. Family History Library, Salt Lake City, Utah.

First Reference Note
1. 1895 Kansas state census, Allen County, population schedule, Carlyle township, p. 5, dwelling [blank], family 27, for Fred Reese in E. E. Cain household; FHL microfilm 570,221.

Subsequent Note
11. 1895 Kansas state census, Allen Co., pop. sch., Carlyle twp., p. 5, dwell. [blank], fam. 27, Fred Reese.

MISSING IDENTIFIERS

When an essential identifier is omitted, such as the dwelling number above, you could replace it with an em dash, but the word "blank" in square editorial brackets is more explicit.

6.47   Statistical Compendiums
Beginning with the 1850 enumeration, the U.S. Bureau of the Census began to compile and publish statistical compendiums to profile the American population by state and county. These volumes are cited in conventional fashion for published books.

Source List Entry
United States. Census Office. *Statistics of the United States (Including Mortality, Property, &c) in 1860.* Washington: Government Printing Office, 1866.

First Reference Note
1. U. S. Census Office, *Statistics of the United States (Including Mortality, Property, &c) in 1860* (Washington: Government Printing Office, 1866), lxi–lxii, "Table OO, Nativity of Americans Residing in Each State and Territory."

Subsequent Note
11. U. S. Census Office, *Statistics of the United States … 1860,* lxi–lxii.

6.48   Statistical Data & Enumeration Instructions, Online
Websites that provide this type of data often request that you include certain elements in your citation. The following models, for two of the sites most often used by history researchers, provide uniform models that include all the requested elements. The IPUMS example cites a text article, a transcription of the instructions given to 1870 enumerators by the Census Bureau. The GeoStat example cites a typical user-defined report—i.e., one created by choosing the specific data items needed for your individual research needs.

Source List Entry

Ruggles, Steven, Matthew Sobek, et al. "1870 Census: Instructions to Assistant Marshals." Article. Minnesota Population Center. *Integrated Public Use Microdata Series: IPUMS-USA*. http://usa.ipums.org/usa/voliii/inst1870.shtml : 2006.

University of Virginia. Geospatial & Statistical Data Center. "Historical Census Browser." Database. *GeoStat Center*. http://fisher.lib.virginia.edu/collections/stats/histcensus/ : 2007.

First Reference Note

1. Steven Ruggles, Matthew Sobek, et al., "1870 Census: Instructions to Assistant Marshals," article, Minnesota Population Center, *Integrated Public Use Microdata Series: IPUMS USA* (http://usa.ipums.org/usa/voliii/inst1870.shtml : accessed 19 October 2006), for "Constitutional Relations: *Indians."*

2. University of Virginia, Geospatial & Statistical Data Center, "Historical Census Browser," database, *GeoStat Center* (http://fisher.lib.virginia.edu/collections/stats/histcensus/ : accessed 23 February 2007), user-defined report for "1850" and "free colored males attending school."

Subsequent Note

11. Ruggles, Sobek, et al., "1870 Census: Instructions to Assistant Marshals," for "Constitutional Relations: *Indians."*

12. University of Virginia, "Historical Census Browser," *GeoStat Center,* user-defined report for "1850" and "free colored males attending school."

IDENTITY OF WEBSITE CREATOR

If the name of the website's creator is different from the website's name, the creator should be identified. In the IPUMS example, two sets of creators have to be cited: one for the database and one for the website. In the GeoStat example, the database creator is the agency itself and the agency's name is replicated in the website name; it would be superfluous to cite that agency again as the creator.

INTERNATIONAL CENSUSES

6.49 Australia

Citations to international censuses follow the same basic rules as those laid out for American censuses. With standard population censuses, generic labels can be used for simplicity—as illustrated below with the 1838 enumeration. However, national-level censuses were not taken in Australia until 1911, and few province-level censuses from earlier years have survived. When citing random documents, particularly when they have nonstandard titles such as the 1836 agricultural census below, it is best to quote the exact title.

If you are standardizing census entries in your Source List, you may wish to place a generic label before that exact title, similar to the phrase "Australia. Victoria Province. 1836 agricultural census" that precedes the title of the document in the first example below.

Microfilm (FHL-GSU)

Source List Entry

Australia. Victoria Province. 1836 agricultural census. "Abstract of the Returns of Stock and Cultivation at Port Phillip, to Accompany the Census Return of 1836." Melbourne Public Library, Sydney. FHL microfilm 209,172, item 1. Family History Library, Salt Lake City, Utah.

Australia. Victoria Province. 1838 population census. Melbourne Public Library, Sydney. FHL microfilm 209,172, item 2. Family History Library, Salt Lake City, Utah.

First Reference Note

1. 1836 agricultural census, Victoria Province, Australia: "Abstract of the Returns of Stock and Cultivation at Port Phillip, to Accompany the Census Return of 1836," p. 1, line 9, C. L. T. de Villiers; Melbourne Public Library, Sydney; FHL microfilm 209,172, item 1.

2. 1838 census of Australia, Victoria Province, Port Phillip, unpaginated 10th page, column 2, George Scarborough; Melbourne Public Library, Sydney; FHL microfilm 209,172, item 2.

Subsequent Note

11. 1836 agricultural census, Victoria Prov., p. 1, line 9, C.L. T. de Villiers.

12. 1838 population census, Victoria Prov., Port Phillip, unpaginated 10th page, col. 2, George Scarborough.

6.50   Canada

Microfilm (FHL-GSU)

Source List Entry

(*National-level copy owned by Library and Archives Canada*)
Canada, Lower. Bellechasse County. 1831 census. Library and Archives Canada, Ottawa. FHL microfilm 1,375,925. Family History Library, Salt Lake City, Utah.

(*Local copy owned by institution other than LAC*)
Canada West. Huron District. 1848 census. University of Western

Ontario, London. FHL microfilm 851,365, item 1. Family History Library, Salt Lake City, Utah.

First Reference Note

1. 1831 census of Lower Canada, Bellechasse County, St. Vallier, p. 3, line 9, Magloire Cotte; Library and Archives Canada, Ottawa; FHL microfilm 1,375,925.

2. 1848 census of Canada West, Huron District, Ashfield Township, folio 3 (penned, circled number), line 9, John Hawkins; University of Western Ontario, London; FHL microfilm 851,365, item 1.

Subsequent Note

11. 1831 census of Canada, Bellechasse Co., Que., p. 3, line 9, Magloire Cotte.

12. 1848 census of Canada, Huron Dist., Ashfield Twp., f. 3 (penned, circled number), line 9, John Hawkins.

IDENTIFICATION OF PAGE OR FOLIO NUMBER

In the preceding Huron District example, each folio of the census has eight "sides" or "pages," each of which are paginated consecutively with printed numbers. Enumerators then added their own folio numbers, numbering them consecutively in the order used. In the Ashfield instance, the enumerator's folio numbers are placed on the first page of each folio and circled. For precise identification, we need to cite that circled folio number, not a specific page within the folio, because each household entry extends across all eight of the print-numbered pages.

Online Database (Ancestry)

Source List Entry

"Cardwell District, Ontario, Canada, 1901 Census." Database. *Ancestry.com.* http://www.ancestry.com : 2007.

First Reference Note

1. "Cardwell District, Ontario, Canada, 1901 Census," database, *Ancestry.com* (www.ancestry.com : accessed 19 January 2007), entry for John H. Smith (b. 1857), Albion, Cardwell District; citing National Archives of Canada microfilm T-6462.

Subsequent Note

11. "Cardwell District, Ontario, Canada, 1901 Census," *Ancestry.com* database entry for John H. Smith (b. 1857), Albion, Cardwell Dist.

IDENTIFICATION OF REPOSITORY WHOSE NAME HAS CHANGED

The Cardwell database above cites the owner-repository as "National

Archives of Canada." After the creation of the database, that facility changed its name to Library and Archives Canada. In citing the database, however, your "source of the source" citation should specify whatever the database gives as its source. If you know that a cited facility has undergone a name change, you may wish to add a note to that effect, but you should place your correction or update in square editorial brackets after the name of the source that is actually cited.

Online Database (Canadian Archives)

See QuickCheck Model *for* DERIVATIVES: DATABASE–ONLINE

Source List Entry
Ontario Genealogical Society. "Federal Census of 1871 (Ontario Index)." Database. Library and Archives Canada, *Canadian Genealogy Centre*. http://www.collectionscanada.ca/genealogy/index-e.html : 2007.

First Reference Note
1. Ontario Genealogical Society, "Federal Census of 1871 (Ontario Index)," database, Library and Archives Canada (LAC), *Canadian Genealogy Centre* (http://www.collectionscanada.ca/genealogy/index-e.html : accessed 21 February 2007), entry for Patrick Lennon (age 67), Ellice, Perth North District; citing division 1, p. 36, LAC microfilm C-9940.

Subsequent Note
11. Ontario Genealogical Society, "Federal Census of 1871 (Ontario Index)," database entry for Patrick Lennon (67), Ellice, Perth North Dist.

Online Database (OntarioGenWeb)

Source List Entry
"1851 Zorra West Twp, Oxford County [Ontario, Canada]." Database. *Ontario GenWeb's Census Project.* http://www.rootsweb.com/~ongenpro/census/: 2007.

First Reference Note
1. "1851 Zorra West Twp, Oxford County [Ontario, Canada]," database, *Ontario GenWeb's Census Project* (http://www.rootsweb.com/~ongenpro/census/ : accessed 1 January 2007), entry for Gorgina Calder (age 12); citing p. 1, line 18 on Library and Archives Canada microfilm T-11744.

Subsequent Note
11. "1851 Zorra West Twp, Oxford County [Ontario, Canada]," database entry for Gorgina Calder (12).

ABBREVIATIONS

At 2.55, you are instructed not to abbreviate words or place names within titles. In the example above, the database title actually presents Zorra West Township as "Zorra West Twp," with no period after the abbreviation. The 2.55 rule applies here, also: *When copying titles, copy the words exactly.* You may amplify the title's punctuation for clarity, but do not alter the words by spelling out what is abbreviated or abbreviating what is spelled out.

Online Database (FamilySearch)

Source List Entry

"1881 Canadian Census." Database. The Church of Jesus Christ of Latter-day Saints. *FamilySearch.* http://www.familysearch.org : 2007.

First Reference Note

1. "1881 Canadian Census," database, The Church of Jesus Christ of Latter-day Saints, *FamilySearch* (http://www.familysearch.org : accessed 18 January 2007), entry for William Stuckey (b. 1819), Verulam, Victoria South, Ontario; citing dist. 129, subdist. E, division 2, p. 19 on Library and Archives Canada microfilm C-13243.

Subsequent Note

11. "1881 Canadian Census," database entry for William Stuckey (b. 1819), Verulam, Victoria South, Ontario.

Online Images (Ancestry.ca)

Source List Entry

Canada. Saskatchewan. Battleford. 1911 census of Canada. Digital images. *Ancestry.ca.* http://www.ancestry.ca : 2007.

First Reference Note

1. 1911 census of Canada, Battleford, Saskatchewan, population schedule, enumeration district (ED) 15, subdistrict 19, p. 2, dwelling 30, family 30, Wm. Leo Jeffcoat; digital image, *Ancestry.ca* (http://www.ancestry.ca : accessed 28 January 2007); citing Library and Archives Canada microfilm T-20326 through T-20460.

Subsequent Note

11. 1911 census of Canada, Battleford, Saskatchewan, pop. sch., ED 15, subdist. 19, p. 2, dwell. 30, fam. 30, Wm. Leo Jeffcoat.

6.51 England (and Wales)

Microfilm (FHL-GSU)

Source List Entry

England. Middlesex. 1841 census of England. PRO HO 107/732/10.

The National Archives of the UK, London. FHL microfilm 438,834. Family History Library, Salt Lake City, Utah.
England. Nottinghamshire. 1851 census of England. PRO HO 107/ 2133. The National Archives of the UK, Kew, Surrey. FHL microfilm 87,763. Family History Library, Salt Lake City, Utah.

First Reference Note

1. 1841 census of England, [county] Middlesex, [city] Westminster, [parish] St. George Hanover Square, folio 44 *recto*, lines 7–8, Charles and Sarah North; PRO HO 107/732/10; FHL microfilm 438,834.

2. 1851 census of England, Nottinghamshire, [city] Nottingham, [parish] St. Mary, folio 483 *verso*, household 13, William Stumbles; PRO HO 107/2133; FHL microfilm 87,763.

Subsequent Note

11. 1841 census of England, Middlesex, Westminster, St. George Hanover Square, fo. 44*r*, lines 7–8, Charles and Sarah North; PRO HO 107/732/10.

12. 1851 census of England, Nottinghamshire, Nottingham, St. Mary, f. 483*v*, household 13, William Stumbles; PRO HO 107/2133.

CITING ENGLISH COUNTIES

See 5.12.

CITING THE HOUSEHOLD

In the 1841 example, no numbers appear for houses, families, or lines. The convention is to cite lines, which can be easily counted. Citing them ensures that the right person is identified on pages with barely legible script or with multiple individuals of the same name

CITING THE ORIGINAL RECORD

As when using other FHL microfilm, your Source List Entry for English censuses should identify the originals and their whereabouts— information you can glean from the beginning of each film roll. As indicated in the foregoing citations, the original census manuscripts for England are held by The National Archives of the UK (also known by the acronym TNA), in the division known as the Public Records Office (PRO).

The 1841 and 1851 censuses are assigned the departmental code *HO,* and the series number *107*. The archives' ID system further identifies the *piece* or *item* number (for 1841: *732*; for 1851: *2133*) and (for 1841, but not for later years), the *book* number (in this example: *10*).

By TNA practice, a space follows the departmental code and the series number. Thereafter, the series, piece, and book numbers are separated by a forward slash (a *virgule*).

CD/DVD Database (LDS)

Source List Entry

1851 British Census: Devon, Norfolk, and Warwick Only. CD-ROM database. Salt Lake City, Utah: The Church of Jesus Christ of Latter-day Saints, 2001.

First Reference Note

1. *1851 British Census: Devon, Norfolk, and Warwick Only,* CD-ROM database (Salt Lake City, Utah: The Church of Jesus Christ of Latter-day Saints, 2001), entry for William Stumbles (age 39), Nottingham St. Mary's Parish, Nottinghamshire, England, folio 483; citing Public Record Office HO 107/1751.

Subsequent Note

11. *1851 British Census: Devon, Norfolk, and Warwick Only,* database entry for William Stumbles (39), Nottingham St. Mary's Par., Nottinghamshire, f. 483; PRO HO 107/1751.

Online Database (Ancestry)

Source List Entry

"1871 England Census." Database. *Ancestry.com.* http://www.ances try.com : 2006.

First Reference Note

1. "1871 England Census," database, *Ancestry.com* (www.ancestry .com : accessed 1 September 2006), entry for George Lucas (age 33), Bromley St. Leonard, London; citing PRO RG 10/571, folio 27, p. 3; Poplar registration district, Bow subdistrict, ED 14, household 9.

Subsequent Note

11. "1871 England Census," *Ancestry.com,* database entry for George Lucas (33), Bromley St. Leonard, London.

Online Database (National Archives/PRO)

See also QuickCheck Model *for* DERIVATIVES: DATABASE, ONLINE

Source List Entry

"1901 Census for England and Wales." Database. *The National Archives.* http://www.1901census.nationalarchives.gov.uk : 2006.

First Reference Note

1. "1901 Census for England and Wales," database, *The National Archives* (http://www.1901census.nationalarchives.gov.uk : accessed 1 September 2006), entry for Freddy Frame (age 10), Glammorgan Mountain Ash, Bedwelty, Monmouthshire, Wales; citing PRO RG 13/4943.

	11. "1901 Census for England and Wales," *The National Archives* database entry, Freddy Frame (10), Glammorgan Mountain Ash, Bedwelty, Monmouthshire.

Online Images (National Archives/PRO)

See QuickCheck Model *for* DIGITAL IMAGES: ONLINE ARCHIVES (U.K., WALES)

Source List Entry
Wales. Monmouthshire. 1901 census of Wales. Digital images. *The National Archives.* http://www.1901census.nationalarchives.gov. uk : 2006.

First Reference Note
	1. 1901 census of Wales, Monmouthshire, Bedwelty, Glammorgan Mountain Ash, p. 5 (stamped), Moses Frame; digital image, *The National Archives* (http://www.1901census.nationalarchives.gov.uk : accessed 1 September 2006); citing PRO RG 13/4943.

Subsequent Note
	11. 1901 census of Wales, Monmouthshire, Bedwelty, Glammorgan Mountain Ash, p. 5 (stamped), Moses Frame.

6.52   France
French decennial censuses from 1836 forward are systematic national enumerations. When working in the English language, you may cite them generically as, say, "1836 census of France" or you may prefer to retain the French nomenclature, *Listes nominatives de recensement de population*. Returns for each *département* (state) are held in its *archives départementales*. However, most copies today are consulted via microfilm held by the Family History Library or digital images offered at the websites of some departmental archives.

Microfilm (FHL-GSU)

Source List Entry
France. Orne. Argentan. Mortrée. La Bellière. 1856 census of France. Listes nominatives de recensement de population, 1836–1896. Cote EDEPOT 286/23. Archives Départementales, Alençon. FHL microfilm 2,267,411, item 2. Family History Library, Salt Lake City, Utah.

First Reference Note
	1. 1856 census of France, Orne (département), Argentan (arrondissement), Mortrée (canton), La Bellière (commune), unnumbered pages, Quartier Tetre-aux-Allains, dwelling 3, family 3, François Roger; FHL microfilm 2,267,411, item 2, frame 423.

Subsequent Note
11. 1856 census of France, Orne, for La Bellière, unnumbered pages, Tetre-aux-Allains, dwell. 3, fam. 3, François Roger.

Online Images (Archives Départementales)

See QuickCheck Model *for* DIGITAL IMAGES: ONLINE ARCHIVES (FRANCE)

Source List Entry
France. La Mayenne. Laval. Évron. 1836 census of France. Digital images. Archives Départementales de la Mayenne. *Archives en ligne.* http://www.lamayenne.fr?SectionId=591&PubliId=2883& Controller : 2007.

First Reference Note
1. 1836 census of France, canton Évron, arrondissement de Laval, La Mayenne, p. 12, no. 314, family 92, Émile Prudhomme; digital image, Archives Départementales de la Mayenne, *Archives en ligne* (http://www.lamayenne.fr?SectionId=591&PubliId=2883&Controller : accessed 24 February 2007); original manuscript not cited.

Subsequent Note
11. 1836 census of France, Évron, Laval, La Mayenne, p. 12, no. 314, fam. 92, Émile Prudhomme.

6.53 Germany

In the German example below, the census is a localized one. There was no German nation in 1799; thus, there was no national enumeration.

Microfilm (FHL-GSU)

Source List Entry
Germany. Mecklenburg-Schwerin. 1799 census of Wismar. Stadtarchiv Wismar. FHL microfilm 1,706,017. Family History Library, Salt Lake City, Utah.

First Reference Note
1. 1799 census of Wismar, Mecklenburg-Schwerin, Germany, p. 8, no. 157, Fiedemann household; Stadtarchiv Wismar; FHL microfilm 1,706,017.

Subsequent Note
11. 1799 census of Wismar, Mecklenburg-Schwerin, p. 8, no. 157, Fiedemann household.

CITING EXACT TITLE VS. TRANSLATED TITLE
Some European census records of earlier centuries carried titles that varied from one year to the next and one locale to the next. The

preceding German example demonstrates using a generic label, translated into your own language. The Italian example below demonstrates how you might preserve the exact wording of the title.

6.54   Italy

Microfilm (FHL-GSU)

Source List Entry
Italy. Palermo. Gratteri. 1815 census. "Riveli di beni e anime [Disclosures of families and property]." Archivio di Stato Palermo. FHL microfilm 2,154,489, item 3. Family History Library, Salt Lake City, Utah.

First Reference Note
1. 1815 census, Gratteri, Palermo, Italy, "Riveli di beni e anime" [Disclosures of families and property], pp. 2 (master list) and 49 (individual sheet), for Giacomo Ilardo; Archivio di Stato Palermo; FHL microfilm 2,154,489, item 3.

Subsequent Note
11. 1815 census, Gratteri, Palermo, Italy, "Riveli di beni e anime," pp. 2 and 49.

CITING EXACT TITLE
When using a foreign-language record with a distinctive title, you may want to cite that title exactly, in quotes. You may also want to add a translation in brackets—for which only the first word should be capitalized. In the example above, because the title of the record would not be readily perceived as a census—and to make the entry fall alphabetically in the expected spot within the PLACE-YEAR arrangement of your Source List—a generic label is added at the beginning of the citation to make its format parallel that of other census records.

6.55   Puerto Rico
See United States, 6.31, 1910–30, Population Schedule.

6.56   Spain

Microfilm (FHL-GSU)

Source List Entry
Spain. Gerona Province. 1720 census of Gerona. Register 12325. "Padrons de veïns." (Census of residents). Arxiu Municipal de Girona, Spain. FHL microfilm 2,290,750. Family History Library, Salt Lake City, Utah.

First Reference Note
    1. 1720 census of Gerona, Gerona Province, Spain: Register 12325, "Padrons de veïns," for Barre, district of Narcis Pont, Carrer nou [Nou Street], unpaginated, unnumbered household of Anna Gaímanya, widow; MS, Arxiu Municipal de Girona; FHL microfilm 2,290,750, frame 710.

Subsequent Note
    11. 1720 census of Gerona, Gerona Prov., for Barre de Narcis Pont, Carrer Nou, Anna Gaímanya, widow; located at microfilm frame 710.

CITING THE HOUSEHOLD
In the above example, the original pages carry no numbers that could be used to narrow down the location of the entry. However, the microfilm itself carries frame numbers. In such situations, you should be careful to attach the frame number to your citation of the microfilm, not to your citation of the census.

6.57   Sweden

Microfilm (FHL-GSU)

Source List Entry
    Sweden. Stockholm. 1862 census of Stockholm. "Mantalslängder" [Population register]. Riksarkivet, Stockholm. FHL microfilm 1,677,806, item 1. Family History Library, Salt Lake City, Utah.

First Reference Note
    1. 1862 census of Stockholm, Sweden, "Mantalslängder" [Population register], Stadens Inre, Quarteret Hippomenes, p. 13, no. 67, A. T. Pettersson; Riksarkivet, Stockholm; FHL microfilm 1,677,806, item 1.

Subsequent Note
    11. Census of 1862, Stockholm, Stadens Inre, Quarteret Hippomenes, p. 13, no. 67, A. T. Pettersson.

6.58   Wales
See England (and Wales), 6.51.

CHURCH RECORDS

7

QuickCheck Models

Guidelines & Examples (beginning page 321)

QuickCheck Model
CHURCH BOOKS: NAMED VOLUME
HELD BY CHURCH
Church as lead element in source list

Source List Entry

CHURCH (AUTHOR)   CHURCH LOCATION   RECORD ...

Immaculate Conception Church (Natchitoches, Louisiana). "Baptisms and

... BOOK TITLE   REPOSITORY   REPOSITORY LOCATION

Confirmations, 1873–1896." Parish rectory, Natchitoches.

First (Full) Reference Note

CHURCH (AUTHOR)   LOCATION   RECORD ...

1. Immaculate Conception Church (Natchitoches, Louisiana), "Baptisms

... BOOK TITLE   PAGE   ITEM OF INTEREST ...

and Confirmations, 1873–1896," p. 259, no. 47, Paul B. Morse baptism

... YEAR   REPOSITORY   REPOSITORY LOCATION

(1890); parish rectory, Natchitoches.

Subsequent (Short) Note

CHURCH   LOCATION   RECORD ...

11. Immaculate Conception Church (Natchitoches), "Baptisms and

... BOOK   PAGE & ITEM

Confirmations, 1873–1896," p. 259, no. 47.

QuickCheck Model
CHURCH BOOKS: NAMED VOLUME
ARCHIVED OFF-SITE
Church & volume as lead elements in Source List

Source List Entry

CHURCH (AUTHOR)   LOCATION   RECORD BOOK ...

Uxbridge Monthly Meeting (Uxbridge, Massachusetts). "Book of Records for

... TITLE ...

Epistles, Certificates, Testimonies of Denial and Acknowledgements

...   COLLECTION   VOL.NO.

[1783–1811]." New England Yearly Meetings of Friends, vol.135.

REPOSITORY   REPOSITORY LOCATION

Friends Historical Library, Swarthmore, Pennsylvania.

First (Full) Reference Note

CHURCH (AUTHOR)   LOCATION   RECORD...

1. Uxbridge Monthly Meeting (Uxbridge, Massachusetts), "Book of

... BOOK TITLE ...

Records for Epistles, Certificates, Testimonies of Denial and Acknowledgements

...   PAGE   COLLECTION   VOL.NO.

[1783–1811]," p. 24; New England Yearly Meetings of Friends, vol.135;

REPOSITORY   REPOSITORY LOCATION

Friends Historical Library, Swarthmore, Pennsylvania.

Subsequent (Short) Note

CHURCH   RECORD BOOK ...

11. Uxbridge (Mass.) Monthly Meeting, "Book of Records for Epistles,

... TITLE ...   PAGE

Certificates, Testimonies of Denial and Acknowledgements," p. 24.

QuickCheck Model
CHURCH BOOKS: NUMBERED VOLUME
ARCHIVED OFF-SITE
Church & series as lead elements in Source List

Source List Entry

CHURCH (AUTHOR)   LOCATION   RECORD SERIES

St. Mary's Church (Charlestown, Massachusetts). Baptismal Registers.

REPOSITORY   REPOSITORY LOCATION

Roman Catholic Chancery Office Archives, Brighton, Massachusetts.

First (Full) Reference Note

CHURCH (AUTHOR)   LOCATION   RECORD BOOK (SERIES & VOL.NO.)

1. St. Mary's Church (Charlestown, Massachusetts), Baptismal Book 1,

PAGE   ITEM OF INTEREST & YEAR   REPOSITORY

p. 42, Mary Elizabeth Kane (1854); Roman Catholic Chancery Office Archives,

REPOSITORY LOCATION

Brighton, Massachusetts.

Subsequent (Short) Note

CHURCH   LOCATION   RECORD BOOK   PAGE

11. St. Mary's Church (Charlestown, Mass.), Baptismal Book 1, p. 42.

QuickCheck Model
IMAGE COPIES: DIGITIZED ONLINE
Church & series as lead elements in Source List

Source List Entry

CHURCH (AUTHOR)	LOCATION	RECORD SERIES ...

St. Lawrence Church (Oxhill, Warwickshire, England). Parish registers,

ITEM TYPE or FORMAT	WEBSITE TITLE	

1568–1840. Digital images. *St. Lawrence Church Oxhill.* http://

URL (DIGITAL LOCATION)	YEAR

www.oxhill.org.uk/ChurchRegisters/Registers.htm : 2006.

First (Full) Reference Note

CHURCH (AUTHOR)	LOCATION	RECORD ...

1. St. Lawrence Church (Oxhill, Warwickshire, England), Banns of

... BOOK I.D. (GENERIC LABEL)	PAGE	ITEM OF INTEREST & ...

Marriage, 1754–1794, unnumbered p. 1, "Mr." Thomas Warde and Martha

... DATE FOR UNPAGINATED ENTRY	ITEM TYPE or FORMAT	WEBSITE TITLE

Rowley , 19 October 1574; digital images, *St. Lawrence Church Oxhill* (http://

... URL (DIGITAL LOCATION)	ACCESS DATE

www.oxhill.org.uk/ChurchRegisters/Registers.htm : accessed 20 September

...

2006).

Subsequent (Short) Note

CHURCH (AUTHOR)	RECORD BOOK

11. St. Lawrence Church (Oxhill, Eng.), Banns of Marriage, 1754–1794,

PAGE	ITEM

unnumbered p. 1, Warde-Rowley, 29 October 1574.

QuickCheck Model
IMAGE COPIES: MICROFILM
FHL-GSU PRESERVATION COPY

Church & series as lead elements in Source List

Source List Entry

CHURCH (AUTHOR)	LOCATION	RECORD SERIES

Midmar Parish (Aberdeenshire, Scotland).Old Parish Registers, 1717–1824.

OWNER/REPOSITORY	REPOSITORY LOCATION	FILM ID ...

General Register Office for Scotland, Edinburgh. FHL microfilm

...	FILM REPOSITORY	FILM REP'Y LOCATION

993,344. Family History Library, Salt Lake City, Utah.

First (Full) Reference Note

CHURCH (AUTHOR)	LOCATION	RECORD BOOK ID (SERIES & VOL.) ...

1. Midmar Parish (Aberdeenshire, Scotland), Old Parish Registers, OPR

... PAGE	ITEM OF INTEREST	FILM ID ...

222/1, p. 65, James Edward baptism (1727); FHL microfilm 993,344,

...

item 1.

Subsequent (Short) Note

CHURCH	RECORD BOOK ID	PAGE

11. Midmar Parish (Aberdeenshire), OPR 222/1, p. 65.

QuickCheck Model
IMAGE COPIES: MICROFILM
LDS RECORDS AT FHL

Church & series as lead elements in Source List

Source List Entry

CHURCH (AUTHOR) ...

Beaver West Ward, The Church of Jesus Christ of Latter-day Saints (Beaver

... LOCATION   SERIES TITLE   REPOSITORY ...

County, Utah). Records of Ward Members, 1905–1947. LDS Church

...   REPOSITORY LOCATION   FILM ID   FILM ...

Archives, Salt Lake City,Utah. FHL microfilm 25,644. Family

... REPOSITORY   FILM LOCATION

History Library, Salt Lake City, Utah.

First (Full) Reference Note

CHURCH (AUTHOR)

1. Beaver West Ward, The Church of Jesus Christ of Latter-day Saints

LOCATION   RECORD BOOK ID (SERIES & VOLUME)

(Beaver County, Utah), Records of Ward Members, 1905–1947, Book

...   PAGE   ITEM OF INTEREST   FILM ID

2, unpaginated, record no. 796, Orvil D. Harris; FHL microfilm 25,644.

Subsequent (Short) Note

CHURCH   RECORD BOOK ID (SHORTENED)   ITEM ...

11. Beaver (Utah) West Ward, Records of Ward Members, Book 2, record

...

796.

QuickCheck Model
IMAGE COPIES: MICROFILM
PUBLICATION

Publication title as lead element in Source List

Source List Entry

FILM TITLE	RECORD TYPE ...

Records of the Diocese of Louisiana and the Floridas. Microfilm publication,

NO. OF ROLLS	PUBLICATION PLACE	PUBLISHER	YEAR

12 rolls. Notre Dame, Indiana: Notre Dame University, 1967.

First (Full) Reference Note

FILM TITLE	RECORD TYPE ...

1. *Records of the Diocese of Louisiana and the Floridas,* microfilm publication,

NO. OF ROLLS	PUBLICATION PLACE	PUBLISHER	YEAR	ROLL USED

12 rolls (Notre Dame, Indiana: Notre Dame University, 1967), roll 1,

PAGE or ARRANGEMENT	RECORD DATE	ITEM OF INTEREST...

arranged by date; see 4–9 June 1798, "Proceedings about the Burial of Diego

Lazaga."

Subsequent (Short) Note

FILM TITLE	ROLL USED	RECORD DATE

11. *Records of the Diocese of Louisiana and the Floridas,* roll 1, 4–9 June 1798,

ITEM

"Proceedings about the Burial of Diego Lazaga."

QuickCheck Model
DERIVATIVES
CHURCH-ISSUED CERTIFICATE

Multiple certificates cited as a collection in Source List
Name of church as lead element

Source List Entry

CHURCH (AUTHOR)   LOCATION   COLLECTION...

Sts. Peter and Paul Catholic Church (Bubach am Forst, Bavaria). Sacramental

... (GENERIC LABEL)   COLLECTION OWNER   OWNER'S ...

Certificates, 1969–75. Privately held by Connie Lenzen, [ADDRESS FOR

YEAR
... LOCATION   OWNED

PRIVATE USE,] Portland, Oregon. 2007.

First (Full) Reference Note

CHURCH (AUTHOR)   LOCATION

1. Sts. Peter and Paul Catholic Church (Bubach am Forst, Bavaria),

COLLECTION (GENERIC LABEL)   COLLECTION OWNER

Sacramental Certificates, 1969–75 (privately held by Connie Lenzen,

YEAR
OWNER'S LOCATION   OWNED   CERTIFICATE ID ...

[ADDRESS FOR PRIVATE USE,] Portland, Oregon, 2007), Johann Andreas

CREDIT LINE
... (WHO, WHEN, WHAT EVENT)   WHEN ISSUED   (SOURCE OF THIS SOURCE)...

Huirass baptismal certificate (1800), issued 1979, citing Book 1, p. 142,

...

no. 8.

Subsequent (Short) Note

CHURCH (AUTHOR)   LOCATION

11. Sts. Peter and Paul Catholic Church (Bubach am Forst, Bavaria),

CERTIFICATE ID   WHEN ISSUED

Johann Andreas Huirass certificate, 1800 baptism, issued 1979.

QuickCheck Model
DERIVATIVES
CHURCH RECORD BOOK, RECOPIED
Church & volume as prime elements in Source List

Source List Entry

CHURCH (AUTHOR)　　　　　　　　　　LOCATION　　　　RECORD ...

St. John the Baptist Catholic Church (Cloutierville, Louisiana). Marriage

... BOOK　　　　　REPOSITORY　　REPOSITORY LOCATION

Book 1 (Latin copy). Parish rectory, Cloutierville.

First (Full) Reference Note

CHURCH (AUTHOR)　　　　　　　　　LOCATION　　　　...

1. St. John the Baptist Catholic Church (Cloutierville, Louisiana), Mar-

... RECORD BOOK　　　　PAGE　　　　ITEM OF INTEREST & ...

riage Book 1 (Latin copy), unpaginated, entry 72, Rogers-Morgan marriage

... YEAR　　REPOSITORY　　REPOSITORY LOCATION

(1848); parish rectory, Cloutierville.

Subsequent (Short) Note

CHURCH　　　　　　　　LOCATION　　RECORD...

11. St. John the Baptist Catholic Church (Cloutierville, La.), Marriage

... BOOK　　　　ITEM

Book 1 (Latin copy), entry 72.

QuickCheck Model
DERIVATIVES
CHURCH RECORDS DATABASE, ONLINE
Compiler as lead element in Source List

Source List Entry

COMPILER   DATABASE TITLE   ITEM TYPE or FORMAT

Lalley, Joseph M., Jr. "Baptismal Records, Wilmington, Delaware." Database.

WEBSITE TITLE ...

19th Century Immigrant Roots:Records for Wilmington, Delaware, USA,

...   URL (DIGITAL LOCATION)   YEAR

and Vicinity. http://www.lalley.com : 2007.

First (Full) Reference Note

COMPILER   DATABASE TITLE

1. Joseph M. Lalley Jr., "Baptismal Records, Wilmington, Delaware,"

ITEM TYPE or FORMAT   WEBSITE ...

database, *19th Century Immigrant Roots: Records for Wilmington, Delaware,*

... TITLE   URL (DIGITAL LOCATION)   DATE

USA, and Vicinity (http://www.lalley.com : accessed 28 January 2007),

ITEM OF INTEREST   CREDIT LINE ...

entry for John Keely, baptized 26 August 1888; citing St. Paul Church

... (SOURCE OF THIS SOURCE)

Baptisms, December 1869–August 1893, p. 214.

Subsequent (Short) Note

COMPILER   DATABASE TITLE   ITEM OF ...

11. Lalley, "Baptismal Records, Wilmington, Delaware," database en-

... INTEREST

try for John Keely, baptized 26 August 1888.

GUIDELINES
& Examples

BASIC ISSUES

7.1 Cultural Differences & Similarities

Different denominations have created different types of records. Some keep sacramental registers (books in which they record the sacraments they have administered—typically, baptisms, marriages, burials, communions, and sometimes confessions and abjurations). Some keep *minutes* that are rich in details on parishioners, such as disciplinary measures; other minutes may treat only business matters. Some hold membership rolls and others have taken censuses. Some keep letters of admission and dismissal. Despite these variations, the formats in which these records are cited are much the same across denominations and nationalities.

7.2 Citation Elements, U.S. vs. International

Regardless of the country in which you work, your citations to church books will have essentially the same elements. An American church register, a Spanish *registro parroquial,* a German *Kirchenbüch*, an Icelandic *kirkjubók,* and a Norwegian *klokkerbók* are all "church books." Similarly, it matters little whether the book is a sacramental register in Poland or a vaccination register in Norway, a register of incoming and outgoing servants such as those kept in Denmark, or a church census such as those found in Italy and Nordic countries. The basic elements for citing them are essentially the same.

The factors that do create variations within citations are usually these:

- whether the register is in the custody of the local church or a central archive;
- whether the register is an original, a transcribed copy, or a translation;

- whether the register carries a distinctive title or whether it is a numbered volume within a named series; and
- whether you are using a manuscript volume, a microcopy, a photocopy, a certificate, a digital image, a database entry, or a published abstract or transcript.

7.3 Citing Church as "Author"

In citing original records created by a church—or images thereof—the church should be treated as the "corporate author." If you are citing abstracts or databases, your source is no longer a set of church records; it is a set of data drawn from those church books. The creator of those derivatives would be the author of the abstracts or database.

7.4 Citing Dates vs. Page Numbers

When registers are paginated, you should cite the page number. The older practice of simply citing the parish and date, then assuming a record can be found in that parish from the date alone, can create problems for you and for others who attempt to find the record again from your incomplete citation. Church entries are frequently recorded out of sequence or in "wrong" registers, pages are rebound out of order, and separate registers often have overlapping dates.

In two situations, you *will* want to include the *full* date of the record:

- when the date method of citation *is* the norm, as with the Scottish records covered at 7.43.

- when a register is unpaginated or does not number individual acts, in which case you should include the *full* date of the record.

When a register is paginated but its title does not include the time frame, you should include in your citation at least the *year* of the entry:

First Reference Note
1.   Santa María Parish (Cée, La Coruña Province, Spain), Marriage Book 2, p. 179, De Mourelle–De Lema marriage (1717).

7.5 Citing Entry vs. Page Numbers

You will need to study the overall arrangement of each register you use and plan your citation to include whatever numbers are needed to identify your entry. In cases in which some types of entries carry numbers and others do not (a situation sometimes found for illegitimate births or sacraments administered to slaves), you will need to cite the entry as, say, "unnumbered entry between 157 and 158."

Many registers that are unpaginated will number individual entries in one fashion or another. Some will number them sequentially within each year (e.g.: 1834:1, 1834:2, etc.), with baptisms, marriages, burials, abjurations, etc., intermingled one after the other in the order they occurred. Other registers number each *type* of act sequentially; for example, "Baptism no. 57" may be followed by "Marriage no.13," which is followed by "Burial no. 29"—all on the same page. Or, the books may be sectioned by type of sacrament, with individual entries numbered consecutively within each section.

7.6   Citing Folio (*Recto* and *Verso*) vs. Page Numbers

The term *page* generally applies to numbering systems in which each side of a sheet of paper has a different number. In many registers, only one number appears on a sheet, usually on the right hand side. In those cases, the front and back of the sheets are distinguished by referring to, say, folio 39 recto (front side) and folio 39 verso (back side) or folio 39*r* and folio 39*v*.

For clarity, with whatever set of numbers you cite, you should indicate whether your numbers represent folios, pages, or entries.

7.7   Identification of Church

The church should be identified precisely—not generically by name of town. Example:

> St. Anne's Church (Prairie de Rocher, Illinois)
> *not* "Prairie de Rocher Church Records"

This principle applies even if an area had only one legal denomination or facility during the period you are researching. It applies even when just one set of church records are known for an area. Many communities had dissenting congregations whose records continue to be discovered. Identifying the specific town and state (or province) is equally important, because researchers frequently find multiple churches of the same name within the same county or diocese.

Many denominations have specific terms that are used to identify their congregations—*chapel, church, meeting, mission, mosque, parish, synagogue, temple,* etc. The term you use to identify the creator or owner of a set of religious records will depend upon the denomination.

Many history researchers use interchangeably the terms *parish* and *church* to identify local records of hierarchy-based denominations such as the Catholic, Episcopalian, and Lutheran churches. However, two potential problems need to be avoided:

- In Louisiana, the term *parish* is also used as a civil jurisdiction comparable to counties in other states. For clarity, when citing Catholic records from that state, it is safer to identify them with the term *church*—i.e., St. James *Church,* rather than St. James *Parish*—or, say, *St. James Catholic Parish.*

- In many locales, historically, some parishes have had mission churches, chapels, or other dependencies in addition to their principal church. Separate record books may have been kept for each facility. In those cases, an identification such as "St. Anne's Parish, Baptismal Book 1" would not suffice if the records belong to St. Rose's Chapel in St. Anne's Parish.

7.8 Identification of Event

Some church registers deal with one specific type of event—e.g., baptisms, confirmations, marriages, or burials. Some registers include more than one event. When using a multipurpose register to cite a specific event, your citation should identify the type of event ("baptism of John Jones, 1 March 1850"). If a register deals with, say, only baptisms and the register carries the word *Baptisms* in its title, you do not need to repeat that when you identify the specific entry.

Caution: Because the abbreviation *b.* could represent birth, baptism, or burial, you should not use those abbreviations in identifying your event within a citation.

7.9 Identification of Individuals

Your First Reference Note should include the name of the key person or persons in the entry if (*a*) they are not identified in the text to which you attach the note; (*b*) the original record spells the name differently from the standardized spelling you use in your text; or (*c*) the names are needed to locate the entry.

7.10 Identification of Record Dates

If your text does not give the date of the record, you will want to include that date in your First Reference Note. If the record book is not paginated, your note will need to include the date of the event, as well as the name of the key person.

7.11 Source List Entries, Options for

Source List Entries may be structured in various ways, each of which affects how you alphabetize the entries. Your choice will also dictate how much data you include in the Source List and how much data reentry you must do to create each Reference Note when using data-management software. Some pros and cons to consider are these:

CITING CREATOR & *COLLECTION* (OR SERIES) AS LEAD ELEMENTS
You will create a leaner, more manageable Source List if it cites the church as the author of the collection of records and then identifies the collection in broad terms. For example:

> **Source List Entry**
> Georgetown Presbyterian Church (Washington, D.C.). Session Minutes, 1879–1946.

If you choose this option, then each time you enter a citation for these records, your source will be this collection (i.e., Session Minutes, 1879–1946). In data entry, each time you select this Master Source, your Reference Note will have to identify the specific volume (which may have a lengthy title and a smaller time frame), along with the page and entry.

CITING CREATOR & *VOLUME* AS LEAD ELEMENTS
In this approach, you also list the church in the Source List as the author of the individual registers, but you create a separate Source List Entry for each register. For example:

> **Source List Entries**
> St. John the Baptist Catholic Church (Cloutierville, Louisiana). "Baptisms of Free Negroes from A.D. 1847 to 1871."
> St. John the Baptist Catholic Church (Cloutierville, Louisiana). "Ecclesiastical Burials, A.D. 1847 to A.D. 1906."
> St. John the Baptist Catholic Church (Cloutierville, Louisiana). "Registre de la Chapelle de Cloutierville, No. 1, 1825–29."

If you choose this option, then each time you enter a citation, your Master Source will be one specific volume created by this church, and you will only have to enter the page and item detail in your Reference Note.

Formatting note—*Three-em dash:* In the St. John the Baptist example above, your working Source List will vary slightly from the format you will use for a published bibliography. When edited for final publication, the name of the church and its location would not be repeated in consecutive entries. Rather, in each instance after the first, the repeated identity of the author/creator would be replaced with a three-em dash, as follows:

St. John the Baptist Catholic Church (Cloutierville, Louisiana). "Baptisms of Free Negroes from A.D. 1847 to 1871."

———. "Ecclesiastical Burials, A.D. 1847 to A.D. 1906."

———. "Registre de la Chapelle de Cloutierville, No. 1, 1825–29."

Caution: Do not enter these three-em dashes in your working Source List. If you do, then the automatic entry that your software makes in the Reference Note template will carry that three-em dash instead of the name of the author/creator. Some software will automatically create appropriate three-em dashes in Source Lists. Others will not. If yours does not, this should be one of the final editing tasks you perform before you create a copy for publication or distribution.

ORIGINAL MATERIALS: BASIC FORMATS

7.12   Record Books, Archived Off-site

Many church registers have been removed to denominational archives or elsewhere for safekeeping, a situation that complicates their citation. By way of comparison: when the register is in the custody of the original church, you have two sets of details to cite:

- the details that identify the original register and its creator;
- the details that identify the specific entry.

When the register has been deposited elsewhere, you have another set of details to add:

- the information that identifies the archive.

Below, the first example uses a *church minute book,* rather than a sacramental register. Also called *vestry books* (by Anglicans and Episcopalians), *actes de fabrique* (by French Catholics), etc., these volumes generally focus on administrative affairs. History researchers typically consult them for records of admissions and dismissals, disciplinary actions, disputes within the congregation, financial matters, and membership lists. The second example uses a typical *sacramental register* where births, marriages, deaths, and confirmations are recorded.

Source List Entry

Second Congregational Church (Newport, Rhode Island). Record Book, 1725–1772. Newport Historical Society, Newport.

St. Mary's Church (New Orleans, Louisiana). Marriage Book 3. Archives of the Catholic Archdiocese of New Orleans.

First Reference Note
 1. Second Congregational Church (Newport, Rhode Island), Record Book, 1725–1772, p. 121; MS 836E, Newport Historical Society, Newport.
 2. St. Mary's Church (New Orleans, Louisiana), Marriage Book 3, p. 91, Guérin-Mailloux; Archives of the Archdiocese of New Orleans.

Subsequent Note
 11. Second Congregational Church (Newport, R.I.), Record Book, 1725–1772, p. 121.
 12. St. Mary's Church (New Orleans), Marriage Book 3, p. 91.

7.13 Record Books, Cited by Exact Title

See QuickCheck Models *for* CHURCH BOOKS: NAMED VOLUME …

When a church book has a distinctly worded title, that title should be copied precisely, with quotation marks around it. Older books may have very long titles or subtitles, in which case you may use just the leading words, so long as the set of words you choose are not identical with that of any other books of that church. Shortened titles must clearly differentiate between similarly named volumes in a series.

Both of the following examples treat the church as the author of the individual volume.

Source List Entry

(*When listing the collection*)
St. John the Baptist Catholic Church (Cloutierville, Louisiana). Parish Registers, 1825–1900. Parish rectory, Cloutierville.

(*When listing a specific record book*)
Uxbridge Monthly Meeting (Uxbridge, Massachusetts). "Book of Records for Epistles, Certificates, Testimonies of Denial and Acknowledgements [1783–1811]." New England Yearly Meetings of Friends, volume 135. Friends Historical Library, Swarthmore, Pennsylvania.

First Reference Note
 1. St. John the Baptist Catholic Church (Cloutierville, Louisiana), "Registre de la Chapelle de Cloutierville, No. 1, 1825–29," entry 176, baptism of Marie Lina Metoyer; parish rectory, Cloutierville.
 2. Uxbridge Monthly Meeting (Uxbridge, Massachusetts), "Book of Records for Epistles, Certificates, Testimonies of Denial and Acknowledgements [1783–1811]," p. 24, disownment of Enoch Philips; New England Yearly Meetings of Friends, vol. 135; Friends Historical Library, Swarthmore, Pennsylvania.

Subsequent Note
11. St. John the Baptist Catholic Church (Cloutierville, La.), "Registre de la Chapelle de Cloutierville, No. 1," entry 176.
12. Uxbridge (Mass.) Monthly Meeting, "Book of Records for Epistles, Certificates, Testimonies of Denial [etc.]," p. 24.

ABBREVIATING THE NAMES OF REPOSITORIES

Researchers frequently shortcut their citations by using acronyms or initialisms for frequently cited libraries. When citing the Friends Historical Library, however, you may prefer not to use its initials, given the ubiquity with which *FHL* is applied to the Family History Library in Salt Lake City.

FHL-GSU Microfilm

When citing Family History Library microfilm of church records, you should first cite the original records in an appropriate format. Then you add the details that identify the film.

Source List Entry
Florida Conference. The Church of Jesus Christ of Latter-day Saints. "Record of Members, 1893–1943." LDS Church Archives, Salt Lake City, Utah. FHL microfilm 1,907. Family History Library, Salt Lake City.

First Reference Note
1. Florida Conference, The Church of Jesus Christ of Latter-day Saints, "Record of Members, 1893–1943," pp. 64–65, entry 1128, birth of Bertha Margaret Kuhle, 1906; FHL microfilm 1,907.

Subsequent Note
11. Florida Conference, The Church of Jesus Christ of Latter-day Saints, "Record of Members, 1893–1943," pp. 64–65, entry 1128.

7.14   Record Books, Cited by Series & Volume Numbers
See QuickCheck Model *for* CHURCH BOOKS: NUMBERED VOLUME

For simplicity, some church archives have consolidated their volumes into series, using numbers for individual registers—e.g., Marriage Register 1, Marriage Register 2, Burial Register 1, Burial Register 2, etc. When you cite these numbered registers, you do not place quotation marks around those generic (series) labels or the volume number. In the example below, the Source List Entry focuses on the series. Then each Reference Note refers to the specific numbered volume in that series.

Source List Entry

St. Mary's Church (Charlestown, Massachusetts). Baptismal Registers.
 Roman Catholic Chancery Office Archives, Brighton, Massachusetts.

First Reference Note

1. St. Mary's Church (Charlestown, Massachusetts), Baptismal
Book 1, p. 42, Mary Elizabeth Kane (1854); Roman Catholic Chancery
Office Archives, Brighton, Massachusetts.

Subsequent Note

11. St. Mary's Church (Charlestown, Mass.), Baptismal Book 1, p. 42.

7.15 Record Books, Sectioned

Many registers are multipurpose books. A Swedish parish register, for
example, may include a *husförhörslängd* (a parish survey akin to a
census) in the same volume with its registrations of christenings,
marriages, and burials. A Canadian register may include abjurations
in the same register with baptisms, burials, or marriages. Early
American registers may have separate sections for those who are free
and those who are enslaved. A register from Mexico or early South-
western parishes in the United States may include marital *diligencias*
(depositions of character witnesses as to the age, parentage, and
marital status of the bridal couple) in the same register in which the
priest reports having blessed the couple's exchange of vows.

Each section may be independently paginated. In some cases, the
section for one record type will run on the right-hand page from front
to back. Then the book will be flipped, and a different section will run
upside down in the other direction on the alternate pages.

However the book is arranged, your reference note should include the
exact title of the section, which you will cite in the same manner that
you cite a chapter within a book or an article within a journal. The
entry or page numbers that you record should also indicate whether
the numbers apply to the whole book or just to that section.

Source List Entry

St. John's Catholic Church (Tuscaloosa, Alabama). "A Marriage, Bap-
 tism, and Obituary Register Kept by the Rev. Patrick B. Hackett."
 Holy Spirit Parish Office, Tuscaloosa.
St. Peter's Parish (Wilmington, Delaware). "Baptisms and Confirma-
 tions, 1829–1849." Roman Catholic Chancery Office Archives,
 Wilmington.

First Reference Note

(*Citing a typical sectioned register*)

    1. St. John's Catholic Church (Tuscaloosa, Alabama), "A Marriage, Baptism, and Obituary Register Kept by the Rev. Patrick B. Hackett," Baptisms: p. 12, Mary O'Sullivan (1846); Holy Spirit Parish Office, Tuscaloosa.

(*Citing a two-sided register*)

    2. St. Peter's Parish (Wilmington, Delaware), "Baptisms and Confirmations, 1829–1849," Confirmations: unnumbered pp. 8–9, Albina Maria Cecilia Lawler (1847); Roman Catholic Chancery Archives, Wilmington. This is a two-sided register. Baptisms are recorded from one direction and separately paginated; confirmations are recorded from the other side and are unpaginated.

Subsequent Note

    11. St. John's Catholic Church (Tuscaloosa, Ala.), "A Marriage, Baptism, and Obituary Register Kept by the Rev. Patrick B. Hackett," Baptisms: p. 12.

    12. St. Peter's Parish (Wilmington, Del.), "Baptisms and Confirmations, 1829–1849," Confirmations: unnumbered pp. 8–9.

7.16   Record Books with Foreign Language Titles
See also 2.23

When the register uses a language other than the one in which you are writing and publishing (as with the San Antonio example below), you may want to add a translation of the title, following these guidelines:

- place the translation in parentheses immediately after the title that it translates;
- capitalize only the first word and proper nouns, if your translation is in English;
- do not italicize your translation, because the register is a manuscript, not a publication;
- do not place quotation marks around the translated words, because you are not quoting anything;
- include that translation in your Source List Entry and your First Reference Note;
- do not repeat the translation in Subsequent Notes.

Source List Entry

(*Untranslated title*)

St. Elizabeth's Catholic Church (East St. Louis, Illinois). "Registrum Defunctorum, 1904–1942." Archives of the Catholic Diocese of Belleville, Illinois.

(*Translated title*)
San Antonio de Valero Parish (San Antonio, Texas). "Libre en que se
    Assientanlos Bautismos de los Indios de esta Mission de S. Ant° de
    Valero" (Book in which there has been entered baptisms of the
    Indians attached to this mission of San Antonio de Valero). Catholic
    Archives, Archdiocese of San Antonio.

First Reference Note

(*Untranslated title*)
    1. St. Elizabeth's Catholic Church (East St. Louis, Illinois),
"Registrum Defunctorum, 1904–1942," p. 87, burial of Mary Hunt
(1923); Archives of the Catholic Diocese of Belleville, Illinois.

(*Translated title*)
    2. San Antonio de Valero Parish (San Antonio, Texas), "Libre en
que se Assientanlos Bautismos de los Indios de esta Mission de S. Ant°
de Valero" (Book in which there has been entered baptisms of the
Indians attached to this mission of San Antonio de Valero), section
Mission de Solano: unpaginated entry 15, X^{tobal} [Christobal] Rangel
(1712); Catholic Archives, Archdiocese of San Antonio.

Subsequent Note

    11. St. Elizabeth's Catholic Church (East St. Louis, Ill.), "Registrum
Defunctorum, 1904–1942," p. 87.
    12. San Antonio de Valero, "Libre ... Bautismos de los Indios de esta
Mission de S. Ant° de Valero," Mission de Solano: entry 15.

IDENTIFYING TYPE OF ACT OR EVENT

In note 1, the reference to the entry for Mary Hunt specifies the type
of event because the title of the register (which explicitly states that it
covers deaths) is not being translated. In note 2, the reader need not
be told that X^{tobal} Rangel's entry is a baptism. Although the title of the
section is a generic label that could cover all types of sacraments, both
the volume's title and its translation identify the type of record.

7.17   Records Created by Diocese

Most church records used by history researchers are generated at the
local level (parish, congregation, meeting, etc.). However, some
denominations have higher levels at which records are kept and can
sometimes be accessed. These records, in their original form, will
generally fit into Basic Format: Documents (archived), 3.14, as
illustrated below.

Source List Entry
Alexandria (Louisiana). Catholic Diocese. Dispensation Files. Chancery
    Office–Archives, Alexandria.

First Reference Note
   1. Jean Gamier Trichel–Marie Louise Aspasie Trichel, dispensation request, June 1877, unpaginated entry; "Marriage Dispensations, Campti, 1856–1876," Dispensation Files; Chancery Office–Archives, Catholic Diocese of Alexandria, Louisiana.

Subsequent Note
   11. Trichel-Trichel dispensation request, "Marriage Dispensations, Campti, 1856–1876," June 1877.

CITING ARCHIVED CHURCH BOOKS VERSUS FILES

In the examples at 7.12–7.16, the First Reference Note follows the basic format for *manuscript volumes*—that is,

AUTHOR, "TITLE" OR GENERIC LABEL, SECTION, PAGE, ENTRY; ARCHIVE, LOCATION

Here at 7.17, the record is a "loose item" in an archived file. Thus the First Reference Note follows the standard format for archived *documents*—from small to largest, i.e.,

ITEM ID, PAGE DATA, "DOCUMENT TITLE," COLLECTION; ARCHIVE, LOCATION

IDENTIFYING PARTIES IN THE SUBSEQUENT NOTE:

In the examples at 7.12–7.17, the name of the sacrament's recipient is not repeated in the Subsequent Note. In the Trichel-Trichel example above, it is. The difference is this: In the earlier examples, you are able to cite an exact page or entry number. In the Trichel example, neither the pages nor the entries are numbered; therefore the parties have to be named to identify the specific item of interest.

IMAGE COPIES

7.18   Church Record Books: Online Images
See QuickCheck Model *for* IMAGE COPIES: DIGITIZED ONLINE

Because the Internet is both a library and a marketplace, it offers image copies of church registers under a variety of conditions. The examples below cover two broad situations: (*a*) image copies offered without charge (by the church itself, by an individual at the network RootsWeb, and by a state archive); and (*b*) image copies available only by subscription. One other factor makes a difference in how the records are cited: whether the website offers images of the *complete* register or whether it offers images of page fragments from an *unidentified register.*

COMPLETE & IDENTIFIED REGISTERS

Source List Entry

(Posted by the church itself)
St. Lawrence Church (Oxhill, Warwickshire, England). Parish registers, 1568–1840. Digital images. *St. Lawrence Church Oxhill.* http://www .oxhill.org.uk/ChurchRegisters/Registers.htm : 2006.

(Posted at RootsWeb)
Shaver/St. Abrahams Lutheran Church (Beckleysville, Maryland). "Kirchen Buch der Evangelisch-Lutherischen Gemeinde an des Barnhardt Hambschers Schulhauss." Digital images. *USGenWeb County Site: Baltimore County, Maryland.* http://www.rootsweb.com/~md baltim/stabrahams/stabrahams.htm : 2006.

(Posted by the State Archives)
Oppland Parish (Sel, Sel, Norway). Death and Burial Records, 1905–19. Digital images. National Archives of Norway. *Digitised Parish Registers.* http://www.arkivverket.no/URN:kb_read : 2006.

First Reference Note

(Posted by the church itself)
1. St. Lawrence Church (Oxhill, Warwickshire, England), Banns of Marriage, 1754–1794, unnumbered p. 1, "Mr." Thomas Warde and Martha Rowley, marriage, 19 October 1574; digital images, *St. Lawrence Church Oxhill* (http://www.oxhill.org.uk/ChurchRegisters/Registers .htm : accessed 20 September 2006).

(Posted at RootsWeb)
2. Shaver/St. Abrahams Lutheran Church (Beckleysville, Maryland), "Kirchen Buch der Evangelisch-Lutherischen Gemeinde an des Barnhardt Hambschers Schulhauss" (Church book of the Protestant Lutheran Congregation at Barnhardt Hambscher's school house in Baltimore County 1805), p. 7, Lydia Schafer baptism, 1 February 1835; digital images, *USGenWeb County Site: Baltimore County, Maryland* (http://www.rootsweb.com/~mdbaltim/stabrahams/stabrahams .htm : accessed 20 September 2006).

(Posted by the State Archives)
3. Oppland Parish (Sel, Sel, Norway), Death and Burial Records, 1905–19, "Deaths" section, p. 139, Bernard Matias Pedersen entry, 5 September 1906; digital images, National Archives of Norway, *Digitised Parish Registers* (http://www.arkivverket.no/URN:kb_read : accessed 20 November 2006).

Subsequent Note
11. St. Lawrence Church (Oxhill, Warwickshire), Banns of Marriage, 1754–1794, unnumbered p. 1, Warde-Rowley, 19 October 1574.

12. Shaver/St. Abrahams Lutheran Church (Beckleysville, Md.), "Kirchen Buch der Evangelisch-Lutherischen Gemeinde," p. 7, Lydia Schafer baptism (1835).

13. Oppland Parish (Sel, Sel), Death and Burial Records, 1905–19, "Deaths" section, p. 139, Bernard Matias Pederson (1906).

IDENTIFYING TITLE OF VOLUME

In the examples above, the images from Shaver Church include the title page showing the exact title of the volume; therefore the exact title appears in the citation, enclosed in quotation marks. For the St. Lawrence and Oppland records, the title page is not shown. Only a generic description appears at the website for the digitized volume; therefore, that generic description appears in the citation without quotation marks.

UNIDENTIFIED & FRAGMENTED VOLUMES

The *Heritage Trail* website, below, provides page images from numerous volumes from multiple churches. For each church, images are filed under a generic label "Death Records" and then by year. The image collection does not show the book's cover. Some page images cover only partial pages. No image carries a formal citation of source. Each full page carries a preprinted heading, "Record of Interments," along with the printed page number. Because the pages are fragmented, it is not possible to determine whether the page heading represents the entire register or just the burial section.

Source List Entry

St. Paul Catholic Church (St. Paul, Oregon). "Record of Interments." Digital images. *Heritage Trail Press.* http://www.heritagetrailpress .com/Church_Records : 2006.

First Reference Note

1. St. Paul Catholic Church (St. Paul, Oregon), "Record of Interments [1909]," p.10, Adam Zorn burial; digital images, *Heritage Trail Press* (http://www.heritagetrailpress.com/Church_Records/parishes/ St_Paul_St_Paul_OR.cfm/ : accessed 18 September 2006), in "Death Records" module.

Subsequent Note

11. St. Paul Catholic Church (St. Paul, Ore.), "Record of Interments [1909]," p. 10, Adam Zorn entry.

7.19 Church Records: Photocopies of Individual Records

When you receive a photocopy of a register page or document—whether from an official or unofficial source—your citation should identify the channel through which you received it. The three examples below illustrate some of the variety your citations might have. Each of them reflects the degree of reliability you might give to that source, based upon the channel. Each case also presumes that you have only this one document from the cited church. When you have multiple documents from a church, your Source List Entry would not typically cite individual documents.

Source List Entry

Jagut, François. Burial record. 15 January 1699, Saint-Denis Parish (Île d'Oléron, France). Photocopy of page from unidentified register and archive. Supplied 4 September 1976 by Maurice Caillebeau, Poitiers.

New Bethel Baptist Church (Lowndes County, Alabama). "Minutes, 1828–1868." Photocopied page, with citation appended. Supplied 23 July 1984 by GeLee Corley Hendrix, CG, FASG, Greenville, South Carolina.

St. Louis Cathedral (New Orleans, Louisiana). Baptismal Book 2. Archives, Catholic Archdiocese of New Orleans. Certified photocopy dated 11 March 1978.

First Reference Note

1. François Jagut burial, 15 January 1699, Saint-Denis Parish (Île d'Oléron, France); photocopy of page from unidentified register and archive, supplied 4 September 1976 by Maurice Caillebeau of Poitiers.

2. New Bethel Baptist Church (Lowndes County, Alabama), "Minutes, 1828–1868," unpaginated entry, 21 November 1835, for dismissal of Isaac Leatherwood and wife Delilah; photocopied page, with citation appended, supplied by GeLee Corley Hendrix, CG, FASG, Greenville, South Carolina, 23 July 1984.

3. St. Louis Cathedral (New Orleans, Louisiana), Baptismal Book 2, p. 180, baptism of Marie Françoise Castel (1750); certified photocopy supplied 11 March 1978 by Alice Forsythe, Archivist, Catholic Archdiocese of New Orleans.

Subsequent Note

11. François Jagut burial record, 15 January 1699, Saint-Denis Parish (Île d'Oléron, France).

12. New Bethel Baptist Church (Lowndes Co., Ala.), "Minutes, 1828–1868," for 21 November 1835 dismissal of Isaac and Delilah Leatherwood.

13. St. Louis Cathedral (New Orleans), Baptismal Book 2, p. 180.

7.20   Church Records: Preservation Film

In the United States, most church registers are private records, not public ones. Consequently, many of the microfilming projects that involve church records are for preservation purposes only. When the register is in the custody of the original church, you have two basic elements to cite:

- the details that identify the original register and its creator;
- the details that identify the specific entry.

When you cite a register held off-site , you have another basic element:
- the details that identify the repository that holds the record book.

When you cite filmed registers, you have yet another element to include:
- the details that identify the film you are actually using.

The following illustrates two different situations: the Beardstown film, in which the preservation copy is archived informally by the diocese; and the Kaskaskia film in which the preservation copy is part of a formal archival series.

Microfilm (Archives, Preservation)

Source List Entry

(*Citing a named volume*)

St. Alexius Congregation (Beardstown, Illinois). "Register and Record of Baptisms, Marriages, Deaths of the R. Cath. Congregation, Beardstown, 1 Nov^br 1859—." Microfilm. Cathedral storage, Diocese of Springfield, Illinois.

(*Citing a series and numbered volume*)

Notre-Dame de L'Immaculée Conception Church (Kaskaskia, Illinois). Sacramental Registers. LAC microfilm C-2899. Library and Archives Canada, Ottawa.

First Reference Note

(*Citing a named volume*)

1. St. Alexius Congregation (Beardstown, Illinois), "Register and Record of Baptisms, Marriages, Deaths of the R. Cath. Congregation, Beardstown, 1 Nov^br 1859—," p. 149, baptism of Edward Grover Malloy (1888); microfilm, Cathedral storage, Diocese of Springfield, Illinois.

(*Citing a series and numbered volume*)

2. Notre-Dame de L'Immaculée Conception Church (Kaskaskia, Illinois), Register 1, p. 13, baptism of Pierre Chabot (1709); LAC microfilm C-2899, Library and Archives Canada, Ottawa.

Subsequent Note

11. Beardstown (Ill.) Congregation, "Register and Record of Baptisms, Marriages, Deaths of the R. Cath. Congregation, Beardstown, 1 Nov^br 1859—," p. 149.

12. Notre-Dame de L'Immaculée Conception Church (Kaskaskia, Ill.), Reg. 1, p. 13.

7.2 I   Church Records: Preservation Film (Duplicate Masters)

See also QuickCheck Model *for* CHURCH BOOKS: NAMED VOLUME … OFF-SITE

In many cases, the archival microfilm you find at a church repository will be preservation film made by the Genealogical Society of Utah. That agency gives one duplicate master to the archive that owns the material and places another at the Family History Library. Rarely will both repositories use the same film identification. If you use the film at the owner-repository, you should cite it by that facility's identification. If you use the Family History Library film, you will cite FHL film but you should also identify the owner repository.

The QuickCheck Model cross-referenced above cites Uxbridge Monthly Meeting records held at the Friends Historical Library. The examples below demonstrate how you would cite that same set of records if you used the archival film at the owner-library *versus* a citation to the film if you used the Family History Library copy. (See also 7.22 for another variation on citing this set of records.)

Microfilm (Archives, Preservation)

OWNER-LIBRARY COPY

(Church & series as lead elements in the Source List)

Source List Entry
> Uxbridge Monthly Meeting (Uxbridge, Massachusetts). New England Yearly Meetings of Friends, volume 135. Friends microfilm MS-NE-135. Friends Historical Library, Swarthmore, Pennsylvania.

First Reference Note
> 1. Uxbridge Monthly Meeting (Uxbridge, Massachusetts), "Book of Records for Epistles, Certificates, Testimonies of Denial and Acknowledgements [1783–1811]," p. 24, disownment of Enoch Philipps; New England Yearly Meetings of Friends, vol. 135; Friends microfilm MS-NE-135; Friends Historical Library, Swarthmore, Pennsylvania.

Subsequent Note
> 11. Uxbridge (Mass.) Monthly Meeting, "Book of Records for Epistles, Certificates, Testimonies of Denial [etc.]," p. 24.

MICROFILM (FHL-GSU COPY)

(Church & collection as lead elements in the Source List)

Source List Entry
> Uxbridge Monthly Meeting (Uxbridge, Massachusetts). Monthly Meeting Records, 1783–1898. Friends Historical Library, Swarthmore,

Pennsylvania. FHL microfilm 1,321–1,324. Family History Library, Salt Lake City, Utah.

First Reference Note
2. Uxbridge Monthly Meeting (Uxbridge, Massachusetts), "Book of Records for Epistles, Certificates, Testimonies of Denial and Acknowledgements [1783–1811]," p. 24, disownment of Enoch Philipps; Family History Library microfilm 1,324, item 3.

Subsequent Note
12. Uxbridge (Mass.) Monthly Meeting, "Book of Records for Epistles, Certificates, Testimonies of Denial [etc.]," p. 24.

USING INITIALISMS FOR LIBRARIES
In the example above, the two libraries have the same initials. Even when you routinely refer to Family History Library as *FHL* in your writings, in cases such as this it is best to write out in full the names of both libraries. That avoids ambiguity as to whose film number you are citing.

7.22 Church Records: Preservation Film (FHL Cataloging)
When you use preservation film at FHL, you will often note two things:

- there will be multiple registers on the same roll;
- FHL's cataloging label for that roll is a *generic* label that gives an overall description of the varied content of the roll. Rarely will it identify the precise name of each register on the roll.

In the preceding example for Uxbridge Monthly Meeting record, FHL microfilm 1,324 is cataloged as:

"Deaths and births, 1783–1881; Marriages, 1799–1896;
Denials and Acknowledgements, 1783–1898"

The film itself actually contains many separate items—not just three as the cataloging implies. FHL cataloging data is *generic* data created by the cataloger to *describe* the entire content of a roll of film

To identify the specific volume you have used, you should *copy the exact title that is on that specific register*. If the register has no title, then you should do one of the following:

- check the beginning frames for that register for identification of a repository and its series name and number; if none is found, then
- copy whatever data appears on the filmer's target at the start of that particular register of file.

If you use the whole span of registers from a particular parish or church, you may decide to use the FHL cataloging label in your Source List as a generic citation to the "collection" (the situation illustrated in note 2 under 7.21). If you do not use all the registers, you may change the generic citation to reflect what you actually use. However, in a Reference Note, you should identify the *exact* register in which you found your information. For example:

FHL-GSU Microfilm

Source List Entry

(Generic Source List Entry using FHL cataloging data for one roll)
Uxbridge Monthly meeting (Uxbridge, Massachusetts). Deaths and births 1783–1881; Marriages, 1799–1896; Denials and Acknowledgements, 1783–1898. Friends Historical Library, Swarthmore, Pennsylvania. Microfilm 1,324. Family History Library, Salt Lake City, Utah.

First Reference Note

1. Uxbridge Monthly Meeting (Uxbridge, Massachusetts), "Book of Records for Epistles, Certificates, Testimonies of Denial and Acknowledgements [1783–1811]," p. 24, disownment of Enoch Philipps; Family History Library microfilm 1,324, item 3.

Subsequent Note

11. Uxbridge (Mass.) Monthly Meeting, "Book of Records for Epistles, Certificates, Testimonies of Denial [etc.]," p. 24.

7.23   Church Records: Published Film

See also QuickCheck Model *for* IMAGE COPIES: MICROFILM PUBLICATION

When church records are filmed and sold as a publication, they are cited much the same as a conventional book citation (See Basic Format: Books, 12.3) . The main difference is that you will cite the number of rolls in the film publication, rather than the number of volumes in a book set.

The owner or creator of the original records will ordinarily be cited as the author/creator of the filmed records. If the title of the filmed collection contains the name of the congregation or diocese that is the creator and owner, then it is not necessary to create an author/creator field to repeat that identity. In the following example, the records were created by a diocese that was, at the time, called "Diocese of Louisiana and the Floridas," seated at New Orleans. That identity appears in the title of the film; hence, no author/creator needs to be cited.

Published Microfilm

Source List Entry

> *Records of the Diocese of Louisiana and the Floridas.* Microfilm publication, 12 rolls. Notre Dame, Indiana: Notre Dame University, 1967.

First Reference Note

> 1. *Records of the Diocese of Louisiana and the Floridas,* microfilm publication, 12 rolls (Notre Dame, Indiana: Notre Dame University, 1967), roll 1, arranged by date; see 4–9 June 1798, "Proceedings about the Burial of Diego Lazaga."

Subsequent Note

> 11. *Records of the Diocese of Louisiana and the Floridas,* roll 1, 4–9 June 1793, "Proceedings about the Burial of Diego Lazaga."

DERIVATIVES: COPIES & COMPILATIONS

7.24 Certificates (Baptism, Burial, Marriage, Membership, etc.)

See QuickCheck Model *for* DERIVATIVES: CHURCH-ISSUED CERTIFICATE

Certificates, which offer bits of information extracted from a register onto a standardized form, are not at all equivalent to photocopies of an actual register entry. You will want to differentiate between the certificates and the original records. The two types can differ radically in reliability, and certificates offer none of the original register's *context* that may be needed for analysis or further clues.

In most cases, a certificate will have been issued long after the fact—as demonstrated below. In other cases, a family has passed down a certificate given by the minister at the time the event occurred. In that case, the certificate would be cited as a family artifact.

In organizing a Source List, some researchers prefer to group church-issued certificates under the name of the church, either as a single item or as a collection of several from that church. Others prefer to group them under the name of the individual or family. The following examples illustrate all these options. Note 1 also demonstrates how to handle a certificate that does not cite the original record for you.

Source List Entry

(Church as lead element in source list)

> St. John the Baptist Catholic Church (Cloutierville, Louisiana). Sacramental Certificates, 1969–75. Privately held by [NAME, ADDRESS FOR PRIVATE USE].

(Certificate as lead element in source list)
Rogers-Morgan marriage certificate (1848 marriage). Issued 1971. St. John the Baptist Catholic Church (Cloutierville, Louisiana). Privately held by [NAME, ADDRESS FOR PRIVATE USE].

(Family collection as lead element in source list)
Rogers Sacramental Certificates, 1969–75. Various churches. Privately held by [NAME, ADDRESS FOR PRIVATE USE].

First Reference Note
1. St. John the Baptist Catholic Church (Cloutierville, Louisiana), Sacramental Certificates, 1969–75 (privately held by [NAME, ADDRESS FOR PRIVATE USE]), Rogers-Morgan marriage certificate (1848 marriage); issued 1971, citing no book or page number.

2. Rogers-Morgan marriage certificate (1848 marriage); issued 1971, St. John the Baptist Catholic Church, Cloutierville, Louisiana; privately held by [NAME, ADDRESS FOR PRIVATE USE].

3. Rogers Sacramental Certificates, 1969–75, privately held by [NAME, ADDRESS FOR PRIVATE USE]; Rogers-Morgan marriage certificate, (1848 marriage); issued 1971, St. John the Baptist Catholic Church, Cloutierville, Louisiana.

Subsequent Note
11. St. John the Baptist Catholic Church (Cloutierville, La.), Rogers-Morgan marriage certificate (1848), issued 1971.

12. Rogers-Morgan marriage certificate (1848), issued 1971.

13. Rogers Sacramental Certificates, 1969–75, Rogers-Morgan marriage certificate (1848), issued 1971.

7.25 Certified Transcriptions & Translations
Transcriptions or translations made by and certified by church personnel are cited much the same as the certificates, with a slight change of wording to indicate that you have the full text of the record rather than an abstract or extract.

Source List Entry
(Church as lead element in Source List)
St. Louis Cathedral (New Orleans, Louisiana). Certified transcripts and translations. Privately held by [NAME, ADDRESS FOR PRIVATE USE].

(Family name as lead element in Source List)
Charleville-Clarisen marriage entry, 1798. Certified translation issued 1937, St. Louis Cathedral, New Orleans, Louisiana. Privately held by [NAME, ADDRESS FOR PRIVATE USE].

First Reference Note
1. Charleville-Clarisen marriage entry (1798); certified translation issued 1937 by John Ray, Archivist, St. Louis Cathedral (New Orleans,

Louisiana), citing vol. 2, p. 120, entry 447; privately held by [NAME, ADDRESS FOR PRIVATE USE].

Subsequent Note
11. Charleville-Clarisen marriage entry (1798); certified translation issued 1937, St. Louis Cathedral (New Orleans).

7.26 Church Brochures, Newsletters, Newspapers, Etc.

Citations to published church periodicals such as newsletters and brochures for weekly services follow Basic Format: Newsletter Articles, 14.21. In the example below, note that the church's name and location are not given in the author's field. When citing periodicals, the sponsor of the periodical is considered to be the *publisher*. The *author's* field is reserved for those who write articles within the periodical. Note 1 below cites one of those articles, but no author is named in the publication; therefore, the author's field is not used in the citation.

Source List Entry
The Linary Lifeline. Weekly brochure. Linary Church of Christ, Crossville, Tennessee. 25 January 2002.

First Reference Note
1. "Our Members in the Military," *The Linary Lifeline*, weekly brochure, Linary Church of Christ (Crossville, Tennessee), 25 January 2002, p. 3.

Subsequent Note
11. "Our Members in the Military," *Linary Lifeline*, 25 January 2002, p. 3.

Online Edition, Church Brochure

Source List Entry
The Linary Lifeline. Weekly brochure. Issue 25 January 2002. Linary Church of Christ, Crossville, Tennessee. http://www.linary.com/bulletin.htm.

First Reference Note
1. "Our Members in the Military," *The Linary Lifeline*, weekly brochure, Linary Church of Christ (Crossville, Tennessee), 25 January 2002, p. 3; PDF image (http://www.linary.com/bulletin.htm).

Subsequent Note
11. "Our Members in the Military," *Linary Lifeline,* 25 January 2002, p. 3.

CITING DATE INFORMATION
When a periodical is reproduced online, you should identify the date of the periodical in the same format you would use for the printed edition. You need not cite the date it was posted online or the date on which you consulted the online edition, because the more meaningful publication date exists on the periodical itself.

CITING IDENTITY & LOCATION OF CHURCH
When a periodical's title would not be generally recognized—as with those issued by churches, organizations, etc.—you should add the name and location of the publisher immediately after the periodical's name. You may also need a one- or two-word identification of the type of periodical.

7.27   Church Databases

See QuickCheck Model *for* DERIVATIVES: CHURCH-RECORDS DATABASE ...

Your citation to online church-records databases will vary, depending upon whether you are citing one with open-access or one available only by subscription. The examples below illustrate each.

Online Databases

Source List Entry

Lalley, Joseph M., Jr. "Baptismal Records, Wilmington, Delaware." Database. *19th Century Immigrant Roots: Records for Wilmington, Delaware, USA, and Vicinity.* http://www.lalley.com : 2007.

Osborn-Ryan, Sharon. "Search the Catholic Church Records Index." Subscription database. *Heritage Trail Press.* http://www.heritage trailpress.com/Church_ Records/ccr_Search.cfm : 2006.

First Reference Note

1. Joseph M. Lalley Jr., "Baptismal Records, Wilmington, Delaware," database, *19th Century Immigrant Roots: Records for Wilmington, Delaware, USA, and Vicinity* (http://www.lalley.com : accessed 28 January 2007), entry for John Keeley, baptized 26 August 1888; citing St. Paul Church, Baptisms, December 1869–August 1893, p. 214.

2. Sharon Osborn-Ryan, "Search the Catholic Church Records Index," subscription database, *Heritage Trail Press* (http://www .heritagetrailpress.com/Church_ Records/ccr_Search.cfm : accessed 18 December 2006), entry for Adam Zorn, buried 1909; citing St. Paul Catholic Church, unnamed register, p. 10.

Subsequent Note
    11. Lalley, "Baptismal Records, Wilmington, Delaware," database entry for John Keeley, baptized 26 August 1888.
    12. Osborn-Ryan, "Search the Catholic Church Records Index," database entry for Adam Zorn, buried 1909.

At 7.18, Image Copies, Online, you will find a citation of the actual record to which the Osborn-Ryan database points. Note the following differences:

CITING AUTHORS/CREATORS
At 7.18, the author is the church because the church created the record book whose images appear at the website. In the two database examples above, the author is the website owner who created the database. The author of each database is *not* the church.

CITING VOLUME & PAGE
At 7.18, the actual book and page is cited because that webpage presents digitized images of the originals. In the two databases cited above, the webpage merely extracts a few details from the original record and tells you where to find the originals. Because you are using only the database, you cite that database. However, you will want to append a note to say what church, book, and page the database cites (i.e., the source of your source).

7.28   Church Directories & Histories
Church publications that are compiled in book form, such as parish histories and membership directories, are treated as publications or authored manuscripts, depending upon whether they have been published. The example below uses a Norwegian *bydebøk* (parish history) that has been published; thus it is cited in Basic Format: Books, 12.3. Unpublished histories would follow the Basic Format: Unpublished Manuscripts, 3.22.

Source List Entry
Rudjord, Kaare. *Oddernes Bydebøk*. Kristiansand, Norway: Kristiansand Kommune, 1968.

First Reference Note
    1. Kaare Rudjord, *Oddernes Bydebøk* (Kristiansand, Norway: Kristiansand Kommune, 1968), 23.

Subsequent Note
    11. Rudjord, *Oddernes Bydebøk*, 23.

7.29   Published Abstracts or Transcriptions

Published versions of sacramental records are cited like any book or article offering derivative records. Using the Basic Format: Books, 12.3, or Journal Articles, 14.16, would create such entries as these:

Source List Entry

(Book citation)

Chamberlayne, Churchill Gibson, transcriber. *Births from the Bristol Parish Register of Henrico, Prince George, and Dinwiddie Counties, Virginia, 1720–1798.* Richmond, Virginia: W. E. Jones, 1898.

(Article citation)

Houston, Jean Young. "Four and Twelve Mile Baptist Churches: Records, 1799–1859, Campbell County, Kentucky," *National Genealogical Society Quarterly,* volume 61 (March 1973): 40–46.

First Reference Note

(Book citation)

1. Churchill Gibson Chamberlayne, transcriber, *Births from the Bristol Parish Register of Henrico, Prince George, and Dinwiddie Counties, Virginia, 1720–1798* (Richmond, Virginia: W. E. Jones, 1898), 29, for Augustus Caesar.

(Article citation)

2. Jean Young Houston, "Four and Twelve Mile Baptist Churches: Records, 1799–1859, Campbell County, Kentucky," *National Genealogical Society Quarterly,* 61 (March 1973): 40–46.

Subsequent Note

11. Chamberlayne, *Births from the Bristol Parish Register,* 29.
12. Houston, "Four and Twelve Mile Baptist Churches," 40–46.

7.30   Recopied Registers

See QuickCheck Model *for* DERIVATIVES: CHURCH RECORD BOOK, RECOPIED

Many original church registers have been recopied as the older volumes deteriorated. In other cases, older sacramental entries were transcribed or abstracted into preprinted, form-type books when standardized registers became popular in the late-nineteenth and early-twentieth centuries. When you recognize that a volume is a copy rather than the original, you should note that point in your citation, because it affects the degree of reliance you might place on information from the register.

Source List Entry

St. John the Baptist Catholic Church (Cloutierville, Louisiana). Marriage Book 1 (Latin copy). Parish rectory, Cloutierville.

First Reference Note
    1. St. John the Baptist Catholic Church (Cloutierville, Louisiana), Marriage Book 1 (Latin copy), unpaginated, entry 72, Rogers-Morgan marriage (1848).

Subsequent Note
    11. St. John the Baptist Catholic Church (Cloutierville, La.), Marriage Book 1 (Latin copy), entry 72.

7.31 Typescripts of Registers

Typescripts are typically cited in Basic Format for Unpublished Manuscripts, 3.22, as illustrated below. When compilers are known, the Source List Entry is alphabetized under the name of the compiler. If no compiler is known and you want to ensure that the Source List Entry stays grouped with other materials from that church, you might use the name of the church as a surrogate author, placed in square editorial brackets.

Source List Entry
Young, Henry James, translator. "Register of York Springs Lutheran Church, Adams County, Pennsylvania." Typescript, 1939. York Historical Society, York.

First Reference Note
    1. Henry James Young, translator, "Register of York Springs Lutheran Church, Adams County, Pennsylvania" (typescript, 1939, York Historical Society, York), 95.

Subsequent Note
    11. Young, "Register of York Springs Lutheran Church," 95.

LDS GENEALOGICAL COMPILATIONS

7.32 Ancestral File

The Family Group Records Collection and related pedigree charts collected since 1978 by The Church of Jesus Christ of Latter-day Saints are combined into LDS's Ancestral File. Because these materials are created by individual LDS members and patrons of the Family History Library, you should identify the compiler of each individual item you cite. LDS itself is cited only as the creator of online databases drawn from these compiled records or as the publisher of the CD-ROM editions of these compiled records.

A style sheet for citing other LDS church collections and products, compatible with *Evidence* Style, is available from FHL. The examples here at 7.32–7.35 cover four of the most common collections.

CD-ROM Edition

Source List Entry
Ancestral File. CD-ROM database. Salt Lake City: The Church of Jesus Christ of Latter-day Saints, 1998.

First Reference Note
1. *Ancestral File,* CD-ROM database (Salt Lake City: The Church of Jesus Christ of Latter-day Saints, 1998), John Shick (FTLN-QK) and Mary Vandament (FTLN-RQ) family group record; submission no. AF95-100470, John Stuart Wammack, La Mesa, California.

Subsequent Note
11. *Ancestral File,* John Shick (FTLN-QK) and Mary Vandament (FTLN-RQ) family group record.

Online Database

Source List Entry
The Church of Jesus Christ of Latter-day Saints. "Ancestral File," database. *FamilySearch.* http://www.familysearch.org : 2007.

First Reference Note
1. The Church of Jesus Christ of Latter-day Saints [LDS], "Ancestral File," database, *FamilySearch* (http://www.familysearch.org : 19 January 2007), John Shick (FTLN-QK) and Mary Vandament (FTLN-RQ) family group record; submission no. AF95-100470, John Stuart Wammack, La Mesa, California.

Subsequent Note
11. LDS, "Ancestral File," database, *FamilySearch,* John Shick (FTLN-QK) and Mary Vandament (FTLN-RQ) family group record.

7.33   Family Group Records Collection
See also the discussion at 7.32.

Microfilm (FHL-GSU)

Source List Entry
The Church of Jesus Christ of Latter-day Saints. "Family Group Records Collection." Salt Lake City: Genealogical Society of Utah, 1993. FHL microfilm 1,394,430. Family History Library, Salt Lake City.

First Reference Note
    1. The Church of Jesus Christ of Latter-day Saints [LDS], "Family Group Records Collection" (Salt Lake City: Genealogical Society of Utah, 1993), FHL microfilm 1,394,430, Ludwig Shick (4H5R-VB) and Sary (PBLX-7b) family group record; submission no. AF83-112153, Mary Ann Cade, Hoopeston, Illinois.

Subsequent Note
    11. LDS, "Family Group Records Collection," Ludwig Shick (4H5R-VB) and Sary (PBLX-7b) family group record.

7.34   International Genealogical Index (IGI)

LDS's International Genealogical Index contains entries extracted from sundry sources. Some, such as the CD-ROM example below, represent genealogical compilations by members and library patrons. Others, such as the online database example, represent information extracted from original records. Given that *an index is not a record,* your citations to the IGI will usually be a temporary citation, pending access to whatever material the IGI entry cites. Therefore, your citation should also include an identity of that "source of the source" that you will need to pursue.

CD/DVD Edition

Source List Entry
International Genealogical Index. CD-ROM database. Salt Lake City: The Church of Jesus Christ of Latter-day Saints, 2000.

First Reference Note
    1. *International Genealogical Index,* CD-ROM database (Salt Lake City: The Church of Jesus Christ of Latter-day Saints, 2000), North American Region, entry for Orion Chase Shown, born 1877; citing FHL microfilm 452,104 (Endowments ... baptisms for the dead, 1943–1970, St. George Temple), reference no. 13849.

Subsequent Note
    11. *International Genealogical Index,* CD-ROM database, North American Region, entry for Orion Chase Shown, born 1877.

Online Database

Source List Entry
The Church of Jesus Christ of Latter-day Saints [LDS]. "International Genealogical Index." Database. *FamilySearch.* http://www.family search.org : 2007.

First Reference Note
    1. The Church of Jesus Christ of Latter-day Saints [LDS], "International Genealogical Index," database, *FamilySearch* (http://www.family search.org : accessed 19 January 2007), Continental Europe Region, entry for Anna Lissabeht Boeni, christened 31 May 1731, Berlingen, Thurgau, Switzerland; citing FHL microfilm 995,205 (Berlingen's Evangelisch Kirchenbuch records, 1604–1875).

Subsequent Note
    11. LDS, "International Genealogical Index," database, *FamilySearch*, Continental European Region, entry for Anna Lissabeht Boeni, christened 31 May 1731, Berlingen.

7.35 Pedigree Resource File

The LDS Pedigree Resource File is a linked database of ancestral data submitted through FamilySearch Internet Genealogy Service. Unlike the older Ancestral File and Family Group Records Collection, this file exists in digital format, online or via CD-ROM. As with those two earlier counterparts, the material is created by individual contributors, not LDS, and your citation should identify the individual who submitted the material.

CD/DVD Edition

Source List Entry
Pedigree Resource File. CD-ROM database. Salt Lake City: The Church of Jesus Christ of Latter-day Saints, 2001.

First Reference Note
    1. *Pedigree Resource File*, CD-ROM database (Salt Lake City: The Church of Jesus Christ of Latter-day Saints, 2001), disc 122, entry for Martin Tschudi (PIN 98522); submitted by Jeffery L. & Lola J. Galloway, The Woodlands, Texas.

Subsequent Note
    11. *Pedigree Resource File*, database, CD-ROM disc 122, entry for Martin Tschudi (PIN 98522).

Online Database

Source List Entry
The Church of Jesus Christ of Latter-day Saints [LDS]. "Pedigree Resource File," database. *FamilySearch*. http://www.familysearch.org : 2007.

First Reference Note

    1. The Church of Jesus Christ of Latter-day Saints [LDS], "Pedigree Resource File," database, *FamilySearch* (http://www.familysearch .org : 19 January 2007), entry for Martin Tschudi (PIN 98522); submitted by Jeffery L. & Lola J. Galloway, The Woodlands, Texas.

Subsequent Note

    11. LDS, "Pedigree Resource File," database, *FamilySearch*, entry for Martin Tschudi (PIN 98522).

INTERNATIONAL EXAMPLES

7.36 Special Issues

Regardless of the country or the type of church book, the essential elements to cite are usually the same. You will need to identify the

- *church:* by its formal name—"Chiesa [Church] di Santa Maria del Gesu, Gratteri, Sicily" not "Gratteri Catholic Church."
- *register:* by exact title —"Matrimoniorum Registrum, ad Mentem Patrum Concilii Provincialis Baltimorensis X"—or by series and volume number, such as Marriage Book 4.
- *entry:* by page or folio, entry number, or date and person receiving the sacrament, according to which system the register uses.
- *archive:* by its full name, city, and state or province.
- *film (or other media)*: if applicable.

If parts of the citation have words in a language other than the one in which you are writing—and if they are words that are not easily recognized in your language—it would be helpful to append, in square editorial brackets, a translation into your language. See, for example, the reference to "Chiesa [Church]" in the first bullet above.

Examples from the records of several countries are used in this section to demonstrate both the common pattern and the differences.

7.37 Canada

Most Canadian church registers, both Protestant and Catholic, can be cited using the basic formats shown in the QuickCheck Models. One common source for sacramental data from Canada's Catholic parishes is a compiled series called the *répertoires* (tables) that is available in several print and digital versions. Typical citations would follow these patterns:

Source List Entry

Charbonneau, Hubert, and Jacques Légaré, eds. *Repértoire des actes de baptême, mariage, sépultre et des recensements du Québec ancien* [Table of baptisms, marriages, burials, and census entries in old Québec]. 47 vols. Montréal: Presses de l'Université de Montréal, ca. 1980–1991.

First Reference Note

1. Hubert Charbonneau and Jacques Légaré, eds., *Repértoire des actes de baptême, mariage, sépultre et des recensements du Québec ancien* [Table of baptisms, marriages, burials, and census entries in old Québec], 47 vols. (Montréal: Presses de l'Université de Montréal, ca. 1980–1991), 1: 301, Galarneau-Greslon marriage (1689).

Subsequent Note

11. Charbonneau and Légaré, *Repértoire ... du Québec ancien,* 1: 301.

CD-ROM Edition

Source List Entry

Charbonneau, Hubert, and Jacques Légaré. *Repértoire des actes de baptême, mariage, et sépultre du Québec ancien, 1621–1799* [Table of baptisms, marriages, and burials in ancient Québec, 1621–1799]. Gaëtan Morin, ed. CD-ROM, vers. 2.0. Montréal: Université de Montreal, 2002.

First Reference Note

1. Hubert Charbonneau and Jacques Légaré, *Repértoire des actes de baptême, mariage, et sépultre du Québec ancien, 1621–1799* [Table of baptisms, marriages, and burials in old Québec, 1621–1799], Gaëtan Morin, ed., CD-ROM, vers. 2.0 (Montréal: Université de Montreal, 2002), entry 453333, baptism of Hélène Martin (1768).

Subsequent Note

11. Charbonneau and Légaré, *Repértoire des actes de baptême, mariage, et sépultre du Québec ancien, 1621–1799,* entry 453333.

Microfilm (Archival)

Source List Entry

(Citing specific parish, then volume by generic label, not exact title)
Saint-Basile Parish (Saint-Basile, New Brunswick). Parish Register, 1792–1838. Microfilm F1332. Provincial Archives of New Brunswick, Fredericton, Canada.

First Reference Note

1. Saint-Basile Parish (Saint-Basile, New Brunswick), Parish Register, 1792–1838, p. 5 *verso*, baptism of Suzanne Roy (1830); microfilm F1332, Provincial Archives of New Brunswick, Fredericton, Canada.

Subsequent Note
11. Saint-Basile (N.B.) Parish Register, 1792–1838, p. 5*v*.

Microfilm Publication (Drouin Collection)

Source List Entry
(Citing published collection by Author/Creator)
Institut Généalogique Drouin. *Drouin Collection* [Parish and Notarial Records]. Microfilm publication, 2,366 rolls. Montreal, Canada. Ca. 1940–50.

First Reference Note
1. Saint-Léonard Parish (Parent, New Brunswick), Parish Register, 1885–1906 (Book 2), p. 198, Lévéque-Corbin marriage (1896); *Drouin Collection,* 2,366 rolls (Montreal: Institut Généalogique, ca. 1940–50), roll 3135.

Subsequent Note
11. Saint-Léonard Parish (Parent, N.B.) Parish Register, 1885–1906 (Book 2), p. 198.

7.38   England

The examples in this section demonstrate citations to two types of Church of England registers that should be differentiated in your notes: parish registers and bishops' transcripts. As a rule, parish registers represent the original entries. Beginning in 1598, parish priests handcopied their registers periodically and sent those copies to their bishops or archdeacons, creating a collection now known as *bishops' transcripts.*

Many of England's ecclesiastical registers have been removed to county record offices where they may or may not be formally cataloged by the coding system represented below. Using the Egloshayle parish record as an example, the citation P52/1/1 denotes the following:

CATALOG REFERENCE CODE .... P52/ (*P* represents *Parish.* Some earlier catalogs use DDP52, wherein *DD* represents *Direct Deposit Registers*)

SERIES NUMBER 1/

PIECE (OR ITEM) NUMBER(S) 1

The Michaelstow example for bishops' transcripts illustrates an archival system used in some county record offices. The material is in loose-sheet form, rather than registers, chronologically filed within folders labeled by the year. However, the cited year is usually *not* the modern calendar year. It may be Old Style (Julian Calendar) year that ran from Ladyday (March 25th) of one year to the eve of Ladyday in the next year (March 24th). Occasionally, it will represent a year running from Easter of one year to Easter Eve of the next.

Source List Entry
Egloshayle Parish (Cornwall, England). Parish Registers, 1600–1680. Cornwall Record Office, Truro.

Michaelstow Parish (Cornwall, England). Bishops' Transcripts, 1677–1772. Cornwall Record Office, Truro.

First Reference Note
1. Egloshayle Parish (Cornwall, England), Parish Registers, vol. P52/1/1, p. 103, Mullis-Anney marriage (1656); Cornwall Record Office, Truro.

2. Michaelstow Parish (Cornwall, England), Bishops' Transcripts, vol. BT151/17, unnumbered 8th p., baptism of Catherine Mullis (1700); Cornwall Record Office, Truro.

Subsequent Note
11. Egloshayle Parish (Cornwall), Parish Register, 1600–1680, p. 103, Mullis-Anney marriage.

12. Michaelstow Parish (Cornwall), Bishops' Transcripts, unnumbered 8th p., baptism of Catherine Mullis.

IDENTIFICATION OF SPECIFIC ENTRY
If the text to which your note is attached identifies the two parties who are being married, you do not have to specifically repeat that identification in your reference notes unless

- the original record spells the names so differently from the consistent spelling you are using that you think the entry might not be recognized otherwise; or
- the volumes carry no pagination, as with Mullis above; or
- the pages are so disorganized or the entries so chaotic that a specific identification of the entry would help to relocate it.

FHL-GSU Microfilm
When you consult the microfilmed bishops' transcripts, you will usually find an arrangement in which the sheets appear to be part of an unpaginated register. Using Michaelstow as an example, a typical citation would be:

Source List Entry
Michaelstow Parish (Cornwall, England). Bishops' Transcripts, 1676–

1773 [1677–1804]. Cornwall Record Office, Truro. FHL micro-film 90,260, item 1. Family History Library, Salt Lake City, Utah.

First Reference Note
1. Michaelstow Parish (Cornwall, England), Bishops' Transcripts, 1676–1773 [1677–1804], unnumbered 8th p., baptism of Catherine Mullis (1700); FHL microfilm 90,260, item 1.

Subsequent Note
11. Michaelstow Parish (Cornwall), Bishops' Transcripts, 1676–1773, unnumbered 8th p., baptism of Catherine Mullis.

CORRECTING AN ERRONEOUS DATE ON A RECORD LABEL
The label to the filmed Michaelstow Bishops' Transcripts states that the series begins in 1676 and ends in 1773. However, the filmed material actually runs from 1677 through 1772, with random entries thereafter, running as late as 1804. In such a case, you would place the corrected dates in square editorial brackets after the dates that are being corrected.

CITING PARISH REGISTERS BY FHL CATALOGING DATA VS. ORIGINAL TITLE
If you use the whole span of registers from a particular parish, you may decide to use the FHL cataloging description in your Source List as a generic citation to all the separate books. However, when you cite one of the registers in a Reference Note, you must identify the exact register in which you found your information.

In the example below, FHL microfilm 588,456 offers nine different registers covering 321 years of baptisms, burials, marriages, and marriage banns from one particular church. The cataloging labels identify the church and the total years spanned, in this fashion:

> Church of England. Parish Church of Husbands-Bosworth. Parish registers, 1567–1888.

Each of the individual registers, however, covers different records and different dates. When you examine each item on the film, in order to decide the best way to cite the material, you will notice three separate situations:

- Some registers are titled.

- Some have no title, but carry an archival stamp that identifies the owner-repository and the archival cataloging number.

- Whether titled or stamped, each register is preceded by a target made by the filmers to identify the material being filmed.

Items 1, 3, and 5 on microfilm 588,456 are used here to illustrate the kind of vagaries you need to consider:

Item 1

ORIGINAL REGISTER TITLE .... None on cover or interior page

ARCHIVAL STAMP READS .... "Leics. Record Office, Acc. [Accession] No. DE-627/1"

LDS TARGET READS .... "Parish Registers for Husbands-Bosworth, volume 1, Baptisms, Marriages, Burials, Years 1567–1686"

Item 3

ORIGINAL REGISTER TITLE .... "Leics. Record Office, Acc. No. DE-627/3"

ARCHIVAL STAMP READS .... "Leics. Record Office, Acc. No. DE-627/3"

LDS TARGET READS .... "Parish Registers for Husbands-Bosworth, volume 2, Baptisms, Marriages, Burials."

Item 5

ORIGINAL REGISTER TITLE .... (A published form-type book with printed title) *A Register-Book for the Publication of Banns of Marriage, According to Act of Parliament of the Twenty Sixth of King George II* (London: Printed for Joseph Fox, Bookseller, 1754).

ARCHIVAL STAMP READS .... "Leics. Record Office, Acc. No. DE-627/5"

LDS TARGET READS .... "Parish Registers for Husbands-Bosworth, volume 5, Banns, Marriages, Years 1754 to 1799."

When a set of parish registers has this much inconsistency from one book to the next, you would look for a common element. In this case, the common element is clear: *All volumes have been cataloged by the Leicestershire Record Office under a uniform cataloging system.* That system uniformly identifies the three as

- Acc. No. DE-627/1
- Acc. No. DE-627/3
- Acc. No. DE 627/5

That archival identification is a logical one to choose for your identification of each volume, when working with the whole series. In the example below:

- the Source List uses a generic entry—one that identifies the parish, type of records, and entire span of years.

- the Reference Note also uses a generic label for the register, rather than the long title of the published form-book that might mislead readers into thinking that you used a published transcription of the register rather than one with manuscript entries. The generic label states the type of records and the span of years—followed by the Leicestershire archival identification for that volume.

For example:

Source List Entry

Husbands-Bosworth Parish (Leicester, England). Parish Registers, 1567–1888. Leicestershire Record Office, Leicester. FHL microfilm 588,456. Family History Library, Salt Lake City, Utah.

First Reference Note

1. Husbands-Bosworth Parish (Leicester, England), Register 5, Banns of Marriages, 1754–1799, p. 14, Burbige-Wilford banns, 1771; Acc. No. DE-627/5, Leicestershire Record Office, Leicester; FHL microfilm 588,456, item 5.

Subsequent Note

11. Husbands-Bosworth Parish (Leicester, Eng.), Register 5, Banns of Marriages, 1754–1799, p. 14.

QUOTATION MARKS AROUND REGISTER LABEL

Because you are using a generic label to identify the register, you should not put quotation marks around your own words.

7.39   France

Historic church records of France, all denominations, were secularized under the Revolutionary government in 1792. Those recorded acts of baptism, marriage, and burial then became France's *état-civil*—its official registry of births, marriages, and deaths.

Consequently, duplicates of pre-1792 parish registers may be found at various levels: one copy may be retained by the parish church; the other will be found in the municipal archive or the mayor's office, and a copy of one of these will typically be found at the departmental (state) archive. It may or may not be possible for you to discern whether the copy you are using is the true original or a post-1791 transcription, short of finding original signatures in the volume you are using.

Archival Copies (Manuscripts)

The examples below illustrate citations to sacramental registers held at three locations: the *ecclesiastical* copy at the church, the état civil copy at the municipal archive, and the *microfilmed état civil* copy at the departmental archive.

Source List Entry

(Church copy, citing the series)
Saint-Projet Parish (Bordeaux, France). Mariages et Sépultures [Burials], 1659–1792, Archives Municipales, Bordeaux.

(État civil copy, citing the series)
Notre-Dame Parish (Dijon, France). Baptismal Registers, pre–1792. Archives Municipales, Dijon.

(Departmental archive copy, citing specific volume)
Saint-Nicolas Parish (Saint-Nicolas, Diocese of Coutances). Burial Register, 1769–1791. Archives Départementales de la Manche, St.-Lo, France.

First Reference Note

1. Saint-Projet Parish (Bordeaux, France), Mariages et Sépultures [Burials], cote [register] GG 639, act 76, Durel-LeBrun marriage (1752); Archives Municipales, Bordeaux.
2. Notre-Dame Parish (Dijon, France), Baptisms, vol. 5, folio 109 verso, Françoise Poissot baptism (1708); Archives Municipales, Dijon.
3. Saint-Nicolas Parish (Saint-Nicolas, Diocese of Coutances), Burial Register, 1769–1791, p. 339, Marie Lemiére burial (1771); microfilm 1Mi EC26, roll 11; Archives Départementales de la Manche, St.-Lo, France.

Subsequent Note

11. St.-Projet Parish (Bordeaux), Mariages et Sépultures, cote GG 639, act 76, 1752 marriage.
12. Notre-Dame Parish (Dijon), Baptisms, vol. 5, folio 109*v*.
13. St.-Nicolas Parish (Diocese of Coutances), Burial Register, 1769–1791, p. 339.

IDENTIFICATION OF DIOCESE

For churches located in large cities such as Bordeaux and Dijon above, you will not need to cite the diocese to which they belong. For smaller cities and towns, particularly those with saint names that are duplicated many times across France (as with Saint-Nicholas Parish above), you should identify the diocese where the parish is located.

FHL-GSU Microfilm

The following example uses the previous Saint-Projet record to illustrate the difference between citing to the original church book (above) and citing to the microfilmed register (below).

Source List Entry

Saint-Projet Parish (Bordeaux, France). Mariages et Sépultures [Burials], 1659–1792. Archives Municipales, Bordeaux. FHL microfilm 1,692,446. Family History Library, Salt Lake City, Utah.

First Reference Note

    1. Saint-Projet Parish (Bordeaux, France), Mariages et Sépultures [Burials], cote GG 639, unpaginated act 76, Durel-LeBrun marriage (1752); FHL microfilm 1,692,446, item 5.

Subsequent Note

    11. St.-Projet Parish (Bordeaux), Mariages et Sépultures, cote GG 639, act 76, 1752 marriage.

CATALOGING DATA VS. SPECIFIC VOLUME

Researchers typically use multiple volumes from a parish. In the example above, the Source List Entry copies the FHL cataloging data for the 1659–1791 period because the researcher used all the volumes within that time frame. Thereafter, the Reference Notes cite the specific volume used.

SILENT TRANSLATIONS OF LABELS AND CATALOGING DATA

In the example above, FHL catalogs the record set in French:

Saint-Projet, Eglise Catholique.
Registres paroissiaux, 1659–1791.

When cataloging data is in a language other than the one you are writing in, you may prefer—in your Source List—to translate the label silently (i.e., without written comment) to create counterparts in your own language (e.g., "Catholic Church," "Parish Registers," or "Marriage Records").

7.40 Germany

German parishes offer two types of registers widely used by family history researchers. The first, *Kirchebüchen* (church books), are frequently subdivided according to the type—e.g.,

Familienbüchen	Family registers
Heiraten & Aufgeboten	Marriages and banns
Kommunionen	Communion
Konfirmationen	Confirmations
Seelen	Church membership rolls
Taufen	Baptisms
Toten (Todten) & Begräbnisse	Deaths and burials

To a lesser extent you can find *Familienbüchen* (literally, family books;

also known by the Latin *Libri de Statu Animarum*) in which families are assembled by household, akin to a genealogical summary.

The registers you cite might be held in the parish's *Kirchenarchives* (church archives), the town's *Standesamt* (civil records office), or the *Stadtarchiv* (state archives) that serves the region.

The examples below illustrate both Catholic (Katholische) and Protestant Evangelical (Evangelische) records, provided by the state archives or consulted on microfilm at the Family History Library. In both cases, the Source List Entry refers to the category of records, while the Reference Notes identify the specific volume or series.

Archival Copies

Source List Entry

(When citing records consulted at or provided by the state archives)
Saschsehausen Evangelische Kirche (Frankfurt, Germany). Taufen, pre-1808. Stadtarchiv, Frankfurt am Main.

(When citing records consulted at or supplied by the church itself)
Westhofen Katholische Kirche (Westhofen, Hessen, Germany). Taufen, 1780–1824. Parish rectory, Westhofen.

First Reference Note

(When citing records consulted at or provided by the state archives)
　　1. Saschsenhausen Evangelische Kirche (Frankfurt, Germany), Taufens [Baptisms], 1755, p. 9, Heinrich Matthias Hertzog baptism (1755); Stadtarchiv, Frankfurt am Main.

(When citing records consulted at or supplied by the church itself)
　　2. Westhofen Katholische Kirche (Westhofen, Hessen, Germany), "Liber Baptismals, Parochia Westhofiesis Mode Capitale Westhofiensis & Annexorum, Incipit ... 1780" [Baptisms beginning 1780], p. 109, baptism of Matthias Ruppert (1817); parish rectory, Westhofen.

Subsequent Note

　　11. Saschsenhausen Evangelische Kirche (Frankfurt), Taufen, 1755, p. 9.
　　12. Westhofen Katholische Kirche (Westhofen), "Liber Baptismals ... Incipit ... 1780," p. 109.

IDENTIFYING A FOREIGN-LANGUAGE REGISTER
The two registers above are handled differently because their titles differ in two significant regards:

- The Saschsenhausen register carries a series title and years (Births, 1755). These do not need to be placed in quotation marks.

- The Westhofen register has a complex title, but no series name or number. That title is copied exactly and placed in quotation marks. Much of the title simply repeats the name of the location, so the "translation" that accompanies the exact title could be just a generic identifier, rather than a complete translation.

IDENTIFYING THE EVENT

When citing a date in a baptismal or burial record, you should specify whether the date represents the date of birth or baptism, on the one hand, or the date of death or burial.

FHL-GSU Preservation Microfilm

The following example uses the previous Westhofen entry to illustrate a difference you may encounter between citing to the original church record book (above) and citing to the microfilmed register (below). On site, the book is identified by its original Latin title, shown in quotation marks in note 2 above. FHL's film of the register includes an image of that register's title. However, to locate the volume, you must use the German-language label created by the filmer. That label (a target filmed immediately before the book) ignores the actual title on the volume and identifies the volume by series (Taufen, Ehen, Tote—i.e., Births, Marriages, and Deaths), assigns a volume number, and adds inclusive dates.

The example below preserves the original Latin title (a clue to the language in which the entries are recorded) but adds the series data so the register can be more easily identified on the film.

Source List Entry

Westhofen Katholische Kirche (Westhofen, Hessen, Germany). Taufen, 1780–1824. Parish rectory, Westhofen. FHL microfilm 948,721, item 3. Family History Library, Salt Lake City, Utah.

Württ-ev-Landes Evangelische Kirche (Mönsheim, Stuttgart). Familienbüchen, vol. 9, 1771–. Pfarramt [Parish rectory], Mönsheim. FHL microfilm 1,056,677. Family History Library, Salt Lake City, Utah.

First Reference Note

1. Westhofen Katholische Kirche (Westhofen, Hessen, Germany), "Liber Baptismals, Parochia Westhofiesis Mode Capitale Westhofiensis & Annexorum, Incipit ... 1780 [Baptismal book, Westhofen Parish ... beginning 1780]," p. 109, Matthias Ruppert, 3 November 1817; filmed as Westhofen Catholic Church, Births, 1780–1824; FHL microfilm 948,721, item 3.

2. Württ-ev-Landes Evangelische Kirche (Mönsheim, Stuttgart), Familienbüchen [Family registers], vol. 9, 1771–, p. 44, family of Johann Georg Rogg (d. 1763) and wife Maria Catharina (d. 1755); FHL microfilm 1,056,677.

Subsequent Note

11. Westhofen Katholische Kirche (Westhofen), "Liber Baptismals ... Incipit ... 1780," p. 109, Matthias Ruppert.

12. Württ-ev-Landes Evangelische Kirche (Mönsheim, Stuttgart), Familienbüchen, 9: 44, family of Johann Georg Rogg (d. 1763) and wife Maria Catharina (d. 1755).

ALPHABETICAL ARRANGEMENTS IN EUROPEAN REGISTERS

The Familienbüch from Württ-ev-Landes illustrates a custom frequently found in early European registers: entries are alphabetized by the first letter of the *given* name (Christian name), not the *family* name (surname). In the Familienbüch above, the Johann George Rogg is not found by looking among families whose surnames begin with *R*. It is found among males who shared the given names *Johann George*—positioned after those with the given names *Johann Frederic* and before those with the given names *Johann Michael*.

DETAILS ESSENTIAL FOR IDENTIFICATION

When citing a family from a Familienbüch, you should include the names of both the husband and the wife, along with an identifying date for each. In many German communities, you will have multiple men of the same name and even multiple couples of the same names.

7.41   Mexico

The pair of examples below illustrates two types of common records. The first is an ordinary baptism. The second is a collection of marriage documents that some Catholic cultures maintained separate and apart from their marriage records. In the Tapalpa example, the collection is simply called "Marriage Information." Elsewhere, it is often called "Marital Inquisitions." Whatever the label, the typical file might include parental consents, depositions by witnesses attesting that the bride and groom were free to marry, and perhaps copies of baptismal records for the two parties.

The example below handles the translation of foreign-language titles differently from the example above at 7.36. The entry above identifies the source in its original language, then provides a translation. The example below uses the translation in lieu of the title in the Source List. As a bilingual researcher, you will set your own policy as to whether, when, and where to translate.

FHL-GSU Preservation Microfilm

Source List Entry

Santiago Apóstol Catholic Church (Monclova, Coahuila, Mexico). Baptisms, 1688–1750. Archivo, Diócesis de Saltillo. FHL microfilm 222,406, item 1. Family History Library, Salt Lake City, Utah.

Tapalpa Iglesia Católica (Jalisco, Guadalajara, Mexico). Informacion Matrimonial. Archivo, Arzobispado de Guadalajara. FHL microfilm 270,221. Family History Library, Salt Lake City, Utah.

First Reference Note

1. Santiago Apóstol Iglesia Católica (Monclova, Coahuila, Mexico), Bautismos, tomo 1-A [Baptisms, vol. 1-A], 1688–1750, unpaginated entry, 26 April 1697, Manuela Sanchez y Mascorro; FHL microfilm 222,406, item 1.

2. Tapalpa Iglesia Católica (Jalisco, Guadalajara, Mexico), Informacion Matrimonial, vol. 51, unpaginated, chronological, 5 March 1842, Margarito Ramirez y Eduarda Morales; FHL microfilm 270,221.

Subsequent Note

11. Santiago Apóstol Iglesia Católica (Monclova), Bautismos, 1688–1750, unpaginated entry, 26 April 1697, Manuela Sanchez y Mascorro.

12. Tapalpa Iglesia Católica (Jalisco), Informacion Matrimonial, vol. 51, unpaginated, chronological documents, 5 March 1842, Margarito Ramirez y Eduarda Morales.

7.42 Norway

The Lutheran Church has been the state church in Norway for nearly four centuries. Since 1812, its recordkeeping has been remarkably systematic. Preprinted registers (*kirkebøker*) have been kept by the ministers since then; and duplicate copies (*klokkerbøker*) have been made intermittently since that year by the parish clerks. Eighty years after the date of a *kirkebøk's* last entry, it is deposited at the State Archives (*statsarkivet*) that serves the parish. Each *klokkerbøk* is deposited there as soon as it is filled.

Citations to these registers will usually fit within the QuickCheck Models for CHURCH BOOKS, if you prefer that style over the one conventionally used in Norway. However, individual registers may not have a distinctive name. They may be identified (on their covers or inside flyleaves) only by their parish, the type of record(s), and the years they cover. You will also find differences in identification and cataloging, depending upon whether you use them at the *statsarkivet* or at FHL.

Regardless of where you use these records, if you understand Norway's archival cataloging system it will be easier for you to decide what specific details to include in your citations. You will also better understand the cryptic citations you may find in the work of other researchers.

When the 1812 decree was implemented, the two types of registers were initially coded as follows:

b   =   *ministerialbøker* (minister's books)
Kl b =   *klokkerbøker* (parish clerk's duplicates)

These codes may or may not appear on the cover or title page of the register you use.

Under Norway's present archival arrangement, church registers are coded into one of seven record groups:

TYPE CODE	TYPE OF REGISTER	ENGLISH TRANSLATION
M	*Ministerialbok*	Minister's book (see below)
K	*Klokkerbok*	Church clerk's duplicate copy
L	*Lysningsbok*	Bann book
FO	*Forlovererklæringer*	Engagement register
FR	*Fødelsregister*	Birth register
S	*Sjeleteregister*	Parish register, 1600s–1700s
D	*Diverse*	Various materials

Within this framework, individual *ministerialbøker* since 1812 have been divided into sections, with some variations. Typically, each section is paginated separately, so the section must be identified in a citation. Each section is also coded, and each page of a register carries the section code and one of the following section names as a header.

TYPE OF RECORDS	ENGLISH TRANSLATION
Døpte (levende fødte)	Christening (Live birth)
Dødfødte	Stillbirth
Ægteviede/exteskap/vigde/viede or *copulerede*	Marriage
Trolovelse	Engagement
Begravede/begravelse (Døde)	Burial (death)
Confirmerede/konfirmerte or *Konfirmasjon*	Confirmation
Vaksinnerte/vaccinerede or *Vaksinasjon*	Vaccination
Innflyttede	Arrival in parish
Uttflyttede	Removal from parish

Thus, if you consult a particular register for Fet Parish, Akershus County, at the Oslo *statsarkivet*, you might find it identified as, say,

TYPE	CATALOG NO.	YEARS	CONTENT	FILM NO.
M	I 12A	1860–66	Konf., Vigde, Døde, Flyttede, Vaksinerte	NO-102

From this, some researchers may cryptically cite a death entry as

M I 12A: Døde, p. 8

meaning:

Fet Prestgejeld [Clerical District], Akershus County, Ministerial Book I 12A, Deaths, p. 8.

However, if you use this same register at the Family History Library, you will find that the cataloging system differs in two ways:

- For the most part, only the *M* and *K* registers have been filmed. However, the film numbers assigned by FHL to these two series are not those of the Norwegian *statsarkivet*.

- The targets or "title boards" that are filmed at the start of each register to identify the contents will carry the *statsarkivet* catalog number, but not the *type* of register.

As a comparison, consider the following citations to another Fet register:

LOCATION	REGISTER ID	TIME SPAN	CONTENTS	FILM NO.
Statsarchivet	M I 10A	1851–1859	Vaksinerte	NOR1-168
FHL	Kirkebøk 10A	1851–1859	Vaksinerte	1,282,652, item 4

Within your research notes, typical citations would be these:

Microfilm (FHL-GSU vs. Norwegian Archives Copies)

Source List Entry

(*If used at the Statsarkivet, Oslo*)
Fet Clerical District (Akershus County). Vaccination records, 1851–1859. Microfilm NOR 1-168. Statsarkivet, Oslo, Norway.

(*If used at the FHL*)
Fet Clerical District (Akershus County, Norway). Vaccination records, 1851–1859. Statsarkivet, Oslo. FHL microfilm 1,282,652, item 4. Family History Library. Salt Lake City, Utah.

First Reference Note

(*Statsarkivet, Oslo*)
1. Fet Clerical District (Akershus County), vol. M I 10A, Section F, Vaccinerede [Vaccinations], unpaginated, entry 94, 3 August 1855,

Otto Pedersen; microfilm NOR 1-168, Statsarkivet, Oslo, Norway.

(FHL)
    1. Fet Clerical District (Akershus County, Norway), vol. M I 10A, Section F, Vaccinerede [Vaccinations], unpaginated, entry 94, 3 August 1855, Otto Pedersen; FHL microfilm 1,282,652, item 4.

Subsequent Note
    11. Fet Clerical District (Akershus Co.), vol. M I 10A, Section F, Vaccinerede [Vaccinations], entry 94.

In other cases, your Norwegian register may have an exact title that is more explicit than the catalog codes. Given that explicit titles are more descriptive than cryptic codes, whose numbers are easily mistyped, you may wish to include the exact title in your citation. The following example from one FHL filmed register illustrates how to incorporate that exact title into the citation:

Source List Entry
Tomter Anex (Romedal Parish, Hedmark County, Norway). Ministerial records, 1861–1869. FHL Microfilm 124,366, item 4. Family History Library. Salt Lake City, Utah.

First Reference Note
    1. Tomter Anex , "Ministerialbog for Tomter Anex, Begyndt [Beginning] 1ste January 1861," Romedal Klokkerbøk 11, p. 28, entry 51, Helmer Kristoffersen christening (1867); FHL microfilm 124,366, item 4.

Subsequent Note
    11. Tomter Anex, "Ministerialbog for Tomter Anex, Begyndt 1ste January 1861," p. 28.

Online Images
See Church Record Books: Online Images, 7.18.

7.43   Scotland
See QuickCheck Model *for* IMAGE COPIES: MICROFILM, FHL-GSU ...

The series known as "Old Parochial Registers" (OPR) is a major source for history researchers working prior to the 1855 enactment of Scotland's civil vital-registration system known as *Statutory Registers.* Existing sporadically and randomly back to 1553, the OPR are often consulted—even in Scotland itself—via the microfilm produced by the Family History Library. The entries below cover not only that film but on-site use of the original register and official extracts provided by the General Register Office for Scotland (GROS).

The cataloging system used by GROS for its centralized records assigns a set of codes conventionally used *in lieu of the titles* that may be on the original records. In the example below, the code "OPR 222/1" represents the following:

OPR	=	Record Group ID (Old Parochial Registers)
222/	=	OPR Code for Midmar Parish, Aberdeenshire
1	=	Volume (Births 1717–1820; Marriages 1718–1824)

Original Registers

Source List Entry
Midmar Parish (Aberdeenshire, Scotland). Old Parish Registers, 1717–1824. General Register Office for Scotland, Edinburgh.

First Reference Note
1. Midmar Parish (Aberdeenshire, Scotland), Old Parish Registers, OPR 222/1, p. 65, James Edward baptism (1727); General Register Office for Scotland, Edinburgh.

Subsequent Note
11. Midmar Parish (Aberdeenshire), OPR 222/1, p. 65.

Microfilm (FHL-GSU)
When you use the filmed registers at the Family History Library, you should find the OPR number on the target at the first of each roll of microfilm.

Source List Entry
Midmar Parish (Aberdeenshire, Scotland). Old Parish Registers, 1717–1824. FHL microfilm 993,344, item 1. Family History Library, Salt Lake City, Utah.

First Reference Note
1. Midmar Parish (Aberdeenshire, Scotland), Old Parish Registers OPR 222/1, p. 65, James Edward baptism (1727); FHL microfilm 993,344, item 1.

Subsequent Note
11. Midmar Parish (Aberdeenshire), OPR 222/1, p. 65.

Online OPR Database
The database below is an official site of the government of Scotland,

created as a partnership between the GROS, the National Archives of Scotland, and the Court of the Lord Lyon. While most government sites credit a particular agency as author, the complexity of citing all three agencies and the fact that this is an official government project justify using only "Scotland" itself as the author.

Most history researchers who use this site will use many of the databases at this website, not just one. Therefore, you may wish to use the website as your Master Source, rather than the database.

Source List Entry

(Database as Master Source)
Scotland. "Search Old Parish Registers (OPR) Births/Christenings (1553–1854)." Database. *ScotlandsPeople.* http://www.scotlands people.gov.uk : 2007.

(Website as Master Source)
Scotland. *ScotlandsPeople.* Databases. http://www.scotlandspeople .gov.uk : 2007.

First Reference Note

1. Scotland, "Search Old Parish Registers (OPR) Births/Christen-ings (1553–1854)," database, *ScotlandsPeople* (www.scotlandspeople .gov.uk : accessed 30 January 2007), entry for James Edward baptism, 1 May 1727, Midmar Parish.

Subsequent Note

11. Scotland, "Search Old Parish Registers," *ScotlandsPeople*, entry for James Edwards baptism, 1 May 1727, Midmar Parish.

Transcribed or Abstracted Scottish Registers

Registers that have been transcribed are cited differently from the original registers. They are a different product, produced by a different person. If you consult them in manuscript form, you cite them as a Recopied Register (7.30) or Typescript (7.31). If you consult a published transcription, then you cite it in the customary form for its particular kind of media—i.e., print (book or article), CD, DVD, online, etc.

The following example illustrates the citation of a transcript prepared like a book but published on CD-ROM in PDF format. In analyzing the example, note three points:

•   The pages of the transcript are not numbered. Instead, entries appear in original order, cited by their original folio numbers.

That folio number is essential to your citation.

- The page/folio field of the citation does not simply state "folio 7 *verso.*" Rather, it states "entry at *original* folio 7 *verso.*" The first phrasing, if it were used here, would imply that you meant folio 7 (or the 7th leaf) of the *transcribed* edition, rather than folio 7 of the original.

- The compiler also identifies the original register by its OPR designation, as well as the microfilm frame numbers on the preservation film made of the original register. The OPR identity and frame numbers are not essential in the sense that they would be needed to relocate an entry on the CD-ROM. However, they would be needed to relocate the entry in the original parish register or on the film. Including this additional data (the source of your source) would make your citation more useful.

CD/DVD Edition

Source List Entry
Nicol, Norman Douglas, transcriber. *Maryculter, Kincardineshire: The Church of Scotland Parish Registers, 1696–1855.* CD-ROM edition. PDF format. Aberdeen, Scotland: Aberdeen & North East Scotland Family History Society, 2004.

First Reference Note
1.   Norman Douglas Nicol, transcriber, *Maryculter, Kincardineshire: The Church of Scotland Parish Registers, 1696–1855,* CD-ROM ed., PDF format (Aberdeen, Scotland: Aberdeen & North East Scotland Family History Society, 2004), entry at original folio 7 *verso*, Robert Strachan (1699); citing OPR 264, General Register Office for Scotland, and frame 36 of FHL microfilm 993,321.

Subsequent Note
11.   Nicol, *Maryculter, Kincardineshire*, entry at folio 7*v*, Robert Strachan.

7.44   Spain
Sacramental *libros* (books) or *registros* (registers) in Spain are, for the most part, still held by the parish churches, although some have been removed to the diocesan archive for safeguarding. Very few have been filmed at this writing.

In comparing the format of the Barcelona and Cée citations below, you will note differences due to the fact that the Barcelona record comes from an archive, while the Cée entry is from the parish church itself. By way of comparison, consider the elements of the Source List Entry for Barcelona and Cée.

TYPE OF ELEMENT	BARCELONA ENTRY	CÉE ENTRY
Largest place	Spain	Spain
Province	*	La Coruña
Municipality	Barcelona	Cée
Identity of archive	Diocesan archive	**
Parish	Santa Cruz Cathedral	Santa María Parish
Collection	Registros de Matrimonios	Libros de Entierros

*   The province need not be named for Barcelona, since it is a major city. The province is cited for Cée, as a village, because names of towns and villages are often repeated across many provinces.

**   No archive is named for Cée; the records are held by the parish church.

Source List Entry
Santa Cruz Cathedral Parish (Barcelona, Spain). Registros de Matrimonios, 1740–44. Archivo Diocesano, Barcelona.
Santa María Parish (Cée, La Coruña Province, Spain). Libros de Entierros [Burial Books], 1700–1900. Parish rectory, Cée.

First Reference Note
1. Santa Cruz Cathedral Parish (Barcelona, Spain), Registros de Matrimonios [Marriage Registers], 1740–44, folio 501, Tomasino-Soler marriage (1743); Archivo Diocesano, Barcelona.
2. Santa María Parish (Cée, La Coruña Province, Spain), Burial Book 2, p. 306, Joséfa de Lema burial (1739); parish rectory, Cée.

Subsequent Note
11. Santa Cruz Cathedral Parish (Barcelona), Matrimonios, 1740–44, folio 501, Tomasino-Soler marriage entry.
12. Santa María Parish (Cée), Burial Book 2, p. 306.

7.45   Sweden
Historically, Swedish parishes (*församling* or *socken*) have maintained nine types of material variously called *böcker* (books) or *längder* (registers, rolls, or lists) that are of particular value to history researchers. In the late 1800s, the nation adopted a uniform system for coding these, and that system is used in each parish archive.

ARCHIVE CODE	TYPE OF REGISTER	ENGLISH TRANSLATION
AI	*Husförhörslängder*	Clerical-survey records
B	*Utflyttningslängder*	Removal records

	Inflyttningslängder	Arrival records
C	*Födelse-* & *Doplängder*	Birth and christening registers
DI	*Kommunionlängder*	Communion lists (first communion)
DII	" "	Communion lists (other than first)
E	*Lysnings-* & *Vigsellängder*	Bann and marriage registers
F	*Döds-* & *Begravningslängder*	Death and burial registers
G	*Avlösningslängder*	Church punishment registers
H	*Flyttningsattest*	Original certificates of removal
	Flyttningsbevis	Exit permits for those going abroad

Microfilm (FHL-GSU)

Citations to the filmed registers typically used by researchers would follow the pattern provided below for *husförhörslängder*. This record type (commonly shortened to HFL in Swedish citations) is more akin to a census than a sacramental register, but the structure of the citation is the same.

Source List Entry
Järna Parish (Dalarnas County, Sweden). Husförhörslängder (Clerical surveys), 1848–1857. Riksarkivet, Stockholm. FHL microfilm 202,853, item 3. Family History Library, Salt Lake City, Utah.

First Reference Note
1. Järna Parish (Dalarnas County, Sweden), Husförhörslängder (Clerical surveys), 1848–1857, vol. AI:13:c, p. 123, Westgård farm, household of Blom Lars Olsson; FHL microfilm 202,853, item 3.

Subsequent Note
11. Järna Parish, 1848–1857, Husförhörslängder, HFL AI:13:c, p. 123, Westgård farm, household of Blom Lars Olsson.

LOCAL & STATE RECORDS

Courts & Governance

8

QuickCheck Models

(See Chapters 9 and 10 for related models)

Guidelines & Examples <inline>(beginning page 383)</inline>

QuickCheck Model
ORIGINAL RECORDS: LOCAL
CASE FILES
Jurisdiction & series as lead elements in Source List

Source List Entry

JURISDICTION	SERIES	REPOSITORY

Florida. Escambia County. Circuit Court Files, 1830–1840. Circuit Clerk's Office,

REPOSITORY
LOCATION
Pensacola.

First (Full) Reference Note

JURISDICTION	SERIES	FILE NO.	...

1. Escambia County, Florida, Circuit Court File 2638-CA-01, L. C.

CASE LABEL	ITEM OF INTEREST ...

Hubbell v. Peter de Alba, for "Reply of Loring C. Hubbell and Emilie, His

...	RECORD DATE	REPOSITORY	REPOSITORY LOCATION

Wife," 1 June 1831; Circuit Clerk's Office, Pensacola.

Subsequent (Short) Note

JURISDICTION	SERIES	FILE NO.	CASE LABEL ...

11. Escambia Co., Fla., Circuit Court File 2638-CA-01, Hubbell v.

(SHORTENED)	ITEM OF INTEREST	RECORD DATE

de Alba, Reply of Hubbell and Wife, 1 June 1831.

QuickCheck Model
ORIGINAL RECORDS: LOCAL
RECORD BOOKS
Jurisdiction & series as lead elements in Source List

Source List Entry

JURISDICTION   SERIES ...

Massachusetts. Hampshire County. Court of Common Pleas Record Books,

                                                      REPOSITORY

...   REPOSITORY   LOCATION

1783–1853. Superior Court Clerk's Office, Northampton.

First (Full) Reference Note

             JURISDICTION   SERIES

1. Hampshire County, Massachusetts, Court of Common Pleas

                                           RECORD

SPECIFIC VOLUME: PAGE   CASE LABEL and/or ITEM OF INTEREST   DATE

Record Book U:218, Benjamin Sibley v. Samuel Hemingway, 1794;

                                REPOSITORY

             REPOSITORY   LOCATION

Superior Court Clerk's Office, Northampton.

Subsequent (Short) Note

        JURISDICTION   SERIES   SPECIFIC VOL. ...

11. Hampshire Co., Mass., Court of Common Pleas Record Book

... & PAGE

U:218.

QuickCheck Model
ORIGINAL RECORDS: LOCAL
RECORD BOOKS, ARCHIVED OFF-SITE
Jurisdiction & series as lead elements in Source List

Source List Entry

JURISDICTION	SERIES	...

New Mexico. Colfax County. District Court Civil Dockets, 1869–1900. History

... REPOSITORY	REPOSITORY LOCATION

Library Museum of New Mexico, Santa Fe.

First (Full) Reference Note

JURISDICTION	SERIES	SPECIFIC VOLUME

1. Colfax County, New Mexico, District Court Civil Docket, 1869–1882,

PAGE or COURT TERM (IF UNPAGINATED)	CASE LABEL and/or ITEM OF INTEREST

unpaginated, April Term 1869, case 16, State v. Samuel Cawker;

REPOSITORY	REPOSITORY LOCATION

History Library Museum of New Mexico, Santa Fe.

Subsequent (Short) Note

JURISDICTION	SERIES	SPECIFIC VOLUME	PAGE ...

11. Colfax Co., N.M., District Court Civil Docket, 1869–1882, unpagi-

... OR COURT TERM	CASE and/or ITEM

nated, April Term 1869, case 16.

QuickCheck Model
ORIGINAL RECORDS: STATE-LEVEL
APPEALS COURT RECORD BOOKS
State & series as lead elements in Source List

Source List Entry

JURISDICTION   SERIES   SERIES NO. ...

Maryland. Court of Appeals Judgments. MSA no. S381-4, Accession

...   REPOSITORY   REPOSITORY LOCATION

no. 683-6. Maryland State Archives, Annapolis.

First (Full) Reference Note

JURISDICTION   SERIES   SPECIFIC BOOK: PAGE   ...

1. Maryland, Court of Appeals Judgments, Book 33: 1–10, Joseph

CASE LABEL and/or ITEM OF INTEREST   RECORD DATE   ARCHIVAL ID ...

Ruppert v. City of Baltimore, April 1865; MSA no. S381-4, accession

...   REPOSITORY   REPOSITORY LOCATION

no. 683-6, Maryland State Archives, Annapolis.

Subsequent (Short) Note

JURISDICTION   SERIES   SPECIFIC BOOK: PAGE   ...

11. Maryland, Court of Appeals Judgments, Book 33:1–10, Ruppert

CASE and/or ITEM   RECORD DATE

v. Baltimore, April 1865.

QuickCheck Model
ORIGINAL RECORDS: STATE-LEVEL
LEGISLATIVE PETITIONS & FILES

State & series as lead elements in Source List

Source List Entry

JURISDICTION	SERIES	RECORD GROUP	REPOSITORY ...

Tennessee. Legislative Petitions. Record Group 50. Tennessee State

...	REPOSITORY LOCATION

Library and Archives, Nashville.

First (Full) Reference Note

ITEM OF INTEREST ...

1. Citizens of Cannon County, Request for Annexation to DeKalb

...	RECORD DATE	SERIES	ARCHIVAL ID or ARRANGEMENT

County, 10 October 1845; Legislative Petitions (chronologically arranged),

RECORD GROUP NO.	REPOSITORY	REPOSITORY LOCATION

Record Group 50; Tennessee State Library and Archives, Nashville.

Subsequent (Short) Note

ITEM OF INTEREST ...

11. Citizens of Cannon County, Request for Annexation to DeKalb

...	RECORD DATE	SERIES	JURISDICTION

County, 10 October 1845; Legislative Petitions, Tennessee.

QuickCheck Model
IMAGE COPIES: CD/DVD
Jurisdiction & series as lead elements in Source List

Source List Entry

JURISDICTION	SERIES	ITEM TYPE or FORMAT

Tennessee. Bedford County. Chancery Court Records. Digital images.

PUBLICATION TITLE ...

Bedford County, Tennessee, Chancery Court Records, Volume 1, Part 1, 1830–

PUBLICATION FORMAT	PUBLICATION PLACE	PUBLISHER	YEAR

1842. CD-ROM. Denver, Colorado: GSC Associates, ca. 2005.

First (Full) Reference Note

JURISDICTION	SERIES	SPECIFIC VOLUME	PAGE(S) or TERM

1. Bedford County, Tennessee, Chancery Court Records 1: 222–24;

CASE LABEL and/or ITEM OF INTEREST	ITEM TYPE or FORMAT ...

Martha A. Cooper v. Abram B. Cooper, divorce; digital images, *Bedford*

... PUBLICATION TITLE

County, Tennessee, Chancery Court Records, Volume 1, Part 1, 1830–1842,

PUBLICATION FORMAT	PUBLICATION PLACE	PUBLISHER	YEAR

CD-ROM (Denver, Colorado: GSC Associates, ca. 2005).

Subsequent (Short) Note

JURISDICTION	SERIES	SPECIFIC VOLUME	PAGE(S) or TERM

11. Bedford County, Tenn., Chancery Court Records 1: 222–24,

CASE LABEL or ITEM

Cooper v. Cooper.

QuickCheck Model
IMAGE COPIES: MICROFILM
ARCHIVAL PRESERVATION COPY

Loose documents—jurisdiction & series as lead elements in Source List

Source List Entry

JURISDICTION	SERIES

Louisiana. Natchitoches. Miscellaneous Archive Records, 1733–1820.

FILM ID	REPOSITORY	REPOSITORY LOCATION

LSA microfilm F.T. 565. Louisiana State Archives, Baton Rouge.

First (Full) Reference Note

CASE ID or ITEM OF INTEREST	RECORD DATE	...

1. Mariotte, f.w.c. v. Bertrand Mailloche, 11 October 1794, Miscella-

... SERIES	ARCHIVAL ID or ARRANGEMENT	RECORD REPOSITORY

neous Archive Records, 1733–1820, unarranged papers; Clerk of Court's

... JURISDICTION/ REP'Y LOCATION	FILM ID	FRAME NOS.

Office, Natchitoches, Louisiana; LSA microfilm F.T. 565, frames 486–87,

FILM REPOSITORY	REPOSITORY LOCATION

Louisiana State Archives, Baton Rouge.

Subsequent (Short) Note

ITEM OF INTEREST	RECORD DATE	...

11. Mariotte, f.w.c. v. Bertrand Mailloche, 11 October 1794, Miscel-

... SERIES	JURISDICTION

laneous Archive Records, 1733–1820, Natchitoches.

QuickCheck Model
IMAGE COPIES: MICROFILM
FHL-GSU PRESERVATION COPY

Bound volume—jurisdiction & series as lead elements in Source List

Source List Entry

JURISDICTION   SERIES ...

England. Cornwall. Week St. Mary. Overseer's Accounts, 1710–42.

RECORD REPOSITORY   REPOSITORY LOCATION   FILM ...

Cornwall County Record Office, Truro. FHL microfilm 1,597,004,

... ID   FILM REPOSITORY   FILM REP'Y LOCATION

item 3. Family History Library, Salt Lake City, Utah.

First (Full) Reference Note

JURISDICTION   SERIES

1. Week St. Mary, Cornwall, England, Overseer's Accounts, 1710–42,

PAGE, ARRANGEMENT or ARCHIVAL I.D   ITEM OF INTEREST ...

unpaginated, chronologically arranged; see 22 April 1731 account of John

...   RECORD REPOSITORY   REPOSITORY LOCATION   FILM ID ...

Colwill Jr.; Cornwall County Record Office, Truro; FHL microfilm 1,597,004,

...

item 3.

Subsequent (Short) Note

JURISDICTION   SERIES

11. Week St. Mary, Cornwall, Eng., Overseer's Accounts, 1710–42,

ITEM

for 22 April 1731.

QuickCheck Model
IMAGE COPIES: ONLINE
Jurisdiction & series as lead elements in Source List

Source List Entry

JURISDICTION	SERIES	REPOSITORY

Missouri. St. Louis, City of. Circuit Court Case Files. Court Clerk's Office,

REPOSITORY LOCATION	ITEM TYPE or FORMAT	WEBSITE CREATOR-OWNER ...

St. Louis. Digital images. St. Louis Circuit Court and Washington

WEBSITE TITLE	

University. *St. Louis Circuit Court Historical Records Project.* http://

... URL (DIGITAL LOCATION) ...	YEAR

library.wustl.edu/vlib/dredscott/exhibits/ds03.html : 2006.

First (Full) Reference Note

JURISDICTION	SERIES	CASE FILE NO.	CASE ...

1. City of St. Louis, Missouri, Circuit Court Case No. 1, Dred Scott

... LABEL	COURT TERM	ITEM OF INTEREST ...

v. Irene Emerson, November Term 1846, "Petition of False Imprisonment for

...	RECORD DATE	ITEM TYPE or FORMAT	WEBSITE OWNER-CREATOR ...

Dred Scott," 6 April 1846; digital images, St. Louis Circuit Court and

WEBSITE TITLE	

Washington University, *St. Louis Circuit Court Historical Records Project* (http://

... URL (DIGITAL LOCATION)	DATE

library.wustl.edu/vlib/dredscott/exhibits/ds03.html : accessed 2 October 2006).

Subsequent (Short) Note

JURISDICTION	SERIES	CASE FILE NO.	CASE LABEL

11. City of St. Louis, Mo., Circuit Court Case No. 1, Scott v. Emerson,

COURT TERM	ITEM

Nov. Term 1846, "Petition of False Imprisonment."

QuickCheck Model
DERIVATIVES: DATABASES, ONLINE
Database as lead element in Source List

Source List Entry

DATABASE TITLE	ITEM TYPE or FORMAT	WEBSITE TITLE (SAME AS CREATOR)

"Oregon Historical Records Index." Database. *Oregon State Archives.*

URL (DIGITAL LOCATION)	YEAR

http://genealogy.state.or.us : 2007.

First (Full) Reference Note

	DATABASE TITLE	ITEM TYPE or FORMAT	WEBSITE TITLE (SAME AS CREATOR)

1. "Oregon Historical Records Index," database, *Oregon State Archives*

URL (DIGITAL LOCATION)	DATE	ITEM OF INTEREST ...

(http://genealogy.state.or.us : accessed 2 February 2007), entry for Lio Ulrich,

...	CREDIT LINE (SOURCE OF THIS SOURCE)

1898; citing insanity commitment case no. 1333, Marion County.

Subsequent (Short) Note

	DATABASE TITLE	RECORD TYPE	ITEM OF INTEREST ...

11. "Oregon Historical Records Index," database entry for Lio Ulrich,

...

1898, Marion Co.

GUIDELINES
& Examples

BASIC ISSUES

8.1 Core Elements

Citations to local government records resemble citations to other localized records such as church registers and cemetery office files. The principles discussed in chapters 5 and 7 can be applied here to civil records at the city and county level. When you consult the original books or files, you have essentially five elements to cite:

- creator of the record (the governmental jurisdiction),
- name/number of the record book or file and series,
- specific item of interest within the book or file,
- record office or repository, and
- location of record office or repository (by city and state).

When you consult image copies or derivatives of the record, you have additional elements to cite:

- format of the copy or derivative,
- creator of the copy or derivative,
- identification of the copy or derivative, and
- location or publication data for the copy or derivative.

8.2 Local Records, Arrangement of Elements

Most users of local government records cite them differently from records maintained at the state and national levels. If you begin your citations to local records with the name of the creator (the city or county) and end with details on the specific item of interest, you will have unlimited space to add as much detail as necessary about that specific item. For example:

> 1. Dutchess County, New York, Court of Common Pleas, Ancient Document no. 13095, Shubael Boughton, plea of trespass, 1791; Dutchess County Archives, Poughkeepsie. Shubael actually filed on behalf of Sarah Boughton, who accused Reuben Sears on a bastardy charge.

In this style of reference note, the location of the repository will typically be cited after the first reference to that county (Dutchess) and that collection (Court of Common Pleas, Ancient Documents). For example, an essay on bastardy cases in Dutchess County might have previously cited this set of records in reference to a 1770 case, using this citation:

First Reference Note

    1. Dutchess County (New York), Court of Common Pleas, Ancient Document no. 5974, Seth Sears Jr., recognizance bond, 1770; Dutchess County Archives, Poughkeepsie.

After this first citation identifies where the Dutchess County Ancient Documents Collection is kept, the archive and city does not have to be repeated every time the Ancient Documents collection is cited.

8.3 State-level Records, Arrangement of Elements

Citations to original resources of the state, provincial, or colonial governments—like those of the federal government—usually follow the traditional arrangement for formally archived materials. First, you identify the specific item of interest, then you record every other element in a smallest-to-largest sequence.

    1. Joseph Ruppert v. City of Baltimore, April 1865; Court of Appeals Judgments, Book 33: 1–10; MSA no. S381-4, accession no. 683-6; Maryland State Archives, Annapolis.

8.4 Use of Image Copies

Often, for preservation of original records, modern researchers must use image copies—microfilm, microfiche, or digital images. Your working citation should identify the original *and* the image version you have used. In some cases, image copies exist in several versions, with varying quality among them. You and others may reach different conclusions about your findings, according to the quality of the version you consulted.

If the record has been consulted on microfilm, the microfilm would also be identified in the Source List Entry and the First Reference Note. To continue the Seth Sears example from 8.2:

Source List Entry

New York. Dutchess County. Court of Common Pleas, Ancient Documents. Dutchess County Archives, Poughkeepsie. FHL microfilm 925,810. Family History Library, Salt Lake City, Utah.

First Reference Note
> 1. Dutchess County, New York, Court of Common Pleas, Ancient Document no. 5974, Seth Sears Jr., recognizance bond, 1770; Dutchess County Archives, Poughkeepsie; FHL microfilm 925,810.

8.5   Use of Record Copies

Many of the "original" court records you consult at the city and county level are *record copies* (see 1.27) rather than *true originals*. Historically, attorneys presented the court with documents critical to the case at hand—contracts, depositions, petitions, etc. Courts then maintained these loose documents in bundles, envelopes, jackets, or packets. Certain items of particular significance from a legal standpoint would be copied into record books, although the original packets would usually be preserved, at least for a certain number of years. If a case was appealed to a higher court, that packet of original papers would be transferred to the appeals court. However, the record books would typically remain with the clerk of the lower court. In other situations, attorneys might borrow a set of case papers and fail to return them.

As a thorough researcher and careful analyst, you would try to use the original or the record copy closest to the original. If a city, county, or state government has preserved the existing original case papers, you would give more weight to the loose documents than to the recorded copies. However, as a legal and practical matter, record copies officially created and maintained by public record offices are treated as "original" records, when the actual original is not known to exist.

8.6   Using Other Derivatives

Abstracts, databases, indexes, transcripts, and translations—whether they are found as typescripts or published in print or digital form—are considered derivatives. You would cite these in the manner of other publications, typescripts, or manuscripts, depending upon the form the derivative takes.

CITATION ISSUES

8.7   Citing Books vs. Files

Whether a record book is labeled "Town Council Minutes" or "Road Assignments" or "Equity Court Record" or "Criminal Court Docket," the basic citation is the same. You have a manuscript volume that carries a specific title or else it is part of a numbered series of volumes. It is usually paginated, so you should include a page citation; if it is not paginated, you should note that fact. If multiple items appear on a page, you may need to flag the specific item of interest.

If you are using loose documents (original bonds, case files, etc.), you are citing a *series* (or *collection*) and the *item* within the series—rather than *book* and *page*. When you use a file or packet containing individual documents, you will need to cite both the *file* (by name and/or number) and the relevant *document* within the file.

8.8 Citing Books vs. Libers

Record books of some early jurisdictions are labeled as Liber 1, etc., rather than Book 1 or Volume 1. When using record series that are referred to locally as *libers*, it is good form to cite them as such.

8.9 Citing Date or Court Term

If the register title or document label carries the year or a narrow range of years, your citation may not need to include the exact date of the record. If the title or label carries no date or cites a wide span of years, you should include at least the year of the record as part of its identification. When a volume of court records is unpaginated, you should cite the *term of court*—typically that term is stated in the record as a *season* or *month* and *year*.

8.10 Citing Exact Titles

When using a large series of civil registers, many researchers prefer to use a generic or series name followed by a number. Local registers are often officially labeled in just this manner: Circuit Court Minutes 1, Circuit Court Minutes 2, etc. However, when an individual volume in the series has distinctive wording—say, volume 8 of a court-minutes series is labeled "Fees"—you should preserve the exact title. For example:

> 1. Whatever County, State, Circuit Court Minutes, Book 8 (Fees): 123; Clerk of Court's Office, Whatever Town.

8.11 Citing Internal Crossreferences

Many civil records offer crossreferences to other files or record books. The case label on a document from a circuit court packet may note that the document was recorded in, say, "Record Book 13, p. 239." Conversely, a court record book may carry a marginal note citing the case number. You should include these internal crossreferences in your research notes. You might choose to include them in your citation—even when the whereabouts of the crossreferenced material is unknown. That could be a clue that could help you or a user of your work discover the referenced material. As an example:

> 1. Whatever County, State, Equity Court Record 5: 234, Spring Term 1840; citing file 13-A.

8.12   Citing Jurisdictions

Any particular type of record could be kept at the city or the county level, depending upon the place and time. Among the jurisdictional quirks you will frequently encounter are the five discussed at length below: independent cities, cities and counties with identical names, cities larger than counties, counties with multiple seats, and defunct jurisdictions or obsolete jurisdictional names.

INDEPENDENT CITIES

Some metropolitan areas are independent cities, entirely separate from surrounding counties, operating their own offices and record-keeping systems. In using records from the City of Richmond, Virginia, for example, you would not cite the creator or location of a public record as "City of Richmond, Henrico County." The creator and the location would both be, simply, "City of Richmond."

CITIES AND COUNTIES WITH IDENTICAL NAMES

When you cite records of an area where there are both a county and an independent city of the same name, you should take special care to identify the specific jurisdiction—e.g., "St. Louis *County*" or "*City of* St. Louis" rather than just "St. Louis."

CITIES LARGER THAN COUNTIES

Other large cities contain several counties within their city bounds. Again, if the record or the record office is part of the city administration, you would not cite the county.

COUNTIES WITH MULTIPLE SEATS

When citing county-level records for counties that have multiple courthouses, each maintaining a different set of records, you will have to identify the specific courthouse that maintains the records you used. The examples below demonstrate one way of handling the situation. Other areas use other ways of differentiating between the seats of government, so your exact words will vary according to the terms used locally. If you are conducting research on-site, the staff can guide you. If you are conducting research via film from the Family History Library, the FHL catalog or the film target itself will usually provide the detail needed to make distinctions.

Source List Entry

Mississippi. Bolivar County. District 1. Wills & Inventories, 1861–1907. Chancery Clerk's Office, Rosedale.

Mississippi. Bolivar County. District 2. Will Records, 1900–1924. Chancery Clerk's Office, Cleveland.

First Reference Note

    1. Bolivar County, Mississippi, District 1, Wills & Inventories, C (1861–1907): 710–11, Will of William Pitts, 1904; Chancery Clerk's Office, Rosedale.

    2. Bolivar County, Mississippi, District 2, Will Records, 1900–1924: 28, Will of Mariah Grier, 1904; Chancery Clerk's Office, Cleveland.

Subsequent Note

    11. Bolivar Co., Miss., Dist. 1, Wills & Inventories, C (1861–1907): 35.

    12. Bolivar Co., Miss., Dist. 2, Will Records, 1900–1924: 28.

DEFUNCT JURISDICTIONS OR OBSOLETE NAMES

Many counties and some cities are no longer functioning jurisdictions or else they have changed their names. Even so, the basic citation pattern remains the same. You would likely add a brief comment to your First Reference Note to explain the situation. If you are using data-management software for your research, you will likely want to store that discussion in your working Source List, so the information will not be lost should you later decide to delete that First Reference Note. Explanations of this type are not commonly included with a published bibliography, unless you are writing a bibliographic essay. The following examples demonstrate typical comments you might need to make.

Source List Entry

Idaho. Alturas County. Declarations of Intention. Idaho State Historical Society, Public Archives and Research Library, Boise.

Virginia. Old Rappahannock County. Order Books. Essex County Circuit Court Clerk's Office, Tappahannock.

First Reference Note

    1. Alturas County, Idaho, Declarations of Intention, Book 1: 39; Idaho State Historical Society, Public Archives and Research Library, Boise. Alturas County was discontinued in 1895.

    2. Old Rappahannock County, Virginia, Order Book 1 (1683–1685): 37; Essex County Circuit Court Clerk's Office, Tappahannock. Old Rappahannock County, which was abolished in 1692, should not be confused with modern Rappahannock County.

Subsequent Note
>   11. Alturas Co., Idaho, Declarations of Intention, Book 1: 39.
>   12. Old Rappahannock Co., Va., Order Book 1: 37.

8.13   Citing Key Parties in the Record

With most local records, if your text identifies the key individuals involved in a document—say, the grantee and the grantor in a deed—you do not have to repeat that identification in your Reference Note. With court cases, the case label *is* included in the citation.

8.14   Citing Nature of the Record

A wide variety of materials are often recorded in court records, aside from the expected litigation. Many of these, because of their special nature, are not indexed in the county's consolidated indexes to civil and criminal suits. Some of the miscellaneous material found in court books are covered in chapter 9—for example, the indentures of minors and the registrations of professional licenses and free people of color. When you cite a record book for a type of record that is different from the label of the book, you will likely want to identify the special nature of the record you found.

8.15   Citing Page Numbers

Page numbers are often handled in different ways, depending upon the type of volume being cited. Typical conventions are these:

DISTINCTIVELY NAMED VOLUMES .... "Name of Volume," p. 123
NUMBERED VOLUME (FROM A SERIES) ..... Chancery Court Minutes 2: 123

8.16   Citing the Record Office

The repository you cite will typically be the name of a record office within the city or county—e.g., Clerk of Court's Office, City Archives Department, etc. That cited repository would rarely be a building (say, Whatever County Courthouse). Many record offices can occupy a building, and record offices often move from one building to another. If you wish to record a building name or a street address in your working Source List, you may; but those are not commonly included in published citations.

In citing Family History Library microfilm for local and state records, your Source List Entry should identify the record office that holds the original. You will usually find that information on a target preceding the register that has been filmed, as well as in the FHL catalog. Because you will often need to go beyond the film to examine the original, identifying the whereabouts of the original, whenever you use film, ensures that you will always know where to turn for deeper research. In your First Reference Note, however, you do not have to cite the original record office, because you did not actually use the original records.

CITY & COUNTY RECORDS

8.17 Background
See also Chapter 9, Licenses, Registrations, Rolls & Vitals
and Chapter 10, Property & Probates

Local courts, across time, have handled a wide variety of needs. In addition to the trial courts that hear criminal cases and civil complaints, you will be citing a wide variety of other actions taken by local governing boards. Within this framework, one finds certain basic materials:

- *Docket books*—a calendar of court cases, giving case numbers, case names, and the court sessions in which the case was to be heard.
- *Fee books*—a log of charges and/or payments for the per diem expenses and mileage of witnesses, printing costs, mileage paid to law enforcement personnel who delivered summons, etc.
- *Minute books*—registers, kept in chronological order, with brief notations as to what transpired in each case, each day of a court session. Minute books kept by supervisory bodies summarize decisions on the region's economic, educational, or social issues deliberated at each meeting.
- *Packets or files*—envelopes or bundles in which all loose papers relating to a case are maintained under the case label, docket number, or some similar system.
- *Record books or Final Record books*—registers kept in chronological order by court term, usually with detailed narratives summarizing past and final actions in a case.

Despite the wide variation in record types, most citations to them will fall within one of two basic types: you will cite a *bound volume* or you will cite *loose documents in a packet or file*.

8.18 Basic Formats: Bound Volumes
See QuickCheck Models *for*
- ORIGINAL RECORDS: LOCAL RECORD BOOKS
- ORIGINAL RECORDS: LOCAL RECORD BOOKS, ARCHIVED OFF-SITE

The four models presented below illustrate four basic points:

- If you use only one book from a series and it carries a distinctive title (as with notes 1 and 3), then you would copy the title of the book exactly, putting it in quotation marks.

- If the series does not number the volumes individually and does not carry a date in its title, then you should add inclusive dates to assure that the correct volume can be relocated, as with note 4.

- If you are citing multiple volumes from a series, you may use a common, generic title (e.g., Will Books) and cite its volume number within the series, as with note 2.

- If you add those inclusive dates inside a quoted title, as in note 1, then you should place those dates in square editorial brackets.

Source List Entry
Kentucky. Marshall County. Board of Supervisors' Minutes, 1886–1908. County Court Clerk's Office, Benton.
Massachusetts. Hampshire County. Court of Common Pleas Record Books, 1783–1853. Superior Court Clerk's Office, Northampton.
Mississippi. Adams County. Circuit Court Record of Judgment Books, 1830–1831. Circuit Court Clerk's Office, Natchez.
New Mexico. Colfax County. District Court Civil Dockets, 1869–1900. History Library Museum of New Mexico, Santa Fe.

First Reference Note
    1. Marshall County, Kentucky, "Board of Tax Supervisor's Minutes [1886–1908]," p. 73, for Bob Hamilton order, 11 January 1890; County Court Clerk's Office, Benton.
    2. Hampshire County, Massachusetts, Court of Common Pleas Record Book U: 218, Benjamin Sibley v. Samuel Hemingway, 1794; Superior Court Clerk's Office, Northampton.
    3. Adams County, Mississippi, "Circuit Court Record of Judgement, NN (May 1830–May 1831)," pp. 458–61, George Mulhollen v. Robert McCullough, slave suit for freedom; Circuit Court Clerk's Office, Natchez.
    4. Colfax County, New Mexico, District Court Civil Docket, 1869–1882, unpaginated, April Term 1869, case 16, State v. Samuel Cawker; History Library Museum of New Mexico, Santa Fe.

Subsequent Note
    11. Marshall Co., Ky., "Board of Tax Supervisor's Minutes [1886–1908]," 73.
    12. Hampshire Co., Mass., Court of Common Pleas Record Book U:218.
    13. Adams Co., Miss., "Circuit Court Record of Judgement, NN," 458–61.
    14. Colfax Co., N. M., District Court Civil Docket, 1869–1882, April Term 1869, case 16.

CITING CASE NAMES, ITALICS VS. ROMAN

The rule *Italic denotes publications* has its counterpart in citations to court cases. The two basic points to keep in mind are these:

- *Published court case (e.g., in a "court reporter, see 13.5)*: place the name of the plaintiff and defendant in italics. The Latin adverb that joins the two (versus or adversus) is abbreviated (v. or adv.) and set in regular type.
- *Unpublished court case:* place the name of the plaintiff and defendant in roman type. Convention no longer requires that v. or adv. be italicized when the case name is in roman.

CD/DVD Database (LDS)

See also QuickCheck Model *for* IMAGE COPIES: CD/DVD

Source List Entry

Tennessee. Bedford County. Chancery Court Records. Digital images. *Bedford County, Tennessee, Chancery Court Records, Volume 1, Part 1, 1830–1842.* CD-ROM. Denver, Colorado: GSC Associates, ca. 2005.

First Reference Note

1. Bedford County, Tennessee, Chancery Court Records 1: 222–24, Martha A. Cooper v. Abram B. Cooper, divorce; digital images, *Bedford County, Tennessee, Chancery Court Records, Volume 1, Part 1, 1830–1842,* CD-ROM (Denver, Colorado: GSC Associates, ca. 2005).

Subsequent Note

11. Bedford Co., Tenn., Chancery Court Records 1: 222–24, Cooper v. Cooper.

Microfilm (FHL-GSU)

See 8.4, 8.24, 8.28–8.29, 8.31, 8.37

8.19 Basic Formats: Loose Papers (Case Files)

See QuickCheck Model *for* ORIGINAL RECORDS: LOCAL CASE FILES

In the examples below, the Source List Entries cite the whole time frame searched, while the Reference Notes cite only the date or year of the specific case being discussed.

Source List Entry

Florida. Escambia County. Circuit Court Files, 1830–1840. Circuit Clerk's Office, Pensacola.

Indiana. Shelby County. Circuit Court Files, 1850–1900. County Clerk's Office, Shelbyville.

Missouri. Clay County. Circuit Court Files, 1835–1900. Clay County Archives, Liberty.

First Reference Note
    1. Escambia County, Florida, Circuit Court File 2638-CA-01, L. C. Hubbell v. Peter de Alba, for "Reply of Loring C. Hubbell and Emilie, His Wife," 1 June 1831; Circuit Clerk's Office, Pensacola.
    2. Shelby County, Indiana, Circuit Court Files, Civil Box 459, Julia Van Horn v. Estate of Elizabeth German, 1887; County Clerk's Office, Shelbyville.
    3. Clay County, Missouri, Circuit Court Files, Box 20, Tapp v. Tapp, Defendant's answer, 9 October 1856; Clay County Archives, Liberty.

Subsequent Note
    11. Escambia Co., Fla., Circuit Court File 2638-CA-01, Hubbell v. de Alba, Reply of Hubbell and Wife, 1 June 1831.
    12. Shelby Co., Ind., Circuit Court Files, Civil Box 459, 1887.
    13. Clay Co., Mo., Circuit Court Files, Box 20, Tapp v. Tapp, Defendant's answer, 9 October 1856.

CITING SPECIFIC DOCUMENTS IN A CASE

The Florida and Missouri examples, above, demonstrate citations to a specific document within a large packet. The Indiana example demonstrates a citation to the whole case. When citing a specific document, you would want to identify three particular elements:

- the key individuals;
- the title or nature of the document, and
- the date of the document.

If it is a lengthy document, you might need to cite a specific page within that document.

Microfilm

See 8.38 *and* QuickCheck Model *for* IMAGE COPIES: MICROFILM, ARCHIVAL ...

Online Images   📇

See also QuickCheck Model *for* IMAGE COPIES: ONLINE

When citing online images of local government records, published at that government's own website, you are citing a legal equivalent to the original. Therefore, you cite the original, then append the essential details for the website at which you accessed the record.

Source List Entry
Missouri. St. Louis, City of. Circuit Court Case Files. Court Clerk's Office, St. Louis. Digital images. St. Louis Circuit Court and Washington University. *St. Louis Circuit Court Historical Records Project.* http://library.wustl.edu/vlib/dredscott/exhibits/ds03.html : 2006.

First Reference Note
　　1. City of St. Louis, Missouri, Circuit Court Case No. 1, Dred Scott v. Irene Emerson, November Term 1846, "Petition of False Imprisonment for Dred Scott," 6 April 1846; digital images, St. Louis Circuit Court and Washington University, *St. Louis Circuit Court Historical Records Project* (http:/library.wustl.edu/vlib/dredscott/exhibits/ds03.html : accessed 2 October 2006).

Subsequent Note
　　11. City of St. Louis, Mo., Circuit Court Case No. 1, Scott v. Emerson, Nov. Term 1846, "Petition of False Imprisonment."

8.20　Basic Formats: Records Archived Off-site

See also QuickCheck Model *for* LOCAL RECORD BOOKS, ARCHIVED OFF-SITE

For preservation, many local records are being deposited in archives off-site—sometimes a local library or historical society, but more commonly the state archives. There, some materials may be kept in their natural arrangement, but others are rearranged by date or sorted into individually named and alphabetized files. The manner in which you cite them will depend upon the organizational scheme of the repository. The following illustrates a variety of situations.

BOUND VOLUMES:

Source List Entry
Georgia. Franklin County. County Court Minutes. Georgia Department of Archives and History, Atlanta.
Rhode Island. Newport. Court of Common Pleas Records. Rhode Island Judicial Archives, Pawtucket.

First Reference Note
　　1. Franklin County, Georgia, County Court Minutes, June 1794–1805, unpaginated, March Term 1799, Cooly v. Strother; Georgia Department of Archives and History, Atlanta.
　　2. Newport, Rhode Island, Court of Common Pleas Records, Book I: 490, May 1774; Rhode Island Judicial Archives, Pawtucket.

Subsequent Note
　　11. Franklin Co., Ga., County Court Minutes, June 1794–1805, unpaginated, March Term 1799, Cooly v. Strother.
　　12. Newport, R.I., Court of Common Pleas Records, Book I: 490.

LOOSE PAPERS:

Source List Entry
North Carolina. Nash County. Nash County Loose Papers. North Carolina State Archives, Raleigh.

North Dakota. Cass County. District Court, Divorce Case Files. North Dakota Institute for Regional Studies, Fargo.

First Reference Note

1. Nash County, North Carolina, Bill in Equity, 1834–35, case no. 6, Delilah Revel v. Nicholas Lewis & Others; Folder: Delilah Revel, Nash County Loose Papers; North Carolina State Archives, Raleigh.

2. Cass County, North Dakota, District Court Divorce Case Files, box 1, case no. 34-2087, 1884, Clara Foster v. Benjamin Foster; North Dakota Institute for Regional Studies, Fargo.

(*Or, as suggested by this particular archive*)
2. Clara Foster v. Benjamin Foster, Case 34-2087, 1884; Box 1, Divorce Case Files; Records of the North Dakota District Court (Cass County); North Dakota Institute for Regional Studies, Fargo.

Subsequent Note

11. Nash Co., N.C., Bill in Equity, 1834–35, case no. 6, Revel v. Lewis & Others.

12. Cass Co., N.D., District Court Divorce Case Files, case no. 34-2087, Foster v. Foster, 1884.

(*Or, as suggested by this particular archive*)
12. Case 34-2087, Cass County Divorce Case File, Institute for Regional Studies.

ALTERNATIVE FORMAT FOR CASS COUNTY

The Cass County District Court records have been removed to an archive that uses the traditional format favored by academic archives and upper-level government archives. Instead of beginning the citation with the name of the records' creator (the county and state), that style calls for beginning your citation with the smallest element and progressing sequentially to the largest. The archive does not suggest a corresponding format for your Source List.

8.21 Bastardy Cases (Presentments)

In most American colonies and states prior to the mid-1800s or so, females who bore a child out of wedlock were expected to name the child's father. If deemed guilty by his peers, that man would be compelled to support the child until it was old enough to be bound out for its own support—thereby sparing the community a financial burden. Males who were charged were usually required to post a bond until the hearing. Depositions were frequently taken and may have survived. Or, in lieu of naming a father from whom support might be extracted, male relatives of the female might have posted a bond, guaranteeing that the child would be supported.

If the original file no longer exists, you may be citing only a *minute* (an official abstract) in a court book. When the case files have survived, they can offer a wide variety of record types to be cited; your citation should identify both the case file and the relevant document within the file. In other situations, archivists may have separated the individual items within a case file and assigned numbers to each document. You will likely need to spend some time evaluating the situation in order to determine precisely what elements you need to cite, to ensure that the valuable facts you found are relocatable.

Source List Entry

New York. Dutchess County. Court of Common Pleas, Ancient Documents. Dutchess County Archives, Poughkeepsie.

Virginia. York County. Deeds, Orders, and Wills, 1677–1684. Circuit Court Clerk's Office, Yorktown.

First Reference Note

1. Dutchess County, New York, Court of Common Pleas, Ancient Document no. 5974, Seth Sears Jr., recognizance bond in bastardy case, 1770; Dutchess County Archives, Poughkeepsie.

2. York County, Virginia, Deeds, Orders, and Wills, 1677–1684, 6: 498, Jane Duncklyn, presentment, 25 June 1683; Circuit Court Clerk's Office, Yorktown.

Subsequent Note

11. Dutchess Co., N.Y., Court of Common Pleas, Ancient Document no. 5974, Seth Sears Jr., recognizance bond.

12. York Co., Va., Deeds, Orders, and Wills, 6: 498.

8.22 Bonds

Historically, bonds have been posted in a variety of matters. In addition to the better-known administration, guardian, and marriage bonds, bonds also guaranteed appearance in court, peaceful conduct toward others, payment of legal obligations, fulfillment of duty as a public officer, financial support for slaves being freed, and much more. Your citation will likely note the type of bond. However, the principal factor that determines the structure of your citation is whether (*a*) you are using a loose bond from a collection, or (*b*) you are citing bond data entered into a record book.

Source List Entry

Georgia. Oglethorpe County. Bond Books, 1799–1830. Ordinary's Office, Lexington.

Missouri. Clay County. Circuit Court Files. Clay County Archives and Historical Library, Liberty.

First Reference Note
 1. Oglethorpe County, Georgia, Bond Book, 1799–1807: 21, John Davenport's guardianship bond; Ordinary's Office, Lexington.
 2. Clay County, Missouri, Circuit Court Box 5, file 355, James Aull and Henry Guess v. Henry Slaughter, for Thomas Pebley's performance bond, 1830; Clay County Archives and Historical Library, Liberty.

Subsequent Note
 11. Oglethorpe Co., Ga., Bond Book 1799–1807: 21, Davenport's guardianship bond.
 12. Clay Co., Mo., Circuit Court Box 5, file 355, Aull and Guess v. Slaughter, for Pebley's performance bond, 1830.

8.23   Coroners' Inquests

Coroners and medical examiners have served a governmental function for centuries. "Minutes" of their activities, during a region's early years, are often found in county order books, supervisors' records, or similar registers. As the population increased, special record books or *evidence books* became common for more or less detailed accounts of coroner actions and findings. In large urban areas, these record books may be within a coroner's office. Elsewhere, they may be kept with probate or court records. In some areas, loose papers created by the coroners—such as affidavits and reports—have survived. The following examples illustrate both bound volumes and loose items.

Source List Entry
California. Calaveras County. Coroner Inquest Papers, 1854–1873.
    Calaveras County Archives, San Andreas.
Kansas. Sedgwick County. Coroner's Inquest Records, 1910–1929.
    County Clerk's Office, Wichita.

First Reference Note
 1. Calaveras County, California, Coroner Inquest Papers, 1854–1873, Box 89, "Inquest on the Body of Vicente Rodriguez," filed 7 December 1854; Calaveras County Archives, San Andreas.
 2. Sedgwick County, Kansas, Coroner's Inquest Records, vol. 2 (1910–1919): 139, for Joseph R. Jackson, 5 March 1913; County Clerk's Office, Wichita.

Subsequent Note
 11. Calaveras Co., Calif., Coroner's Inquest Papers, 1854–1873, Box 89, "Inquest on the Body of Vicente Rodriguez," filed 7 December 1854.
 12. Sedgwick Co., Kans., Coroner's Inquest Records, 2:139, Joseph R. Jackson.

CITING DATES IN THE SHORT FORM

The short form used for note 11 carries the exact date of the document. The short form at note 12 does not. The difference is this: note 12 is a paginated book, in which the document can be located by citing the book and page number. Note 11 is a set of loose items in a box of papers that are chronologically filed. The date is essential to relocating the document and should not be dropped from the short form.

8.24 County Commissioners' Records

Early governments typically included a board that handled a variety of social problems from elections to indigent care to road building. This governing agency has gone by a variety of names. Whether it be called a town council, a board of supervisors, or a parish police jury, it typically created registers that chronicle the issues it debated and the actions it took. The following sampling should provide a model representative of your research area.

Source List Entry

Alabama. Clarke County. Commissioners' Court, 1813–1832. Probate Judge's Office, Grove Hill.

Colorado. Arapahoe County. Road Records, 1867–1900. County Clerk's Office, Littleton.

Mississippi. Hancock County. Supervisors' Minutes, 1866–1900. Circuit Clerk's Office, Bay St. Louis.

Tennessee. White County. County Court Minutes, 1806–1841. County Clerk's Office, Sparta.

First Reference Note

1. Clarke County, Alabama, Commissioners' Court, vol. A (1813–1832): 127–29, road appointments, May 1823; Probate Judge's Office, Grove Hill.

2. Arapahoe County, Colorado, Road Records, vol. 1, chronologically arranged: see August 1867 for Cherry Creek Road; County Clerk's Office, Littleton.

3. Hancock County, Mississippi, Supervisors' Minutes, vol. 1: 28, appointment of R. R. Breland as election inspector, March Term 1867; Circuit Clerk's Office, Bay St. Louis.

4. White County, Tennessee, County Court Minutes, 1812–1814: 74, Abner Rose road appointment; County Clerk's Office, Sparta.

Subsequent Note

11. Clarke Co., Ala., Commissioner's Court, A: 127–29.

12. Arapahoe Co., Colo., Road Records, 1: August 1867.

13. Hancock Co., Miss., Supervisors' Minutes, 1:28.

14. White Co., Tenn., County Court Minutes, 1812–1814: 74.

Microfilm (FHL/GSU)

See QuickCheck Model *for* IMAGE COPIES: MICROFILM, FHL-GSU …

Source List Entry

England. Cornwall. Week St. Mary. Overseers' Accounts, 1710–42.
  Cornwall County Record Office, Truro. FHL microfilm 1,597,004,
  item 3. Family History Library, Salt Lake City, Utah.

First Reference Note

  1. Week St. Mary, Cornwall, England, Overseers' Accounts, 1710–
42, unpaginated, chronologically arranged; see 22 April 1731 account of
John Colwill Jr.; Cornwall County Record Office, Truro; FHL microfilm 1,597,004, item 3.

Subsequent Note

  11. Week St. Mary, Cornwall, Eng., Overseers' Accounts, 1710–
42, for 22 April 1731.

8.25   Divorce & Separation Cases

Divorce cases have typically been handled as civil suits. In some
colonies and early states, however, divorce petitions introduced at the
local level were remanded to the state legislature for a decision. In such
times and places, you will also be citing legislative petitions, files, and
decisions (see 8.42). In some locales, divorces were not permitted, but
spouses could legally sue for *separation of bed and board*. In other
cases, spouses sued for *separation of property* even when they continued to share a residence. When you encounter a legal separation, as
opposed to a divorce, your citation should note the type of separation.
For suits settled by a local court, citations to case files or record books
typically follow one of the patterns below.

Source List Entry

Illinois. Cook County. Superior Court in Chancery. Divorce Records.
  Cook County Archives, Chicago.
Louisiana. Natchitoches Parish. District Court Files, 1805–1900. Office
  of the Clerk of Court, Natchitoches.

First Reference Note

  1. Cook County, Illinois, Superior Court in Chancery, divorce file
36535 (1921), Mary F. Apgar v. William Apgar, final decree; Cook
County Archives, Chicago.
  2. Natchitoches Parish, Louisiana, District Court Files, bundle
194, case 3485 (1851), Melite Anty v. Her Husband, separation of
property; Office of the Clerk of Court, Natchitoches.

Subsequent Note
11. Cook Co., Ill., Superior Court in Chancery, divorce file 36535 (1921), Apgar v. Apgar, final decree.
12. Natchitoches Par., La., District Court Files, bundle 194, case 3485 (1851), Anty v. Husband, separation of property.

DATES IN PARENTHESES
When citing legal cases, the convention is to place the year of the case in parentheses after the case number or after the citation to the volume: page where proceedings are discussed.

Online Databases & Indexes

See also QuickCheck Model *for* DERIVATIVES: DATABASES, ONLINE

Source List Entry
"Louisiana, Parish Court (Orleans Parish): Index to the Suit Records, 1813–1835." Database. New Orleans Public Library. *Nutrias.* http://nutrias.org/~nopl/inv/vcp/parish1.htm : 2007.

First Reference Note
1. "Louisiana, Parish Court (Orleans Parish): Index to the Suit Records, 1813–1835," database, New Orleans Public Library, *Nutrias* (http://nutrias.org/~nopl/inv/vcp/parish1.htm : 14 January 2007), entry for H. Lefebre Jr. v. Marie Eliza Borne, separation of bed and board [no date given]; citing case 4189.

Subsequent Note
11. "Louisiana, Parish Court (Orleans Parish): Index to the Suit Records, 1813–1835," database entry for Lefebre v. Borne.

8.26 Election Certificates & Returns
The term *certificates of election* implies the existence of loose certificates. However, what you typically find are narrative accounts—more aptly called *certifications*—recorded in bound registers. These certificates or certifications are also variously called *election returns*. Terminology varies by jurisdiction.

Source List Entry
Kentucky. Marshall County. Certificates of Election, 1884–1898. County Court Clerk's Office, Benton.

First Reference Note
1. Marshall County, Kentucky, "Certificates of Election, 1884–1898," p. 57, certification of H. W. Heath, County Attorney, elected 4 August 1890; County Court Clerk's Office, Benton.

Subsequent Note
11. Marshall County, Ky., "Certificates of Election, 1884–1898," 57, certification of H. W. Heath.

8.27   Indigent Records

Poorhouse accounts, commitments to poor farms, pauper rolls, welfare files, warnings out—across time and place, society has dealt with the impoverished and the unfortunate in many ways. Regardless of the label that a record bears, the essential issue is whether you found your information in a record book or in a file of loose papers. Both are illustrated below, together with a situation in which loose items are informally inserted in a bound book.

Source List Entry
California. Sonoma County. Indigent Records, 1876–1919. Sonoma County History and Genealogy Library, Santa Rosa.
Illinois. Cass County. Almshouse Register, 1887–1945. County Clerk's Office, Virginia, Illinois. Accession no. 4/0226/12. Illinois Regional Archives Depository, University of Illinois, Springfield.
Tennessee. Lincoln County. Poor Farm Records, 1874–1961. Lincoln County Archives, Fayetteville.

First Reference Note
1. Sonoma County, California, Indigent Records, 1876–1919, unnumbered applications in alphabetical order, Frederick Parker Application, 1916; Sonoma County History and Genealogy Library, Santa Rosa.
2. Cass County, Illinois, "Almshouse Register, 1887–1945," unpaginated, chronological entries, page covering 1887–89, entry no. 18, Eligh Schnider, 23 May 1888; accession no. 4/0226/12; Illinois Regional Archives Depository, University of Illinois, Springfield.
3. Cass County, Illinois, "Applications for Admission to the County Home," L. J. Reed, 18 May 1932; unnumbered loose papers, alphabetized and inserted in the volume labeled "Almshouse Register, 1887–1945"; accession no. 4/0226/12; Illinois Regional Archives Depository, University of Illinois, Springfield.
4. Lincoln County, Tennessee, Poor Farm Records, 1874–1961, unnumbered items, admission of Lou Ella Neugeant, 12 February 1917; Lincoln County Archives, Fayetteville.

Subsequent Note
11. Sonoma Co., Calif., Indigent Records, 1876–1919, Frederick Parker Application, 1916.
12. Cass Co., Ill., "Almshouse Register, 1887–1945," unpaginated, chronological entries, page covering 1887–89, entry no. 18, Eligh Schnider, 23 May 1888.

      13. Cass Co., Ill., "Applications for Admission to the County Home," L. J. Reed, 18 May 1932.

      14. Lincoln Co., Tenn., Poor Farm Records, 1874–1961, Lou Ella Neugeant, 12 February 1917.

CREATING SHORTENED CITATIONS

On occasion, as in the Cass County examples above, the details that need to be cited in order for material to be located in a register are so complicated that it is best not to attempt to shorten anything in a subsequent note except the physical location.

RECORDS HELD OFF-SITE

All four resources above reflect a growing trend: the removal of historic county and city governmental records from their original office to a historical repository. In some cases, as with the California and Tennessee examples, the material is cataloged and held informally. In the Illinois example, the material has been removed to a university that now serves as a regional depository of the state archive. There, the record book is formally cataloged under the system's accession numbers. When accession, document or manuscript, or series numbers have been assigned, you should include those in your First Reference Note.

8.28   Insanity Hearings

Variously known as lunacy, *non compos mentis,* and interdiction proceedings, hearings to determine sanity have been dealt with in various ways across time. Some states have assigned them to the probate courts, particularly when property was involved. In other locales, hearings and commitments were handled by one of the civil courts, in which case the records usually are intermixed with all types of other civil suits. As cities and counties increased in size and the number of these cases grew, special registers or file collections were often created specifically for these proceedings. The following examples illustrate both loose and bound records in a variety of situations.

BOUND VOLUMES:

Source List Entry

(*Citing one random book in Source List*)
Georgia. Hancock County. "Lunacy Book, 1845–1858." Ordinary's Office, Sparta.

(*Citing a record series in Source List*)
Tennessee. Marshall County. County Court Minutes, 1836–1900. County Court Clerk's Office, Lewisburg.

First Reference Note

    1. Hancock County, Georgia, "Lunacy Book, 1845–1858," p. 17, Daniel McCook commitment, 16 April 1853; Ordinary's Office, Sparta.

    2. Marshall County, Tennessee, County Court Minutes, vol. A (1836–1840): 49, August Term 1837, court order for William Richie, lunatic; County Court Clerk's Office, Lewisburg.

Subsequent Note

    11. Hancock Co., Ga., "Lunacy Book, 1845–1858," 17.

    12. Marshall Co., Tenn., County Court Minutes, A: 49.

LOOSE PAPERS:

Source List Entry

Louisiana. Natchitoches Parish. Succession Files, 1805–1900. Office of
    the Clerk of Court, Natchitoches.

First Reference Note

    1. Natchitoches Parish, Louisiana, Succession File no. 1575, Interdiction of Delphine Gallien, ca. 1870; Office of the Clerk of Court, Natchitoches.

Subsequent Note

    11. Natchitoches Par., La., Succession File no. 1575, Interdiction of Delphine Gallien, ca. 1870.

Microfilm (FHL-GSU)

Source List Entry

Arizona. Pima County. Records of Habeas Corpus and Insanity, 1887–
    1913. Superior Court Clerk's Office, Tucson. FHL microfilm
    2,171,023, item 4. Family History Library, Salt Lake City, Utah.

First Reference Note

    1. Pima County, Arizona, Records of Habeas Corpus and Insanity, 1887–1913, vol. 1-A: 21–22, George T. Griffin, citing case no. 636; FHL microfilm 2,171,023, item 4.

Subsequent Note

    11. Pima Co., Ariz., Records of Habeas Corpus and Insanity, vol. 1-A: 21–22.

Online Databases & Indexes

See QuickCheck Model *for* DERIVATIVES: DATABASES, ONLINE

Source List Entry

"Oregon Historical Records Index." Database. *Oregon State Archives.*
    http://genealogy.state.or.us : 2007.

First Reference Note
    1. "Oregon Historical Records Index," database, *Oregon State Archives* (http://genealogy.state.or.us : accessed 2 February 2007), entry for Lio Ulrich, 1898; citing insanity commitment case no. 1333, Marion County.

Subsequent Note
    11. "Oregon Historical Records Index," database entry for Lio Ulrich, 1898, Marion Co.

CITING THE SOURCE OF YOUR SOURCE

The "source of the source" cited by databases such as this one could refer to the original numbering scheme of the court that created the record or it could refer to a new number assigned by the archive that created the database. In the above instance, the number is the original case number assigned by the Marion County Court, and the records of that court have been redeposited in the Oregon State Archives. In these situations, you might need the assistance of the archival staff to locate the original file using the cited number. However, the case number cited in the database is still an essential starting point.

8.29   Jail Records

A jail register, by whatever name, is usually a log that can be simply cited by Basic Formats: Bound Volumes, 8.18. When consulted on FHL microfilm, your citation might be constructed like this:

Microfilm (FHL-GSU)

Source List Entry
> South Carolina. Lexington County. Jail Books, 1873–1900. Sheriff's Office, Lexington. FHL microfilm 1,027,259. Family History Library, Salt Lake City, Utah.

First Reference Note
    1. Lexington County, South Carolina, "Sheriff's Jail Book, 1873–1883," p. 25, State v. Pickens Giles, Larceny, committed to jail 13 February 1875; FHL microfilm 1,027,259.

Subsequent Note
    11. Lexington Co., S.C., "Sheriff's Jail Book, 1873–1883," 25.

8.30   Jury Lists

Occasionally, you will find a county or city in which jury lists are kept in special registers. You may even find a packet of loose lists. As a rule, however, jury lists are recorded intermittently in the record books or minutes of the court to which the jury was called. As illustrated in the example below, you should cite the register and page, then note that the item of interest is a jury list rather than a specific court case.

Source List Entry
Georgia. Richmond County. Court of Ordinary Minutes, 1791–1818. Ordinary's Office, Augusta.

First Reference Note
1. Richmond County, Georgia, Court of Ordinary Minutes, 1791–1818: 74–75, for jury list; Ordinary's Office, Augusta.

Subsequent Note
11 Richmond Co., Ga., Court of Ordinary Minutes, 1791–1818: 74–75.

8.31 Naturalization Records, Local

Prior to 1906, U.S. residents who met legal requirements for naturalization could obtain their citizenship through any court at any level. You will find declarations of intent and naturalization oaths recorded in city and county courts, district circuit courts, and appellate courts. The models that follow demonstrate citations to bound records and loose files created at the local level, as well as local records that have been transferred to the state archive. Federal naturalization records are handled in chapter 11, National Government Records.

Source List Entry
Maryland. Baltimore. City Court. Naturalization Records. Maryland State Archives, Annapolis.
Pennsylvania. Allegheny County. Naturalization Declarations and Petitions. Prothonotary's Office, Pittsburgh.
Wisconsin. Milwaukee County. Third Judicial District Court Files. Milwaukee County Historical Society, Milwaukee.

First Reference Note
1. Baltimore, Maryland, City Court Naturalization Record Book 7:302, Arthur F. Appeltofft, 1884; Maryland State Archives, Annapolis.
2. Allegheny County, Pennsylvania, Naturalization Declarations and Petitions, 1840–1844: loose items arranged chronologically by court term; see October Term 1840, for 2 October 1838 declaration of intention by George Parks; Prothonotary's Office, Pittsburgh.
3. Milwaukee County, Wisconsin, Third Judicial District Court Files, no. 2574, Mathew Cawker, 1846, declaration of intention; Milwaukee County Historical Society, Milwaukee.

Subsequent Note
11. Baltimore, Md., City Court Naturalization Record Book 7:

302, Arthur F. Appeltofft, 1884.

    12. Allegheny Co., Penn., Naturalization Declarations and Petitions, 1840–1844, October Term 1840, for George Parks' 1838 declaration of intention.

    13. Milwaukee Co., Wisc., Third Judicial District Court Files, no. 2574, Mathew Cawker, 1846, declaration of intention.

CITING THE TERM OF COURT

Note 2 points to the need to carefully analyze the situation in which your record is recorded. Those loose documents from the Allegheny County Prothronotary records are filed in chronological order by court term, but may contain documents bearing earlier dates. When the item of interest carries the earlier date, you should include both the court term and the document date in both the full citation and the short form.

Microfilm (FHL-GSU)

Source List Entry

Ohio. Lucas County Board of Collections. Naturalization Records. Center for Archival Collections, Bowling Green State University, Bowling Green. FHL microfilm 1,991,417. Family History Library, Salt Lake City, Utah.

First Reference Note

    1. Lucas County, Ohio, Board of Collections, Naturalization Records, City of Toledo, ward 1, precinct A, p. 55, no. 109, Henry Lehr, naturalized 19 October 1896; Center for Archival Collections, Bowling Green State University, Bowling Green, Ohio; FHL microfilm 1,991,417.

Subsequent Note

    11. Lucas Co., Ohio, Naturalization Records, City of Toledo, ward 1, precinct A, p. 55, no. 109, Henry Lehr, 1896.

CITATION REQUESTS BY REPOSITORIES

When using filmed records, you should check the beginning of the reel for special instructions or requests. In the case above, the register has been removed from Lucas County and is now part of a university-based public-records preservation program. Preceding the first page of the register is a special "Note to Researchers" that explains the provenance of the book and states: "Any publication or other public use of materials reproduced from the holdings of the Center must credit the Center for Archival Collections." When you encounter requirements of this type, you should record them in your working Source List, so you will not overlook compliance when you publish or distribute your research. *This is an exception to the rule given in the last sentence at 8.16, paragraph 2.*

CITING AGENCY AS AUTHOR

For county records still maintained by the agency that created them, you do not have to include the agency's name in the "author" field. Most examples in this chapter follow that principle. However, when county records have been removed to a different repository, as with the Lucas County example above, the identity of the creator/agency *should* be added to the author field to preserve that element of the record's provenance.

Online Databases & Indexes

Source List Entry

Delaware. "Naturalization Records Database." *State of Delaware: The Official Website*. http://www.state.de.us/sos/dpa/collections/nat rlzndb/ : 2007.

First Reference Note

1. Delaware, "Naturalization Records Database," *State of Delaware: The Official Website* (http://www.state.de.us/sos/dpa/collections/natrlzndb/ : accessed 1 February 2007), entry for Jakob Abramovitz of Romania, 1903; citing New Castle County Declarations of Intent, Naturalizations, First Papers.

Subsequent Note

11. Delaware, "Naturalization Records Database," entry for Jakob Abramovitz of Romania, 1903 declaration of intent.

8.32   Orphans' Court Records

See Chapter 10, Local & State Records: Property & Probates.

8.33   Pension Affidavits

See also 9.14 for Veterans, Widows, and Orphan Rolls, Local

Local affidavits that pension applicants made before a duly appointed board or official are sometimes recorded in special registers set aside for that purpose. Often, they are intermingled with other matters in court record books. Citations in either case usually follow the Basic Citation Formats for court records, 8.18–8.20. When quirks exist, you should add a comment to explain them.

In the following example, the particular volume cited in the Reference Notes carries a distinct label that is different from others in its series.

Therefore, that title is copied exactly and placed in quotation marks. Inside the register, the lack of pagination or consistent arrangement are irregularities that need to be noted. Because there are multiple widows of the same name as the cited person, her age and the name of her late husband are added as identifiers.

Source List Entry

Mississippi. Attala County. Confederate Pension Applications, 1898–1924. Chancery Clerk's Office, Kosciusko.

First Reference Note

1. Attala County, Mississippi, Confederate Pension Records, Book 3 (1898–1904), unpaginated, 1898 application of Elizabeth Boyd, aged 74, widow of Cyrus Boyd; Chancery Clerk's Office, Kosciusko. This register appears to be a later consolidation of information from loose applications; entries are neither alphabetical nor chronological.

Subsequent Note

11. Attala County, Mississippi, "Confederate Pension Records, Book 3," unpaginated, 1898 application of Elizabeth Boyd, aged 74, widow of Cyrus Boyd.

8.34 Poor-farm Records

See Indigent Records, 8.27.

8.35 Probate Court Records

See Chapter 10, Local & State Records: Property & Probates

8.36 Town Records

New England and New York have "towns" as the basic local unit of government. Some records that would be maintained at the county level in other American states are administered by these Northeastern towns. As with the large metropolitan independent cities, when citing council records, selectmen's records, treasurer's records, etc., from the "towns" of New England and New York, you should not assign the records to the *county* in which the town lies.

Moreover, a "town" in these states can contain several other "towns" (i.e., named settlements or municipalities), each with its own name and its own post office. In the Newport, Rhode Island, example below, records of Newport are maintained at Newport—thus Newport is both the creator of the record and the location of the record. However, in the Glocester, Rhode Island, example, town records created by the "town" of Glocester are physically maintained in its smaller "town" of Chepachet.

Source List Entry

New Hampshire. Richmond. Town Records, 1770–1806. Town Clerk's Office, Richmond.

Rhode Island. Glocester. Land Evidences. Town Clerk's Office, Chepachet.

Rhode Island. Newport. Town Council Records. Newport Historical Society, Newport.

Vermont. Bennington. Town Records, 1741–1809. Town Clerk's Office, Bennington.

First Reference Note

1. Richmond, New Hampshire, Town Records 1: 7, for clearing of road past James Shafter's residence; Town Clerk's Office, Richmond.

2. Glocester, Rhode Island, Land Evidences 5:434; Town Clerk's Office, Chepachet.

3. Newport, Rhode Island, Town Council Records 18: 103, for Nathaniel Taylor; Newport Historical Society, Newport.

4. Bennington, Vermont, Town Records, vol. A-1 (1741–1809): 290; Town Clerk's Office, Bennington.

Subsequent Note

11. Richmond, N.H., Town Records, 1: 7.

12. Glocester, R.I., Land Evidences, 5: 434.

13. Newport, R.I., Town Council Records, 18: 103.

14. Bennington, Vt., Town Records, A-1: 290.

CITING NATURE OF INFORMATION

If the cited page of a town record book explicitly treats an individual you discussed in the text, the citation does not need to tell users exactly what to look for on the cited page. However, let us say that in the New Hampshire example above (notes 1 and 11), the discussion in the text treats a man whose name does *not* appear on the cited page. Therefore, the note alerts the reader to the specific passage that is of value.

COLONY & STATE RECORDS

8.37   Archival Inventories

Most state archives create in-house finding aids such as calendars, inventories, or registers. Because most organize their holdings by *record group* (see 3.1), the inventories are usually keyed to specific record groups and are typically maintained in one of five ways:

- unpublished guides in binders that are shelved and open to users;
- unbound typescripts stored in folders, within file cabinets maintained in the reference room—an arrangement often called *vertical files* (see 3.23);

- bound or unbound typescripts archived in the record group itself;
- an essay or list microfilmed at the beginning of roll one of a film series; or
- digitized copies posted online.

An inventory from the Tennessee state archive is used below to demonstrate typical citations to all five forms:

BOUND TYPESCRIPTS

Source List Entry

McGrath, Vincent G. "Tennessee Supreme Court Clerk's Records, 1810–1955; Record Group 191." Typescript. Tennessee State Library and Archives, Nashville. 1992.

First Reference Note

1. Vincent G. McGrath, "Tennessee Supreme Court Clerk's Records, 1810–1955; Record Group 191" (Typescript, Tennessee State Library and Archives, Nashville, 1992), unnumbered pp. 2–3, "Historical Sketch."

Subsequent Note

11. McGrath, "Tennessee Supreme Court Clerk's Records, 1810–1955," unnumbered pp. 2–3.

UNBOUND TYPESCRIPTS IN REFERENCE-STYLE "VERTICAL FILES"

Source List Entry

McGrath, Vincent G. "Tennessee Supreme Court Clerk's Records, 1810–1955; Record Group 191." Typescript. Tennessee State Library and Archives, Nashville. 1992.

First Reference Note

1. Vincent G. McGrath, "Tennessee Supreme Court Clerk's Records, 1810–1955; Record Group 191" (1992), unnumbered pp. 2-3, "Historical Sketch"; Folder: Supreme Court Clerk's Records, 1810–1955, RG 191; Vertical Files: Record Group Registers; Tennessee State Library and Archives, Nashville.

Subsequent Note

11. McGrath, "Tennessee Supreme Court Clerk's Records, 1810–1955," unnumbered pp. 2–3.

TYPESCRIPTS ARCHIVED WITH THE RECORD GROUP ITSELF

Source List Entry

McGrath, Vincent G. "Tennessee Supreme Court Clerk's Records, 1810–1955; Record Group 191." Typescript, 1992. Series 1, Record Group 191. Tennessee State Library and Archives, Nashville.

First Reference Note
　　1. Vincent G. McGrath, "Tennessee Supreme Court Clerk's Records, 1810–1955; Record Group 191" (typescript, 1992), unnumbered pp. 2-3, "Historical Sketch"; Series 1, Tennessee Supreme Court Clerk's Records, RG 191; Tennessee State Library and Archives, Nashville.

Subsequent Note
　　11. McGrath, "Tennessee Supreme Court Clerk's Records, 1810–1955," unnumbered pp. 2–3.

Microfilm (State Archives)

Source List Entry
McGrath, Vincent G. "Tennessee Supreme Court Clerk's Records, 1810–1955; Record Group 191." Microfilm RG 191, roll 3. Tennessee State Library and Archives, Nashville.

First Reference Note
　　1. Vincent G. McGrath, "Tennessee Supreme Court Clerk's Records, 1810–1955; Record Group 191" (typescript, 1992), unnumbered pp. 2-3, "Historical Sketch"; microfilm RG 191, roll 3; Tennessee State Library and Archives, Nashville.

Subsequent Note
　　11. McGrath, "Tennessee Supreme Court Clerk's Records, 1810–1955," unnumbered pp. 2–3.

Online Image

Source List Entry
McGrath, Vincent G. "Tennessee Supreme Court Clerk's Records, 1810–1955; Record Group 191." Digital image. *Tennessee State Library and Archives*. http://www.tennessee.gov/tsla/history/state/recordgroups/alphalist.htm : 2007.

First Reference Note
　　1. Vincent G. McGrath, "Tennessee Supreme Court Clerk's Records, 1810–1955; Record Group 191," unnumbered pp. 2-3, "Historical Sketch," PDF, *Tennessee State Library and Archives* (http://www.tennessee.gov/tsla/history/state/recordgroups/alphalist.htm : accessed 1 February 2007), select "Supreme Court Clerk's Records, 1810–1955" to view the PDF.

Subsequent Note
　　11. McGrath, "Tennessee Supreme Court Clerk's Records, 1810–1955," unnumbered pp. 2–3.

8.38   Courts: Colony Level

In some American colonies, the court seated at the capital was the only court in the colony. In others, it was the principal court, or it served only an appellate function. (For appellate courts, see 8.39.) In the Maryland example, below, the case label carries a quaint notation seldom seen in later years: the use of the symbol @ as a substitute for *against* (i.e., *versus*). The Louisiana example illustrates the difference between citing an original file vis à vis the microfilm image.

BOUND VOLUMES

Source List Entry

Maryland. Provincial Court Judgments, 1679–1778. Maryland State Archives, Annapolis.

First Reference Note

1.   Maryland, Provincial Court Judgments, vol. 58: 99–102, Peregrine Frisby @ Alexander Calder, May Term 1768.

Subsequent Note

11.   Maryland, Provincial Court Judgments, 58: 99–102.

LOOSE PAPERS

Source List Entry

Louisiana. Spanish Judiciary Records, 1769–1804. Louisiana Historical Center, New Orleans.

First Reference Note

1.   Louisiana, Spanish Judiciary Records, 1769–1804, doc. 1777-03-13-01, Rex v. Cesario, for testimony of Margarita, 17 March 1777; Louisiana Historical Center, New Orleans.

Subsequent Note

11.   Louisiana, Spanish Judiciary Records, doc. 1777-03-13-01, Rex v. Cesario, testimony of Margarita, 17 March 1777.

Microfilm (FHL-GSU)

Source List Entry

Louisiana. Spanish Judicial Records, 1769–1804. Louisiana Historical Center, New Orleans. FHL microfilm, 239 rolls. Family History Library, Salt Lake City, Utah.

First Reference Note

1.   Louisiana, Spanish Judicial Records, 1769–1804, doc. 1777-03-13-01, Rex v. Cesario, for testimony of Margarita, 17 March 1777; FHL microfilm 1,033,277.

Subsequent Note

11. Louisiana, Spanish Judicial Records, doc. 1777-03-13-01, *Rex v. Cesario*, for testimony of Margarita, 17 March 1777.

FILM SERIES, NOT CONSECUTIVELY NUMBERED

If the FHL film series above were consecutively numbered, you might want to record the beginning and ending numbers. When the series is not consecutively numbered, as with the 239 rolls of the Spanish Judicial Records, your Source List Entry might cite the specific roll you used or, if you used multiple rolls, it might simply state the number of rolls in the series.

Online Databases & Indexes

Source List Entry

South Carolina. "Criminal Journals, 1769–1776." Database. *South Carolina Department of Archives and History.* http://www.archive index.sc.gov/ : 2007.

First Reference Note

1. South Carolina, "Criminal Journals, 1769–1776," database, *South Carolina Department of Archives and History* (http://www. archiveindex.sc.gov/ : accessed 2 February 2007), entry for King v. John Smith, Stealing Negroes, 1769.

Subsequent Note

11. South Carolina, "Criminal Journals, 1769–1776," entry for King v. Smith, Stealing Negroes, 1769.

CITING A COMMON NAME

When citing a database entry for a common name, you should include enough detail to identify the specific case.

CITING NATURE OF CASE

When citing court cases, it is usually not necessary to identify the charges, unless the detail is needed to identify an entry for a man with a common name.

8.39   Courts: State (or Provincial) Appellate Cases

See also QuickCheck Model *for* ORIGINAL RECORDS: STATE-LEVEL: APPEALS COURT...

When a case is appealed from a local court to a district, state, provincial, or federal court, the file generated at the local level is transmitted to the higher court, where it is assigned a new docket number or case number. The case name may also be reversed. For example, a case might originate locally as John Brown v. Sam Smith. If the case was decided in favor of Brown, then Smith appealed, the name of the new case before the appellate court would be Sam Smith v. John Brown. Your citation to the appellate case should carry the label and the case number used in the appellate court, not the label and number of the original case at the local level.

Source List Entry

Maryland. Court of Appeals Judgments. MSA no. S381-4, accession no. 683-6. Maryland State Archives, Annapolis.

Nova Scotia. Supreme Court. Case Files, 1930. Nova Scotia Archives and Records Management, Halifax.

First Reference Note

1. Maryland, Court of Appeals Judgments, Book 33: 1–10, Joseph Ruppert v. City of Baltimore, April 1865; MSA no. S381-4, accession no. 683-6; Maryland State Archives, Annapolis.

2. Nova Scotia, Supreme Court Case Files, no. D159 (1930), Charles Albert White v. Mae Ada White, divorce; RG 39, Nova Scotia Archives and Records Management, Halifax.

Subsequent Note

11. Maryland, Court of Appeals Judgments, Book 33: 1–10, Ruppert v. City of Baltimore, April 1865.

12. Nova Scotia, Supreme Court case files, no. D159 (1930), Charles Albert White v. Mae Ada White, divorce.

Online Databases & Indexes

Source List Entry

"Missouri Supreme Court Historical Database." *Missouri Secretary of State.* http://www/sos.mo.gov/archive/judiciary/supremecourt : 2007.

First Reference Note

1. "Missouri Supreme Court Historical Database," *Missouri Secretary of State* (http://www/sos.mo.gov/archive/judiciary/supremecourt : accessed 1 February 2007), entry for George A. Christmann et al. v. Aurora Charleville, 1865; citing "location 15B/6/6, box 533, folder 8," Missouri State Archives.

Subsequent Note

11. "Missouri Supreme Court Historical Database," entry for Christmann v. Charleville, 1865.

8.40 Governors' Papers

The official papers of state or colonial governors typically offer appointment and commission records, correspondence, memoranda, and petitions on an endless variety of subjects. Citing them will vary according to two main factors:

- the cataloging system of the archive; and
- whether the item of interest appears in a bound book or whether it is a loose item in a file.

The following citations to a single folio within a collection demonstrate the differences between citing an individual document or a passage from a bound volume.

Source List Entry
Colorado. Territorial Governors Collection. John Evans Papers. Colorado State Archives, Denver.

First Reference Note
1. John Evans to H. B. Morse, appointment, 26 December 1862; folio 93, FF6, John Evans Papers, Colorado Territorial Governors Collection; Colorado State Archives, Denver.
2. John Evans to W. P. Dole, 29 July 1863; Letter Press Book, pp. 491–95, John Evans Papers, Colorado Territorial Governors Collection; Colorado State Archives, Denver.

Subsequent Note
11. John Evans to H. B. Morse, appointment, 1862, folio 93, FF6, John Evans Papers.
12. John Evans to W. P. Dole, 29 July 1863; Letter Press Book, pp. 491–95, John Evans Papers.

USE OF IBID.
When you edit your manuscript for publication, if you were to have two consecutive references to the John Evans Papers—as in the situation above—your second note would use *ibid.* (meaning *in the same place*) to replace the repetitive wording. However, you would not make this substitution until you reach final-draft stage, because the insertion of added material could separate the *ibid.* reference from the note that should immediately precede it. If you are using a relational database to maintain your research files, printouts from that database might make the appropriate *ibid.* substitution for you automatically.

8.41 Legislative Acts
Legislative acts are typically consulted in published form. See chapter 13, Publications: Legal Works & Government Documents.

8.42 Legislative Petitions & Files
See also QuickCheck Model *for* ORIGINAL RECORDS: STATE-LEVEL: LEGISLATIVE ...

Historically, when a private act was passed by the legislature to benefit an individual or a subset of people—as in a divorce case, a slave manumission, or a request for pension, etc.—legislative files will contain a copy of the original petition and other supporting papers. These documents are typically cited in the classic manner for formally archived materials—i.e., smallest to largest. If the material has been filmed or extracted into a database, there are other considerations, as illustrated by comparing these two citations:

Source List Entry
Tennessee. Legislative Petitions. Record Group 50. Tennessee State
    Library and Archives, Nashville.

First Reference Note
    1. Citizens of Cannon County, Request for Annexation to DeKalb County, 10 October 1845; Legislative Petitions (chronologically arranged), Record Group 50; Tennessee State Library and Archives, Nashville.

Subsequent Note
    11. Citizens of Cannon County, Request for Annexation to DeKalb County, 10 October 1845, Legislative Petitions, Tennessee.

Microfilm (State Archives)

Source List Entry
Tennessee. Legislative Petitions. TSLA microfilm RG 50. Tennessee
    State Library and Archives, Nashville.

First Reference Note
    1. Citizens of Cannon County, Request for Annexation to DeKalb County, 10 October 1845; Legislative Petitions, TSLA microfilm RG 50, roll 17, chronologically arranged; Tennessee State Library and Archives, Nashville.

Subsequent Note
    11. Citizens of Cannon County, Request for Annexation to DeKalb County, 10 October 1845, Legislative Petitions, Tennessee.

Online Databases & Abstracts

When you cite a database entry—even from the state archive that holds the original files—you are not citing a document itself. You are citing a newly created finding aid. Whereas the above microfilm citation began with an identification of the original record, the database entry below begins with the name of the database, cited as a publication in which you have found a reference to an original document.

Source List Entry

South Carolina. "Legislative Papers, 1782–1866." Database. *South Carolina Department of Archives and History*. http://www.archives index.sc.gov/ : 2007.

First Reference Note

1. South Carolina, "Legislative Papers, 1782–1866," database, *South Carolina Department of Archives and History* (http://www.archives index.sc.gov/ : accessed 2 February 2007), abstract, petition of Elijah Jefcoat and others, ca. 1811; citing Series S165015, item 00901.

Subsequent Note

11. South Carolina, "Legislative Papers, 1782–1866," abstract, petition of Elijah Jefcoat and others, ca. 1811.

8.43   Pension Application Files (State-level)

Across time, pensions to military veterans and their widows have been granted, or hearings have been held, at almost every governmental level. Section 8.33 covers *affidavits* recorded at the city or county level. Section 9.12 covers *rolls* maintained at the state level. At section 11.40 you will find pension *files* maintained at the federal level. *State-level application files* also exist. As a rule, they are cited in the same way as other state-level files such as legislative petitions (8.42).

When you consult online images of these state-level files, accessed through a state-sponsored website, you will be citing both the original document and the web publication. You have a choice as to where you wish to place your emphasis:

Emphasis on the original document

If your citation emphasizes the original, as in the first option on the following page, you will need to study the website carefully to glean full details for an archival citation. Typically, this means you must search for links to other pages that provide a description or inventory of that record group. After citing, as fully as possible, the document, file, collection, series, and archive, you will then identify fully the website at which you accessed the material. In the case at hand, the website identifies the record group and record group number but does not provide a specific label for the series or collection. There, the collection name that introduces the citation is a generic one.

Emphasis on the website (i.e., the publication)

This approach is usually more feasible for digitized state-level and national-level files that you access through a government-operated website. Simply cite the website as you would in the database example at 8.42. However, instead of identifying your source as a "database" or "abstract," you identify it as a digital image. Then you add the appropriate description of the document and file, together with whatever citation the website provides.

Online Databases & Images

Source List Entry

(To emphasize the original files)

Florida. Confederate Pension Files. Records of the State Board of Pensions, Record Group 137. State Library and Archives of Florida, Jacksonville. Digital images. "Florida Confederate Pension Application Files." State Library and Archives of Florida. *The Florida Memory Project.* http://www.floridamemory.com/Collections/Pension Files/ : 2007.

(To emphasize the website)

"Florida Confederate Pension Application Files." Database and images. State Library and Archives of Florida. *The Florida Memory Project.* http://www.floridamemory.com/Collections/Pension Files/ : 2007.

First Reference Note

(To emphasize the original files)

1. Widow's Pension Claim, 26 July 1910, application no. A01208, Elizabeth Harper Ortegas, widow of John Ortegas, 2nd Regiment, Florida Infantry; Confederate Pension Files; Records of the State Board of Pensions, RG 137; State Library and Archives of Florida, Jacksonville; digital images, "Florida Confederate Pension Application Files," State Library and Archives, *The Florida Memory Project* (http://www.floridamemory.com/Collections/Pension Files/ : accessed 1 February 2007).

(To emphasize the website)

2. "Florida Confederate Pension Application Files," database and images, State Library and Archives of Florida, *The Florida Memory Project* (http://www.floridamemory.com/Collections/Pension Files/ : accessed 1 February 2007), entry for Elizabeth Harper, widow of John Ortegas, "2nd Regt. Inf., application no. A01208."

Subsequent Note

11. Widow's Pension Claim, 26 July 1910, application no. A01208, Elizabeth Harper Ortegas, widow of John Ortegas, 2nd Regt. Inf., Confederate Pension Files, Florida.

12. "Florida Confederate Pension Application Files," digital images, Widow's Pension Claim, 26 July 1910, Elizabeth Harper Ortegas, widow of John Ortegas, "2nd Regt., Inf., application no. A01208."

LOCAL &
STATE RECORDS
Licenses, Registrations, Rolls & Vital Records

9

QuickCheck Models

(See Chapters 8 and 10 for related models)

Guidelines & Examples (beginning page 433)

QuickCheck Model
LOCAL RECORDS: FILE ITEMS
Jurisdiction & series as lead elements in Source List

Source List Entry

JURISDICTION	SERIES or COLLECTION	...

Alabama. Dallas County. Child Labor Affidavits, 1908–1914. Probate

... REPOSITORY	REPOSITORY LOCATION

Judge's Office, Selma.

First (Full) Reference Note

JURISDICTION	SERIES or COLLECTION	...

1. Dallas County, Alabama, Child Labor Affidavits, 1908–1914, alpha-

... ITEM NO. or ARRANGEMENT	ITEM OF INTEREST

betically arranged by name of child; see Harvey Dodd (born 22 May 1901),

... RECORD DATE	REPOSITORY	REPOSITORY LOCATION

filed 23 May 1913; Probate Judge's Office, Selma.

Subsequent (Short) Note

JURISDICTION	SERIES or COLLECTION	ITEM OF ...

11. Dallas Co., Ala., Child Labor Affidavits, 1908–1914, affidavit for

... INTEREST	RECORD DATE

Harvey Dodd, filed 23 May 1913.

QuickCheck Model
LOCAL RECORDS
FILES MOVED TO STATE ARCHIVES
Jurisdiction & series as lead elements in Source List

Source List Entry

JURISDICTION · RECORD SERIES

New Jersey. Sussex County. Applications for Tavern Licenses, 1753–1769.

COLLECTION · REPOSITORY · REPOSITORY LOCATION

County Government Records. New Jersey State Archives, Trenton.

First (Full) Reference Note

JURISDICTION · RECORD SERIES ...

1. Sussex County, New Jersey, Applications for Tavern Licenses, 1753–

... FILE · ITEM NO. or ARRANGEMENT

1769, file: "Sussex County Tavern Licenses, 1754," alphabetically arranged,

ITEM OF INTEREST · * · COLLECTION · REPOSITORY ...

see Joseph Walling;   County Government Records; New Jersey State

... REPOSITORY LOCATION

Archives, Trenton.

Subsequent (Short) Note

JURISDICTION · FILE

11. Sussex Co., N.J., file: "Sussex County Tavern Licenses, 1754,"

ITEM OF INTEREST

Joseph Walling.

---

* *After the identification of the item, you should add the year or date of the record, if that information is not embedded in the title of the record (as in the case above).*

QuickCheck Model
LOCAL RECORDS
REGISTERS: NAMED VOLUME

Jurisdiction & series as lead elements in Source List

Source List Entry

JURISDICTION   SERIES   ...

Missouri. St. Louis, City of. Record of Druggists' Licenses, 1893–1909. City

... REPOSITORY   REPOSITORY LOCATION

Board of Pharmacy, St. Louis.

First (Full) Reference Note

JURISDICTION   SPECIFIC VOLUME ...

1. City of St. Louis, Missouri, "To Record Druggists' Licenses,

...   PAGE NO. or ARRANGEMENT

1898," registrations semi-alphabetical by first letter of surname, p. N,

ITEM OF INTEREST   *   REPOSITORY   REPOSITORY LOCATION

no. 1041, Oscar F. Nitzschmann;   City Board of Pharmacy, St. Louis.

Subsequent (Short) Note

JURISDICTION   SPECIFIC VOLUME   PAGE

11. St. Louis, Mo., "To Record Druggists' Licenses, 1898," p. N,

CASE and/or ITEM

no. 1041, Oscar F. Nitzschmann.

* *After the identification of the item, you should add the date or year of the record, if that information is not embedded in the title of the record (as in the case above).*

QuickCheck Model
LOCAL RECORDS
REGISTERS: NUMBERED VOLUME
Jurisdiction & series as lead elements in Source List

Source List Entry

JURISDICTION   SERIES ...

Illinois. Chicago. Record and Index of Persons Registered and of Poll Lists

REPOSITORY
...   REPOSITORY   LOCATION

of Voters, 1888–1892. Board of Election Commissioners, Chicago.

First (Full) Reference Note

JURISDICTION   SERIES ...

1. Chicago, Illinois, Record and Index of Persons Registered and

ITEM OF
...   SPECIFIC VOLUME   PAGE   INTEREST   *   ...

of Poll Lists of Voters, vol. AA-CU (1888): 78, Olaf Aune   ; Board

REPOSITORY
... REPOSITORY   LOCATION

of Election Commissioners, Chicago.

Subsequent (Short) Note

JURISDICTION   SERIES ...

11. Chicago, Ill., Record and Index of Persons Registered and of

ITEM OF
...   SPECIFIC VOLUME   PAGE   INTEREST

Poll Lists of Voters, vol. AA-CU (1888): 78, Olaf Aune.

---

* *After the identification of the item, you should add the date or year of the record, if that information is not embedded in the title of the record (as in the case above).*

QuickCheck Model
LOCAL RECORDS
VITAL-RECORDS CERTIFICATE

Jurisdiction & series as lead elements in Source List

Source List Entry

JURISDICTION	SERIES	REPOSITORY ...

Florida. Polk County. Marriage Certificates. Polk County Central Bureau

...	REPOSITORY LOCATION

of Vital Statistics, Bartow.

First (Full) Reference Note

JURISDICTION	CERTIFICATE TYPE & NO.	CERT. DATE	ID OF ...

1. Polk County, Florida, marriage certificate no. 6745 (1940), Garland-

PERSON(S)	REPOSITORY	REPOSITORY LOCATION

Davis; Polk County Central Bureau of Vital Statistics, Bartow.

Subsequent (Short) Note

JURISDICTION	CERTIFICATE TYPE & NO.	CERT. DATE	ID OF ...

11. Polk Co., Fla., marriage certificate no. 6745 (1940), Garland-

PERSON(S)

Davis.

QuickCheck Model
LOCAL RECORDS
VITAL-RECORDS REGISTER
Jurisdiction & volume as lead elements in Source List

Source List Entry

JURISDICTION	SPECIFIC VOLUME	REPOSITORY ...

Kentucky. Pendleton County. "Births, 1852–1859." Office of the Clerk of

...	REPOSITORY LOCATION

County Court, Falmouth.

First (Full) Reference Note

JURISDICTION	SPECIFIC VOLUME	SECTION

1. Pendleton County, Kentucky, "Births, 1852–1859," 1855 section,

PAGE	ITEM OF INTEREST ...

p. 1, for "Alexander," black child attributed to "Father or Owner," W.

...	REPOSITORY	REPOSITORY LOCATION

G. Woodson; Office of the Clerk of County Court, Falmouth.

Subsequent (Short) Note

JURISDICTION	SPECIFIC VOLUME	SECTION & PAGE

11. Pendleton Co., Ky., "Births, 1852–1859," 1855 section, p. 1, for

ITEM OF INTEREST

"Alexander," black child attributed to W. G. Woodson.

QuickCheck Model
LOCAL RECORDS
VITAL RECORDS, AMENDED
Jurisdiction & series as lead elements in Source List

Source List Entry

JURISDICTION   SERIES   REPOSITORY ...

Texas. Limestone County. Amended Birth Records. County Clerk's Office,

REPOSITORY
LOCATION

Groesbeck.

First (Full) Reference Note

JURISDICTION   CERTIFICATE TYPE ...

1. Limestone County, Texas, amended birth certificate, local file

... & NO.   CERT. DATE   ID OF PERSON ...

no. 1982 (issued 1983), Johnnie LaVerne Grooms, formerly "Unknown

...   CREDIT LINE (SOURCE OF THE SOURCE) ...

Grooms"; citing the 1927 registration in "Book 7, page 61D, Birth

...   REPOSITORY   REPOSITORY LOCATION

Records of Limestone County"; County Clerk's Office, Groesbeck.

Subsequent (Short) Note

JURISDICTION   CERTIFICATE TYPE & NO.

11. Limestone Co., Tex., amended birth certificate, local file no.

...   CERT. DATE   ID OF PERSON

1982 (issued 1983), Johnnie LaVerne Grooms.

QuickCheck Model
LOCAL RECORDS
VITAL RECORDS, DELAYED
Jurisdiction & series as lead elements in Source List

Source List Entry

JURISDICTION   SERIES   REPOSITORY

Illinois. Cass County. Delayed Birth Records. County Clerk's Office,

REPOSITORY LOCATION

Virginia, Illinois.

First (Full) Reference Note

                                                    CERT.

JURISDICTION   CERTIFICATE TYPE & NO.   DATE   ID ...

1. Cass County, Illinois, delayed birth certificate no. 4071 (1942), Mary

... OF PERSON   REPOSITORY   REPOSITORY LOCATION

Rose Hunt; County Clerk's Office, Virginia, Illinois.

Subsequent (Short) Note

                                                 CERT.

JURISDICTION   CERTIFICATE TYPE & NO.   DATE   ...

11. Cass Co., Ill., delayed birth certificate no. 4071 (1942), Mary

ID OF PERSON

Rose Hunt.

QuickCheck Model
STATE-LEVEL RECORDS
MISCELLANEOUS FILES
State & series as lead elements in Source List

Source List Entry

JURISDICTION   SERIES   RECORD GROUP NAME ...

Pennsylvania.   Military Accounts: Militia. Records of the Comptroller

         ... & NO.   REPOSITORY   REPOSITORY LOCATION

General, Record Group 4. Pennsylvania State Archives, Harrisburg.

First (Full) Reference Note

ITEM OF INTEREST

1. George Widdows (3d. Company, Capt. John Young, Philadelphia),

DOCUMENT   RECORD DATE   SERIES ...

Absentee Return, 7th Battalion: 1778–1779, undated; Military Accounts:

...   RECORD GROUP NAME & NO.   REPOSITORY ...

Militia; Records of the Comptroller General, Record Group 4; Pennsylvania

...   REPOSITORY LOCATION

State Archives, Harrisburg.

Subsequent (Short) Note

ITEM OF INTEREST   DOCUMENT ...

11. George Widdows (3d. Co., Philadelphia), Absentee Return, 7th Battn.,

...

1778–79.

QuickCheck Model
STATE-LEVEL RECORDS
VITAL-RECORDS CERTIFICATE
Jurisdiction, agency & series as lead elements in Source List

Source List Entry

JURISDICTION   AGENCY / CREATOR   SERIES

Delaware. Department of Health and Social Services. Birth Certificates.

        REPOSITORY
    REPOSITORY   LOCATION

Office of Vital Statistics, Dover.

First (Full) Reference Note

JURISDICTION   AGENCY / CREATOR   CERTIFICATE ...

1. Delaware Department of Health and Social Services, birth certificate

       CERT.   REPOSITORY
...TYPE & NO.   DATE   ID OF PERSON   REPOSITORY   LOCATION

107-53-001504 (1953), Edward Devine; Office of Vital Statistics, Dover.

Subsequent (Short) Note

                                 CERT.
JURISDICTION   CERTIFICATE TYPE & NO.   DATE   ID OF ...

11. Delaware birth certificate no. 107-53-001504 (1953), Edward

PERSON

Devine.

QuickCheck Model
STATE-LEVEL RECORDS
VITAL-RECORDS REGISTER
Jurisdiction, agency & series as lead elements in Source List

Source List Entry

JURISDICTION   AGENCY / CREATOR   SERIES   REPOSITORY ...

Rhode Island. Department of Health. State Death Registers. Office of Vital

   ...   REPOSITORY LOCATION

Records, Providence.

First (Full) Reference Note

JURISDICTION   AGENCY/CREATOR   SERIES   BOOK ...

1. Rhode Island Department of Health, State Death Registers, 1875:

& PAGE ENTRY ID OF PERSON   *   REPOSITORY   REPOSITORY LOCATION

1290, no. 28, Lucy J. DeHaro;   Office of Vital Records, Providence.

Subsequent (Short) Note

JURISDICTION   SERIES   BOOK & PAGE ENTRY ID OF ...

11. Rhode Island State Death Registers, 1875: 1290, no. 28, Lucy J.

PERSON

Deharo.

---

* *After the identification of the person(s), you should add the date or year of the record, if that information is not embedded in the title of the volume (as in the case above).*

QuickCheck Model
STATE-LEVEL RECORDS
VITAL RECORDS, AMENDED
Jurisdiction, agency & series as lead elements in Source List

Source List Entry

JURIS-
DICTION   AGENCY / CREATOR   SERIES

Texas. Department of State Health Services. Amended birth records.

             REPOSITORY
     REPOSITORY   LOCATION

Vital Statistics Office, Austin.

First (Full) Reference Note

         JURIS-
         DICTION   AGENCY / CREATOR   CERTIFICATE ...

1. Texas Department of State Health Services, amended birth

               CERT.
...TYPE & NO.   DATE   ID OF PERSON ...

certificate no. 5129 (1927), Johnnie LaVerne Grooms, formerly "Unknown

              REPOSITORY
      ...   REPOSITORY   LOCATION

Grooms"; Vital Statistics Office, Austin.

Subsequent (Short) Note

         JURIS-
         DICTION   CERTIFICATE TYPE & NO.   DATE   ID OF ...

11. Texas amended birth certificate no. 5129 (1927), Johnnie

... PERSON

LaVerne Grooms.

GUIDELINES
& Examples

BASIC ISSUES

9.1 Background

Governments have long felt a need to license or register certain classes of its people. In addition to the birth, marriage, and death registrations most researchers know well, governments also have kept rolls of *freemen* (free of servitude, regardless of race) who were qualified to vote, *free people of color* who were not necessarily enfranchised but needed "protection papers" to prevent their being reenslaved, and children employed at hazardous jobs. Governments have required the licensing of dogs, guns, knives, boats, cars, and many other items. They have maintained rolls and registers of militia, pensioners, and citizens engaged in critical professions such as law, medicine, and the ministry.

Most of the principles discussed at 8.1–8.16 for the use of local and state records also apply to licenses and registrations at the county and town levels. Some key points will be reiterated where appropriate in this chapter. The basic issues that determine the structure of your citations in this record category will be

- whether the record was created at the local or state level;
- whether the *original* record you are citing is a "loose" document from an agency file, an official copy recorded in a clerk's record book, or an image copy consulted in filmed or digitized form; and
- whether the *derivative* record you are citing is an official certificate issued by an agency, or whether it is a database or index.

9.2 Citing Key Parties in the Record

Because registrations and related records are intrinsically personal and individual, your citation to a record usually needs to identify the key person or persons involved. You should also render each name exactly as it appears in the original record. If you feel a correction of the spelling is needed, you should place your correction in square editorial brackets immediately after the official spelling.

9.3 Citing Local vs. State Records

Records held at the *local level* are typically cited as authored works. That is, you begin your Reference Note by citing the local agency or jurisdiction that created (authored) the record, followed by identification of the record book or file, the page or file number, and the specific item of interest. In your First Reference Note, you close out the basic citation by identifying the repository and its location.

Records held at the *state level* are typically cited in classic format for formally archived records. Your Reference Note begins by identifying the smallest element (the item of interest) and proceeds through the various file, collection, series, and record-group designations until you reach the largest element (the repository and its location).

MARRIAGE LICENSES, REGISTRATIONS, ETC.

9.4 Basic Formats: Bound Volumes

Civil marriage registrations typically begin with the filing of an *intent* (in some regions), the purchase of a *license,* and (in former times) the signing of a *bond* to ensure that the parties were legally qualified to marry. Official copies of the intents, bonds, and licenses were maintained by the local clerk. The license was typically provided to the groom, who surrendered it to the minister or civil official when the ceremony occurred. That official was then to *return* the license with details of the time, place, and parties involved.

Often, the license issued to the groom carried a preprinted section for the minister or other designated official to fill in the marriage details. This part of the form was sometimes called the *minister's certificate,* in the sense that the officiating party was *certifying* the facts. This "certification" returned to the court by the minister or civil official should not be confused with modern certificates, discussed at 9.31.

In some locales, only the *returns* were registered by the town or county clerk. In other locales, the clerks maintained registers of all these record types. Many kept files of the bonds and licenses. As states began to require formal registration of all vital events, copies of the marriage returns were forwarded to the designated state agency, which then responded to record requests by supplying certificates attesting the basic details. For these certificates, see 9.41, State-level Certificates.

The bonds, intents, licenses, and returns created at the local level are cited in one of two ways—as a record in a bound volume or as a loose document. The basic examples, below, illustrate a range of terminology used by various states.

Source List Entry
Alabama. Mobile County. Colored Marriage Records, 1865–1900. Probate Judge's Office, Mobile.

Mississippi. Leake County. Marriage Books, 1837–1900. Chancery Clerk's Office, Carthage.

Pennsylvania. Allegheny County. Marriage License Dockets, 1885–1905. Office of the Orphans' Court Clerk, Pittsburgh.

First Reference Note
1. Mobile County, Alabama, Colored Marriage Records, 4:378, Hubbell-Clark, 1874; Probate Judge's Office, Mobile.

2. Leake County, Mississippi, Marriage Book B:72, James Boyd and Mary Smith, 1853, recorded bond and license (with original signatures) and return; Chancery Clerk's Office, Carthage.

3. Allegheny County, Pennsylvania, Marriage License Dockets 1899, vol. 48:646, Joseph Sebastian Kim–Katharine Page; Office of the Orphans' Court Clerk, Pittsburgh.

Subsequent Note
11. Mobile Co., Ala., Colored Marriage Licenses, 4:378.

12. Leake Co., Miss., Marriage Book B:72.

13. Allegheny Co., Penn., Marriage License Dockets, 48:646.

IDENTIFYING SPOUSES IN MARRIAGE RECORDS
In citing marriage records, you may choose to identify spouses by surnames only, as in note 1, or by full names (as in notes 2 and 3). If you have a specific book and page from a well-organized series, and if your research is thorough enough that you know for certain only one such couple by that pair of surnames got married in that year, then surnames-only can suffice. However, in many communities you will find certain families repeatedly intermarrying, even in the same year.

IDENTIFYING DATE OR YEAR OF MARRIAGE
As a rule, the exact date of marriage does not have to be cited in a reference note *if* you can identify a specific book and page or if the record is part of a numbered and sequentially arranged series. Unpaginated registers and loose documents, however, are typically arranged in chronological order and exact dates are necessary.

If the title of the register does not carry a year, you should include the year of marriage after the identity of the parties, to place the register in a proper time sequence. A numbered register, if the number is mistyped—or a named volume in a set with similar titles—might result in an entry that is unidentifiable without a referenced year.

Two patterns for citing the year appear in the above examples. Notes 1 and 2 place the year immediately after the spousal names. Note 3 places the year in the title of the register, before the volume number. In the note 3 instance, "vol. 48" refers to the forty-eighth volume for the year 1899. The year is an essential part of the label. In notes 1 and 2, Marriage Records 4 and Marriage Book B each cover a number of years, and neither book carries a date in its title. Therefore, the year is added to the identity of the spouses to give the citation a time reference. The microfiche example below further illustrates the point with a different variant.

Microfiche (Local) ▪▪

Source List Entry
Pennsylvania. Pittsburgh. Ministers' Returns of Marriages, 1850–1880. Register of Wills Office, Pittsburgh.

First Reference Note
    1. Pittsburgh, Pennsylvania, Ministers' Returns of Marriages, vol. 2 (1870–1879): 159, Falloon–Hann, 1871 (microfiche copy); Register of Wills Office, Pittsburgh.

Subsequent Note
    11. Pittsburgh, Pa., Ministers' Returns of Marriages, 2:159.

IDENTIFYING A REGISTER BY DATE & VOLUME
This ministers' return citation illustrates a common situation in using courthouse and townhall registers: the identification of the register contains three parts: the series name, the volume number, and the years covered by the volume you are citing. Consider the following possible options for the arrangement of these three elements

    Ministers' Returns of Marriages, vol. 2 (1870–1879): 159
    Ministers' Returns of Marriages, 1870–1879, vol. 2: 159

- The first option would tell your reader the name of the series, the volume number within that series, and the dates covered by that volume.

• The second options would tell your reader the name of the series, the years covered by the series, and the volume number within that span of years.

Obviously, there is a difference. In that example, the series actually covers 1850–1880. That whole series is cited in the Source List Entry. The First Reference Note then cites the specific volume (2) and the years covered by that specific volume (1870–1879).

Microfilm (FHL-GSU)

Source List Entry
Ohio. Hocking County. Marriage Records, 1850–1880. Probate Judge's Office, Logan. FHL microfilm 912,319. Family History Library, Salt Lake City, Utah.

First Reference Note
1. Hocking County, Ohio, Marriage Records, C: 46, Strawser-Leisure, 1861; FHL microfilm 912,319.

Subsequent Note
11. Hocking Co., Ohio, Marriage Records, C: 46.

9.5   Basic Formats: Loose Papers (Bonds & Licenses)

Source List Entry
Illinois. St. Clair County. Marriage Licenses and Returns. County Clerk's Office, Belleville.
Massachusetts. Boston. Marriage Intents. City Registrar's Office, Boston.

First Reference Note
1. St. Clair County, Illinois, Marriage Licenses and Returns, no. 3538, Malloy-Keating, 1895; County Clerk's Office, Belleville.
2. Boston, Massachusetts, Marriage Intents, 1856, no. 1721, Lawrence Woodfork to Jane Johnson; City Registrar's Office, Boston.

Subsequent Note
11. St. Clair Co., Ill., Marriage Licenses and Returns, no. 3538, 1895.
12. Boston, Mass., Marriage Intents, 1856: no. 1721.

9.6   Basic Formats: Online Resources
As discussed more fully at 2.33–2.34, your citation to an online database, or a set of posted abstracts, will be constructed differently from a citation to image copies.

Online Abstracts, Databases & Indexes

Online abstracts, databases, and indexes can usually be cited like any authored article at a website. The key issue is that you are not citing original records. You are citing a derivative work created by someone other than the original creator. Therefore, your emphasis will be on the derivative. Whatever data your derivative provides about the original will be cited only as the source of your source.

Source List Entry

(*To cite abstracts*)

Ratay, Nancy, "Marriages from the Day Book of Thompson Barron, Unitarian Minister, 1838–1860, Windsor County, VT [and] Cheshire and Merrimack Counties, NH." Abstracts. USGenWeb. *USGenWebArchives: New Hampshire.* http://ftp.rootsweb.com/pub/usgenweb/nh/state/vitals/marriages/marriagesbarron.txt : 2007.

(*To cite a database or index*)

"Idaho Marriages, 1842–1996." Database. *Ancestry.com.* http://www.ancestry.com/search/ : 2007.

First Reference Note

1. Nancy Ratay, "Marriages from the Day Book of Thompson Barron, Unitarian Minister, 1838–1860, Windsor County, VT [and] Cheshire and Merrimack Counties, NH," abstracts, *USGenWebArchives: New Hampshire* (http://ftp.rootsweb.com/pub/usgenweb/nh/state/vitals/marriages/marriagesbarron.txt : accessed 3 February 2007), chronologically arranged, entry for Rufus Bullard to Harriett C. Ripley, 1 September 1842.

2. "Idaho Marriages, 1842–1996," database, *Ancestry.com* (http://www.ancestry.com/search/ : accessed 3 February 2007), entry for William E. Sebring–Mable Shown, 19 February 1900; citing Ada County, Idaho, [Marriages] Vol. 4: 280.

Subsequent Note

11. Ratay, "Marriages from the Day Book of Thompson Barron," Bullard-Ripley, 1842.

12. "Idaho Marriages, 1842–1996," database, *Ancestry.com,* entry for Sebring-Shown, 1900.

ONLINE REPUBLICATION FROM A PRINTED SOURCE

If the abstract, database, or index is a republication of material previously published in printed form, you have an added layer of identification: the original source of the material. In the following case, the online compiler is identified only in her copyright line at the end of the material; the compiler of the information in the original publication is not identified. RootsWeb is the agency whose website *California Statewide* hosts Melton's material.

Source List Entry

Nancy Pratt Melton, "Overland Monthly & Out West Magazine, 1872: Record of Marriages." Database. RootsWeb, *California Statewide.* http://freepages.genealogy.rootsweb.com/~npmelton/marr72.htm : 2006.

First Reference Note

1.   Nancy Pratt Melton, compiler, "Overland Monthly & Out West Magazine, 1872: Record of Marriages," abstracts, RootsWeb, *California Statewide* (http://freepages.genealogy.rootsweb.com/~npmelton/ marr72.htm : accessed 4 October 2006), A. J. Stiles to Mary A. Jennings, Nevada City, 1872; citing *Overland Monthly & OutWest Magazine*, vol. 8, issues 5–6, and vol. 9, issues 1–6 (March–October 1872).

Subsequent Note

11.   Melton, "Overland Monthly & Out West Magazine, 1872: Record of Marriages," RootsWeb, *California Statewide,* Stiles-Jennings, Nevada City, 4 March 1872.

Online Images

When you cite a digital image of a record, you are citing the record— albeit in surrogate form. With local records, you may cite that digital image in the same manner you would the original. Then you append the identification of the web publication, including the details outlined at 2.33.

Source List Entry

Indiana. Vigo County. Marriage Licenses, 1923. Digital images. Vigo County Public Library, *Vigo County Marriage Record Project.* http:// marriage.vigo.lib.in.us/marriage/ : 2007.

First Reference Note

1.   Vigo County, Indiana, Marriage Licenses [vol. 62?], p. 16, Lee Shick–Alice Taylor, 28 March 1923; digital images, Vigo County Public Library, *Vigo County Marriage Record Project* (http://marriage .vigo.lib.in.us/marriage/5907/0072a.pdf : accessed 1 February 2007).

Subsequent Note

11.   Vigo Co., Ind., Marriage Licenses [vol. 62?], p. 16, Shick– Taylor, 1923.

IDENTIFYING MISSING SOURCE DATA

Some digitizing projects provide full information for their sources. Others will omit some detail critical to your citation. This Vigo record illustrates how the needed information might be obtained and cited. The online image of the marriage license clearly suggests that it came from a register, in which it appears on page 16; the identity of the register is not provided. However, a search of the Family History Library catalog reveals that March 1923 marriage records for Vigo County appear at the end of volume 61 and the beginning of volume 62. The "page 16" data the website gives for that marriage at the end of March suggests that the online image was taken from volume 62. Having tentatively identified the probable volume, you are justified in adding it to your citation—placing it in square editorial brackets with a question mark. You might then order the appropriate FHL microfilm to verify your deduction. The FHL catalog entry also identifies the location of the original register, another piece of information omitted from the online image and database.

9.7   Records Removed to State Archives

Local files of bonds, intents, and licenses are often transferred to the state archives, where they are typically maintained in a "county records collection." There, they are usually organized under the county name and then by name of the bridal couple, as in this example:

Source List Entry
North Carolina. Alamance County. Original Marriage Bonds. County Records Collection. North Carolina State Archives, Raleigh.

First Reference Note
1. Alamance County, North Carolina, Original Marriage Bonds, File: "Merritt, Joseph to Kizzie Murray, 1866"; County Records Collection; North Carolina State Archives, Raleigh.

Subsequent Note
11. Alamance Co., N.C., Original Marriage Bonds, File: "Merritt, Joseph to Kizzie Murray, 1866."

9.8   Stray Marriage Records

When working with old registers, one frequently encounters items recorded in places where they would not be expected. To eliminate a later question as to whether you have cited your source erroneously, your citation needs to note the aberration in some way—as illustrated by this marriage record recorded in an animal register.

Source List Entry
Massachusetts. Sutton. "Sutton's Book of Records of Estrays & Marks, Dom. 1732–Dom. 1816." Town Clerk's Office, Sutton.

First Reference Note
> 1. Sutton, Massachusetts, "Sutton's Book of Records of Estrays & Marks, Dom. 1732–Dom. 1816," unnumbered page between part 1 (estray records) and part 2 (marks and brands), marriage intent for Samuel Marble and Patience Gale Booth, 23 July 1743.

Subsequent Note
> 1. Sutton, Mass., "Sutton's Book of Records of Estrays & Marks, Dom. 1732–Dom. 1816," unnumbered page between part 1 (estray records) and part 2 (marks and brands), marriage intent for Marble-Booth, 1743.

MILITARY/PENSION ROLLS & REGISTRATIONS

9.9   Militia Rolls: Local

While city and county offices maintain a variety of records related in some fashion to military service, *rolls* or *rosters* at the county level typically cover local militia units. Their organization varies widely across time and place. Many will fit into the Basic Formats previously illustrated for bound or loose marriage registrations (9.4–9.5). In other cases, such as the entry below, you will need to study the register and devise your own description of what you have found and where you found it.

Source List Entry
> Vermont. Hubbardton. Militia Rolls, 1861–1867. Town Clerk's Office, Hubbardton.

First Reference Note
> 1. Hubbardton, Vermont, "Enrolled Militia [1864–1867]," unpaginated lists arranged in semi-alphabetical order by first letter of surname, see Charles H. Petter; Town Clerk's Office, Hubbardton.

Subsequent Note
> 11. Hubbardton, Vt., "Enrolled Militia [1864–1867]," see Charles H. Petter.

REGISTER TITLES, CLARIFICATION ADDED
In the above example, the cited register is not part of a series. It is cited by its exact title, "Enrolled Militia." However, that title gives no clue to the time period. For future reference you would want to add, in square editorial brackets, the years covered by the volume—information you would get by scanning the volume.

9.10 Militia Rolls: Local, Moved to State Archives

When local militia rolls are removed to a state or regional archive, they are usually cataloged in a county-records collection. As such, they are cited differently from the state-level militia or military rolls created by the state's adjutant-general's office (or its counterpart in states that used other terminology). A typical citation to a roll of local origin that is now in a state archives system would be this:

Source List Entry

Illinois. Cass County. Militia Roll Record, 1861. Accession no. 4/0226/
11. Illinois Regional Archives Depository. University of Illinois,
Springfield.

First Reference Note

1. Cass County, Illinois, Militia Roll Record, 1861: 9, for Michael
Connell; accession no. 4/0226/11, Illinois Regional Archives Depository; University of Illinois, Springfield.

Subsequent Note

11. Cass Co., Ill., Militia Roll Record, 1861: 9.

9.11 Military Rolls: State level

See also QuickCheck Model *for* STATE-LEVEL RECORDS: MISCELLANEOUS FILE

Military rolls created by the state and maintained by the state archives are cited differently from rolls created at the local level that have been removed to the state archives as part of a county-records collection. As discussed at 9.3, state-agency records are typically cataloged in the traditional archival manner, in which the Source List Entry empha-sizes the state and the collection, while the First Reference Note begins with the smallest element of the citation and progresses to the largest, in the manner below.

Source List Entry

North Carolina. Military Collection. Treasurer and Comptroller's
Records. North Carolina State Archives, Raleigh.

First Reference Note

1. Demsey Goodman entry, Capt. John Sumner's Company, Chowan County Muster Roll, 1754; Military Collection, Box 2; Treasurer
and Comptroller's Records; North Carolina State Archives, Raleigh.

Subsequent Note

11. Demsey Goodman, Capt. Sumner's Co., Chowan County
Muster Roll, 1754.

Microfilm (FHL-GSU)

Source List Entry

Rhode Island. Adjutant General's Office. "Muster Roll of Company A, Ninth Regiment of Infantry, U.S.A.; War with Mexico, 1847–48." Rhode Island State Archives, Providence. FHL microfilm 1,976,500, item 1. Family History Library, Salt Lake City, Utah.

First Reference Note

1. Rhode Island Adjutant General's Office, "Muster Roll of Company A, Ninth Regiment of Infantry, U.S.A.; War with Mexico, 1847–48," unpaginated p. 1, Rufus Collins; FHL microfilm 1,976,500, item 1.

Subsequent Note

11. R.I. Adjutant General's Office, "Muster Roll of Company A, Ninth Regiment of Infantry, U.S.A ... 1847–48," p. 1, Rufus Collins.

Online Databases

Source List Entry

Illinois. Secretary of State. "Illinois Civil War Muster and Descriptive Rolls Database." *CyberDriveIllinois*. http://www.cyberdriveillinois .com/departments/archives/databases.html : 2007.

First Reference Note

1. Illinois Secretary of State, "Illinois Civil War Muster and Descriptive Rolls Database," *CyberDriveIllinois* (http://www.cyberdrive illinois.com/departments/archives/databases.html : accessed 1 February 2007), entry for George Day, "PVT [Co.] K, 61 IL US INF," Lucan, Lawrence County.

Subsequent Note

11. Illinois Secretary of State, "Illinois Civil War Muster and Descriptive Rolls Database," entry for George Day, "PVT, [Co.] K, 61 IL US INF," Lucan, Lawrence County.

9.12   Pension Rolls: Local

See also 8.33, Pension Affidavits (City and County) and 11.40, Pension Files (Federal).

For the major wars, you will frequently find pension rolls or registers in the county courthouse or town hall. Some rolls may be semi-alphabetical, listing individuals under the "A," "B," etc., sections as they became eligible—together with the date of eligibility. Other jurisdictions may have created a new roll each year, sometimes subdividing those rolls into several lists according to the "classes" of pensions authorized by state law. The following example treats a register with different types of lists, whereon *the same individual appears more than once.* Whatever record book you consult, you will need to analyze it to decide the best way to identify your material.

Source List Entry
Mississippi. Leake County. "Register of Confederate Pensioners, 1893–1925." Chancery Court Clerk's Office, Carthage.

First Reference Note
1. Leake County, Mississippi, "Register of Confederate Pensioners, 1893–1925," p. 1, Frank Boyd, granted 5 September 1893, and p. 4, "List of Servants Applications for 1893"; Chancery Court Clerk's Office, Carthage.

Subsequent Note
11. Leake Co., Miss., "Register of Confederate Pensioners, 1893–1925," 1, 4.

9.13 Soldiers' Discharge Registers: Local

By and large, this class of record begins in the twentieth century and relates to all branches of the military, even though the volumes may be labeled as *soldiers'* registers. Your Source List Entry could cite the *series* of discharge registers (as in the Arizona example), or it could cite the *particular register* that you use (as in the Alabama example). Listing individual discharges in your Source List Entry would unduly bloat your bibliography. Service number, rank, and unit are key elements to include in your Reference Notes.

Source List Entry
Alabama. Chilton County. "Soldiers' Discharge Records, 1917–." Probate Judge's Office, Clanton.
Arizona. Pinal County. Military Discharges and Index, 1944–1973. County Recorder's Office, Florence.

First Reference Note
1. Chilton County, Alabama, "Soldiers' Discharge Records, 1917–," p. 8, Reuben L. Reynolds, service no. 98848, Private, Headquarters Company, 167th U.S. Infantry, discharged 1919; Probate Judge's Office, Clanton.
2. Pinal County, Arizona, Military Discharges, volume 1: 24, Oliver Perry Harding, service no. 9740569, Seaman 2nd class, discharged 1944; County Recorder's Office, Florence.

Subsequent Note
11. Chilton Co., Ala., "Soldiers' Discharge Records, 1917–," 8, Reuben L. Reynolds, serv. no. 98848.
12. Pinal Co., Ariz., Military Discharges, 1: 24.

9.14   Veteran, Widow & Orphan Rolls: Local

See also 8.33, Pension Affidavits

Precise language should be used when citing veterans' rolls (or those of widows and orphans) as opposed to pension rolls. Not all veterans or dependents received pensions. Veterans' and dependents' lists often were compiled in fiscal preparation for anticipated pension expenses. Thus, individuals will appear on the veterans' rolls earlier than their first appearance on pension rolls. Some then died before going on the pension rolls or were otherwise ineligible for a pension. Also, when citing a dependent on a veterans' roll, you should identify that person as widow or orphan, as the case may be. Otherwise a male child could be assumed to be a veteran. Conversely, while pre-twentieth-century females are typically assumed to be widows, a few did see military service of their own.

Source List Entry
Mississippi. Newton County. "Roster of Confederate Soldiers and Sailors, 1909–1910." Chancery Court Clerk's Office, Decatur.

First Reference Note
1. Newton County, Mississippi, "Roster of Confederate Soldiers and Sailors, 1909–1910," p. 102, for Rolla Wallace, CSA servant; Chancery Court Clerk's Office, Decatur.

Subsequent Note
11. Newton Co., Miss., "Roster of Confederate Soldiers and Sailors, 1909–1910," 102, Rolla Wallace.

9.15   Veteran, Widow & Orphan Rolls: State

See also 8.43, Pension Application Files (State Level)

The guidance at 9.14 applies here as well. Whether citing local or state rolls, those of veterans and their dependents should be distinguished from pension rolls. The rolls are also a different entity from applications and affidavits, and the correct terminology should be applied to the record you are using if it is to be properly interpreted by you and relocated by your readers.

Veterans' and dependents' rolls, when created by the state government, are cited in the traditional archival manner discussed at 9.3.

Source List Entry
Alabama. "Widows of Confederate Soldiers." Card file. Alabama Department of Archives and History, Montgomery.

First Reference Note
    1. Card entry, Sarah Thornton, widow of J. W. Thornton, Dadeville (citing "Claims, 2nd Aud. C.S. Treas. 1862–'64"); "Widows of Confederate Soldiers," alphabetical card file; Alabama Department of Archives and History, Montgomery,

Subsequent Note
    11. Card entry, Sarah Thornton, widow of J. W. Thornton, Dadeville; "Widows of Confederate Soldiers," card file.

CITING THE SOURCE OF THE SOURCE

Citing the source of a source is easier when you use a Reference Note format that places the smallest element at the *end* of the citation. In the example above, the standard archival format is used for material held by state archives and that places the smallest element at the *beginning*. The source of the source relates to that smallest element. Therefore, to create separation between the details that identify the card you actually used from those of the unconsulted original, the source-of-the-source information is placed in parentheses. It is preceded by the word *citing* to clarify the point that you are copying that source identity from the card and have not actually consulted that source of the source.

MISCELLANEOUS ROLLS & REGISTRATIONS

9.16   Child Labor Affidavits & Licenses

See QuickCheck Model *for* LOCAL RECORDS: FILE ITEMS

The early twentieth century saw much political lobbying for restrictions on child labor. Legislation in many states called for affidavits to be filed by employers who hired children within certain age brackets or licenses to be issued to adolescents who sought employment. A typical citation to these records, when found locally, would be this:

Source List Entry
Alabama. Dallas County. Child Labor Affidavits, 1908–1914. Probate Judge's Office, Selma.

First Reference Note
    1. Dallas County, Alabama, Child Labor Affidavits, 1908–1914, alphabetically arranged by name of child; see Harvey Dodd (born 22 May 1901), filed 23 May 1913; Probate Judge's Office, Selma.

Subsequent Note
    11. Dallas Co., Ala., Child Labor Affidavits, 1908–1914, affidavit for Harvey Dodd, filed 23 May 1913.

9.17   Free Papers, Licenses & Registrations

See also Slavery & Servitude Records, 9.24–9.29.

Nearly a half-million free people of color resided in the United States on the eve of the Civil War—almost half in the South, slightly more in the North. Some states, North and South, required these men and women to register with a county official. Even when registration was not required, cautious free people of color often created a public record of their free status whenever they moved into a new area. In some regions, the population was large enough to warrant the maintenance of special registers. In other jurisdictions, the registrations might appear in any kind of county or city record book.

Source List Entry

Missouri. Clay County. Order Books, 1822–65. Clay County Archives, Liberty.

South Carolina. Kershaw County. Deed Records. Clerk of Court's Office, Camden.

Virginia. Fairfax County. Registrations of Free Negroes, 1822–1861. Clerk of Court's Office, Fairfax.

First Reference Note

1. Clay County, Missouri, Order Book 12: 192–93, Mary Austin, license to remain in Missouri, 1854.

2. Kershaw County, South Carolina, Deed Book A: 132, registration of free paper, Onach Kampae, Oneyda [Oneida Indian]; Clerk of Court's Office, Camden.

3. Fairfax County, Virginia, "Registration of Free Negroes Commencing September Court 1822, Book No. 2," entry 148, Armistead Gantt; Clerk of Court's Office, Fairfax.

Subsequent Note

11. Clay Co., Mo., Order Book 12: 192–93.

12. Kershaw Co., S.C., Deed Book A: 132.

13. Fairfax Co., Va., "Registration of Free Negroes … Book No. 2," entry 148.

Online Databases

Source List Entry

Indiana. "Registry of Negroes and Mulattos, 1853–54, Vigo County, Indiana." Database. *Indiana State Archives.* http://www.in.gov/icpr/archives/databases/vigo_reg.html : 2007.

First Reference Note

1. Indiana, "Registry of Negroes and Mulattos, 1853–54, Vigo County, Indiana," database, *Indiana State Archives* (http://www.in.gov/

icpr/archives/databases/vigo_reg.html : accessed 1 February 2007), entry for Amanda Brooks, age 11.

Subsequent Note

    11. Indiana, "Registry of Negroes and Mulattos, 1853–54, Vigo County, Indiana," database entry for Amanda Brooks, age 11.

9.18   Jury Lists

In smaller towns and counties, early jury lists were typically recorded as a court minute in the record books of that court (see 8.30). In larger locales and later times, special jury-list registers have been kept. In either case, they fit within the Basic Citation Format for most types of bound county record books:

Source List Entry

Alabama. Mobile County. "Orphan's Court Docket Book & Jury List Book, 1839–44." Probate Judge's Office, Mobile.

First Reference Note

    1. Mobile County, Alabama, "Orphan's Court Docket Book & Jury List Book," p. 191, jury list of 25 June 1839; Probate Judge's Office, Mobile.

Subsequent Note

    11. Mobile Co., Ala., "Orphan's Court Docket Book & Jury List Book," 191.

9.19   Licenses, Miscellaneous

See QuickCheck Model *for* LOCAL RECORDS: REGISTERS: NAMED VOLUME

Across time, local governments have required citizens to purchase licenses to own or operate an endless array of personal items, activities, and businesses. Occasionally, specific registers were set aside for items or activities that were especially significant to the economy or the social environment—licenses to peddle or to operate taverns are historically common examples. More often, the licenses are scattered in local court records or miscellaneous books.

Most matters of this type fit the Basic Model for citing county- or city-level record books (9.3). The examples below illustrate two types of licenses, as well as two technical points.

CITING SINGLE VOLUME VS. SERIES

The Mobile dog-license book, in the next set of models, is the only such register in that repository. Its exact title is cited in both the Source List Entry and the First Reference Note. The St. Louis registry of pharmacy licenses is just one of numerous volumes in a pharmacy-license series. Thus, the St. Louis Source List Entry cites the whole period that was searched. The St. Louis Reference Notes cite the exact name of the register for the item of interest.

CITING UNPAGINATED REGISTRIES

The St. Louis example also illustrates the handling of an unpaginated but semi-alphabetized registry.

Source List Entry

Alabama. Mobile County. "Dog Licenses, vol. 1, 1888–1926." Probate Judge's Office, Mobile.

Missouri. St. Louis, City of. Record of Druggists' Licenses, 1893–1909. City Board of Pharmacy, St. Louis.

First Reference Note

1. Mobile County, Alabama, "Dog Licenses, vol. 1, 1888–1926," p. 19, registration of "Flip Flap" by E. F. Ladd, 11 November 1902; Probate Judge's Office, Mobile.

2. City of St. Louis, Missouri, "To Record Druggists' Licenses, 1898," registrations semi-alphabetical by first letter of surname, p. N, no. 1041, Oscar F. Nitzschmann; City Board of Pharmacy, St. Louis.

Subsequent Note

11. Mobile Co., Ala., Dog Licenses, 1: 19.

12. St. Louis, Mo., "To Record Druggists' Licenses, 1898," p. N, no. 1041, Oscar F. Nitzschmann.

9.20   Licenses: Moved to State Archives

See QuickCheck Model *for* LOCAL RECORDS: FILES MOVED TO STATE ARCHIVES

Original licenses, when and where preserved, are among the papers frequently transferred from the county or town to the state archives for preservation. There, they are typically arranged in the manner of the tavern licenses cited below—by county, then record type, and thereunder by file folders in annual or alphabetical sequence. When you are citing a file of loose papers such as this, you should clearly identify it as a *file*. Otherwise, those who seek the record you cite will often assume they are searching for a bound volume.

Source List Entry

New Jersey. Sussex County. Applications for Tavern Licenses, 1753–1769. County Government Records. New Jersey State Archives, Trenton.

First Reference Note

1. Sussex County, New Jersey, Applications for Tavern Licenses, 1753–1769, file: "Sussex County Tavern Licenses, 1754," alphabetically

arranged, see Joseph Walling; County Government Records; New Jersey State Archives, Trenton.

Subsequent Note
    11. Sussex Co., N.J., file: "Sussex County Tavern Licenses, 1754," Joseph Walling.

9.21 Marks & Brands Registrations
See Chapter 10, Property & Probates

9.22 Pauper Records or Rolls
See Chapter 8, Courts & Governance

9.23 Voter Rolls
See QuickCheck Model *for* LOCAL RECORDS : REGISTERS: NUMBERED VOLUME

Across time and place, voter rolls have been maintained in many different ways. Some offices kept annual registers. Others used the same register for many years, with unpaginated leaves for each letter of the alphabet; names would be entered there semi-alphabetically by first letter of surname, in chronological sequence, and then struck off as voters died or moved away. Entries of the latter type may or may not carry a date of registration or removal. With this type of record you will need to analyze the circumstances and study your item of interest in context with other entries throughout the book, to determine what information might be needed to relocate the item.

In the Pinal County citation, for example, the undated entry states that the voter filed his declaration of intent to become a U.S. citizen on 2 November 1878. It does not reference an oath of allegiance, a proceeding that usually followed the declaration by at least three years. If your citation notes the filing date for the declaration, then it brackets the record, timewise, between 2 November 1878 and (likely) November 1881.

Source List Entry
Arizona. Pinal County. Great Registers, 1876–1920. County Recorder's Office, Florence.
Illinois. Chicago. Record and Index of Persons Registered and of Poll Lists of Voters, 1888–1892. Board of Election Commissioners, Chicago.

First Reference Note
    1. Pinal County, Arizona, Great Registers, vol. 1, p. B for Martin Bracamonte, age 25, undated entry; citing declaration of intent filed 2 November 1878; County Recorder's Office, Florence.

2. Chicago, Illinois, Record and Index of Persons Registered and of Poll Lists of Voters, vol. AA-CU (1888): 78, Olaf Aune; Board of Election Commissioners, Chicago.

Subsequent Note
11. Pinal Co., Ariz., Great Registers, vol. 1, p. B for Martin Bracamonte.

12. Chicago, Ill., Record and Index of Persons Registered and of Poll Lists of Voters, vol. AA-CU (1888): 78, Olaf Aune.

SLAVERY & SERVITUDE RECORDS

9.24   Background

Rolls and registers of the enslaved take a multitude of forms. Lists were compiled for lawsuits and probate cases, and these appear in many of the court records whose citation forms appear in chapters 8 and 10. Sales of titles to slaves and bonded servants of all races appear in the deeds, mortgages, and probate records covered in chapter 10. Slaveholders were regularly taxed on their bondsmen, and those records (also treated in chapter 10) occasionally name the individual slaves. Special registers were sometimes created—especially for manumissions. The examples here at 9.25–9.29 provide a cross-section of rolls and registrations that relate to slavery and servitude. If you do not find an appropriate model here, you should be able to find one that fits your situation in those other chapters.

9.25   Indentureships

Agreements by youth or the poor to serve a master for a certain number of years in return for their support or training in a trade were common in the past. Some indentureships appear in court minute books and record books; citations to these could follow the Basic Format for bound volumes at 8.18. In other jurisdictions they were recorded among deeds, mortgages, and miscellaneous local registers. The following model follows the Basic Format for bound volumes in a numbered series, as shown at 8.18 and 9.4.

Source List Entry
Pennsylvania. Franklin County. Mortgage Books, 1800–1850. Register of Deeds Office, Chambersburg.

First Reference Note
1. Franklin County, Pennsylvania, Mortgage Book B: 83–84, indenture of Lord Dunmore, 8 September 1822; Register of Deeds Office, Chambersburg.

> *Subsequent Note*
> 11. Franklin Co., Pa., Mortgage Book B: 83–84.

9.26   Inventories & Other Lists

By their nature, inventories and lists come in many types. The three examples below cover lists found within legal suits, tax records, and estate files. In each case, you will need to cite both the individual document and the file or volume, as well as the series in which you found the document.

Source List Entry

Louisiana. Natchitoches Parish. Parish Court Files, 1805–1850. Clerk of Court's Office, Natchitoches.

New York. Minisink. Assessment Rolls, 1798–1804. Town Assessor's Office, Minisink.

North Carolina. Alamance County. Inventories of Estates, 1859–1863. Superior Court Clerk's Office, Graham.

First Reference Note

   1. Natchitoches Parish, Louisiana, Parish Court Files, alphabetically arranged by year: Dupré Heirs v. Alexis Cloutier, 1825, for "Slaves Mentioned in Bte. Dupré's Inventory [1785] and Their Increase."

   2. Walkill, New York, "1798 Assessment Roll—Third Division, N.Y., Towns of Minisink and Dearfork," unpaginated section: "Slaveowners, Town of Walkill," for Thomas Eager; Town Assessor's Office, Minisink.

   3. Alamance County, North Carolina, Inventories of Estates, vol. 1 (1859–1863): 217, inventory of slaves of John Murray, 1860.

Subsequent Note

   11. Natchitoches Par., La., Parish Court Files, Dupré Heirs v. Cloutier, for "Slaves Mentioned in Bte. Dupré's Inventory [1785] and Their Increase."

   12. Walkill, N.Y., "1798 Assessment Roll—Third Division, N.Y., Towns of Minisink and Dearfork," section: "Slaveowners, Town of Walkill."

   13. Alamance Co., N.C., Inventories of Estates, 1: 217.

TOWNS SITUATED WITHIN TOWNS

See 8.36, for a discussion of New York and New England "towns" that fall within other "towns," as in the case of Walkill and Minisink above.

9.27   Manumissions (Emancipations)

See also 9.17, Free Papers, Licenses & Registrations

Prior to the Emancipation Proclamation of 1863, individual masters granted freedom to slaves in many ways. Some were manumitted by legislative act, in which case you will cite that legislative act (see 13.13, Session Laws, State) and, perhaps, supporting legislative files that have survived (8.42). Some were manumitted by wills, in which case you will cite the will in Basic Citation Format for probate records (10.30–10.34). Other manumissions are registered randomly in local court record books or deed books, as with the example below.

Note: Manumissions or emancipations from *slavery* should not be confused with emancipations of free youth from the disability of minority. The latter typically required a court proceeding and would be cited as such (see 8.18–8.19).

Source List Entry
Alabama. Mobile County. Deed Records, 1813–1865. Probate Judge's Office, Mobile.

First Reference Note
1. Mobile County, Alabama, Deed Book E: 163, George Baptiste to Laurentine, manumission, 1847; Probate Judge's Office, Mobile.

Subsequent Note
11. Mobile Co., Ala., Deed Book E: 163.

Online Databases

Source List Entry
Illinois. "Servitude and Emancipation Records Database, 1722–1863." Database. *Illinois State Archives.* http://www.ilsos.gov/Genealogy MWeb/servfrm.html : 2007.

First Reference Note
1. Illinois, "Servitude and Emancipation Records Database, 1722–1863," database, *Illinois State Archives* (http://www.ilsos.gov/ GenealogyMWeb/servfrm.html : accessed 2 April 2007), entry for George W. James, St. Clair County, 5 April 1855.

Subsequent Note
11. Illinois, "Database of Servitude and Emancipation Records (1722–1863)," entry for George W. James, St. Clair Co., 1855.

IDENTIFICATION OF DATABASE BY RECORD FORMAT
When citing a database whose title identifies it as a database—you do not have to enter "database" in the position where the record type is usually cited (see the grayed text above). To do so would be redundant. If the title of this database had simply been "Servitude and Emancipation Records, 1722–1863," then it would be appropriate to add the identification "database," in the position shown above.

9.28 Mortgages & Sales of Servants

Slaves were typically classed as *chattel*. They could be mortgaged and sold. While sales of chattel did not have to be publicly recorded in most jurisdictions, the recording of chattel *mortgages* was almost always required. When citing a mortgage, if the title of the register does not include the word *mortgage* (or *deed of trust* as it might be variously called), you should add that detail to your First Reference Note.

Source List Entry

Florida. Escambia County. Deed Records, 1821–1865. Comptroller's Office, Pensacola.

First Reference Note

1. Escambia County, Florida, Deed Book G: 32, Christin to de Rioboo, mortgage of Joe, 1839; Comptroller's Office, Pensacola.

Subsequent Note

11. Escambia Co., Fla., Deed Book G:32.

9.29 Slave Passes for Travel

Most slave passes were documents used temporarily and locally, allowing slaves to travel within their neighborhood without being taken up as a runaway. Permanent recording in county or city registers was not the practice. When a master did choose to record a pass for out-of-state travel, it usually represented de facto manumission to circumvent a state's anti-manumission laws. A typical citation might be constructed like this one:

Source List Entry

Louisiana. Natchitoches Parish. Conveyance Records, 1857. Clerk of Court's Office, Natchitoches.

First Reference Note

1. Natchitoches Parish, Louisiana, Conveyance Book 53:23, John Payne to Jane et al., free pass to slaves for interstate travel; Clerk of Court's Office, Natchitoches.

Subsequent Note

11. Natchitoches Par., La., Conveyance Book 53: 23.

VITAL REGISTRATIONS (BIRTHS, DEATHS, ETC.)

9.30 Background

Across time, maintaining vital registrations (aka *vital records*) has been a function of both civil and church authorities. In some cases, historic church registers of baptisms, marriages, and burials were appropriated by the state to create an archive of civil registrations. (The first *état civil* records of France, covered at 9.49, are a prominent example.) In other cases where church sacramental records were the only form of vital registrations—as in the parts of the United States that originated as French and Spanish colonies—those records have not been secularized. They remain private and are treated in chapter 7, Church Records.

One fundamental rule should be observed when citing vital records. *The name of a principal party should be cited exactly as it appears in the record or the index*, whichever you cite. Otherwise the entry may not be relocatable in the databases now used for most sets of vital registrations. Your narrative may discuss an individual by his or her "family call name," but your corresponding citation must render that name as your source has it. Your family may spell its surname in a distinctive fashion, but if the registration or database spells it otherwise, you must cite the exact spelling used in your source. If you wish to "correct" the spelling of a record, you would do so by placing your spelling in square editorial brackets after the spelling used by the source.

When using registers from prior centuries, you should not make assumptions about surnames or apply modern conventions. If the child's name is rendered with no surname and the record does not specifically say that the parents are married, you should not assign the father's surname to that child. A child born outside of marriage may not have used the name of the father cited in the registration. Or that culture may have followed different naming conventions.

Other key issues to consider, when citing U.S. vital records, are these:

- Is your resource a *register* or a *certificate*?
- Was your certificate created at the time the event occurred or does it represent a modern extraction of data from an earlier record?
- Does your certificate represent a *full* extraction from an earlier record or is it a *short-form certificate* (9.40)?
- Was this record created by a local, state, or national agency?

The elements you include in the citation can vary according to the nature of the record and your own need. Fundamental rules are these:

- If the document is locatable by book and page number, as with the Kansas City record at 9.32 below, you do not need to cite the date.
- If the record set includes the year as part of the file number, you

must include that year in the citation. Each year, many cities and states begin renumbering, starting with the base number *1*. If you do not cite the year, the record may not be relocatable without an extensive search. The New York City example at 9.32 demonstrates this situation. In some locales, the year will be part of the number, as in 1930:12345—signifying certificate no. 12345 for the year 1930—or 107-53-001504 for a 1953 certificate.

- When citing online databases, the exact date should always be included to ensure that the correct entry is identified.

9.31 Certificates vs. Registrations

In common parlance, the term *certificate* is often used in reference to all types of birth, marriage, and death records. Historians, however, need to identify their materials precisely. If you are citing an entry in a *register*, you are usually not citing a *certificate*. (An exception would be a form-type register in which each page is preprinted with multiple "certificates.") If you are citing a photocopy or digital image of a page from a register, you are not citing a certificate. A vital-records certificate is typically a loose piece of paper, preprinted as a form with blanks to be filled in. In some cases, particularly with marriage records, the certificates represent bits of data abstracted from a more complete record that was created at an earlier point in time.

9.32 City Certificates & Registrations

See also 9.31, Certificates vs. Registrations *and* 9.43, Town Registers

Many researchers associate vital registration at the town level with New England and New York. However, larger towns and cities in many states have created and maintained registration systems separate from those maintained at the county level. In citing city or town records, you should clearly identify the creator as the city or town, rather than the county. When cities encompass more than one county—as with New York City, below—you may also need to include the county name.

Source List Entry
Kansas. Kansas City. Record of Births, 1892–1911. City Clerk's Office, Kansas City.

New York. Manhattan County. New York City. Death Certificates, 1866–1919. Municipal Archives, New York City.

First Reference Note
1. Kansas City, Kansas, Record of Births, Book A: 121, Arthur Millsap, 1902; City Clerk's Office, Kansas City.

2. New York City, Manhattan County, death certificate no. 1917-29300, Dmytro Samarez; Municipal Archives, New York City.

Subsequent Note
11. Kansas City, Kans., Record of Births, A: 121, Arthur Millsap, 1902.
12. New York City, Manhattan Co., death certificate no. 1917-29300, Dmytro Samarez.

Kansas City and Manhattan records appear again in the microfilm models below, to demonstrate differences in citing material you use on-site and material you consult via an image copy. The Manhattan record also illustrates citing database entries *vis à vis* the originals.

Microfilm (FHL-GSU)

Source List Entry
Kansas. Kansas City. Record of Mortality, 1892–1903. City Clerk's Office, Kansas City. FHL microfilm 475,917, item 1. Family History Library, Salt Lake City, Utah.
New York. Manhattan County. New York City. Death Certificates, 1866–1919. Municipal Archives, New York City. FHL microfilm 1,322,415. Family History Library, Salt Lake City, Utah.

First Reference Note
1. Kansas City, Kansas, Record of Mortality, Book A: 121, Julia Ann Tapp; FHL microfilm 475,917, item 1.
2. New York City, Manhattan County, death certificate no. 1917-29300, Dmytro Samarez; FHL microfilm 1,322,415.

Subsequent Note
11. Kansas City, Kans., Record of Mortality, A: 121.
12. New York City, Manhattan Co., death certificate no. 1917-29300, Dmytro Samarez.

Online Databases

Source List Entry
Italian Genealogical Group. "NYC Death Records." Database. http://www.italiangen.org/NYCDEATH.STM : 2007.

First Reference Note
1. Italian Genealogical Group. "NYC Death Records," database (http://www.italiangen.org/NYCDEATH.STM : accessed 1 February 2007), entry for Dmytro Samarez; citing death certificate no. 1917-29300, New York City, Manhattan County.

Subsequent Note
11. Italian Genealogical Group, "NYC Death Records," database entry for Dmytro Samarez, 1917, Manhattan County.

9.33 County-level Certificates

See also

- QuickCheck Model *for* LOCAL RECORDS: VITAL-RECORDS CERTIFICATE
- 9.31 for Certificates vs. Registrations

In citing county-level *certificates* of birth, marriage, and death you can usually follow the Basic Format at 9.5. Given that these vital-records certificates are often maintained by a different office than the one that maintains marriage bonds, licenses, and returns, you will need to adapt the Basic Format to identify the appropriate office and its record arrangement or numbering scheme. The examples below demonstrate several common variants. The Source List Entry in each case cites the county's *collection* of records, while the Reference Notes cite the *specific volume* and/or *item of interest*. Listing individual certificates in the Source List could make the list too unmanageable.

Source List Entry
Alabama. Perry County. Birth Certificates, 1908–1909. Probate Judge's Office, Marion.
Alabama. Bibb County. Death Certificates, 1908–1911. Probate Judge's Office, Centerville.
Florida. Polk County. Marriage Certificates. Polk County Central Bureau of Vital Statistics, Bartow.
Montana. Yellowstone County. Marriage Certificates. District Court Clerk's Office, Billings.

First Reference Note
1. Perry County, Alabama, Birth Certificates, 1908–1909, alphabetized collection, unnumbered certificates, for Charles Leslie Harrison, 1908; Probate Judge's Office, Marion.
2. Bibb County, Alabama, death certificate no. 1908-28, Vernice Bledsow; Probate Judge's Office, Centerville.
3. Polk County, Florida, marriage certificate no. 6745 (1940), Garland-Davis; Polk County Central Bureau of Vital Statistics, Bartow.
4. Yellowstone County, Montana, marriage certificate no. 2885 (1912), Ferguson-Webb; District Court Clerk's Office, Billings.

Subsequent Note
11. Perry Co., Ala., birth certificate, Charles Leslie Harrison, 1908.
12. Bibb Co., Ala., death certificate no. 1908-28, Vernice Bledsow.
13. Polk Co., Fla., marr. certificate no. 6745 (1940), Garland-Davis.
14. Yellowstone Co., Mont., marr. certificate no. 2885 (1912), Ferguson-Webb.

Online Databases & Images (County Level)   🖥

Many local-level databases include multiple types of vital records, as illustrated below. Shelby County's database title, which generically refers to "death records," is a mix of death certificates and burial permits. Whatever kind of item you use, you should identify it precisely. For the essential difference in citing image copies versus database entries at the same website, see 9.6, Online Resources.

Source List Entry

Tennessee. Shelby County. "Death Record Search (1848–1954)." Database and images. *Shelby County Register of Deeds.* http://register .shelby.tn.us/deathSearch.php : 2007.

First Reference Note

(*Citing database entries*)

1. Shelby County, Tennessee, "Death Record Search (1848–1954)," database, *Shelby County Register of Deeds* (http://register.shelby .tn.us/deathSearch.php : accessed 7 February 2007), entry for burial permit no. 1956, Arthur S. Watson, 9 December 1902.

2. Shelby County, Tennessee, "Death Record Search (1848–1954)," database, *Shelby County Register of Deeds* (http://register .shelby.tn.us/deathSearch.php : accessed 7 February 2007), entry for death certificate no. 114 (file no.) 116 (reg. no.), "Infant Day," 11 May 1922.

(*Citing image copies of certificates*)

3. Shelby County, Tennessee, death certificate no. 114 (file no.) 116 (reg. no.), "Infant Day," 11 May 1922; digital image, *Shelby County Register of Deeds* (http://register.shelby.tn.us/deathSearch.php : accessed 7 February 2007).

Subsequent Note

11. Shelby Co., Tenn., "Death Record Search (1848–1954)," database entry for burial permit no. 1956, Arthur S. Watson, 9 December 1902.

12. Shelby Co., Tenn., "Death Record Search (1848–1954)," database entry for death certificate no. 114 (file no.) 116 (reg. no.), "Infant Day," 11 May 1922.

13. Shelby Co., Tenn., death certificate no. 114 (file no.) 116 (reg. no.), "Infant Day," 11 May 1922.

9.34   County-level Registrations

See also

- QuickCheck Model *for* LOCAL RECORDS: VITAL-RECORDS REGISTER
- 9.31 for Certificates vs. Registrations.

In most locales, the earliest civil registrations of births and deaths appear in registers that, theoretically, enter the details of an event shortly after it occurred. The information would typically be given by a family member, a midwife, or a doctor. (New England town records can be an exception to the time element, as discussed under 9.43.) The timeliness of the material in these early local registers makes them a valued source. However, immediate registrations also meant that a child's birth might be recorded before the child was named, as with "Infant Day" immediately above and "Is not baptized" below.

Source List Entry
Ohio. Ottawa County. Record of Births, 1867–1890. Probate Court Clerk's Office, Port Clinton.

First Reference Note
1. Ottawa County, Ohio, Record of Births, vol. 1 (1867–1890): 4, 1868 entry for "Is not baptized," female child of Albert Witcher; Probate Judge's Office, Port Clinton.

Subsequent Note
11. Ottawa Co., Ohio, Record of Births, 1: 4, 1868 entry for "Is not baptized," female child of Albert Witcher.

ADDING EXPLANATORY NOTES

When a register ambiguously identifies key pieces of information, you should be careful to quote the exact wording of the record. You may later form an opinion about the interpretation, but you should not make that interpretation prior to constructing your citation, unless you add an explanation that covers alternate possibilities. The following example illustrates the point in two ways.

* First, the register includes both free and slave births. The column that would normally contain parental data in other jurisdictions is headed "Father or Owner." You might presume that this child was a slave and identify W. G. Woodson as his owner, but without information from other sources, you would not know whether Woodson was a slave owner, a free African-American father, or both. Therefore, the precise column header is added to his identification and the issue is left open for a later decision.

* Second, notice that the name of the child is also open to interpretation. In that case, the Reference Note presents both possibilities and explains the interpretation that has been made.

Source List Entry
Kentucky. Pendleton County. "Births, 1852–1859." Office of the Clerk of County Court, Falmouth.

First Reference Note

> 1. Pendleton County, Kentucky, "Births, 1852–1859," 1855 section, p. 1, for "Alexander," a black child attributed to "Father or Owner," W. G. Woodson; Office of the Clerk of County Court, Falmouth. *Note:* The entry in the name column appears to read "B. Alexander." However, a close analysis of the recording pattern reveals that every child whose race is entered as black in the race column also has a "B" in front of his or her given name. The child's name should be simply "Alexander."

Subsequent Note

> 11. Pendleton Co., Ky., "Births, 1852–1859," 1855 section, p. 1, for "Alexander," black child attributed to W. G. Woodson.

Online Databases & Indexes

The Shelby County, Tennessee, example at 9.33 illustrates an official website that offers images of death certificates accessible through a database. The North Dakota example, below, illustrates a privately created database of registrations without images.

Source List Entry

> Barron, George L. "Stutsman County [North Dakota]—Old Death Index." Database. *USGenWeb Archives: Stutsman County, North Dakota, Genealogy.* http://www.rootsweb.com/~usgenweb/nd/stutsman/earsdhx1.html : 2007.

First Reference Note

> 1. George L. Barron, "Stutsman County [North Dakota]—Old Death Index," database, *USGenWeb Archives: Stutsman County, North Dakota, Genealogy* (http://www.rootsweb.com/~usgenweb/nd/stutsman/earsdhx1.html : accessed 1 February 2007), entry for Gulleck Abby, 20 September 1921.

Subsequent Note

> 11. Barron, "Stutsman County [North Dakota]—Old Death Index," database entry for Gulleck Abby, 20 September 1921.

9.35   Delayed & Amended Birth Certificates

See also

- QuickCheck Model *for* LOCAL RECORDS: VITAL RECORDS, AMENDED
- QuickCheck Model *for* LOCAL RECORDS: VITAL RECORDS, DELAYED

This class of records, which typically begins in the twentieth century, offers loose certificates or registers whose pages are designed as certificates. The citations in this section are appropriate when you consult these certificates onsite or when you receive an image copy of the original certificate. See also 9.40 for Short-form Certificates.

Source List Entry
Illinois. Cass County. Delayed Birth Records. County Clerk's Office, Virginia, Illinois.

Texas. Limestone County. Amended Birth Records. County Clerk's Office, Groesbeck.

First Reference Note
1. Cass County, Illinois, delayed birth certificate no. 4071 (1942), Mary Rose Hunt; County Clerk's Office, Virginia, Illinois.

2. Limestone County, Texas, amended birth certificate, local file no. 1982 (issued 1983), Johnnie LaVerne Grooms, formerly "Unknown Grooms"; citing the 1927 registration in "Book 7, page 61D, Birth Records of Limestone County"; County Clerk's Office, Groesbeck.

Subsequent Note
11. Cass Co., Ill., delayed birth certificate no. 4071 (1942), Mary Rose Hunt.

12. Limestone Co., Tex., amended birth certificate, local file no. 1982 (issued 1983), Johnnie LaVerne Grooms.

CITING DATE OF CERTIFICATE
Typically, as with Note 1, when you cite the year of the certificate you can simply place that date in parentheses after the number. However, if that practice were applied to Note 2 above—i.e., *no. 1982 (1983)*—the similarity in the two sets of digits could create confusion. Therefore, the word *issued* is inserted before the year, even though it is not used in other citations. *Clarity* always trumps *consistency*.

CITING STATE NAME REPETITIOUSLY IN SOURCE LIST ENTRY
When the Source List Entry begins with a state name, as creator, you do not have to repeat that state name in the "location data" at the end of the entry. However, in the Cass County example above, the state name is repeated in the location field because the name of the town alone (Virginia) could be confusing.

CITING THE SOURCE OF A SOURCE
When the certificate cites an original volume and page at which a registration was first recorded (as in the Limestone County example, above), it is helpful to note the whereabouts of the original in your citation. However, you should not cite the original in lieu of the certificate. Your wording should clearly indicate it is the certificate that identifies the original, which you have not consulted.

Online Databases & Indexes

Source List Entry
Oregon. "Oregon Historical Records Index." Database. *Oregon State Archives.* http://genealogy.state.or.us : 2007.

First Reference Note
1. Oregon, "Oregon Historical Records Index," database, *Oregon State Archives* (http://genealogy.state.or.us : accessed 13 January 2007), entry for Harry Herbert Shown, delayed birth certificate 0108, citing 1896 birth.

Subsequent Note
11. Oregon, "Oregon Historical Records Index," database entry for Harry Herbert Shown, delayed birth certificate 0108, citing 1896 birth.

CITING CERTIFICATE YEAR VS. BIRTH YEAR
In the Illinois example first given in this section 9.35, the cited document is a delayed birth certificate issued in the year 1942. That year is appropriately positioned next to the certificate number. In the Oregon example, immediately above, the database does not state the year in which the delayed certificate was issued; rather, it states the year of birth. Therefore, the Oregon citation specifically states that the date represents the birth year rather than the year of the registration.

9.36   Divorce Records
Divorce suits, as a rule, begin and end in a local court. They are cited like any other local court suit. (See 8.25, Divorce & Separation Cases.) In some early states, prior to the mid-1800s or so, divorce petitions submitted to local courts were forwarded to the state legislature for a decision; if approved, a special act of the legislature would grant the divorce. In those cases, you will be citing the legislative act (see 13.13). If the original petitions to the state legislature still exist, you would cite that record according to 8.42, Legislative Petitions. For databases to divorce certificates issued by state-level registrars, see 9.42.

9.37   Negative-search Certificates
Negative evidence—the absence of evidence one would expect to find—can be as critical as positive evidence in historical research. When a search within a specific body of records yields negative results, your citation needs to identify not only the party conducting the search but also the date of the search and the parameters of the search. In some states, the practice is to issue a formal "failure to find" certificate.

In other instances, you may be citing only a letter from the official who conducted the search. Both formats are illustrated below.

Source List Entry

Alabama. Death Certificates. Bureau of Vital Statistics, Montgomery.
Illinois. Richland County. Delayed Birth Records. County Clerk, Olney.

First Reference Note

1. Alabama, Certificate of Failure to Find Record, 9 August 1983; citing death search for "L. Columbus 'Lum' Harrison, 1917–1921, Perry County"; Bureau of Vital Statistics, Montgomery.

2. Richland County, Illinois, County Clerk, 10 January 1975 letter reporting negative birth-record search for Floyd Finley Shown, 1888–93.

Subsequent Note

11. Alabama, Certificate of Failure to Find Record, death search for "L. Columbus 'Lum' Harrison, 1917–1921, Perry County."

12. Richland Co., Ill., County Clerk, 10 January 1975 letter reporting negative birth-record search for Floyd Finley Shown, 1888–93.

9.38 Permits (Certificates): Burial or Transportation

A technical difference exists between *permits* and *certificates* for both burials and the transporting of bodies, although all these may be interfiled. A *permit* was a document issued prior to burial or transportation. Some jurisdictions that issued permits also logged the issuance into a register, in which case the original permit might then be kept by the funeral home. (See 4.8–4.9, Funeral Home Records.) Some jurisdictions requested the return of the permit once the body was transported or interred. Others called for funeral homes to complete a *certificate of burial* that would be filed after the burial, usually with the department that maintained vital records for that jurisdiction. The following offers typical citations to varied circumstances.

Source List Entry

(When issued by the state)
Florida. Removal and Burial Permits. State Board of Health. Bureau of
    Vital Statistics. Jacksonville.

(When issued by the city or county)
Missouri. St. Louis, City of. Burial Certificates. City Clerk's Office, St.
    Louis.

First Reference Note

1. Florida State Board of Health, removal and burial permit no. 5524, Albert Franklin Firestone, issued 19 January 1933; Bureau of

Vital Statistics, Jacksonville.

    2. City of St. Louis, Missouri, burial certificate no. 4545, Susanna Stamm, issued 28 June 1895; City Clerk's Office, St. Louis.

Subsequent Note

    11. Florida removal and burial permit no. 5524, Albert Franklin Firestone, issued 19 January 1933.

    12. City of St. Louis burial certificate no. 4545, Susanna Stamm, issued 28 June 1895.

Archival Microfilm

The examples below use the St. Louis certificate from above to illustrate citing a microfilmed preservation copy of a collection of certificates. In this case, the microfilm is available in two locations, each of which use different archival identification for the film. When you use unpublished microfilm in one archive and attribute it to that archive only, you should use that facility's identification.

In the example below, when you use the film at the Missouri State Archives (MSA), and examine its opening frames carefully, you will find that film identified there as a production by the St. Louis County Library (SLCL). That note of attribution also carries SLCL's identification number. *If you choose to identify the film by the name of this producer* rather than the repository (state archives) in which you use it, *then you must cite that producer's microfilm identification number.* If, however, you choose to cite the archival repository for that preservation copy, rather than the producer, *then you must use the repository's microfilm identification number.*

Source List Entry

Missouri. St. Louis, City of. Burial Certificates. City Clerk's Office, St. Louis. MSA microfilm C10469 (Certificates 3712–4765). Missouri State Archives, Jefferson City.

(*or*)

Missouri. St. Louis, City of. Burial Certificates. City Clerk's Office, St. Louis. SLCL microfilm BC SL-53. St. Louis County Library, St. Louis.

First Reference Note

    1. City of St. Louis, Missouri, burial certificate no. 4545, Susanna Stamm, issued 28 June 1895; MSA microfilm C10469 (Certificates 3712–4765), Missouri State Archives, Jefferson City.

(*or*)

    1. City of St. Louis, Missouri, burial certificate no. 4545, Susanna

Stamm, issued 28 June 1895; SLCL microfilm BC SL-53, St. Louis County Library, St. Louis.

Subsequent Note
11. City of St. Louis burial certificate no. 4545, Susanna Stamm, issued 28 June 1895.

9.39 Published Vital Records
See also 9.43, Town Registers: New England

When birth, marriage, and death records are abstracted, compiled, or transcribed and then published, you are no longer citing the original vital records, you are citing a publication. You should use the standard format for printed books, journal articles, or electronic data, depending upon the medium in which it appears. (See chapters 12 and 14.) For example:

Source List Entry
Kardell, Caroline Lewis, and Russell A. Lovell Jr. *Vital Records of Sandwich, Massachusetts, to 1885*. 3 vols. Boston: New England Historic Genealogical Society, 1996.

First Reference Note
1. Caroline Lewis Kardell and Russell A. Lovell Jr., *Vital Records of Sandwich, Massachusetts, to 1885*, 3 vols. (Boston: New England Historic Genealogical Society, 1996), 1: xxvii.

Subsequent Note
11. Kardell and Lovell, *Vital Records of Sandwich*, 1: xxvii.

The once-common practice of generically citing published vital records as "Sandwich VR" does not meet modern standards. It fails to distinguish between the use of original records and that of a derivative work. When you use a published compilation rather than the original records, you should cite your source for what it is, a publication.

9.40 Short-form Certificates (Local or State)
See also QuickCheck Model *for* STATE-LEVEL RECORDS : VITAL RECORDS, AMENDED

Modern concerns about privacy cause many local and state agencies to issue short-form certificates of birth, marriage, and death events—with various pieces of personal information omitted. When your citation refers to a short-form certificate (or modern counterparts stamped "heirloom copy" or "for genealogical purposes"), rather than a photocopy of the original, you should identify the record's abridged nature.

Source List Entry

Texas. Department of State Health Services. Birth Certificates. Vital Statistics Office, Austin.

First Reference Note

1. Texas Department of State Health Services, birth certificate (short form), no. 5129-27 (1927), Johnnie LaVerne Grooms; Vital Statistics Office, Austin.

Subsequent Note

11. Texas birth certificate (short form) no. 5129-27, Johnnie LaVerne Grooms.

9.41   State-level Certificates

See QuickCheck Model *for* STATE-LEVEL RECORDS : VITAL-RECORDS CERTIFICATE

State registrars of vital statistics may maintain file copies of loose certificates or they may retain bound registers only (see 9.42). When citing an individual certificate, the following formats usually suffice:

Source List Entry

Delaware. Department of Health and Social Services. Birth Certificates. Office of Vital Statistics, Dover.
Oregon. Department of Human Services. Death Certificates. Center for Health Statistics, Portland.

First Reference Note

1. Delaware Department of Health and Social Services, birth certificate 107-53-001504 (1953), Edward Devine; Office of Vital Statistics, Dover.
2. Oregon Department of Human Services, death certificate no. 79-006405, Tzilla Lilah Miller (1979); Center for Health Statistics, Portland.

Subsequent Note

11. Delaware birth certificate no. 107-53-001504 (1953), Edward Devine.
12. Oregon death certificate no. 79-006405 (1979), Tzilla Lilah Miller.

9.42   State-level Registers

See (also)

- QuickCheck Model *for* STATE-LEVEL RECORDS: VITAL RECORDS REGISTER
- 9.4–9.8 *for* Marriage Licenses, Registrations, Etc.
- 9.41 *for* State-level Certificates

Some states maintain registrations in volumes, typically labeled by year, rather than individual certificates. Sometimes they are numbered consecutively, with multiple volumes for a single year or a single volume for several years. In either mode, the pages may be numbered sequentially, with multiple entries on a page, or the registrations may be a bound collection of numbered but unpaginated certificates. If you are able to consult the registers on microfilm, you should study the arrangement to create an appropriate citation. If you receive a photocopy, the registrar's office should identify for you a book and page or certificate number.

Source List Entry

Massachusetts. *Massachusetts Vital Records, 1841–1910.* Massachusetts Archives, Boston.

Rhode Island. Department of Health. *State Death Registers.* Office of Vital Records, Providence.

Vermont. Department of Health. *Marriage Registrations, 1870.* Vital Records Division, Middlesex.

First Reference Note

1. *Massachusetts Vital Records,* 453: 293, no. 5262, Joseph A. Anglin–Mary Ann Fitzsimmons, marriage, 1895; Massachusetts Archives, Boston.

2. Rhode Island Department of Health, *State Death Registers,* 1875: 1290, no. 28, Lucy J. DeHaro; Office of Vital Records, Providence.

3. Vermont Department of Health, *Marriage Registrations,* 1870: no. 907, Alexander Phillips–Catherine Burke; Vital Records Division, Middlesex.

Subsequent Note

11. *Massachusetts Vital Records,* 453: 293, no. 5262, Anglin-Fitzsimmons marriage, 1895.

12. Rhode Island *State Death Registers,* 1875: 1290, no. 28, Lucy J. DeHaro.

13. Vermont *Marriage Registrations,* 1870: no. 907, Phillips-Burke.

Online Databases & Indexes (State Level)

When citing online databases and indexes to state-level vital records, you will have variances, depending upon the amount of data supplied by the site. The three samples below illustrate these variations:

AUTHOR/CREATOR..... In the Illinois and North Dakota examples, you have an identified database compiler (the state). For the Kentucky example, the detail supplied at the website does not make clear whether the database was the creation of the state vital-records office or the university. In that case, your citation can omit the compiler's identity and lead with the name of the database.

DATABASE NAME ...... In the Illinois and Kentucky examples, the database is located at a website that carries a variety of offerings. Therefore, you cite the database as you would a chapter in a book or an article in a journal—i.e., you put the database name in quotation marks and the website name in italics. In the North Dakota example, the database and the website are one and the same. Therefore, only the website name needs citing. Italics are used for the website's name, because it is a stand-alone publication, not a mere part of a larger whole.

Source List Entry

Illinois. "Illinois Statewide Marriage Index, 1763–1900." Database. *Illinois State Archives.* http://www.cyberdriveillinois.com/depart ments/archives/marriage.html : 2007.

"Kentucky Divorce Index, 1973–1993." Database. *Kentucky Vital Records Index.* http://ukcc.uky.edu/~vitalrec/ : 2007.

North Dakota. Department of Health. *Public Death Index.* Database. https://secure.apps.state.nd.us/doh/certificates/death CertSearch.htm : 2007.

First Reference Note

1. Illinois, "Illinois Statewide Marriage Index, 1763–1900," database, *Illinois State Archives* (http://www.cyberdriveillinois.com/depart ments/archives/marriage.html : accessed 7 February 2007), entry for Finley Shown and Delenna [Dulcena] Witters, 15 September 1888; citing Lawrence County Marriages, vol. 2: 131, license no. 95.

2. "Kentucky Divorce Index, 1973–1993," database, *Kentucky Vital Records Index* (http://ukcc.uky.edu/~vitalrec/ : accessed 13 February 2007), entry for Shown v. Shown, Daviess County, 8 June 1979 decree.

3. North Dakota Department of Health, *Public Death Index,* database (https://secure.apps.state.nd.us/doh/certificates/deathCertSearch .htm : accessed 1 March 2007), entry for Horace A. Day, 11 January 1905.

Subsequent Note

11. Illinois, "Illinois Statewide Marriage Index, 1763–1900," database, *Illinois State Archives,* entry for Finley Shown and Delenna [Dulcena] Witters, 15 September 1888.

12. "Kentucky Divorce Index, 1973–1993," database, *Kentucky Vital Records Index,* entry for Shown v. Shown, Daviess Co., 8 June 1979 decree.

13. North Dakota, *Public Death Index*, database entry for Horace A. Day, 11 January 1905.

9.43   Town Registers: New England

Births, marriages, and deaths have been registered in New England towns since the mid-seventeenth century, although a town's collections may not be complete. As a rule, registrations occurred shortly after the event. However, researchers also encounter registrations of whole families of children on a single day—a situation suggesting that the family had just arrived in the town. When the internal characteristics of a record persuade you this was the case, you should include a comment to that effect in your First Reference Note, because the issue of timeliness can affect your analysis of the evidence. Most entries in early town-level vital registers, however, can be cited by this model:

Source List Entry

Rhode Island. Providence. Births, Marriages, and Deaths, 1699–1856. City Registrar's Office, Providence.

First Reference Note

1. Providence, Rhode Island, Births, Marriages, and Deaths, 5: 201, John James–Catherine Downing marriage, 1817; City Registrar's Office, Providence.

Subsequent Note

11. Providence, R.I., Births, Marriages, and Deaths, 5: 201, James-Downing marriage, 1817.

CD/DVD Database & Images

Source List Entry

Early Vital Records of Bristol County, Massachusetts, to about 1850. Database and images. CD-ROM. Wheat Ridge, Colorado: Search & ReSearch, ca. 1998.

First Reference Note

1. *Early Vital Records of Bristol County, Massachusetts, to about 1850*, digital images, CD-ROM (Wheat Ridge, Colorado: Search & ReSearch, ca. 1998), Town of Bristol, DeWolf–Bourn marriage, 1839; database entries are linked to images that are not in a book and page arrangement.

Subsequent Note

11. *Early Vital Records of Bristol County, Massachusetts, to about 1850*, digital image, Town of Bristol, DeWolf–Bourn marriage, 1839.

Microfilm (FHL-GSU)

Source List Entry
Rhode Island. Providence. Births, Marriages, and Deaths, 1699–1856. City Registrar, Providence. FHL microfilm 915,075. Family History Library, Salt Lake City, Utah.

First Reference Note
1. Providence (Rhode Island), Births, Marriages, and Deaths, 5: 201, James-Downing marriage, 1817; FHL microfilm 915,075.

Subsequent Note
11. Providence (R.I.), Births, Marriages, and Deaths, 5: 201, James-Downing marriage, 1817.

9.44   Tribal Registrations
Vital registrations created by Indian agencies are organized by tribe, rather than state, county, or town. Most of these records are under the jurisdiction of the National Archives. See 11.19–11.21, Indian Affairs Records.

VITAL REGISTRATIONS: INTERNATIONAL

9.45   Background
Considering the breadth of records available internationally, it is not possible to cover all types in all countries. This section focuses upon representative examples from the most commonly used resources.

9.46   Canada: Birth, Marriage & Death Registrations
See also 7.37, Church Records: Canada

Across Canada, civil vital records are maintained by the provinces, although a few early ones have been transferred to Library and Archives Canada. Within Québec (as in France), civil registrations of births, marriages, and deaths are known by the term the *état civil.* The Catholic baptisms, marriages, and burials that constituted the earliest vital registration in Canada are covered at 7.37. A typical citation to civil registrations at Library and Archives Canada would be this:

Microfilm (Library and Archives Canada)

Source List Entry
Ontario. Department of Agriculture. Civil Registration of Births, Marriages, and Deaths; Waterloo County, 1855. Volume 2429,

Series A-IV-4. Record Group 17. LAC microfilm C-15758. Library and Archives Canada, Ottawa.

First Reference Note
1.   Ontario Department of Agriculture, Civil Registration of Births, Marriages, and Deaths, Waterloo County, 1855: file 1, return 6, p. 1, entry 11, Claussen-Pierreault marriage; microfilm C-15758, Library and Archives Canada, Ottawa.

Subsequent Note
11.   Ontario Department of Agriculture, Civil Registration of Births, Marriages, and Deaths, Waterloo County, 1855: file 1, return 6, p. 1, entry 11, Claussen-Pierreault marriage.

Death registrations for the Province of Ontario illustrate the need for careful identification when citing microfilmed records. The originals are held by the Archives of Ontario and have been filmed for preservation purposes. Most researchers use the preservation film. Whether you consult the film at FHL or the Archives of Ontario, the film will be identical. However, each facility catalogs the film by its own numbering scheme. The following pair of citations, to a single record, illustrates the difference.

Microfilm (FHL-GSU)

Source List Entry
Ontario. Registrar General. Death Registrations, 1869–1933. RG 80-8. Archives of Ontario. FHL microfilm 1,846,464. Family History Library, Salt Lake City, Utah.

First Reference Note
1.   Ontario Registrar General, Death Registrations, 1869–1933, Nicholas B. Gustin registration no. 2668 (1869); FHL microfilm 1,846,464.

Subsequent Note
11.   Ontario Registrar General, Death Registrations, 1869–1933, Nicholas B. Gustin registration no. 2668 (1869).

In the example above, when using FHL film, most researchers begin their First Reference Note with an identification of the creator, then the record, then the specific item—after which they identify the FHL film number.

In contrast, the example below features preservation microfilm consulted at the archive that owns the actual records. Thus, it follows that archive's preferred style. The First Reference Note cites the elements from smallest to largest—beginning with the specific item, progressing through the identification of the collection and the microfilm for that collection, then ending with the identity of the archive.

Microfilm (Provincial Archives)

Source List Entry

Ontario. Registrar General. Registrations of Deaths: 1869–. Microfilm MS 935, 455 rolls. Archives of Ontario, Toronto.

First Reference Note

1.   Nicholas B. Gustin death registration no. 2668 (1869); Ontario Registrations of Deaths, 1869–; microfilm MS 935, roll 1, Archives of Ontario, Toronto.

Subsequent Note

11.   Nicholas B. Gustin death registration no. 2668 (1869), Ontario Registrations of Deaths, 1869–1933.

9.47   Canada: Divorce Records

Prior to 1968 a Canadian divorce was obtainable by a special act of the Canadian Parliament, as well as from the provincial courts. In the former case, a brief notice of the matter would appear amid the parliamentary acts published for each year in *Statutes of Canada*. An entry gleaned from the online database maintained by Library and Archives Canada might be cited as follows:

Online Databases

Source List Entry

Canada. "Divorce in Canada (1841–1968)." Database. Library and Archives Canada, *Canadian Genealogy Centre*. http://www .collectionscanada.ca/genealogy/index-e.html : 2007.

First Reference Note

1.   Canada, "Divorce in Canada (1841–1968)," database, Library and Archives Canada, *Canadian Genealogy Centre* (http://www.col lectionscanada.ca/genealogy/index-e.html : accessed 13 February 2007), entry for Vicgor [Victor?] Eccles Blackhall v. Blanche Mabel Jackson; citing no. 47, *Statutes of Canada,* 1909.

Subsequent Note

11.   Canada, "Divorce in Canada (1841–1968)," database entry for Vicgor [Victor?] Eccles Blackhall v. Blanche Mabel Jackson, 1909.

9.48   England: Vital Records Databases & Indexes

See also 7.38, Church Records: England, for parish-level baptismal, marriage, and burial entries.

Original Certificates

Civil registrations of births, marriages, and deaths have existed in England since 1837. As a rule, they are not open for public use. You will likely cite certificates acquired from either a local registry office or from the General Registry Office at Southport, which maintains a national index. In some cases, your certificate will be a photocopy of the original registry entry. In other cases, you may be working with a newly printed form on which a clerk has handcopied details from the original. Or, you may have a short form certificate on which the clerk has extracted only the name of the child and the date and place of birth. If the registration you are citing represents an offshore birth, marriage, or death of an English citizen, you would be citing an "Overseas Events" certificate. Your citation should identify the type of certificate you are using.

A typical certificate also carries three sets of numbers. On the Melville Williams certificate that is cited below, the three numbers that appear are as follows:

XCZ044848	This preprinted number represents the unique number of the certificate issued to the inquirer. It is not the record's file number, and it need not be cited.
W004481	This "W" number represents the number on the application form you would have filled in; it is added there by the staff, as a double-check to ensure that all requests are filled. It need not be cited.
5C/96/459	This is the essential number for you to cite—the number that allows someone to retrieve the same record again. In this case, *5C* represents the registry district, *96* the volume number, and *459* the page number.

Source List Entry

England. Registrar General. Birth Certificates. General Registry Office, Southport.

First Reference Note
　　1.　England, birth certificate (short form) for Melville Williams, 1897; citing 5C/96/459, St. Austel registration district and subdistrict; General Registry Office, Southport.

Subsequent Note
　　11.　England, birth certificate (short form), Melville Williams, 1897, citing 5C/96/459, St. Austel registration district and subdistrict.

CD-DVD Index

Source List Entry
British Isles Vital Records Index. Database. 2d ed. CD-ROM. Salt Lake
　　City: The Church of Jesus Christ of Latter-day Saints, 2002.

First Reference Note
　　1.　*British Isles Vital Records Index,* database, CD-ROM, 2d ed. (Salt Lake City: The Church of Jesus Christ of Latter-day Saints, 2002), entry for Nicholas Mills, christened 18 September 1636, Hurst, Berkshire, England; citing FHL microfilm 1,279,460.

Subsequent Note
　　11.　*British Isles Vital Records Index,* database entry for Nicholas Mills, christened 18 September 1636, Hurst, Berkshire, England.

Online Databases

Numerous databases exist to British vital records. Some are free (open-access) sites, while others are subscription based, as in note 3, below. When you know that a site is by subscription, your citation might include that detail. However, many researchers consider this detail optional because databases that are free one day might be subscriber-based the next—or vice-versa—rendering your data obsolete in either case.

Source List Entry
"England & Wales, FreeBMD Index: 1837–1983." Database. *FreeBMD.*
　　http://freebmd.rootsweb.com/cgi/search.pl : 2007.
"England & Wales, Free BMD Index: 1837–1983." Database.
　　Ancestry.co.uk. http://search.ancestry.co.uk : 2007.
Treequest. "Births, 1837–2003." Database. *Familyrelatives.org.* http://
　　www.familyrelatives.org/treequest/jsp/customer/index.jsp : 18
　　December 2006.

First Reference Note
　　1.　"England & Wales, FreeBMD Index: 1837–1983," database, *FreeBMD* (http://freebmd.rootsweb.com/cgi/search.pl : accessed 20

February 2007), death entry for Daniel Dendy; citing June [quarter] 1846, Hambledon, vol. 4: 138.

    2. "England & Wales, Free BMD Index: 1837–1983," database. *Ancestry.co.uk* (http://search.ancestry.co.uk : accessed 20 February 2007), marriage entry for Daniel Dendy [bride unidentified]; citing Surrey County, June [quarter] 1841, vol. 4: 77.

    3. Treequest, "Births, 1837–2003," subscription database, *Familyrelatives.org* (http://www.familyrelatives.org/treequest/jsp/cus tomer/index.jsp : accessed 18 December 2006), birth entry for Ainissa Hemming Jones; citing G[reat] Boughton, January–March 1838, vol. 19: 44.

Subsequent Note

    11. "England & Wales, FreeBMD Index: 1837–1983," database death entry for Daniel Dendy, Hambledon, June [quarter] 1846.

    12. "England & Wales, Free BMD Index: 1837–1983," database marriage entry for Daniel Dendy, Surrey County, June [quarter] 1841.

    13. Treequest, "Births, 1837–2003," database birth entry for Ainissa Hemming Jones, G[reat] Boughton, January–March 1838.

CITING DATES FROM ENGLISH VITAL REGISTERS

The indexes to English vital records, as a rule, are *quarterly* indexes. In the compilations made from these quarterly records, when an index cites a month, it refers to the month in which the quarter ended. The marriage might have occurred at any time during that quarter. If your reference note reports the month and year cited by the database, it should indicate that the month represents a full quarter; otherwise, it would appear to be the actual month of the marriage. In the above examples, that explanation is handled by placing the word *quarter* in square editorial brackets immediately after the word *June*.

9.49   France: États-Civil

See also 7.39 for Church Records: France

In 1792, France's Revolutionary government secularized all existing church registrations of births, marriages, and deaths to create a civil registration system known as its *états-civil*. Civil clerks or *greffes* in each town were required by law to make copies of the existing church record. The *copie greffe* was to then be abstracted into an *état civil* (civil report) for fiscal planning and taxation purposes. Copies of those civil lists are typically found at the local level. Worldwide, these records are more likely to be consulted via the Family History Library microfilm.

In the example below, the Source List Entry covers the whole collection and time frame, while the Reference Notes cite the specific volume (with the exact title in quotation marks) and identifies the act. This Stürtzelbronn register does not use act *numbers;* entries are located by date. In other cases where an act number exists, you would want to include it.

Microfilm (FHL-GSU)

Source List Entry
France. Moselle. Sarreguemines. Stürtzelbronn. États-civil (Births, Adoptions, Marriages, Divorces, and Deaths), 1792–1877. Archives départementales de la Moselle, Saint-Julien-lès-Metz. FHL microfilm 2,003,446. Family History Library, Salt Lake City, Utah.

First Reference Note
1. Stürtzelbronn, Sarreguemines, Moselle, "État-civil de l'an XII de la République," naissance (birth), Jacque Arbogast, 6 Nivose an XII (28 December 1803); FHL microfilm 2,003,446.

Subsequent Note
11. Stürtzelbronn, Sarreguemines, "État-civil de l'an XII de la République," naissance, Jacque Arbogast, 6 Nivose XII (28 December 1803).

CITING DATES FROM THE FRENCH REVOLUTIONARY CALENDAR
French vital records dated between 22 September 1792 and 1 January 1806 follow the Revolutionary calendar that was adopted in October 1793 and applied retroactively to the start of the Revolutionary government thirteen months earlier. When you record these calendar dates, you will likely want to express the Gregorian calendar equivalents in parentheses.

CITING TITLES IN FOREIGN LANGUAGES
See 2.23.

9.50   Germany: Emigration Registers

Prior to the creation of the German nation in 1871, records on internal migration and emigration to other countries were created at a local level—that of the *oberamt,* analogous to a U.S. county. Most surviving records today are held by the state archives, some of whom require that citations to their records credit their facility. The Staatsarchiv at Ludwigsburg, cited below, is one which sets that policy. Therefore, the First Reference Note below includes the location of the original records, as well as the identity of the microfilm.

FHL-GSU Microfilm

Source List Entry

Württemberg. Geislingen. Auswanderungsakten [Emigration documents], 1817–1900. Geislingen Oberamt [Governmental district]. Staatsarchiv [State Archives], Ludwigsburg, Germany. FHL microfilm 577,786. Family History Library, Salt Lake City, Utah.

First Reference Note

1. Geislingen, Württemberg, Auswanderungsakten [Emigration documents], vol. 189a (1817–1893): year 1888, entry 124, Wilh. Schwarz; Staatsarchiv [State Archives], Ludwigsburg, Germany; FHL microfilm 577,786.

Subsequent Note

11. Geislingen, Württemberg, Auswanderungsakten [Emigration documents], vol. 189a, 1817–1893: year 1888, entry 124, Wilh. Schwarz.

9.5 I   Germany: Vital Registrations

See also 7.40 Church Records: Germany, for baptismal, marriage, and burial sacramental entries, as well as *Familienbuch* entries.

Researchers who work with Germany's civil registrations commonly consult three forms: *Ansässigmachungsakten* (citizenship records); *Verehlichungsakten* (marriage records); and *Zivilstandsregisters* (registers of births, marriages, and deaths). The following example can be used for any of those types by substituting the appropriate register title or description.

FHL-GSU Microfilm

Source List Entry

Germany. Passau. Bayern. Verehlichungsakten und Ansässigmachungsakten [Marriages and citizenship], 1800–1910. Stadtarchiv Passau. FHL 1,710,296, item 2. Family History Library, Salt Lake City, Utah.

First Reference Note

1. Bayern, Passau, Verehlichungsakten [Marriages], 1800–1910, section R, no. 304, Anton Reiter–Kreszenz Wimmer, 1913; FHL microfilm 1,710,296, item 2.

Subsequent Note

11. Bayern, Passau, Verehlichungsakten [Marriages], 1800–1910, section R, no. 304, Anton Reiter–Kreszenz Wimmer, 1913.

9.52   Ireland: Vital Registrations

Civil registration of births, marriages, and deaths date back to 1845–64, as an extension of Ireland's Poor Law legislation that created a public-health system. The new registration districts overlapped the Poor Law Unions into which counties already had been divided. Because these registration district bounds correspond to neither counties nor unions, *you will need to cite the **registration district** in your "creator" field*. All registration districts have been supervised by the General Register Office (GRO) in Dublin, where master indexes have been compiled. Although some records from older jurisdictions are maintained by Ireland's Department of Health, most records are obtained from the GRO. A typical citation to a birth, marriage, or death record might be this:

BOUND VOLUMES:

Source List Entry

Ireland. Cookstown District. Death Records. General Register Office, Dublin.

First Reference Note

1. Cookstown District, Ireland, Death Records, 1871, vol. 1:408, no. 133, Samuel Geddes; General Register Office, Dublin.

Subsequent Note

11. Cookstown Dist. Death Records, 1871, 1:408, no. 133.

9.53   Israel: Holocaust Victims Database

Begun in 1955, the Hall of Names created by Yad Vashem, the Holocaust Martyrs' and Heroes' Remembrance Authority, offers biographical data on more than three million victims of the Holocaust. Materials at its online registry might be cited as follows:

Online Database & Images

Source List Entry

Yad Vashem. *The Central Database of Shoah Victims' Names*. Database and images. http://www.yadvashem.org : 2007.

First Reference Note

(*To cite the database*)

1. Yad Vashem, *The Central Database of Shoah Victims' Names* (http://www.yadvashem.org : accessed 1 February 2007), entry for Henryk Sperber, b. 1921, Cracow, Poland.

(To cite images)
    2. Eugenia Halbreich (Sperber), contributor, "Page of Testimony" and photograph for Henryk Sperber, b. 1921, Cracow, Poland; digital images, Yad Vashem, *The Central Database of Shoah Victims' Names* (http://www.yadvashem.org : accessed 1 February 2007).

Subsequent Note
    1. Yad Vashem, *The Central Database of Shoah Victims' Names,* entry for Henryk Sperber, b. 1921, Cracow, Poland.
    2. Halbreich (Sperber), "Page of Testimony" and photograph for Henryk Sperber, b. 1921, Cracow, Poland; Yad Vashem, *The Central Database of Shoah Victims' Names.*

9.54   Italy: Vital Registrations

Civil vital registration has existed in Italy since the Napoleonic era, although records were not consistently created during much of the 1800s and have randomly survived. Duplicate originals were to be kept by the *commune* (town or township) and the province. As a rule citations are to the local copy held by the *ufficio di stato civile* (office of civil vital registration) or to the microfilm made by the Genealogical Society of Utah. Typically, registers are preprinted volumes with formal titles. Most are sequentially numbered, although the number is not always visible on the filmed copy. In citing these registers, you have two basic options:

- you may cite the exact title from the title page (as in notes 1 and 3), in which case you do not need to include the year of the act in your citation *if* the title of the volume cites only one year (as with note 1); or

- you may cite the series and volume number (as in notes 2 and 4), in which case you should add the year of the act to your citation.

On occasion, you may need to cite an entry from a decennial index, pending access to the original volume in which the act is registered. Notes 3 and 4 illustrate both the exact-title format and the series: volume format. The Source List Entry covers the full series searched.

FHL-GSU Microfilm

Source List Entry
Italy. Palermo. Gratteri. Registri degli Atti di Nascita [Registers of the Acts of Birth], 1862–1910. Ufficio dello Stato Civile, Gratteri. FHL microfilm 1,965,163–1,965,164. Family History Library, Salt Lake City, Utah.

First Reference Note

(*To cite the actual register*)

1. Gratteri, Palermo, "Registro degli Atti di Nascita [Register of the Acts of Birth; or Birth Registrations], 1882": entry 56, Sebastiano Sammarco; FHL microfilm 1,965,164, item 1.

2. Gratteri, Palermo, Birth Registrations, vol. 23: entry 56, Sebastiano Sammarco, 1882; FHL microfilm 1,965,164, item 1.

(*To cite an index entry*)

3. Gratteri, Palermo, "Indice decennale del Registri degli Atti di Nascita, Corso dai 1 Gennaro 1886 a tutto l'anno 1895" [Decennial Index to Birth Registrations from 1 January 1886 through all of the year 1895], unpaginated, for Guisseppe Talamo di Guiseppe, 1891, entry 25; FHL microfilm 1,965,164, item 2.

4. Gratteri, Palermo, Birth Registrations, vol. 30 [Decennial Index, 1886–1895], unpaginated, for Guisseppe Talamo di Guiseppe, 1891, entry 25; FHL microfilm 1,965,164, item 2.

Subsequent Note

11. Gratteri, Palermo, "Registro degli Atti di Nascita, 1882": entry 56, Sebastiano Sammarco.

12. Gratteri, Palermo, Birth Registrations, vol. 23: entry 56, Sebastiano Sammarco, 1882.

13. Gratteri, Palermo, "Indice decennale del Registri degli Atti di Nascita ... 1886[–]1895," for Guisseppe Talamo di Guiseppe, 1891, entry 25.

14. Gratteri, Palermo, Birth Registrations, vol. 30 [Decennial Index, 1886–1895], for Guisseppe Talamo di Guiseppe, 1891, entry 25.

9.55   Mexico: LDS Vital Records Index

Online Databases

Source List Entry

Church of Jesus Christ of Latter-day Saints, The. "Vital Records Index." Database. *FamilySearch.* http://www.familysearch.org/Eng/default.asp : 2007.

First Reference Note

1. The Church of Jesus Christ of Latter-day Saints (LDS), "Vital Records Index," database, *FamilySearch* (http://www.familysearch.org/Eng/default.asp : accessed 20 February 2007), entry for Manuela de la Trenidad Sanches de Herrera of Atlixco (Puebla, Mexico), born 2 June 1697; citing FHL microfilm 703,444.

Subsequent Note

11. LDS, "Vital Records Index," database, *Family Search,* entry for

Manuela de la Trenidad Sanches de Herrera of Atlixco (Puebla, Mexico), born 2 June 1697.

9.56 Scotland: Statutory Registers

See also 7.43 Church Records: Scotland

Beginning in 1855, Scotland instituted the systematic and mandatory registration of births, marriages, and deaths on a secular level. For records prior to that date, you will turn to the not-so-regularly kept (or preserved) records of the Church of Scotland known as the OPR or Old Parish Records (7.43).

The Statutory Registers that began in 1855 are organized by parish and county but are in the domain of the Registrar General at Edinburgh. Researchers commonly consult them as microfilm copies or as online images made available through *ScotlandsPeople,* the subscription-based website of the General Record Office for Scotland (GROS). The following samples cover both media, as well as the online database created by GROS.

Microfilm (FHL-GSU)

Source List Entry

> Scotland. Berwick County. Coldstream Parish. Registers of Births, Marriages, and Deaths. Statutory Registers, Registrar General, Edinburgh. FHL microfilm 280,594, item 8. Family History Library, Salt Lake City, Utah.

First Reference Note

> 1.   Coldstream Parish, Berwick County, Register of Births, 1859, entry 14, Ralph Wallace; citing Reg. no. 733, Coldstream District; FHL microfilm 280,594, item 8.

Subsequent Note

> 11.   Coldstream Parish, Berwick Co., Register of Births, 1859, entry 14, Ralph Wallace.

Online Databases

See 9.6 for differences in citing online image and online databases.

Source List Entry

> Scotland. "Search the Records." Database. *ScotlandsPeople.* http://www.scotlandspeople.gov.uk : 2007.

First Reference Note
    1. Scotland, "Search the Records," database, *ScotlandsPeople* (http: //www.scotlandspeople.gov.uk : accessed 6 February 2007), birth entry for Ralph Wallace, 1859, Coldstream in Berwick; citing Statutory Registers no. 733/00/00144.

Subsequent Note
    11. Scotland, "Search the Records," database birth entry for Ralph Wallace, 1859, Coldstream in Berwick.

Online Images 🖳

Source List Entry
Scotland. Berwick County. Coldstream Parish. Registers of Births, Marriages, and Deaths. Digital images. Scotland, *ScotlandsPeople*. http://www.scotlandspeople.gov.uk : 2007.

First Reference Note
    1. Coldstream Parish, Berwick County, Register of Births, 1859: entry 14, Ralph Wallace; digital image, *ScotlandsPeople* (http://www .scotlandspeople.gov.uk : accessed 6 February 2007).

Subsequent Note
    11. Coldstream Parish, Berwick Co., Register of Births, 1859: entry 14, Ralph Wallace.

SCOTLAND'S CATALOGING SYSTEM
For an explanation of the cataloging system used by GROS, see 7.43.

9.57   Switzerland: Familienregisters

Many of the early civil registers of Switzerland and some other European countries are random volumes, rather than part of any series, and they typically carry complex titles. So that these registers can be more easily located in your Source List, you may prefer to use a generic category such as the one below for Buchackern, *Familienregisters*. Your Reference Notes would then cite , in quotation marks, the exact title of each individual register. Because the volume is undated, a date is added to the title in square editorial brackets.

In the example below, the volume extends over a number of years and a closing date is not easily discernible from the content. Therefore, the date that is added to the title cites the beginning year, followed by an en-dash to indicate an "open" time frame.

Microfilm (FHL-GSU)

Source List Entry

Switzerland. Thurgau. Buchackern. Familienregisters. Staatsarchiv Luzern. FHL microfilm 958,407, item 2. Family History Library, Salt Lake City, Utah.

First Reference Note

1. Buchackern, Canton Thurgau, "Haushaltungs-Register in der Ortsgemeinde Buchakern, Zivilstandskreis Erlen, Verbürgerten Familien [1786–]," [Householders register at Buchakern, Erlen District, authenticating families], p. 27, family of Konrad Stump and Elisabetha Rudishauser; FHL microfilm 958,407, item 2.

Subsequent Note

11. Buchackern, Canton Thurgau, "Haushaltungs-Register," p. 27, Konrad Stump and Elisabetha Rudishauser family.

9.58   Scandinavia: LDS Vital Records Index (Denmark, Finland, Norway, Sweden)

Online Databases

Source List Entry

Church of Jesus Christ of Latter-day Saints, The. "Vital Records Index." Database. *FamilySearch*. http://www.familysearch.org/Eng/default .asp : 2007.

First Reference Note

1. The Church of Jesus Christ of Latter-day Saints (LDS), "Vital Records Index," database, *FamilySearch* (http://www.familysearch.org/ Eng/default.asp : 2 February 2007), marriage entry for Thomas Andraea and Stina Christophori at Kangasala, Hame, Finland, 26 December 1789; citing FHL microfilm 56,538.

Subsequent Note

11. LDS, "Vital Records Index," database, *FamilySearch*, marriage entry for Thomas Andraea and Stina Christophori, 26 December 1789.

LOCAL &
STATE RECORDS

Property & Probates

10

QuickCheck Models

(See Chapters 8 and 9 for related models)

Guidelines & Examples (beginning page 497)

QuickCheck Model
ORIGINAL RECORDS: LOCAL
CASE FILES
(Jurisdiction & series as lead elements in Source List)

Source List Entry

JURISDICTION	SERIES	REPOSITORY ...

Missouri. St. Louis, City of. Probate case files. Probate Court Clerk's

...	REPOSITORY LOCATION

Office, St. Louis.

First (Full) Reference Note

JURISDICTION	SERIES	FILE NO. & ...

1. City of St. Louis, Missouri, probate case files, no. 26469, Landry

... NAME	FILE DATE	ITEM OF INTEREST	RECORD DATE	...

Charleville (1900), deposition of Mary T. Mason, 24 September 1901; Probate

... REPOSITORY	REPOSITORY LOCATION

Court Clerk's Office, St. Louis.

Subsequent (Short) Note

JURISDICTION	SERIES	FILE NO. & ...

11. City of St. Louis, Mo., probate case files, no. 26469, Landry

... NAME	FILE DATE	ITEM OF INTEREST	RECORD DATE

Charleville (1900), deposition of Mary T. Mason, 24 September 1901.

QuickCheck Model
ORIGINAL RECORDS: LOCAL
REGISTERS
(Jurisdiction & series as lead elements in Source List)

Source List Entry

JURISDICTION	SERIES	...

Tennessee. Franklin County. Deed Records, 1807–1882. Office of the

... REPOSITORY	REPOSITORY LOCATION

Register of Deeds, Winchester.

First (Full) Reference Note

	JURISDICTION	SERIES	VOLUME & PAGE(S)	ITEM OF INTEREST ...

1. Franklin County, Tennessee, Deeds, C: 305–06, Alexander Suiter to

... (PARTIES & TYPE OF DOCUMENT)	RECORD DATE	REPOSITORY ...

James McFarland, power of attorney, 28 October 1811; Office of the Register

...	REPOSITORY LOCATION

of Deeds, Winchester.

Subsequent (Short) Note

JURISDICTION	SERIES	VOLUME & PAGE(S)

11. Franklin Co., Tenn., Deeds, C: 305–06.

QuickCheck Model
ORIGINAL RECORDS: LOCAL
TRACT BOOK
(Jurisdiction & series as lead elements in Source List)

Source List Entry

JURISDICTION	SERIES	REPOSITORY

Alabama. Perry County. Tract Books, 1819–. Probate Judge's Office,

REPOSITORY
LOCATION

Marion.

First (Full) Reference Note

JURISDICTION	SERIES	VOLUME & PAGE NO. ...

1. Perry County, Alabama, Tract Books, 1: unpaginated entries arranged

... or ARRANGEMENT	ITEM OF ...

by legal land description; see Township 21 North, Range 8 East, Section 35,

... INTEREST	RECORD DATE	REPOSITORY	REPOSITORY LOCATION

W½ NE¼, James J. Harrison, 1833; Probate Judge's Office, Marion.

Subsequent (Short) Note

JURISDICTION	SERIES	VOLUME: PAGE(S)	ITEM ...

11. Perry Co., Ala., Tract Books, 1: T21N, R8E, Sect. 35, W½ NE¼,

... OF INTEREST	DATE

James. J. Harrison, 1833.

QuickCheck Model
ORIGINAL RECORDS: STATE-LEVEL
LAND-GRANT REGISTER
(Jurisdiction/agency & series as lead elements in Source List)

Source List Entry

JURISDICTION/ AGENCY	SERIES	...

Maryland. Land Office. Patent Records, 1637–Present, Series S11. Mary-

... REPOSITORY	REPOSITORY LOCATION

land State Archives, Annapolis.

First (Full) Reference Note

ITEM OF INTEREST	RECORD DATE	SPECIFIC ...

1. Warrant to "Mr. Edward Booker," 26 October 1662, "Maryland

... VOLUME	PAGE	SERIES ...

Patends [*sic*], Certificates & Warrants, 1662–1664," p. 18; Maryland Land

... or RECORD GROUP	REPOSITORY

Office Patent Records, 1637–Present, Series S11; Maryland State Archives,

REPOSITORY LOCATION

Annapolis.

Subsequent (Short) Note

ITEM OF INTEREST	RECORD DATE	SPECIFIC ...

11. Warrant to "Mr. Edward Booker," 26 October 1662, "Maryland

... VOLUME	PAGE

Patends [*sic*], Certificates & Warrants, 1662–1664," 18.

QuickCheck Model
ORIGINAL RECORDS: STATE-LEVEL
LAND WARRANTS: LOOSE
(Jurisdiction & series as lead elements in Source List)

Source List Entry

JURISDICTION   SERIES   RECORD GROUP ...

Kentucky. Certificates of Settlement and Preemptions. Non-military Reg-

...   REPOSITORY   REPOSITORY LOCATION

isters and Land Records. Kentucky Land Office, Louisville.

First (Full) Reference Note

ITEM OF INTEREST   RECORD DATE

1. Preemption Warrant no. 1085, James Wallace, 26 February 1780;

SERIES   RECORD GROUP ...

Certificates of Settlement and Preemption, Non-military Registers and Land

...   REPOSITORY   REPOSITORY LOCATION

Records; Kentucky Land Office, Louisville.

Subsequent (Short) Note

ITEM OF INTEREST   RECORD DATE

11. Preemption Warrant no. 1085, James Wallace, 26 February 1780,

SERIES, ETC. (SHORTENED)

Certificates of Settlement and Preemption, Kentucky.

QuickCheck Model
IMAGE COPIES: CD/DVD
(Jurisdiction/agency & series as lead elements in Source List)

Source List Entry

JURISDICTION / AGENCY	SERIES	RECORD ...

Pennsylvania. Surveyor General. Old Rights Registers. Records of the

... GROUP	REPOSITORY ...

Pennsylvania Land Office, Record Group 17. Pennsylvania State

REPOSITORY LOCATION	ITEM TYPE or FORMAT	PUBLICATION ...

Archives, Harrisburg. Digital images. *First Landowners of Pennsylvania:*

... TITLE ...

Colonial and State Warrant Registers in the PA Archives, Harrisburg, 1682–ca.

PUBLICATION FORMAT	PUBLICATION PLACE	PUBLISHER	YEAR

1940. CD-ROM. Alexandria, Virginia: Ancestor Tracks, 2005.

First (Full) Reference Note

JURISDICTION / AGENCY	SPECIFIC VOLUME	PAGE

1. Pennsylvania Surveyor General, "Old Rights, Bucks & Chester," p. 6,

ITEM OF INTEREST	ITEM TYPE or FORMAT	PUBLICATION ...

entry 85, John Bainbridge; digital images, *First Landowners of Pennsylvania:*

... TITLE

Colonial and State Warrant Registers in the PA Archives, Harrisburg, 1682–ca. 1940,

PUBLICATION FORMAT	PUBLICATION PLACE	PUBLISHER	YEAR

CD-ROM (Alexandria, Virginia: Ancestor Tracks, 2005).

Subsequent (Short) Note

JURISDICTION / AGENCY	SPECIFIC VOLUME	PAGE

11. Pennsylvania Surveyor General, "Old Rights, Bucks & Chester," p. 6,

... ITEM OF INTEREST

entry 85, John Bainbridge.

QuickCheck Model
IMAGE COPIES: MICROFILM
(Jurisdiction & series as lead elements in Source List)

Source List Entry

JURISDICTION (AUTHOR)   SERIES ...

Massachusetts. Sutton. Record of Strays and Marks and Miscellaneous

    ...   RECORD REPOSITORY   REPOSITORY LOCATION ...

Town Records, 1732–1822. Town Clerk's Office, Sutton. FHL

    ... FILM ID   FILM REPOSITORY   FILM LOCATION ...

microfilm 858,541, item 1. Family History Library, Salt Lake City,

...

Utah.

First (Full) Reference Note

        JURISDICTION   SPECIFIC ...

1. Sutton, Massachusetts, "Sutton's Book of Records of Estrays &

    ... VOLUME   PAGE   ITEM OF INTEREST   ...

Marks, Dom. 1732–Dom. 1816," part 3: p. 6, Ebenezer Harwood entry, 1

    ... RECORD DATE   FILM ID

November 1737; FHL microfilm 858,541, item 1.

Subsequent (Short) Note

        JURISDICTION   SPECIFIC VOLUME ...

11. Sutton, Mass., "Sutton's Book of Records of Estrays & Marks,

    ...   PAGE

Dom. 1732–Dom. 1816," pt. 3: p. 6.

QuickCheck Model
IMAGE COPIES: ONLINE
(Jurisdiction & series as lead elements in Source List)

Source List Entry

JURISDICTION	SERIES	REPOSITORY

Florida. Miami–Dade County. Old Plat Books. County Recorder's Office,

REPOSITORY LOCATION	ITEM TYPE or FORMAT	WEBSITE CREATOR-OWNER	WEBSITE ...

Miami. Digital images. Miami-Dade County Clerk. *County Recorder's*

... TITLE	URL (DIGITAL LOCATION) ...

Record Search. http://www.miami-dadeclerk.com/public-records/

...	YEAR

oldpbimage.asp : 2007.

First (Full) Reference Note

JURISDICTION	SPECIFIC VOLUME	PAGE	ITEM ...

1. Miami–Dade County, Florida, Old Plat Book 1: 11, "Perrine Grant,

... OF INTEREST	RECORD DATE	ITEM TYPE or FORMAT ...

Subdivision of Section 4 T^P 56^S R40^E," March 1909; digital image, Miami-

WEBSITE CREATOR-OWNER	WEBSITE TITLE	URL ...

Dade County Clerk, *County Recorder's Record Search* (http://www.miami

... (DIGITAL LOCATION)	DATE

-dadeclerk.com/public-records/oldpbimage.asp : accessed 2 February 2007).

Subsequent (Short) Note

JURISDICTION	SPECIFIC VOLUME	PAGE	ITEM OF INTEREST

11. Miami-Dade Co., Fla., Old Plat Book 1: 11, "Perrine Grant,"

RECORD DATE

March 1909.

QuickCheck Model
DERIVATIVES: ABSTRACTS, ONLINE
(Compiler & article title as lead elements in Source List)

Source List Entry

CREATOR OF DATABASE	ARTICLE TITLE

Crawford, Nancy Gay, compiler. "Camden County [Georgia] Deed Ab-

...	ITEM TYPE*	SITE OWNER or CREATOR*	WEBSITE TITLE

stracts." *Welcome to Camden County GAGenWeb Project.*

URL (DIGITAL LOCATION)	YEAR

http://www.rootsweb.com/~gacamden/deedabs.html : 2007.

First (Full) Reference Note

CREATOR / ABSTRACTOR	ARTICLE TITLE

1. Nancy Gay Crawford, compiler, "Camden County [Georgia] Deed

...	WEBSITE TITLE	...

Abstracts," *Welcome to Camden County GAGenWebProject* (http://

... URL (DIGITAL LOCATION)	DATE

www.roots.web.com/~gacamden/deedabs.html : accessed 2 February 2007),

ITEM OF INTEREST	RECORD DATE ...

Elihu Atwater, Certificate of Admission to Connecticut Bar, 19 December

...	CREDIT LINE (SOURCE OF THIS SOURCE)

1801; citing Deed Book E: 295.

Subsequent (Short) Note

CREATOR	DATABASE TITLE	...

11. Crawford, "Camden County [Georgia] Deed Abstracts," *Welcome*

... WEBSITE TITLE	ITEM OF INTEREST (SHORTENED)

to Camden County GAGenWeb Project, Elihu Atwater Certificate, E: 295.

---

* The article's title identifies the type of record; you do not have to repeat that item type in the Record Type Field. Similarly, the website's title includes the name of its creator (GAGenWeb); that detail does not have to be repeated in a separate Owner/Creator field.

QuickCheck Model
DERIVATIVES: DATABASE, ONLINE
(*Database as lead element in Source List*)

Source List Entry

DATABASE TITLE	ITEM TYPE *	WEBSITE TITLE (SAME AS CREATOR)

"Names Listed on General Land Office Database." *Indiana Commission*

...	URL (DIGITAL LOCATION) ...

on Public Records. http://www.in.gov/icpr/archives/databases/land/

...	YEAR

general_.html : 2007.

First (Full) Reference Note

DATABASE TITLE	...

1. "Names Listed on General Land Office Database," *Indiana Commis-*

... WEBSITE TITLE (SAME AS CREATOR)	URL (DIGITAL LOCATION) ...

sion on Public Records (http://www.in.gov/icpr/archives/databases/land/

...	DATE	ITEM OF INTEREST ...

general_.html : accessed 10 February 2007), entry for Henry Bickel,

...	CREDIT LINE (SOURCE OF THIS SOURCE) ...

T25N, R3E, S20 & 21; generically citing "land office plat maps and field

...

notes" as the sources of the database.

Subsequent (Short) Note

DATABASE TITLE	...

11. "Names Listed on General Land Office Database," *Indiana Com-*

... WEBSITE TITLE	ITEM OF INTEREST

mission on Public Records, entry for Henry Bickel, T25N, R3E, S20 & 21.

* *"Database" is explicitly stated in the title. You do not have to repeat it in the Record Type field.*

GUIDELINES
& Examples

BASIC ISSUES

10.1 Background
Many issues relating to property and probate records are handled the same as those for local court and governance records. See discussions in chapters 8 and 9 for additional guidance.

10.2 Citing Key Parties in the Record
When citing deeds, if your text identifies the key individuals involved in a document—say, the grantee and the grantor—you do not have to repeat that identification in your citation. On the other hand, if your text states, say, that Jonathan Turner lived on Neal's Creek and your source for that piece of information is a deed between other parties in which Turner is merely mentioned as a landowner adjacent to the property being sold, it would be appropriate for your Reference Note to name the key parties of the deed. For example:

> 1. Anderson County, South Carolina, Conveyance Book T: 457, John Poor Sr. to Hugh Poor, mentioning Jonathan Turner; Clerk of Court's Office, Anderson.

When citing wills, tax rolls, and similar records, it is best to identify the individual(s) of interest in your note, spelling the name(s) exactly as spelled in the record.

10.3 Citing Property & Probate Records
Two fundamental factors determine how you cite property and probate records: their form (bound or loose) and the governmental level at which they are created and now maintained. Most U.S. probate materials are local records; but in some colonies, probates were handled at the colony or province level. Unclaimed lands in regions controlled by European-American governments have been dispensed to individuals by the Crown, the colony, the state, and the

497

federal government. For land transactions at the national level, see chapter 11. The present chapter treats property and probate records maintained at the state, county, and town levels.

10.4 Using Originals vs. Record Copies

Many of the property and probate records you consult at the city and county level are *record copies* rather than "true originals." Historically, citizens have created deeds, marriage contracts, probate inventories, and a host of related records in the private office of an attorney, a notary, or a justice of the peace. On those occasions, duplicate originals were typically made—one to be kept by the official who created the record and one or more *duplicate originals* for the key parties involved (say, the grantor and grantee in a land sale). Depending upon the law in effect at the time and place, either the official who created the document or one of the parties to the transaction might bring one of the duplicate originals to the town or county record office. There, the document would be recopied into a record book. Depending upon law and custom, the originals might be returned to the individual who submitted them for recording or they might be kept by the clerk. Retaining the original was a common early practice for probate records, less so for deeds.

As a careful researcher, you will want to use the original or the copy closest to the original (the so-called "most original"). If a city or county has preserved probate *files,* you would give more weight to the documents kept therein than to the record-book copies. However, as a legal and practical matter, record copies officially created and maintained by public record offices are treated as *original records*, unless a "more original" version exists.

DEEDS & CONVEYANCES

10.5 Basic Formats: Original Registers

See also QuickCheck Model *for* ORIGINAL RECORDS: LOCAL REGISTERS ...

Most property records for transfers between individuals are recorded at the city, town, or county level. The registers for them carry an endless variety of labels. Even so, their citations usually follow a basic pattern with six parts:

- creator's name (the local jurisdiction);
- label on the volume you are using;
- page(s) where you found the item of interest;

- identification of the item of interest (if not identified in your text);
- office where the record is kept;
- city where the office is found.

Optionally, you may need to include three other elements:
- key parties to the record (illustrated at note 4, below; *see also* 10.2)
- type of record (*see also* 10.10)
- date of record (illustrated at note 4 below; *see also* 10.8)

Regardless of the type of deed you are citing—a quitclaim deed, a fee-simple deed, a deed of trust, a donation, etc.—one basic pattern should fit. The following examples illustrate that basic pattern by using a range of titles found across the United States for variously named registers and officials.

Source List Entry

(To list only one volume from a series)
Idaho. Elmore County. "Homesteads, 1898–1946." County Court Clerk's Office, Mountain Home.

(To list a full series)
Maryland. Baltimore. Superior Court Land Records. City Archives, Baltimore.

New Jersey. Sussex County. Mortgages, 1766–1868. County Clerk's Office, Newton.

Pennsylvania. Franklin County. Deeds, 1810–1850. Register of Deeds Office, Chambersburg.

Vermont. Pownal. Land Records, 1821–1831. Town Clerk's Office, Pownal.

First Reference Note

1. Elmore County, Idaho, "Homesteads, 1898–1946," p. 23; County Court Clerk's Office, Mountain Home.

2. Baltimore, Maryland, Superior Court Land Records, Liber TR 11: 144–45; City Archives, Baltimore.

3. Sussex County, New Jersey, Mortgage Book G: 404, John Bescherer to Gersham Coursen; County Clerk's Office, Newton.

4. Franklin County, Pennsylvania, Deed Book 18: 155, William Timmons and wife & Samuel Witter and wife to John Gouter, 8 April 1839; Register of Deeds Office, Chambersburg.

5. Pownal, Vermont, Land Records, vol. 9: 25; Town Clerk's Office, Pownal.

Subsequent Note

11. Elmore Co., Idaho, "Homesteads, 1898–1946," 23.

12. Baltimore, Md., Superior Court Land Records, Liber TR 11: 144–45.

13. Sussex Co., N.J., Mortgage Book G: 404.
14. Franklin Co., Pa., Deed Book 18: 155.
15. Pownal, Vt., Land Records, 9: 25.

PUNCTUATION TIPS

Note 1 cites a volume that covers an unusually long period of time for a land book. Using quotation marks around the exact title will forestall later questions about the accuracy of the date span or whether the citation refers to just one or multiple books.

Notes 3 and 4 each cite a specific book: Mortgage Book G and Deed Book 18. Their citations carry no comma between the elements in the volume's label. In contrast, the other notes first cite a *series* ("Homesteads," "Land Records," and "Superior Court Land Records"—all in plural form), then single out one specific volume by either its number or its date. When the whole series is cited in the Reference Note, a comma separates the name of the series from the specific volume.

All these approaches are equally correct. Your choice might depend upon whether the cited volume or series has a simple or complex title.

10.6   Basic Formats: Microfilm Images

When using preservation copies of local courthouse records, you would expand upon the Basic Format to identify the film and its creator. In most cases for this class of record, you will be working with preservation film produced by the Genealogical Society of Utah and deposited at the Family History Library.

Microfilm (FHL-GSU)

Source List Entry

Pennsylvania. Franklin County. Deeds. 1784–1883. Register of Deeds Office, Chambersburg. FHL microfilm, 91 rolls. Family History Library, Salt Lake City.

First Reference Note

1. Franklin County, Pennsylvania, Deed Book 9:123–34; FHL microfilm 323,799.

Subsequent Note

11. Franklin Co., Pa., Deed Book 9: 123–34.

CITING MICROFILM NUMBERS
See 2.26.

IDENTIFYING THE RECORD OFFICE FOR FILMED VOLUMES
See 2.31 and 8.16, paragraph 2.

10.7 Deed Books, Miscellanea in

A wide variety of materials may appear in deed records. Many items, because of their special nature, are not indexed in the modern "consolidated" index to conveyances that researchers often consult. That consolidated index typically focuses upon transfers of real estate.

Among the miscellaneous records often found in deed books are marriage contracts and settlements, powers of attorney, registrations of free people of color, slave sales, wills, and the hiring of substitutes for military service. You may also find frontier claims for wolf bounties, partnership agreements, articles of incorporation for businesses, and even post–Civil War oaths of allegiance. When you cite a deed book for a miscellaneous type of record one would not normally expect to find in a deed book, you should add a note mentioning the special nature of the record you found. Otherwise, you or others may later question whether the citation to a deed book for that type of record is correct.

10.8 Delayed Recordings

Deeds often were not recorded promptly. The date of the deed you are discussing in your text can be much earlier than the dates on the record book you cite, causing users of your work (or yourself at a later date) to question the accuracy of the dates you are reporting. In such situations—particularly in counties whose records are known to have been destroyed long after the date you give for the deed—you may wish to add a note explaining the delayed recording.

Source List Entry
Alabama. Calhoun County. Deed Records, 1868–1900. Probate Judge's Office, Anniston.

First Reference Note
1. Calhoun County, Alabama, Deed Records, B3 (1868–1872): 17–18, Crow to Boozer; Probate Judge's Office, Anniston. This 1847 deed was re-recorded after the 1868 fire.

Subsequent Note
11. Calhoun Co., Ala., Deed Records, B3: 17–18.

10.9 Documents Online, Random Items

Although most research in probate and property records involves the use of whole *sets* of registers of files, you will also encounter random materials posted online. Sometimes they are image copies, sometimes transcripts or abstracts. The following examples cover both types.

Online Images (Random Items)

Source List Entry
"Test Your Skills." Digital images. *Board for Certification of Genealogists*. http://www.bcgcertification.org/tests/index.html : 2007.

First Reference Note
1. "Test Your Skills," digital images, *Board for Certification of Genealogists* (http://www.bcgcertification.org/tests/index.html : accessed 6 February 2007), Herman Greve to Dorchen Greve, deed, 7 July 1870; citing Monroe County, Wisconsin, Deed Book 24: 433.

Subsequent Note
11. "Test Your Skills," digital images, *Board for Certification of Genealogists*, Greve to Greve, deed, 7 July 1870.

Online Transcripts or Abstracts (Random Items)

Source List Entry
"Test Your Skills," *Board for Certification of Genealogists*. http://www.bcg certification.org/tests/index/html : 2007.

First Reference Note
1. "Test Your Skills," *Board for Certification of Genealogists* (www.bcgcertification.org/tests/index.html : 6 February 2007), deed transcription and abstract, Herman Greve to Dorchen Greve, 7 July 1870; citing Monroe County, Wisconsin, Deeds 24:433.

Subsequent Note
11. "Test Your Skills," *Board for Certification of Genealogists*, deed transcription and abstract, Greve to Greve, 7 July 1870.

See also QuickCheck Model *for* DERIVATIVES: ABSTRACTS, ONLINE for material that represents a full run of records, rather than random items.

10.10 Lease & Release Conveyances

Some American colonies used a pair of documents called a *lease* and *release* to convey land—a subterfuge designed to evade Crown taxes or prohibitions on outright sales. By this practice, the owner/lessor would, on Day 1, execute a *lease,* under which the lessee would pay some token such as a peppercorn or an ear of Indian corn. In exchange, the document would grant him all rights to the property for an unusually long period of time—say, ninety-nine years—after which the property was to revert to the lessor. On Day 2, the parties would execute a *release,* in which the lessor would cancel the clause requiring

an eventual return of the land (i.e., a *reversion* of the property). The sum paid for that release usually reflected the property's true value.

These two-part conveyances follow the Basic Format for Deeds & Conveyances at 10.5. If you want your deed references to identify the grantor, grantee, and date of the conveyance, then your basic structure might be as follows:

Source List Entry
South Carolina. Charleston. Deed Books, 1719–1782. Office of the
    Register of Mesne Conveyances, Charleston.

First Reference Note
    1. Charleston, South Carolina, Deed Book A (1719–1721): 202–
11, Jacob Satur to William Wallace, Lease and Release, 18 and 19 April
1721; Office of the Register of Mesne Conveyances, Charleston.

Subsequent Note
    11. Charleston, S.C., Deed Book A: 202–11.

10.11 Mortgages or Deeds of Trust
Deeds in which the grantor put up certain property as collateral for debt, whether those records were called *mortgages* or *deeds of trust,* are cited using the Basic Format for Deeds & Conveyances at 10.5. If the title of the volume explicitly states *Mortgages* or *Deeds of Trust,* as illustrated there in note 3, your citation does not have to explicitly state that the document is a mortgage or a deed of trust. If, however, the title of the register is a generic *Deeds* or *Conveyances,* and the document is a mortgage or a deed of trust rather than an outright sale, your citation should say so, as illustrated in the two examples below.

When a release from a mortgage (variously called a cancellation) is subsequently recorded, that document may be overwritten atop the mortgage or it may be penned into the margin beside the mortgage itself. In either case, you should note that the cited book and page covers both the mortgage and the release. Elsewhere, you may find releases or cancellations recorded separately from the mortgages, in which case your citation should clearly state that the document you are citing is the release and not the actual mortgage.

Source List Entry
Louisiana. Natchitoches Parish. Conveyance Records, 1803–1900. Clerk
    of Court's Office, Natchitoches.
Texas. Victoria County. Deed Records, 1838–1890. County Clerk's
    Office, Victoria.

First Reference Note
　　1. Natchitoches Parish, Louisiana, Conveyance Book 74: 574–75, Anatole J. Forstall to Leopold and Mortimer Perot, cancellation of mortgage, 14 March 1881.
　　2. Victoria County, Texas, Deed Book 6: 140, James Hogan to James D. Wright, mortgage, 4 January 1854; County Clerk's Office, Victoria.

Subsequent Note
　　11. Natchitoches Par., La., Conv. Book 74: 574–75.
　　12. Victoria Co., Tex., Deed Book 6: 140.

10.12 Multiple Deeds Cited Together

Section 2.5 gives a basic rule for source citation: each statement of fact in your narrative or database—unless it represents "common knowledge"—should be keyed to a specific source. On occasion, however, a single statement of fact will have multiple sources (see 2.20). At other times, for a single statement about property, it may be necessary to cite multiple deeds from the same volume or from more than one volume. When those multiple citations are from the same county, they can usually be consolidated in the following manner:

Source List Entry
New York. Cayuga County. Deed Records, 1822–1828. County Records
　　Retention Center, Auburn.

First Reference Note
　　1. Cayuga County, New York, Deed Books Z: 103–4; EE: 226, 237; and GG: 336; County Records Retention Center, Auburn.

Subsequent Note
　　11. Cayuga Co., N.Y., Deed Books Z: 103–4; EE: 226, 237; and GG:336.

PUNCTUATION TIP
When citing multiple deeds from multiple volumes, punctuation helps to maintain clarity in three ways:

- Semicolons separate the deed books, making it unnecessary to repeat the phrase "Deed Book" before the reference to each separate book.
- Commas separate page references when there are multiple citations to the same book.
- En-dashes separate a range of consecutive page numbers, when relevant material appears on every page within the sequence.

10.13 Records Archived Off-site

When using local land and property records that have been removed to the state archives or another facility for preservation, you would cite them by the same Basic Format shown at 8.20 for local court records archived off-site.

10.14 State or Colony Deeds

At various times, some areas required deeds to be recorded at the state or colony level rather than at the local town or county. In these cases, the state or the colony is the "creator" of the collection. The county may not be mentioned in the citation at all, unless you add a special reference to that effect. In citing these statewide deeds, if your text's discussion or your database entry does not identify the specific county involved, then you would want to add that identification to the note.

Source List Entry

South Carolina. Deed Books, 1719–1782. Office of the Register of Mesne Conveyances, Charleston.

First Reference Note

1. South Carolina, Deed Book G (1727–1729): 230–31, Rachel Braggains to William Braggains, both of Colleton County; Office of the Register of Mesne Conveyances, Charleston.

Subsequent Note

11. South Carolina, Deed Book G: 230–31.

LAND GRANTS

10.15 Background

Two systems have dominated the formal settlement of land within the United States. Each of the early colonies made grants to its own settlers. Sometimes this was done directly, sometimes through *proprietors* or *concessionaires* who were allotted vast tracts and given the authority to parcel them among settlers as they pleased.

After the formation of the United States, the states created from the first thirteen English colonies claimed title to all unsettled land within their bounds and continued to distribute that land to settlers. As those first thirteen states split, the seven new states cut from them also held the right to distribute previously unclaimed lands that lay within their boundaries. All twenty states are known as *state land states*.

Within the regions that comprised England's Fourteenth and Fifteenth Colonies (East and West Florida) and within the French and Spanish provinces taken over by the United States, a different system prevailed. As the United States acquired each region, they were designated *public lands*, to be distributed by the federal government. However, within the thirty states created from the "public lands," significant tracts were ceded to the state governments for one reason or another. Those state governments then distributed the land to qualifying residents.

Consequently, in every American state, land records are maintained at the state level in addition to the person-to-person transactions that took place at the local level (10.5 through 10.17). Land records at each level are cited differently. Local conveyances are covered at 10.5– 10.14. Federal land records are covered at 11.22–11.31. State-level land records are handled below at 10.16–10.21.

10.16 State or Colony Grants: Bound Volumes

See also QuickCheck Model *for* ORIGINAL RECORDS: STATE LEVEL: LAND-GRANT REGISTER

In some instances, you will have multiple patents to cite from a state series across a broad swath of time. In other cases, you may only have one patent or one volume to cite. The four examples below demonstrate both situations and two particular differences between them:

DIFFERENT NEEDS

In the Maryland and Pennsylvania examples, each Source List Entry cites a specific register, alphabetizing it under the name of the agency that created it. In the South Carolina and Virginia examples, the Source List Entry cites nothing smaller than the series or collection, again alphabetizing it under the name of the agency that created it. Either approach applies in any state; you should choose the approach that fits your particular need.

DIFFERENT ARCHIVAL LANGUAGE

The Pennsylvania land office organizes its collections into *record groups*. The Maryland and South Carolina archives arrange theirs by *series*. Hence, different terms are used below. Although all the cited registers are part of a state's land-office records, the states may habitually credit different "authors." In the Pennsylvania example below, the Land Office itself is credited with creation of the registers. In the Pennsylvania example at 10.18, the state assigns the "creator" role to a specific officer within that Land Office: the Surveyor-

General. When you use any original register from an archive, you should note the precise identity of the agency that created it—as it is identified in the register or in the cataloging data—and cite it exactly. Preciseness will help to ensure that it can be located again amid many similarly titled volumes.

As with other formally archived and cataloged records of state-level governments, the Reference Notes below are cited in traditional smallest-to-largest format, beginning with the item of interest.

Source List Entry

(*To list only one volume from a series*)

Maryland. Land Office. "Maryland Patends [*sic*], Certificates & Warrants, 1662–1664." Patent Records, 1637–Present, Series S11. Maryland State Archives, Annapolis.

Pennsylvania. Land Office. Warrant Register 14 [undated]. Pennsylvania Warrant Application Registers, 1765–Present. Records of the Pennsylvania Land Office, Record Group 17. Pennsylvania State Archives, Harrisburg.

(*To list a whole series, when you use more than one volume*)

South Carolina. Auditor General. Memorial Books, 1731–1778. State Department of Archives and History, Columbia.

Virginia. Land Office. Military Certificates nos. 1–9926, 1782–1786. Library of Virginia, Richmond.

First Reference Note

1. Warrant to "Mr. Edward Booker," 26 October 1662, "Maryland Patends [*sic*], Certificates & Warrants, 1662–1664," p. 18 (cross-referenced to Liber AA: 317); Maryland Land Office Patent Records, 1637–Present, Series S11; Maryland State Archives, Annapolis.

2. John Culbertson's Warrant, 5 May 1817; Pennsylvania Warrant Register 14: Franklin County section, warrant no. C1421; Pennsylvania Land Office Records, Record Group 17; Pennsylvania State Archives, Harrisburg.

3. Abraham Odam's Memorial, 1761; Memorial Books, 1731–1778, volume 14: 67; Auditor General Series S111001; South Carolina Department of Archives and History, Columbia.

4. Grant to Heirs of Thomas Dunn, 15 April 1831; Virginia Land Office Military Certificates nos. 1–9926, vol. 3: certificate no. 6897; Land Office Inventory entry no. 89; Library of Virginia, Richmond.

Subsequent Note

11. Warrant to "Mr. Edward Booker," 26 October 1662, "Maryland Patends [*sic*], Certificates & Warrants, 1662–1664," 18.

12. John Culbertson's Warrant, 5 May 1817, Pennsylvania Warrant Register 14: Franklin County warrant no. C1421.

13. Abraham Odam's Memorial, 1761, South Carolina Auditor General, Memorial Books, 1731–1778, vol. 14:67.

14. Grant to Heirs of Thomas Dunn, 1831, Virginia Land Office Military Certificates nos. 1–9926, vol. 3: no. 6897.

CITING A SECTIONED REGISTER
In the Pennsylvania example, the register is not consecutively paginated from start to finish. The register is sectioned by county and warrants are arranged under the county.

CITING CROSS-REFERENCE
The Maryland example contains a situation frequently found in early state and colonial records: the record you are consulting carries a cross-reference to another volume or set of files. When you encounter these, you should include them; that other source may provide or lead to additional information.

CITING HONORIFICS
All four entries above involve males. In one, the name is prefaced by the honorific *Mr.* By modern conventions, you would not use that honorific in citations. However, the appearance of the title *Mr.* before a man's name in a seventeenth-century record is an important identifier that should be preserved.

10.17 State or Colony Grants: Loose Records
See QuickCheck Model *for* ORIGINAL RECORDS, STATE LEVEL: LAND WARRANTS...

Source List Entry
Kentucky. Certificates of Settlement and Preemptions. Non-military Registers and Land Records. Kentucky Land Office, Louisville.

First Reference Note
1. Preemption Warrant no. 1085, James Wallace, 26 February 1780; Certificates of Settlement and Preemption, Non-military Registers and Land Records; Kentucky Land Office, Louisville.

Subsequent Note
Preemption Warrant no. 1085, James Wallace, 26 February 1780, Certificates of Settlement and Preemption, Kentucky.

10.18 State or Colony Grants: CD/DVD & Microfilm Images
See QuickCheck Model *for* IMAGE COPIES: CD/DVD

Citing a CD or DVD that offers *image* copies of an original register is analogous to citing a microfilm that offers image copies of that same original. Within that framework, there are two variations:

- When you cite microfilm of a register, you typically focus upon the creator of the record, the identity of the record, and the item of interest within that record. Secondarily, you cite the microfilm that provided the image copy. That pattern is followed for the CD-ROM citation at notes 1 and 11, below.

- When you cite modern material prepared by the creators of the CD-ROM—perhaps a database or an introduction as in notes 2 and 12—then your citation would be comparable to that of a print book publication that offers an introduction or chapters by different authors.

CD/DVD Editions

Source List Entry

(Jurisdiction/agency and series as lead elements of the Source List Entry)
Pennsylvania. Surveyor General. Old Rights Registers. Records of the Pennsylvania Land Office, Record Group 17. Pennsylvania State Archives, Harrisburg. Digital images. *First Landowners of Pennsylvania: Colonial and State Warrant Registers in the PA Archives, Harrisburg, 1682–ca. 1940*. CD-ROM. Alexandria, Virginia: Ancestor Tracks, 2005.

(Publication and its new material as lead elements of the Source List Entry)
MacInnes, Sharon Cook, and Angus MacInnes. "Introduction." *First Landowners of Pennsylvania: Colonial and State Warrant Registers in the PA Archives, Harrisburg 1682–ca. 1940*. Digital images. CD-ROM. Alexandria, Virginia: Ancestor Tracks, 2005.

First Reference Note

1. Pennsylvania Surveyor General, "Old Rights, Bucks & Chester," p. 6, entry 85, John Bainbridge; digital images, *First Landowners of Pennsylvania: Colonial and State Warrant Registers in the PA Archives, Harrisburg, 1682–ca. 1940*, CD-ROM (Alexandria, Virginia: Ancestor Tracks, 2005).

2. Sharon Cook MacInnes and Angus MacInnes, "Introduction," p. 3, *First Landowners of Pennsylvania: Colonial and State Warrant Registers in the PA Archives, Harrisburg 1682–ca. 1940*, CD-ROM (Alexandria, Virginia: Ancestor Tracks, 2005).

Subsequent Note

11. Pennsylvania Surveyor General, "Old Rights, Bucks & Chester," p. 6, entry 85, John Bainbridge.

12. MacInnes and MacInnes, "Introduction," p. 3, *First Landowners of Pennsylvania*.

Microfilm (FHL-GSU)

Source List Entry

Pennsylvania. Surveyor General. Old Rights Registers. Records of the
    Pennsylvania Land Office, Record Group 17. Pennsylvania State
    Archives, Harrisburg. FHL microfilm 1,028,678, item 3. Family
    History Library, Salt Lake City, Utah.

First Reference Note

    1. Pennsylvania Surveyor General, "Old Rights, Bucks & Chester,"
p. 6, entry 85, John Bainbridge; FHL microfilm 1,028,678, item 3.

Subsequent Note

    11. Pennsylvania Surveyor General, "Old Rights, Bucks & Chester,"
p. 6, entry 85, John Bainbridge.

Microfilm (State Archives)

Source List Entry

Virginia. Land Office. Military Certificates [Revolutionary War Bounty
    Land Warrants]. LVA microfilm, Land Office Records reels 347–
    349. Library of Virginia, Richmond.

First Reference Note

    1. Virginia Land Office, Military Certificates [Revolutionary War
Bounty Land Warrants], vol. 3: no. 6897, Heirs of Thomas Dunn (15
April 1831); LVA microfilm, Land Office Records reel 347; Library of
Virginia, Richmond.

Subsequent Note

    11. Virginia Land Office, Military Certificates, vol. 3: no. 6897,
Heirs of Thomas Dunn, 1831.

10.19 State or Colony Grants: Online Materials

Both of the databases below were created by a state agency to offer
records held by the state archives and library. Both agencies offer
image copies as well. If you prefer, your Source List Entry can cover
both the databases and the images. However, your Reference Notes
can take different forms, because they represent two different types of
material.

Databases: These do not represent the original documents. They are
a modern derivative. Thus, the Reference Note citation of a database
begins with an identification of that derivative creation in the Basic
Format for published articles and databases—i.e., Author, "Database

Title," *Website Title* and publication data (in parentheses)—and ends with the specific item to which that database refers.

Images: These depict the original records. They may be the "most original" form you are allowed to use. You may wish to make those originals the primary focus of your Reference Notes, with a secondary reference to the website at which they are published, as in note 2 under "Online Images," below. See also 8.43.

Online Databases

Source List Entry
South Carolina. "Plats for State Land Grants, 1784–1868." Database and digital images. *South Carolina Department of Archives and History*. http://www.archivesindex.sc.gov/ : 2007.

First Reference Note
1. South Carolina, "Plats for State Land Grants, 1784–1868," database, *South Carolina Department of Archives and History* (http://www.archivesindex.sc.gov/ : accessed 2 February 2007), entry for Samuel Jefcoat, 1792; citing series S213190, vol. 29: 301, item 2.

Subsequent Note
11. South Carolina, "Plats for State Land Grants, 1784–1868," database entry for Samuel Jefcoat, 1792.

Online Images

Source List Entry
(*To list by name of the database through which you access the images*)
Virginia. "Advanced Search: Archives/Manuscripts." Database and digital images. *The Library of Virginia*. http://ajax.lva.lib.va.us : 2007.

(*To list by name of record series*)
Virginia. Revolutionary War Bounty Warrants. Executive Department Office of the Governor, Record Group 3. Virginia State Archives. Digital images. The *Library of Virginia*. http://ajax.lva.lib.va.us : 2007.

First Reference Note
(*To cite as a published source accessed through the website*)
1. "Advanced Search: Archives/Manuscripts," digital images, *The Library of Virginia* (http://ajax.lva.lib.va.us : accessed 8 January 2007), Thomas Dunn file, Revolutionary War Bounty Warrants; citing Execu-

tive Department Office of the Governor, Record Group 3; Virginia State Archives.

(*To emphasize the original document*)

2. Thomas Dunn file, Revolutionary War Bounty Warrants; Executive Department Office of the Governor, Record Group 3; Virginia State Archives; digital images, *The Library of Virginia* (http://ajax.lva.lib.va.us : accessed 8 January 2007).

Subsequent Note

11. "Advanced Search: Archives/Manuscripts," digital images, *The Library of Virginia*, Thomas Dunn file, Revolutionary War Bounty Warrants.

(*or*)

12. "Thomas Dunn" file, Revolutionary War Bounty Warrants, digital images, *The Library of Virginia*.

Online Images (Card Files)

Source List Entry

"Maryland Indexes (Patents, Index), MSA S1426." Card file, digital images. *Maryland State Archives: Reference and Research*. http://www.msa.md.gov/msa/stagser/s1400/s1426/html/index54.html : 2007.

First Reference Note

1. "Maryland Indexes (Patents, Index), MSA S1426," card file, digital images, *Maryland State Archives: Reference and Research* (http://www.msa.md.gov/msa/stagser/s1400/s1426/html/index54.html : accessed 2 February 2007), entry for Thomas Scudamore, 1687, "Scudamores Last."

Subsequent Note

11. "Maryland Indexes (Patents, Index), MSA S1426," card file, digital image for Thomas Scudamore, 1687, "Scudamores Last."

10.20 State Land Office Records for U.S. Public Lands: Original Records

Although the United States claimed original domain over the land in all territories acquired after 1787, Congress passed acts ceding parts of the public domain to the state governments of the thirty states known as *public land states*. Those state governments maintained their own land offices, creating a variety of materials from tract books to plats to copies of colonial grants made by Britain, France, and Spain. Your citations to this material will be governed primarily by one issue—whether you have used a bound volume or a loose document. Both types are illustrated below.

Source List Entry

Indiana. State Land Office. U.S. Land Office Tract Books, Indianapolis District. Indiana State Archives, Indianapolis.

Indiana. State Land Office. U.S. Land Office Register's and Receiver's Records, Indianapolis District. Correspondence and Miscellaneous Loose Records. Indiana State Archives, Indianapolis.

First Reference Note

1. David Gearman entry, 1834; U.S. Land Office Tract Books, Indianapolis District, vol. 5: 61; Indiana State Land Office Records, Indiana State Archives, Indianapolis.

2. David Gearman Receipt 15733, U.S. Land Office Register's and Receiver's Records, Indianapolis District; Correspondence and Miscellaneous Loose Records; Indiana State Land Office Records, Indiana State Archives, Indianapolis.

Subsequent Note

1. David Gearman entry, 1834; U.S. Land Office Tract Books, Indianapolis Dist., vol. 5: 61; Indiana State Land Office Records.

2. David Gearman Receipt 15733, U.S. Land Office Register's and Receiver's Records, Indianapolis Dist.; Correspondence and Miscellaneous Loose Records; Indiana State Land Office Records.

CREATING SHORTENED CITATIONS

The short-form examples at 10.16–10.18, State or Colony Grants, identify the person, date (if needed), book or file, and entry number in that book or file. The state agency or collection is not named because the state is already named in the title of the book or file. However, in the Gearman examples above, the book's title and the file title both refer to the United States—Indianapolis District. If your short form stopped there, users would logically anticipate finding the record in the *federal* land office, not the state one. Therefore, the short form for the U.S. records held by the state should explicitly connect the records to the *state* land office.

10.21 State Land Office Records for U.S. Public Lands: Image Copies

Microfilm (FHL-GSU)

Source List Entry

Alabama. General Land Office. "Alabama Land Grants & Land Patents, ca. 1819–1850." Loose certificates. Alabama Department of Archives and History. FHL microfilm 1,769,330. Family History Library, Salt Lake City, Utah.

First Reference Note

1. Alabama, General Land Office, "Alabama Land Grants & Land

Patents, ca. 1819–1850," loose certificates, alphabetically arranged, certificate 13537, Harris S. Evans, Wilcox County, Alabama; FHL microfilm 1,769,330.

Subsequent Note

11. Alabama, General Land Office, "Alabama Land Grants & Land Patents, ca. 1819–1850, certificate 13537, Harris S. Evans.

Online Databases

See also QuickCheck Model *for* DERIVATIVES: DATABASE, ONLINE

Source List Entry

Indiana. "Names Listed on General Land Office Database." *Indiana Commission on Public Records.* http://www.in.gov/icpr/archives/data bases/land/general_.html : 2007.

(*or*)

"Names Listed on General Land Office Database." *Indiana Commission on Public Records.* http://www.in.gov/icpr/archives/databases/land/ general_.html : 2007.

First Reference Note

1. "Names Listed on General Land Office Database," *Indiana Commission on Public Records* (http://www.in.gov/icpr/archives/data bases/land/general_.html : accessed 10 February 2007), entry for Henry Bickel, T25N, R3E, S20 & 21; generically citing "land office plat maps and field notes" as the source of the database.

Subsequent Note

11. "Names Listed on General Land Office Database," *Indiana Commission on Public Records*, entry for Henry Bickel, T25N, R3E, S20 & 21.

CITING THE DATABASE AUTHOR/CREATOR

Above, the state commission identified in the website title is the creator of the website and the creator of the database. Therefore you do not have to repeat its identity in the Author or Creator Field for either the database or the website. You may, as in the first Source List example, put the jurisdiction at the start of the entry if you specifically want all the Indiana entries to be together in your Source List.

MISCELLANEOUS RECORDS

10.22 Building Permits

In smaller counties and early urban areas, building permits appear in a variety of miscellaneous books. Twentieth-century metropolitan areas tend to maintain separate registers. In either case, they can usually be cited using the Basic Format for deeds (10.5) or town records (8.36). If the label on the volume does not identify the record as a building permit, you might want to add a note to that effect.

Source List Entry
Massachusetts. Yarmouth. Town Records, 1849–1892. Town Clerk's Office, Yarmouth.

First Reference Note
1. Yarmouth, Massachusetts, Town Records, Book 2 (1880–1892): 161, permission to build blacksmith shop, 17 April 1886.

Subsequent Note
11. Yarmouth, Mass., Town Records, 2:161.

10.23 Estray (Ranger) Books

Historically, landowners fenced their crops but allowed their livestock to forage for food in the woods. Animals that strayed beyond the domain of the owners could be taken up by anyone whose property they wandered onto. However, that "taking up" was to be reported to a local authority who would record the incident, identify the finder, and provide a description of the animal. By the twentieth century, the record might also state that the finder was under bond. Registers of this type are commonly known as Estray Books or Ranger Books, although other labels were used across place and time.

The following illustrate basic citations to town- and county-level registers. If the text to which your reference is attached identifies the parties involved and the time frame of the document, you may—as in the Massachusetts example—cite just the creator (the county or town), the book's name, and the page on which the entry appears. If your text discusses an incident without specifically identifying the parties or the time frame, then you might follow the Alabama model.

Source List Entry
Alabama. Mobile County. Estray Book 1, 1891–1923. Probate Judge's Office, Mobile.
Massachusetts. Sutton. "Sutton's Book of Records of Estrays & Marks, Dom. 1732–Dom. 1816." Town Clerk's Office, Sutton.
Tennessee. Williamson County. Ranger Books, 1834–1872. County Clerk's Office, Franklin.

First Reference Note
1. Mobile County, Alabama, Estray Book 1: 61–62, report and bond of Walter Williams, 28 June 1923; Probate Judge's Office, Mobile.

    2. Sutton, Massachusetts, "Sutton's Book of Records of Estrays & Marks, Dom. 1732–Dom. 1816," part 3: p. 6; Town Clerk's Office, Sutton.

    3. Williamson County, Tennessee, Ranger Book 1, unpaginated, chronological entries, for 11 November 1830, Jacob Carl; County Clerk's Office, Franklin.

Subsequent Note

    11. Mobile Co., Ala., Estray Book 1: 61–62.

    12. Sutton, Mass., "Sutton's Book of Records of Estrays & Marks, Dom. 1732–Dom. 1816," pt. 3: p. 6.

    13. Williamson Co., Tenn., Ranger Book 1, unpaginated, 11 November 1830, Jacob Carl.

EXACT REGISTER TITLE VS. FHL CATALOGING LABEL

The Source List Entry for Sutton, above, assumes that this is the only estray or marks-and-brands register that you are using for Sutton. Therefore, it cites the individual volume rather than a series, and it cites the title exactly as it appears on the register cover. The First Reference Note does the same.

The FHL film example below demonstrates how you might construct your citations in the event that you were to use multiple books of this type from Sutton. The Source List Entry below identifies the series as it appears in FHL cataloging, while the First Reference Note cites the exact title of the book in which the Harwood entry is found—a title that differs markedly from the FHL cataloging entry. Without having the exact title in the Reference Note, a user of your work might have to examine several Sutton registers to find the one that carried the Harwood entry at page 6 of part 3.

Microfilm (FHL-GSU)

See also QuickCheck Model *for* IMAGE COPIES: MICROFILM

Source List Entry

Massachusetts. Sutton. Record of Strays and Marks and Miscellaneous Town Records, 1732–1822. Town Clerk's Office, Sutton. FHL microfilm 858,541, item 1. Family History Library, Salt Lake City, Utah.

First Reference Note

    1. Sutton, Massachusetts, "Sutton's Book of Records of Estrays & Marks, Dom. 1732–Dom. 1816," part 3: p. 6, Ebenezer Harwood entry, 1 November 1737; FHL microfilm 858,541, item 1.

10.24 Homestead Exemption Records

The word *homestead* is used in various ways insofar as property is concerned. Most usages have specific meanings peculiar to that class of record. In chapter 11, National Records, you will encounter materials relating to *homestead allotments* made to Native Americans (11.9) and *homestead grants* made to settlers under the federal Homestead Act of 1862 (11.22). Below, this section treats a type of record created by local authorities—not by the federal government—to *exempt* homeowners from taxes on their personal dwelling, usually up to a certain value.

This type of record book can be cited using the Basic Format for Deeds & Conveyances (10.5). For example:

Source List Entry
New York. Cayuga County. Homestead Exemptions, 1851–1966. Cayuga County Records Retention Center, Auburn.

First Reference Note
1. Cayuga County, New York, Homestead Exemptions, 1851–1966 [1 volume], p. 75, for David Whipple, 26 February 1904; Cayuga County Records Retention Center, Auburn.

Subsequent Note
11. Cayuga Co., N.Y., Homestead Exemptions, 1851–1966, 75.

CITING REGISTERS WITH UNUSUAL DATE SPANS
This Cayuga example is one in which a single volume covers an inordinate number of years. If you were to merely copy the dates as written, odds are you (or someone else) would later suspect a copying error. Second-guessing can be prevented by flagging unusual situations. In this example, it is handled by placing the note "1 volume" in square editorial brackets after the identification of the records. It could also be handled by placing the exact title in quotation marks.

10.25 Marks & Brands Books

Historic registers that record livestock marks and brands (and occasionally the identifying marks local craftsmen used on their products) can be handled using the Basic Format for Deeds & Conveyances (10.5).

The examples below demonstrate a common record quirk: *registers that have lost their covers*. In such cases, you may create a generic label that describes the contents and the time frame. You will also want to note the situation in square editorial brackets. Aside from this quirk, the dates shown in the Source List Entry reflect the record series and the full span of years searched. The dates shown in the First Reference Note are for the specific book in which Emanuel Odom's entry appears.

Source List Entry
Mississippi. Madison County. Marks and Brands Registers, ca. 1828–1900. Circuit Clerk's Office, Canton.

First Reference Note
1. Madison County, Mississippi, Marks and Brands Register, ca. 1828–1860 [no cover]: unpaginated entries arranged chronologically; see entry for 7 July 1842, Emanuel Odom; Circuit Clerk's Office, Canton.

Subsequent Note
11. Madison Co., Miss., Marks and Brands Register, ca. 1828–1900, entry for 7 July 1842, Emanuel Odom.

10.26 Mining Records
Regardless of whether you cite an assessment, a deed, a plat, a recorded permit, or an entry in a claims register, in most instances you will be citing a record book by the Basic Format for Deeds & Conveyances (10.5). The citation below, for a local register that has been removed to the state archives, corresponds to the Basic Formats for county records that are archived off-site, as covered at 8.20, 9.7, 9.10, and 10.36.

Source List Entry
Idaho. Ada County. Placer Claims, Book 1 (1864–). Idaho State Archives, Boise.

First Reference Note
1. Ada County, Idaho, Placer Claims, Book 1 (1864–): 96–97, Mason Chapman, 23 February 1877; Idaho State Archives, Boise.

Subsequent Note
11. Ada Co., Idaho, Placer Claims, 1: 96–97.

CITING OPEN-ENDED DATES ON REGISTERS
Many record volumes are labeled with only the beginning date. If you cited only that date, you would leave an erroneous impression that the

volume contained records only for that year. The convention in these cases is to use an en dash (not a hyphen and not an em dash) after the year to indicate that the cited year was not the final one.

10.27 Notarial Books & Files

In the French and Spanish colonies of America, as in many European countries even today, legal recordkeeping was a function of the notary public. Whenever someone needed a deed, a marriage contract, a will, an estate inventory, or other legal document, they visited or called the community notary, who would not only draft the document for them but maintain a copy in his notarial archive. At his retirement or death, that archive would pass to his successor. As recordkeeping became more formalized, provisions were sometimes made for centralizing these archives in a notarial office. In the rural areas of America that had been settled by the French and Spanish, notaries often kept their own archives after the regions were acquired by the United States, although copies or abstracts usually were filed at the local courthouse.

The examples below and on the following page demonstrate handling several situations encountered by modern researchers: notarial acts that have been centralized locally (New Orleans), volumes that appear randomly in a local courthouse (Kaskaskia, Illinois; and Natchitoches, Louisiana), and collections that have been microfilmed by the Family History Library. In the Natchitoches example, because the volume is not part of a series, it is identified by its exact title placed in quotation marks. For a situation in which original, loose, notarial acts have been acquired by a private archive and made available on preservation microfilm, see 3.19.

Source List Entry

Illinois. Randolph County. Kaskaskia Notarial Records, ca. 1717–1765. County Clerk's Office, Chester.

Louisiana. Natchitoches Parish. "Frederick Williams, Notarial, April 24, 1836 to July 25, 1837." Clerk of Court's Office, Natchitoches.

Louisiana. Orleans Parish. Acts of Rafaël Perdoma, 1783–1790. Notarial Archives, New Orleans.

First Reference Note

1. Randolph County, Illinois, Kaskaskia Notarial Records, ca. 1717–1765, Act K-352, Henry Biron and Marie Maurice Medar, marriage contract, 24 April 1724; County Clerk's Office, Chester.

2. Natchitoches Parish, Louisiana, "Frederick Williams, Notarial, April 24, 1836 to July 25, 1837," 47–48, Samuel Houston of Texas to

John P. Dunn of Natchitoches, power of attorney, 26 June 1836; Clerk of Court's Office, Natchitoches.

  3. Orleans Parish, Louisiana, Acts of Rafaël Perdoma, 7: 160–61, Noriega–LeSassier dowry receipt; Notarial Archives, New Orleans.

Subsequent Note
  11. Randolph Co., Ill., Kaskaskia Notarial Records, Act K-352.
  12. Natchitoches Par., La., "Frederick Williams, Notarial, April 24, 1836 to July 25, 1837," 47–48.
  13. Orleans Par., La., Acts of Rafaël Perdoma, 7: 160–61.

Microfilm (FHL-GSU)

Source List Entry
Québec. Île Montréal. Actes de notaire, Michel Gamelin-Gaucher, 1772–1779. Library and Archives Canada, Ottawa. FHL microfilm 1,420,476, item 4.

First Reference Note
  1. Île Montréal, Québec, Actes de notaire, Michel Gamelin-Gaucher, 1772–1779 , no. 72, cession by J^n B^{te} Giroux and wife to J^n B^{te} Giroux, *fils,* 7 October 1773; FHL microfilm 1,420,476, item 2

Subsequent Note
  11. Ile Montréal, Qué., Actes de notaire, Michel Gamelin-Gaucher, 1772–1779, no. 72.

MARRIAGE CONTRACT VS. MARRIAGE RECORD

When citing a marriage *contract* or marriage *settlement* filed amid notarial records, you should be careful not to call the document a marriage *record.* Contracts were executed prior to marriage, to establish a division of property and the terms that would apply to heirship after the death of one of the parties. Within a contract a couple merely promised to marry at a later date, and not all contracts resulted in an actual marriage.

10.28 Plat Books, County Level

See also QuickCheck Model *for* IMAGE COPIES: ONLINE

Plat books at the local level provide scaled renderings of surveys for towns, subdivisions, and other special tracts. Most, but not all, are paginated. They are typically cited as a register—meaning that you identify the jurisdiction that created them, the title of the register, and the specific page. Beyond that, your citation should also identify the subject of the plat and its date, as well as the record office and location.

Source List Entry

Florida. Miami–Dade County. Old Plat Books. County Recorder's Office, Miami.

First Reference Note

1. Miami–Dade County, Florida, Old Plat Book 1: 11, "Perrine Grant, Subdivision of Section 4 T^P 56^S R40^E," March 1909; County Recorder's Office, Miami.

Subsequent Note

11. Miami–Dade Co., Fla., Old Plat Book 1: 11, "Perrine Grant," March 1909.

10.29 Tract Books, County Level

See also QuickCheck Model *for* ORIGINAL RECORDS: LOCAL: TRACT BOOK

In the thirty American states that are considered public-land states (see 10.15), county offices maintain land registers that are generically called *tract books*. Arranged by legal land description—township, range, section, and fraction thereof—the register records the details from the original patent for each individually patented tract within the county. Specific data is cited by that legal land description and date, not by page number (which may or may not exist and can be altered by the insertion of new pages). The exact titles of these registers vary from state to state and from county to county, as do the names of the offices that keep these records. The following provides typical patterns.

Source List Entry

Alabama. Perry County. Tract Books, 1819–. Probate Judge's Office, Marion.

Mississippi. Madison County. "Original U.S. Land Entries." Chancery Clerk's Office, Canton.

First Reference Note

1. Perry County, Alabama, Tract Books, 1: unpaginated entries arranged by legal land description; see Township 21 North, Range 8 East, Section 27, "SW Fraction E of Cahaba," James J. Harrison, 1833; Probate Judge's Office, Marion.

2. Madison County, Mississippi, "Original U.S. Land Entries," unpaginated entries arranged by legal land description; see Township 11 North, Range 3 East, Section 23 entries, William J. Balfour, 1835; Chancery Clerk's Office, Canton.

Subsequent Note

11. Perry Co., Ala., Tract Books, 1: T21N, R8E, Sec. 27 (frac.), James J. Harrison, 1833.

> 12. Madison Co., Miss., "Original U.S. Land Entries," T11N, R3E, S23, William J. Balfour.

NON-STANDARD LEGAL DESCRIPTION

The Mississippi example cites the specific land location in standard terms and abbreviations. The purchaser acquired multiple tracts all in the same section; it is not necessary for your citation to enumerate all the parcels of that section. The Alabama example identifies a single parcel taken out by the purchaser, but it carries a non-standard element in its legal description—a "fraction" rather than the typical parcel of a quarter section or a quarter-of-a-quarter. The legal description of that non-standard element is copied exactly with quotation marks.

TITLE OF BOOK IN QUOTATION MARKS

The Alabama record book uses the generic label *tract book*. It does not need to carry quotation marks. The Mississippi example carries a non-standard label. In such cases, quoting the exact label will help to ensure that the cited reference can be found again by yourself or others.

PROBATES

10.30 Basic Formats: Bound Volumes

Probate (aka estate or succession) books and files carry many labels across time and place. Regardless of the label, however, a record typically falls into one of two categories: (*a*) a clerk's copy recorded in a bound volume or (*b*) a loose document, usually found as part of a packet. As an occasional oddity, you might find a bound volume in a probate packet—often a doctor's ledger or a merchant's account book. In that case, the personal book would be cited as any other item within the estate packet. The following samples cover a variety of labels and situations you encounter when working with probate records.

Source List Entry

(*Citing an individual volume*)
Alabama. Chilton County. "Exemptions to Widows & Orphans, Vol. 1." Probate Judge's Office, Clanton.

(*Citing a probate series*)
Massachusetts. Bristol County. Probate Records. Probate Registry Office, Taunton.
Michigan. Wayne County. Wills, 1880–1920. Office of the County Probate Court Clerk, Detroit.
New York. Putnam County. Old Estates and Wills, 1812–1875. Surrogate Court Clerk's Office, Carmel.

First Reference Note

(*Citing an individual volume*)

    1. Chilton County, Alabama, "Exemptions to Widows & Orphans, Vol. 1," 13–15, estate of T. E. Gilchrist, 1897; Probate Judge's Office, Clanton.

(*Citing a probate series*)

    2. Bristol County, Massachusetts, Probate Record Book 61: 327, Charles DeWolf; Probate Registry Office, Taunton.

    3. Wayne County, Michigan, Will Book 3176: 112, Josephine Gutowski; Office of the County Probate Court Clerk, Detroit.

    4. Putnam County, New York, Old Estates and Wills, A: 232, Sarah Sears Will, 1816 (citing file 191); Surrogate Court Clerk's Office, Carmel.

Subsequent Note

    11. Chilton Co., Ala., "Exemptions to Widows & Orphans, Vol. 1" 13–15.

    12. Bristol Co., Mass., Probate Record Book 61: 327.

    13. Wayne Co., Mich., Will Book 3176: 112.

    14. Putnam Co., N.Y., Old Estates and Wills, A: 232.

CITING EXACT TITLE VS. SERIES

The Alabama example, above, cites the exact title of a register that carries a distinctive name; even though it is labeled "Vol. 1," it is not part of a general series with many similarly titled volumes. Therefore its title is copied exactly and the phrase "Vol. 1" that appears on its cover is considered part of its unique title. The Massachusetts and Michigan examples illustrate situations in which a series with a generic label contains hundreds to thousands of volumes.

CITING CROSSREFERENCES

Entries in probate record books often carry cossreferences to the case file from which the record was copied. When these appear, as in the New York example above, you may wish to include the reference in your citation. Doing so may help you or a user of your work to locate the appropriate original file.

10.31 Basic Formats: Loose Papers

Source List Entry

Connecticut. Norwich. Probate District Files. Probate Court. Norwich.

Missouri. Clay County. Probate Files, Old Series. Probate Division, Clay County Archives and Historical Library, Liberty.

Ohio. Ross County. Probate Files. Clerk of Court's Office, Chillicothe.

First Reference Note
1. Norwich, Connecticut, Norwich Probate District, file 10590, Hannah A. and Henry Thomas; Probate Court, Norwich.
2. Clay County, Missouri, William Tapp probate file CF-15-42, Box 58, Old Series, Probate Division; Clay County Archives and Historical Library, Liberty.
3. Ross County, Ohio, probate file 8009, Johann Heinrich Strasser; Clerk of Court's Office, Chillicothe. This file currently cannot be found at the courthouse; a photocopy of the original will was supplied by Jimmie D. Rude, [ADDRESS FOR PRIVATE USE,] Portland, Oregon, to Cameron Allen, J.D., FASG, [ADDRESS FOR PRIVATE USE,] Columbus, Ohio, prior to 1997.

Subsequent Note
11. Norwich, Conn., Norwich Probate Dist., file 10590.
12. Clay Co., Mo., probate file CF-15-42, Box 58, Old Series.
13. Ross Co., Ohio, probate file 8009.

CITING PRIVATE COPIES OF MISSING DOCUMENTS
Given that record loss continues to occur in local archives, researchers occasionally acquire copies of records no longer found in the official repository. The Ohio example above illustrates one manner of treating those situations.

10.32 Basic Formats: Microfilm Images

Microfilm (FHL-GSU)

BOUND VOLUMES:

Source List Entry
Tennessee. Lincoln County. Wills [and Inventories], 1809–1863. County Court Clerk's Office, Fayetteville. FHL microfilm 968,737. Family History Library, Salt Lake City, Utah.

First Reference Note
1. Lincoln County, Tennessee, Wills [and Inventories], Book 1: 27, inventory of the estate of William Frame, 1813; FHL microfilm 968,737.

Subsequent Note
11. Lincoln Co., Tenn., Wills [and Inventories], Book 1: 27.

CLARIFYING THE TITLE OF AN ORIGINAL REGISTER
Registers labeled "Wills" often contain other documents. The above example demonstrates how to clarify a title to better identify the contents. When you alter the title, you should put your added detail in square editorial brackets.

LOOSE PAPERS:
See also QuickCheck Model *for* ORIGINAL RECORDS: LOCAL: CASE FILES ...

Source List Entry
Missouri. St. Louis, City of. Probate case files. Probate Court Clerk's Office, St. Louis. FHL microfilm 2,296,637. Family History Library, Salt Lake City, Utah.

First Reference Note
1. City of St. Louis, Missouri, probate case files, no. 26469, Landry Charleville (1900), deposition of Mary T. Mason, 24 September 1901; FHL microfilm 2,296,637.

Subsequent Note
11. City of St. Louis, Mo., probate case files, no. 26469, Landry Charleville (1900), deposition of Mary T. Mason, 24 September 1901.

CITING SPECIFIC DOCUMENTS WITHIN THE FILE
The film example above and the digital-image example on the following page both demonstrate citing one specific document within a large probate file.

Microfilm (State Archives)

Source List Entry
Maryland. Baltimore, City of. Orphans' Court Proceedings, 1850–1900. MSA microfilm CR 298. Maryland State Archives, Annapolis.

First Reference Note
1. City of Baltimore (Maryland), Orphans' Court Proceedings, Liber 58: 489, Minors of Charles Ruppert; Maryland State Archives microfilm CR 298.

Subsequent Note
11. City of Baltimore, Md., Orphans' Court Proceedings, 58: 489.

CITING REPOSITORIES BY ACRONYMS OR INITIALISMS
The two microfilm examples in this section 10.32 handle the identity of the filmer differently. The distinction is this: The FHL-GSU example for Tennessee follows the pattern used throughout this guide: the creator and holder of the microfilm is identified in full and by acronym in the Source List Entry—but only by acronym in the Reference Note. The Maryland example applies the same rule to the Source List Entry, but then writes out the name in full in Reference Notes. This manual uses the acronym-only short form in Reference Notes *only* for citations to the Family History Library and the U.S.

National Archives—those being two facilities whose acronym is almost universally recognized by historical researchers.

10.33 Basic Formats: Online Materials

Online Databases & Indexes

Source List Entry
Illinois Regional Archives Depository System. Illinois State University. "Livingston County Probate Case Files Index, 1837–1958." *Illinois State Archives.* http://www.cyberdriveillinois.com/departments/archives/pontiac.html : 2007.

First Reference Note
    1. Illinois Regional Archives Depository System, Illinois State University, "Livingston County Probate Case Files Index, 1837–1958," *Illinois State Archives* (http://www.cyberdriveillinois.com/departments/archives/pontiac.html : accessed 13 February 2007), entry for Edwin Eugene Smith, record type "P," case 7422.

Subsequent Note
    11. Illinois Regional Archives Depository System, "Livingston County Probate Case Files Index, 1837–1958," entry for Edwin Eugene Smith, record type "P," case 7422.

CITING DATABASE ENTRY VS. IMAGE COPY
The Illinois example above does not cite an *original* county record. It cites a *database* created by a state agency (the Illinois Regional Archives Depository System, Illinois State University). Therefore, the material appears in the Source List Entry under the name of the agency.

The Missouri example, below, cites image copies of original case files created at the county level. Therefore, you would cite that original case file in the manner that is customary for county- or town-level case files. Then, instead of stating the physical location of the original case, you would state the virtual location of the digital files.

Online Images

Source List Entry
Missouri. St. Louis, City of. Probate case files. "St. Louis Probate Court Digitization Project, 1802–1900." Digital images. *Missouri Secretary of State.* http://www.sos.mo.gov/archives/stlprobate : 2007.

First Reference Note

    1. City of St. Louis, Missouri, probate case file 26469, Landry Charleville (1900), for deposition of Mary T. Mason, 24 September 1901; "St. Louis Probate Court Digitization Project, 1802–1900," digital images, *Missouri Secretary of State* (http://www.sos.mo.gov/archives/stlprobate : accessed 6 February 2007); the Mason document is imaged as p. 3 of Collection 4 of documents within the Charleville file.

Subsequent Note

    11. City of St. Louis, Mo., probate file 26469, Landry Charleville (1900), deposition of Mary T. Mason, 24 September 1901.

10.34 Bonds

Extant bond records at the local level typically exist in one of two forms. Most are clerical copies entered into record books. In some locales, the loose original bonds survive and may be arranged alphabetically or chronologically—or not at all. Occasionally, the original bonds have been removed to the state archives (see 8.20, 9.7, 9.10, and 10.35). A common citation to a county-level, probate-bond book would be as follows:

Source List Entry

Georgia. Hancock County. Wills and Estate Records, 1794–1804. Court of Ordinary, Sparta.

First Reference Note

    1. Hancock County, Georgia, Wills and Estate Records, 1794–1807: 1, administrators' bond, Jane Strother and Richard Strother.

Subsequent Note

    11. Hancock Co., Ga., Wills and Estate Records, 1794–1807: 1.

10.35 Orphans' Court Records

In some jurisdictions, a special court operated for the probating of estates with minor heirs, even if one parent still lived. As a rule, probate courts did not concern themselves with the oversight of propertyless orphans. (For records of the latter class, see 9.24–9.25, Slavery & Servitude Records.) As the following example illustrates, the citation of Orphans' Court records fits the Basic Format; only the labels differ. In this example, two different dates are cited because the different pages represent different records.

Source List Entry

Pennsylvania. Bedford County. Orphans' Court Dockets, 1772–1814. Prothonotary's Office, Bedford.

First Reference Note
1. Bedford County, Pennsylvania, Orphans' Court Dockets, Book 2:182, 237, Jacob Whitmer, administrator, estate of Abraham Witter, April 1810 and August 1811; Prothonotary's Office, Bedford.

Subsequent Note
11. Bedford Co., Penn., Orphans' Court Dockets, 2:182, 237.

10.36 Records Removed to State Archives

Probate records removed from the local level to the state archives may be cataloged there separately from the records created by state agencies (as with the North Carolina example below). Or, they may be part of a collection "gathered" by the state agency, but still attributed to the county (as with the New Jersey example below).

In both cases, the county continues to be identified as the creator of the records, and materials are cited in much the same manner as when they were held locally. The key difference is that you will substitute the name and location of the state archives for the name and location of the local agency. In citing the state archival system, you may also have file and/or accession numbers to cite.

BOUND VOLUMES:

Source List Entry
Illinois. McLean County. Will Records. 1838–1940. Accession 3/0096/
01. Illinois Regional Archives Depository System. Illinois State
University, Normal.

First Reference Note
1. McLean County, Illinois, Will Records, vol. 9 (1895–1898):
61, will of Martha M. Dayloymple; accession no. 3/0096/01; Illinois
Regional Archives Depository System, Illinois State University, Normal.

Subsequent Note
11. McLean County, Ill., Will Records, vol. 9: 61.

LOOSE PAPERS:

Source List Entry
New Jersey. Morris County. Wills and Inventories, 1740–1820
[subseries]; Wills and Inventories, ca. 1670–1900 [series], control
no. SSTSE033. Secretary of State's Office, Department of State
Record Group. New Jersey State Archives, Trenton.
North Carolina. Granville County. Original Estate Records. North
Carolina State Archives, Raleigh.

First Reference Note
    1. Morris County, New Jersey, Wills and Inventories, 1740–1820: file 850N, Trustrim Hull; Wills and Inventories, ca. 1670–1900, control no. SSTSE033; Secretary of State's Office, Department of State Record Group; New Jersey State Archives, Trenton.
    2. Granville County, North Carolina, Original Estate Records: file "Kittrell, Jonathan, 1802"; North Carolina State Archives, Raleigh.

Subsequent Note
    11. Morris Co., N.J., Wills and Inventories, 1740–1820: file 850N, Trustrim Hull.
    12. Granville Co., N.C., Original Estate Records: file "Kittrell, Jonathan, 1802."

Microfilm (FHL-GSU)

Source List Entry
Alabama. Tuscaloosa County. Estate Case Files, 1830–1930. Alabama Department of Archives and History, Montgomery. FHL microfilm 2,114,516 and 2,114,618–2,114,620. Family History Library, Salt Lake City, Utah.

First Reference Note
    1. Tuscaloosa County, Alabama, Estate Case Files, folder: "Douglas Aikin, 1874," for Appraisement Bill, 15 January 1874; FHL microfilm 2,114,516.

Subsequent Note
    11. Tuscaloosa Co., Ala., Estate Case Files, folder: "Douglas Aikin, 1874," Appraisement Bill.

CITING WHOLE FILM SERIES VS. INDIVIDUAL ROLL

Your Source List will be trimmer if your Source List Entry cites a film series as an aggregate, rather than creating separate entries for individual rolls within a series. With large series of FHL film, this is often not possible, because each roll of a series is individually numbered and the numbers often are not consecutive. The case above illustrates an aggregate citation to a series that contains only one break in its numerical sequence. More breaks in the sequence might be more difficult to cite. (See also 2.26.)

10.37 State or Colony Records

Some early jurisdictions required the filing of probates or wills at the colony or state level. When you cite these state-level documents, the county is not cited as creator. The document or file is cited formally in the manner of most state and federal agency records. Elements of the Reference Note should appear in smallest-to-largest sequence.

Source List Entry
North Carolina. Records of Probate, Will Books. State Records Collection, Secretary of State Records. North Carolina State Archives, Raleigh.

First Reference Note
1. Nathaniel Chevin Will, 1719–20, Pasquotank Precinct; Will Book 1712–1722: 219; Records of Probate; State Records Collection, Secretary of State Records; North Carolina State Archives, Raleigh.

Subsequent Note
11. Nathaniel Chevin Will, Will Book 1712–1722: 219, Secretary of State Records, N.C. State Archives.

TAX RECORDS

10.38 Basic Formats
Tax rolls for most American locales can exist at three levels. Historically, most assessments originated at the county or town level. The appropriate agency there would collect not only the county or town levy but also whatever levy had been imposed by the state. Local officials would then submit a copy of the return to the state treasurer, auditor, or other appropriate office. Additionally, various federal assessments have been levied.

How you cite a tax roll will depend primarily upon whether you have used the local, state, or federal record. Chapter 11 treats federal tax levies at 11.56. The examples below cover assessment and payment rolls maintained locally, while 10.42 covers the state-level tax rolls.

Source List Entry
Alabama. Perry County. "1865 Assessment of Taxes on Real Estate." Tax Assessor's Office, Marion.

First Reference Note
1. Perry County, Alabama, "1865 Assessment of Taxes on Real Estate," p. 56, W. D. Washburn; Tax Assessor's Office, Marion.

Subsequent Note
11. Perry Co., Ala., "1865 Assessment of Taxes on Real Estate," 56, W. D. Washburn.

Microfilm (FHL-GSU)

Source List Entry

Kentucky. Christian County. Tax Books, 1797–1875. Kentucky State Historical Society, Frankfort. FHL microfilm 7,926–7,929. Family History Library, Salt Lake City, Utah.

Pennsylvania. Bedford County Assessment Books, 1841–1844. Board of County Commissioners, Bedford. FHL microfilm 149,113. Family History Library, Salt Lake City, Utah.

First Reference Note

1. Christian County, Kentucky, 1799 Tax Book, List 2, unpaginated entries arranged chronologically, entry for John Frame, 12 August 1799; FHL microfilm 7,926.

2. Bedford County, Pennsylvania, 1842 Assessment Book, Dublin Township, p. 8, William Henesy, farmer; FHL microfilm 149,113.

Subsequent Note

11. Christian Co., Ky., 1799 Tax Book, List 2, John Frame, 12 August 1799.

12. Bedford Co., Penn., 1842 Assessment Book, Dublin Township, p. 8, William Henesy, farmer.

IDENTIFICATION OF INDIVIDUALS ON TAX ROLL

In the Kentucky example, above, only one John Frame appears on the cited page. Thus, it suffices to simply give his name. In the Pennsylvania example, *two* men named William Henesy appear on the same page—one called *farmer* and one called *laborer*. Thus, the citation includes the occupation as part of this William Henesy's identification.

10.39 Citing a Run of Tax Records

Ideally, citations to tax rolls will follow the full treatments shown at 10.38. Certainly, your working files should use the full treatments. However, when you prepare a manuscript for publication it can be impractical to give a full treatment to the citation of every tax roll on which a person appears over the course of a lifetime. As a compromise, researchers often cite the *run* of tax rolls for the person(s) of interest.

Microfilm (State Archives)

Source List Entry

Georgia. Jefferson County. Tax Digests, 1796–1828. Microfilm rolls RHS 953–957. Georgia Department of Archives and History, Atlanta.

First Reference Note

    1. Jefferson County, Georgia, 1799–1828 Tax Digests, unpaginated entries arranged chronologically; all years read for all entries relating to Boyd, Gawley, McBride, Millen, Sampson, and Ware/Weir; microfilm rolls RHS 953–957, Georgia Department of Archives and History, Atlanta.

Subsequent Note

    11. Jefferson Co., Ga., 1799–1828 Tax Digests, all entries for Boyd, Gawley, McBride, Millen, Sampson, and Ware/Weir.

10.40 Quit-rent Rolls

Rent rolls, quit-rent rolls, and *debt books* maintained by early proprietors in some American colonies and the British Isles can usually be cited by one of the basic models for local- or colony-level tax rolls. Your choice of style will depend upon three factors: (*a*) whether the roll is a loose document or a record-book copy; (*b*) whether it was created by a local agency or by the colony; and (*c*) whether a local record is still held by the local jurisdiction or has been archived off-site.

10.41 Records Removed to State Archives

When locally generated tax rolls have been transferred to the state archives for preservation, they are typically cataloged in the archives' county-records collection. Most can be cited using the county-level arrangement as in 10.36. The principal difference is that you cite the state archives as the repository rather than the local office.

10.42 State or Colony Tax Rolls

When you cite original tax records created by the state or colony and maintained by the archives as part of *state-government* records, most archives prefer that you use the traditional structure for citing formally cataloged materials. Your source list emphasis will be upon the state and its agency (not the county), and your reference note will begin with the smallest element (the entry) and work up to the largest. Often it will include multiple series and collection names and numbers that will have to be included in your citation.

Source List Entry

New York. State Treasurer Records. Accounts and Tax Assessment Lists, 1722–1788, Albany County. Manuscripts and Special Collections Department. New York State Library, Albany.

First Reference Note

    1. Enoch Phillips tax entry, Saratoga District, unpaginated entries

arranged semi-alphabetically, 1786 Albany County Tax Roll; folder 5, box 1, Accounts and Tax Assessment Lists, 1722–1788; State Treasurer Records, Manuscripts and Special Collections Department; New York State Library, Albany.

Subsequent Note
11. Enoch Phillips tax entry, Saratoga Dist., 1786 Albany Co. [N.Y.] Tax Roll.

CITING THE COUNTY IN THE SOURCE LIST
If you use state-level tax rolls of just one county, you may wish to cite that county in your Source List Entry. If you use the state-level collection for multiple counties, you would likely cite the whole collection rather than naming each and every county in the source list. Your Reference Notes would then identify each specific county at the point at which that county's records were used.

Microfilm (State Archives)

Source List Entry
Tennessee. Jackson County. Tax lists. Manuscript Tax Lists Microfilm, roll 5. Tennessee State Library and Archives, Nashville.

First Reference Note
1. Jackson County, Tennessee, 1803 Tax List, p. 1, Captain Hay's District, entries for John and George Frame; Manuscript Tax Lists Microfilm, roll 5; Tennessee State Library and Archives, Nashville.

Subsequent Note
11. Jackson Co., Tenn., 1803 Tax List, p. 1, John and George Frame.

Online Databases & Indexes

Source List Entry
Oregon. "Oregon Historical Records Index.." *Oregon State Archives.* http://genealogy.state.or.us : 2007.
South Carolina. "Combined Index to 30 Record Series, 1675–1929" Database. *South Carolina Department of Archives and History.* http://www.archivesindex.sc.gov/ : 2007.

First Reference Note
1. Oregon, "Oregon Historical Records Index," *Oregon State Archives* (http://genealogy.state.or.us : accessed 1 February 2007), undated entry for "F. G. Shown, Assessment, Crook County, Vol. 1, pg. 38."

2. South Carolina, "Combined Index to 30 Record Series, 1675–1929," database, *South Carolina Department of Archives and History* (http://www.archivesindex.sc.gov/ : accessed 2 February 2007), entry for Samuel Bruton tax return, 23 April 1825, All Saints Parish, Horry District.

Subsequent Note

11. Oregon, "Oregon Historical Records Index," database, *Oregon State Archives,* undated entry for "F. G. Shown, Assessment, Crook County, Vol. 1, pg. 38."

12. South Carolina, "Combined Index to 30 Record Series, 1675–1929," database, *South Carolina Department of Archives and History*, entry for Samuel Bruton tax return, 1825, All Saints Parish, Horry Dist.

INTERNATIONAL

10.43 Basic Formats

As with U.S. records, citations to national-level probate and property records often have a different structure from records created at the local level. See chapter 11 for national-level records not covered in this section.

10.44 Canada: Provincial Land Records

See also 10.27, Notarial Books & Files.

FHL Microfilm

Source List Entry

Saskatchewan Homestead Records, 1870–1930. Dominion Lands, Department of the Interior. Ottawa, Canada. FHL microfilm, 1,641 rolls. Family History Library, Salt Lake City, Utah.

First Reference Note

1. "Certificate for Homestead Patent," no. 15346, William Henry Whitney, 3 August 1886; Saskatchewan Homestead Records, 1870–1930; FHL microfilm 1,017,377, frames 10–11.

Subsequent Note

11. "Certificate for Homestead Patent," no. 15346, William Henry Whitney, 3 August 1886, Saskatchewan Homestead Records.

Online Databases

Source List Entry

Nova Scotia. "Land Petitions: Nova Scotia Petitions, 1769–1799 &

Cape Breton Island Petitions, 1787–1843." Database. *Nova Scotia Archives & Records Management.* http://www.gov.ns.ca/nsarm/data bases/land/ : 2007.

First Reference Note
1. Nova Scotia, "Land Petitions: Nova Scotia Petitions, 1769–1799 & Cape Breton Island Petitions, 1787–1843," database, *Nova Scotia Archives & Records Management* (http://www.gov.ns.ca/nsarm/databases/land/ : accessed 1 February 2007), entry for Elisha Budd, 1788.

Subsequent Note
11. Nova Scotia, "Land Petitions: Nova Scotia Petitions, 1769–1799 & Cape Breton Island Petitions, 1787–1843," database entry for Elisha Budd, 1788.

10.45   England: Tax Rolls, Local
Internationally, tax records will carry labels that are peculiar to the time and place. As with American tax rolls, however, differences in the citation of these rolls will depend chiefly upon whether they are created locally or at the national level and whether they exist as bound volumes or loose documents. The example below uses a "highway rate [tax] book" that is part of a filmed series of local parish chest records. For national-level tax records in England, see chapter 11.

FHL-GSU Microfilm

Source List Entry
England. Norfolk, county of. Brisley. East Beckham and West Beckham. Parish Chest Records. Norfolk Record Office, Norwich. FHL microfilm 2,262,678, item 1. Family History Library, Salt Lake City, Utah.

First Reference Note
1. East Beckham and West Beckham, County of Norfolk, "Highway Rate Book, 1838–1851," unnumbered pages, unalphabetized entries, arranged by date: 8 October 1838, Susan Akers, West Beckham; FHL microfilm 2,262,678, item 1.

Subsequent Note
11. East Beckham and West Beckham, Co. Norfolk, "Highway Rate Book, 1838–1851," 8 October 1838, Susan Akers.

10.46   France: Notarial Records
By legislative act of 1928, many of France's early notarial records have been transferred from the local level to the archives départementales

(or, for the Châtelet de Paris, to the Archives Nationales). There, they are cataloged within Series E under the uniform cataloging system followed by France's national and departmental archives. A typical citation to a notarial record would follow the pattern below:

Source List Entry

France. Gironde. Bordeaux. Acts of Bois de Fauquier, Royal Notary. Série E. Archives Départementales de Gironde, Bordeaux.

First Reference Note

1. Bordeaux, Gironde, Acts of Bois de Fauquier, Royal Notary; 1 September 1752, folio 41, Jean Durel–Cécile Le Brun, marriage contract; doc. 3E 12185, Archives Départementales de Gironde, Bordeaux.

Subsequent Note

11. Bordeaux, Gironde, Notarial Acts of Bois de Fauquier, 1 September 1752, folio 41, Durel–Le Brun marriage contract.

10.47 Ireland: Property & Probate Records

Land registrations, wills, and estate administrations in Ireland are maintained on the national level. See chapter 11, National Government Resources, 11.64 (Land Registrations) and 11.66 (Wills & Administrations). Two major series of tax-related records for Ireland (Griffith's Valuations and Tithe Applotments) are covered at 11.63 and 11.65.

NATIONAL GOVERNMENT RECORDS

11

QuickCheck Models

Guidelines & Examples (beginning page 557)

QuickCheck Model
AUDIO RECORDINGS: NATIONAL ARCHIVES
Series as lead element in Source List

Source List Entry

SERIES   RECORD GROUP ...

General Radio Programs and Recordings, 1941–1993. Records of the

... TITLE   RECORD GROUP NO.

Office of the Secretary of Agriculture, 1839–, Record Group 16.

REPOSITORY   REPOSITORY LOCATION

National Archives, College Park, Maryland.

First (Full) Reference Note

                                                          SPECIFIC

             FILE UNIT   DATE   DATA ...

1. Interview with Charlie Smith, former slave, November 1961, minute

...   FILE UNIT NO.   SERIES ...

8, audio tape NWDNM(s)-16.332B; General Radio Programs and Recordings,

        ...   RECORD GROUP TITLE ...

1941–1993; Records of the Office of the Secretary of Agriculture, 1839–,

    RG NO.   REPOSITORY   REPOSITORY LOCATION

Record Group 16; National Archives, College Park, Maryland.

Subsequent (Short) Note

                                                SPECIFIC

            FILE UNIT   DATE   DATA   FILE ...

11. Interview with Charlie Smith, November 1961, minute 8, audio

   ... UNIT NO.   RG NO.   REPOSITORY

tape NWDNM(s)-16.332B, RG 16, NA–College Park.

QuickCheck Model
MANUSCRIPTS: LIBRARY OF CONGRESS
Series as lead element in Source List

Source List Entry

SERIES	COLLECTION ...

District of Columbia Miscellany, 1790–1808, Series 3. Thomas Jefferson

...	DIVISION	REPOSITORY	REPOSITORY LOCATION

Papers. Manuscripts Division, Library of Congress, Washington, D.C.

First (Full) Reference Note

DOCUMENT ID...

1. Letter of introduction for Collen Williamson, Daniel Carroll to

...	DOCUMENT DATE	SERIES ...

Thomas Jefferson, 10 May 1792; Series 3, District of Columbia Miscel-

...	COLLECTION	DIVISION	...

lany, 1790–1808; Thomas Jefferson Papers; Manuscript Division, Library

... REPOSITORY	REPOSITORY LOCATION

of Congress, Washington, D.C.

Subsequent (Short) Note

DOCUMENT ID	DOCUMENT DATE

11. Letter of introduction for Collen Williamson, 10 May 1792,

SERIES / COLLECTION	REPOSITORY

Series 3, Thomas Jefferson Papers, Library of Congress.

QuickCheck Model
MANUSCRIPTS: NATIONAL ARCHIVES
Series as lead element in Source List

Source List Entry

SERIES	...

Southern Claims Commission, 1871–1880, Allowed Case Files. Settled Ac-

... SUBGROUP	RECORD GROUP ...

counts and Claims, Third Auditor. Records of the Treasury Department

... TITLE	RECORD GROUP NO.	REPOSITORY	REP'Y ...

Accounting Officers, Record Group 217. National Archives, Washing-

... LOCATION

ton, D.C.

First (Full) Reference Note

	DOCUMENT ID	DOCUMENT DATE	FILE UNIT ...

1. Cross-examination of Moses White, undated; Minerva Boyd (Warren

...	FILE UNIT NO.	SUBSERIES	SERIES ...

Co., Mississippi), claim no. 6,942, Allowed Case Files, Southern Claims

...	SUBGROUP

Commission, 1871–1880; Settled Accounts and Claims, Third Auditor;

RECORD GROUP TITLE	RG NO. ...

Records of the Treasury Department Accounting Officers, Record Group

...	REPOSITORY	REPOSITORY LOCATION

217; National Archives, Washington, D.C.

Subsequent (Short) Note

DOCUMENT ID	FILE UNIT ID...

11. Cross-examination of Moses White, Minerva Boyd claim no. 6,942

...	SERIES	RG NO.	REPOSITORY

(Allowed), Southern Claims Commission, RG 217, NA-Washington.

QuickCheck Model
MANUSCRIPTS: NATIONAL ARCHIVES–REGIONAL
Subgroup as lead element in Source List

Source List Entry

SUBGROUP

U.S. District Court, Arkansas, Western Division, Fort Smith, 1866–1900.

SERIES   RECORD GROUP ...

Criminal Defendant Jacket Files. Records of the District Courts of the

... TITLE   RECORD GROUP NO.   REPOSITORY ...

United States, 1685–1991. Record Group 21. National Archives–South-

...   REPOSITORY LOCATION

west Region, Fort Worth, Texas.

First (Full) Reference Note

DOCUMENT ID   DOCUMENT DATE   FILE UNIT   ...

1. Writ of arrest, 1 April 1871; John Shawn and Wyatt Earp, Larceny

FILE UNIT NO.   SERIES   SUBGROUP ...

Jacket no. 59; Criminal Defendant Jacket Files, U.S. District Court, Western

...   RECORD GROUP ...

District of Arkansas, Fort Smith, 1866–1900; Records of the District Courts

... TITLE   RG NO.   REPOSITORY ...

of the United States, 1685–1991, Record Group 21; National Archives–

...   REPOSITORY LOCATION

Southwest Region, Fort Worth, Texas.

Subsequent (Short) Note

DOCUMENT ID   FILE UNIT   FILE UNIT NO.

11. Writ of arrest, Shawn and Earp, Larceny Jacket no. 59, U.S. Dist.

SUBGROUP   RG NO.   REPOSITORY

Court, West. Dist. of Ark., Fort Smith, RG 21, NA–Fort Worth.

QuickCheck Model
MAPS: NATIONAL ARCHIVES
Specific item as lead element in Source List

Source List Entry

FILE UNIT	DATE ...

"Map of the Battle Field of Gettysburg, July 1st, 2nd, 3rd, 1863." Published

...	SERIES	RECORD GROUP ...

1876. Civil Works Map File, 1800–1947. Records of the Office of the

... TITLE	RECORD GROUP NO.	REPOSITORY

Chief of Engineers, 1789–1988, Record Group 77. National Archives,

REPOSITORY LOCATION

College Park, Maryland.

First (Full) Reference Note

FILE UNIT

1. "Map of the Battle Field of Gettysburg, July 1st, 2nd, 3rd, 1863,"

DATE	SERIES	RECORD GROUP ...

published 1876; Civil Works Map File, 1800–1947; Records of the Office of

... TITLE	RG NO.	REPOSITORY

the Chief of Engineers, 1789–1988, Record Group 77; National Archives,

REPOSITORY LOCATION

College Park, Maryland.

Subsequent (Short) Note

FILE UNIT

11. "Map of the Battle Field of Gettysburg, July 1st, 2nd, 3rd, 1863,"

DATE	SERIES	RG NO.	REPOSITORY

1876, Civil Works Map File, RG 77, NA–College Park.

QuickCheck Model
PHOTOGRAPHS: LIBRARY OF CONGRESS
Subseries as lead element in Source List

Source List Entry

SUBSERIES   SERIES ...

Contrabands, Freedmen, and Refugees. Photographs of African Americans

...   COLLECTION   LIBRARY ...

during the Civil War. Civil War Photograph Collection. Prints and

... DIVISION   REPOSITORY   REPOSITORY LOCATION

Photographs Division, Library of Congress, Washington, D.C.

First (Full) Reference Note

PHOTOGRAPH TITLE   PHOTOGRAPH NO.

1. "Freedman's Barracks, Alexandria, Va.," no. LOT 4161-H,

SUBSERIES   SERIES ...

Contrabands, Freedmen, and Refugees, Photographs of African Americans

...   COLLECTION   LIBRARY ...

during the Civil War; Civil War Photograph Collection; Prints and Photo-

... DIVISION   REPOSITORY   REPOSITORY LOCATION

graphs Division, Library of Congress, Washington, D.C.

Subsequent (Short) Note

PHOTOGRAPH TITLE   PHOTOGRAPH NO.   ...

11. "Freedman's Barracks, Alexandria, Va.," no. LOT 4161-H, Civil

COLLECTION   REPOSITORY

War Photograph Collection, Library of Congress.

QuickCheck Model
RAILROAD RETIREMENT BOARD
PENSION FILE

Individual file as lead element in Source List

Source List Entry*

FILE ID	FILE NO.	FILE YEAR	...

Anderson, Leonard Ray. Pension file. SS no. 702-07-8940, 1941. Records

NARA RECORD GROUP TITLE	NARA RECORD GROUP ...

of the Railroad Retirement Board, 1934–. National Archives Record

... NO.	AGENCY / REPOSITORY	REPOSITORY LOCATION

Group 184. RRB–Congressional Inquiry Section, Chicago, Illinois.

First (Full) Reference Note*

FILE ID ...	FILE NO.	FILE YEAR

1. Leonard Ray Anderson pension file, SS no. 702-07-8940, 1941;

NARA RECORD GROUP TITLE	NARA RECORD GROUP ...

Records of the Railroad Retirement Board, 1934–, National Archives

... NO.	AGENCY / REPOSITORY	REPOSITORY LOCATION

Record Group 184; RRB–Congressional Inquiry Section, Chicago, Illinois.

Subsequent (Short) Note*

FILE ID	FILE NO.	FILE YEAR

11. Leonard Ray Anderson pension file, SS no. 702-07-8940, 1941,

AGENCY / REPOSITORY

Railroad Retirement Board.

* *A citation to RRB files differs from the format used for materials in other NARA record groups. See 11.53 for an explanation.*

QuickCheck Model
SOCIAL SECURITY ADMINISTRATION
FORMS SS-5

Agency as lead element in Source List

Source List Entry

AGENCY	SERIES ...

Social Security Adminstration. Applications for Account Numbers, Form

...	AGENCY OFFICE / REPOSITORY	REPOSITORY LOCATION

SS-5. Social Security Administration, Baltimore, Maryland.

First (Full) Reference Note

NAME	SOCIAL SECURITY NO.	DATE

1. Theresa Boggus Sammarco, SS no. 116-05-4655, 23 May 1937,

ITEM (FROM THE SERIES OF THE SAME NAME)	AGENCY / REPOSITORY

Application for Account Number (Form SS-5), Social Security Administra-

...	REPOSITORY LOCATION

tion, Baltimore, Maryland.

Subsequent (Short) Note

NAME	SOCIAL SECURITY NO.	DATE	...

11. Theresa Boggus Sammarco, SS no. 116-05-4655, 1937, Application

... ITEM	AGENCY / REPOSITORY

for Account No. (Form SS-5), Social Security Administration.

QuickCheck Model
DATABASES: CD-ROM PUBLICATONS
Agency/creator as lead element in Source List

Source List Entry

CREATOR	TITLE

Bureau of Land Management. *Minnesota, 1820–1908: Cash and Homestead*

...	ITEM TYPE or FORMAT	PUBLICATION PLACE	PUBLISHER ...

Entries. CD-ROM. Springfield, Virginia: General Land Office Auto-

...	YEAR

mated Records Project, 1995.

First (Full) Reference Note

CREATOR	TITLE ...

1. Bureau of Land Management, *Minnesota, 1820–1908: Cash and*

...	ITEM TYPE or FORMAT	PUBLICATION PLACE	PUBLISHER

Homestead Entries, CD-ROM (Springfield, Virginia: General Land Office

...	YEAR	ITEM OF INTEREST ...

Automated Records Project, 1995), database entry for Adelbert L. Warren,

...

Cass Lake land office, certificate no. 181.

Subsequent (Short) Note

CREATOR	TITLE (SHORTENED)	ITEM ...

11. Bureau of Land Management, *Minnesota, 1820–1908,* database

... OF INTEREST

entry for Adelbert L. Warren, Cass Lake land office, certificate no. 181.

QuickCheck Model
DATABASES ONLINE
NATIONAL ARCHIVES (AUSTRALIA)
Source List arranged geographically by country, then database as lead element

Source List Entry

COUNTRY	DATABASE TITLE	ITEM TYPE or FORMAT	WEBSITE TITLE (SAME AS CREATOR-OWNER)	URL ...

Australia. "Record Search." Database. *National Archives of Australia.* http://

... (DIGITAL LOCATION)	YEAR

www.naa.gov.au/The_Collection/recordsearch.html : 2007.

First (Full) Reference Note

	DATABASE TITLE	ITEM TYPE or FORMAT	WEBSITE TITLE	URL ...

1. "Records Search," database, *National Archives of Australia* (http://

... (DIGITAL LOCATION)	DATE

www.naa.gov.au/The_Collection/recordsearch.html : accessed 1 March 2007),

ITEM OF INTEREST	CREDIT LINE ...

entry for Pvt. J. W. C. Andrews, Court-Martial, 1942; citing barcode

... (SOURCE OF THIS SOURCE)

7871766, series A471, control no. 26755.

Subsequent (Short) Note

	DATABASE TITLE	ITEM TYPE or FORMAT	WEBSITE TITLE	...

11. "Record Search," database, *National Archives of Australia,* entry

... OF INTEREST

for Pvt. J. W. C. Andrews, Court-Martial, 1942.

NOTE

The Australian example above does not cite an agency as creator in the "author" field because the website's title self-identifies the creator/owner of both the website and its database. In the Canadian example at right and the English example on the subsequent page, the website titles do not identify a creator/owner; therefore one must be named in the author field immediately before the website. In the Canadian example, the database is the product of an outside entity that should be credited also.

QuickCheck Model
DATABASES ONLINE
NATIONAL ARCHIVES (CANADA)
Source List arranged geographically by country, then creator as lead element

Source List Entry

COUNTRY	CREATOR OF DATABASE	DATABASE TITLE	ITEM TYPE or FORMAT

Canada. Pier 21 Society. "Immigration Records (1925–1935)." Database.

WEBSITE CREATOR-OWNER	WEBSITE TITLE	...

Library and Archives Canada. *Canadian Genealogy Centre.* http://

... URL (DIGITAL LOCATION)	YEAR

www.collectionscanada.ca/genealogy/index-e.html : 2007.

First (Full) Reference Note

CREATOR OF DATABASE	DATABASE TITLE	ITEM TYPE or FORMAT

1. Pier 21 Society, "Immigration Records (1925–1935)," database,

WEBSITE CREATOR-OWNER	WEBSITE TITLE	URL ...

Library and Archives Canada, *Canadian Genealogy Centre* (http://

... (DIGITAL LOCATION)	DATE ...

www.collectionscanada.ca/genealogy/index-e.html : accessed 17 February

...	ITEM OF INTEREST

2007), entry for Frank A. Chilcote, arrived 1926/03/15, Emerson, Manitoba;

CREDIT LINE (SOURCE OF THIS SOURCE) ...

citing RG 76-Immigration, series C-5, register 1926: vol. 1, p. 260, microfilm

...

reel T-15350.

Subsequent (Short) Note

CREATOR OF DATABASE	DATABASE TITLE	ITEM TYPE or FORMAT

11. Pier 21 Society, "Immigration Records (1925–1935)," database,

WEBSITE TITLE	ITEM OF INTEREST

Canadian Genealogy Centre, entry for Frank A. Chilcote, 1926/03/15.

QuickCheck Model
DATABASES ONLINE
NATIONAL ARCHIVES (U.K.)

Source List arranged geographically by country, then creator as lead element

Source List Entry

COUNTRY	CREATOR-OWNER OF DATABASE & WEBSITE	DATABASE TITLE

England. The National Archives. "Death Duty Registers, 1796–1811."

ITEM TYPE or FORMAT	WEBSITE TITLE	URL ...

Database. *DocumentsOnline.* http://www.nationalarchives.gov.uk/

... (DIGITAL LOCATION)	YEAR

documentsonline : 2007.

First (Full) Reference Note

CREATOR-OWNER OF DATABASE & WEBSITE	DATABASE TITLE

1. The National Archives (U.K.), "Death Duty Registers, 1796–1811,"

ITEM TYPE or FORMAT	WEBSITE TITLE	URL (DIGITAL ...

database, *DocumentsOnline* (http://www.nationalarchives.gov.uk/

... LOCATION)	DATE	ITEM ...

documentsonline : accessed 5 February 2007), entry for Mary Bomford,

... OF INTEREST	CREDIT LINE (SOURCE OF THIS SOURCE)

parish of Hadbury, Worcestershire, 1859; citing catalog reference IR 26/423.

Subsequent (Short) Note

DATABASE TITLE	ITEM TYPE or FORMAT	WEBSITE TITLE

11. "Death Duty Registers, 1796–1811," database, *DocumentsOnline*,

ITEM OF INTEREST

entry for Mary Bomford, Hadbury, Worcestershire, 1859.

QuickCheck Model
DATABASES ONLINE
NATIONAL ARCHIVES (U.S.)
Database as lead element in Source List

Source List Entry

"Archival Research Catalog (ARC)." Database and images. *The National*

Archives. http://www.archives.gov/research/arc : 2007.

First (Full) Reference Note

1. "Archival Research Catalog (ARC)," database, *The National Archives*

(http://www.archives.gov/research/arc : accessed 26 February 2007),

entry for Larceny Jacket no. 59, John Shawn and Wyatt Earp, 1871, ARC

Identifier 242166; citing Criminal Defendant Jacket Files, 1866–1900;

Western District of Arkansas, Fort Smith Division; Records of District Courts

of the United States, Record Group 21; National Archives–Southwest Re-

gion, Fort Worth, Texas.

Subsequent (Short) Note

11. "Archival Research Catalog (ARC)," database, *The National Archives,*

entry for Larceny Jacket no. 59, Shawn and Earp, 1871.

QuickCheck Model
IMAGE COPIES: NARA MICROFILM
NARA STYLE CITATION

Series as lead element in Source List

Source List Entry

SERIES   MICROFILM ID (ABBREVIATED) ...

Despatches from Colon, Panama, 1852–1906 (NARA microfilm publication

... PUB'N NO. & TOTAL ROLLS   SUBGROUP   RECORD GROUP ...

T193, 19 rolls). Consular Despatches, 1785–1906. General Records of

... TITLE   RECORD GROUP NO.   REPOSITORY

the Department of State, Record Group 59. National Archives,

REPOSITORY LOCATION

Washington, D.C.

First (Full) Reference Note

FILE UNIT   DATE ...

1. Geo. W. Fletcher to Hon. Lewis Cass, Secretary of State, 19 April

...   SERIES   FILM ID (NO TITLE)

1857; Despatches from Colon, Panama, 1852–1906 (NARA microfilm

... PUB'N NO. & SPECIFIC ROLL)   SUBGROUP ...   RECORD GROUP ...

publication T193, roll 1); Consular Despatches, 1785–1906; General Records

... TITLE   RG NO.   REPOSITORY

of the Department of State, Record Group 59; National Archives,

REPOSITORY LOCATION

Washington, D.C.

Subsequent (Short) Note

FILE UNIT   DATE   SERIES

11. Fletcher to Cass, 19 April 1857; Despatches from Colon, Panama,

...   FILM ID   RG NO.   REPOSITORY

1852–1906 (T193, roll 1), RG 59, NA–Washington.

QuickCheck Model
IMAGE COPIES: NARA MICROFILM
PUBLICATIONS STYLE CITATION

Publication title as lead element in Source List

Source List Entry

PUBLICATION TITLE	PUB'N ...

Record of Appointment of Postmasters, 1832–September 30, 1971. Microfilm

... NO.	TOTAL ROLLS	PUBLICATION PLACE	PUBLISHER ...

publication M841, 145 rolls. Washington, D.C.: National Archives

...	YEAR

and Records Service, 1973.

First (Full) Reference Note

PUBLICATION TITLE	FILM ...

1. *Record of Appointment of Postmasters, 1832–September 30, 1971*, micro-

... ID (PUBLICATION NO.)	PUB'N PLACE	PUBLISHER ...

film publication M841 (Washington, D.C.: National Archives and Records

...	YEAR	SPECIFIC ROLL	ITEM OF INTEREST (COUNTY, STATE, DATE & PO.) ...

Service, 1973), roll 68, Newton County, Mississippi, 25 March 1854, New

...

Ireland.

Subsequent (Short) Note

PUBLICATION TITLE	FILM ...

11. *Record of Appointment of Postmasters, 1832–September 30, 1971*, NARA

... ID & ROLL NO.	ITEM OF INTEREST

M841, roll 68, Newton Co., Miss., 25 March 1854, New Ireland.

QuickCheck Model
IMAGES ONLINE: LIBRARY OF CONGRESS
Creator of database/website as lead element in Source List

Source List Entry

CREATOR-OWNER
OF DATABASE & WEBSITE   TITLE OF DATABASE ...

Library of Congress. "Born in Slavery: Slave Narratives from the Federal

               ...   ITEM TYPE or FORMAT   WEBSITE TITLE

Writers' Project, 1936–1938." Database and images. *American Memory*.

           URL (DIGITAL LOCATION)   YEAR

http://memory.loc.gov/ammem/snhtml/snhome.html : 2007.

First (Full) Reference Note

          CREATOR-OWNER
       OF DATABASE & WEBSITE   TITLE OF DATABASE ...

1. Library of Congress, "Born in Slavery: Slave Narratives from the

             ...   ITEM TYPE or FORMAT   WEBSITE ...

Federal Writers' Project, 1936–1938," digital image of typescript, *American*

... TITLE   URL (DIGITAL LOCATION)   DATE ...

Memory (http://memory.loc.gov/ammem/snhtml/snhome.html : accessed 6

         ...   ITEM OF INTEREST ...

March 2007), memoir of Rachael Goings (née Rachal Exelina Mayberry or

         ...   DIGITAL ID   CREDIT LINE ...

Mabry), Cape Girardeau, Missouri, digital ID mesn 100/12612; citing WPA

         ... SOURCE OF THIS SOURCE ...

Federal Writers' Project, Missouri Narratives, vol. 10, p. 121.

Subsequent (Short) Note

        CREATOR / OWNER
      OF DATABASE & WEBSITE   TITLE OF DATABASE (SHORTENED)   WEBSITE ...

11. Library of Congress, "Born in Slavery: Slave Narratives," *American*

...TITLE   ITEM OF INTEREST

Memory, memoir of Rachael Goings, digital ID mesn 100/12612.

QuickCheck Model
IMAGES ONLINE: NATIONAL ARCHIVES (U.S.)
Citing as a published item, with database title as lead element in Source List

Source List Entry

DATABASE TITLE   ITEM TYPE or FORMAT   WEBSITE ...

"Archival Research Catalog (ARC)." Database and images. *The National*

... TITLE   URL (DIGITAL LOCATION)   YEAR

Archives. http://www.archives.gov/research/arc : 2007.

First (Full) Reference Note

ITEM TYPE
DATABASE TITLE   or FORMAT   WEBSITE ...

1. "Archival Research Catalog (ARC)," digital image, *The National*

... TITLE   URL (DIGITAL LOCATION)   DATE ...

Archives (http://www.archives.gov/research/arc : accessed 13 January 2007),

ITEM ...

"Immigration Identification Photo of Gung Chun Fooey, ca. 1912," file unit:

... OF INTEREST   DIGITAL ID ..

Sue Kee Lung and Gung Chun Fooey, 1912, NAIL control no. NRIS-85-

... NO.   CREDIT LINE ...

PORTOLDSERIES-2779-GUNGPHOTO; citing Records of the Immigration

... (SOURCE OF YOUR SOURCE) ...

and Naturalization Service, 1787–1998, RG 85, National Archives–Pacific

... (SOURCE OF YOUR SOURCE)

Alaska Region, Seattle.

Subsequent (Short) Note

DATABASE TITLE   DIGITAL FILE TYPE   WEBSITE TITLE ...

11. "Archival Research Catalog (ARC)," digital image, *The National*

...   ITEM OF INTEREST

Archives, photo of Gung Chun Fooey, ca. 1912.

QuickCheck Model
IMAGES ONLINE
PATENT & TRADEMARK OFFICE (U.S.)

Citing as a published item, with database title as lead element in Source List

Source List Entry

DATABASE TITLE	ITEM TYPE or FORMAT*	...

"USPTO Patent Full-Text and Image Database." . *United States*

... WEBSITE TITLE (SAME AS CREATOR-OWNER)	URL (DIGITAL LOCATION) ...

Patent and Trademark Office. http://www.uspto.gov/main/sitesearch.htm

YEAR
: 2007.

First (Full) Reference Note

DATABASE TITLE	ITEM TYPE or FORMAT	...

1. "USPTO Patent Full-Text and Image Database," digital images, *United*

... WEBSITE TITLE (SAME AS CREATOR-OWNER)	URL (DIGITAL LOCATION)

States Patent and Trademark Office (http://www.uspto.gov/main/sitesearch.htm

DATE	SPECIFIC ITEM ...

: accessed 6 March 2007), Robert C. Russell, sound-based indexing system,

... OF INTEREST	CREDIT LINE (SOURCE OF THIS SOURCE)

patent file no. 1,261,167 (1918); original file location not cited.

Subsequent (Short) Note

DATABASE TITLE	SPECIFIC ...

11. "USPTO Patent Full-Text and Image Database," Robert C. Russell

... ITEM OF INTEREST	

patent file no. 1,261,167 (1918).

The title of the source explicitly says that it offers both a database and images, so that information does not have to be repeated in the "Item Type or Format" field of the Source List Entry. In the First Reference Note, the type is specified because the title offers two options and only one is being cited.

GUIDELINES
& Examples

U.S. RECORDS
(Basic Issues)

11.1 Citing Federal Records (U.S.)

The archival materials held by the U.S. National Archives and its branches within the National Archives and Records Administration (both commonly known as NARA) are divided into *record groups*. Each of those record groups represent an agency, a bureau, a commission, a department, etc. Their contents are traditionally cited by the formal structure discussed at 3.1, although NARA uses some special terms for its record levels. Citations to material at the National Archives are lengthy. Once you have cited a record in full, your subsequent citations to that record can be shortened somewhat. However, in the first reference to a record, you should include all the elements needed to relocate the record. Typically, these elements (with the corresponding punctuation that would be used in a Reference Note citation) are as follows:

- *Item of interest*, with relevant names, item description, dates, page numbers;
- *File Unit Name*, date (or inclusive dates);
- *Series Name,* inclusive dates;
- *Subgroup Name,* inclusive dates;
- *Record Group Name,* inclusive dates, record group number; and
- *Archive*, location.

PUNCTUATION

To ensure clarity within long archival citations, semicolons are used to divide the major elements, as demonstrated above. Commas are then used between semicolons, as needed. When you quote a document title exactly, you should use quotation marks around the words you are quoting. When an item lacks a title and you create a generic description, you do not use quotation marks around your own words.

SEQUENCE OF THE ELEMENTS

SOURCE LIST ENTRIES ... The first element you cite in your Source List Entry will usually be the series (or subseries) name, rather than the individual document or file. From that point, you proceed in smallest-to-largest sequence, citing the subgroup, the record group name and number, then the archive and its location.

Attempting to list materials in the Source List by the individual document or file unit will radically bloat your Source List. At the other extreme, citing only the record group in the Source List would provide too little identification.

REFERENCE NOTES .... The first element you cite in your Reference Note will be the specific item of interest. You will then proceed in smallest-to-largest order, following the sequence of the items bulleted on the prior page.

CITING ARCHIVE BOX NUMBERS

NARA requests that you not use box numbers in citing its materials. Those change as documents are reprocessed for better preservation or service. For a notable exception, see 11.44, Congressional Records.

CITING "ENTRY" OR "SECTION" NUMBERS FROM NARA FINDING AIDS

NARA provides many finding aids, from guides to the archives at large to inventories and preliminary inventories that catalog individual record groups. In its major guides, NARA typically uses *chapter* and *section* numbers to organize discussions (e.g., 11.1.3). Within inventories, it typically subdivides the catalog descriptions into numbered *entries*. When you cite from those publications, it is appropriate to cite their section or entry number. However, those numbers relate *only* to the finding aid in which you find them. They are not meant to be part of a manuscript citation, because the manuscripts are organized differently. NARA's recommended style for manuscripts does not include entry and section numbers from the finding aids.

Even so, the entry numbers used within the inventories are important to the retrieval process. When you conduct research personally at NARA and seek records for which an inventory or preliminary inventory (PI) exists, the request forms you fill out will ask for the specific entry number within the inventory. For this reason, experienced NARA researchers routinely record the entry number *in their working notes*, in a fashion similar to this:

Source List Entry
Emigration Rolls, 1817–38 (**PI 163: entry 220**). Cherokee Removal
    Records, 1817–1884. Records of the Bureau of Indian Affairs,
    Record Group 75. National Archives, Washington, D.C.

(*or*)

First Reference Note
    Captain John Page, "Muster Roll of Cherokees to Emigrate West
of the Mississippi River," 31 December 1838; Emigration Rolls, 1817–
38 (**PI 163: entry 220**); Cherokee Removal Records, 1817–1884;
Records of the Bureau of Indian Affairs, Record Group 75; National
Archives, Washington, D.C.

11.2   Citing NARA Style

For more guidance in citing NARA records, see *Citing Records in the
National Archives of the United States,* General Information Leaflet
(GIL) no. 17, available in print or at NARA's website. *Evidence* follows
NARA Style for the citation of manuscript materials, adding models
for Source List Entries and Subsequent Notes that are not covered in
GIL 17. For microfilm and database images accessed through NARA's
online catalog ARC, *Evidence* illustrates the NARA Style citation at
11.8 and 11.11. Otherwise, *Evidence* citations to published film and
digital images follow the traditional and more concise format for
published film and online offerings.

11.3   Creating Short Citations

Reference Notes to manuscript material in the U.S. National Archives
(as discussed at 11.1) begin with the smallest element. Similarly, when
you create a short citation for Subsequent Notes, it should also begin
with that smallest element, phrased the same as in the full note (or
pulled from the first few words of the full note) so that it can be easily
matched to the first full citation.

11.4   Identifying the Archives

The U.S. National Archives has long been known simply as "the
National Archives." However, that name is also used by the national
archives of the United Kingdom—formerly called the Public Record
Office (PRO)—and by archives of some other English-speaking
countries. Because subject matter can overlap among these facilities,
your citations should distinguish between them.

U.S. FACILITIES
The U.S. National Archives has two principal facilities in the Capital
Area, the original facility in downtown Washington and the newer

facility popularly known as Archives II, located in the suburb of College Park, Maryland. Outside the D.C. area, there exist a number of NARA regional archives and record centers. Because different material is housed in different locations, when you cite *unfilmed* manuscripts you should identify the specific facility that holds them.

COMMON ACRONYMS

Three acronyms have been widely used for the U.S. National Archives (NA) and the agency that administers it, the National Archives and Records Administration (NARA), whose name appears on older publications as National Archives and Records Service (NARS). NARA is the common acronym when referring to the archive system and its publications. When you cite unpublished material used in one of the regional facilities of the National Archives, the common acronym would be *NA–* followed by the name of the particular facility where the record is housed (e.g., NA–College Park, NA–Denver, NA–Fort Worth, etc.).

AFFILIATED ARCHIVES

Several non-NARA institutions are considered *affiliated archives*—e.g., the U.S. Military Academy, U.S. Naval Academy, Oklahoma Historical Society, and the Yellowstone National Park Archives. Original NARA material deposited with these institutions should be cited in the same manner as material at the National Archives, with one exception. In lieu of identifying the repository as "National Archives–[location]," NARA requests that you identify it as

> "... National Archives—Affiliated Archives: record on deposit at [name of affiliate, city, state]."

11.5 Identifying the Author or Creator

Many government compilations credit no individual. In those cases, the author is typically the agency. If the agency is also the publisher, you may leave the "author" or "creator" field blank to avoid redundancy. When citing websites, if the title of the website contains the name of the agency, you do not have to duplicate that identity in the author or creator field, for the same reason. If the creator of the government-sponsored database is *not* the same as the agency that created the website, you should identify both the database creator and the website creator. (For example, see QuickCheck Model: Databases Online—National Archives [Canada]) In all cases, the phrase *website creator* refers to the creator of the *content*—i.e., the sponsoring agency or owner—not the graphic designer who might be credited at the site.

BASIC FORMATS

11.6   Basic Formats: Audio & Video Recordings
See also QuickCheck Model *for* AUDIO RECORDINGS: NATIONAL ARCHIVES

The U.S. federal government has created or collected many types of sound recordings that are now maintained at the National Archives. Some were acquired as evidence in court cases. Others represent speeches, memoirs, interviews, or depositions for congressional hearings. In each case, you will need to thoughtfully analyze the nature of the item in order to identify it correctly at the Item or File Unit level. Past that point, the structure of the citation will follow the framework outlined at 11.1. The examples below illustrate that principle with two types of items, an oral memoir and an interview, both from the same record set.

> *Source List Entry*
> Sound Recordings of California Desert Oral Histories, 1977–1978. Records of the Bureau of Land Management, Record Group 49. National Archives, College Park, Maryland.

> *First Reference Note*
>   1. Avda Haenszel, "Early Memories of Searchlight, Nevada," recorded 18 October 1977, minute 23, audio tape NWDNM (s)-49.6; Sound Recordings of California Desert Oral Histories, 1977–1978; Records of the Bureau of Land Management, Record Group 49; National Archives, College Park, Maryland.
>   2. Edmund Jaeger, desert naturalist, interview by Eric J. Rudd and Paul Clark, 19 October 1977, minute 15, audio tape NWDNM(s)-49.7 (7" reel-to-reel); Sound Recordings of California Desert Oral Histories, 1977–1978; Records of the Bureau of Land Management, Record Group 49; National Archives, College Park, Maryland.

> *Subsequent Note*
>   11. Haenszel, "Early Memories of Searchlight, Nevada," minute 23, audio tape NWDNM(s)-49.6, RG 49, NA–College Park.
>   12. Edmund Jaeger interview, 19 October 1977, minute 15, audio tape NWDNM(s)-49.7, RG 49, NA–College Park.

CITING MEDIA FORMAT

You may wish to include in your citation an identification of the mechanical record format, especially if the medium is now antiquated. The Jaeger example illustrates the inclusion of mechanical format; the Haenszel example omits it.

11.7 Basic Format: Manuscript (Textual) Materials

See also QuickCheck Model *for* MANUSCRIPTS: NATIONAL ARCHIVES

Regardless of the agency or record type, most manuscript material will fit into the basic format illustrated below and the QuickCheck Model cited above. The example below represents a situation in which all the records used from the subgroup "Carded Medical Records" are part of a small series called "Carded Marriage Records." Because this series is the only one used from that subgroup, the Source List Entry makes the series the lead element. If you used material from several series within the subgroup, you might want to make that subgroup the lead element in the Source List Entry.

Source List Entry
Carded Marriage Records, 1884–1912. Carded Medical Records, 1812–1912. Records of the Adjutant General's Office, Record Group 94. National Archives, Washington, D.C.

First Reference Note
1. Carey O. Diehl and Pilar Carasco y Diaz, 5 August 1907, Cienfuegos, Cuba; Carded Marriage Records, 1884–1912; Carded Medical Records, 1812–1912; Records of the Adjutant General's Office, 1780s–1917, Record Group 94; National Archives, Washington, D.C.

Subsequent Note
11. Diehl and Carasco y Diaz, marriage, 5 Aug. 1907, Cienfuegos, Carded Medical Records, RG 94, NA–Washington.

11.8 Basic Formats: Microfilm Records

See QuickCheck Models *for* IMAGE COPIES: NARA MICROFILM ...

NARA films that carry the prefix *M* or *T* are considered publications and should be cited as a publication. In addition, each NARA facility may also film or fiche material that is not treated as a publication and does not carry the M or T prefix. Examples appear in this chapter at 11.9 and 11.20. When you use a film or fiche at a regional archive, you should note whether the film is a regional project or a publication of NARA itself. For example:

NARA MICROFILM PUBLICATION
If you consult NARA's M208, *Records of the Cherokee Agency in Tennessee, 1801–1835,* at the Southwest (Fort Worth) branch of the National Archives, you would not cite M208 as a NA–Fort Worth publication. It is a NARA publication. Again, a basic rule for citing publications applies here: *Publications are attributed to the publisher, not to the library or archive in which you use the publication.*

PRESERVATION FILM

If you are at the Fort Worth branch and you consult that facility's preservation film identified as Project no. AMID 5-004, Registers of Vital Statistics, Kaw Reservation, 1931–1951, you do not cite it as a NARA publication. You cite it as a preservation microfilm project of the National Archives–Southwest at Fort Worth. (See 11.9.)

MICROFILM & FICHE CITED NARA STYLE

NARA's citation guide (see 11.2) suggests that when its microfilm is used, the citation can be constructed as though you used the original records. You would then insert in parentheses a brief reference to the microfilm publication *number* (but not its name) and the roll or fiche number. That parenthetical addition would be placed after the series or subgroup (whichever applies in that particular case) that is represented on the film. That recommendation presents a problem for many researchers, particularly for two reasons:

PRACTICALITY. .... When using NARA microfilm, you may not find enough explicit information there to identify the series, subseries, entries, and other elements required for a full and correct citation of those originals, which were not actually consulted.

PRECISION. .... A principle of sound historical research holds that we should cite only what we have used. Thus, many researchers feel that when they use a publication (print, film, or digital), it is the publication that should be fully cited and that their citations should not imply that they personally consulted the more complete original files. While a NARA microfilm publication does represent an official image of a document held by NARA, image copies are not always equal to the original in quality. Differences in legibility can affect one's interpretation of what the original says. By citing only the microfilm, if that is indeed what you have used, you create no ambiguity as to what you actually consulted.

The Basic Formats for NARA microfilm, illustrated below, provide two options. The first is modeled after NARA's preferred citation to the original records, with a brief parenthetical mention of the microfilm. The second is a citation directly to the microfilm publication, following standard format for published books and film.

Microfilm (NARA)

Source List Entry

(To cite both the original and the film, NARA Style)

Despatches from Colon, Panama, 1852–1906 (NARA microfilm publication T193, 19 rolls). Consular Despatches, 1785–1906. General Records of the Department of State, Record Group 59. National Archives, Washington, D.C.

(To cite the film as a publication, Evidence Style)

Despatches from U.S. Consuls in Colon, Panama, 1852–1906. Micropublication T193, 19 rolls. Washington, D.C.: National Archives and Records Service, 1965.

First Reference Note

(To cite both the original and the film, NARA Style)

    1. Geo. W. Fletcher to Hon. Lewis Cass, Secretary of State, 19 April 1857; Despatches from Colon, Panama, 1852–1906 (NARA microfilm publication T193, roll 1); Consular Despatches, 1785–1906; General Records of the Department of State, Record Group 59; National Archives, Washington, D.C.

(To cite the film as a publication, Evidence Style)

    2. *Despatches from U.S. Consuls in Colon, Panama, 1852–1906,* microfilm publication T193, 19 rolls (Washington, D.C.: National Archives and Records Service, 1965), roll 1, for 19 April 1857, Geo. W. Fletcher to Hon. Lewis Cass.

Subsequent Note

(To cite both the original and the film, NARA Style)

    11. Fletcher to Cass, 19 April 1857; Despatches from Colon, Panama, 1852–1906 (T193, roll 1), RG 59, NA–Washington.

(To cite the film as a publication, Evidence Style)

    12. *Despatches from U.S. Consuls in Colon, Panama, 1852–1906,* NARA T193, roll 1, 19 April 1857, Fletcher to Cass.

Microfilm models in the rest of this chapter will follow *Evidence*'s Publications Style, for simplicity and to conserve space.

CITING NARA MICROFILM AS A PUBLICATION (*EVIDENCE* STYLE)

When citing NARA's published microfilm as a publication, most researchers begin the citation with the name of the film, leaving the "author" field blank. NARA is then identified as the publisher. Using this format, the roll number, frame number, and the item of interest is usually cited *after* the publication data, in the fashion commonly used for citing the volume and pages from a standard print publication. All needed information for a full Publications Style citation should appear on the film's title page at the start of the roll.

CITING NARA MICROFILM USED ELSEWHERE

Many non-federal libraries offer copies of NARA film or fiche. When you use a NARA publication at another repository, you should still cite it as a NARA publication, using NARA's title and publication facts. If you want to add into your working files an identification of the library where you found the film and that library's call number, that can be helpful to you as research continues. However, library call numbers are not a standard part of a published citation.

IDENTIFYING ORIGINAL MANUSCRIPTS WHEN USING FILM—A PROCESS

Paragraph 4 of this section ("Microfilm & Fiche Cited NARA Style," page 563) points to one difficulty in following NARA Style for micropublications: finding, on the *film,* the specific information needed to fully and correctly cite the *original* record. At least part of the information may be gleaned through a two-step process:

Step One: Study the Microfilm Carefully

Read the "Introduction" that appears at the start of the film roll or at the start of Roll 1 of the series.* There, you will typically find a passage that refers to the subseries, series, and subgroup, although the text rarely identifies the items by these terms. There will also be a passage that explicitly identifies the record group.

To illustrate, consider the post office appointments covered by the QuickCheck Model for Image Copies: NARA MICROFILM—PUBLICATIONS STYLE CITATION, which provides this format:

Microfilm (NARA)

Source List Entry
Record of Appointment of Postmasters, 1832–September 30, 1971. Microfilm
   publication M841, 145 rolls. Washington, D.C.: National Archives
   and Records Service, 1973.

First Reference Note
   1. *Record of Appointment of Postmasters, 1832–September 30, 1971*,
microfilm publication M841 (Washington, D.C.: National Archives

---

* These introductory discussions of filmed materials are also posted at the NARA website as notes attached to its online microfilm catalog, and many are separately published as special NARA finding aids called *descriptive pamphlets.* See 13.44.

and Records Service, 1973), roll 68, Newton County, Mississippi, 25 March 1854, New Ireland.

Subsequent Note

11. *Record of Appointment of Postmasters, 1832–September 30, 1971*, NARA M841, roll 68, Newton Co., Miss., 25 March 1854, New Ireland.

When you analyze the film to decide what needs to be cited, you would first read the introduction, which tells you several critical things about the organization of the material:

- The film is made from 181 manuscript volumes divided into six time periods. Each original volume typically covers multiple states and territories, and the arrangement of those regions is *not* alphabetical, as a rule.

- Under each state or territory, the entries are arranged by county (parish, district, etc.), by time frame, and then by post office.

- For the microfilm publication, filmers took the pages and volumes out of their original sequence and created a new arrangement that is first by state, then county, then time period. Consequently, the film series does not present whole registers. As an example: for Newton County, Mississippi, you find one page from volume 17, then one page from volume 45, then one page from volume 258, etc. The page number is shown on the filmed image. The volume number is shown on the filmer's "target" that precedes the image.

- The film itself does not carry frame numbers.

Considering these issues, your citation to the microfilm would logically identify the elements needed to relocate the record on the microfilm: publication title, the publication number (prefaced by M or T), roll number, state, county, date, and post office. If you choose to cite your microfilm NARA Style, then—from the target and the filmed page itself—you can extract the exact *volume* and *page* for each individual entry.

The *series* and the *subgroup* can be tentatively identified from the film's Introduction. In the present case, the first paragraph of the Introduction states:

> On the 145 rolls of this microfilm publication is reproduced the Post Office Department record of appointment of postmasters for the approximate period 1832–September 30, 1971. This record was prepared in the offices of the Junior Assistant to the Postmaster General from 1832 to January 2,

> 1835, the Second Assistant Postmaster General from July 2, 1836, to 1851, the First Assistant Postmaster General from 1851 to 1950, and the Bureau of Post Office Operations from 1950 to September 30, 1971.

From this paragraph, you might conclude that the *subgroup* is *probably* the subject "appointment of postmasters." From the title of the film, you can conclude that the time frame which should be included in the subgroup title is "1832–September 30, 1971."

You can also hypothesize from this paragraph of the Introduction that the *series* you need to cite would be one of the three time frames assigned to the bureaucratic offices. The Newton County appointment cited in the foregoing model is dated 25 March 1854. Thus, it should be part of the material identified above as "[Records of] the First Assistant Postmaster General from 1851 to 1950."

However, you cannot *assume* which piece of information represents the series and which represents the subgroup. In some of NARA's record groups, "Records of [a particular office]" would represent the subgroup, while "appointments," "correspondence," and similar material would represent series within that subgroup. In other cases, "Appointments" might be a subgroup itself, one that is subdivided into time frames similar to those given above.

The identity of the *record group* is explicitly stated in the next-to-last paragraph of M841's "Introduction":

> The records reproduced in this microfilm publication are part of the National Archives of the United States designated as Records of the Post Office Department, Record Group 28.

Step Two: Confirm your Presumptions

Using the published guides to the National Archives—in print and online—you *might* be able to test your reconstructed citation. The major archival guides will tell you whether an inventory or a preliminary inventory exists for the record group of interest. If it does, then you should obtain a copy for study. There, you will find brief descriptions of the material within that record group, arranged by subgroups, series, and (sometimes) subseries. At each level, you will be given the "title" that was in service at the time the inventory was compiled. If you are consulting an online inventory, you should have the current working title of the subgroup, series, and subseries. If you are consulting a printed inventory, then—before you go to print—you may wish to contact the National Archives and ensure that you have, indeed, created a correct citation to the current identity and location of the original material whose image you consulted on film.

Citing NARA microfilm as a publication eliminates the need for this process to identity the archival hierarchies of the original record. However, regardless of the citation format you choose, studying the introduction to the microfilm publication is still essential to a sound interpretation of what you are using.

11.9 Basic Formats: NA–Regional Holdings

See also QuickCheck Model *for* MANUSCRIPTS: NATIONAL ARCHIVES–REGIONAL

Many federal records have been dispersed from the Capital Area to a more geographically convenient regional facility. A citation to these manuscript materials typically follows the Basic Format for National Archives manuscripts (11.7), with one difference: rather than citing the Washington facility, you cite the regional facility.

Source List Entry
Kaw Reservation. Vital Statistics, Registers, 1931–1951. Pawnee Agency Records. Records of the Bureau of Indian Affairs, Record Group 75. National Archives–Southwest Region, Fort Worth, Texas.

First Reference Note
1. Death entry, Peggy J. Bowker, 27 November 1941, "Register of Vital Statistics for Kaw Reservation," p. 51; Pawnee Agency Records; Records of the Bureau of Indian Affairs, Record Group 75; National Archives–Southwest Region, Fort Worth, Texas.

Subsequent Note
11. Death entry, Peggy J. Bowker, "Register of Vital Statistics for Kaw Reservation," p. 51, RG 75, NA–Fort Worth.

The regional archives have also microfilmed some of their frequently used records for preservation purposes. NARA does not consider that film to be a publication. As with other preservation film, you would cite the document by the standard format for original materials, drawing the information from the identification of the original record found in the film's introduction or from the identification targets that the film crews prepared and filmed at the start of the roll. Then you would add the specifics for the preservation film.

Film created by a regional facility should be attributed to that region, not to NARA. If you consult the film at a library, you should still identify it as a NA–regional project. You may also add the library's film number for quick reference in your working files. For example:

Microfilm (Regional Facilities, Preservation Film)

Source List Entry
Pawnee Agency. Homestead Allotments, 1923. Microfilm project AMID
   5-004. National Archives–Southwest Region, Fort Worth, Texas.

First Reference Note
   1. Entry 201, "Andrew Pappan, dead," Homestead Allotments,
1923, Pawnee Agency (microfilm project AMID 5-004, roll 81);
Records of the Central Superintendency; Records of the Bureau of
Indian Affairs, Record Group 75; National Archives–Southwest Region, Fort Worth, Texas.

Subsequent Note
   11. Entry 201, "Andrew Pappan, dead," Homestead Allotments,
1923, Pawnee Agency, AMID 5-004, roll 81, NA–Fort Worth.

Microfilm (FHL Copies of NA–Regional film)

Source List Entry
Pawnee Agency. Homestead Allotments, 1923. Microfilm project AMID
   5-004. National Archives–Southwest Region, Fort Worth, Texas.
   Consulted as FHL microfilm 1,249,780, item 2. Family History
   Library, Salt Lake City, Utah.

First Reference Note
   1. Entry 201, "Andrew Pappan, dead," Homestead Allotments,
1923, Pawnee Agency (microfilm project AMID 5-004, roll 81);
Records of the Central Superintendency; Records of the Bureau of
Indian Affairs, Record Group 75; National Archives–Southwest Region, Fort Worth, Texas; consulted as FHL microfilm 1,249,780, item 2.

Subsequent Note
   11. Entry 201, "Andrew Pappan, dead," Homestead Allotments,
1923, Pawnee Agency, AMID 5-004, roll 81, NA–Fort Worth.

CITING REGIONAL ARCHIVES WEBSITES
See 11.37.

11.10 Basic Format: Online Databases or Indexes
See QuickCheck Model *for* DATABASES ONLINE: NATIONAL ARCHIVES (U.S.)

Online databases to NARA records are finding aids that provide
selected details and point you to the original records. Some are linked

to image copies (see 11.11), but the databases are not equivalent to the originals. Therefore, your citation needs to specifically state whether you are citing the database information or the digital image. The primary focus of your database citation is the database itself; after that, you (*a*) identify the specific data of interest in the database, and (*b*) add whatever citation the database provides for its own source.

Online Databases (or Indexes)

Source List Entry
"Archival Research Catalog (ARC)." Database and images. *The National Archives.* http://www.archives.gov/research/arc : 2007.

First Reference Note
1. "Archival Research Catalog (ARC)," database, *The National Archives* (http://www.archives.gov/research/arc : accessed 26 February 2007), entry for Larceny Jacket no. 59, John Shawn [Shown] and Wyatt Earp, 1871, ARC Identifier 242166; citing Criminal Defendant Jacket Files, 1866–1900; Western District of Arkansas, Fort Smith Division; Records of District Courts of the United States, Record Group 21; National Archives–Southwest Region, Fort Worth, Texas.

Subsequent Note
11. "Archival Research Catalog (ARC)," database, *The National Archives,* entry for Larceny Jacket no. 59, Shawn and Earp, 1871.

CORRECTING LABEL ERRORS
Archives personnel who create file labels, indexes, and databases may have trouble reading names in historic documents. When a modern label carries a reading you feel is erroneous, you still need to cite the label exactly so the record can be retrieved. You may also want to "correct" the reading in your notes or your citation. To do so, place the correction in square editorial brackets, as demonstrated above with the surname "Shawn [Shown]."

11.11 Basic Formats: Online Images

See also QuickCheck Model *for* IMAGES ONLINE: NATIONAL ARCHIVES (U.S.)

When you cite a digital image accessed via NARA's ARC database, you have two choices:

EMPHASIS ON THE WEBSITE
For simplicity you may prefer to cite ARC images as an online pub‐lication, in the same way you cite database entries from ARC. In the publications format, the database and website are the key elements,

followed by a citation to the specific item, then its digital ID number. NARA prefers that you then add the citation of the original, as provided in the ARC cataloging data that accompanies the image.

EMPHASIS ON THE ORIGINAL

If you choose to cite the record as an original, you may be able to glean most or all of the needed series, subgroup, and record group identification from the catalog description that accompanies the image. Following that citation to the original, NARA's GIL 17 asks that you append the URL, with some specific verbiage to introduce it. That verbiage is boldfaced in note 2 of the example that follows.

Both approaches are demonstrated below. This manual recommends a Publications Style citation for ARC images for four reasons:

- to adhere to the policy of citing original files only if you have researched those files (based on the premise that the use of an isolated document extracted from a database is not equivalent to actual study of a full record set);

- to specifically identify the digital document so it can be relocated at the website with some degree of certainty;

- to fully identify the website and its sponsor, given the frequency with which URLs change in the digital world; and

- to be consistent with the manner in which you cite databases and digital images by other online providers.

Online Images

Source List Entry

(Publications Style citation to the website and image)
"Archival Research Catalog (ARC)." Database and images. *The National Archives.* http://www.archives.gov/research/arc: 2007.

(NARA Style citation—full citation of original; minimal ID of website
Post and Reservation Maps, 1820–1905. Records of the War Department, Office of the Quartermaster General, Record Group 92. National Archives, College Park, Maryland. At http://www.archives .gov/research/arc/ : 2007.

First Reference Note

(Publications Style citation to the website and image)
    1. "Archival Research Catalog (ARC)," digital image, *The National Archives* (www.archives.gov/research/arc: 13 February 2007), "Contraband Quarters, Mason's (Roosevelt) Island, Washington, D.C.," ARC

Identifier 305820; citing Post and Reservation Maps, 1820–1905; Records of the War Department, Office of the Quartermaster General, Record Group 92; National Archives, College Park, Maryland.

(NARA Style citation—full citation of original; minimal ID of website)
    2. "Contraband Quarters, Mason's (Roosevelt) Island, Washington, D.C.," Post and Reservation Maps, 1820–1905; Records of the War Department, Office of the Quartermaster General, Record Group 92; National Archives, College Park, Maryland; **online version on** 13 February 2007, available through the online catalog at http://www.archives.gov/research/arc.

Subsequent Note

(Publications Style citation to the website and image)
    11. "Archival Research Catalog (ARC)," digital image, *The National Archives*, "Contraband Quarters, Mason's (Roosevelt) Island, Washington, D.C."

(NARA Style citation—full citation of original; minimal ID of website)
    12. "Contraband Quarters, Mason's (Roosevelt) Island," Post and Reservation Maps, 1820–1905, RG 92, NA–College Park.

IMMIGRATION, PASSENGER & SEAMEN RECORDS

See also Naturalization Records 11.49.

11.12 Background

The U.S. National Archives offers a variety of immigration lists, manifests, and passenger records, as well as custom collector's abstracts made from those materials. Some of the lists are created at the port of debarkation and deposited with U.S. Customs upon arrival. Others are U.S. documents created at portside on incoming passengers. Some are passenger manifests for coastwise U.S. vessels, whose voyages both originated and ended at U.S. ports. Some are manifests of slaves being transported coastwise or entries for slaves whose masters are listed on the passenger manifests. Other lists itemize the crews or protection certificates issued to crewmen. While the core citation to NARA files will remain the same (Basic Format for National Archives manuscripts, 11.7), you will want to ensure that your description of the item makes clear the type of record you have used. Several of these types are illustrated at 11.13 through 11.18.

11.13 Crew Records: Lists for Ships, Incoming or Departing

Since 1803, each ship master arriving at or departing from American ports has been required to file a crew list with the customs collector of that port. Few of the surviving nineteenth-century lists have been filmed by the National Archives. Therefore, your citations to this type of record will typically be to an original manuscript—some of which are now in a regional archive, as with the example below.

Source List Entry
Crew Lists, 1803–07, New London, Connecticut. Records of the U.S. Customs Service, Record Group 36. National Archives–Northeast Region, Boston, Massachusetts.

First Reference Note
1. Enoch Hubbard, crew list of the schooner *Sally*, 3 August 1803, departing for Barbados; New London Crew Lists, 1803–1807; Records of the U.S. Customs Service, Record Group 36; National Archives–Northeast Region, Boston, Massachusetts.

Subsequent Note
11. Enoch Hubbard, crew list of the schooner *Sally*, 3 August 1803, RG 36, NA–Boston.

CITING PORT OF DESTINATION
In the New London example above, the identification of the crew list includes the vessel's name, date of departure, and *destination*. On occasion (particularly in larger ports) more than one vessel of the same name may have been in port at the same time. Citing the destination may be necessary to distinguish between ship lists.

11.14 Crew Records: Seamen Protection Certificates
This class of records exists in three basic types. Under a Congressional Act of 1796, American seamen have periodically carried protection certificates attesting their citizenship to curtail their illegal impressments by ships from other nations. Seamen applied for these certificates at the office of the collector of customs and took the certificates with them. The collector was to record the details in his register and retain both the applications and the proofs of citizenship that the seamen provided. Access to the originals and citation formats vary between these three types, as follows:

REGISTERS
Most of the registers today exist in local historical societies, where they can be cited by the Basic Format for documents held in nongovernmental archives (3.13). The registers held by the National Archives can be cited in Basic Format for National Archives manuscripts (11.7).

APPLICATIONS

Most surviving applications are arranged chronologically, not alphabetically, although indexes exist for several major ports. You can cite these by Basic Format for National Archives manuscripts (11.7). If the material is not chronologically or alphabetically arranged, you should note the arrangement so the record can be easily retrieved. A small percentage of these have been microfilmed and can be cited in the Basic Formats for National Archives microfilm (11.8).

CERTIFICATES

Few original certificates exist in customs' records. Those that do typically reflect unusual circumstances such as a sailor returning a damaged certificate to have a new one issued. If you have found an actual certificate (the loose document) at NARA, you can cite it in Basic Format for National Archives manuscripts (11.7). If you find the document in an archive elsewhere, you would use the Basic Format for archived documents (3.13). Wherever you find the record, you should identify it precisely as a register, an application, or a certificate.

11.15 Passenger Manifests: Manuscripts & Microfilm

In citing passenger manifests held by NARA, the data you enter in your "item" field should have two parts. First you cite the specific passenger, together with whatever identifying information is needed. Then you cite the ship and the date. When citing slave manifests, you will also need to identify the slave master. Sometimes that master is named as part of the slave's entry. At other times, masters who have paid passage for numerous slaves will have submitted lists of their own that have been copied into the manifests, as with Hubbell below.

Source List Entry

Outward Slave Manifests, 1820–1860. Records of the U.S. Customs Service, Record Group 36. National Archives, Washington, D.C.

First Reference Note

1. Entry for Matilde, age 28, on list of L. C. Hubbell, slave owner; *Champion* manifest, 12 November 1839; Port of Mobile, 1839–1840; Outward Slave Manifests, 1820–1860; Records of the U.S. Customs Service, Record Group 36; National Archives, Washington, D.C.

Subsequent Note

11. Entry for Matilde, 28, on list of L. C. Hubbell; *Champion* manifest, 12 November 1839, Mobile; RG 36, NA–Washington.

CITING SHIP NAMES

Convention calls for italicizing the names of vessels. When (as in the example below) the name of the vessel is preceded by initials that identify the type of vessel—e.g., SS or S.S. for steamship—those initials are not italicized. A vessel's description is not part of its name.

NARA Microfilm

When citing manifest data from a microfilmed publication, the order of elements differs from the order used for manuscripts. As shown above, the manuscript format goes from the smallest element (the item of interest) to the largest (the archive and its location). When citing a publication, your elements will go from largest (the publication title) to smallest (the item of interest).

Source List Entry
Registers of Vessels Arriving at the Port of New York from Foreign Ports, 1789–1919. Microfilm publication M1066, 27 rolls. Washington: National Archives and Records Service, 1980.

First Reference Note
1. *Registers of Vessels Arriving at the Port of New York from Foreign Ports, 1789–1919,* microfilm publication M1066 (Washington: National Archives and Records Service, 1980), roll 27, alphabetical by ship; SS *Königin Luise,* 23 June 1905, for Rosaria Furia, p. 58, line 2.

Subsequent Note
11. *Registers of Vessels Arriving at the Port of New York from Foreign Ports, 1789–1919,* NARA M1066, roll 27, SS *Königin Luise,* 23 June 1905, for Rosaria Furia, p. 58, line 2.

11.16 Passenger Manifests: Online Derivatives

Online offerings for incoming passenger lists are typically of three types: databases (or indexes), images, and transcriptions. Structures of the sites vary widely. At some, you will find identification of the creator of the derivative, the website title, and a database title. More often, one or more of these will be missing, as illustrated by the models below. In the Ellis Island example, the database (at this writing) carries the title "Passenger Record." In the Castle Garden case (at this writing), the database carries no title at the website's home page and the retrieved entry carries no title. Obviously, your formats will vary.

Online Databases & Indexes

Source List Entry
"Atlantic Ports, Gulf Coasts, and Great Lakes Passenger Lists, Roll 8: 1845–1849." Database. *Ancestry.com.* http://www.ancestry .com : 2007.

CastleGarden.org: America's First Immigration Center. Database. http://
www.castlegarden.org : 2007.
Statue of Liberty—Ellis Island Foundation. Database and images. http://
www.ellisisland.org : 2007.

First Reference Note

1. "Atlantic Ports, Gulf Coasts, and Great Lakes Passenger Lists,
Roll 8: 1845–1849," database, *Ancestry.com* (http://www.ancestry
.com : accessed 2 February 2007), entry for J. Hely, age 36, arrived
Passamaquoddy, Maine, 1845 [no ship stated].

2. *CastleGarden.org: America's First Immigration Center,* untitled
database (http://www.castlegarden.org : accessed 2 February 2007),
entry for Ernesto Spadini, age 43, arrived 5 September 1902 aboard the
Massilia.

3. "Passenger Record," database, *Statue of Liberty—Ellis Island
Foundation* (http://www.ellisisland.org : accessed 1 February 2007), entry
for Tekla Wyczenska, age 20, arrived 23 February 1901 on the *Rhein.*

Subsequent Note

11. "Atlantic Ports, Gulf Coasts, and Great Lakes Passenger Lists,
Roll 8: 1845–1849," database, *Ancestry.com,* entry for J. Hely, 36,
Passamaquoddy, Maine, 1845.

12. *CastleGarden.org: America's First Immigration Center,* database
entry for Ernesto Spadini, 43, arrived 5 Sept. 1902, *Massilia.*

13. "Passenger Record," database, *Statue of Liberty—Ellis Island
Foundation,* entry for Tekla Wyczenska, 20, arrived 23 Feb. 1901, *Rhein.*

CITING PORT OF ARRIVAL

As illustrated at 11.15, when citing *original* ship rolls you should
include the port of arrival, because those records are arranged by port.
When citing databases, however, you can only cite what the database
provides. If a database does not identify the port of arrival, your
citation will not identify the port.

SEQUENCE OF ELEMENTS

The basic elements and their sequence are the same when citing
database entries (above) and online typescripts (below). In both cases,
you are citing modern creations derived from an original source—not
the original itself. Therefore, the derivative and its creators are the
focus of your citation. In your Reference Note, whatever information
your source supplies for its source should be added at the end of your
citation. You do not cite the unconsulted original in your Source List.

The examples below offer two models for citations to the website of
the Immigrant Ships Transcribers Guild. Note the differences in the
pieces of data needed for the Guild's extracts from NARA film as
compared to the Guild's extracts from newspapers.

Online Typescripts (Transcriptions)   🖥

Source List Entry

Immigrant Ships Transcribers Guild. Database. http://www.immigrant
　　ships.net : 2007.
Statue of Liberty—Ellis Island Foundation. Database and images. http://
　　www.ellisisland.org : 2007.

First Reference Note

　　1. "Brig Franklin: Gothenburg, Sweden to New Bedford, Massachusetts, 19 September 1831," database, *Immigrant Ships Transcribers
Guild* (http://www.immigrantships.net : accessed 2 February 2007),
line 8, Kalvin Kneuttson, age 31; citing "National Archives and Records
Administration, Film M575, Reel 5."

　　2. "Halifax, Nova Scotia, Ship Arrivals and Departures, Index,
1851–1872," *Immigrant Ships Transcribers Guild* (http://www
.immigrantships.net : accessed 2 February 2007), 1852 link, newspaper
abstract from *Novascotian* (Halifax), 1 March 1852, plate 67, column 4,
for passenger list of newly arrived R. M.S.*Cambria*.

　　3. "Ship Manifest: Manifest for Lombardia," typescript, *Statue of
Liberty—Ellis Island Foundation* (http://www.ellisisland.org : accessed 1
March 2007), entry for Barbara Basiaglia, age 18, arrived 17 April 1902.

Subsequent Note

　　11. "Brig Franklin ... New Bedford, Massachusetts, 19 September
1831," *Immigrant Ships Transcribers Guild*, line 8, Kalvin Kneuttson, 31.

　　12. "Halifax, Nova Scotia, Ship Arrivals and Departures, Index,
1851–1872," *Immigrant Ships Transcribers Guild*, 1852 link, newspaper
abstract for *Novascotian* (Halifax), 1 March 1852.

　　13. "Ship Manifest: Manifest for Lombardia," typescript, *Statue of
Liberty—Ellis Island Foundation*, entry for Barbara Basiaglia, 18, arrived
17 April 1902.

CITING THE SOURCE OF THE SOURCE

Typescripts at the official Ellis Island website are obviously made from
the manifest to which they are attached. However, the website of the
Immigrant Ships Transcribers Guild offers ship lists from many
sources. Your Guild citation should note where the transcriber
acquired the data, in some fashion similar to the two variants in notes
1 and 2 above. If your online source does not identify its own source,
you would state that fact in your citation.

CREATING SHORTENED CITATIONS

If you choose to shorten the title of a database, as in note 11, you
should keep (*a*) the initial words and (*b*) any reference to the *arrival*
port, ship, and date.

11.17 Passenger Manifests: Online Images

When you cite online *images* of ship manifests, you should clearly indicate that you have viewed an image of the original, not a database or an online transcription. Because URLs for both manifest images and ship photos can be exceedingly long, you may wish to cite only the website's home page and database, with any necessary instructions about key words to follow, as demonstrated at 11.18. Conventionally, the short form citation for a manifest will directly reference the manifest.

Online Images

Source List Entry

Statue of Liberty—Ellis Island Foundation. Database and images. http://www.ellisisland.org : 2007.

First Reference Note

(*To emphasize the database and website*)
   1. "Passenger Record," digital images, *Statue of Liberty—Ellis Island Foundation* (http://www.ellisisland.org : accessed 22 January 2007), manifest, S. S. *Rhein,* February 1901, stamped p. 290, line 16, Tekla Wyczenska, age 20.

(*To emphasize the original manifest*)
   1. Manifest, S. S. *Rhein,* February 1901, stamped p. 290, line 16, Tekla Wyczenska, age 20; "Passenger Record," digital images, *Statue of Liberty—Ellis Island Foundation* (http://www.ellisisland.org : accessed 22 January 2007).

Subsequent Note

   11. Manifest, S.S. *Rhein,* 23 February 1901, stamped p. 290, line 16, Tekla Wyczenska, 20.

11.18 Ship Images, Online

Online Images

Source List Entry

Statue of Liberty—Ellis Island Foundation. Database and images. http://www.ellisisland.org : 2007.

First Reference Note

   1. Photo of S. S. *Rhein* (built 1899), digital image, *Statue of Liberty—Ellis Island Foundation* (http://www.ellisisland.org : accessed 22 January 2007), retrieve by choosing the "ship" link attached to the "Passenger Record" database search results for Tekla Wyczenska, age 20, arrived 23 February 1901 aboard the S.S. *Rhein.*

Subsequent Note
11. Photo of S.S. *Rhein* (built 1899), digital image, *Statue of Liberty—Ellis Island Foundation*.

CITING THE WEBSITE IN THE SHORT FORM
The short form for the manifest at 11.17 cites the original document, which is part of a major National Archives series and can be easily located and widely accessed. Therefore, the website does not *have* to be cited in the short form. The digital photograph of the ship, cited here at 11.18, presents a different situation. The website brings together random images from many locations. Therefore, the website's identity is essential in the shortened reference.

INDIAN AFFAIRS RECORDS
See also 6.36 and 6.40 for enumerations by the Bureau of Indian Affairs and the Census Bureau's special Indian schedules.

11.19 Indian Affairs: Manuscript Materials
The first set of examples below illustrates citations to three different series or subseries (emigration rolls, spoilation claims, and citizenship petitions) from one major subgroup (Cherokee Removal Records) within the Bureau of Indian Affairs record group. A single Source List Entry can serve all three types of records, if the Source List Entry uses the *series* as the lead element. Each Reference Note thereafter begins by citing the specific item of interest and its file identification, before adding the other elements cited in the Source List Entry.

Source List Entry
Cherokee Removal Records, 1817–1884. Records of the Bureau of Indian Affairs, Record Group 75. National Archives, Washington, D.C.

First Reference Note
1. Captain John Page, compiler, "Muster Roll of Cherokees to Emigrate West of the Mississippi River," 31 December 1838; Emigration Rolls; Cherokee Removal Records, 1817–1884; Records of the Bureau of Indian Affairs, Record Group 75; National Archives, Washington, D.C.
2. Moses Daniell claim, June 1838, "Original Record of Spoilations, No. 2," pp. 262–63; Decisions on Spoilation Claims, 1838; Records of the First Board of Cherokee Commissioners; Cherokee Removal Records, 1817–1884; Records of the Bureau of Indian Affairs, Record Group 75; National Archives, Washington, D.C.
3. William Blyth et al., petition for citizenship, 1838; Muster Rolls, 1835–1838; Emigration Rolls, 1817–1838; Cherokee Removal

Records, 1817–1884; Records of the Bureau of Indian Affairs, Record Group 75; National Archives, Washington, D.C.

Subsequent Note

11. Page, "Muster Roll of Cherokees to Emigrate West of the Mississippi River," 31 December 1838, Cherokee Removal Records, RG 75, NA–Washington.

12. Daniell claim, June 1838, "Original Record of Spoilations, No. 2," pp. 262–63, Cherokee Removal Records, RG 75, NA–Washington.

13. Blyth et al., petition for citizenship, 1838, Cherokee Removal Records, RG 75, NA–Washington.

CREATING IBID. REFERENCES

The Reference Notes above contain much duplication of detail from one to the next. That is necessary in your database or any manuscript in progress. When you reach a final draft stage, you should convert the above sequence of notes to appropriate *ibid.* references. In the examples that follow, note that the first citation covers the record from the smallest unit all the way through to the repository and its location. The second citation also starts with the smallest unit and proceeds only to the point that it would begin to duplicate the note before it. The third citation follows the pattern of the second.

1. Captain John Page, compiler, "Muster Roll of Cherokees to Emigrate West of the Mississippi River," 31 December 1838; Emigration Rolls; Cherokee Removal Records, 1817–1884; Records of the Bureau of Indian Affairs, Record Group 75; National Archives, Washington, D.C.

2. Moses Daniell claim, June 1838, "Original Record of Spoilations, No. 2," pp. 262–63; Decisions on Spoilation Claims, 1838; Records of the First Board of Cherokee Commissioners; Cherokee Removal Records, ibid.

3. William Blyth et al., petition for citizenship, 1838; Muster Rolls, 1835–1838; Emigration Rolls, 1817–1838; Cherokee Removal Records, ibid.

You should not attempt this level of shortening, however, until you reach that final draft stage. If, in your working files, you were to convert parts of notes 2 and 3 to *ibid.,* then the insertion of new material as you continue your research would likely separate the *ibid.* reference from the note that should precede it.

11.20 Indian Affairs: Microfilm Publications

Manuscripts from the Bureau of Indian Affairs record group have been microfilmed for distribution in at least two different ways. Those considered publications carry an M or T number and have a formal title that you italicize when citing it in Publications Style. Unpublished microfilm of BIA records is typically a project of NARA regional archives (see 11.9) and will not carry an M or T in its film series number. In the two models below, note 1 demonstrates citing a single document; note 2, a particular record from a large file. No frame number is cited in either because the film carries none.

Microfilm Publications (NARA)

Source List Entry
Letters Received by the Office of Indian Affairs, 1800–1823. Microfilm publication M271, 4 rolls. Washington, D.C.: National Archives and Records Service, 1959.

Special Files of the Office of Indian Affairs, 1807–1904. Microfilm publication M574, 85 rolls. Washington, D.C.: National Archives and Records Service, 1971.

First Reference Note
1. *Letters Received by the Office of Indian Affairs, 1800–1823,* microfilm publication M271 (Washington, D.C.: National Archives and Records Service, 1959), roll 1, frames 1103–07, Benjamin Hawkins, "Report on the Petition of the Halfbreeds Resident on Alabama, Sufferers by the Civil War among the Creek," 15 January 1816.

2. *Special Files of the Office of Indian Affairs, 1807–1904,* microfilm publication M574, 85 rolls (Washington, D.C.: National Archives and Records Service, 1971), roll 4, frames 255–56, N. Smith to J. Van Horne, 13 November 1837, in Special File 31, Williamson Smith claim.

Subsequent Note
11. *Letters Received by the Office of Indian Affairs, 1800–1823,* NARA M271, roll 1, frames 1103–07.

12. *Special Files of the Office of Indian Affairs, 1807–1904,* NARA M574, roll 4, frames 255–56, Smith to Van Horne, 13 November 1837, in Special File 31, Williamson Smith claim.

CREATING SHORTENED CITATIONS
In the two Subsequent Notes above, after citing the frame number, far more detail is intentionally given in 12 than in 11. How much detail to include in the shortened citation is a decision you will make on a case-by-case basis, as you assess the material you are citing.

For models to Indian Affairs records filmed by regional archives, see 11.9, Basic Formats: NA–Regional Holdings, Microfilm.

11.21   Indian Affairs: Online Derivatives
Many film series published by NARA are offered as databases and

images by independent vendors. The example below provides a format usable for most online offerings. For online databases and image copies offered at NARA's own website, see 11.10–11.11.

Online Databases & Indexes

Source List Entry

"Dawes Final Rolls of the Five Civilized Tribes." Database. *Access Genealogy: Indian Tribal Records*. http://www.accessgenealogy.com/native/finalindex.php : 2007.

First Reference Note

1. "Dawes Final Rolls of the Five Civilized Tribes," database, *Access Genealogy: Indian Tribal Records* (http://www.accessgenealogy .com/native/finalindex.php : accessed 2 February 2007), entry for Silwee Tubbee, age 39, full-blood; citing card 1722, [Dawes] roll no. 4867, Dawes Commission [no citation to NARA originals or film].

Subsequent Note

11. "Dawes Final Rolls of the Five Civilized Tribes," *Access Genealogy: Indian Tribal Records,* database entry for Silwee Tubbee, age 39, full-blood; citing card 1722, roll no. 4867.

LAND RECORDS

See also 10.20–10.21, State Land Office Records for U.S. Public Lands.

11.22 Background

The store of federal records created by the U.S. General Land Office and its successor, the Bureau of Land Management, is vast and complex. In addition to the land entry files that are most frequently sought by history researchers, there are patent certificates, plats, and a wide range of administrative records such as applications, correspondence, scrip files, and registers of many types.

Most administrative records can be cited by the Basic Format for National Archives manuscripts (11.7). However, when you cite land entry files, your citation will need to identify the particular type of file and should contain certain information, depending upon that type. The basic types of land entry files, in brief, are these:

CASH ENTRY FILES

Almost all land sold after 30 June 1820 was for cash. Those *cash entry files* are arranged by land office, then by patent number.

CREDIT ENTRY FILES

Prior to 30 June 1820, most public land was sold by the United States on credit. These credit files are arranged by land office, thereunder numerically by one of two types:

- *Credit prior files*: land that was purchased and entirely paid for prior to 30 June 1820.
- *Credit under files*: land that was purchased on credit prior to 30 June 1820, but paid off after that date under the credit terms.

DONATION FILES
To encourage settlement of certain territories—Arkansas, Florida, Oregon, and Washington, specifically—Congress offered free land to those willing to meet certain conditions. The resulting files are organized by state. Thereunder, the arrangements (and the details you need to include in your citation) differ by state. Florida's donation claims are arranged numerically. Files for Oregon and Washington state are subdivided by land office, then further divided into approved claims (arranged by final certificate number) and unapproved claims that are generally in chronological order.

HOMESTEAD FILES
The Homestead Act of 1862, which offered free land in exchange for making specified improvements, created a different set of records. Loose documents for each applicant are centralized in *homestead files.* Their arrangement (hence, the data you should record) varies according to time frame.

- *1863–30 June 1908:* Files are arranged by state, then land office, then subdivided according to whether the land was eventually *patented* or left *unpatented* (i.e., *canceled homestead applications*).
- *1 July 1908–16 May 1973:* These files, called *serial patent files*, are arranged numerically by patent number nationwide.

For sample citations to these four types of land entry files, see 11.23–27. For some other types of land records held by the National Archives, see 11.28–31.

11.23 Land Entry Files: Manuscripts
The following examples cover six types of land entry files from the four series discussed at 11.22.

Source List Entry

(*Cash entry file*)
St. Louis, Missouri, Land Office. Cash entry files. Records of the Bureau of Land Management, Record Group 49. National Archives, Washington, D.C.

(Credit under file)
Washington, Mississippi, Land Office. Credit under files. Records of the
   Bureau of Land Management, Record Group 49. National Ar-
   chives, Washington, D.C.

(Homestead files, pre-1908, citing whole file)
Bloomington, Nebraska, Land Office. Homestead files. Records of the
   Bureau of Land Management, Record Group 49. National Ar-
   chives, Washington, D.C.
Lincoln, Nebraska, Land Office. Homestead files. Records of the
   Bureau of Land Management, Record Group 49. National Ar-
   chives, Washington, D.C.

First Reference Note

(Cash entry file)
   1. Batiste Charleville (St. Genevieve County) cash entry file,
certificate no. 7429, St. Louis, Missouri, Land Office; Land Entry
Papers, 1800–1908; Records of the Bureau of Land Management,
Record Group 49; National Archives, Washington, D.C.

(Credit under file)
   2. John Warren (Pike County) credit under file, certificate no. 43,
Washington, Mississippi, Land Office; Land Entry Papers, 1800–1908;
Records of the Bureau of Land Management, Record Group 49;
National Archives, Washington, D.C.

(Homestead file, pre-1908, citing a particular document)
   3. Application no. 5928, 26 November 1878, in John H. Rowland
(Franklin County) homestead file bearing final certificate no. 5780, 16
May 1885, Bloomington, Nebraska, Land Office; Land Entry Papers,
1800–1908; Records of the Bureau of Land Management, Record
Group 49; National Archives, Washington, D.C.

(Homestead file, pre-1908, citing whole file)
   4. Robert Vandament (Chase County) homestead file, final certificate no. 328, Lincoln, Nebraska, Land Office; Land Entry Papers,
1800–1908; Records of the Bureau of Land Management, Record
Group 49; National Archives, Washington, D.C.

Subsequent Note

   11. Batiste Charleville cash entry file no. 7429, St. Louis, Mo., Land
Office, RG 49, NA–Washington.
   12. John Warren credit under file no. 43, Washington, Miss., Land
Office, RG 49, NA–Washington.
   13. Application no. 5928 in John H. Rowland homestead file
bearing final certificate no. 5780, Bloomington, Neb., Land Office, RG
49, NA–Washington.
   14. Robert Vandament homestead file no. 328, Lincoln, Neb.,
Land Office, RG 49, NA–Washington.

CITING DOCUMENT NUMBERS

As illustrated by the Rowland example in note 3 above, many U.S. land office files have multiple document numbers—application numbers, claim numbers, register and receiver numbers, final certificate numbers, patent numbers, etc. When you cite a number, you should include any descriptive words that are attached to that number.

11.24 Land Entry Files: Microfilm

Few U.S. land entry files have been microfilmed. Most of those available on film can be cited by the following model:

Source List Entry

Oregon and Washington Donation Land Files, 1851–1903. Microfilm publication M815, 108 rolls. Washington, D.C.: National Archives, 1970.

First Reference Note

1. *Oregon and Washington Donation Land Files, 1851–1903,* microfilm publication M815 (Washington, D.C.: National Archives, 1970), roll 2, "Oregon City Land Office, Donation Certificates 75–149," Alex^r Vaughan file (Linn County), certificate no. 78, issued 18 January 1854.

Subsequent Note

11. *Oregon and Washington Donation Land Files, 1851–1903,* NARA M815, roll 2, Alex^r Vaughan file, certificate no. 78.

11.25 Land Office Records: CD/DVD Databases

See also QuickCheck Model *for* DATABASES: CD-ROM PUBLICATIONS

The United States Bureau of Land Management has published electronic databases and images in several formats. Its CD-ROM version offers a database to many *patents*, but not to the *land entry files* held by NARA. When citing entries from that database, you will find no field actually labeled "patent." Instead, you find two fields labeled "ACCESS_NR" and "IMAGE_NAME." The "IMAGE_NAME" field carries the patent number you should cite so that the original files can be retrieved from the National Archives.

In the two examples below, you will note two other differences:

- *Land Office or Warrant Type*: Citations to a General Land Office patent should also include the land office (the regional jurisdiction, expressed as City, State) through which the entry was processed. However, some lands were distributed through programs that do not carry a city/state land-office name. The Ohio example below illustrates this situation, using a United Brethren Warrant issued within the district called the U.S. Military Survey.

- *Title:* Each state CD carries a distinctive title because content varies. Not all state CDs deal with the same records. When you use multiple CDs from this series, you should not automatically assign the same subtitle to every state CD.

CD/DVD Databases (General Land Office)

Source List Entry
Bureau of Land Management. *Ohio: Homesteads, Cash Entry Patents, Virginia Military Warrants, Canadian Refugee and United Brethren Patents from 1790 to 1907.* CD-ROM. Springfield, Virginia: General Land Office Automated Records Project, 1996.

First Reference Note
1. Bureau of Land Management, *Ohio: Homesteads, Cash Entry Patents, Virginia Military Warrants, Canadian Refugee and United Brethren Patents from 1790 to 1907,* CD-ROM (Springfield, Virginia: General Land Office Automated Records Project, 1996), database entry for Frederick Shick, U.S. Military Survey: United Brethren Warrant, image name [patent no.] 23990.

Subsequent Note
11. Bureau of Land Management, *Ohio ... 1790–1907,* database entry for Frederick Shick, U.S. Military Survey: United Brethren Warrant, image name [patent] no. 23990.

This CD-ROM series can also be consulted at the Family History Library, where it carries an FHL catalog number. You may wish to include that FHL number in your working notes, but you should still fully identify the CD-ROM by its original publication data.

CD-ROM Databases (GLO Publication, FHL Copy)

Source List Entry
Bureau of Land Management. *Minnesota, 1820–1908: Cash and Homestead Entries.* CD-ROM. Springfield, Virginia: General Land Office Automated Records Project, 1995. FHL CD-ROM 39. Family History Library, Salt Lake City, Utah.

First Reference Note
1. Bureau of Land Management, *Minnesota, 1820–1908: Cash and Homestead Entries,* CD-ROM (Springfield, Virginia: General Land Office Automated Records Project, 1995), database entry for Adelbert L. Warren, Cass Lake land office, certificate no. 181; FHL CD-ROM 39.

Subsequent Note
11. Bureau of Land Management, *Minnesota, 1820–1908,* database entry for Adelbert L. Warren, Cass Lake land office, certificate no. 181. See also 11.27 for online databases based on this CD-ROM series.

11.26 Land Office Records: Microfilm

When you cite land records filmed from National Archives holdings, you will typically cite one of three types:

- Film published by NARA;
- FHL copies of film made by NARA;
- Film made for preservation, usually by a regional facility.

The first two types are modeled below. For the regional film, see 11.9.

Microfilm (NARA)

Source List Entry
Letters Sent by the Surveyor General of the Territory Northwest of the Ohio River, 1797–1854. Microfilm publication M477, 10 rolls. Washington, D.C.: National Archives and Records Service, 1963.

First Reference Note
1. *Letters Sent by the Surveyor General of the Territory Northwest of the Ohio River, 1797–1854,* microfilm publication M477 (Washington, D.C.: National Archives and Records Service, 1963), roll 1, frames 71–73, Jared Mansfield to Albert Gallatin, 10 February 1806.

Subsequent Note
11. *Letters Sent by the Surveyor General of the Territory Northwest of the Ohio River, 1797–1854,* NARA M477, roll 1, frames 71–73.

Microfilm (NARA Film, FHL Copy)

Source List Entry
Records of the Bureau of Land Management, Prescott General Land Office, 1871–1908. Microfilm publication M1629, 16 rolls. Washington, D.C.: National Archives and Records Administration, 1989. FHL microfilm 1,639,158. Family History Library, Salt Lake City, Utah.

First Reference Note
1. *Records of the Bureau of Land Management, Prescott General Land Office, 1871–1908,* microfilm publication M1629, 16 rolls (Washington, D.C.: National Archives and Records Administration, 1989), roll 14 for "Abstracts of Valentine Scripp," p. 14, statement no. 17, filed 13 April 1905 by Dick Wick Hall, certificate no. 213; consulted as FHL microfilm 1,639,158.

Subsequent Note
11. *Records of the Bureau of Land Management, Prescott General Land Office, 1871–1908,* NARA M1629, roll 14, "Abstracts of Valentine Scripp," p. 14, statement no. 17, Dick Wick Hall.

CITING FRAME NUMBERS

For the *Prescott General Land Office* papers, the microfilm does not show frame numbers. Therefore, none could be cited. For the *Letters Sent*, frame numbers do appear. Therefore, frame numbers are cited to help relocate the material.

11.27 Land Office Records: Online Materials

The standard source for accessing land patents online is presently the database offered by the Bureau of Land Management, with links to image copies of the patents. For your Source List, you may create a single entry that generically covers both the database and images. For your Reference Notes, you will want to distinguish between the two, as demonstrated below.

Online Database & Images (BLM)

Source List Entry

Bureau of Land Management. "Land Patent Search." Database and images. *General Land Office Records.* http://www.glorecords.blm .gov/PatentSearch : 2007.

First Reference Note

(*To cite the database*)

1. Bureau of Land Management, "Land Patent Search," database, *General Land Office Records* (http://www.glorecords.blm.gov/Patent Search : accessed 2 February 2007), entry for George W. Day, Platte County, Wyoming, no. 644032.

(*To cite the image, with emphasis on the website*)

2. Bureau of Land Management, "Land Patent Search," digital images, *General Land Office Records* (http://www.glorecords.blm.gov/ PatentSearch : accessed 2 February 2007), George W. Day (Platte County, Wyoming), homestead patent no. 644032.

(*Or, to cite the image, with emphasize on the original document*)

2. George W. Day (Platte County, Wyoming), homestead patent no. 644032; "Land Patent Search," digital images, *General Land Office Records* (http://www.glorecords.blm.gov/PatentSearch : accessed 2 February 2007).

Subsequent Note

11. Bureau of Land Management, "Land Patent Search," database, *General Land Office Records,* entry for George W. Day, Platte Co., Wyo., no. 644032.

12. George W. Day (Platte Co., Wyo.), homestead patent no. 644032.

The Bureau of Land Management's Automated Records Project, covered at 11.25, is also available online through a subscription site, in which case your citation will differ significantly from the CD-ROM citation. The following example uses the Minnesota example cited at 11.25 to demonstrate the differences.

Online Database (Commercial)

Source List Entry
"Minnesota Land Records." Database. *Ancestry.com.* http://www .ancestry.com : 2007.

First Reference Note
1. "Minnesota Land Records," database, *Ancestry.com* (http:// www.ancestry.com : accessed 1 February 2007), entry for Adelbert L. Warren, Cass Lake land office, doc. no. 181; citing *Minnesota Pre-1908 Homestead and Cash Entry Patents,* General Land Office Automated Records Project, 1995.

Subsequent Note
1. "Minnesota Land Records," database entry for Adelbert L. Warren, Cass Lake land office, doc. no. 181.

CITING COUNTY LOCATION
The sample citation for George Day's entry at the BLM website, above, and the samples for Land Entry Files: Manuscripts at 11.23 all cite the county location to help distinguish between same-name individuals. The above example for the Warren entry in the *Ancestry.com* database does not include the county location because the database does not give it.

11.28 Special Land Files: Bounty Land Records
From the close of the Revolution through 1855, many veterans and their widows, as well as some civilians, qualified for bounty land from the public domain. Case files typically include the application and records submitted to prove service. Many of the files are organized not just by war but also by the year of the act under which the veteran qualified for bounty land.

For some wars, the number provided on the file jacket is a code that indicates whether the application was approved, how many acres a successful applicant was granted, and the year of the Congressional act under which the claim was submitted. (Example: File 12345-5580, signifying the act of 1855 under which applicant number 12345 received 80 acres.)

However, that coded number does not appear on every jacket or every bounty land document, as illustrated by the two models below. Also, a veteran or widow may have qualified for land under multiple acts, in which case documents from earlier applications may be folded into later applications bearing later numbers. Moreover, applications dealing with Revolutionary War and War of 1812 service have been removed from the General Land Office records (RG 49) and interfiled with pension cases in Veterans Affairs (RG 15).

All things considered, it is essential that a bounty-land citation include not only the applicant's file number, but also the veteran's military unit and rank, as well as the war and the specific record group. If the file jacket states the *year of the legislative act,* that year should be noted after the warrant number.

Typical citations would be as follows:

Source List Entry

Military Bounty Land Warrants and Related Papers. Records of the Bureau of Land Management, Record Group 49. National Archives, Washington, D.C.

Pension and Bounty Land Application Files Based on Service between 1812 and 1855. Department of Veterans Affairs, Record Group 15. National Archives, Washington, D.C.

First Reference Note

(*To cite an entire file*)

1. Stephen Nolen (Pvt., Boyd's Ala. Volunteers, Creek War 1837), bounty land warrant file 8594 (Act of 1850); Military Bounty Land Warrants and Related Papers; Records of the Bureau of Land Management, Record Group 49; National Archives, Washington, D.C.

(*To cite one document from the file*)

2. Power of attorney to James W. Lansing of Albany, New York, 3 August 1815; James Ball (Sgt., Danver's Co., 29th Inf. Regt., War of 1812), bounty land warrant file 1115; Case Files of Pension and Bounty Land Applications Based on Service between 1812 and 1855; Pension and Bounty Land Warrant Application Files, 1800–1960; Department of Veterans Affairs, Record Group 15; National Archives, Washington, D.C.

Subsequent Note

11. Stephen Nolen Creek War bounty land warrant file 8594 (Act of 1850), RG 49, NA–Washington.

12. Power of attorney to Lansing, 1815; James Ball, War of 1812 bounty land warrant file 1115; RG 15, NA–Washington.

11.29 Special Land Files: Private Land Claims

At the close of the American Revolution, the United States claimed all lands to the west of it that were not already claimed by one of the original states or occupied by France or Spain. As the U.S. eventually acquired the French and Spanish domains, the General Land Office faced a problem. Thousands of settlers already held titles by grant from the French, Spanish, or British Crown, or they claimed land by right of occupation.

The body of paperwork created in the settlement of those preexisting titles and claims is known as *private land claims,* materials primarily held by the National Archives. The files are arranged by state, thereunder by docket number. Your citation should include both pieces of information, as well as the name of the claimant.

Source List Entry
Private Land Claim Files, 1789–1908. Records of the Bureau of Land
  Management, Record Group 49. National Archives, Washington, D.C.

First Reference Note
    1. Survey of 24 March 1804, William Hunt claim, Alabama no. 381;
Private Land Claim Files, 1789–1908; Records of the Bureau of Land
Management, Record Group 49; National Archives, Washington, D.C.

Subsequent Note
    11. Survey of 24 March 1804, William Hunt claim, Alabama, 381,
Private Land Claim Files, RG 49, NA–Washington.

11.30 Special Land Files: Survey Plat Maps

For every township of the public domain, surveyors created a plat map after all the land was surveyed and titles were settled within the bounds of that township. In areas that were settled prior to the U.S. surveys (see 11.29), those plat maps show the exact bounds of each settler's approved lands, making them valuable research tools for reconstructing neighborhoods. When citing such a map, you may want to include in your citation the names of the specific parties of interest, as well as their legal land description(s).

If you consulted a printed or photostatic copy at a library, be certain to cite the exact title of the map and whatever date it carries. Across time, there have been multiple surveys of all townships and ranges.

Source List Entry
(*To cite a T-R plat obtained from the Bureau of Land Management*)
General Land Office. Township-Range Survey Plats: Louisiana. Bureau
  of Land Management–Eastern States Office, Springfield, Virginia.

(To cite a T-R plat map from an archive or library)
General Land Office. Township-Range Maps Collection. Hoole Library, University of Alabama, Tuscaloosa.

First Reference Note

(To cite a T-R plat obtained from the Bureau of Land Management)
    1. General Land Office, Township-Range Survey Plat: Township 6 North, Range 4 West, Northwestern District of Louisiana, 1848; Bureau of Land Management–Eastern States Office, Springfield, Virginia.

(To cite a T-R plat map from an archive or library)
    2. General Land Office, "Alabama N & E, St. Stephens' Meridian, Part of T^P 1 North, Range 1 East, Land District: St. Stephens, Ala.," 1839 plat map; item no. 1993, Township-Range Maps Collection; Hoole Library, University of Alabama, Tuscaloosa.

Subsequent Note

    11. General Land Office, Township-Range Survey Plat: T6N, R4W, NW District of Louisiana, 1848.
    12. General Land Office, "Alabama N & E, St. Stephens' Meridian, Part of T^P 1 North, Range 1 East ... St. Stephens, Ala.," 1839.

CITING TOWNSHIP & RANGE

As a rule, the Bureau of Land Management and its predecessor, the General Land Office, have surveyed only the thirty states that are part of the public domain. For those states you would identify a plat by township, range, land office district, and state. The remaining states are not part of the public domain and (a few tracts excepted) have not been surveyed by the federal government. Where the BLM website offers plats of federal sites in non-BLM states, as with Cape Hatteras at note 3, below, you will usually have no township and range to cite.

Online Images

Digital images of many original survey plats, as well as modern supplements and some special plats from states that are not part of the public domain, are available at the Bureau of Land Management's website. When using a plat from this source, your citation should include the *type* of plat, as illustrated below with an "Original Survey," a "Townsite Survey," and a "Dependent Resurvey."

Source List Entry

Bureau of Land Management. "Survey Search." Database and images. *General Land Office Records.* http://www.glorecords .blm.gov/PatentSearch : 2007.

First Reference Note

(*To cite the database*)
1. Bureau of Land Management, "Survey Search," database, *General Land Office Records* (http://www.glorecords.blm.gov/PatentSearch : accessed 1 February 2007), entry for Original Survey DM ID 34041 (1874), Township 5N, Range 10W, Caddo County, Oklahoma.

(*To cite the plat-map image, with emphasis on the website*)
2. Bureau of Land Management, "Survey Search," digital images, *General Land Office Records* (http://www.glorecords.blm.gov/PatentSearch : accessed 1 February 2007), Dependent Resurvey DM 71756 (1978), Cape Hatteras National Seashore, Wake County, North Carolina.

(*To cite the plat-map image, with emphasis on the document*)
3. Townsite Survey DM 37964 (1909), Township 44 N, Range 5W (town of Desmet), Benewah County, Idaho; Bureau of Land Management, "Survey Search," digital images, *General Land Office Records* (http://www.glorecords.blm.gov/Patent Search : accessed 1 February 2007).

(*To cite the plat-map image, with specific reference to landowner*)
4. Rhoda Stanly, section 77; Original Survey DM 74165, ca. 1820 [date torn away], Township 7N, Range 1W, Adams County, Mississippi; Bureau of Land Management, "Survey Search," digital images, *General Land Office Records* (http://www.glorecords.blm.gov/Patent Search : accessed 1 February 2007).

Subsequent Note
11. Bureau of Land Management, "Survey Search," Original Survey DM ID 34041 (1874), T5N, R10W, Caddo Co., Okla.
12. Dependent Resurvey DM 71756 (1978), Cape Hatteras National Seashore, Wake Co., N.C.
13. Townsite Survey DM 37964 (1909), Township 44N, Range 5W (town of Desmet), Benewah Co., Idaho.
14. Rhoda Stanly, section 77; Original Survey DM 74165, ca. 1820 [date torn away], Township 7N, Range 1W, Adams Co., Miss.

CITING LAND DESCRIPTIONS
Survey maps for areas settled prior to U.S. acquisition of the land will show irregularly shaped parcels with section numbers that often exceed the customary thirty-six sections per township. Note 4, above, is a case at point.

11.31 Special Land Files: Tract Books
Chapter 9 introduced tract books held at the local and state levels. These registers, arranged by legal land description, record each piece

of land within their bounds, together with details such as when it was patented, to whom, and under what laws the land was acquired.

Tract books were also created at the federal level by the General Land Office. These volumes are *not organized by county.* Rather, they are arranged by state and thereunder by the name of the district land office. Within each district, registers are set up by township and range.

The land office identity is a vital piece of information that you will need to extract from records you use elsewhere (deeds, mortgages, tax rolls, etc.), and it must be included in your citations to federal tract books. Because many purchasers of the public land obtained multiple tracts, your citation also needs to identify the specific entry by township, range, section, and fractional section. Even though tract book entries carry a certificate number, the book is *arranged by that land description,* not by any entry number.

The standard source for federal-level microfilm is the 1957 film series of the Bureau of Land Management, which covers all thirty of the public land states. The examples below demonstrate a basic citation to the series and an expanded citation for the FHL film copy. Two quirks should be noted here:

- *BLM film:* The title, *Records Improvement,* is not self-explanatory. Thus, it is appropriate to add further identification in square editorial brackets, as in note 1. Do not italicize the addition; your words are not part of the official title of the published film.

- *FHL copy of the BLM film:* FHL catalogs this film by record type ("U.S. Tract Book") not by the name of the film publication. Nonetheless, the film was still produced by BLM and you are citing the BLM film, regardless of where you used it. To clarify the vague BLM title, you may add FHL's alternate identity in square editorial brackets, as in note 2 below.

Microfilm Publications (BLM Film & FHL Copy)

Source List Entry

Bureau of Land Management. *Records Improvement* [U.S. Tract Books]. Microfilm, 1,265 rolls. Washington, D.C.: BLM, 1957.

(Or, for FHL copy)

Bureau of Land Management. *Records Improvement* [U.S. Tract Books]. Microfilm, 1,265 rolls. Washington, D.C.: Department of the Interior, 1957. FHL microfilm 1,445,686, Family History Library, Salt Lake City, Utah.

First Reference Note
    1. Bureau of Land Management, *Records Improvement* [U.S. Tract Books], microfilm, 1,265 rolls (Washington, D.C.: Department of the Interior, 1957), Mississippi roll 10, Jackson Land Office, volume M2, page 24, cancelled entry for Sarah Prentiss, 1896, SE¼ of NE¼, Section 11, Township 3N, Range 7W, certificate of purchase no. 30743.

(Or, for FHL copy)
    1. Bureau of Land Management, *Records Improvement* [U.S. Tract Books], microfilm, 1,265 rolls (Washington, D.C.: Department of the Interior, 1957), Mississippi roll 10, Jackson Land Office, vol. M2, p. 24, cancelled entry for Sarah Prentiss, 19 October 1896, SE¼ of NE¼, Section 11, Township 3N, Range 7W, certificate of purchase no. 30743; FHL microfilm 1,445,686.

Subsequent Note
    11. Bureau of Land Management, *Records Improvement* [U.S. Tract Books], Miss. roll 10, Jackson Land Office, vol. M2: 24, Sarah Prentiss, SE¼ of NE¼, S11, T3N, R7W.

MILITARY & PENSION RECORDS

11.32 Military: Compiled Service Records

To research soldiers in a particular war, researchers frequently begin with carded records maintained by the National Archives. As their name implies, these Compiled Military Service Records (CMSR) abstract the service of each *volunteer* soldier, drawing from a number of record series. Comparable carded records do not exist for regular military personnel. Some of the carded records have been microfilmed. Some are being abstracted into online databases. The examples in this section cover all three categories, across a variety of wars.

In creating your own citations, note especially the following:

SOURCE LIST ENTRY
The series name for these cards typically begins with the phrase "Carded Records, Volunteer Organizations ...." You may use that formal title of the series in your Source List Entry if you wish. Many researchers, however, prefer to alphabetize the entry under a more intuitive generic label prefaced by the word "Military" or by the name of the war. The following examples use the inverted phrase "Military, Compiled Service Records," followed by the name of the conflict.

REFERENCE NOTES
When citing military records at the federal level, you typically need to identify the soldier by rank, unit, and war or time frame (as applicable), as well as by personal name.

Source List Entry

Military, Compiled Service Records. Civil War. Carded Records, Volunteer Organizations. Records of the Adjutant General's Office, 1780s–1917, Record Group 94. National Archives, Washington, D.C.

Military, Compiled Service Records. "Indian Wars," 1817–58. Carded Records, Volunteer Organizations. Records of the Adjutant General's Office, 1780s–1917, Record Group 94. National Archives, Washington, D.C.

First Reference Note

    1. Compiled service record, David Kiepler, Pvt., Co. C, 131 New York Inf.; Carded Records, Volunteer Organizations, Civil War; Records of the Adjutant General's Office, 1780s–1917, Record Group 94; National Archives, Washington, D.C.

    2. Compiled service record, Henry Jethcoate, Pvt., McDugald's Co., Alabama Militia Regt., Creek War; Carded Records, Volunteer Organizations, "Indian Wars," 1817–58; Records of the Adjutant General's Office, 1780s–1917, Record Group 94; National Archives, Washington, D.C.

Subsequent Note

    11. Compiled military service record, David Kiepler, Pvt., Co. C, 131 N.Y. Inf., Civil War, RG 94, NA–Washington.

    12. Compiled service record, Henry Jethcoate, Pvt., McDugald's Co., Ala. Mil. Reg't, Creek War, RG 94, NA–Washington.

CITING "INDIAN WARS" RECORDS

Records of some conflicts involving Native Americans have been consolidated by time frame at NARA—as with the Jethcoate example above. The series "Indian Wars" covers assorted actions across the frontier. When citing this series, you also need to cite the particular conflict the soldier served in—e.g., Black Hawk War, Creek War, etc.

Note above, that the RG 94 series title places "Indian Wars" in quotation marks, in the *so-called* sense, because there was no one conflict called "Indian Wars." However, in the 11.40 "Indian Wars" example, the title to the series in RG 15 does not place quotation marks around the phrase *Indian Wars*. It is best to copy series and collection titles exactly, even when they appear to be inconsistent—especially as databases become increasingly common. Not copying a title precisely can stymie a new search for that record.

Microfilm (NARA)

Source List Entry

Index to Compiled Service Records of Volunteer Soldiers Who Served from 1784 to 1811. Microfilm publication M694, 9 rolls. Washington, D.C.: National Archives and Records Service, 1967.

Index to Compiled Service Records of Volunteer Soldiers Who Served during the War of 1812. Microfilm publication M602, 234 rolls. Washington, D.C.: National Archives and Records Service, 1966.

First Reference Note

1. *Index to Compiled Service Records of Volunteer Soldiers Who Served from 1784 to 1811,* microfilm publication M694, 9 rolls (Washington, D.C.: National Archives and Records Service, 1967), roll 5, index card for Michael Hockersmith, Pvt., Huston's Battalion, Kentucky Mounted Volunteers, 1794.

2. *Index to Compiled Service Records of Volunteer Soldiers Who Served during the War of 1812,* microfilm publication M602, 234 rolls (Washington, D.C.: National Archives and Records Service, 1966), roll 21, index card for John Boyd, Pvt., Russell's Separate Battalion, Tennessee Mounted Gunmen.

Subsequent Note

11. *Index to Compiled Service Records of Volunteer Soldiers Who Served from 1784 to 1811,* NARA M694, roll 5, index card for Michael Hockersmith, Pvt., Huston's Battn., Ky. Mtd. Vols., 1794.

12. *Index to Compiled Service Records of Volunteer Soldiers Who Served during the War of 1812,* NARA M602, roll 21, index card for John Boyd, Pvt., Russell's Separate Battn., Tenn. Mtd. Gunmen.

Online Databases & Indexes

Source List Entry

National Park Service. *Civil War Soldiers & Sailors System.* http://www.itd.nps.gov/cwss/ : 2007.

"Records of World War II Prisoners of War, Created 1942–1947, Documenting the Period 12/7/1941–11/19/1946." Database. *The National Archives.* http://www.archives.gov/aad/ : 2007.

First Reference Note

(*Civil War Service Database*)

1. National Park Service, "Soldiers," database, *Civil War Soldiers & Sailors System* (http://www.itd.nps.gov/cwss/ : accessed 1 February 2007), entry for Joseph Chess, Pvt., Co. 4, 28th Iowa Inf., Union.

(*Civil War Medals of Honor Database*)

2. National Park Service, "Medals of Honor," database, *Civil War Soldiers & Sailors System* (http://www.itd.nps.gov/cwss/Medal.cfm : accessed 1 February 2007), entry for Joseph S. Smith, Lt. Col., 2nd Army Corps, Union.

(*WW II POW Database*)

3. "Records of World War II Prisoners of War, Created 1942–1947, Documenting the Period 12/7/1941–11/19/1946," database, *The*

National Archives (http://www.archives.gov/aad/ : accessed 16 March 2006), entry for Edmond L. Rachal, Army serial number 38385568.

Subsequent Note
   11. National Park Service, *Civil War Soldiers & Sailors System,* service database entry for Joseph Chess, Pvt., Co. 4, 28th Iowa Inf., Union.
   12. National Park Service, *Civil War Soldiers & Sailors System,* Medals of Honor database entry for Joseph S. Smith, Lt. Col., 2nd Army Corps, Union.
   13. "Records of World War II Prisoners of War," database, *The National Archives,* entry for Edmond L. Rachal, Army serial no. 38385568.

CITING AGENCIES AS AUTHORS
NARA's website carries the agency name as the website name. You do not need to repeat it in the author field, although you may, if you wish. In contrast, the name of the website *Civil War Soldiers & Sailors System* does not identify its creator. Therefore, the author field needs to identify the agency that created the website and its databases.

11.33 Military: Draft Registrations
Registration cards completed by draft-age males during World Wars I and II are usually consulted as NARA microfilm (which can be cited by the Basic Format at 11.8) or by online database and image copies. A typical citation to an online image would be this:

Online Databases & Images

Source List Entry
"World War I Draft Registration Cards, 1917–1918." Database and
   images. *Ancestry.com.* http://www.ancestry.com : 2007.

First Reference Note
   1. "World War I Draft Registration Cards, 1917–1918," digital images, *Ancestry.com* (http://www.ancestry.com : accessed 1 February 2007), Christopher Ferraci, serial no. 1251, order no. 367, Draft Board 7, Rochester, Monroe County, New York; citing *World War I Selective Service System Draft Registration Cards, 1917–1918,* NARA microfilm publication M1509; no specific roll cited.

Subsequent Note
   11. World War I draft registration card for Christopher Ferraci, serial no. 1251, order no. 367, Draft Board 7, Rochester, Monroe County, New York.

CITING DRAFT CARD NUMBER
Whether or not you need to cite a draft card number would depend

upon how common the name might be and whether you are dealing with a rural or urban area. Ferraci, in the entry above, was the only individual of that name in his draft board district; an identification number is not really essential in his case. Had his name been more common, a card number *would* have been essential to distinguish him from others of the same name. When choosing a number to cite, you may choose either the serial number (at top left of card) or the order number (at top right of card). Frequently, one or the other number is illegible. On many of the cards, these two numbers appear but are not labeled.

11.34 Military: Employees, Civilian

Civilians employed by U.S. military forces are not covered by the carded records at 11.32 or the military databases cited at 11.33. By and large, your citations to civilian employees will be to original registers or files. As shown below, these easily fit into Basic Format for National Archives manuscripts (11.7).

Source List Entry
"Wagonmasters and Forage Masters Serving during the Civil War." Claims 1839–1914. Records of the Office of the Quartermaster General, Record Group 92. National Archives, Washington, D.C.

First Reference Note
1. William Bloomer entry, "List of Wagonmasters and Forage Masters Serving during the Civil War"; Claims 1839–1914; Records of the Office of the Quartermaster General, Record Group 92; National Archives, Washington, D.C.

Subsequent Note
11. William Bloomer entry, "List of Wagonmasters and Forage Masters Serving during the Civil War," Claims 1839–1914, RG 92, NA–Washington.

11.35 Military: Enlistment Papers

Enlistment papers for Army *volunteers* who joined after about 1863 (but not *regular* military personnel) will usually be found in the Compiled Military Service Records. Therefore, those records are typically cited as a particular document from the soldier's carded records. Enlistment papers for regular Army personnel exist separately in two Enlistment Papers series. Typically, they include a variety of materials, often beginning with the prospective soldier's medical examination that is used in the model below, and may include several types of enlistments for the same soldier—a substitute enlistment, a volunteer enlistment, etc. In citing any enlistment paper, you should identify its type as specifically as possible.

As noted at 11.32, when citing documents from the Compiled Military Service Records maintained for *volunteers,* you would cite the serviceman by rank and unit. However, when using enlistment papers for members of the *regular* army, as with the examples below, rank and unit data will often not be found on the record. In those cases, you would want to note the place of enlistment, the attesting officer, and officer's unit.

Source List Entry

Enlistment Papers, 1798 to October 31, 1912. Records of the Adjutant General's Office, 1780s–1917, RG 94. National Archives, Washington, D.C.

First Reference Note

1. Joseph Davis, Medical Examination of Recruits, 31 May 1848, Lexington, Kentucky, attested by Capt. R. A. Arnold, 2nd U.S. Dragoons; File No. 2 (113); Enlistment Papers, 1798 to October 31, 1912; Records of the Adjutant General's Office, 1780s–1917, Record Group 94; National Archives, Washington, D.C.

Subsequent Note

11. Joseph Davis, Medical Examination of Recruits, 31 May 1848, Lexington, Kentucky, File No. 2 (113); Enlistment Papers, 1798 to October 31, 1912; RG 94, NA–Washington.

Microfilm (NARA)

Source List Entry

Registers of Enlistments in the United States Army, 1798–1914. Microfilm publication M233, 81 rolls. Washington, D.C.: National Archives and Records Service, 1956.

First Reference Note

1. *Registers of Enlistments in the United States Army, 1798–1914,* microfilm publication M233, 81 rolls (Washington, D.C.: National Archives and Records Service, 1956), roll 13, vol. 26, p. 123, entry no. 3951, Samuel Witter, Pvt., 17th U.S. Inf., enlisted 181_ [illegible].

Subsequent Note

11. *Registers of Enlistments in the United States Army, 1798–1914,* NARA M233, roll 13, vol. 26: 123, Samuel Witter, Pvt., 17th U.S. Inf., enlisted 181_ [illegible].

11.36 Military: Headstone & Burial Records

Applications by veterans for a military headstone can follow the Basic Format for National Archives manuscripts (11.7). The examples below demonstrate the differences between citing the original files *vis a vis* the online database that covers some veterans' graves.

Source List Entry
Headstone Applications, 1909–1962. Memorial Division. Records of the Quartermaster General's Office, Record Group 92. National Archives, Washington, D.C.

First Reference Note
1. Application for Headstone for Robert Morton alias Tapp, 17 October 1909; Headstone Applications, 1909–1962, Memorial Division; Records of the Quartermaster General's Office, Record Group 92; National Archives, Washington, D.C.

Subsequent Note
11. Application for Headstone for Robert Morton alias Tapp, 17 October 1909, Headstone Applications, RG 92, NA–Washington.

Online Databases & Indexes

Source List Entry
Department of Veterans Affairs, "Nationwide Gravesite Locator." Database. *Burial & Memorial Benefits.* http://gravelocator.cem.va.gov : 2007.

First Reference Note
1. Department of Veterans Affairs, "Nationwide Gravesite Locator," database, *Burial & Memorial Benefits* (http://grave locator.cem.va.gov : accessed 2 February 2007), entry for Willie A. Metoyer (1895–1963), Golden Gate National Cemetery, San Bruno, California.

Subsequent Note
11. Dept. of Veterans Affairs, "Nationwide Gravesite Locator," database, *Burial & Memorial Benefits,* entry for Willie A. Metoyer (1895–1963).

IDENTIFICATION OF PRINCIPAL PARTY
When working with a nationwide database, you might find many same-name individuals with similar personal detail. To ensure that the correct entry is flagged, you will likely have to include some of that personal detail in your citation. The above example adds the years of birth and death and the place of burial.

11.37 Military: Imprisonments

Manuscript records for imprisonments within the military system can be cited in Basic Format for National Archives manuscripts (11.7). An online database to Fort Leavenworth inmates is also offered by NA–Central Plains. In citing this database, note that the website is not *The National Archives,* as with other examples in this chapter. Each regional archive hosts its own website.

Online Databases & Indexes

Source List Entry

"Name Index to Inmate Case Files, U.S. Penitentiary, Leavenworth, Kansas, 1895–1931." Database. *National Archives in the Central Plains.* http://www.archives.gov/central-plains/ : 2007.

First Reference Note

1. "Name Index to Inmate Case Files, U.S. Penitentiary, Leavenworth, Kansas, 1895–1931," database, *National Archives in the Central Plains* (http://www.archives.gov/central-plains/ : accessed 7 February 2007), entry for Charles Quagon, inmate 7733.

Subsequent Note

11. "Name Index to Inmate Case Files, U.S. Penitentiary, Leavenworth, Kansas, 1895–1931," database entry for Charles Quagon, inmate 7733.

11.38 Military: Muster Rolls

NARA's muster rolls for regular military units are typically grouped by time frame and thereunder by arm of service. For volunteer units, they are commonly arranged by war (or time-frame) and state. Beyond that, they are filed numerically by regiment, then alphabetically or numerically by company or troop, and then chronologically. Your citation to any muster roll needs to include all these details.

In the example below, the citation is to the roll itself, not to any particular individual on the roll. If you wish to cite an individual, put that name at the start of the First Reference Note, to conform to the smallest-to-largest pattern for elements in a Reference Note citation of a manuscript.

Source List Entry

Muster Rolls of Regular Army Organizations, 1784–1912. Records of the Adjutant General's Office, 1780s–1917, Record Group 94. National Archives, Washington, D.C.

First Reference Note
1.   Muster rolls of Co. C, 8th Infantry, 19 February–30 June 1856; Inspection Returns, 1821–1860, Recruits, Fort Columbus, New York; Muster Rolls of Regular Army Organizations, 1784–1912; Records of the Adjutant General's Office, 1780s–1917, Record Group 94; National Archives, Washington, D.C.

Subsequent Note
11. Muster rolls of Co. C, 8th Inf., 19 February–30 June 1856, Regular Army Organizations, 1784–1912, RG 94, NA–Washington.

11.39 Military: Navy & Other Branches

Military records created by the U.S. Navy and other military branches can be cited by the same models used for Army records under 11.32–11.38. Several of the databases covered there include personnel from all the services. Manuscript materials follow the Basic Format for National Archives manuscripts (11.7), as illustrated with this example:

Source List Entry
Naval Apprentices, 1838–40. Bureau of Naval Personnel, Record Group 24. National Archives, Washington, D.C.

First Reference Note
1.   George H. Duren apprenticeship, parental certificate of consent, 3 September 1838; Naval Apprentices, 1838–40; Bureau of Naval Personnel, Record Group 24; National Archives, Washington, D.C.

Subsequent Note
11. George H. Duren apprenticeship, parental certificate, 1838, Naval Apprentices, RG 24, NA–Washington.

11.40 Pension Files

The essential details for pension files are much the same as those for bounty land records (11.28). When you cite a pension file's number, you should include the letters that preface the number (S.C., W.C., Inv., etc.). These designate the type of file—Soldiers' Certificate, Widows' Certificate, Invalid (i.e., disabled), etc.

When citing a pension for a *widow* or the *eligible children* of a deceased veteran, your citation to their file must also fully identify the *veteran* by service name and unit. Even though the files carry separate numbers and are bundled in separate envelopes, they share a common jacket that carries the veteran's identity. When the veteran or the widow submit multiple applications—say, first under one act and then under another—you will again have multiple, but still separate, files and file numbers within a common jacket. The key exception to the rule that all files are jacketed with the veteran is the case of eligible children of veterans whose mothers have remarried a man who is also a pensioner; in those cases, the children's file may be jacketed with the stepfather.

The following examples cover typical citations to

- Civil War veterans (Union Army);
- Indian Wars pensioners;
- widows and remarried widows;
- rejected applicants;
- microfilmed pension indexes; and
- online databases.

Source List Entry

Civil War and Later Pension Files. Department of Veterans Affairs, Record Group 15. National Archives, Washington, D.C.

Indian Wars, Case Files of Rejected Pension Applications. Records of the Bureau of Pensions and Its Predecessors, 1805–1935. Department of Veterans Affairs, Record Group 15. National Archives, Washington, D.C.

First Reference Note

(Civil War veteran)

1. John W. Witters (Pvt., Co. E, 154th Ill. Inf., Civil War), pension no. S.C. 283,321, Case Files of Approved Pension Applications ..., 1861–1934; Civil War and Later Pension Files; Department of Veterans Affairs, Record Group 15; National Archives, Washington, D.C.

(Civil War widow, approved application)

2. Deposition of Claimant, 16 May 1902, Mary Scoville, widow's pension application no. 748,632, certificate no. 543,796; service of Frank Scoville (Pvt., Co. M, 22nd N.Y. Vol. Cav., Civil War); Case Files of Approved Pension Applications ..., 1861–1934; Civil War and Later Pension Files; Department of Veterans Affairs, Record Group 15; National Archives, Washington, D.C.

(Indian Wars widow, rejected application)

3. Mary A. Morse, widow's pension application no. 2156 (Rejected), for service of Daniel Morse (Pvt., Capt. H. P. Hill's Co., Ga. Vols., 1836); Case Files of Rejected Pension Applications, Indian Wars; Records of the Bureau of Pensions and Its Predecessors, 1805–1935; Department of Veterans Affairs, Record Group 15; National Archives, Washington, D.C.

Subsequent Note

11. John W. Witters Civil War pension no. S.C. 283,321, RG 15, NA–Washington.

12. Deposition of Claimant, Mary Scoville, widow's pension no. 748,632, Civil War, RG 15, NA–Washington.

13. Mary A. Morse, widow's pension application no. 2156 (Rejected), Indian Wars, RG 15, NA–Washington.

Microfilm (NARA)

Source List Entry

Index to Pension Application Files of Remarried Widows Based on Service in the Civil War and Later Wars and in the Regular Army after the Civil War. Microfilm publication M1785, 7 rolls. Washington, D.C.: National Archives and Records Administration, 1993.

First Reference Note

1. *Index to Pension Application Files of Remarried Widows Based on Service in the Civil War and Later Wars and in the Regular Army after the Civil War,* microfilm publication M1785, 7 rolls (Washington, D.C.: National Archives and Records Administration, 1993), roll 6, for Adelaide Shown, now Kocher, widow of John O. Shown, Co. K, 64th Ill. Inf.

Subsequent Note

11. *Index to Pension Application Files of Remarried Widows Based on Service in the Civil War and Later Wars,* NARA M1785, roll 6, for Adelaide Shown, now Kocher, widow of John O. Shown, Co. K, 64th Ill. Inf.

Online Databases & Images

Source List Entry

"Civil War Pension Index: General Index to Pension Files, 1861–1934." Database and images. *Ancestry.com.* http://www.ancestry.com : 2007.

First Reference Note

1. "Civil War Pension Index: General Index to Pension Files, 1861–1934," database, *Ancestry.com* (http://www.ancestry.com : accessed 1 February 2007), entry for John A. Shown and widow Adelaide, Montana.

2. "Civil War Pension Index: General Index to Pension Files, 1861–1934," digital images, *Ancestry.com* (http://www.ancestry.com : accessed 1 February 2007); John A. Shown (Co. K, 64th Ill. Inf.) index card; imaged from *General Index to Pension Files, 1861–1934,* T288 (Washington, D.C.: National Archives [n.d.]), no roll number cited.

Subsequent Note

11. "Civil War Pension Index: General Index to Pension Files,

1861–1934," database, *Ancestry.com*, entry for John A. Shown and widow Adelaide, Montana.

12. John A. Shown (Co. K, 64th Ill. Inf.) index card; "Civil War Pension Index: General Index to Pension Files, 1861–1934."

IDENTIFICATION OF SOLDIER
In the two examples above, the same soldier is identified differently because the two resources provide different details. The database supplies only the place from which the widow applied for her pension. The image copy of NARA's file card provides the soldier's company and rank data. Your citation should be to the data you actually find, although you may add any clarifications you feel are needed, so long as it is clear that the clarification comes from you and not the source.

MISCELLANEOUS U.S. RECORDS

11.41 Captured Confederate Records
Many records of the Confederate government that survived the Civil War are now held by the U.S. National Archives. Their materials can be cited in the Basic Format for National Archives manuscripts (11.7), as illustrated below.

Source List Entry
Register of Memorials and Petitions, 1861–65. Legislative Records. War Department Collection of Confederate Records, Record Group 109. National Archives, Washington, D.C.

First Reference Note
1. Memorial to the CSA Congress, pleading an exemption from combat duty for editors, 5 February 1864; Register of Memorials and Petitions, 1861–65; Legislative Records; War Department Collection of Confederate Records, Record Group 109; National Archives, Washington, D.C.

Subsequent Note
11. Memorial to the CSA Congress, pleading an exemption from combat duty for editors, 5 February 1864, Register of Memorials and Petitions, RG 109, NA–Washington.

11.42 Civil War Claims: International Commissions
America's conflict of 1861–65 caught many alien residents in the cross-fire economically and politically, even when they did not serve militarily. At the close of the war, the governments of Great Britain and France negotiated with the United States to create claims commissions through which their citizens could seek compensation for

property officially confiscated or destroyed by U.S. forces. The examples below treat these two particular commissions, but they can also be followed for similar commissions created after other conflicts.

Source List Entry
British and American Claims, Mixed Commission, 1871–1873. Case files. Records of Boundary and Claims Commissions and Arbitrations, Record Group 76. National Archives, College Park, Maryland.
French and American Claims Commission, 1880–1883. Case files. Records of Boundary and Claims Commissions and Arbitrations, Record Group 76. National Archives, College Park, Maryland.

First Reference Note
(To cite an entire case file)
1. Samuel Goodman Levey claim, no. 61, Mixed Commission of British and American Claims, 1871–1873, case files; Records of Boundary and Claims Commissions and Arbitrations, Record Group 76; National Archives, College Park, Maryland.

(To cite an individual document from a case file)
2. "Acte de Naissance, Louis Joseph Poète," in Pierre Poète claim, no. 399, French and American Claims Commission, 1880–1883, case files; Records of Boundary and Claims Commissions and Arbitrations, Record Group 76; National Archives, College Park, Maryland.

(To cite from a card index to claims)
3. Pierre Poète card, Index to Docketed French Claims, 1881, French and American Claims Commission; Boundary and Claims Commissions and Arbitrations, Record Group 76; National Archives, College Park, Maryland

Subsequent Note
11. Samuel Goodman Levey claim, no. 61, Mixed Commission of British and American Claims, case files, RG 76, NA–College Park.
12. "Acte de Naissance, Louis Joseph Poète, " Pierre Poète claim, no. 399, French and American Claims Commission, case files, RG 76, NA–College Park.
13. Pierre Poète card, Index to Docketed French Claims, 1881, French and American Claims Commission, RG 76, NA–College Park.

11.43 Civil War Claims: Southern Claims Commission
The case files for this claims commission well illustrate the complexities of citing bureaucratic records. The Commission, which operated between 1871 and 1880, created millions of documents in some 22,298 case files—in addition to its own administrative records.

Because the Commission operated under the Treasury Department, the *administrative* records are part of that department's Record Group

56. The *case files,* however, have been moved to other record groups. Their current location depends upon whether the individual case was allowed, barred (because it immediately failed to meet a requirement), or disallowed after considerable investigation. Among the disallowed cases, the file location then depends upon whether the claimant accepted the ruling or pursued the case to the U.S. Court of Claims. In brief, the differences in location and citation details are as follows:

Allowed case files—The allowed claims have been assigned to RG 217, which represents records created by the Third Auditor of the Treasury. The files are arranged by state, thereunder by county, and then alphabetically by the name of the claimant. Your First Reference Note should include all these elements.

Barred or disallowed cases, not appealed—These files are now held by the House of Representatives (RG 233), where the barred files are arranged alphabetically by the name of the claimant, and the disallowed files are arranged by office number and case number. When citing the disallowed files, you will have to include these numbers. However, both barred and disallowed cases have been microfiched; you will typically cite that media. State and county identification is not necessary, although you may include it for consistency, if you wish.

Barred or disallowed cases, appealed—These are now held within U.S. Court of Claims materials. See 11.45.

Source List Entry
Southern Claims Commission, 1871–1880, Allowed Case Files. Settled Accounts and Claims, Third Auditor. Records of the Treasury Department Accounting Officers, Record Group 217. National Archives, Washington, D.C.

Southern Claims Commission, 1871–1880. Barred and Disallowed Case Files. Records of the U.S. House of Representatives, Record Group 233. National Archives, Washington, D.C.

First Reference Note
(*Citing a particular document from the case file*)
1. Report of Enos Richardson, 1 March 1876; St. Ville St. André (Natchitoches Parish, Louisiana) claim, no. 18532, Allowed Case Files, Southern Claims Commission, 1871–1880; Settled Accounts and Claims, Third Auditor; Records of the Treasury Department Accounting Officers, Record Group 217; National Archives, Washington, D.C.

(*Citing an entire case file*)
2. Franklin Sessions claim, no. 5004, Barred and Disallowed Case Files, Southern Claims Commission, 1871–1880; Records of the U.S.

House of Representatives, Record Group 233; National Archives, Washington, D.C.

Subsequent Note
11. Report of Enos Richardson, 1 March 1876; St. Ville St. André claim, no. 18532 (allowed), Southern Claims Commission, RG 217, NA–Washington

12. Franklin Sessions claim, no. 5004, (barred/disallowed), Southern Claims Commission, RG 233, NA–Washington.

Microfiche (NARA)

Source List Entry
Barred and Disallowed Case Files of the Southern Claims Commission, 1871–1880. Microfiche publication M1407, 4,829 cards. Washington, D.C.: National Archives and Records Administration, 1987.

First Reference Note
1. *Barred and Disallowed Case Files of the Southern Claims Commission, 1871–1880,* microfiche publication M1407, 4,829 cards (Washington, D.C.: National Archives and Records Administration, 1987), fiche card 4345, Shandy Jones claim, no. 18680, for claimant's petition, 19 October 1871.

Subsequent Note
11. *Barred and Disallowed Case Files of the Southern Claims Commission, 1871–1880,* NARA M1407, fiche card 4345, Shandy Jones claim, no. 18680, for claimant's petition, 19 October 1871.

CITING A CLAIM'S LOCATION

At 11.29, Private Land Claims, you are instructed to include in your citation the state where the claim was centered, because those records are arranged by state. The Civil War claims cases covered at 11.42 and 11.43 are *not* arranged by state or county. Therefore, it is not necessary to include either in your Reference Note for a particular claim. Many researchers still wish to do so. The QuickCheck Model for MANU-SCRIPTS: NATIONAL ARCHIVES demonstrates how you could handle the inclusion of state and county identification in an SCC claims citation.

Online Images

Case files for the Southern Claims Commission are among the NARA records now offered online in digital format by private industry. If you consulted the online image copy of the approved claim file of St. Ville St. André (cited above), you have two style choices:

- *NARA Style:* Like most archives, NARA prefers that you cite its material in full, as though you consulted the original, regardless of the form in which you use it. This may or may not be possible for digital images, depending upon whether the digital provider supplies all the detail necessary to cite the original records. NARA's style guide then gives you the option of (*a*) stating in brackets that you have used "Electronic Records," or (*b*) citing the digital provider in full. The NARA Style citation below provides the full citation to the provider.

- *Publications Style:* If—as is likely the case—you have a number of digitized records from multiple case files, you could more efficiently handle these by creating one Source List Entry for the provider's image database, then specifically identify each record in your Reference Notes, as follows:

Source List Entry

(NARA Style)
Southern Claims Commission, 1871–1880, Allowed Case Files. Settled
　　Accounts and Claims, Third Auditor. Records of the Treasury
　　Department Accounting Officers, Record Group 217. National
　　Archives, Washington, D.C. iArchives. "Southern Claims Com-
　　mission Case Files." Database and images. *Footnote.com.* http://
　　www.footnote.com : 2006.

(Publications Style)
iArchives. "Southern Claims Commission Case Files." Database and
　　images. *Footnote.com.* http://www.footnote.com : 2006.

First Reference Note

(NARA Style)
　　1. Report of Enos Richardson, 1 March 1876; St. Ville St. André
(Natchitoches Parish, Louisiana) claim no. 18532, Allowed Case Files,
Southern Claims Commission, 1871–1880; Settled Accounts and Claims,
Third Auditor; Records of the Treasury Department Accounting Offic-
ers, Record Group 217, National Archives, Washington, D.C.; digital
images, "Southern Claims Commission Case Files," iArchives,
Footnote.com (http://www.footnote.com : accessed 1 September 2006).

(Publications Style)
　　1. iArchives, "Southern Claims Commission Case Files," digital
images, *Footnote.com* (http://www.footnote.com : accessed 1 September
2006), Report of Enos Richardson, 1 March 1876, St. Ville St. André
(Natchitoches Parish, Louisiana) claim no. 18532, Allowed Case Files.

Subsequent Note

　　11. Report of Enos Richardson, 1 March 1876, St. Ville St. André
claim no. 18532, Allowed Case Files, Southern Claims Commission.

11.44 Congressional Records

Historical files of the U.S. Congress are held primarily in three record groups—RG 46 (Senate), RG 233 (House), and RG 128 (Joint Committees). Within each record group, materials are subdivided by Congress (i.e., the subgroup), by activity or record type (the series), and then by Committee (the subseries). Although the National Archives, as a rule, suggests that box numbers and file numbers not be cited (because these can change in a reorganization of files), an exception exists for Senate records prior to 1947 and House records prior to 1962. Those record sets are conventionally cited by an alphanumeric scheme. Whenever you find this number-letter combination attached to a legislative document or penned onto NARA's stamp on the reverse of a photocopied document, you should include it in your citation.

In the Senate example below, the alphanumeric code for the cited document is SEN 24A-G14, bundle 2. This code is read as follows:

SEN 24   identifies the legislative branch and the Congress.

A   identifies the type of record—i.e.,

           SENATE: A=legislative proceedings, B=executive proceedings, C=impeachments, and D=records of the Secretary of the Senate;

           HOUSE: A=legislative proceedings, B=impeachments, C=Clerk of the House.

G14   At this level, a number of letter codes designate the type of record. The letter *G,* in this example, represents petitions and various other letters for journals, committee reports, papers attached to bills and resolutions, etc.

For both examples below, the lead element in the Source List Entries is the Congress (expressed as an ordinal), not the series. Leading with the Congress gives you the flexibility to cite various Congressional series under a single Source List Entry. If you use only one series of records from a particular Congress, you may wish your Source List Entry to be more specific.

Source List Entry
U.S. Congress. Sixth Congress. Records of the House of Representatives, Record Group 233. National Archives, Washington, D.C.

U.S. Congress. Twenty-Fourth Congress. Records of the Senate, Record Group 46. National Archives, Washington, D.C.

First Reference Note

    1. Petition to Congress by Citizens of Hamilton County (Territory Northwest of River Ohio), 22 October 1800; series HR 6A-F4.3, box 6, 6th Congress; Records of the House of Representatives, Record Group 233; National Archives, Washington, D.C..

    2. Remonstrance of Citizens of Mississippi against the Manner of Executing the Fourteenth Article of the Treaty of Dancing Rabbit Creek with the Choctaw Indians ... communicated to the Senate, February 24, 1836; series SEN 24A-G14, bundle 2, 24th Congress; Records of the Senate, Record Group 46; National Archives, Washington, D.C..

Subsequent Note

    11. Petition to Congress by Citizens of Hamilton County, 22 October 1800; HR 6A-F4.3, Sixth Cong.; RG 233, NA–Washington.

    12. Remonstrance of Citizens of Mississippi ... Fourteenth Article ... Treaty of Dancing Rabbit Creek ... 1836; SEN 24A-G14, bundle 2; 24th Cong., RG 46, NA–Washington.

IDENTIFYING A CONGRESSIONAL PETITION

Congressional petitions and similar documents often have no formal title by which to identify them. They usually begin with generic words such as "To the Senate and House of Representatives in Congress assembled...." Because such preambles are so common, you cannot use those first few words to serve as a label. Instead, you should create a generic label based upon the content of the petition.

In some cases, a generic label or title may already be in use. Often these petitions are discovered by means of published government documents such as *American State Papers,* Clarence Edwin Carter's *Territorial Papers,* or the *CIS Serial Set Index* (see Bibliography, Appendix B), whose editors may have created titles to the documents they published. If one of those resources led you to the record, you might want to use the document title assigned by the editor whenever you cite the photocopied original you obtain from the National Archives—as demonstrated by the two examples above.

11.45 Court of Claims Case Files

Congressional acts of 1883 and 1887 created a U.S. Court of Claims to hear cases of a type that had previously been brought before Congress: i.e., the appeals of American citizens who felt their claims against a government agency had not been handled fairly. When cases moved from an agency or a commission into the Court of Claims they were assigned a CC (Court of Claims) docket number that must be identified in citations to the cases. When citing cases appealed from the Southern Claims Commission, it is also necessary to include two other numbers assigned by the SCC: the *office* number and the *report* number.

The following models continue the examples presented under the Southern Claims Commission, 11.43. In the case cited below, when Standifer's claim was disallowed and he appealed the SCC decision to the U.S. Court of Claims, his file was moved from the Records of the U.S. House of Representatives (RG 233) for permanent archiving in the Records of the U.S. Court of Claims (RG 123).

Source List Entry
U.S. Court of Claims. Congressional Jurisdiction Case Records, 1884–1952. Record Group 123. National Archives, Washington, D.C.

First Reference Note
1. Affidavit of William J. Haralson, 15 November 1872, p. 2; Lemuel J. Standifer v. United States, Records of the Southern Claims Commission, disallowed claim no. 625, Office no. 69, Report no. 3; appealed as Court of Claims no. 4789, Congressional Jurisdiction Case Records, 1884–1952; Records of the U.S. Court of Claims, Record Group 123; National Archives, Washington, D.C.

Subsequent Note
11. Affidavit of William J. Haralson, 15 November 1872, *Standifer v. U.S.*, Court of Claims no. 4789, RG 123.

The microfilm example below cites the alphabetized docket cards you will have used first to identify Standifer's CC claim number, in order to access the case file itself.

Microfilm (NARA)

Source List Entry
U.S. Court of Claims Docket Cards for Congressional Case Files, ca.1884–1937. Microfilm publication M2007, 5 rolls. Washington, D.C. : National Archives and Records Administration, 1994.

First Reference Note
1. *U.S. Court of Claims Docket Cards for Congressional Case Files, ca.1884–1937,* microfilm publication M2007, 5 rolls (Washington, D.C.: National Archives and Records Administration, 1994), roll 5, Lemuel J. Standifer card, citing CC claim no. 4789.

Subsequent Note
11. *U.S. Court of Claims Docket Cards for Congressional Case Files, ca.1884–1937,* NARA M2007, roll 5, Lemuel J. Standifer card.

11.46 Court Records: Circuit & District

The U.S. federal circuit and district courts have jurisdiction over both civil and criminal matters that involve federal laws or cross state bounds—for example, bankruptcy, copyright, and admiralty cases. They deviate from the Basic Format for National Archives manuscripts (11.7) in one critical way: most have been dispersed to the regional archives that serves their district. Therefore, your citation to original records held by a branch should identify it as the repository, as illustrated in the example below.

Source List Entry

U.S. District Court, Northern District of California. Civil Case Files, 1853–1912. Records of the District Courts of the United States, Record Group 21. National Archives–Pacific Region, San Bruno, California.

First Reference Note

1. Satisfaction and Order of Judgment, 23 February 1875; Levi Strauss et al. v. A. B. Elfelt, 1874–75, case no. 1211; Civil Case Files, U.S. District Court, Northern District of California, 1853–1912; Records of the District Courts of the United States, Record Group 21; National Archives–Pacific Region, San Bruno, California.

Subsequent Note

11. Strauss v. Elfelt, 1874–75, case no. 1211, U.S. Dist. Court, Northern District of California, RG 21, NA–San Bruno.

NARA Microfilm

Source List Entry

Prize and Related Records for the War of 1812 of the U.S. District Court for the Southern District of New York, 1812–1816. Microfilm publication M928, 9 rolls. Washington, D.C.: National Archives and Records Service, 1973.

First Reference Note

1. *Prize and Related Records for the War of 1812 of the U.S. District Court for the Southern District of New York, 1812–1816*, microfilm publication M928, 9 rolls (Washington, D.C.: National Archives and Records Service, 1973), roll 1, frames 1262–1336, combined cases: *United States of America* v. *Brig Caledonia* (1812) and *390 Packages of Skins, J. J. Astor* v. *United States* (1813), see particularly frames 1318–20, for deposition of William J. Johnson, 8 September 1814.

Subsequent Note

11. *Prize and Related Records for the War of 1812 of the U.S. District*

Court for the Southern District of New York, 1812–1816, NARA M928, roll 1, frames 1318–20, deposition of William J. Johnson.

Online Database & Images (ARC)

The Strauss v. Elfelt case that is cited to original records above is also accessible through NARA's Archival Research Catalog database. As demonstrated below, there are both differences and similarities in citing the different media. In both situations, you cite the case in full. For an online publication, however, your emphasis is on the publication (e.g., ARC). Secondarily you identify the item of interest within that publication (the case and its documents). When citing the electronic database or image *vis a vis* the original, there are also differences in the order of elements within the citation to the case itself.

ORIGINAL FILE

The First Reference Note follows manuscript format, beginning with the smallest element—a specific document and its date—then identifies the case, the case number, and the other elements up to the largest (the archive and its location).

ONLINE DATABASE AND IMAGE

Below—after identifying the database, the website, and the publication data—the First Reference Note to the image identifies the case name and number *before* identifying the specific document. This is necessary so that the digital ID can be attached to the specific item it belongs with. The NAIL (National Archives Information Locator) control number for that digitized document is not the same as the number for the whole file; thus, the individual number should not be positioned next to the reference to the whole file.

Source List Entry

"Archival Research Catalog (ARC)." Database and images. *The National Archives.* http://www.archives.gov/research/arc : 2006.

First Reference Note

(*Citing database for the full case file*)

1. "Archival Research Catalog (ARC)," database, *The National Archives* (http://www.archives.gov/research/arc : accessed 17 February 2007), entry for Levi Strauss et al. v. A. B. Elfelt, 1874–75, case no. 1211, NAIL control no. NRHS-21-CCSFCIVCAS-1211; citing Civil Case Files, U.S. District Court, Northern District of California, 1853–1912; Records of the District Courts of the United States, 1685 [*sic*]–1991, Record Group 21; National Archives–Pacific Region, San Bruno, California.

(Citing a specific digitized image from the case file)
2. "Archival Research Catalog (ARC)," digital image, *The National Archives* (http://www.archives.gov/research/arc : accessed 17 February 2007), Levi Strauss et al. v. A. B. Elfelt, 1874–75, case no. 1211, for Satisfaction and Order of Judgment, 23 February 1875, NAIL control no. NRHS-21-CCSFCIVCAS-1211-JUDGMENT; citing [etc.]

Subsequent Note
11. "Archival Research Catalog (ARC)," database, *The National Archives*, entry for Strauss v. Elfelt, 1874–75, case no. 1211.
12. "Archival Research Catalog (ARC)," digital image, *The National Archives*, Strauss v. Elfelt, case no. 1211, for Satisfaction and Order of Judgment.

Examples at 11.48 and 11.52 demonstrate simpler citation of images accessed through the ARC database.

11.47 Freedmen's Bureau Records

The most commonly used files of the Freedmen's Bureau and its auxiliary, the Freedman's [*sic*] Bank, can be consulted on film or online. The following uses the bank's records to model both media formats. Both examples illustrate special problems or circumstances that often need to be discussed in a citation.

Microfilm (NARA)

Source List Entry
Registers of Signatures of Depositors in Branches of the Freedman's Savings and Trust Company, 1865–1874. Microfilm publication M816, 27 rolls. Washington, D.C.: National Archives and Records Service, 1970.

First Reference Note
1. *Registers of Signatures of Depositors in Branches of the Freedman's Savings and Trust Company, 1865–1874,* microfilm publication M816, 27 rolls (Washington, D.C.: National Archives and Records Service, 1970), roll 11, for Louisville, Kentucky, bank card no. 384, S. Martin, white male, age 16.

Subsequent Note
1. *Registers of Signatures of Depositors in Branches of the Freedman's Savings and Trust Company, 1865–1874,* NARA M816, roll 11, Louisville, Ky., bank card no. 384.

Online Databases & Images

Source List Entry
"Freedman's Bank Records, 1865–1874." Database and images. *Ancestry.com.* http://www.ancestry.com : 2007.

First Reference Note
    1. Mrs. Zelphire Edwards, bank card no. 696 [bank not identified but context suggests the New Orleans branch]; "Freedman's Bank Records, 1865–1874," digital images, *Ancestry.com* (http://www .ancestry.com : 6 March 2007); citing *"Registers of Signatures of Depositors in Branches of the Freedman's Savings and Trust Company, 1865–1874,* M816, 27 rolls" [exact roll not cited, but should be 11].

Subsequent Note
    11. Mrs. Zelphire Edwards, bank card no. 696 [New Orleans], "Freedman's Bank Records, 1865–1874."

CITING FULL IDENTITIES

In the microfilm example, the record only partially identifies the person of interest (i.e., only the first initial and surname). To more fully identify that person, especially since his physical description distinguishes him in this set of records, that example includes that physical identifier.

CITING MISSING PARTS OF A REFERENCE

In the database example above, the details provided by the database include the depositor's card number but not the bank's location. Because every local Freedman's Bank started numbering its cards with "1," the name of the bank is an essential identifier. You may have to study surrounding cards, as well as the card of interest, for clues to the bank's identity.

CITING THE SOURCE OF A SOURCE

The database's citation identifies the NARA film publication from which the images are made and states the number of rolls in that publication. It does not state *which* roll contains the information for the unnamed bank. After you identify that bank name (see paragraph above), you would then consult a NARA microfilm guide to identify the specific NARA roll on which the record can be found.

11.48 Maps

See also QuickCheck Model for MAPS: NATIONAL ARCHIVES

Most maps found at the National Archives can be cited using the Basic Format for National Archives manuscripts (11.7) or the QuickCheck Model referenced above. *Topographical* maps, however, are highly specialized and have other citation needs; therefore, they must be cited differently than manuscripts. See 12.68.

Because many researchers prefer to cite maps as individual items in their Source List, that option is demonstrated below.

Online Images

Source List Entry

"Archival Research Catalog (ARC)." Database and images. *The National Archives*. http://www.archives.gov/research/arc : 2007.

First Reference Note

1. "Archival Research Catalog (ARC)," digital image, *The National Archives* (http://arcweb.archives.gov/arc : accessed 1 February 2007), "Map of the Battle Field of Gettysburg, July 1st, 2nd, 3rd, 1863," published 1876, NAIL control no. NWDNC-77-CWMF-E119; citing Civil Works Map File, 1800–1947; Records of the Office of the Chief of Engineers, 1789–1988, Record Group 77; National Archives, College Park, Maryland.

Subsequent Note

11. "Archival Research Catalog (ARC)," digital image, *The National Archives,* "Map of the Battle Field of Gettysburg, July 1st, 2nd, 3rd, 1863," published 1876.

11.49 Naturalization Records

Between 1782 and 1906, naturalization proceedings in the United States could take place in any court of law. There was no uniform procedure that was nationally applied. A federal act that took effect on 27 September 1906 standardized the process and created a Bureau of Immigration and Naturalization (presently, the U.S. Citizenship and Immigration Services) to oversee its administration. However, naturalizations could still take place in any court of record, as well as (under the 1906 policy) U.S. federal district courts.

Chapter 8, Local & State Records: Courts & Governance, covers naturalization materials created at the local levels. This section provides models for the national-level court records. The first model below calls attention to one particular document in a typical file: the certificate of arrival form that individuals were supposed to complete when they filed their petitions for naturalization between 1906 and 1924. The second model demonstrates the citing of a second document from a file that has already been fully referenced.

Source List Entry

U.S. District Court, New York, Eastern District. Naturalization records, 1865–1990. Records of District Courts of the United States, Record Group 21. National Archives–Northeast Region, New York City.

First Reference Note
    1. Abraham Minowitz certificate of arrival (1937), naturalization file no. 309123, Eastern District of New York; Records of the District Courts of the United States, Record Group 21; National Archives–Northeast Region, New York City.
    2. Abraham Minowitz declaration of intention (1938), naturalization file no. 309123, Eastern District of New York.

Subsequent Note
    11. Abraham Minowitz certificate of arrival (1937), naturalization file no. 309123, Eastern District of New York.
    12. Abraham Minowitz declaration of intention (1938), naturalization file no. 309123, Eastern District of New York..

11.50 Passport Records

The passport records below illustrate a common problem you will face in working with governmental records such as those at the National Archives. Intuitively, you might want the key words "Passports" or "U.S. Passports" to be the lead element in your Source List Entries. However, the United States had no Passport Office at the time these cited records were created. Using the actual agency name, "Department of State," as the author or creator would not place these passport records in the spot you would intuitively look for them in your Source List. The following models illustrate two ways to handle that issue.

- For the file label "Card Index to U.S. Passports, 1850..." the parts of the label are inverted in the Source List, as one would do to a personal name. Thus, the key thought—U.S. Passports, Card Index—will be the words under which the entry is alphabetized.

- For "Letters Relating to Passports, 1793–1828," a generic lead was created—U.S. Passport Records—followed by the precise name of the series.

If you wish, you might combine them both under the generic lead, "U.S. Passport Records." The principle that applies in both cases is this: the Source List Entry for manuscript collections can create a generic description—whatever best describes the material you used—so long as it is augmented by precise details to identify the collection or series and archive.

Source List Entry
U.S. Passports, Card Index, 1850–1852 [and] 1860–1880. General Records, Department of State, Record Group 59. National Archives, Washington, D.C.

U.S. Passport Records. Letters Relating to Passports, 1793–1828, April 1, 1829, to February 1, 1836. General Records of the Department of State, Record Group 59. National Archives, Washington, D.C.

First Reference Note

1. Charles Bertram card, 21 February 1865; Card Index to U.S. Passports, 1850–1852 [and] 1860–1880; General Records, Department of State, Record Group 59; National Archives, Washington, D.C.

2. Thomas Alston Jr. to Hon. Martin van Buren, 21 May 1829; folder "May 1829—Philadelphia Applications," Letters Relating to Passports, 1793–1828, April 1, 1829 to February 1, 1836; General Records of the Department of State, RG 59; National Archives, Washington, D.C.

Subsequent Note

11. Charles Bertram card, 21 February 1865; Card Index to U.S. Passports, 1850–1852, 1860–1880; RG 59, NA–Washington.

12. Alston to van Buren, 21 May 1829; folder "May 1829—Philadelphia Applications," Letters Relating to Passports; RG 59, NA–Washington.

11.51 Patents & Trademark Records

Original patent materials from the U.S. Patent and Trademark Office (USPTO) that are held by NARA can be cited by the Basic Format for National Archives manuscripts (11.7) and the QuickCheck Model for Manuscripts: National Archives). However, citations to USPTO's *online* databases and images do not follow the NARA model for online materials, because patents are not part of NARA's ARC database. USPTO's own databases and images—both the online material and its DVD-ROMs—follow the standard online and CD-DVD models used throughout this manual, as the following examples illustrate.

Source List Entry

Patent Specifications and Drawings. Records Relating to Numbered Patents, 1836–1973. Records of the Patent and Trademark Office, Record Group 241. National Archives, Washington, D.C.

First Reference Note

1. Robert C. Russell, sound-based indexing system, patent file no. 1,261,167 (1918); Records Relating to Numbered Patents, 1836–1973; Records of the Patent and Trademark Office, Record Group 241; National Archives, Washington, D.C.

Subsequent Note

11. Robert C. Russell patent 1,261,167 (1918), RG 241, NA–Washington.

DVD Databases & Images

Source List Entry

U.S. Patent and Trademark Office. *USAPat: Facsimile Images of United States Patents Issued 1790 to Present.* DVD-ROM, 52 discs. Washington, D.C.: Office for Patent and Trademark Information : 2006.

First Reference Note

1. U.S. Patent and Trademark Office, *USAPat: Facsimile Images of United States Patents Issued 1790 to Present,* DVD-ROM, 52 discs (Washington, D.C.: Office for Patent and Trademark Information, 2006), disc vol. USP 2006 W06, Robert C. Russell, sound-based indexing system, patent file no. 1,261,167 (1918).

Subsequent Note

11. Patent and Trademark Office, *USA PAT: Facsimile Images of United States Patents,* disc W06, Robert C. Russell, patent 1,261,167 (1918).

Online Databases & Images

See also QuickCheck Model for IMAGES ONLINE: PATENT & TRADEMARK ...

Source List Entry

"USPTO Patent Full-Text and Image Database." *United States Patent and Trademark Office.* http://www.uspto.gov/main/sitesearch.htm : 2007.

First Reference Note

1. "USPTO Patent Full-Text and Image Database," *United States Patent and Trademark Office,* database (http://www.uspto.gov/main/sitesearch.htm : accessed 6 March 2007), entry for Robert C. Russell, patent no. 1,261,167 (1918), for a sound-based indexing system.

2. "USPTO Patent Full-Text and Image Database," digital images, *United States Patent and Trademark Office* (http://www.uspto.gov/main/sitesearch.htm : accessed 6 March 2007), Robert C. Russell, sound-based indexing system, patent file no. 1,261,167 (1918), original file location not cited.

Subsequent Note

11. "USPTO Patent Full-Text and Image Database," database entry for Robert C. Russell, patent no. 1,261,167 (1918).

12. Robert C. Russell, patent file 1,261,167 (1918).

CITING THE DATE OR YEAR

Most examples in this manual use the standard comma to separate the elements that describe a document. However, when an element ends in a number and is immediately followed by a year, placing that year in parentheses will help to set it apart from the preceding number.

Using a standard comma to separate the two would create a confusing sequence: 1,261,167, 1918.

11.52 Photographic Files

Photographic files at NARA are cited with either the Basic Format for National Archives manuscripts (11.7) or for online images (11.11), depending upon how you accessed the material. Again, *Evidence* recommends that you cite the original files in your Source List only if you have actually researched the original files. If you have only extracted random images from the database, your Source List should credit that database. The following examples demonstrate citing the original files versus an online image.

Source List Entry

Kodak Negative File, 1933–1976. Records of the Tennessee Valley Authority, 1918–, Record Group 142. National Archives–Southeast, Atlanta, Georgia.

First Reference Note

1. "Higgins' home, interior, 1937," Kodak Negative File, 1933–1976; Records of the Tennessee Valley Authority, 1918–, Record Group 142; National Archives–Southeast, Atlanta, Georgia.

Subsequent Note

11. "Higgins' home, interior, 1937," Kodak Negative File, 1933–1976, RG 142, NA–Atlanta.

Online Images

Source List Entry

"Archival Research Catalog (ARC)." Database and images. *The National Archives.* http://www.archives.gov/research/arc : 2007.

First Reference Note

1. "Archives Research Catalog (ARC)," digital images, *The National Archives* (http://www.archives.gov/research/arc : accessed 3 March 2007), photo, "Higgins' home, interior, 1937," NAIL control no. NRCA-142-INF001-C924D; Kodak Negative File, 1933–1976; Records of the Tennessee Valley Authority, 1918–, Record Group 142; National Archives–Southeast, Atlanta, Georgia.

Subsequent Note

11. "Archival Research Catalog (ARC)," digital image, *The National Archives,* photo, "Higgins' home, interior, 1937."

11.53 Railroad Retirement Board Files

See also QuickCheck Model *for* ORIGINAL RECORDS: RAILROAD RETIREMENT BOARD

Records of the federally administered Railroad Retirement Board are part of the National Archives system (Record Group 184). However, many historical records used by researchers are maintained by the Chicago office of the Board—not to be confused with the Chicago branch of the National Archives. Citations to documents within an RRB pension file usually include (*a*) the name of the employee; (*b*) the form number; and (*c*) the Social Security number of the employee, which serves as the file number. Each of the examples below cite one specific document from a file. The QuickCheck Model for the Railroad Retirement Board demonstrates a citation to a full file.

Source List Entry
(To list a group of similar files under the Board name)
Railroad Retirement Board, 1934–. Pension files. National Archives Record Group 184, RRB–Congressional Inquiry Section; Chicago, Illinois.

(To list an individual file under a personal name)
Graves, Jess. Pension file. Social Security no. 544-05-9766, 1951. Records of the Railroad Retirement Board, 1934–. National Archives Record Group 184; RRB–Congressional Inquiry Section, Chicago, Illinois.

First Reference Note
(To cite a particular document from an individual file)
    1. "Record of Employee's Prior Service" (Form AA-2P), filed 3 March 1941, Leonard Ray Anderson pension file, Social Security no. 702-07-8940, 1941; Records of the Railroad Retirement Board, 1934–, National Archives Record Group 184; RRB–Congressional Inquiry Section, Chicago, Illinois.
    2. "Employee's Statement of Compensated Service" (Form AA-15), filed 7 June 1951, Jess Graves pension file, Social Security no. 544-05-9766, 1951; Records of the Railroad Retirement Board, 1934–, National Archives Record Group 184; RRB–Congressional Inquiry Section, Chicago, Illinois.

Subsequent Note
    11. "Record of Employee's Prior Service" (Form AA-2P), 1941, Leonard Ray Anderson pension file, SS no. 702-07-8940, Railroad Retirement Board.
    12. "Employee's Statement of Compensated Service" (Form AA-15), 1951, Jess Graves pension file, SS no. 544-05-9766, Railroad Retirement Board.

IDENTIFICATION OF RECORD GROUP
In all other NARA examples within this chapter, the phrase "National

Archives" is not placed before the phrase " Record Group ___." In the RRB examples above, it does appear. The difference is this: in all other cases, the National Archives is cited as the repository. In the RRB examples, the repository is the RRB–Congressional Inquiry Section, Chicago. Unless you identify "Record Group 184" as a National Archives record group, the link between the RRB and the National Archives will be lost.

11.54 Slave Narratives

See also QuickCheck Model *for* IMAGES ONLINE: LIBRARY OF CONGRESS

Traditionally, the interviews of ex-slaves conducted by the Depression-era Work Projects Administration (aka Works Progress Administration) have been consulted and cited as print publications. (See 13.49–13.51.) More recently, they—along with corresponding interviews of elderly whites—have been digitized and are available online from the Library of Congress and elsewhere. A typical citation to the online transcriptions would be this:

Online Databases & Transcriptions

Source List Entry

Library of Congress. "Born in Slavery: Slave Narratives from the Federal Writers' Project, 1936–1938." Database and images. *American Memory.* http://memory.loc.gov/ammem/snhtml/snhome.html : 2006.

First Reference Note

(*To cite a typescript memoir*)

    1. Library of Congress, "Born in Slavery: Slave Narratives from the Federal Writers' Project, 1936–1938," digital image of typescript, *American Memory* (http://memory.loc.gov/ammem/snhtml/snhome .html : 6 March 2007), memoir of Rachael Goings (née Rachal Exelina Mayberry or Mabry), Cape Girardeau, Missouri, digital ID mesn 100/ 12612; citing WPA Federal Writers' Project, Missouri Narratives, vol. 10, p. 121.

(*To cite a photographic image*)

    2. Library of Congress, "Born in Slavery: Slave Narratives," digital images, *American Memory* (http://memory.loc.gov/ammem/ snhtml/snhome.html : 6 March 2007), photo, "James Boyd, Age about 100, Texas," digital ID mesnp 16117b; citing WPA Federal Writers' Project, 1936–1938.

Subsequent Note

    11. Library of Congress, "Born in Slavery: Slave Narratives," *American Memory,* memoir of Rachael Goings, digital ID mesn 100/ 12612.

12. Library of Congress, "Born in Slavery: Slave Narratives," photo, "James Boyd, Age about 100, Texas," digital ID mesnp 16117b.

11.55 Social Security Records

See also QuickCheck Model *for* SOCIAL SECURITY ADMINISTRATION ...

Administrative records of the Social Security Administration, National Archives Record Group 47, are handled by the Basic Format for National Archives manuscripts (11.7). SSA records that relate to individual Americans are not open to the public, although one document can be an exception: a deceased person's application for account number, available by request from the SSA. This Form SS-5 is not cited in the standard form for NARA records because it is not part of the SSA files held by NARA.

Source List Entry

Social Security Administration. Applications for Account Numbers, Form SS-5. Social Security Administration, Baltimore, Maryland.

First Reference Note

1. Theresa Boggus Sammarco, SS no. 116-05-4655, 23 May 1937, Application for Account Number (Form SS-5), Social Security Administration, Baltimore, Maryland.

Subsequent Note

11. Theresa Boggus Sammarco, SS no. 116-05-4655, 1937, Application for Account No. (Form SS-5), Social Security Administration.

The SSA maintains an official Master Death File that is available from the administration on DVD under certain conditions. Various websites also offer a derivative of the master file that is commonly known as the "Social Security Death Index" (SSDI). While these unofficial databases are conventionally attributed to the SSA, you will also want to note which publisher's "edition" you used because different websites offer different content as well as variations in search engine technology that can affect the results of a search.

The following examples use the same file cited above to illustrate handling both the official DVD and one of its derivatives.

Official SSA Database-DVD

Source List Entry

Social Security Administration. *Death Master File*. DVD database. Springfield, Virginia: National Technical Information Service, 2006.

First Reference Note
    1. U.S. Social Security Administration, *Death Master File,* DVD database (Springfield, Virginia: National Technical Information Service, 2006), entry for Theresa Sammarco, 1978, SS no. 116-05-4655.

Subsequent Note
    11. U.S. Social Security Administration, *Death Master File,* DVD database entry for Theresa Sammarco, SS no. 116-05-4655.

Online Databases

Source List Entry
Social Security Administration. "Social Security Death Index." Database. *FamilySearch.org.* http://www.familysearch.org : 2007.

First Reference Note
    1. Social Security Administration, "U.S. Social Security Death Index," database, *FamilySearch.org* (http://www.familysearch.org : accessed 6 March 2007), entry for Theresa Sammarco, 1978, SS no. 116-05-4655.

Subsequent Note
    11. Social Security Administration, "U.S. Social Security Death Index," database, *FamilySearch.org*, entry for Theresa Sammarco, SS no. 116-05-4655.

IDENTIFYING THE URL
At some websites (as with the Library of Congress example at 11.54, Slave Narratives) the search screen can be accessed via a relatively short URL. In other situations, such as the Social Security Death Index search engine at *FamilySearch.org* above, the URL is inordinately long. In such cases, you may prefer to cite only the URL for the website's home page. Users of your citation can then navigate the site map or use its menus to access the database you have named.

11.56 Tax Records (Federal Level)
Federal-level taxation of individual Americans occurred only intermittently prior to the U.S. Revenue Act of 1913 that instituted a permanent income tax. Records of earlier levies are scattered in many facilities. Some have been microfilmed. Those in custody of the National Archives can be handled using the Basic Format for National Archives manuscripts or microfilm (11.7–11.8).

The following provides typical citations to the two most commonly used sets of tax records, the 1798 Direct Tax on land and slaves (for which most records are held by nongovernmental repositories) and the Civil War–era Internal Revenue Assessment Lists (which are held by the National Archives and typically consulted on microfilm).

Source List Entry
U.S. Direct Tax of 1798. Massachusetts. New England Historic Genealogical Society Library, Boston, Massachusetts.

First Reference Note
1. U.S. Direct Tax of 1798, Franklin County, Massachusetts; New Salem, Division 8, Collection District 2; Massachusetts vol. 16: 711, for Benjamin Sibley; New England Historic Genealogical Society Library, Boston, Massachusetts.

Subsequent Note
11. U.S. Direct Tax of 1798, Franklin Co., Mass.; New Salem, Div. 8, Dist. 2; Mass. vol. 16: 711, for Benjamin Sibley.

Microfilm (NARA)

Source List Entry
Internal Revenue Assessment Lists for Alabama, 1865–1866. Microfilm publication M754, 6 rolls. Washington, D.C.: National Archives and Records Administration, 1987.

First Reference Note
1. *Internal Revenue Assessment Lists for Alabama, 1865–1866,* microfilm publication M754, 6 rolls (Washington, D.C.: National Archives and Records Administration, 1987), roll 3, division 14, collection district 2 (Tuscaloosa County), p. 212, Rich[d] P. Baugh.

Subsequent Note
11. *Internal Revenue Assessment Lists for Alabama, 1865–1866,* NARA M754, roll 3, div. 14, dist. 2 (Tuscaloosa Co.), p. 212, Rich[d] P. Baugh.

11.57 WPA Records
Administrative records of the Depression-era Work Projects Administration (also known as the Works Progress Administration) and its Federal Writers' Project can be handled using the Basic Format for National Archives manuscripts (11.7). Interviews conducted with ex-slave and elderly whites are treated at 11.54, Slave Narratives. Most of the record inventories and repository guides that the WPA created are accessed as bound manuscripts or publications (see 13.49–13.51).

INTERNATIONAL RECORDS

11.58 Australia: Military & Naturalization Records

See QuickCheck Model *for* DATABASES ONLINE: NATIONAL ARCHIVES (AUSTRALIA)

Australia's National Archives offers a single database that covers a number of major record types. The examples below treat two of the most commonly consulted categories.

Online Databases

Source List Entry

Australia. "Record Search." Database. *National Archives of Australia.*
    http://www.naa.gov.au/The_Collection/recordsearch.html : 2007.

First Reference Note

(Military records)
    1. "Record Search," database, *National Archives of Australia* (http://www.naa.gov.au/The_Collection/recordsearch.html : accessed 1 March 2007), entry for Pvt. J. W. C. Andrews, Court-Martial, 1942; citing barcode 7871766, series A471, control no. 26755.

(Naturalization records)
    2. "Record Search," database, *National Archives of Australia* (http://www.naa.gov.au/The_Collection/recordsearch.html : accessed 1 March 2007), entry for Clara Johanna Anderson, 1909 naturalization, Canberra; citing series A1, control symbol 1909/7399.

Subsequent Note

    11. "Record Search," database, *National Archives of Australia,* entry for Pvt. J. W. C. Andrews, Court-Martial, 1942.
    12. "Record Search," database, *National Archives of Australia,* entry for Clara Johanna Anderson, 1909 naturalization, Canberra.

CITING COUNTRY & AGENCY

In the Source List Entry above, the word Australia is placed before the entry so that the entry will be grouped geographically with other materials of the Australian government. In the Reference Note, that initial geographic notation is not needed. No agency needs to be cited as "author" or "creator" because the name of that agency is the name of the website itself.

11.59 Canada: Immigration Records

See also QuickCheck Model *for* DATABASES ONLINE: NATIONAL ARCHIVES (CANADA)

National-level governmental records for Canada are fairly recent in origin. Prior to the formation of Canada's national government in 1867, records were created in the various colonies belonging to France and Britain. For your citations to properly attribute Canada's governmental records, you need a basic familiarity with the geopolitical landscape and the changes that occurred in 1763, 1841, and 1867 particularly. You cannot expect microfilmed records to provide this basic detail, and the cataloging for manuscript materials may leave jurisdictional matters equally murky.

Library and Archives Canada (LAC), like the U.S. National Archives, is the primary filmer of its own materials. However, LAC does not consider its film to be *publications*. Its films are not titled and may not provide sufficient cataloging data for you to create a complete citation to the original records. Instead (as with FHL microfilm), you would typically identify the material by whatever label appears on a filmed register or whatever data appears on the filmer's target for a set of loose files. You would then add the LAC film number.

The examples below illustrate the handling of two types of situations:

- The Chinese immigration register is a film project of Library and Archives Canada; thus, you should cite LAC's film number.

- The alien declaration of 1794 (a colonial rather than national record) is a film project of the Genealogical Society of Utah, deposited with the Family History Library. A LAC film number is not required if FHL film is consulted at FHL.

Microfilm (LAC film, FHL copy)

Source List Entry

(To cite LAC)
Canada. "General Register of Chinese Immigration, 1885–1889." Chinese Immigration Records, Record Group 76, Records of the Immigration Branch. LAC microfilm C-9510. Library and Archives Canada, Ottawa.

(To cite FHL)
Canada. Declaration of Aliens, Lower Canada, 1794–1811. Series B, volume/file 45, Record Group 4. Library and Archives Canada, Ottawa. FHL microfilm 1,312,081, item 1. Family History Library, Salt Lake City, Utah.

First Reference Note

1. "General Register of Chinese Immigration, 1885–1889," serial no. 240, port no. 236, Ma Fook, certificate 25 June 1888; Chinese

General Registers, 1885–1903, Chinese Immigration Records; microfilm C-9510, Library and Archives Canada, Ottawa.

2. "Declarations Made by Persons Resident in Lower Canada in Compliance with ... Alien Act ... 1794," Heth Baldwin declaration, 21 June 1794, no. 13; FHL microfilm 1,312,081, item 1.

Subsequent Note

11. "General Register of Chinese Immigration, 1885–1889," serial no. 240, port no. 236, Ma Fook, certificate 25 June 1888.

12. Heth Baldwin declaration, 21 June 1794, no. 13.

11.60 England: Military, Probate & Taxation Records

See QuickCheck Model *for* DATABASES ONLINE: NATIONAL ARCHIVES (U.K.)

The National Archives of the United Kingdom at Kew offers individual databases for various record types, some with images. Citations to these electronic records are similar to those offered by the U.S. National Archives, although the United Kingdom's cataloging system creates a more concise reference in your source-of-the-source field.

Online Databases

Source List Entry

(Military records)

England. The National Archives. "Registers of Seamen's Services." Database. *DocumentsOnline.* http://www.nationalarchives.gov.uk/documentsonline : 2007.

(Probate records)

England. The National Archives. "Family History: Wills." Database. *DocumentsOnline.* http://www.nationalarchives.gov.uk/documents online : 2007.

(Taxation records)

England. The National Archives. "Death Duty Registers, 1796–1811." Database. *DocumentsOnline.* http://www.nationalarchives.gov .uk/documentsonline : 2007.

First Reference Note

1. The National Archives (U.K.), "Registers of Seamen's Services," database, *DocumentsOnline* (http://ww.nationalarchives.gov.uk/documentsonline : accessed 5 February 2007), entry for William Dendy, no. 124927, October 1865; citing catalog reference ADM 188/164.

2. The National Archives (U.K.), "Family History: Wills," database, *DocumentsOnline* (http://www.nationalarchives.gov.uk/documents online : accessed 5 February 2007), entry for will of John Peace, Petersfield, Hampshire, 1725; citing catalog reference IR PROB 11/601.

3. The National Archives (U.K.), "Death Duty Registers, 1796–1811," database, *DocumentsOnline* (http://www.nationalarchives.gov.uk/documentsonline : accessed 5 February 2007), entry for Mary Bomford, Hadbury parish, Worcestershire, 1859; citing catalog reference IR 26/423.

Subsequent Note

11. "Registers of Seamen's Services," database, *DocumentsOnline,* entry for William Dendy, no. 124927, October 1865.

12. "Family History: Wills," database, *DocumentsOnline,* entry for will of John Peace, Petersfield, Hampshire, 1725.

13. "Death Duty Registers, 1796–1811," database, *Documents Online,* entry for Mary Bomford, Hadbury, Worcestershire, 1859.

Online Images

When citing digital images you access through an archive's online database, as discussed at 11.10, you have two options:

EMPHASIS ON THE WEBSITE

For simplicity you may prefer to cite the website in the same way you cite database entries—i.e., as an online publication. In this format, the database and the website are the key elements, followed by a citation to the specific item, its digital ID number, and whatever information the image description may supply for its source.

EMPHASIS ON THE ORIGINAL

If you choose to cite the record as an original, you may be able to glean the needed series, subgroup, and record group number from the description that accompanies the image. Following that citation, you would add the identification of the website and the digital ID number of the document. Both approaches are illustrated below:

Source List Entry

(To cite the image, Publications Style)
England. The National Archives. "Registers of Seamen's Services." Database and images. *DocumentsOnline.* http://www.national archives.gov.uk/documentsonline : 2007.

(To cite the original record)
England. The National Archives. Board of Inland Revenue ... Registers of Legacy Duty [Etc.]. Records of the Boards of Stamps, Taxes, Excise, Stamps and Taxes, and Inland Revenue. London. Database and images. *DocumentsOnline.* http://www.nationalarchives.gov.uk/documentsonline : 2007.
England. The National Archives. Will Registers. Records of the Prerogative Court of Canterbury. London. Database and images. *DocumentsOnline.* http://www.nationalarchives.gov.uk/documents online : 2007.

First Reference Note

(To cite the image, Publications Style)
    1. The National Archives (U.K.), *DocumentsOnline* (http://www .nationalarchives.gov.uk/documentsonline : accessed 5 February 2007), William Dendy, official no. 124927, digital image 422/402; citing Admiralty Registers of Seamen's Services, catalog reference ADM 188/ 16; Records of the Admiralty, Naval Forces, Royal Marines, Coastguard, and Related Bodies.

(To emphasize the original records rather than the image)
    2. Mary Bomford, recorded will, parish of Hadbury, Worcestershire, 1859; Board of Inland Revenue ... Registers of Legacy Duty, catalog reference IR 26/423; Records of the Boards of Stamps, Taxes, Excise, Stamps and Taxes, and Inland Revenue; The National Archives, London; digital images, *DocumentsOnline* (http://www .nationalarchives.gov.uk/documentsonline : accessed 5 February 2007), digital no. 228.
    3. Johannis [John] Peace, recorded will, Petersfield, Hampshire, 1725; "Romney Quire Numbers 1–48," catalog reference PROB 11/ 601; Records of the Prerogative Court of Canterbury; The National Archives, London; digital images, *DocumentsOnline* (http://www.national archives.gov.uk/documentsonline : accessed 5 February 2007), digital no. 129/129.

Subsequent Note

(To cite the image, Publications Style)
    11. The National Archives (U.K.), "Registers of Seamen's Ser-vices," *DocumentsOnline*, William Dendy, official no. 124927.

(To emphasize the original record rather than the image)
    12. Mary Bomford, recorded will, Hadbury, Worcestershire, 1859; Board of Inland Revenue ... Registers of Legacy Duty, catalog reference IR 26/423; National Archives, London.
    13. Johannis [John] Peace, recorded will, Petersfield, Hampshire, 1725; "Romney Quire Numbers 1–48," catalog reference PROB 11/ 601; National Archives, London.

11.61 France: Military & Emigration Rolls

Records in the Archives Nationales of France and its auxiliary centers are cataloged and cited by a formal archival scheme that codes groups of records by a combination of letters and numbers. To use part of the citation from the troop list below, in the following citation

Colonies, Series D^{2C} 54, Archives d'Outre-Mer

"Colonies" identifies the *record group*, "D" identifies the *series*, the superscript "2C" identifies the subseries, and "54" identifies the carton. Archives d'Outre Mer is the branch (or "center") of the Archives Nationales that holds the record.

Traditionally, many historical researchers who cite the records of France's national archives have omitted an identification of the archive center (e.g., Archives d'Outre-Mer) or simply attributed the record to the parent archive (Archives Nationales). Because the Archives Nationales system has greatly expanded and records are being dispersed, *Evidence* recommends that you identify the precise archive center where the record is found.

Manuscripts held by France's Bibliothèque Nationale and its branches such as the Bibliothèque de l'Arsenal use a different cataloging scheme. Nonetheless, the Reference Notes are constructed in a similar fashion, as these two examples demonstrate:

Source List Entry
Archives de la Bastille. Bibliothèque de l'Arsenal, Paris, France.
Colonies, Series D, Matériel. Archives d'Outre-Mer, Aix-en-Provence, France.

First Reference Note
   1. "Personnes renfermées en la maison de force de la Salpêtrière, bonnes pour les isles," 27 June 1719, doc. 12692, Archives de la Bastille; Bibliothèque de l'Arsenal, Paris, France.
   2. "Rolle General des Trouppes de la Loüisianne, commencé en 1744" [filed 1771]; Colonies D^{2C} 54; Archives d'Outre-Mer, Aix-en-Provence, France.

Subsequent Note
   11. "Personnes renfermées en la maison de force de la Salpêtrière, bonnes pour les isles," 27 June 1719, doc. 12692, Archives de la Bastille.
   12. "Rolle General des Trouppes de la Loüisianne, commencé en 1744," [filed 1771], Colonies D^{2C} 54, Archives d'Outre-Mer.

ERRORS IN FILE LOCATIONS
Many early documents are now filed or bound in locations a researcher would not expect. The 1744 roll is an example. Because most documents in the series are grouped chronologically, one would not ordinarily look for it amid materials of three decades later. When you discover a document in this situation, you should note the aberrant location. That can usually be handled with a simple comment in square editorial brackets, as in notes 2 and 12.

11.62 Germany: Emigration Rolls

Germany's extant emigration lists are local rather than national records. German principalities were not unified into a nation-state until 1871. See 9.50 for German emigration lists.

11.63 Ireland: Griffith's Valuations

The national assessment of property that took place between 1847 and 1864—the "Primary Valuation of Tenements," commonly known as "Griffith's Valuation"—exists today in numerous forms. The results of the original assessment were printed contemporaneously in 290 or so volumes, each covering an individual "poor law union." Copies are found, piecemeal, in many repositories; none seems to hold them all. Typically, those volumes are organized (and titled) by union and county. When you consult one of the printed volumes, you would cite it in Basic Format for published books (see 12.3).

Major collections of these volumes have been reproduced on microfilm, CD-ROM, and online. The following example demonstrates citations to both database extracts from the original volumes and online image copies of the original volumes.

Online Databases and Images

Source List Entry

Griffith, Richard. *General Valuation of Rateable Property in Ireland … Union of Ballycastle … County of Antrim*. Dublin: Alex. Thom and Sons, for Her Majesty's Stationery Office, 1861. Digital images available at "Griffith's Valuation," *The Origins Network*. http://www.originsnetwork.com : 2007.

"Griffith's Valuation." Database and images. *The Origins Network*. http://www.originsnetwork.com : 2007.

First Reference Note

(*Citing images of original publication*)

1. Richard Griffith, *General Valuation of Rateable Property in Ireland … Union of Ballycastle … County of Antrim* (Dublin: Her Majesty's Stationery Office, 1861), 79, for William Donovan, occupier, Fair Hill Street, Ballycastle (town), Townparks (townland), Ramoan (parish); "Griffith's Valuation," digital images, *The Origins Network* (http://www.originsnetwork.com : 20 February 2007).

(*Citing database extracts*)

2. "Griffith's Valuation," database, *The Origins Network* (http://www.originsnetwork.com : accessed 20 February 2007), transcribed "details" for William Donovan, occupier, Ballycastle (town), Townparks

(townland), Ramoan (parish), County Antrim; citing "barony of Cary, union of Ballycastle, page 89" [*sic*, should be 79].

Subsequent Note

(*Citing images of original publication*)
    11. Griffith, *General Valuation ... Union of Ballycastle,* 79.

(*Citing database extracts*)
    12. "Griffith's Valuation," database, *The Origins Network*, transcribed "details" for William Donovan, occupier, Townparks, Ramoan, County Antrim.

IDENTIFYING LOCATIONS

Griffith's Valuation identifies up to eight geographic jurisdictions for each individual—county, barony, poor law union, parish, townland, municipality (with street in urban areas), and individual landholding. To ensure that any entry can be relocated among many of the same name, you should note all of those jurisdictions.

IDENTIFYING THE VOLUME

The online resource above offers images of individual pages from the original printed volume. Each image usually displays a printed page number but not the name of the volume. As with all printed works, you will need to move backward to its title page to identify the title and, sometimes, the publication data. You should also examine the title page to determine whether the volume represents a "general valuation" (aka "primary valuation," meaning the initial assessment) or a later "appeals printing" that reflects some revisions in the identity of occupiers. Where both versions exist, they were sometimes printed in the same year.

SEQUENCE OF GEOGRAPHIC NAMES

In comparing the two models above, you will note that the arrangement of the geographic names, when citing the original volumes, differs from when you cite the database. That is due to the differences inherent in those two creations (i.e., the book and the database). The book's title names the union and county; you do not need to repeat that in the personal detail that identifies the individual of interest. The database, however, identifies its locations differently and does not identify the title of the book from which data is taken. Therefore your citation to the database needs to contain fuller data.

In situations such as this—whatever the source or the provider—you will need to thoughtfully study the structure of the resource you are using. To use this website as a further example, it offers not only images from the original (unnamed) books but also two database pages for each person of interest.

Master List—The first database page is a master list of all individuals of that name. The elements from that master list are used in the model citation above. You need to include those particular details so that the proper person can be located again in the database.

Individual Details—The second database page, accessible from this master list, is a "detail" page for each individual. There, you find a transcription of all detail from the original image. A page number is cited and you are told that the publication was printed in 1861, but the volume is not named. (The volume was identified for this citation from the header on its first page and fuller library cataloging elsewhere.) This "detail" page also adds three place names not found in the master database—i.e., the county, barony, and union.

In short, even when pieces of a citation appear to be missing, by carefully analyzing your resource, you are often able to ferret out enough details for an adequate citation.

11.64 Ireland: Land Registrations

In 1708, the Registry of Deeds was established in Dublin as a central record office for conveyances that affected Irish lands—deeds, leases, marriage contracts, etc.—although recording was optional. Beginning in 1892, registration became mandatory, with four separate registry offices (three of them in Dublin) handling different regions of the republic. The following demonstrate typical citations to (*a*) a county-level index from a regional office; (*b*) a deed recorded in the national register.

> *Source List Entry*
> Ireland. "Transcripts of Memorials of Deeds, Conveyances & Wills,
> 1763–1765." Registry of Deeds, Dublin.
> Monaghan, county of. Lands Index, 1739–1810. Registry of Deeds,
> Dublin.
>
> *First Reference Note*
> 1. Ireland, "Transcripts of Memorials of Deeds, Conveyances &
> Wills, 1763–1765," vol. 228: 40–41, Andrew Clarke of Castlebair,
> County Mayo, to Edwd Shields, town of Galloway, citing doc. no.
> 1406666; Registry of Deeds, Dublin.
> 2. County Monaghan, Lands Index, 1739–1810, "B" section:

"Ballaghnaman—Morrison to Morrison," citing Book 145, p. 493, doc. 99589; Registry of Deeds, Dublin. Entries are indexed under the name of the property (e.g. "Ballaghnaman") rather than the name of the buyer (Morrison) or seller (Morrison).

Subsequent Note
11. Ireland, "Transcripts of Memorials of Deeds, Conveyances & Wills, 1763–1765, vol. 228: 40–41.
12. Co. Monaghan, Lands Index, 1739–1810, "B" section: "Ballaghnaman—Morrison to Morrison."

11.65   Ireland: Tithe Applotment Survey
Between 1827 and 1845, a countrywide tax assessment was made of agricultural land for the support of the Protestant Church of Ireland, in place of the long-established practice of collecting in-kind tithes from crops. The resulting set of records, known as the Tithe Applotment Survey, set a taxable value on agricultural land (urban and industrial land was not included), to be paid in cash by landlords. Today, the extant rolls are held by the National Archives of Ireland at Dublin and the Public Records Office of Northern Ireland at Belfast. They are commonly consulted on microfilm.

FHL-GSU Microfilm

Source List Entry
Ireland. Land Commission. Tithe Applotment Books and Indexes for Northern Ireland, ca. 1822–1837. Public Record Office of Northern Ireland, Belfast. FHL microfilm 258,444–258,470. Family History Library, Salt Lake City, Utah.

First Reference Note
1. Ireland, Land Commission, Tithe Applotment Books and Indexes for Northern Ireland: Kildress, p. 22, Gaddis entries; Public Record Office of Northern Ireland, Belfast; FHL microfilm 258,460.

Subsequent Note
11. Ireland, Tithe Applotment Books and Indexes: Kildress, p. 22.

10.66   Ireland: Wills & Administrations
Prior to 1858, the Church of Ireland oversaw the proving of wills and the administrations of the estates of those who died without wills. Procedures might have been conducted in either the consistorial court of a diocese (for residents of the diocese who left property there) or the prerogative court of the diocese (for residents whose property

straddled diocesan lines or was valued at more than £5). The records of wills and administrations surviving the 1922 fire at the Public Record Office, where these records were consolidated, can usually be cited by the following model.

Source List Entry
Ireland. Archdiocese of Armagh. Consistorial and Metropolitical Court. Public Record Office of Northern Ireland, Belfast.

First Reference Note
1. John Geddes will, dated 1798, proved 1808; Archdiocese of Armagh, Consistorial and Metropolitical Court; MS T/1762/2, Public Record Office of Northern Ireland, Belfast.

Subsequent Note
11. John Geddes will; Archdiocese of Armagh, Consistorial and Metropolitical Court; MS T/1762/2, Public Record Office of Northern Ireland.

11.67 Mexico: Colonial Post Records
Many of Mexico's colonial records that pertain to the United States have been microfilmed by the U.S. Library of Congress. The examples below demonstrate citations to two major collections from the archive. The first represents use of the original record books (*tomos*). The second represents use of the microfilmed images.

Source List Entry
Mexico. Ramo de Provincias. Colleción: Historia. Archivo General de la Nación, Mexico City.

First Reference Note
1. "Hendrique" [Henri Trichel] of Natchitoches to Governor of Los Adayes, petition, 2 June 1737; tomo [vol.] 524, folio 306/123; Series: Historia, Ramo de Provincias; Archivo General de la Nación (AGN), Mexico City.

Subsequent Note
11. "Hendrique" [Henri Trichel] to Governor of Los Adayes, petition, 2 June 1737; tomo 524: 306/123; Historia, Provincias, AGN.

Microfilm (Preservation film)

Source List Entry
Mexico. Ramo de Provincias. Colleción: Historia. Archivo General de la Nación, Mexico City. Library of Congress Photoduplication Service in Mexico, 1950.

First Reference Note
1. Santhiago de Xalpa Mission, "Memoria y Padron de los Indios," 22 April 1744; tomo 249, folios 92–100, particularly folio 99, family 363; Provincias Internas, 1662 à 1762; Archivo General de la Nación roll 228, Library of Congress Photoduplication Service in Mexico.

Subsequent Note
11. Santhiago de Xalpa Mission, "Memoria y Padron de los Indios," 22 April 1744; tomo 249, folios 92–100, particularly f. 99, family 363.

11.68 Scotland: Title Deeds

Despite its 1607 union with England, Scotland has maintained its own national-level recordkeeping system for many record classes. The principal repositories for these materials are the National Archives of Scotland and the three facilities maintained by the General Register Office. Materials preserved by the latter are variously handled in other chapters. Materials identified through the commonly consulted online database of the National Archives can be cited by the model below.

When citing entries from any national database, you should include whatever basic detail is provided for name, place, and date, as well as the archival citation to the manuscript file. In the archival citation below, "GD1/61" is said (at a deeper level in the online catalog) to be the series number for Title Deeds of Properties in Forfar Burgh, 1595–1739. Your citation will be more meaningful to others—and to yourself in the future—if you include that more explicit identity of the collection in your First Reference Note.

Online Databases

Source List Entry
Scotland. "NAS Public Catalogue." Database. *The National Archives of Scotland*. http://www.nas.gov.uk: 2007.

First Reference Note
1. "NAS Public Catalogue," database, *The National Archives of Scotland* (http://www.nas.gov.uk/ : 8 February 2007), entry for William Hunter, Instrument of Cognition and Sasine, 5 June 1650; citing reference number GD1/61/4 (Title Deeds of Properties in Forfar Burgh, 1595–1739).

Subsequent Note
11. "NAS Public Catalogue," database, *National Archives of Scotland,* entry for William Hunter, Instrument of Cognition and Sasine, 5 June 1650.

11.69 Spain: Emigration Lists

No centralized national resource exists, at this writing, for Spain's tens of thousands of records listing emigrants to other parts of the world. Your citations to those lists will vary according to the type of collection, series, or archive in which you found a particular list. The following model focuses upon one set of records commonly used by historians working on Spanish emigrants to colonial America.

The vast series known as Papeles Procedentes de Cuba (aka "Papers Coming from Cuba" or "Cuban Papers") is arranged by the archive into *edicións* (series), for which you need to cite *legajos* (bundles) and folios (sheets).

Source List Entry
Spain. Papeles Procedentes de Cuba. Archivo General de Indias, Seville.

First Reference Note
1. Passenger list, *El Sagrado Corazón de Jesús,* 1779; Papeles Procedentes de Cuba, edición 141, legajo 689, folio 414; Archivo General de Indias, Seville, Spain.

Subsequent Note
11. Passenger list, *El Sagrado Corazón de Jesús,* 1779; PPC ed. 141, leg. 689, f. 414.

Microfilmed copies of the Papeles Procedentes de Cuba are widely available in the United States. However, the edición and roll numbers are not identical from one facility to another. When you attribute an edition, legajo, and folio to a specific roll of microfilm, you should identify the film by its cataloging identity at the facility where you consulted it.

Microfilm (Library Copy)

Source List Entry
Spain. Papeles Procedentes de Cuba. Archivo General de Indias, Seville. Microfilm, 1,361 rolls. Clayton Library, Houston, Texas.

First Reference Note
1. Passenger list, *El Sagrado Corazón de Jesús,* 1779; Papeles Procedentes de Cuba, edición 141, legajo 689, folio 414; Archivo General de Indias, Seville, Spain; consulted as microfilm PPC roll 68, Clayton Library, Houston.

Subsequent Note
11. Passenger list, *El Sagrado Corazón de Jesús,* 1779; Papeles

Procedentes de Cuba, ed. 141, leg. 689, f. 414; PPC roll 68, Clayton Library.

(*Or, if edition is not cited*)

    11. Passenger list, *El Sagrado Corazón de Jesús,* 1779; Papeles Procedentes de Cuba, leg. 689, f. 414.

11.70 Wales: Crime and Punishment Records

Since it formally united with England in 1536, Wales has been subject to many of Britain's governmental systems that created records on the general population. Unlike England, Ireland, Northern Ireland, and Scotland, Wales does not have a national archive to serve as a central repository for national-level governmental records, although it does have a National Library. Some major record categories, such as civil registrations and censuses, are available through the U.K.'s national archive and its databases (see 11.60, England). Other filmed records available through the Family History Library in Salt Lake City may be cited by Basic Format for FHL microfilm (see 3.19). The following model provides a pattern for citing national-level databases offered by the National Library of Wales.

Online Databases

Source List Entry
Wales. "Crime and Punishment." Database. *The National Library of Wales.* http://www.llgc.org.uk/: 2007.

First Reference Note
    1. Wales, "Crime and Punishment," database, *The National Library of Wales* (http://www.llgc.org.uk/ : 8 February 2007), entry for Thomas Jones of Wrexham, Denbigh County, 1730; citing file no. 4/44/6, document no. 14.

Subsequent Note
    11. Wales, "Crime and Punishment," database entry for Thomas Jones of Wrexham, Denbigh Co.; citing file no. 4/44/6, doc. no. 14.

11.71 Worldwide: Patent Databases

Online Database & Images

Source List Entry
    European Patent Office. http://ep.espacenet.com : 6 January 2007.

First Reference Note

1. *European Patent Office* (http://ep.espacenet.com : 6 January 2007), database entry for Robert C. Russell, patent no. 1,261,167 (1918, U.S.), for a sound-based indexing system.

2. G. Vacherat, patent certificate no. 1497 (1889, France), système de maillons pour chaînes [A system of links for chains]; digital images, *European Patent Office* (http://ep.espacenet.com : 6 January 2007); citing prior publication in Confédération Suisse, *Bureau Fedéral de la Propriété Intellectuelle.*

Subsequent Note

11. *European Patent Office,* database entry for Robert C. Russell, patent no. 1,261,167 (1918, U.S.).

12. G. Vacherat patent certificate no. 1497 (1889, France).

PUBLICATIONS 12
(Books, CDs, Maps, Leaflets & Videos)

QuickCheck Models

Guidelines & Examples (beginning page 662)

Guidelines & Examples

QuickCheck Model
PRINT PUBLICATIONS
BOOK: BASIC FORMAT

Source List Entry

AUTHOR	MAIN TITLE	SUBTITLE	PLACE OF PUBLICATION

Nickell, Joe. *Detecting Forgery: Forensic Investigation of Documents*. Lexington:

PUBLISHER	YEAR

University Press of Kentucky, 1996.

First (Full) Reference Note

AUTHOR	MAIN TITLE	SUBTITLE

1. Joe Nickell, *Detecting Forgery: Forensic Investigation of Documents*

PLACE OF PUBLICATION	PUBLISHER	YEAR	PAGE

(Lexington: University Press of Kentucky, 1996), 123.

Subsequent (Short) Note

AUTHOR	SHORT TITLE	PAGE

11. Nickell, *Detecting Forgery*, 123.

QuickCheck Model
PRINT PUBLICATIONS
BOOK: CHAPTER

Source List Entry

AUTHOR   CHAPTER TITLE ...

Brady, Patricia. "Free Men of Color as Tomb Builders in the Nineteenth

...   BOOK TITLE   BOOK EDITOR   ...

Century." *Cross, Crozier, and Crucible*. Glenn R. Conrad, ed. New

PLACE OF PUB'N   PUBLISHER   YEAR   CHAPTER PAGES

Orleans: Archdiocese of New Orleans, 1993. Pages 478–88.

First (Full) Reference Note

AUTHOR   CHAPTER TITLE ...

1. Patricia Brady, "Free Men of Color as Tomb Builders in the Nineteenth

...   BOOK TITLE   BOOK EDITOR   ...

Century," *Cross, Crozier, and Crucible,* Glenn R. Conrad, editor (New

PLACE OF PUB'N   PUBLISHER   YEAR   PAGES

Orleans: Archdiocese of New Orleans, 1993), 478–88, particularly 481.

Subsequent (Short) Note

AUTHOR   CHAPTER TITLE   PAGE

11. Brady, "Free Men of Color as Tomb Builders," 481.

QuickCheck Model
PRINT PUBLICATIONS
BOOK: EDITED

Source List Entry

EDITOR	MAIN TITLE	SUBTITLE	PLACE ...

Miller, Randall M., editor. *"Dear Master": Letters of a Slave Family*. Ithaca,

... OF PUB'N	PUBLISHER	YEAR

New York: Cornell University Press, 1978.

First (Full) Reference Note

EDITOR	TITLE

1. Randall M. Miller, editor, *"Dear Master": Letters of a Slave Family*

PLACE OF PUBLICATION	PUBLISHER	YEAR	PAGE

(Ithaca, New York: Cornell University Press, 1978), 152.

Subsequent (Short) Note

EDITOR	SHORT TITLE	PAGE

11. Miller, *"Dear Master,"* 152.

QuickCheck Model
PRINT PUBLICATIONS
BOOK: MULTIVOLUME SET

Source List Entry

ABSTRACTOR	TITLE	VOLUME DATA
Langley, Clara A.	*South Carolina Deed Abstracts, 1719–1772.*	4 volumes.

PLACE OF PUBLICATION	PUBLISHER	YEAR(S)
Easley, South Carolina:	Southern Historical Press,	1983–84.

First (Full) Reference Note

ABSTRACTOR	TITLE	VOL. DATA
1. Clara A. Langley,	*South Carolina Deed Abstracts, 1719–1772,*	4 vols.

PLACE OF PUBLICATION	PUBLISHER	YEAR(S)	VOL. & PAGE
(Easley, South Carolina:	Southern Historical Press,	1983–84),	4:17.

Subsequent (Short) Note

ABSTRACTOR	TITLE	VOL. & PAGE
11. Langley,	*South Carolina Deed Abstracts, 1719–1772,*	4:17.

QuickCheck Model
PRINT PUBLICATIONS
BOOK: REPRINT
(No new material added)

Source List Entry

AUTHOR	TITLE	ORIGINAL PUB'N YEAR	NEW FORMAT

O'Beirne, H. F. *Leaders and Leading Men of the Indian Territory.* 1891. Reprint,

PLACE OF PUBLICATION	PUBLISHER	YEAR

Conway, Arkansas: Oldbuck Press, 1993.

First (Full) Reference Note

AUTHOR	TITLE	ORIGINAL PUB'N YEAR

1. H. F. O'Beirne, *Leaders and Leading Men of the Indian Territory* (1891;

NEW FORMAT	PLACE OF PUBLICATION	PUBLISHER	YEAR	PAGE

reprint, Conway, Arkansas: Oldbuck Press, 1993), 123.

Subsequent (Short) Note

AUTHOR	TITLE	PAGE

11. O'Beirne, *Leaders and Leading Men of the Indian Territory,* 123.

QuickCheck Model
PRINT PUBLICATIONS
BOOK: REVISED EDITION

Source List Entry

AUTHOR	TITLE

Heinegg, Paul. *Free African Americans of North Carolina and Virginia.*

EDITION DATA	PLACE OF PUBLICATION	PUBLISHER	YEAR

Third edition. Baltimore: Clearfield Co., 1997.

First (Full) Reference Note

AUTHOR	TITLE

1. Paul Heinegg, *Free African Americans of North Carolina and Virginia,*

EDITION DATA	PLACE OF PUBLICATION	PUBLISHER	YEAR	PAGE

3d ed. (Baltimore: Clearfield Co., 1997), 256.

Subsequent (Short) Note

AUTHOR	TITLE*	PAGE

11. Heinegg, *Free African Americans of North Carolina and Virginia,* 256.

*It might appear that this title could be shortened to *Free African Americans.* However, Heinegg has produced several different volumes that begin with those same three words. Before shortening any title, one should be certain the author has not produced similarly titled works.

QuickCheck Model
PRINT PUBLICATIONS
LEAFLET

Source List Entry

AUTHOR   TITLE ...

National Archives and Records Administration. *The Washington National*

...   FORMAT   PLACE OF PUBLICATION   PUBLISHER   YEAR

Records Center. Leaflet. Washington, D.C.: NARA, 2002.

First (Full) Reference Note

AUTHOR   TITLE ...

1. National Archives and Records Administration, *The Washington*

...   FORMAT   PLACE OF PUBLICATION   PUBLISHER   YEAR   PAGE ...

National Records Center, leaflet (Washington, D.C.: NARA, 2002), outside

...

panel 2.

Subsequent (Short) Note

AUTHOR   TITLE ...

11. National Archives and Records Administration, *Washington National*

...   PAGE

Records Center, outside panel 2.

QuickCheck Model
PRINT PUBLICATIONS
MAP

Source List Entry

<u>AUTHOR</u>   <u>TITLE ...</u>

Mouzon, Henry. *An Accurate Map of North and South Carolina with Their*

<u>...</u>   <u>PLACE OF
PUB'N</u>   <u>PUBLISHER</u>   <u>YEAR</u>

Indian Frontiers. London: Thomas Jeffreys, 1775.

First (Full) Reference Note

<u>AUTHOR</u>   <u>TITLE ...</u>

1. Henry Mouzon, *An Accurate Map of North and South Carolina with*

<u>...</u>   <u>PLACE OF
PUB'N</u>   <u>PUBLISHER</u>   <u>YEAR</u>

Their Indian Frontiers (London: Thomas Jeffreys, 1775).

Subsequent (Short) Note

<u>AUTHOR</u>   <u>SHORT TITLE</u>   <u>YEAR</u>

11. Mouzon, *An Accurate Map of North and South Carolina* (1775).

QuickCheck Model
ELECTRONIC PUBLICATIONS
AUDIO BOOK

Source List Entry

AUTHOR	MAIN TITLE	SUBTITLE	FORMAT / ...
Dunn, Jane.	*Elizabeth and Mary: Cousins, Rivals, Queens.*		Audio cassette

... EDITION	PLACE OF PUB'N	PUBLISHER	YEAR
edition.	New York:	Random House Audio Publishing Group,	2004.

First (Full) Reference Note

AUTHOR	MAIN TITLE	SUBTITLE	...
1. Jane Dunn,	*Elizabeth and Mary:*	*Cousins, Rivals, Queens,*	audio

FORMAT/ EDITION	PLACE OF PUBLICATION	PUBLISHER	YEAR
cassette ed.	(New York:	Random House Audio Publishing Group,	2004),

SPECIFIC LOCATION

minute 35.

Subsequent (Short) Note

AUTHOR	SHORT TITLE	SPECIFIC LOCATION
11. Dunn,	*Elizabeth and Mary,*	minute 35.

QuickCheck Model
ELECTRONIC PUBLICATIONS
CD/DVD BOOK (TEXT)

Source List Entry

AUTHOR (TRANSLATOR)	TITLE

Burgoyne, Bruce E., translator. *A Hessian Diary of the American Revolution.*

FORMAT	PLACE OF PUBLICATION	PUBLISHER	YEAR

CD-ROM. Westminster, Maryland: Heritage Books, 2005.

First (Full) Reference Note

AUTHOR (TRANSLATOR)	TITLE ...

1. Bruce E. Burgoyne, transl., *A Hessian Diary of the American Revo-*

...	FORMAT	PLACE OF PUBLICATION	PUBLISHER	YEAR	PAGE

lution, CD-ROM (Westminster, Maryland: Heritage Books, 2005), 123.

Subsequent (Short) Note

AUTHOR (TRANSLATOR)	TITLE	PAGE

11. Burgoyne, *A Hessian Diary of the American Revolution,* 123.

QuickCheck Model
ELECTRONIC PUBLICATIONS
VIDEO

Source List Entry

PRESENTER	TITLE	SERIES ...

Wells, Spencer, host. *Journey of Man: A Genetic Odyssey*. PBS documen-

...	FORMAT	PLACE OF PUB'N	PUBLISHER	YEAR

tary. DVD video. N.p.: Warner Home Video, 2003.

First (Full) Reference Note

PRESENTER	TITLE	...

1. Spencer Wells, host, *Journey of Man: A Genetic Odyssey*, PBS

... SERIES	FORMAT	PLACE OF PUB'N	PUBLISHER	YEAR	SPECIFIC LOCATION

documentary, DVD video (N.p.: Warner Home Video, 2003), minute 37.

Subsequent (Short) Note

PRESENTER	SHORT TITLE	SPECIFIC LOCATION

11. Wells, *Journey of Man*, minute 37.

QuickCheck Model
ELECTRONIC PUBLICATIONS
WEBSITE AS "BOOK"
(Website devoted to one single item)

Source List Entry

AUTHOR	TITLE OF WEBSITE	URL (DIGITAL LOCATION) ...

Kestenbaum, Larry. *The Political Graveyard.* http://politicalgraveyard

...	YEAR

.com : 2007.

First (Full) Reference Note

AUTHOR	WEBSTITE TITLE	URL (DIGITAL ...

1.   Larry Kestenbaum, *The Political Graveyard* (http://political

... LOCATION)	DATE	ITEM OF INTEREST

graveyard.com : accessed 25 March 2007), "Matteo, Salvatore T."

Subsequent (Short) Note

AUTHOR	WEBSITE TITLE	ITEM OF INTEREST

11.   Kestenbaum, *The Political Graveyard,* "Matteo, Salvatore T."

QuickCheck Model
IMAGE COPIES
CD/DVD PUBLICATION

Source List Entry

AUTHOR	TITLE	ORIGINAL PUB'N YEAR

Fox, William F. *Regimental Losses in the Civil War, 1861–1865.* 1889.

NEW FORMAT	DVD TITLE

Image reprint, DVD-ROM. *The Complete Civil War on DVD-ROM.*

PLACE OF PUBLICATION	PUBLISHER	YEAR

Carmel, Indiana: CivilWarAmerica.com, 2005.

First (Full) Reference Note

AUTHOR	TITLE

1.   William F. Fox, *Regimental Losses in the Civil War, 1861–1865*

ORIGINAL PUBL'N YEAR	NEW FORMAT	DVD TITLE

(1889), image reprint, DVD-ROM, *The Complete Civil War on DVD-ROM*

PLACE OF PUBLICATION	PUBLISHER	YEAR	PAGE

(Carmel, Indiana: CivilWarAmerica.com, 2005), 23.

Subsequent (Short) Note

AUTHOR	SHORT TITLE	PAGE

11.   Fox, *Regimental Losses in the Civil War*, 23.

QuickCheck Model
IMAGE COPIES
MICROFILM, FHL-GSU (PRESERVATION COPY)
(Unpublished film of a published book)

Source List Entry

AUTHOR	TITLE	TRANSLATION OF TITLE

Martín, Jesús Larios. *Dinastías reales de España* [Royal dynasties of Spain].

ORIGINAL PUBLICATION DATA (PLACE: PUBLISHER, YEAR)	FILM ID	POSITION ON FILM

Madrid, Spain: Hidalguía, 1963. FHL microfilm 1,181,722, item 9.

FILM REPOSITORY	FILM REP'Y LOCATION

Family History Library, Salt Lake City, Utah.

First (Full) Reference Note

AUTHOR	TITLE	TRANSLATION OF ...

11. Jesús Larios Martín, *Dinastías reales de España* [Royal dynasties

... TITLE	ORIGINAL PUBLICATION DATA (PLACE: PUBLISHER, YEAR)	PAGE	FILM ID	POSITION ON FILM

of Spain] (Madrid: Hidalguía, 1963), 23; FHL microfilm 1,181,722, item 9.

Subsequent (Short) Note

AUTHOR	TITLE	PAGE

11. Martín, *Dinastías reales de Espaóa*, 23.

659

QuickCheck Model
IMAGE COPIES
MICROFILM PUBLICATION
(Commercially published microfilm)

Source List Entry

AUTHOR	TITLE	ORIGINAL ...

Bligh, Reginald. *A Case of Extreme and Unparalleled Hardship*. London:

... PUBLICATION DATA (PLACE: PUBLISHER, YEAR)	FILM PUBLICATION SERIES	ROLL & ...

Printed for the Author, 1799. *Early English Book Series*. Roll 6400,

... ITEM	PLACE OF FILM PUBLICATION	FILM PUBLISHER	YEAR

no. 15. Woodbridge, Connecticut: Research Publications, 1986.

First (Full) Reference Note

AUTHOR	TITLE

11. Reginald Bligh, *A Case of Extreme and Unparalleled Hardship*

ORIGINAL PUBLICATION DATA (PLACE: PUBLISHER, YEAR)	PAGE	FILM PUBLICATION SERIES

(London: Printed for the Author, 1799), 34; *Early English Book Series*

PLACE OF FILM PUBLICATION	FILM PUBLISHER	YEAR	ROLL & ITEM

(Woodbridge, Connecticut: Research Publications, 1986), roll 6400, no. 15.

Subsequent (Short) Note

AUTHOR	TITLE	PAGE

11. Bligh, *A Case of Extreme and Unparalleled Hardship*, 15.

QuickCheck Model
IMAGE COPIES
ONLINE PUBLICATION

Source List Entry

AUTHOR	TITLE ...

Gardiner, Samuel Rawson. *Reports of Cases in the Courts of the Star*

...	ORIGINAL PUB'N YEAR	NEW FORMAT	WEBSITE ...

Chamber and High Commission. 1886. Digital images. *Cornell University*

... TITLE	URL (DIGITAL LOCATION)	YEAR

Library Historical Monographs. http://historical.library.cornell.edu : 2007.

First (Full) Reference Note

AUTHOR	TITLE ...

1. Samuel Rawson Gardiner, *Reports of Cases in the Courts of the Star*

...	ORIG. PUB'N YEAR	PAGE	NEW FORMAT	...

Chamber and High Commission (1886), 139; digital images, *Cornell*

... WEBSITE TITLE	URL (DIGITAL LOCATION)

University Library Historical Monographs (http://historical.library.cornell.edu :

... DATE

accessed 20 February 2007).

Subsequent (Short) Note

AUTHOR	SHORT TITLE	PAGE

11. Gardiner, *Reports of Cases in the Courts of the Star Chamber,* 139.

GUIDELINES
& Examples

BASIC ISSUES

12.1   Abbreviations in Book Citations

History writers rarely abbreviate amid their narrative or text but often do so in their citations, within certain parameters. Basic principles of abbreviation are covered at 2.55–2.56. In working with publications specifically, the following guidelines apply:

AUTHOR'S NAME .... Spell out in full, as it appears on the book's title page. If initials appear in lieu of given names but those names are known, you may state the full name, so long as you place square editorial brackets around the added information.

AUTHOR'S ROLE .... (Abstractor, compiler, editor, transcriber, translator, etc.) Spell out in full in Source List Entry; abbreviate in Reference Notes, if desired.

TITLE OF BOOK .... Copy exactly from the title page—not the cover or spine. Do not abbreviate words that are spelled out in the title, and do not spell out words the title abbreviates. Be especially careful in rendering words or phrases that are commonly written in multiple ways.

Example—If a title refers to "World War II," do not write it as WW II or World War Two. Doing so can cause negative searches when you or your readers attempt to relocate the title in electronic catalogs. Even an added or dropped space between the elements of *WW II* will negate a search.

PUBLICATION PLACE ..... Spell out the city name in full. State or country names may be abbreviated, so long as you use standard abbreviations.

PUBLISHER .... Names of commercial firms are usually spelled out, except for the word *Company,* which may be abbreviated as *Co.* Suffixes that denote the *kind* of company, such as *Inc.* and *Ltd.,* are commonly dropped. *University,* when it appears in the name of a publisher, is frequently abbreviated as *Univ.*

12.2   Basic Citation Forms: Source Lists vs. Reference Notes

Citations to published works differ in several regards from citations to the manuscript materials covered in previous chapters. In addition to the basic citation principles discussed in Chapter 2, the following guidelines apply when citing books and other "stand-alone" publications such as leaflets, pamphlets, and videos.

With works of this class, the Source List Entry and the First Reference Note are quite similar in form. The primary differences are in (*a*) the arrangement of the author's name, (*b*) punctuation, and (*c*) page references. Basic guidelines are as follows:

AUTHOR NAMES, GIVEN VS. SURNAME

SOURCE LIST .... Arrange entries alphabetically by author's last name. Position suffixes immediately after the surname, with no intervening punctuation.

SOURCE LIST ENTRY ...... Invert names (Last, First Middle), so entries can be alphabetically arranged by surname.

FIRST REFERENCE NOTE .. Write author's name in normal sequence. In Western style, that is: First Middle Last.

SUBSEQUENT NOTE .... Use last name only, unless you are citing multiple authors with the same last name. In that case, you may wish to repeat the given name(s) to distinguish between authors.

PAGE NUMBERS

SOURCE LIST ENTRY ...... Page numbers are typically not cited in a Source List Entry. However, when your reference is to an individually authored chapter within an edited work, your Source List should cite inclusive pages for that chapter.

REFERENCE NOTES .... Typically, you will cite only the page or pages that support what you say in your text. If your reference is to one individually authored chapter

663

in a larger edited work, you may wish to cite the full chapter, then add "specifically, p. ___" or similar language to focus upon the exact page.

PUNCTUATION

SOURCE LIST ENTRY ...... Each major element of the citation is separated by a *full stop* (a *period*).

FIRST REFERENCE NOTE .. Most major elements are separated by *commas*. However, complex citations to a single source may require *semicolons* to separate major parts, in which case commas are used to separate smaller items within each major part. These situations are not typically an issue when citing books, although exceptions exist such as those at 12.33–12.34.

Publication data for print publications are set off by *parentheses*, with a *colon* separating the place of publication from the name of the publisher. *A comma will not appear immediately before a parenthesis in a correctly punctuated citation.*

Publication data for web-based works are also set off by *parentheses*, with a *colon* separating the URL from the date of publication or access.

When citing multiple sources in a single note, place a *full stop* (a *period*) between each cited source to clearly indicate where one source stops and another starts.

Note: Some manuals recommend that all sources cited in a reference note be combined into one sentence, with semicolons separating each publication from the other. However, history researchers who use original, manuscript material will have many complex sources that require internal semicolons. Using a full stop (a period) to separate each source will prevent confusion as to where one source ends and the next one starts.

SUBSEQUENT NOTE .... *Commas* typically separate (*a*) individual elements in a citation to a single source or (*b*) the smallest level in a complex citation.

12.3 Basic Format: Books & Other "Stand-alone" Publications
See also QuickCheck Model *for* PRINT PUBLICATIONS: BOOK, BASIC FORMAT

Source List Entry
Fogleman, Aaron Spencer. *Hopeful Journeys: German Immigration, Settlement, and Political Culture in Colonial America, 1717–1775.* Philadelphia: University of Pennsylvania Press, 1996.

First Reference Note
1. Aaron Spencer Fogleman, *Hopeful Journeys: German Immigration, Settlement, and Political Culture in Colonial America, 1717–1775* (Philadelphia: University of Pennsylvania Press, 1996), 147.

Subsequent Note
11. Fogleman, *Hopeful Journeys,* 147.

12.4 Ibid. References
See also 2.69

Ibid., as the abbreviation for *ibidem* (meaning "in the same place" or "in the same source"), is appropriate only when

- two consecutive notes cite the same source; and
- the first of those consecutive notes contains just one source.

First Reference Note
1. Frank Ching, *Ancestors: 900 Years in the Life of a Chinese Family* (New York: William Morrow, 1988), 156.
2. Russell Jones, *Chinese Names: The Traditions Surrounding the Use of Chinese Surnames and Personal Names* (Petaling Jaya, Malaysia: Pelanduk Publications, ca. 1997), 133.

Subsequent Note
11. Ching, *Ancestors,* 156.
12. Ibid., 178.
13. Ibid., 239; Jones, *Chinese Names,* 133.
14. Ching, *Ancestors,* 180.

At notes 12 and 13, ibid. is appropriately used because each note refers to the same one source that precedes it. In note 14, ibid. cannot be used because the preceding note cites two different sources.

MULTIPLE SOURCES IN SAME CITATION
Section 12.2 instructs you to use a period (full stop) to separate the sources, when creating full citations to complex sources. However, in note 13 above, the citation is so simple that both sources can be cited in the same "sentence," separated by a semicolon, without diminishing clarity.

CITATION PARTS

AUTHORS & CREATORS

12.5 **Author, Defined**

In a literary sense, *authors* of nonfiction are those who accumulate a body of knowledge through research and/or practical experience, then

- analyze that knowledge;
- weigh the usefulness of each part;
- determine how to link the most relevant information; and
- use their conclusions to create new and original narratives.

When you cite works that fit this description, you need cite only the author's name. Your readers will take it for granted that you are referencing an authored book.

12.6 **Author's Role**

In library catalogs, the word *author* is often used synonymously with *creator*. Many works used by historical writers involve other creative roles, as with *abstractor, compiler, editor, indexer, translator,* and *transcriber.* (See Glossary for definitions of each.) As a researcher who must analyze every element of a source, you will want to note the exact role of the creator of each published source you use. For example:

> ### Source List Entry
> Taylor, Maureen, compiler. *Register of Seamen's Protection Certificates from the Providence, Rhode Island Custom District, 1796–1870.* Baltimore: Clearfield Company, 1995.

> ### First Reference Note
> 1. Maureen Taylor, compiler, *Register of Seamen's Protection Certificates from the Providence, Rhode Island Custom District, 1796–1870* (Baltimore: Clearfield Co., 1995), 145.

> ### Subsequent Note
> 1. Taylor, *Register of Seamen's Protection Certificates ... Providence, Rhode Island,* 145.

If the title of a publication makes clear the role of the creator, then it need not be repeated after that person's name. In the following example, the title clearly identifies the publication as a book of abstracts. It would therefore be redundant to add "abstractor" after the creator's name.

Source List Entry
Moore, Caroline T. *Abstracts of Records of the Province of South Carolina, 1692–1721.* Columbia, South Carolina: R. L. Bryan Co., 1978.

First Reference Note
1. Caroline T. Moore, *Abstracts of Records of the Province of South Carolina, 1692–1721* (Columbia, South Carolina: R. L. Bryan Co., 1978), 27.

12.7   Author's Role: Abstractor or Transcriber

These terms may be used, or used incorrectly, or not used at all on a book's title page. As a researcher, you will want to evaluate the work and describe it appropriately. For example, consider these two works and the data provided on their title pages:

Mays, Edith. *Amherst Papers, 1756–1763, The Southern Sector: Despatches from South Carolina, Virginia, and His Majesty's Superintendent of Indian Affairs.* Bowie, Maryland: Heritage Books, 1999.
Ritter, Kathy A. *Apprentices of Connecticut, 1637–1900.* Salt Lake City: Ancestry Publishing, 1986.

Neither Mays nor Ritter states her role on her title page. It is clear from examining each book that Mays transcribed documents in full, while Ritter prepared abstracts. That distinction is important to evaluating the information you take from their books.

The title of Ritter's book is also one appropriate for a general history of apprenticeships in Connecticut. By identifying her as *abstractor,* rather than *author,* you clarify the nature of the book. Careful notetaking would produce the following:

Source List Entry
Mays, Edith, transcriber. *Amherst Papers, 1756–1763, The Southern Sector: Despatches from South Carolina, Virginia, and His Majesty's Superintendent of Indian Affairs.* Bowie, Maryland: Heritage Books, 1999.
Ritter, Kathy A., abstractor. *Apprentices of Connecticut, 1637–1900.* Salt Lake City, Utah: Ancestry Publishing, 1986.

First Reference Note
1. Edith Mays, transcriber, *Amherst Papers, 1756–1763, The Southern Sector: Despatches from South Carolina, Virginia, and His Majesty's Superintendent of Indian Affairs* (Bowie, Maryland: Heritage Books, 1999), 295–99.
2. Kathy A. Ritter, abstractor, *Apprentices of Connecticut, 1637–1900* (Salt Lake City, Utah: Ancestry Publishing, 1986), 49.

Subsequent Note

    11. Mays, *Amherst Papers ... Southern Sector,* 132.

    12. Ritter, *Apprentices of Connecticut,* 49.

12.8   Author's Role: Compiler or Author

Family histories have often been called *compiled* works, language left over from the days when many genealogies presented only bare-bones begats listing names, dates, and places for people grouped into family clusters. By today's expectations, however, a well-done genealogy consists of far more than mere names and dates. It includes considerable biographical information, historical context, and evidence analysis—all of which make it an *authored* work.

Consider, for example, the following Source List Entries whose details are taken from the title pages of each book.

> Andrews, John Lennell Jr. *South Carolina Revolutionary War Indents: A Schedule*. Columbia, South Carolina: SCMAR, 2001.
> Fiske, Jane Fletcher, compiler. *Thomas Cooke of Rhode Island*. 2 vols. Boxford, Massachusetts: Privately printed, 1987.

Although Fiske's title page identifies her as "compiler," your evaluation of the book informs you that it is not a mere assembly of raw facts. Fiske did, indeed, produce a book that fits the definition of an *authored* work. Therefore, to help with your future analysis of material from that source, your research notes would *not* label her a "compiler."

By comparison, the Andrews book is clearly a *compiled* work—a database listing names, dates, volumes, etc.—rather than an authored work. His title page does not call him a compiler. However, as an analytical researcher you would want to add that information to your citation to clearly identify the nature of his book.

All points considered, careful notetaking would produce the following Source List Entries:

> Andrews, John Lennell Jr., compiler. *South Carolina Revolutionary War Indents: A Schedule*. Columbia, South Carolina: SCMAR, 2001.
> Fiske, Jane Fletcher. *Thomas Cooke of Rhode Island*. 2 vols. Boxford, Massachusetts: Privately printed, 1987.

12.9   Author's Role: Translator or Transcriber

Guides to abbreviations often recommend *trans.* for both *transcriber* and *translator*. However, history researchers use works of both types and need to distinguish one abbreviation from the other. If you prefer to abbreviate these terms in your citations, *transcr.* and *transl.* would preserve critical distinctions. For example:

Source List Entry
Costa, Myldred Masson, translator. *The Letters of Marie Madeleine Hachard, 1727–28.* New Orleans: Laborde Printing Co., 1974.

Osborne, Francis Mardon, transcriber. *The Church Wardens' Accounts of St. Michael's Church, Chagford, 1480–1600.* Chagford, England: Redwood Burn, ca. 1979.

First Reference Note
1. Myldred Masson Costa, transl., *The Letters of Marie Madeleine Hachard, 1727–28* (New Orleans: Laborde Printing Co., 1974), 17.

2. Francis Mardon Osborne, transcr., *The Church Wardens' Accounts of St. Michael's Church, Chagford, 1480–1600* (Chagford, England: Redwood Burn, ca. 1979), 37.

Subsequent Note
11. Costa, *Letters of Marie Madeleine Hachard,* 17.

12. Osborne, *Church Wardens' Accounts of St. Michael's Church, Chagford, 1480–1600,* 37.

12.10   Authors, Multiple
See also Edited Works, 12.63–12.66

When a book has two authors, both are cited. In the Source List Entry, only the first author's name is inverted. In a Subsequent Note, both authors are cited by surname only. If both authors have the same surname, convention prefers that they not be coupled under the one surname. Each name should appear independently.

Source List Entry
Salmon, John S., and Emily J. Salmon. *Franklin County, Virginia, 1786–1986: A Bicentennial History.* Rocky Mount, Virginia: Franklin County Bicentennial Commission, 1993.

First Reference Note
1. John S. Salmon and Emily J. Salmon, *Franklin County, Virginia, 1786–1986: A Bicentennial History* (Rocky Mount, Virginia: Franklin County Bicentennial Commission, 1993), 234.

Subsequent Note
11. Salmon and Salmon, *Franklin County, Virginia,* 234.

When a book has three or more authors, you may name all or just the first one, replacing the other names with *et al.* (i.e., the abbreviation for *et alii,* meaning *and others*). The term is frequently used in cases such as the "with Alexander Sharon" example below, in which an additional author is assigned a subordinate role.

Source List Entry

Huerta, Herrera; Juan Manuel; and Vicente San Vicente Tello. *Archivo General de la Nación, México: Guía General.* Mexico City: Archivo General, 1990.

Mokotoff, Gary, and Sallyann Amdur Sack; with Alexander Sharon. *Where Once We Walked: A Guide to the Jewish Communities Destroyed in the Holocaust.* Bergenfield, New Jersey: Avotaynu, 2002.

First Reference Note

1. Herrera Huerta, Juan Manuel, and Vicente San Vicente Tello, *Archivo General de la Nación, México: Guía General* (Mexico City: Archivo General, 1990), 37–42.

2. Gary Mokotoff, Sallyann Amdur Sack, et al., *Where Once We Walked: A Guide to the Jewish Communities Destroyed in the Holocaust* (Bergenfield, New Jersey: Avotaynu, 2002), 32–37.

Subsequent Note

11. Huerta, Manuel, and Tello, *Archivo General de la Nación,* 38.

12. Mokotoff, Sack, et al., *Where Once We Walked,* 33.

PUNCTUATION BETWEEN MULTIPLE AUTHORS

Items in a series are separated by commas, as with the names of the three authors in notes 1 and 11. However, in the Source List Entry above, inverting the name of the main author invokes a different rule, because it requires a comma to separate Huerta's last name from his first. In that case, the three main items in the series—the names of the three authors—are separated by semicolons rather than commas.

12.11 Authors, Unidentified

When a book's title page fails to identify an author, you might find that identity in a library catalog or it may be common knowledge. In such cases, you may choose to credit the author in your notes, placing the added material in square editorial brackets to signify that you are adding an identity not provided by the source itself.

Source List Entry

[Colket, Meredith B., Jr., and Frank E. Bridgers]. *Guide to Genealogical Records in the National Archives.* Washington, D.C.: National Archives and Records Service, 1982.

First Reference Note

1. [Meredith B. Colket Jr. and Frank E. Bridgers], *Guide to*

Genealogical Records in the National Archives (Washington, D.C.: National Archives and Records Service, 1982), 11.

Subsequent Note
11. [Colket and Bridgers], *Guide to Genealogical Records in the National Archives*, 11.

12.12 Authors, Unknown
When you do not know the author's identity, you may substitute *Anonymous* or simply leave blank the Author Field of your citation.

Source List Entry
American Indians: A Select Catalog of National Archives Microfilm Publications. Washington, D.C.: National Archives Trust Fund Board, 1995.

[Anonymous]. *Guide to the National Archives of the United States.* Washington, D.C.: National Archives and Records Service, 1974.

First Reference Note
1. *American Indians: A Select Catalog of National Archives Microfilm Publications* (Washington, D.C.: National Archives Trust Fund Board, 1995), 39.

2. [Anonymous], *Guide to the National Archives of the United States* (Washington, D.C.: National Archives and Records Service, 1974), 237.

Subsequent Note
11. *American Indians: A Select Catalog of National Archives Microfilm Publications*, 39.

12. [Anonymous], *Guide to the National Archives of the United States*, 237.

PAGE & ENTRY NUMBERS

12.13 Citing Pages vs. Entries
Many compiled works organize their material by entry numbers or by named entries. Identifying the specific entry can be useful when the material on a page is particularly dense or when names are rendered under peculiar variations. As a careful notetaker, you will likely use this practice during research, even if you choose to drop the entry identification in your published citations.

When citing pages, modern writers rarely use *page, p.,* or *p. no.* before the number. However, if you are referencing works that have other numbers to be cited, then each number set needs to be specifically identified. In your citation, you may spell out *page* or you may abbreviate it. However, abbreviating the less common term *entry* could confuse readers. A typical citation using both sets of numbers would follow this pattern:

Source List Entry

Mills, Elizabeth Shown. *Natchitoches, 1800–1826: Translated Abstracts of Register Number Five of the Catholic Church Parish of St. François des Natchitoches in Louisiana.* New Orleans: Polyanthos, 1980.

First Reference Note

1. Elizabeth Shown Mills, *Natchitoches, 1800–1826: Translated Abstracts of Register Number Five of the Catholic Church Parish of St. François des Natchitoches in Louisiana* (New Orleans: Polyanthos, 1980), page 96, entry 595, for "Maria Clara Eslect" [Chelette].

Subsequent Note

11. Mills, *Natchitoches, 1800–1826,* p. 96, entry 595.

CLARIFYING AN ENTRY

Square editorial brackets are used around the name *Chelette*, above, because that spelling correction is added for clarification. The brackets tell readers that the added name does not appear in the original.

12.14 Page Numbers, Missing

Most published books are paginated. When you use one that is not, you should state the absence of pagination and look for some means by which the specific page can be identified. For example:

Source List Entry

St. James Catholic Church, Gadsden, Alabama, 1876–1976. Gadsden: The parish, 1976.

First Reference Note

1. *St. James Catholic Church, Gadsden, Alabama, 1876–1976* (Gadsden: The parish, 1976), unpaginated, 10th page.

Subsequent Note

11. *St. James Catholic Church, Gadsden,* unpaginated, 10th page.

Special items tipped into books (photos, maps, etc.) often are not paginated. An unnumbered item can be cited by identifying the pages before and after it.

Source List Entry

Biographical and Historical Memoirs of Northwest Louisiana. Nashville, Tennessee: Southern Publishing Co., 1890.

First Reference Note
> 1. *Biographical and Historical Memoirs of Northwest Louisiana* (Nashville, Tennessee: Southern Publishing Co., 1890), "Photograph of Wm. F. Moreland," unnumbered page tipped between 456 and 457.

Subsequent Note
> 11. *Biographical and Historical Memoirs of Northwest Louisiana,* unnumbered page between 456 and 457.

PUBLICATION FACTS

12.15   Details, Missing

Three notations are common when standard publication data does not appear in the book and cannot be located in a cataloging database.

PUBLICATION PLACE ..... No place *or* n.p.
PUBLISHER .... No publisher *or* n.p.
              (*See also* **12.20,** Self-published Works)
PUBLICATION DATE .... No date *or* n.d.

If a piece of information is known, though not printed in the book, it may be inserted in the proper place in square editorial brackets, as with the City of Louisville example, below.

Source List Entry
> Blankenship, Bob. *Cherokee Roots.* Gatlinburg, Tennessee: Buckhorn Press, no date.
> Gerling, Juanita. *The Poly Family History.* No place: No publisher, 1989.
> *Official Commemorative Book for the Sesquicentennial of Louisville, Ohio.* Louisville: [City of Louisville], 1984.

First Reference Note
> 1. Bob Blankenship, *Cherokee Roots* (Gatlinburg, Tennessee: Buckhorn Press, n.d.), 7.
> 2. Juanita Gerling, *The Poly Family History* (N.p.: n.p., 1989), 9.
> 3. *Official Commemorative Book for the Sesquicentennial of Louisville, Ohio* (Louisville: [City of Louisville], 1984), 10.

Subsequent Note
> 11. Blankenship, *Cherokee Roots,* 7.
> 12. Gerling, *Poly Family History,* 9.
> 13. *Official Commemorative Book for the Sesquicentennial of Louisville,* 10.

12.16   Places of Publication, Multiple

Major publishers often have multiple locations. You need cite only one. If you wish to cite both in your Source List Entry, you need not repeat both in your First Reference Note.

Source List Entry
Malone, Ann Patton. *Sweet Chariot: Slave Family & Household Structure in Nineteenth-Century Louisiana.* Chapel Hill, North Carolina, and London, England: University of North Carolina Press, 1992.

First Reference Note
1. Ann Patton Malone, *Sweet Chariot: Slave Family & Household Structure in Nineteenth-Century Louisiana* (Chapel Hill: University of North Carolina Press, 1992), 123.

12.17 Publishers, Identification of

Many academic presses omit the names of publishers from their citations. That economy works for them because academic citations to published works are theoretically limited to vetted works issued by publishing houses that are easily identified and located.

Omitting publishers, however, creates problems when using the thousands of works issued each year by small presses or self-publishers. To help researchers identify and locate more obscure works, this manual recommends that citations include all three publication facts that are traditional for Humanities Style—i.e., place of publication, publisher, and date.

12.18 Publishers, Multiple

When a book has different publishers in different countries, citing just one is commonplace, although citing both in the Source List Entry or the First Reference Note will benefit international readers.

Source List Entry
Grenham, John. *Tracing Your Irish Ancestors: The Complete Guide.* Dublin: Gill and Macmillan, 1992. Baltimore: Genealogical Publishing Co., 1993.

First Reference Note
1. John Grenham, *Tracing Your Irish Ancestors: The Complete Guide* (Dublin: Gill and Macmillan, 1992), 40.

Subsequent Note
11. Grenham, *Tracing Your Irish Ancestors,* 40.

12.19 Publishers, Name Changes

When a publisher changes its name or merges into another publishing house, the name change is immaterial to your citation. You cite the publisher as identified on the title page of the book you use. For multivolume sets or series that have a change in publishers from one volume to the next, see 12.85, for "Multiple Editors and Publishers."

12.20 Self-published Works

When a book's title page indicates it is privately published, that fact may be reported in several ways. Placing "The Author," "Privately printed," or *p.p.* in the publisher's field are all common practices.

Because self-published works seldom appear in publishing directories, the Library of Congress now follows a practice you may wish to adopt: placing the author-publisher's address (as shown on the title page or its reverse) amid your publication data. The LC format uses square brackets around the street or postal address.

Source List Entry

Brandt, Edward R. *Learning and Deciphering the Gothic Script*. Minneapolis, Minnesota: Edward R. Brandt [13 Twenty-Seventh Avenue S.E., 55414-3101], 1990.

First Reference Note

1. Edward R. Brandt, *Learning and Deciphering the Gothic Script* (Minneapolis: Edward R. Brandt [13 Twenty-Seventh Avenue S.E., 55414-3101], 1990), 21.

Subsequent Note

11. Brandt, *Learning and Deciphering the Gothic Script*, 21.

TITLES

12.21 Titles, Citing Full vs. Shortened
See also 2.22, 2.43, and 2.45

Copy each title *precisely* in your research notes, making no alterations in spellings or abbreviations. When you begin writing your narrative—or when you enter records and sources into a data-management program—you have choices to make between the use of *full* titles or *short* titles. The basic rules are these:

SOURCE LIST ENTRY ...... Use full title.

FIRST REFERENCE NOTE .. Use full title. (*But see* 12.56 for an exception.)

SUBSEQUENT NOTE .... You may shorten a long title after your First Reference Note cites it fully.

Creating short titles for publications involves several considerations:

BASIC PRINCIPLES
Your short title should

- draw from the first few words of the title;
- clearly convey the subject of the book; and
- distinguish that book from other works with similar titles or other works by the same author.

Consider this basic example:

First Reference Note
1. Henry Putney Beers, *The Confederacy: A Guide to the Archives of the Government of the Confederate States of America* (Washington, D.C.: National Archives and Records Administration, 1986), 36.

Subsequent Note
11. Beers, *The Confederacy,* 36.

In a well-punctuated book title, the colon typically represents the break between the main title and the subtitle. That break is commonly a stopping point for the shortened title. However, if the main title does not clearly identify the focus of the book, words from the subtitle should be included in the shortened citation. For example:

First Reference Note
1. Leonard Mosley, *Blood Relations: The Rise and Fall of the duPonts of Delaware* (New York: Atheneum, 1980), 165.

Subsequent Note
11. Mosley, *Blood Relations ... duPonts of Delaware,* 165.

USING ELLIPSES IN SHORTENED TITLES
See also 2.67

If you shorten a title by leaving out words in its middle, as in the Mosley example above, you would indicate the omission with three evenly spaced dots (ellipsis points) carrying a space before and after. If you shorten a title by leaving out words at the end of the title, as with the Beers example, you omit the ellipsis points entirely.

SHORTENING TITLES, WHEN USING MULTIPLE WORKS OF SIMILAR TITLES
When an author or compiler issues multiple books with similar titles but differing dates, the short title should include those dates to distinguish that book from others of similar title. The next example demonstrates how to shorten a title in situations of this type. Both publications are cited in the Source List Entry for comparison.

Source List Entry

Green, Karen Mauer, compiler. *The Kentucky Gazette, 1787–1800: Genealogical and Historical Abstracts*. Baltimore: Gateway Press, 1986.
————. *The Kentucky Gazette, 1801–1820: Genealogical and Historical Abstracts*. Baltimore: Gateway Press, 1985.

First Reference Note

1. Karen Mauer Green, compiler, *The Kentucky Gazette, 1801–1820: Genealogical and Historical Abstracts* (Baltimore: Gateway Press, 1985), 117.

Subsequent Note

11. Green, *Kentucky Gazette, 1801–1820,* 117.

(*not*)

11. Green, *Kentucky Gazette,* 117.

12.22 Titles, Correcting & Clarifying

If you add words within the title to clarify it, you should place the addition or correction in square editorial brackets. In the first example below, a place was added because neither the book's title nor its place of publication gives a clue to the location of the "Public Records Office." In the second example, a typo on the title page is corrected by placing the missing letter in square editorial brackets.

Source List Entry

Colwell, Stella. *Family Roots: Discovering the Past in the Public Record Office* [London]. Rutland, Vermont: Charles E. Tuttle Co., 1991.
Wright, May B. *Abbots of Abilene, Texas, and [T]heir Kin: My Families from the Wrong Side of Blanket*. Blanket, Texas: Rootingaround Press, 1960.

12.23 Titles, Inconsistencies within

When the title on a book cover differs from that on the title page, use the wording on the title page.

12.24 Titles, Italics vs. Quotation Marks

See also 2.72 and 2.76

Titles of some published works appear in italics, while others are placed in quotation marks. The guiding principles are these:

Book Titles .... Set in italics.

"Chapter Titles" .... Set in quotation marks.

Series Titles .... Do not use either unless you cite the whole series *instead of* individual volumes (*cf.*

12.85. In that case, the series title should be italicized.

12.25 Titles, Multiple by Same Author
See also 2.65

When you use multiple works by the same author, your Working Source List should write the author's name in full in each entry. In the final draft of the bibliography you plan to publish, you should not repeat the author's name in every entry. You should spell it out in full in the first entry, then substitute a 3-em dash for the name in each subsequent entry.

If the author's name changes at some point amid his or her publishing career, the different names are not consolidated. You should retain the author's identity as it was when each book was published.

Source List Entry
Barefield, Marilyn Davis, compiler. *The Old Mardisville, Lebanon & Centre Land Office Records & Military Warrants, 1834–1860.* Greenville, South Carolina: Southern Historical Press, 1990.

Hahn, Marilyn Davis, compiler. *Old Cahaba Land Office Records & Military Warrants, 1817–1853.* Birmingham, Alabama: Southern University Press, 1986.

———. *Old St. Stephen's Land Office Records & American State Papers, Public Lands, Vol. 1, 1768–1888.* Greenville, South Carolina: Southern Historical Press, 1983.

ITALICIZING VOLUME NUMBERS
As a rule, when a volume number appears between a title and a subtitle, the volume number is not italicized because it is not part of the title. In the last Hahn example above, the volume reference *is* part of Hahn's title because it specifies which volume of *ASP* she abstracted.

12.26 Titles, Punctuation & Capitalization
See also 2.22–2.23, 2.59–2.61

Book titles often do not follow standard rules of punctuation or capitalization. Many typesetters omit punctuation marks at the ends of lines when they set a title on the cover or the title page. If you convert that layout to a citation without adding the punctuation, the result would be poor grammar or syntax. In other cases, the author may have used personal preferences rather than standard conventions.

You may silently correct punctuation and capitalization problems in your source citation. Simply use correct procedures for the language in which you are writing. For example, the Wright citation at 12.22 contains two corrections, one of them silent. First, Wright's title page carries the expected comma *before* Texas but it does not place the matching comma *after* Texas. The punctuation has been silently corrected. Second, an obvious typo is corrected in the word *Their;* the missing *T* appears in square editorial brackets to flag the correction. The two corrections are handled differently for two reasons:

- Punctuation requires correction so often that the use of brackets around added punctuation would be excessive and distracting.

- Punctuation is usually ignored when title searches are run in catalogs and databases, but the *wording* of the title must be exact. An added letter or a dropped letter can nullify a search. Any additions or corrections must be clearly flagged.

English capitalizes more liberally than most other Western languages—each of which has its own rules. Conventionally, English book titles capitalize every word except articles, prepositions, and conjunctions; if one of these appears at the start of a title or subtitle, it is also capitalized. French titles typically capitalize only proper nouns and the first word of the title and subtitle, while German titles capitalize first words and every noun. *The Chicago Manual of Style,* cited in the bibliography, offers extensive capitalization rules for titles in other languages.

12.27 Titles, Translated
See 2.23

12.28 Titles within a Title
Italics are used for book titles, as noted under 2.68 and 12.24. However, when a title contains the title of another publication, the type on the internal title is reversed from italics to roman typeface.

Source List Entry
Bloom, Harold, editor. *Kate Chopin's* The Awakening. Broomall, Pennsylvania: Chelsea House, 1999.

First Reference Note
1.   Harold Bloom, editor, *Kate Chopin's* The Awakening (Broomall, Pennsylvania: Chelsea House, 1999), 72.

Subsequent Note
11.   Bloom, *Kate Chopin's* The Awakening, 72.

SPECIAL PUBLICATION TYPES

ANTHOLOGIES

12.29   Anthology vs. New Edition

Anthologies are special publications that assemble items selected from a much larger body of work. They are new works and are cited as such—with an added reference to the original publication data for the specific item you have used. When a full run of a journal is reproduced and offered in a different medium, it constitutes a *new edition* of the same work. See 14.16 for the CD-ROM example.

12.30   Anthologies, Dual Credit Needed

Citing an anthology usually means citing two separate works in both the Source List Entry and the First Reference Note:

- the anthology that is being used; and
- the original publication.

Many anthologies are published long after the material was created. Therefore, the original date of publication is an important factor to consider in your evidence analysis. As demonstrated below, you first cite what you have actually consulted (the item in the anthology). Then you briefly identify the original publication by time and place:

Source List Entry

Halbert, Henry S. "Okla Hannali; or, the Six Towns District of the Choctaws." *A Choctaw Sourcebook.* John H. Peterson Jr., editor. New York: Garland Publishing Co., 1985. Originally published, *American Antiquarian and Oriental Journal* 15 (1893): 146–49.

First Reference Note

1. Henry S. Halbert, "Okla Hannali; or, the Six Towns District of the Choctaws," *A Choctaw Sourcebook,* John H. Peterson Jr., editor (New York: Garland Publishing Co., 1985), unpaginated; originally published, *American Antiquarian and Oriental Journal* 15 (1893): 146–49.

Subsequent Note

11. Halbert, "Okla Hannali; or, the Six Towns District of the Choctaws," 146–49.

12.31   Anthologies, Citing Author vs. Editor, Etc.

Your handling of the Author Field of your citation will depend upon

- what you are using from the anthology; and
- whether the anthology has an editor.

EMPHASIS ON AUTHOR OF ARTICLE

In the Halbert example at 12.30, the specific article is the item you have used. The primary creator is the person who wrote the article. This anthology has an editor who wrote an introduction, but you are not citing from that introduction. Therefore, you credit the editor for assembling the anthology, citing his name immediately after the name of the book, but your emphasis is upon the original author and the article that author wrote.

EMPHASIS ON INTRODUCTION BY EDITOR OR GUEST WRITER

The example below assumes that the material of interest to you is actually written by the editor who assembled the anthology, and that you are citing nothing else from this publication. Therefore, the editor who wrote the introduction becomes your primary author.

Source List Entry

Don Yoder, "Introduction," *Pennsylvania German Church Records of Births, Baptisms, Marriages, Burials, Etc., from The Pennsylvania German Society Proceedings and Addresses.* 3 volumes. Baltimore: Genealogical Publishing Co., 1983. Volume 1, pages v–xii.

First Reference Note

1. Don Yoder, "Introduction," *Pennsylvania German Church Records of Births, Baptisms, Marriages, Burials, Etc., from The Pennsylvania German Society Proceedings and Addresses,* 3 vols. (Baltimore: Genealogical Publishing Co., 1983), 1: v–xii.

Subsequent Note

11. Yoder, "Introduction," *Pennsylvania German Church Records,* 1: vii.

12.32 Anthologies, Complex Punctuation for

Because anthologies create a more complex citation, a semicolon is typically needed in the First Reference Note:

1. Arthur M. Schlesinger Sr., "Social Class," *The Social Fabric: American Life from 1607 to the Civil War,* John H. Cary and Julius Weinberg, editors (Boston: Little, Brown and Co.), 83–97; originally published as "The Aristocracy in Colonial America," Massachusetts Historical Society *Proceedings,* vol. 74 (1962).

The citation for the anthology itself ends with the inclusive page numbers (83–97) on the third line. The rest of the citation identifies the original publication, as cited in the anthology. Because you are citing just one source (the anthology), to which you add a notation that it was originally published elsewhere, both parts of this citation should be in the same sentence. A semicolon is used to separate the source you have used (the anthology) from the source of your source.

ATLASES

12.33 Atlases: Print Editions

An atlas, being a book of maps, follows Basic Format: Books (12.3). Variations occur when the maps are numbered as plates rather than pages—sometimes with several plates to a page—or when a book is reprinted or issued in a new edition. Differences in the particulars you need to cite can also occur when you use specialized atlases. The following sampler covers several types of atlases commonly used by history researchers: a historical atlas in its original edition, a reprint, a county atlas that features townships and ranges, and a collection of topographical maps.

Source List Entry

(Historical atlas, original edition)
The Official Atlas of the Civil War. Introduction by Henry Steele Commager. New York: Thomas Yoseloff, 1958.

(Historical atlas, reprint edition)
Robinson's Atlas of Morris County, New Jersey. 1887. Reprint, Morristown, New Jersey: Morris County Historical Society, 1990.

(County atlas)
Indiana's County Maps. Lyndon Station, Wisconsin: Thomas Publications–County Maps, n.d.

(Topographical atlas)
North Carolina Atlas & Gazetteer: Topo Maps of the Entire State. Third edition. Yarmouth, Maine: Delorme, 1997.

First Reference Note

1. *The Official Atlas of the Civil War,* introduction by Henry Steele Commager (New York: Thomas Yoseloff, 1958), plate XL, map 2, "Map of the Battle-Field of Gettysburg, Pa., July 1, 2, and 3, 1862."

2. *Robinson's Atlas of Morris County, New Jersey* (1887; reprint, Morristown, New Jersey: Morris County Historical Society, 1990), plate 25, "Plan of Port Oram, Randolph Township."

3. *Indiana's County Maps* (Lyndon Station, Wisconsin: Thomas Publications–County Maps, n.d), 19, Daviess County, for T4N, R30E.

4. *North Carolina Atlas & Gazetteer: Topo Maps of the Entire State,* 3d ed. (Yarmouth, Maine: Delorme, 1997), 73, for Red Springs.

Subsequent Note

11. *Official Atlas of the Civil War,* plate XL map 2.

12. *Robinson's Atlas of Morris County, New Jersey,* plate 25.
13. *Indiana's County Maps,* 19, Daviess County.
14. *North Carolina Atlas & Gazetteer,* 73.

12.34 Atlases: Reprints Online

Citing online reprints of atlases that first appeared as print publications requires two separate identifications. First, you identify the original work (for which the details should appear at the website that offers the images), together with the specific item of interest. Then you identify the website itself by creator-owner, name, and URL. The model below provides a full citation to the original atlas. Citation rules for reprints would allow you to shorten this slightly, if you prefer, by omitting the original publisher and place of publication but retaining the original publication date. Again, a semicolon separates the original publication from the details about its new digital location.

Dictionary, Standard (Online)

Source List Entry

Schwartzberg, Joseph E. *A Historical Atlas of South Asia.* 2d impression. New York: Oxford University Press, 1992. Digital images. http:// dsal.uchicago.edu/reference/schwartzberg : 2006.

First Reference Note

1. Joseph E. Schwartzberg, *A Historical Atlas of South Asia,* 2d impression (New York: Oxford University Press, 1992), 64, "Territorial and Administrative Changes, 1800–1947"; digital images, University of Chicago, *Digital South Asia Library* (http://dsal.uchicago.edu/reference/schwartzberg : accessed 25 October 2006).

Subsequent Note

11. Schwartzberg, *Historical Atlas of South Asia,* 64.

BIBLES & SACRED TEXTS

12.35 Bible Passages, Quoted

Reference Note citations for Biblical passages, as with dictionaries and other universally known reference works, are typically concise. Their Source List Entries, however, are complete citations.

Source List Entry

The Holy Bible, with the Confraternity Text. Thomas B. McDonough, editor. Catholic Family Bible, Papal edition. Chicago: Catholic Press, 1969.

First & Subsequent Note
        1. Proverbs 19: 2, Catholic Family Bible.
    (*or*)
        1. Prov. 19: 2, Catholic Family Bible.

12.36   Bible Versions, Identified

Because differences exist between Bible versions—e.g., King James, New Revised Standard Version (NRSV), Catholic Family, etc.—the version should be cited.

12.37   Bibles, Family Heirlooms with Personal Data

When your emphasis is on the family data recorded in a family Bible, you should follow the model provided at 3.27.

12.38   Other Sacred Texts

The citation forms and practices recommended in this section for the Christian Bible apply to all sacred texts, such as the *Qu'ran*, the *Torah*, the *Book of Mormon*, etc.

BOOK CHAPTERS, FOREWORDS, ETC.

See also QuickCheck Model *for* PRINT PUBLICATIONS: BOOK: CHAPTER

12.39   Chapters, When to Cite

If a book has only one author, you will typically cite to the book and page, not the chapter. If a book has multiple authors, each writing a different chapter, you will typically cite both the chapter author and the editor; for that situation, see Edited Works, 12.63–12.66.

12.40   Foreword by Guest Writer

Many books have not only an author (or compiler, etc.) but also a guest author who writes a foreword or introduction.

If you are referring to the main body of the book, then you need not cite the individual who wrote the foreword. Simply cite the publication using Basic Format: Books (12.3).

If your reference is to the foreword or introduction itself, then you will cite both writers, giving the lead position to the author of the foreword.

Source List Entry
Pares, Richard. "Introduction." *A History of Russia*. By Bernard Pares. Definitive edition. New York: Vintage Books, 1965. Pages viii–xxi.

First Reference Note
1. Richard Pares, "Introduction," *A History of Russia,* by Bernard Pares, definitive ed. (New York: Vintage Books, 1965), viii–xxi, particularly xi.

Subsequent Note
11. Pares, "Introduction," *History of Russia,* xi.

12.41 Preface by Book's Author

Many authors begin their books with a preface, an introduction, or a foreword that they personally wrote. You would typically use Basic Format: Books (12.3) to cite them, although your citation may want to call attention to the introduction specifically, as illustrated here:

Source List Entry
Powell, Lawrence N. *New Masters: Northern Planters during the Civil War and Reconstruction.* New Haven, Connecticut: Yale University Press, 1980.

First Reference Note
1. Lawrence N. Powell, *New Masters: Northern Planters during the Civil War and Reconstruction* (New Haven, Connecticut: Yale University Press, 1980), xi–xiv, "Preface."

Subsequent Note
11. Powell, *New Masters,* xii, 39.

BROADSIDES, FOLDERS & LEAFLETS

12.42 Authors, Identification of

Individual authors often are not identified on historic broadsides or modern brochures, folders, leaflets, and pamphlets. You may credit the sponsoring agency as the author, as with the examples below. Or, you may leave that space blank, given that the agency will be identified as the publisher. If you cite the agency fully as author, you may use its common acronym in the publisher field.

Source List Entry
National Archives and Records Administration. *The Washington National Records Center.* Leaflet. Washington, D.C.: NARA, 2002.

First Reference Note
1. National Archives and Records Administration, *The Washington National Records Center,* leaflet (Washington, D.C.: NARA, 2002), outside panel 2.

Subsequent Note
 11. National Archives and Records Administration, *Washington National Records Center,* outside panel 2.

12.43 Broadsides: Originals & Reprints

Historic broadsides, in their original form, are typically found in archival collections. In those cases, the citation will include references to both the publication and the archival collection in which it is found, as illustrated by the New Orleans example below. Modern reproductions are cited in Basic Format: Books. For a more precise identification of your source, you would probably want to include in your citation the fact that it is a broadside, in which case that piece of data would go in the Edition Field of your citation template.

Source List Entry
> *An Account of Some of the Bloody Deeds of Gen. Jackson*. Broadside. N.p.: n.p., 1928. William Cook['s] War of 1812 in the South Collection. Williams Research Center, The Historic New Orleans Collection. New Orleans, Louisiana.
> *Proclamation against Ill-treatment of "Informers," 10 November 1756*. Broadside. Reprint, Amsterdam: Theatrum Orbis Terrarum, 1971.

First Reference Note
 1. *An Account of Some of the Bloody Deeds of Gen. Jackson*, broadside (N.p.: n.p., 1928); William Cook['s] War of 1812 in the South Collection; Williams Research Center, The Historic New Orleans Collection; New Orleans, Louisiana.
 2. *Proclamation against Ill-treatment of "Informers," 10 November 1756*, broadside (reprint, Amsterdam: Theatrum Orbis Terrarum, 1971).

Subsequent Note
 11. *An Account of Some of the Bloody Deeds of Gen. Jackson*, broadside, William Cook['s] War of 1812 in the South Collection.
 12. *Proclamation against Ill-treatment of "Informers," 10 November 1756*, broadside.

12.44 Missing Data

Broadsides, brochures, folders, leaflets, pamphlets, and the like often are not paginated and they may not be dated. The examples above demonstrate the handling of material that lacks pagination or information on the publisher and the place of publication. The example below at 12.45 illustrates the treatment of an undated item.

12.45 Publication Number

See also QuickCheck Model *for* PRINT PUBLICATIONS: LEAFLET

Some leaflets carry a special publication number whose data is placed in roman type between the title and the publication facts.

Source List Entry

The Military System of Pennsylvania during the Revolutionary War. Information Leaflet 3. Harrisburg: Pennsylvania Historical and Museum Commission, no date.

First Reference Note

1. *The Military System of Pennsylvania during the Revolutionary War,* Information Leaflet 3 (Harrisburg: Pennsylvania Historical and Museum Commission, n.d.), 2.

Subsequent Note

11. *Military System of Pennsylvania during the Revolutionary War,* 2.

CONFERENCE & INSTITUTE PAPERS

12.46 Papers: Basic Differences

Variances in your citations to conference or institute syllabi will depend upon three factors:

- whether you are citing a printed syllabus or an electronic one;
- whether you need to cite the full syllabus or an individual item; and
- whether the conference consolidates all contributions into a single volume or presents each separately as a bound "paper."

Section 12.47 covers consolidated papers; 12.48 covers individual presentations.

12.47 Papers: Consolidated (Syllabi)

Most published conference syllabi carry a specific title. As a rule, you should pull that title from the title page, rather than the often-stylized cover. The complexity of the citation will vary from one instance to another. In both examples below, the presenter's material is treated as a chapter within a book. The Federation example can entirely follow QuickCheck Model: BOOK CHAPTER, because the publication's title identifies it as a syllabus. The Samford University example, however, calls for added information after the title to identify it as a syllabus—a detail analogous to a series title, as discussed at 12.84–12.89. The Samford example also illustrates one other quirk: pages that are numbered by individual session rather than being sequentially numbered throughout the syllabus.

Source List Entry

(To cite the full syllabus)

Course 4: *Advanced Research Methodology & Evidence Analysis.* 2006
Syllabus, Samford University Institute of Genealogy & Historical
Research. Birmingham, Alabama: IGHR, 2006.

Federation of Genealogical Societies. *Legends Live Forever: Researching
the Past for Future Generations—A Conference for the Nation's Genealogists, 2004 Syllabus.* Austin, Texas: FGS, 2004.

(To cite material by individual presenter)

Jones, Thomas W. "Probate Records: Analysis, Interpretation, and
Correlation." *Course 4: Advanced Research Methodology & Evidence
Analysis.* 2006 Syllabus, Samford University Institute of Genealogy
& Historical Research. Birmingham, Alabama: IGHR, 2006. Ses-
sion 4TH2, pp. 1–11.

Milner, Paul. "Effective Internet Use of England's National Archives."
Federation of Genealogical Societies. *Legends Live Forever: Research-
ing the Past for Future Generations—A Conference for the Nation's
Genealogists, 2004 Syllabus.* Austin, Texas: FGS, 2004. Pages 278–81.

First Reference Note

(To cite the full syllabus)

1. Course 4: *Advanced Research Methodology & Evidence Analysis,*
2006 Syllabus, Samford University Institute of Genealogy & Historical
Research (Birmingham, Alabama: IGHR, 2006).

2. Federation of Genealogical Societies, *Legends Live Forever: Researching the Past for Future Generations—A Conference for the Nation's
Genealogists, 2004 Syllabus* (Austin, Texas: FGS, 2004).

(To cite material by individual presenter)

3. Thomas W. Jones, "Probate Records: Analysis, Interpretation,
and Correlation," *Course 4: Advanced Research Methodology & Evidence
Analysis,* 2006 Syllabus, Samford University Institute of Genealogy &
Historical Research (Birmingham, Alabama: IGHR, 2006), session
4TH2, p. 11.

4. Paul Milner, "Effective Internet Use of England's National
Archives," Federation of Genealogical Societies, *Legends Live Forever:
Researching the Past for Future Generations—A Conference for the Nation's
Genealogists, 2004 Syllabus* (Austin, Texas: FGS, 2004), 278–81.

Subsequent Note

11. Course 4: *Advanced Research Methodology & Evidence Analysis,*
2006 Syllabus, IGHR.

12. Federation of Genealogical Societies, *Legends Live Forever ...
2004 Syllabus.*

13. Jones, "Probate Records: Analysis, Interpretation, and Correlation," 11.

14. Milner, "Effective Internet Use of England's National Archives," 279.

Conference Syllabi (CD-ROM)

Source List Entry

(To cite the full syllabus)

Genealogy & Family Heritage Jamboree, St. George, Utah, 2006: Syllabus. CD-ROM. Morgan, Utah: My Ancestors Found, 2006.

(To cite material by an individual presenter)
Johnson, Baerbel K. "Civil Registration in Germany." *Genealogy & Family Heritage Jamboree, St. George, Utah, 2006: Syllabus.* CD-ROM. Morgan, Utah: My Ancestors Found, 2006.

First Reference Note

(To cite the full syllabus)
1. *Genealogy & Family Heritage Jamboree, St. George, Utah, 2006: Syllabus,* CD-ROM (Morgan, Utah: My Ancestors Found, 2006).

(To cite material by an individual presenter)
2. Baerbel K. Johnson, "Civil Registration in Germany," *Genealogy & Family Heritage Jamboree, St. George, Utah, 2006: Syllabus,* CD-ROM (Morgan, Utah: My Ancestors Found, 2006), 4.

Subsequent Note

11. *Genealogy & Family Heritage Jamboree, St. George, Utah, 2006: Syllabus.*
12. Johnson, "Civil Registration in Germany," 4.

12.48 Papers: Individually Distributed

Source List Entry

Rutman, Darrett B. "Community Study." *The Newberry Papers in Family and Community History.* Paper 77-4J. Newberry Library Conference on Quantitative and Social Science Approaches in Early American History. Chicago: Newberry Library, 1977.

First Reference Note

1. Darrett B. Rutman, "Community Study," *The Newberry Papers in Family and Community History,* Paper 77-4J, Newberry Library Conference on Quantitative and Social Science Approaches in Early American History (Chicago: Newberry Library, 1977), 17 for "mass prosopography."

Subsequent Note

11. Rutman, "Community Study," p. 17 and p. 22, fig. 2.

DICTIONARIES & ENCYCLOPEDIAS

12.49 Basic Issues

The details essential to a dictionary or encyclopedia citation depend upon the characteristics of (*a*) the publication's content and (*b*) its publication medium. Well-known, standard, reference works that are regularly revised are typically cited in an abbreviated format. Specialized, one-time publications that present topical essays in alphabetical order are cited fully, with credit to both the essay authors and the editors. The examples at 12.50–12.54 illustrate a variety of works that have been issued as print publications, digital reprints, and first-edition electronic books.

12.50 Biographical Works

See also QuickCheck Model *for* ELECTRONIC PUBLICATIONS: WEBSITE AS "BOOK"

Variously called biographical *directories,* biographical *dictionaries,* and even *encyclopedias,* these works typically offer brief biographies of people prominently involved with a certain subject or place. How you cite a publication of this type depends upon its medium—i.e., whether it is printed, posted online, or published on CD or DVD. Typical citations to a printed biographical work follow Basic Format: Books (12.3), producing entries such as this:

Source List Entry
Boatner, Mark M., III. *The Biographical Directory of World War II.* Novato, California: Presidio Press, 1999.

First Reference Note
   1. Mark M. Boatner III, *The Biographical Directory of World War II* (Novato, California: Presidio Press, 1999), 2, "Abe Nobuyuki."

Subsequent Note
   11. Boatner, *Biographical Directory of World War II,* 2.

(*or*)
   11. Boatner, *Biographical Directory of World War II,* "Abe Nobuyuki."

Biographical Works (CD/DVD)

A citation to a book whose first edition is published solely on CD or DVD will cover essentially the same elements as the Basic Format: Books (12.3). However, you will need to add a notation that it is an electronic edition.

Electronic publications have far more vagaries than print publications, and most need to be addressed in some way. You should examine the publication thoughtfully to identify special issues. In the example below, the biographies are arranged in sections that correspond to book chapters—e.g., "Administrators," "Cadets," etc. The first time an entry is cited from a particular section, you would need to identify both the section and the page, as well as the item of interest. Thereafter, only the item need be cited. If, as in note 12, you cite a new item from the publication, you would again need to reference the section and page, as well as the item.

Source List Entry

Brasseaux, Carl A. *France's Forgotten Legion: Service Records of French Military and Administrative Personnel Stationed in the Mississippi Valley and Gulf Coast Region, 1699–1769.* CD-ROM. Baton Rouge: Louisiana State University Press, 2000.

First Reference Note

1. Carl A. Brasseaux, *France's Forgotten Legion: Service Records of French Military and Administrative Personnel Stationed in the Mississippi Valley and Gulf Coast Region, 1699–1769,* CD-ROM (Baton Rouge: Louisiana State University Press, 2000), section: "Administrators, M–V," 2, "Maraffret Layssard."

Subsequent Note

11. Brasseaux, *France's Forgotten Legion,* "Maraffret Layssard."
12. Ibid., section: "Cadets," 17, "DeMézières, Athanase."

PUNCTUATING NAMES

In the DeMézières example, a comma appears between the two names of the biographee. In the Maraffret Layssard example, it does not. The difference is this: In most entries, the biographee's names are inverted (*Surname, Given Name*) to permit alphabetizing under the surname. When those names are inverted, they are separated by a comma. In the Maraffret Layssard example, however, no comma appears because "Maraffret Layssard" is a double surname, and the biographer did not use a given name at all in the title of the sketch.

12.51 Dictionary, Standard

See also QuickCheck Model *for* PRINT PUBLICATIONS: BOOK, BASIC FORMAT

For a traditional dictionary by a major publisher, your Reference Notes need only cite the name of the dictionary, its edition, and the word being defined. Page numbers are not needed because word entries are in alphabetical sequence. Your Source List might carry a full citation to the dictionary following the Basic Format.

Source List Entry
American Heritage Dictionary of the English Language. Fourth edition. Boston: Houghton Mifflin, 2000.

First Reference Note
1. *American Heritage Dictionary of the English Language,* 4th ed., "mitachondria."

Subsequent Note
11. *American Heritage Dictionary of the English Language,* 4th ed., "mitachondria."

Dictionary, Standard (Online)

Source List Entry
Merriam-Webster Online Dictionary. http://www.m-w.com : 2007.

First Reference Note
1. *Merriam-Webster Online Dictionary* (http://www.m-w.com : accessed 15 February 2007), "agnate."

Subsequent Note
11. *Merriam-Webster Online Dictionary* (2007), "agnate."

CITING DICTIONARY ENTRIES
The Latin *s.v.* (abbreviation for *sub verbo,* meaning *under the word*) was long used to introduce dictionary words within citations. Modern researchers tend to simply cite the word.

12.52 Dictionary, Specialized

See also QuickCheck Model *for* PRINT PUBLICATIONS: BOOK: EDITED

Specialized dictionaries are of two basic types:

- word-definition dictionaries that focus on a specific field; and
- books of an encyclopedic nature that offer essays rather than definitions.

The principal difference between these two types, from the standpoint of citations, is that the first usually has just a compiler, while the second has both essay authors and editors who need to be credited. Whether your reference emphasizes the editors or an individual author depends upon whether you are referring to the entire volume or to one essay therein.

SPECIALIZED "ESSAY" DICTIONARIES

Source List Entry

(*When citing the entire publication*)
Miller, Randall M., and John David Smith, editors. *Dictionary of Afro-American Slavery*. New York: Greenwood Press, 1988.

(*When citing an individual essay*)
Mills, Elizabeth Shown. "Afro-American Slave Genealogy." *Dictionary of Afro-American Slavery*. Randall M. Miller and John David Smith, editors. New York: Greenwood Press, 1988. Pages 287–90.

First Reference Note

1. Elizabeth Shown Mills, "Afro-American Slave Genealogy," in *Dictionary of Afro-American Slavery,* Randall M. Miller and John David Smith, editors (New York: Greenwood Press, 1988), 287–90.

Subsequent Note

11. Mills, "Afro-American Slave Genealogy," 288.

SPECIALIZED "WORD" DICTIONARIES

Source List Entry

Picken, Mary Brooks. *A Dictionary of Costume and Fashion*. Mineola, New York: Dover Publications, 1999.

First Reference Note

1. Mary Brooks Picken, *A Dictionary of Costume and Fashion* (Mineola, New York: Dover Publications, 1999), 26, "bavolets."

Subsequent Note

11. Picken, *Dictionary of Costume and Fashion*, 26.

Dictionary, Specialized (Online)

Source List Entry

Bouvier, John. *A Law Dictionary Adapted to the Constitution and Laws of the United States of America and of the Several States of the American Union*. Revised sixth edition. 1856. HTML reprint. *The Constitution Society*. http://www.constitution.org/bouv/bouvier.htm : 2007.

First Reference Note

1. John Bouvier, *A Law Dictionary Adapted to the Constitution and Laws of the United States of America and of the Several States of the American Union*, rev. 6th ed. (1856); HTML reprint, *The Constitution Society* (http://www.constitution.org/bouv/bouvier.htm : accessed 2 February 2007), "a vinculo matrimonii."

Subsequent Note
11. Bouvier, *Law Dictionary* (1856), "a vinculo matrimonii."

12.53   Encyclopedia, Standard
A traditional encyclopedia need only be cited by its name, edition (the year or an ordinal such as "4th ed."), and the title of the essay.

Source List Entry
World Book Encyclopedia. Chicago: World Book, 1998.

First Reference Note
1. *World Book Encyclopedia* (1998), "John Wesley."

Subsequent Note
11. *World Book Encyclopedia* (1998), "Francis Asbury" and "John Wesley."

Encyclopedia, Standard (Online)   🖳
Researchers who use online encyclopedias frequently encounter two offerings: brief articles, available at no charge; and complete articles that are available only by subscription. The following illustrates how each can be handled.

Source List Entry
Encyclopædia Britannica Concise. http://www.concisebritannica.com : 2007.
Encyclopædia Britannica Online. http://www.britannica.com : 2007.

First Reference Note
1. *Encyclopædia Britannica Concise* (http://www.concise britannica.com : accessed 15 January 2007), "DNA Fingerprinting."
2. *Encyclopædia Britannica Online*, Encylopaedia Britannica Premium Service (http://www.britannica.com : accessed 15 January 2007), "Heredity."

Subsequent Note
11. *Encyclopædia Britannica Concise* (2007), "DNA Fingerprinting."
12. *Encyclopædia Britannica Online* (2007), "Heredity."

12.54   Encyclopedia, Specialized
Many encyclopedias are one- or two-volume publications that treat a narrow subject. Most are quite akin to specialized dictionaries. Often the difference simply lies in the word the editor chose to use in the title. The essays may or may not be signed. The following example demonstrates four variations:

- a basic citation to the volume and its editors;
- a citation to a specific essay, unsigned;
- the manner in which ibid. is used with works of this type; and
- the manner in which Subsequent Notes are handled for each First Reference Note to a particular entry.

Source List Entry

Schmidt, Patricia Brady, et al., editors. *Encyclopædia of New Orleans Artists, 1718–1918.* New Orleans, Louisiana: Historic New Orleans Collection, 1987.

First Reference Note

(*To cite the entire volume*)
  1. Patricia Brady Schmidt et al., editors, *Encyclopædia of New Orleans Artists, 1718–1918* (New Orleans: Historic New Orleans Collection, 1987).

(*To cite particular entries*)
  2. Ibid., 238–39, see "Jules Lion."
  3. Ibid.

Subsequent Note

  11. Schmidt et al., *Encyclopædia of New Orleans Artists.*
  12. Ibid., 239, "Jules Lion," and 294, "Oliver Peirce."
  13. Ibid., 238–39, "Jules Lion."

DIRECTORIES

12.55 Directories: Basic Format

Historical researchers use a variety of directories—business or professional, church, and city or county directories being the most common. In printed form, they are typically cited by Basic Format: Books (12.3), with occasional modifications as discussed at 12.56–12.59.

Directories (Published Microfilm)

Directories that have been reprinted as microfilmed images involve dual publications: (*a*) the original directory; and (*b*) the microfilm publication. As with reprints published in paper form, your citation does not have to supply all the original publication information. You need only supply the *original date,* along with the current publication data. In your Source List, you may choose to create entries for one or both. In your First Reference Note, you will need to identify both.

Source List Entry

(*To cite all directories for one locale*)
City Directories of the United States, 1902–1935, Chicago, Illinois, reel 15,
    1915. Woodbridge, Connecticut: Research Publications, 1990.

(*To cite one specific directory on the film*)
Donnelley, Reuben H., compiler. *The Lakeside Annual Directory of the
    City of Chicago, 1915*. Microfilm reprint. *City Directories of the United
    States, 1902–1935, Chicago, Illinois*, roll 15, *1915*. Woodbridge,
    Connecticut: Research Publications, 1990.

First Reference Note

    1. Reuben H. Donnelley, compiler, *The Lakeside Annual Directory
of the City of Chicago, 1915*, microfilm reprint, *City Directories of the
United States, 1902–1935, Chicago, Illinois*, roll 15, *1915* (Woodbridge,
Connecticut: Research Publications, 1990), 1427, "Jos. Samarka."

Subsequent Note

    1. Donnelley, *Lakeside Annual Directory ... Chicago, 1915*, 1427,
"Jos. Samarka."

CITING SUBTITLES & MICROFILM ROLLS

In the above citations to the microfilm, note that the roll number is *not*
italicized because it is not part of the title. However, the year that
follows the roll number *is* italicized because it is a subtitle to the main
title that appears on every roll—i.e., *City Directories of the United States,
1902–1935, Chicago, Illinois*. In a citation of this type, do not move the
year (the subtitle) to a position in front of the roll number. If you did
so, you would imply that you used the fifteenth roll for the year 1915.

IDENTIFYING THE COMPILER

If the identity of the compiler is cited on the title page, include it in the
citation. Often no compiler is named.

IDENTIFYING THE INDIVIDUAL

Typically, your text will identify the person of interest. Your note,
then, does not have to repeat the name. However, when the directory
abbreviates the name or uses an unexpected spelling of the name, your
citation should note the variant.

12.56 Directories: Citing Multiple Years

When you need to cite a long run of directories by the same publisher,
your handling of the citation will depend upon whether or not the title
and publisher remain the same through the span of years. If only the
years and page numbers differ, you can create a generic citation.

Source List Entry
Polk, R. L., compiler. *Colorado Springs, Colorado, City Directory.* Colorado Springs: R. L. Polk Directory Co., 1924, 1927, 1929, 1931.

First Reference Note
1. R. L. Polk, compiler, *Colorado Springs, Colorado, City Directory* (Colorado Springs: R. L. Polk Directory Co., 1924), 52; also subsequent years by the same title: (1927) 57, (1929) 63, (1931) 68.

Subsequent Note
11. Polk, *Colorado Springs, Colorado, City Directory,* for (1924) 52, and (1929) 63.

For directories that have the same compiler and publisher across a span of years, with slight variation in titles, you might use this approach:

Source List Entry
Jones, John Q., compiler. *Badlands City Directory, with Listings for Adjacent Wetlands, Marshlands, and Arid City* [varying subtitles]. Badlands: Jones Press, 1924–27.

First Reference Note
1. John Q. Jones, compiler, *Badlands City Directory, with Listings for Adjacent Wetlands, Marshlands, and Arid City* (Badlands: Jones Press, 1924), 52, for "Wily Urp." See also Wily's entries under "Erp" in Jones's directories for subsequent years with varying subtitles, specifically: (1924) 37, (1925) 63, (1927) 48.

Subsequent Note
11. Jones, *Badlands City Directory* [and Adjacent Areas], (1924) 52.

SHORTENING A DIRECTORY TITLE
In the Jones example, above, the Subsequent Note shortens the title, but adds a three-word summary of the omitted portion to preserve the fact that the volume is not restricted to just Badlands City. It places the addition in square editorial brackets to flag the alteration.

12.57 Directories: Page Numbers Missing
Directories compiled by local organizations frequently are not paginated. As an alternate system of location, you might choose to count the *folios* (leaves), specifying whether the item of interest appears on the *recto* (right side) of the bound leaf or the *verso* (back side).

Source List Entry
Church of the Holy Child. *Parish Photographic Directory.* Bethlehem, Maryland: The parish, 1973.

First Reference Note
1. Church of the Holy Child, *Parish Photographic Directory* (Bethlehem, Maryland: The parish, 1973), unpaginated, folio 6 verso, portrait of "John and Mary Reilly."

Subsequent Note
11. Church of the Holy Child, *Parish Photographic Directory*, 6v.

12.58 Directories: Titles, Clarified

In the Cohen example at 12.59, the last portion of the subtitle is missing a word that is needed for clarity, *Deaths*. When added, it is placed in square editorial brackets to clearly indicate that the word is not part of the original title.

As with the Jones Directory at 12.56, the severely shortened form of the Cohen Directory in the Subsequent Note below needs a clarification to indicate that the volume covers more than just the central city. Again, the added word appears in square editorial brackets.

12.59 Directories: Titles, Overlong

Old directories often have exceedingly long subtitles. Even in the First Reference Note, you may need to shorten a title by replacing some of the wording with ellipsis points. In this example, even with the ellipsis used, the title remains uncommonly long. However, much of the subtitle is retained because it notes the volume's inclusion of special items that have significant research value.

Source List Entry
Cohen, H. A. *Cohen's New Orleans Directory, Including Jefferson City, Carrollton, Gretna, Algiers, and McDonough, for 1854; ... Portraits of the Citizens of New Orleans, with Their Biographies; Also, A Tableau of the Yellow Fever* [Deaths] *of 1853*. New Orleans: The Picayune, 1854.

First Reference Note
1. H. A. Cohen, *Cohen's New Orleans Directory, Including Jefferson City, Carrollton, Gretna, Algiers, and McDonough, for 1854; ... Portraits of the Citizens of New Orleans, with Their Biographies; Also, A Tableau of the Yellow Fever* [Deaths] *of 1853* (New Orleans: The Picayune, 1854), 19.

Subsequent Note
11. Cohen, *Cohen's New Orleans* [Area] *Directory, 1854*, 19.

E-BOOKS

12.60 E-Books: Basic Issue, Citing According to Media

Electronic books and their online equivalents generally take one of four forms:

- audio versions of books issued in print;
- text publications solely released on CD-ROM or online;
- digital image editions of books previously published in print; and
- reformatted digital editions of books previously appearing in paper form.

This section treats narrative works (not manipulatable databases) that are issued in electronic form at their first publication—i.e., types 1 and 2 above. Image editions and reprints are handled at 12.79.

12.61 E-Books: Audio

See QuickCheck Model *for* ELECTRONIC PUBLICATIONS: AUDIO BOOK

E-books may be issued as an audio edition of a book that is also released in print, or they may be a text-based stand-alone publication as demonstrated at 12.62. The two are cited similarly, with only a difference in the description of the format and/or edition.

Cassette, CD, or DVD ∩

Source List Entry

Dunn, Jane. *Elizabeth and Mary: Cousins, Rivals, Queens.* Audio cassette edition. New York: Random House Audio Publishing Group, 2004.

First Reference Note

1. Jane Dunn, *Elizabeth and Mary: Cousins, Rivals, Queens*, audio cassette edition (New York: Random House Audio Publishing Group, 2004), minute 35.

Subsequent Note

11. Dunn, *Elizabeth and Mary*, minute 35.

12.62 E-Print Books: New Publications

See QuickCheck Model *for* ELECTRONIC PUBLICATIONS: CD/DVD BOOK

CD or DVD ✎

Source List Entry

Burgoyne, Bruce E., translator. *A Hessian Diary of the American Revolution.* CD-ROM. Westminster, Maryland: Heritage Books. 2005.

First Reference Note

1. Bruce E. Burgoyne, translator, *A Hessian Diary of the American Revolution*, CD-ROM (Westminster, Maryland: Heritage Books, 2005), 123.

Subsequent Note
> 11. Burgoyne, *A Hessian Diary of the American Revolution,* 123.

Online Book, New Publication 🖥

A book issued solely in an electronic edition for online marketing will typically have eight elements to cite:

- author
- title
- publication date
- download format

- website name
- URL
- download date
- specific page

Source List Entry
> Vale, Barry. *A History of the Church of England, 1529–1662.* No publication date. PDF download. *Authors OnLine.* http://www.authors online.co.uk/viewbook.php?bid=505 : 2006.

First Reference Note
> 1. Barry Vale, *A History of the Church of England, 1529–1662,* no publication date; PDF download, *Authors OnLine* (http://www.authors online.co.uk/viewbook.php?bid=505 : downloaded 5 August 2006), 27.

Subsequent Note
> 11. Vale, *History of the Church of England,* 27.

EDITED WORKS

12.63   Edited Works: Basic Format

See QuickCheck Model *for* PRINT PUBLICATIONS: BOOK: EDITED

Historical editors fill a variety of roles. Some select documentary material and prepare it for publication, with valuable annotations clearly identified as editorial additions. Other editors silently polish the writings of contemporary authors—sometimes a volume by a single author, sometimes a work in which several authors have written individual chapters. The role an editor plays will determine how you cite the publication.

When citing an editor who prepares historical documents for press, rather than editing the work of others, your citation follows Basic Format: Books (12.3).

Source List Entry
> Miller, Randall M., editor. *"Dear Master": Letters of a Slave Family.* Ithaca, New York: Cornell University Press, 1978.

First Reference Note
    1.   Randall M. Miller, editor, *"Dear Master": Letters of a Slave Family* (Ithaca, New York: Cornell University Press, 1978), 152.

Subsequent Note
    11.   Miller, *"Dear Master,"* 152.

12.64   Edited Works: Citing Chapter Authors

In this type of volume, you may choose to emphasize the individual chapter authors or the editor. As a rule, your choice of emphasis would follow these guidelines.

AUTHOR .... if you are referring to material in only one chapter.
EDITOR .... if you are referring to the entire volume, not to any
                                specific page therein.

When you cite a specific chapter, you will have two individuals to credit—first the author and then the editor.

Source List Entry

(When citing a chapter author)
Bell, Mary McCampbell. "Transcripts and Abstracts." Elizabeth Shown
    Mills, editor. *Professional Genealogy: A Manual for Researchers, Writers, Editors, Lecturers, and Librarians.* Baltimore: Genealogical Publishing Co., 2001. Chap. 16, pp. 291–326.

(When citing the entire book)
Mills, Elizabeth Shown, editor. *Professional Genealogy: A Manual for
    Researchers, Writers, Editors, Lecturers, and Librarians.* Baltimore: Genealogical Publishing Co., 2001.

First Reference Note
    1.   Mary McCampbell Bell, "Transcripts and Abstracts," in Elizabeth Shown Mills, editor, *Professional Genealogy: A Manual for Researchers, Writers, Editors, Lecturers, and Librarians* (Baltimore: Genealogical Publishing Co, 2001), chap. 16, pp. 291–326.
    2.   Elizabeth Shown Mills, editor, *Professional Genealogy: A Manual for Researchers, Writers, Editors, Lecturers, and Librarians* (Baltimore: Genealogical Publishing Co., 2001).

Subsequent Note
    11.   Bell, "Transcripts and Abstracts," 292.
    12.   Mills, ed., *Professional Genealogy.*

CHAPTER NUMBER VS. PAGE NUMBERS
Some researchers prefer to cite the chapter number as well as the chapter name and page numbers, when referencing individually

authored chapters. If you cite both chapter numbers and page numbers, you should specify what each number set represents, to avoid possible misinterpretation.

12.65   Edited Works: Citing Editor as Author

In many collections of edited essays, the editor will write a preface or key chapters. In the Source List Entry, you need not cite an individual chapter written by the editor. In your Reference Notes, you might cite the specific portion that you use.

Source List Entry

Wheaton, Robert, and Tamara K. Hareven, editors. *Family and Sexuality in French History*. Philadelphia: University of Pennsylvania Press, 1980.

First Reference Note

1.   Robert Wheaton, "Recent Trends in the Historical Study of the French Family," in *Family and Sexuality in French History,* Robert Wheaton and Tamara K. Hareven, editors (Philadelphia: University of Pennsylvania Press, 1980), 3–20, especially 7.

Subsequent Note

11.   Wheaton, "Recent Trends in the Historical Study of the French Family," 7.

12.66   Edited Works: Citing Editor as Well as Author

The title page of some works credits both the author and an editor who has worked extensively to enhance the manuscript. When an author shares credit with an editor, you should also credit both individuals. The following example illustrates Source List Entries for both parties; you may choose either or both forms. However, your Note entries will generally credit the author and give secondary placement to the editor.

Source List Entry

Sanborn, Melinde Lutz, editor. *The Ancestry of Emily Jane Angell*. By Dean Crawford Smith. Boston: New England Historic Genealogical Society, 1992.
Smith, Dean Crawford. *The Ancestry of Emily Jane Angell*. Melinde Lutz Sanborn, editor. Boston: New England Historic Genealogical Society, 1992.

First Reference Note

1.   Dean Crawford Smith, *The Ancestry of Emily Jane Angell,* Melinde Lutz Sanborn, editor (Boston: New England Historic Genealogical Society, 1992), 234.

Subsequent Note
> 11. Smith, *Ancestry of Emily Jane Angell*, 234.
> (*or*)
> 11. Smith and Sanborn, *Ancestry of Emily Jane Angell*, 234.

MAPS

12.67 Historic Maps

See QuickCheck Model *for* PRINT PUBLICATIONS: MAP

Individually published maps are cited the same as published books, except for the need to include page numbers. (For paginated atlases, see 12.33–12.34.) With individual maps, you may or may not have a cartographer to cite in the Author Field. If the title to the map does not include a date or time frame, your shortened citation in the Subsequent Note should include the year of publication.

Source List Entry
> *Map of the State of New York, with Part of Upper Canada*. London: I. T. Hinton, 1831.
> Mouzon, Henry. *An Accurate Map of North and South Carolina with Their Indian Frontiers*. London: Thomas Jeffreys, 1775.

First Reference Note
> 1. *Map of the State of New York, with Part of Upper Canada* (London: I. T. Hinton, 1831).
> 2. Henry Mouzon, *An Accurate Map of North and South Carolina with Their Indian Frontiers* (London: Thomas Jeffreys, 1775).

Subsequent Note
> 11. *Map of the State of New York, with Part of Upper Canada* (1831).
> 12. Mouzon, *An Accurate Map of North and South Carolina* (1775).

Historic Maps, Online

Source List Entry
> *Bancroft's Map of California, Nevada, Utah & Arizona*. San Francisco: A. L. Bancroft & Co., 1873. Digital image. *David Rumsey Map Collection*. http://www.davidrumsey.com/dec_15_01add.html : 2007.

First Reference Note
> 1. *Bancroft's Map of California, Nevada, Utah & Arizona* (San Francisco: A. L. Bancroft & Co., 1873); digital image, *David Rumsey Map Collection* (http://www.davidrumsey.com/dec_15_01add.html : accessed 25 January 2007).

Subsequent Note
> 11. *Bancroft's Map of California, Nevada, Utah & Arizona,* 1873.

12.68 Topographic Maps

The most commonly used topographic maps for the United States are produced by the Geological Survey of the Department of Interior. However, some other government agencies issue topographic maps that incorporate details from elsewhere. In citing this form of map you should note the specific agency that created it. The descriptive details given in the two citations below differ because the maps are compiled and serialized differently.

Source List Entry
> United States. Mississippi River Commission, Corps of Engineers. *Topographic Maps.* Series 95072. 1960.
> United States. Department of the Interior. *Geological Survey Topographic Maps.* 15' Series. Photorevised 1957.

First Reference Note
> 1. U.S. Mississippi River Commission, Corps of Engineers, *Topographic Map: Little Rock,* Map NI 15-5, series 95072, 1960.
> 2. U.S. Department of the Interior, *Geological Survey Topographic Map: Louisiana, Montgomery Quadrangle,* 15' series, photorevised 1957.

Subsequent Note
> 11. U.S. Mississippi River Commission, *Topographic Map: Little Rock,* Map NI 15-5, Series 95072, 1960.
> 12. U.S. Dept. of the Interior, *Geological Survey Topographic Map: Louisiana, Montgomery Quadrangle,* 15' Series, 1957.

MULTIVOLUME WORKS

12.69 Multivolume Works: Basic Format

See also QuickCheck Model *for* PRINT PUBLICATIONS: BOOK: MULTIVOLUME

When citing a multivolume work, you should state the total number of volumes immediately after the title, setting the information in roman type. Your page citation will then include both the specific volume number and its page number. Whether you choose to leave a space between the volume number and the page number is a matter of preference; whichever style you choose, use it consistently.

Source List Entry
> Jones, Henry Z, Jr. *The Palatine Families of New York, 1710.* 2 volumes. Universal City, California: The author, 1986.

First Reference Note

    1. Henry Z Jones Jr., *The Palatine Families of New York, 1710,* 2 vols. (Universal City, California: The author, 1985), 1: 379–82.

Subsequent Note

    11. Jones, *Palatine Families of New York, 1710,* 1: 379–82.

CITING NON-STANDARD NAMES

When a single letter appears in a given name, it is not always an abbreviation. If an author's name does not carry a period after a single letter, as with Henry Z Jones above, you should not add a period.

12.70   Multivolume Works: Date Ranges

With multivolume works, individual volumes are frequently issued in different years. How you handle the situation depends upon (*a*) whether the set consists of just two volumes, as opposed to three or more; and (*b*) whether the volumes are issued in consecutive years or intermittently. As rule of thumb:

Two volumes, consecutive years—use an en dash to separate the two years, as with Appel, below.

Two volumes, nonconsecutive years—use a comma and a space to separate the two years, as with Davidson, below.

Three or more volumes—cite only the first and last year, separated by an en dash, as with Jordan, below.

Source List Entry

Appel, Paul B. *Seeds of Change: Transplanting America.* 2 volumes. Brainerd, Minnesota: Blue Ox Press, 1880–81.

Davidson, William H. *A Rockaway in Talbot: Travels in an Old Georgia County.* 2 volumes. West Point, Georgia: Hester Printing, 1983, 1985.

Jordan, Jerry Wright. *Cherokee by Blood: Records of Eastern Cherokee Ancestry in the U.S. Court of Claims, 1906–1910.* 8 volumes. Baltimore: Heritage Books, 1987–91.

First Reference Note

    1. Paul B. Appel, *Seeds of Change: Transplanting America,* 2 vols. (Brainerd, Minnesota: Blue Ox Press, 1880–81), 1: 123.

    2. William H. Davidson, *A Rockaway in Talbot: Travels in an Old Georgia County,* 2 vols. (West Point, Georgia: Hester Printing, 1983, 1985), 2: 137.

    3. Jerry Wright Jordan, *Cherokee by Blood: Records of Eastern Cherokee Ancestry in the U.S. Court of Claims, 1906–1910,* 8 vols. (Baltimore: Heritage Books, 1987–91), 1: 126–81, Sizemore claims.

Subsequent Note
   11. Appel, *Seeds of Change,* 1:123.
   12. Davidson, *A Rockaway in Talbot,* 2:137.
   13. Jordan, *Cherokee by Blood,* 1:126.

12.71 Multivolume Works: Different Subtitles

Many compilations use a different subtitle for each volume in the set. Even if you use just one volume of a set, your Source List Entry should note the total number of volumes. Your Reference Note does not have to cite the total number, but the note should include the specific subtitle for the volume you are citing.

The following examples cite a popular set in both its original and reprint forms. In both cases, you will note three points with regard to the identification of the specific volume you are using:

• When your First Reference Note cites only the specific volume used, that volume's identification is placed *before* the publication data, and the page number appears alone after the publication data.

• When your First Reference Note cites the total number of volumes, the specific volume is identified *after* the publication data.

• When you cite the title of the set, the volume number, and the specific volume's subtitle, you do not italicize the volume number. It is not part of the official title of the publication.

Source List Entry

(When citing the original series)
Hinshaw, William Wade, et al., compilers. *Encyclopedia of American Quaker Genealogy.* 6 volumes. Ann Arbor, Michigan: Edwards Brothers, 1936–50.

(When citing the reprint series)
Hinshaw, William Wade et al., compilers. *Encyclopedia of American Quaker Genealogy.* 6 vols. 1936–50. Reprint, Baltimore, Maryland: Genealogical Publishing Co., 1991–94.

First Reference Note

(When citing a single volume)
   1. William Wade Hinshaw et al., compilers, *Encyclopedia of American Quaker Genealogy,* vol. 4, *Ohio* (Ann Arbor, Michigan: Edwards Brothers, 1946), 111.

(or)
   1. William Wade Hinshaw et al., compilers, *Encyclopedia of American Quaker Genealogy,* 6 vols. (1936–50; reprint, Baltimore: Genealogical Publishing Co., 1991–94), vol. 4, *Ohio* (1946), 111.

Subsequent Note
11. Hinshaw et al., *Encyclopedia of American Quaker Genealogy*, vol. 4, *Ohio*, 24.

12.72 Multivolume Works: Ongoing Volumes
If the set is still ongoing, state the number of volumes to date. In the date field of your citation, state the first year of publication followed by an en dash to indicate that its publication period is open-ended.

Source List Entry
Anderson, Robert Charles, et al. *The Great Migration: Immigrants to New England, 1634–1635.* 4 volumes to date. Boston: New England Historic Genealogical Society, 1999–.

First Reference Note
1. Robert Charles Anderson et al., *The Great Migration: Immigrants to New England, 1634–1635,* 4 vols. to date (Boston: New England Historic Genealogical Society, 1999–), 3: 33.

Subsequent Note
11. Anderson, *The Great Migration ... 1634–1635,* 3: 33.

CREATING SHORT TITLES
When creating short titles for Subsequent Notes, the most common practice is to use the main title and drop the subtitle. In some cases, however, authors have separate works whose main titles are the same or nearly so—as with Anderson, who produced an earlier series titled *The Great Migration Begins: Immigrants to New England, 1620–1633.* Including the dates in the short title helps to distinguish one series from the other.

12.73 Multivolume Works: Single Volume Split into Several
Some multivolume sets assign a single volume number to several separately bound volumes. A convenient example is Heiss's supplement to the six-volume set by Hinshaw, at 12.71 above. Heiss produced seven additional volumes treating the state of Indiana. However, because the original intent was for him to prepare "volume 7" of the Hinshaw series, he used the label "volume 7" for all seven volumes he eventually produced, and he assigned "part numbers" to each of his separately bound books.

Source List Entry
Heiss, Willard C., compiler. *Encyclopedia of American Quaker Genealogy.* Volume 7. *Abstracts of Records of the Society of Friends in Indiana.* 7 parts. Indianapolis: Indiana Historical Society, 1962–77.

First Reference Note
 1. Willard C. Heiss, compiler, *Encyclopedia of American Quaker Genealogy*, vol. 7, *Abstracts of Records of the Society of Friends in Indiana*, 7 parts (Indianapolis: Indiana Historical Society, 1962–77), part 1: 74.

Subsequent Note
 11. Heiss, *Encyclopedia of American Quaker Genealogy*, vol. 7, *Indiana*, part 1: 74.

12.74 Multivolume Works: Successive Authors or Editors

Multivolume sets that continue for years frequently have a succession of authors or editors. If you use multiple volumes, you may wish to cite the full set. If you use only one volume by one author or editor, then you may prefer to cite that one individual. The following examples illustrate the options.

Source List Entry

(*To cite a single volume from the set*)
Salzman, L. F., editor. *Victoria History of the County of Warwick*. Volume 6. London: A. Constable, 1951.

(*To cite the whole set*)
Victoria History of the County of Warwick. 8 volumes. London: A. Constable, 1904–59.

First Reference Note
 1. L. F. Salzman, editor, *Victoria History of the County of Warwick*, vol. 6 (London: A. Constable, 1951), 155–60.

 (*or*)
 1. *Victoria History of the County of Warwick*, 8 vols. (London: A. Constable, 1904–59), L. F. Salzman, editor, vol. 6 (1951): 155–60.

Subsequent Note
 11. Salzman, *Victoria History of the County of Warwick*, 6: 155.

REPRINTS & REVISIONS

12.75 Reprints & Revisions: Basic Format
See also QuickCheck Models *for*
• PRINT PUBLICATIONS: BOOK: REPRINT
• PRINT PUBLICATIONS: BOOK: REVISED EDITION

Many works continue to be republished long after their initial release. Some are reissued as facsimile reprints (exact page images), some as reprints (often retypeset), and some as new editions that have been revised or amplified. As a careful researcher, you will want your citation to show the exact type of source you used, because faithfulness to the original or the quality of revision can affect the reliability of the information you use from that source. A reprint that offers no enhancements or updates would typically be cited this way:

Source List Entry
Torrence, Clayton. *Virginia Wills and Administrations, 1632–1800: An Index.* 1930. Reprint, Baltimore: Genealogical Publishing Co., 1995.

First Reference Note
1. Clayton Torrence, *Virginia Wills and Administrations, 1632–1800: An Index* (1930; reprint, Baltimore: Genealogical Publishing Co., 1995), 113.

Subsequent Note
11. Torrence, *Virginia Wills and Administrations*, 113.

12.76   Reprints & Revisions: Citing Dates
When a revised edition updates the content of a book, it is not necessary to include the publication date of the original edition. (See 12.82.) However, when you cite a reprint of unrevised material, you *should* include the original publication date (12.79–12.81). The fact that a book was researched and written at an earlier time, without updating, often makes a difference in your analysis of its information.

12.77   Reprints & Revisions: Facsimile (Image) Reproductions
When a publication presents a facsimile of *original, manuscript records*, that fact should be added to the citation. Viewing the information in its original or manuscript form also carries weight in the evaluation of its evidence.

Source List Entry
Wiltshire, Betty C. *Register of Choctaw Emigrants to the West, 1831 and 1832.* Facsimile edition. Carrollton, Mississippi: Pioneer Publishing Co., 1993.

First Reference Note
1. Betty C. Wiltshire, *Register of Choctaw Emigrants to the West, 1831 and 1832* (Carrollton, Mississippi: Pioneer Publishing Co., 1993), 17; Wiltshire's *Register* presents facsimiles of the original roll, with an introduction and index.

Subsequent Note
11. Wiltshire, *Register of Choctaw Emigrants ... 1831 and 1832,* 17.

12.78 Reprints, Basic Issues

Reprints may offer images of the original publication (see 12.79) or they may be retypeset into a new and different reprint edition (12.81). When citing a reprint, it is not necessary to identify the original *publisher* or original *place* of publication. However, the original *date* of publication should be noted.

12.79 Reprints: Image Editions

Reprints that offer image copies of earlier publications are called facsimile *reprints* (as opposed to facsimile *reproductions* of original records, covered at 12.77). However, the modern terms *image copy* or *image reprint* are better understood today.

When using an image reprint edition, do not assume that the content is exactly the same from the old volume to the new. Many reprints have added matter. If you initially use the original edition, but decide to cite a more accessible reprint, you should consult the reprint to be certain the page numbers have not been altered by deletions or by additions of new material.

Source List Entry

Wilson, John. *The Gazetteer of Scotland.* 1882. Image reprint, Lovettsville, Virginia: Willow Bend Books, 1996.

First Reference Note

1. John Wilson, *The Gazetteer of Scotland* (1882; image reprint, Lovettsville, Virginia: Willow Bend Books, 1996), 31.

Subsequent Note

11. Wilson, *Gazetteer of Scotland,* image reprint, 31.

Digital Reprints (CD or DVD) ☉

Because electronic discs have such a large storage capacity, CD and DVD book reprints typically offer several books on the same disc, usually with a common theme. Therefore, you will have a two-part citation: (*a*) an identification of the original book; and (*b*) a citation to the disc itself, which typically carries a new and broader title. As noted under 12.76, your citation to the original does not have to include the original *publisher* or *place of publication*—only the original publication *date.*

Source List Entry

Pendell, Lucille H., and Elizabeth Bethel. *Preliminary Inventory of the Records of the Adjutant General's Office.* National Archives Preliminary Inventory 17. 1949. CD-ROM reprint. *Military Preliminary*

Inventory Record Groups. Westminster, Maryland: Heritage Books, 2005.

First Reference Note
    1. Lucille H. Pendell and Elizabeth Bethel, *Preliminary Inventory of the Records of the Adjutant General's Office*, National Archives Preliminary Inventory No. 17 (1949), 35; CD-ROM reprint, *Military Preliminary Inventory Record Groups* (Westminster, Maryland: Heritage Books, 2005).

Subsequent Note
    11. Pendell and Bethel, *Preliminary Inventory of the Records of the Adjutant General's Office,* 35.

PLACEMENT OF PAGE NUMBERS
Note, above, that the page number is placed at the end of the citation to the original book. It is not placed after the CD citation, because the CD has no pagination of its own. The pagination exists within each individual book on the CD.

Image Reprints (FHL-GSU Microfilm)
See also 2.29 and 12.55

Books reproduced as microfilmed images also require a two-part citation—one to the original book, another to the microfilm edition. At 12.55, you will find examples of citing a standard microfilmed reprint that has been published commercially. The following treats *preservation* microfilm that functions as an image reprint.

Source List Entry
Hartopp, Henry. *Leicestershire Lay Subsidy Roll, 1 James 1, 1603–1604.* Lincoln, England: James Williamson, n.d. FHL microfilm 990,094, item 17. Family History Library, Salt Lake City, Utah.

First Reference Note
    1. Henry Hartopp, *Leicestershire Lay Subsidy Roll, 1 James 1, 1603–1604* (Lincoln, England: James Williamson, n.d.), 26; FHL microfilm 990,094, item 17.

Subsequent Note
    11. Hartopp, *Leicestershire Lay Subsidy Roll,* 26.

PLACEMENT OF PAGE NUMBERS
As with citing page numbers on CD reprints, note that the page number in this microfilm example is also placed immediately after the citation to the original book. If the book were not paginated but the microfilm carried frame numbers, then the frame number would be placed after the microfilm.

12.80 Reprints: Multivolumes Bound as One

Many modern reprints of multivolume sets will bind the reproduced books into a smaller number of volumes. The situation is typically handled as follows:

Source List Entry

Gannett, Henry. *A Gazetteer of Virginia and West Virginia.* 1904. Reprint, 2 volumes in 1. Baltimore: Genealogical Publishing Co., 1980.

First Reference Note

1. Henry Gannett, *A Gazetteer of Virginia and West Virginia,* 2 vols. in 1 (1904; reprint, Baltimore: Genealogical Publishing Co., 1980), 2 (West Virginia): 35.

Subsequent Note

11. Gannett, *Gazetteer of Virginia and West Virginia,* 2: 35.

12.81 Reprints: New Editions

A reprint that adds enhancements without revising the original text varies only slightly from the basic format at 12.75. The usual variance is a need to acknowledge the writer of the new material. Note 1, below, acknowledges the introduction that has been added, but the original editors of the journal remain the primary "authors." Note 2 demonstrates how the new contributor would be cited if you were explicitly referencing something in his contribution.

Source List Entry

Hogan, William Ransom, and Edwin Adams, editors. *William Johnson's Natchez: The Ante-Bellum Diary of a Free Negro.* 1951. Reprint, with introduction by William L. Andrews. Baton Rouge: Louisiana State University Press, 1993.

First Reference Note

1. William Ransom Hogan and Edwin Adams, editors, *William Johnson's Natchez: The Ante-Bellum Diary of a Free Negro* (1951), reprint, with introduction by William L. Andrews (Baton Rouge: Louisiana State University Press, 1993), 5.

2. William L. Andrews, "Introduction to the 1993 Edition," William Ransom Hogan and Edwin Adams, editors, *William Johnson's Natchez: The Ante-Bellum Diary of a Free Negro* (1951; reprint, Baton Rouge: Louisiana State University Press, 1993), xiii.

Subsequent Note

11. Hogan and Adams, *William Johnson's Natchez,* 5.

12. Andrews, "Introduction to the 1993 Edition," *William Johnson's Natchez,* xiii.

Reprints: New Editions (CD/DVD) 🖘

Some CD or DVD publishers prefer to totally restructure the data. Some will eliminate the original title page and copyright page, making it more difficult for you to construct a thorough citation to the original. In some cases, you can ferret out the detail by reading the introduction added by the electronic publisher (a wise practice in any case). If you still do not see the needed data for the original publisher, you can usually find it in a major library catalog such as that of the Library of Congress.

The following example, from the Brøderbund catalog of CDs, is one in which the original title pages have been dropped and all pagination has been eliminated. A close reading of the CD's preface yields the essential publication data, but only in scattered pieces. An examination of the structure of the material reveals that specific data on the CD can be relocated by referring to the date and the individual—not by page number as with the original print publication. From your analysis of the CD, you could construct the following citation:

Source List Entry
Coldham, Peter Wilson. *The Complete Book of Emigrants, 1607–1660.* 1987. CD-ROM edition. *Family Tree Maker's Family Archives: The Complete Book of Emigrants, 1607–1776.* N.p.: Brøderbund, 2000.

First Reference Note
1. Peter Wilson Coldham, *The Complete Book of Emigrants, 1607–1660* (1987), CD-ROM ed. *Family Tree Maker's Family Archives: The Complete Book of Emigrants, 1607–1776,* part 2 (N.p.: Brøderbund, 2000), for 3 December 1683, George Ivory.

Subsequent Note
11. Coldham, *Complete Book of Emigrants, 1607–1660,* CD-ROM ed., for 3 December 1683, George Ivory.

PUBLISHER'S PRODUCT NUMBERS
When a publisher issues many CD-ROM or DVD products, those products are often numbered. In the above case, the CD-ROM carries the product number 350. However, whether you are working with publications in print or electronic form, a publisher's product number, stock number, or catalog number is not an essential part of your citation. In your working files, you are free to include any additional information about a source that you feel might help you. In a published citation, however, the critical elements for identification and analysis are those illustrated by the model above.

12.82 Revised Editions

See also QuickCheck Model *for* PRINT PUBLICATIONS: REVISED EDITION

As a rule, researchers want to consult the latest edition of a book, for updated information and corrections of earlier errors. Occasionally, as with Black's below, you will want to cite an earlier edition for data deleted from the later editions. In such cases, your note might also explain why you are not using the latest edition.

When research notes are taken from an earlier edition and you have at hand a citation to the new edition, *you should not change the edition data in your notes without examining that new edition.* The referenced material may or may not appear on the same page.

The original publication date is not normally cited when the contents of the book are being kept up-to-date.

Source List Entry

Black, Henry Campbell. *Black's Law Dictionary: Definitions of the Terms and Phrases of American and English Jurisprudence, Ancient and Modern.* Fourth edition. St. Paul, Minnesota: West Publishing Co., 1951.

Booth, Wayne C.; Gregory G. Colomb; and Joseph M. Williams. *The Craft of Research.* Second edition. Chicago: University of Chicago Press, ca. 2003.

First Reference Note

1. Henry Campbell Black, *Black's Law Dictionary: Definitions of the Terms and Phrases of American and English Jurisprudence, Ancient and Modern,* 4th ed. (St. Paul, Minnesota: West Publishing Co., 1951), 321. Although Black's is now in its eighth edition, the fourth edition offers the most extensive treatment of historic terms.

2. Wayne C. Booth, Gregory G. Colomb, and Joseph M. Williams, *The Craft of Research,* 2d ed. (Chicago: University of Chicago Press, ca. 2003), 159.

Subsequent Note

11. Black, *Black's Law Dictionary,* 321.

12. Booth, Colomb, and Williams, *The Craft of Research,* 159.

Revised Edition, Online

Source List Entry

Hancock, Ian. *The Pariah Syndrome.* Revised online edition. *Patrin: The Patrin Web Journal, Romani Culture and History.* http://www.geocities.com/~patrin : 2007.

First Reference Note
> 1. Ian Hancock, *The Pariah Syndrome,* rev. online ed., *Patrin: The Patrin Web Journal, Romani Culture and History* (http://www.geocities.com/~patrin : accessed 12 January 2007), chap. 8, para. 2.

Subsequent Note
> 11. Hancock, *The Pariah Syndrome,* online edition, chap. 8, para. 2.

12.83 Revisions, Posthumous

Classic reference works may continue to be revised long after the death of the original author. *Black's Law Dictionary* above is an example of one such work that is regularly revised by the publisher without identification of the individual who performed the revision.

Other works are so extensively revised that the new contributors should be identified. The quality of the new work does rest upon the level of expertise the new contributors bring to the task. When multiple parties participate in the revision, as with the Weis book below, the title page's description of their contribution may assign them different levels of responsibility—a point of reference that careful researchers also preserve.

Source List Entry
> Weis, Frederick Lewis. *Ancestral Roots of Certain American Colonists Who Came to America before 1700.* Seventh edition. Additions and corrections by Walter Lee Sheppard Jr., assisted by David Faris. Baltimore: Genealogical Publishing Co., 1995.

First Reference Note
> 1. Frederick Lewis Weis, *Ancestral Roots of Certain American Colonists Who Came to America before 1700,* 7th ed., additions and corrections by Walter Lee Sheppard Jr., assisted by David Faris (Baltimore: Genealogical Publishing Co., 1995), 221.

Subsequent Note
> 11. Weis, Sheppard, and Faris, *Ancestral Roots of Certain American Colonists,* 221.

SERIES & OCCASIONAL WORKS

12.84 Series: Basic Issues

Many agencies have issued special publication series—sometimes annually, sometimes on an occasional basis—that are indispensable to historical research. Most are rarely easy to cite. As a genre, they have complicated titles, titles within titles, a mixed-bag of publishers, and various subseries within the overall series. Some are commonly known by a series name that may or may not appear on the title page of the volume you use. Sections 12.85–12.86 present a range of examples, grouped by type, from which you can select the model most similar to the source you have used.

12.85 Series: "Archives" of the Various States

Numerous states have published early records in series that are generically called *[State name] Archives*. Many are issued in several consecutive series, in which case you must cite the exact series. Some have "volumes" that consist of multiple parts, each of which is also called a "volume" (see 12.73). The *Pennsylvania Archives* example below illustrates the handling of both of these situations in a single instance. Here, "Volume 8" of Series 2 consists of two bound books that are individually labeled "Volume 1" and "Volume 2."

Source List Entry

Linn, John B., and Wm. H. Egle, editors. *Record of Pennsylvania Marriages prior to 1810. Pennsylvania Archives,* 2d series, volume 8, volume [part] 1. Harrisburg, Pennsylvania: Clarence M. Busch, 1895.

First Reference Note

1.   "Marriages Recorded by the Registrar General of the Province, 1685–1689," *Record of Pennsylvania Marriages prior to 1810,* John B. Linn and William. H. Egle, editors, *Pennsylvania Archives,* 2d ser., vol. 8, vol. [part] 1 (Harrisburg: Clarence M. Busch, 1895), 5.

Subsequent Note

11.   "Marriages Recorded by the Registrar General of the Province, 1685–1689," Linn and Egle, *Pennsylvania Archives,* 2d ser., 8:1:5.

SHORT CITATIONS

Many researchers shortcut the complexity of these volumes with a "simple" citation such as

Pennsylvania Archives, Ser. 2, 8:5

Cryptic citations of this type, however, do not tell readers the type of record the author is relying upon. Nor would it inform users that volume 8 of this second series consists of multiple volumes itself—or explain which of those multiple volumes contains this particular page 5, considering that each "volume" of "volume" 8 has a page 5.

TYPEFACE FOR SERIES NAME

Because the series name *Pennsylvania Archives* is considered a formal title for this set of material, it is typeset in italics. However, the ordinal number that is used to identify the series—"second series" or "2d series"—is not part of the title and is rendered in roman type.

WHOLE SERIES OR SETS, HOW TO CITE
The above example focuses explicitly upon one book within the series or set known as *Pennsylvania Archives*. If you use multiple volumes from the set or if you need to cite the entire set, as in a bibliography to accompany a lecture, your citation will be significantly different:

> *Source List Entry*
> Hazard, Samuel, et al., editors. *Pennsylvania Archives.* 120 volumes. Philadelphia and Harrisburg, Pennsylvania: [various publishers], 1852–56, 1874–1919.

> *First Reference Note*
> 1. Samuel Hazard et al., editors, *Pennsylvania Archives,* 120 vols. (Philadelphia and Harrisburg: [various publishers], 1852–56, 1874–1919).

> *Subsequent Note*
> 11. Hazard et al., *Pennsylvania Archives,* previously cited.

INCLUSIVE VOLUMES AND YEARS
A citation to the entire set should note the number of volumes in the set and the inclusive dates of publication.

MULTIPLE EDITORS AND PUBLISHERS
Series that extend over many years frequently have multiple editors, publishers, and places of publication. When citing the entire series, these inconsistencies are handled by (*a*) citing the first or primary editor, followed by "et al."; and (*b*) citing the publisher as "various," with that term placed in square editorial brackets.

12.86   Series: "Occasional Publications" by Societies
Many societies issue "occasional publications" similar to the [*State Name*] *Archives* series treated at 12.85. The Colonial Society of Massachusetts series, below, illustrates a common, confusing issue: where to position a volume number so that its meaning is clear. Consider:

> *Source List Entry*
> Colonial Society of Massachusetts. *Transactions, 1917–1919.* Volume 20 of *Publications of the Colonial Society of Massachusetts.* Boston: The society, 1920.

> (*or*)
> Colonial Society of Massachusetts. *Publications of the Colonial Society of*

> *Massachusetts,* vol. 20, *Transactions, 1917–1919.* Boston: The society, 1920.

The difference is this:

Individual volume cited before the series—As illustrated in the first option, if you place the volume number before naming the series, you should note that this is "vol. 20 *of*" the whole series.

Volume number cited between the series title and the individual volume title—If you use the sequence in the second option above, the volume number needs no added word of explanation.

However, if you were to cite the series and then use the individual volume as a subtitle, *followed* by the volume number—i.e.,

> Colonial Society of Massachusetts. *Publications of the Colonial Society of Massachusetts: Transactions, 1917–1919,* vol. 20. Boston: The society, 1920.

then you would be implying that there were 20 or more volumes of transactions for the 1917–1919 period, rather than saying that those three years were all in volume 20.

SERIES ARRANGED BY COLLECTIONS

Other societies issue "occasional" publications keyed to certain collections they hold. For example, the Wisconsin Historical Society (previously, State Historical Society of Wisconsin) has a publications program that draws from its Draper Collection and is subdivided into smaller series, such as the one below. The pattern for citing this series follows the one used for *Pennsylvania Archives,* with one exception. Because the name of the series is not self-explanatory (as *Pennsylvania Archives* is), Wisconsin's Calendar Series has not taken on a distinctive identity of its own. Therefore, the words "Calendar Series" are not typeset in italics, as if that phrase were a formal title.

Source List Entry
Quaife, M. M., editor. *The Preston and Virginia Papers of the Draper Collection of Manuscripts.* Publications of the State Historical Society of Wisconsin, Calendar Series, vol. 1. Madison: The Society, 1915.

First Reference Note
1. M. M. Quaife, ed., *The Preston and Virginia Papers of the Draper Collection of Manuscripts,* Publications of the State Historical Society of Wisconsin, Calendar Series, vol. 1 (Madison: The Society, 1915), 43.

Subsequent Note
11. Quaife, *Preston and Virginia Papers,* 43.

12.87   Series: With Multiple Authors

Many serial books represent a collection of historical materials, with each item credited to an individual author or editor. Some will also have a general editor. As with any book that has both chapter authors and a general editor, you will need to credit both in one fashion or another. The general rules are these:

- If your interest lies in one particular item—say, the Salem Congregation records from the Moravian series in the example below—you would cite John Michael Graff, the bishop who kept the diary of that church.

- If you are referring to the whole volume generically, you would cite the editor (Fries) and the volume title.

- Your Source List might carry dual entries: one for the diarist Graff, and one for the whole volume under the name of its editor.

Source List Entry
(*When citing the entire volume*)
Fries, Adelaide L., editor. *Records of the Moravians in North Carolina.* Volume 2, *1752–1775.* Publications of the North Carolina Historical Commission. Raleigh: Edwards & Broughton Printing Co., 1925.

(*When citing material from a specific article*)
Graff, John Michael. "Diary of Salem Congregation, 1775." Adelaide L. Fries, editor. *Records of the Moravians in North Carolina.* Volume 2, *1752–1775.* Publications of the North Carolina Historical Commission. Raleigh: Edwards & Broughton Printing Co., 1925. Pages 862–894.

First Reference Note
(*When citing the entire volume*)
   1. Adelaide L. Fries, editor, *Records of the Moravians in North Carolina,* vol. 2, *1752–1775* (Raleigh: Edwards & Broughton Printing Co., 1925).

(*When citing material from a specific article*)
   2. John Michael Graff, "Diary of Salem Congregation, 1775," Adelaide L. Fries, editor, *Records of the Moravians in North Carolina,* vol. 2, *1752–1775* (Raleigh: Edwards & Broughton Printing Co., 1925), 862.

Subsequent Note
   11. Fries, *Records of the Moravians in North Carolina,* vol. 2, previously cited.
   12. Graff, "Diary of Salem Congregation, 1775," 864.

12.88 Series: With Named Parts

A still-more complex situation exists when serial books are divided into named "parts." In the example below, Kinnaird's work represents volumes 2–4 of the annual report of a sponsoring organization. Here, the Source List Entry illustrates how to cite all three volumes as a single source, while the Reference Note examples illustrate how to cite each volume specifically.

Source List Entry

Kinnaird, Lawrence. *Spain in the Mississippi Valley, 1765–1794*. 3 parts; being volumes 2–4 of *Annual Report of the American Historical Association for the Year 1945*. Washington, D.C.: Government Printing Office, 1946.

First Reference Note

1. Lawrence Kinnaird, *Spain in the Mississippi Valley, 1765–1794*, part 1, *The Revolutionary Period, 1765–1781;* vol. 2 of *Annual Report of the American Historical Association for the Year 1945* (Washington, D.C.: Government Printing Office, 1946), 33.

2. Lawrence Kinnaird, *Spain in the Mississippi Valley, 1765–1794*, part 2, *Post-War Decade;* vol. 3 of *Annual Report of the American Historical Association for the Year 1945* (Washington, D.C.: Government Printing Office, 1946), 66.

3. Lawrence Kinnaird, *Spain in the Mississippi Valley, 1765–1794*, part 3, *Problems of Frontier Defense, 1792–1794;* vol. 4 of *Annual Report of the American Historical Association for the Year 1945* (Washington, D.C.: Government Printing Office, 1946), 99.

Subsequent Note

11. Kinnaird, *Spain in the Mississippi Valley*, part 1:33.
12. Ibid., part 2: 66.
13. Ibid., part 3: 99.

PUNCTUATION WITHIN CITATIONS

The Kinnaird example, above, illustrates how clarity is served by following the semicolon *vs.* period guidelines at 2.74 and 12.2. There you are advised that, when citing multiple sources in the same note, you should put a period (full stop) at the end of each source before presenting a new source. Complex sources such as Kinnaird require internal semicolons. When citing sources of this type, if your notes were to follow the once-standard practice of putting many sources into a single sentence, all linked by semicolons, it would be difficult to determine where the details for one source stops and another starts.

12.89 Series: With Titles Cited as a Courtesy

Citing the series title for "occasional publications" is sometimes considered more a courtesy than a necessity. These individual situations are ones most researchers learn with experience, as they study citations used by major journals and presses. The three examples below illustrate the point with a privately published series, a society series, and an academic series.

Source List Entry

Holmes, Jack D. L. *Honor and Fidelity: The Louisiana Infantry Regiment and the Louisiana Militia Companies, 1766–1821.* Louisiana Collection Series. Birmingham, Alabama: Privately printed, 1965.

Lenzen, Connie. *Research in Oregon.* Research in the States Series, NGS special publication no. 62. Arlington, Virginia: National Genealogical Society, 1992.

Reed, Sheldon. *Reactivation of the Dight Institute, 1947–1949: Counseling in Human Genetics.* Bulletin no. 6, Charles Fremont Dight Institute for the Promotion of Human Genetics. Minneapolis: University of Minnesota, for the Dight Institute, 1949.

First Reference Note

(*Conventional citations that omit the series name*)

   1. Jack D. L. Holmes, *Honor and Fidelity: The Louisiana Infantry Regiment and the Louisiana Militia Companies, 1766–1821* (Birmingham, Alabama: Privately printed, 1965), 63.

   2. Connie Lenzen, *Research in Oregon* (Arlington, Virginia: National Genealogical Society, 1992), 13.

   3. Sheldon Reed, *Reactivation of the Dight Institute, 1947–1949: Counseling in Human Genetics* (Minneapolis: University of Minnesota for the Dight Institute, 1949), 3.

(*Full citations, with series name included*)

   1. Jack D. L. Holmes, *Honor and Fidelity: The Louisiana Infantry Regiment and the Louisiana Militia Companies, 1766–1821,* Louisiana Collection Series (Birmingham, Alabama: Privately printed, 1965), 63.

   2. Connie Lenzen, *Research in Oregon,* Research in the States Series, NGS special publication no. 62 (Arlington, Virginia: National Genealogical Society, 1992), 13.

   3. Sheldon Reed, *Reactivation of the Dight Institute, 1947–1949: Counseling in Human Genetics. ,* Bulletin no. 6, Charles Fremont Dight Institute for the Promotion of Human Genetics (Minneapolis: University of Minnesota for the Dight Institute, 1949), 3.

Subsequent Note

   11. Holmes, *Honor and Fidelity,* 63.

   12. Lenzen, *Research in Oregon,* 13.

   13. Reed, *Reactivation of the Dight Institute,* 3.

TYPEFACE, ITALIC VS. ROMAN

In all the examples above, the series name is not considered part of the publication's formal title. Therefore, the series name is not italicized.

VIDEOS & AUDIO PRESENTATIONS

12.90   Documentaries, Etc.: Digital or Analog
See also QuickCheck Model *for* ELECTRONIC PUBLICATIONS: VIDEO

Citations to videos follow Basic Format: Books, with only a slight modification. Whether you cite a digital or taped publication, you will want to identify the format, but the nature of that format rarely affects the structure of your citation. In the example below, the Series Field of your citation template is used to identify the publication as a PBS documentary; the Edition or Format Field is used to identify it as a DVD video.

CD/DVD

Source List Entry

> Wells, Spencer, host. *Journey of Man: A Genetic Odyssey.* PBS documentary. DVD video. N.p.: Warner Home Video, 2003.

First Reference Note

> 1. Spencer Wells, host, *Journey of Man: A Genetic Odyssey,* PBS documentary, DVD video (N.p.: Warner Home Video, 2003), minute 37.

Subsequent Note

> 11. Wells, *Journey of Man,* minute 37.

12.91   Lectures: CD/DVD or Internet Download

Citations to audio lectures vary according to whether you are citing a physical publication such as a CD-ROM or an electronic download from the Internet. If the presentation was part of a conference program, the conference should also be identified by sponsor and year. The following pair demonstrate the differences when citing the two media types.

CD/DVD

Source List Entry

> Beidler, James M. "Duplicate Documents That Aren't the Same." Lecture 172. Federation of Genealogical Societies Annual Conference: Boston, 2006. *New England Research.* Audio CD-ROM. Austin, Texas: Federation of Genealogical Societies, 2006.

First Reference Note
 1. James M. Beidler, "Duplicate Documents That Aren't the Same," lecture 172, Federation of Genealogical Societies Annual Conference: Boston, 2006, *New England Research,* audio CD-ROM (Austin, Texas: Federation of Genealogical Societies, 2006), minute 25.

Subsequent Note
 11. James M. Beidler, "Duplicate Documents That Aren't the Same," minute 25.

Internet Download

Source List Entry
Warren, Paula Stuart. *Railroad Records and Railroad History: Methods for Tracking.* Lecture T-173. Federation of Genealogical Societies Annual Conference: Boston, 2006. Audio download. *FGS Storefront.* http://www.lulu.com/content/405412 : 2006.

First Reference Note
 1. Paula Stuart Warren, *Railroad Records and Railroad History: Methods for Tracking,* lecture T-173, Federation of Genealogical Societies Annual Conference, Boston, 2006; audio download, *FGS Storefront* (http://www.lulu.com/content/405412 : 26 October 2006), minute 30.

Subsequent Note
 11. Warren, *Railroad Records and Railroad History,* minute 30.

VITAL-RECORD INDEXES & COMPENDIUMS

12.92 Vital Records, Published

Published vital records—whether they are official publications of a local governmental agency or local compendiums assembled from various sources—are simply publications.

In regions such as New York City, terms such as *printed originals* refer to the yearly indexes of local registrars that were typeset and published. As a class, these indexes are *derivatives* not actual originals. Hence, they are cited as one would any local governmental publications. See chapter 13.

For New England towns, records of birth, marriage, and death have long been referred to generically as *VRs*—e.g., Ipswich VR, Sandwich VR. In the past, researchers have used that term indiscriminately for several types of material that carry significantly different evidentiary weight:

- original registers of births, marriages, and deaths in the town hall;

- published volumes that precisely transcribe or abstract those original, official records;

- published volumes that abstract data from the official records, then rearrange them into an alphabetical sequence that obscures their context; and

- published volumes in which compilers assemble data from a variety of sources, both original and derivative—often with their own interpretations and conclusions silently interjected.

You should distinguish between the original records and derivatives, by citing each one according to their type. Chapter 9: Licenses, Registrations, Rolls & Vital Records, illustrates citations to a variety of original documents that record vital events. If you are using abstracts or transcripts of vital records that have been published in book form, you would follow Basic Format: Books (12.3). You will also help yourself and others if you note whether the work is a compendium created from sources of mixed value or whether the compiler has faithfully rendered a set of originals in their native context. As an example:

Source List Entry
Joslyn, Roger D., compiler. *Vital Records of Charlestown, Massachusetts, to 1850.* 2 volumes in 3. Boston: New England Historic Genealogical Society, 1984–1995.

First Reference Note
1. Roger D. Joslyn, compiler, *Vital Records of Charlestown, Massachusetts, to 1850,* 2 vols. in 3 (Boston: New England Historic Genealogical Society, 1984–95), 1:84; Joslyn's work presents abstracts from the original town, city, and county registers, preserving the original arrangements and spellings.

Subsequent Note
11. Joslyn, *Vital Records of Charlestown, Massachusetts,* 1:84.

PUBLICATIONS

13

Legal Works & Government Documents

QuickCheck Models

Guidelines & Examples <inline>(beginning page 740)</inline>

QuickCheck Model
BOOK: BASIC FORMAT
(Citing from title page)

Source List Entry

<table>
<tr><td>AUTHOR (COMPILER)</td><td>TITLE ...</td></tr>
</table>

Smyth, Constantine Joseph. *A Complete Abstract of the Statutes of Nebraska,*

<table>
<tr><td>...</td><td>PLACE OF PUB'N</td><td>PUBLISHER</td><td>YEAR</td></tr>
</table>

with Legal Forms. Omaha: Rees Printing Co., 1905.

First (Full) Reference Note

<table>
<tr><td>AUTHOR (COMPILER)</td><td>TITLE ...</td></tr>
</table>

1. Constantine Joseph Smyth, *A Complete Abstract of the Statutes of*

<table>
<tr><td>...</td><td>PLACE OF PUB'N</td><td>PUBLISHER</td><td>YEAR</td><td>PAGE</td></tr>
</table>

Nebraska, with Legal Forms (Omaha: Rees Printing Co., 1905), 123.

Subsequent (Short) Note

<table>
<tr><td>AUTHOR</td><td>TITLE</td><td>PAGE</td></tr>
</table>

11. Smyth, *Complete Abstract of the Statutes of Nebraska,* 123.

QuickCheck Model
CASE REPORTERS
SERIES NAMED FOR EDITOR
(Citing individual volume from title page)

Source List Entry

EDITOR	TITLE ...

Martin, François X. *Term Reports of Cases Argued and Determined in the*

...	TOTAL VOLUMES

Superior Court of the Territory of Orleans, 1809–1823. 12 volumes.

PLACE OF PUBLICATION	PUBLISHER	YEAR

New Orleans: F. X. Martin, 1854.

First (Full) Reference Note

EDITOR	TITLE ...

1. François X. Martin, *Term Reports of Cases Argued and Determined in*

...	TOTAL VOLS.	PLACE OF PUBLICATION

the Superior Court of the Territory of Orleans, 1809–1823, 12 vols. (New Orleans:

PUBLISHER	PUB'N YEAR	VOL./ PAGE	CASE	YEAR	...

F. X. Martin, 1854), 1: 183, *Adelle* v. *Beauregard* (1810); hereinafter cited as

... CASE LABEL (LEGAL STYLE)

Adelle v. *Beauregard*, 1 Martin La. 183 (1810).

Subsequent (Short) Note

CASE LABEL (LEGAL STYLE)

11. *Adelle* v. *Beauregard*, 1 Martin La. 183 (1810).

QuickCheck Model
CASE REPORTERS
STANDARDIZED SERIES
(Citing individual volume from title page)

Source List Entry

<u>TITLE ...</u>

West's Supreme Court Reporter: Cases Argued and Determined in the United

...	SPECIFIC VOL(S)	COURT TERM / SUBTITLE	PLACE OF PUBLICATION

States Supreme Court. Volume 1. *October Term 1882.* St. Paul, Minnesota:

PUBLISHER	YEAR

West Publishing Co., 1883.

First (Full) Reference Note

<u>TITLE ...</u>

1. *West's Supreme Court Reporter: Cases Argued and Determined in the*

...	SPECIFIC VOL.	COURT TERM / SUBTITLE	PLACE OF PUBLICATION

United States Supreme Court, vol. 1, *October Term 1882* (St. Paul, Minnesota:

PUBLISHER	PUB'N YEAR	PAGES	CASE	...

West Publishing Co., 1883), 80–82, *Waples* v. *Hays, Tutrix;* hereinafter cited

<u>... CASE LABEL (LEGAL STYLE)</u>

as *Waples* v. *Hays,* 1 S.Ct. 80 (1882).

Subsequent (Short) Note

<u>CASE LABEL (LEGAL STYLE)</u>

11. *Waples* v. *Hays,* 1 S.Ct. 80 (1882).

QuickCheck Model
CODES & STATUTES, ONLINE
STATE DATABASE

Source List Entry

<u>DATABASE ...</u>

"Georgia Legislative Documents: Acts and Resolutions of the General Assem-

<u>... TITLE</u>   <u>ITEM TYPE or FORMAT</u>   <u>WEBSITE CREATOR-OWNER</u>

bly of the State of Georgia, 1910." Database. University System of Georgia.

<u>WEBSITE TITLE</u>   <u>URL (DIGITAL LOCATION)</u>

Galileo. http://dlg.galileo.usg.edu/CollectionsA-Z/zlgl_information.html

<u>YEAR</u>

: 2007.

First (Full) Reference Note

<u>DATABASE ...</u>

1. "Georgia Legislative Documents: Acts and Resolutions of the General

<u>... TITLE</u>   <u>ITEM TYPE or FORMAT</u>   <u>WEBSITE CREATOR-OWNER ...</u>

Assembly of the State of Georgia, 1910," database, University System of

<u>... WEBSITE TITLE</u>   <u>URL (DIGITAL LOCATION)</u>

Georgia, *Galileo* (http://dlg.galileo.usg.edu/CollectionsA-Z/zlgl_infor

<u>... DATE PUBLISHED, UPDATED or ACCESSED</u>   <u>PAGE</u>   <u>PART & ...</u>

mation.html : accessed 2 March 2007), p. 26, Part I (Public Laws), Title

<u>... TITLE OF ACT (or ARTICLE, SECTION NO.)</u>

II (Taxation), Act: "Method of Assessing and Collecting Taxes."

Subsequent (Short) Note

<u>DATABASE ...</u>

11. "Georgia Legislative Documents: Acts and Resolutions of the General

<u>... TITLE</u>   <u>PAGE</u>   <u>TITLE OF ACT</u>

Assembly ... 1910," p. 26, "Method of Assessing and Collecting Taxes."

QuickCheck Model
CODES & STATUTES, ONLINE
U.S. CODE

Source List Entry

AUTHOR	NAME OF CODE	EDITION	WEBSITE CREATOR-OWNER

United States. Congress. *United States Code*. Web edition. Cornell Law School.

WEBSITE TITLE	URL (DIGITAL LOCATION)	EDITION YEAR

U.S. Code Collection. http://www.law.cornell. edu/uscode/ : 2007.

First (Full) Reference Note

NAME OF ACT	TITLE NO.	NAME OF CODE

1. "National Cemeteries and Memorials," Title 38, *United States Code,*

PART / CHAPTER / SECTION	EDITION	WEBSITE CREATOR-OWNER	WEBSITE ...

part 2, chapter 24, § 2402; Web edition, Cornell Law School, *U.S. Code*

... TITLE	URL (DIGITAL LOCATION)	DATE

Collection (http://www.law.cornell.edu/uscode/ : accessed 1 February 2007).

Subsequent (Short) Note

NAME OF ACT	SHORT CITATION (LEGAL STYLE)

11. "National Cemeteries and Memorials," 38 U.S.C. 2402.

QuickCheck Model
SLIP LAW: FEDERAL

Source List Entry

<table>
<tr><td>AUTHOR</td><td>TITLE OF ACT</td><td>ACT ...</td></tr>
</table>

United States. Congress. *National Cemetery Systems Act of 1973.* Public Law

<table>
<tr><td>... NO.</td></tr>
</table>

94–43.

First (Full) Reference Note

<table>
<tr><td>TITLE OF ACT</td><td>ACT NO.</td></tr>
</table>

1. *National Cemetery Systems Act of 1973,* Public Law 94–43.

Subsequent (Short) Note

<table>
<tr><td>TITLE OF ACT</td><td>ACT NO.</td></tr>
</table>

11. *National Cemetery Systems Act of 1973,* Public Law 94–43.

QuickCheck Model
STATUTES: FEDERAL
(Citing volume from title page)

Source List Entry

AUTHOR	TITLE OF SERIES	SPECIFIC VOL.	PLACE OF PUBLICATION ...
United States. Congress.	*U.S. Statutes at Large.*	Volume 19.	Washington,

...	PUBLISHER	YEAR
D.C.:	Government Printing Office,	1877.

First (Full) Reference Note

	AUTHOR	TITLE OF SERIES	SPECIFIC VOL.	PLACE OF PUBLICATION ...
1.	United States Congress,	*U.S. Statutes at Large,*	vol. 19	(Washington,

...	PUBLISHER	YEAR	PAGE	TITLE OF ACT ...
D.C.:	Government Printing Office,	1877),	377,	"An Act to Provide for the

...

Sale of Desert Lands."

Subsequent (Short) Note

SHORTENED CITATION (ACADEMIC STYLE)	
TITLE VOL.: PAGE (YEAR)	TITLE OF ACT ...
11. *U.S. Statutes at Large* 19: 377 (1877),	"An Act to Provide for the

...

Sale of Desert Lands."

QuickCheck Model
STATUTES: STATE
(Citing volume from title page)

Source List Entry

AUTHOR (COMPILER)   TITLE ...

Henning, Wilbur Fisk. *Insolvency and Assignment Laws of California,*

           PLACE OF
     ...   PUBLICATION   PUBLISHER   YEAR

Annotated. Los Angeles: Chas. W. Palm Co., 1895.

First (Full) Reference Note

AUTHOR (COMPILER)   TITLE ...

1. Wilbur Fisk Henning, *Insolvency and Assignment Laws of California,*

        PLACE OF
   ...   PUBLICATION   PUBLISHER   YEAR   PAGE

Annotated (Los Angeles: Chas. W. Palm Co., 1895), 123.

Subsequent (Short) Note

AUTHOR   TITLE   PAGE

11. Henning, *Insolvency and Assignment Laws of California,* 123.

QuickCheck Model
CONGRESSIONAL RECORDS
(*Citing volume from title page*)

Source List Entry

AUTHOR   TITLE ...

United States. Congress. *Memorial of the State of Missouri and Documents in*

...   CONGRESS ...

Relation to Indian Depredations upon Citizens of That State. 19th Congress,

... SESSION   DOC. ID   PLACE OF PUBLICATION   PUBLISHER

1st session, Senate Document 55. Washington, D.C.: Gales and Seaton,

YEAR

1826.

First (Full) Reference Note

AUTHOR   TITLE ...

1. U.S. Congress, *Memorial of the State of Missouri and Documents in*

...   CONGRESS & SESSION

Relation to Indian Depredations upon Citizens of That State, 19th Cong., 1st sess.,

DOC. ID   PLACE OF PUBLICATION   PUBLISHER   YEAR   PAGE

Senate Document 55 (Washington, D.C.: Gales and Seaton, 1826), 48.

Subsequent (Short) Note

AUTHOR   TITLE

11. U.S. Cong., *Memorial of the State of Missouri ... Indian Depredations,*

PAGE

48.

QuickCheck Model
CONGRESSIONAL RECORDS
(*Traditional academic style*)

Source List Entry

AUTHOR	SERIES TITLE	CONGRESS	SESSION	YEAR

United States. Congress. *Senate Documents.* 19th Congress, 1st session. 1826.

First (Full) Reference Note

AUTHOR	DOCUMENT TITLE ...

1. U. S. Congress, *Memorial of the State of Missouri and Documents in*

...	CONGRESS & ...

Relation to Indian Depredations upon Citizens of That State, 19th Cong.,

...SESSION	YEAR	DOC. ID	PLACE OF PUBLICATION	PUBLISHER	YEAR	PAGE

1st sess., 1826, S. Doc. 55 (Washington, D.C.: Gales and Seaton, 1826), 48.

Subsequent (Short) Note

AUTHOR	CONGRESS & SESSION	YEAR	DOC. ID

11. U. S. Cong., 19th Cong., 1st sess., 1826, S. Doc. 55.

QuickCheck Model
CONGRESSIONAL RECORDS
ONLINE IMAGES

Source List Entry

AUTHOR	SERIES TITLE	FORMAT	WEBSITE CREATOR

United States. Congress. *Annals of Congress.* Digital images. Library of Congress.

WEBSITE TITLE ...

A Century of Lawmaking for a New Nation: U.S. Congressional Documents

...	URL (DIGITAL LOCATION)	YEAR

and Debates, 1774–1875. http://memory.loc.gov/ammem/amlaw/ : 2007.

First (Full) Reference Note

AUTHOR	SERIES TITLE	CONGRESS & SESSION	YEAR

1. U.S. Congress, *Annals of Congress,* 14th Cong., 2d sess. (1817),

PAGES	ITEM	FORMAT	WEBSITE CREATOR

939–40, "Colonization of Free Negroes"; digital images, Library of Congress,

WEBSITE ...

A Century of Lawmaking for a New Nation: U.S. Congressional Documents and

... TITLE	URL (DIGITAL LOCATION)	DATE ...

Debates, 1774–1875 (http://memory.loc.gov/ammem/amlaw/ : accessed 30

...

April 2007).

Subsequent (Short) Note

AUTHOR	SERIES TITLE	CONG. & SESS.	PAGES

11. U.S. Cong., *Annals of Congress,* 14th Cong., 2d sess., 939–40.

QuickCheck Model
NATIONAL ARCHIVES (U.S.) GUIDES
DESCRIPTIVE PAMPHLET, ONLINE

Source List Entry

AUTHOR   TITLE OF ...

United States. National Archives. *Registers of Vessels Arriving at the Port of New*

... PAMPHLET   SERIES ID   ...

York from Foreign Ports, 1789–1919. Descriptive Pamphlet M1066. Web

EDITION   WEBSITE TITLE (SAME AS CREATOR-OWNER)   URL ...

edition. *The National Archives.* http://www.archives.gov/genealogy/

... (DIGITAL LOCATION)   YEAR

immigration/microfilm/customs-records-1820-1891.html : 2006.

First (Full) Reference Note

AUTHOR   TITLE OF ...

1. U.S. National Archives, *Registers of Vessels Arriving at the Port of*

... PAMPHLET   SERIES ID   ...

New York from Foreign Ports, 1789–1919, Descriptive Pamphlet M1066, Web

EDITION   WEBSITE TITLE   URL ...

edition, *The National Archives* (http://www.archives.gov/genealogy/immigra

... (DIGITAL LOCATION)   DATE   PAGE

tion/microfilm/customs-records-1820-1891.html : accessed 5 April 2007), 2.

Subsequent (Short) Note

AUTHOR   TITLE OF ...

11. National Archives, *Registers of Vessels Arriving at the Port of New York*

... PAMPHLET   SERIES ID   PAGE

from Foreign Ports, 1789–1919, DP M1066, 2.

QuickCheck Model
NATIONAL ARCHIVES (U.S.) GUIDES
PRELIMINARY INVENTORY, MICROFILMED

Source List Entry

AUTHOR	BOOK TITLE ...
Ulibarri, George S.	*Preliminary Inventory of Records Relating to International*

...	SERIES ID	PLACE OF PUBLICATION	PUBLISHER ...
Claims.	Preliminary Inventory 177.	Washington, D.C.:	National Archives

...	YEAR
and Records Service,	1974.

First (Full) Reference Note

AUTHOR	BOOK TITLE ...
1. George S. Ulibarri,	*Preliminary Inventory of Records Relating to Interna-*

...	SERIES ID	PLACE OF PUBLICATION	PUBLISHER ...
tional Claims,	PI 177	(Washington, D.C.:	National Archives and Records

...	YEAR	PAGE	ITEM
Service,	1974),	p. 38,	entry 225.

Subsequent (Short) Note

AUTHOR	BOOK TITLE ...
11. Ulibarri,	*Preliminary Inventory of Records Relating to International*

...	PAGE	ITEM
Claims,	p. 38,	entry 225.

GUIDELINES
& Examples

BASIC ISSUES

13.1 Background

Legal and governmental publications are among the most complex sources to cite. There is no one-size-fits-all pattern. Every nation, every U.S. state, and every law journal has its own preferred style. Moreover, the rapid conversion of society from print media to electronic libraries has created a demand for legal citations that does not depend upon time-honored printed works.

The traditional variants have one factor in common: they originated under circumstances alien to modern historical researchers. In brief:

- These systems developed within the legal profession, designed by and for those who practiced law. Publications were relatively few by today's standards and were well known to practitioners. A "shorthand" evolved for citing those books—one that often bears little resemblance to the information carried on their title pages. Even library catalogs may not match their data to the title pages of individual books.

- Legal-style citations evolved in an era when citations were constructed manually. No virtual software laid out preset bounds. No source templates standardized each field into a consistent pattern for all types of records. Thus, citations for *case law* did not have to match those for, say, *statute law*.

As a history researcher and writer, you face a dilemma. Most of your readers will not be trained in law. If you prefer to use legal-style citations, many of your readers will have difficulty using that shorthand to find the actual volumes you consulted. Your challenge is to construct citations that will be usable by all readers, regardless of their training and experience.

13.2   Citation Style Options: Legal Style & Academic Style

UNITED STATES

In many U.S. legal forums, citation practices follow the *Bluebook* Style developed by several leading law-review journals. Some states have issued their own guides. The *ALWD Citation Manual* of the Association of Legal Writing Directors is also gaining favor. (All are identified fully in the bibliography, Appendix B.) If you work extensively in legal records, you will want to study all of them. As a brief introduction:

BLUEBOOK STYLE, BASIC PATTERN

The legal shorthand used by the *Bluebook* disregards the formal title and publication data that appear on the title page of legal works. Instead, it refers to all statutes using what is called the *tripartite* (three-part) system:

VOL. NO. • NAME OF REPORTER (SERIES) • PAGE NO.

As an example:

2 Stat. 139

refers to volume 2 of *U.S. Statutes at Large* (laws passed by the U.S. Congress) and the act that starts on page 139.

INTERNATIONALLY

Each country has its own style. You should consult a guide to the practices of the country whose records you are using.

13.3   Citation Style Options: Layman's Style

Other U.S. style guides such as *Chicago Manual of Style* offer a somewhat simplified academic style for citing published laws and court cases in nonlegal publications. Both traditional legal citations and modified citations for laymen are currently recommended by the Library of Congress at its website *A Century of Lawmaking for a New Nation* (http://memory.loc.gov/ammem/amlaw/lawhome.html), where you will find digitized images of the 1789–1875 U.S. statutes and many other published government documents. Studying these materials can help you learn the basics of citing in traditional legal and academic styles.

Your simplest option would be to cite the published volume by the QuickCheck Model for BOOK: BASIC FORMAT, taking your data from the title page. If you are new to legal research or if you have difficulty making *Bluebook* citations fit into your software's current templates, this option will likely appeal to you.

As an introduction to legal-style citations, this chapter
- provides a brief synopsis of published legal resources and governmental works that follow those citation patterns;
- offers a combination of legal and traditional citations; and
- adapts some complex citations so they will be more compatible with data-management software.

The basic pattern this guide follows is this:

SOURCE LIST ENTRY ..... Use bibliographic data from title page, to construct an entry in Basic Format: Book.

FIRST NOTE .... Use this same bibliographic data to construct a full note citation, to which you may choose to append "hereinafter cited as ..." and then provide the appropriate (cryptic) legal citation.

SUBSEQUENT NOTES .... In this shortened form of the full note, you might choose to use the legal citation or use a common short citation in Book: Basic Format.

ABBREVIATIONS .... *Bluebook* Style strongly encourages abbreviations and lays out explicit rules for them. If you are writing for a nonlegal audience, it is better to follow the more general rule of writing: spell out everything at first use.

LEGAL REFERENCE WORKS

BACKGROUND

13.4 Case Law vs. Statutory Law

The decisions reached in significant trial cases are known as *case law.* These represent certain cases appealed to the state or federal superior courts, whose rulings interpret unclear areas of the statutory law. Section 13.5 covers the *case reporters* that chronicle case law and the *digests,* which serve as a finding aid to the printed reporters.

Laws passed by governing bodies at the local, state, or national levels are collectively called *statutory law.* Section 13.6, below, follows these records in their natural progression from *slip laws* to *statutes* and eventually to *codes.*

13.5   Reporters & Digests

CASE REPORTERS

Periodically (usually annually), details and decisions from significant cases heard by appeals courts of a state or nation are compiled into volumes called *case reporters*.

DIGESTS

Printed indexes to names of plaintiffs and defendants are found in publications generally called *digests,* which are periodically compiled extracts from the cases, arranged topically. However, also see 13.6 for another legal use of the term *digest*.

13.6   Statutory Law: Slip Laws, Statutes & Codes

SLIP LAWS

Individual laws, after they are passed and before they are consolidated into bound collections, are known as *slip laws*.

STATUTES

The laws passed during each legislative session are, at the end of the session, compiled into volumes called *session laws* or *statutes*.

CODES (SOMETIMES, DIGESTS)

Periodically, the accumulated laws and amendments are consolidated into a *code*—a summary of existing laws. Laws that once existed but had been dropped prior to the compilation of the code would not be included. Sometimes the label *digest* is used in lieu of *code,* but you should note that the term *digest* also has another legal meaning discussed under 13.5.

13.7   Titles of Laws: Punctuation & Typeface

SESSION LAWS OR CODES .... Because these laws are published as bound volumes, the titles of the volumes follow the common practice of using italics for book titles. The titles of the individual laws are placed in roman type, with quotation marks around the exact words of the law's title, as you would do when citing a chapter within a book or an article within a journal.

SLIP LAWS .... Because these are published individually, their exact titles are set in italics, without quotation marks.

CODES, STATUTES & SLIP LAWS

(Codes)

13.8 **Federal Codes**

See also QuickCheck Model *for* CODES & STATUTES, ONLINE: U.S. CODE

The *U.S. Code*, which summarizes all existing federal laws, is a massive set of volumes that is most easily used in an online version. The QuickCheck Model cited above provides a full citation to the current *Code* and a website provider—a model that can be used for all comparable codes. Within the legal field, however, current recommendations lean toward a shorter model for the *U.S. Code*—suggesting that you cite your provider/publisher (LexisNexis, Cornell, WestLaw, etc.) only in your Source List. The law itself would then be cited generically in your notes, without reference to any particular website or book. For example:

Codes, U.S. (Online)

Source List Entry

United States. Congress. *U.S. Code*. Web edition. Cornell Law School. *U.S. Code Collection*. http://www.law.cornell.edu/uscode/ : 2007.

First Reference Note

1. "National Cemeteries and Memorials," Title 38, *U.S. Code*, part 2, chapter 24, § 2402 (2007 edition).

(or, legal style)

1. 38 U.S.C. 2402.

Subsequent Note

[Repeat either of the First Reference Note styles. If you wish, you may abbreviate *part* (pt.), *chapter* (chap.), and *edition* (ed.).]

13.9 **Municipal Codes**

See also QuickCheck Model *for* BOOK: BASIC FORMAT

Most publications by local governments—codes, ordinances, etc.—can be cited using Book: Basic Format. When citing municipal codes or laws, as with those at the state and federal level, you may need to add the law and its chapter, section, or paragraph number—depending upon the complexity of the code.

Source List Entry

Varnum, Charles W., and J. Frank Adams, compilers. *The Municipal*

Code of the City and County of Denver, Approved April 12, 1906, Containing ... Liquor Ordinances of Annexed Towns and Cities. Denver: Smith-Brooks Co., 1906.

First Reference Note
1. Charles W. Varnum and J. Frank Adams, comps., *The Municipal Code of the City and County of Denver, Approved April 12, 1906, Containing ... Liquor Ordinances of Annexed Towns and Cities* (Denver: Smith-Brooks Co., 1906), 722–23, South Denver Ordinance No. 60, Sect. 2.

Subsequent Note
11. Varnum and Adams, *Municipal Code of ... Denver ... 1906*, 722.

IDENTIFICATION OF "AUTHOR"
The "author" of municipal codes is often the municipality. In some cases, such as the one above, compilers are identified.

CORRECTING & AMPLIFYING TITLES
If the title of the municipal code or statutes cites only the city and not the state, as in this Denver example, you may wish to add the state in square editorial brackets—especially if the municipality is not well-known.

13.10 State Codes
Historic state-level codes are typically consulted in their original print format or as online images. For a standard printed work, your citation would be similar to this:

Source List Entry
Clay, C. C. *A Digest of the Laws of the State of Alabama*. Tuskaloosa: Marmaduke J. Slade, 1843.

First Reference Note
1. C. C. Clay, *A Digest of the Laws of the State of Alabama* (Tuskaloosa: Marmaduke J. Slade, 1843), 267–272, "Guardians," § 10.

Subsequent Note
11. Clay, *Digest of the Laws of ... Alabama* [1843], 267–72, § 10.

CITING THE CHAPTER AND/OR SECTION
In the case of lengthy laws such as the one above, you will want to cite the chapter and/or section (§).

CITING THE DATE
Although Subsequent Note citations for books rarely include the year of publication, a date is needed in the above case because the title of

the publication yields no clue to when these laws were in effect. You would add the year of the *code* (not the year of publication) in square editorial brackets after the title.

Codes, State (Online)

See QuickCheck Model *for* CODES & STATUTES ONLINE: STATE DATABASE

Online versions of historic codes typically take one of two formats: searchable database-style editions (as with the Georgia example below) or digital images (as with the Maryland example).

Source List Entry

"Georgia Legislative Documents: Acts and Resolutions of the General Assembly of the State of Georgia, 1910." Database. University System of Georgia. *Galileo.* http://dlg.galileo.usg.edu/CollectionsA-Z/zlgl_information.html : 2007.

Scott, Otho, and Hiram M'Cullough, compilers. *The Maryland Code: Public General Laws.* Second edition. Baltimore: John Murphy & Co., 1860. Digital images. *Archives of Maryland Online.* http://www.mdarchives.state.md.us/megafile/msa/speccol/sc2900/sc2908/html/codes.html : 2007.

First Reference Note

1. "Georgia Legislative Documents: Acts and Resolutions of the General Assembly of the State of Georgia, 1910," database, University System of Georgia, *Galileo* (http://dlg.galileo.usg.edu/CollectionsA-Z/zlgl_information.html : 2 February 2007), p. 26, Part I (Public Laws), Title II (Taxation), Act: "Method of Assessing and Collecting Taxes."

2. Otho Scott and Hiram M'Cullough, comps., *The Maryland Code: Public General Laws,* 2d ed. (Baltimore: John Murphy & Co., 1860), "Bastardy & Fornication," p. 62, art. 13, § 4; digital images, *Archives of Maryland Online* (http://www.mdarchives.state.md.us/megafile/msa/speccol/sc2900/sc2908/html/codes.html : accessed 1 March 2007).

Subsequent Note

11. "Georgia Legislative Documents: Acts and Resolutions of the General Assembly ... 1910," p. 26, "Method of Assessing and Collecting Taxes."

12. Scott and M'Cullough, *Maryland Code* [1860], p. 62, art. 13, § 4.

CITING NAME OF ACT

In the Maryland example, the shortened title does not cite the name of the act, because the format of the publication allows you to identify the specific act by page, article, and section number. In the Georgia example, the shortened title includes the name of the act because there is no article or section number to otherwise identify which act you were citing from Title II (which covers all areas of taxation). Each time you use these codes, digests, or statutes, you will have to thoughtfully appraise the situation to determine the essential elements.

(Session Laws, Legislative Acts, Statutes)

13.11   Session Laws vs. Codes

The statutes published for each session of Congress or the state legislatures contain laws that did not eventually make their way into the code books. Some were left out of the codes because they were repealed or overturned before the code was compiled. Others were left out because they are private acts for individuals or resolutions passed to honor individuals or occasions. Therefore, you will frequently need to cite session laws, as well as code books.

13.12   Session Laws: Federal

See also QuickCheck Model *for* STATUTES: FEDERAL

U.S. statutes have been published in several series, bearing different names. The following two examples cover an 1873 set that consolidated all the prior statutes and the current series, begun in 1874.

Source List Entry

United States. Congress. *The Public Statutes at Large of the United States of America, 1789–1873.* 17 volumes. Washington, D.C.: [various publishers], 1845–73.

———. *U.S. Statutes at Large, 1874—*. Washington, D.C.: Government Printing Office. Published biennially.

First Reference Note

1. U.S. Congress, *The Public Statutes at Large of the United States of America, 1789–1873,* 17 vols. (Washington, D.C.: [various publishers], 1845–73), 2: 139, 30 March 1802, "An Act to Regulate Trade and Intercourse with the Indian Tribes," chap. 13.

2. U.S. Congress, *U.S. Statutes at Large,* vol. 19 (Washington, D.C.: Government Printing Office, 1877), 377, "An Act to Provide for the Sale of Desert Lands."

Subsequent Note

11. *U.S. Statutes at Large* 2: 139 (1802), "An Act to Regulate Trade and Intercourse with the Indian Tribes," chap. 13.

12. *U.S. Statutes at Large* 19: 377 (1877), "An Act to Provide for the Sale of Desert Lands."

(or, legal style)

11. 2 Stat. 139, chap. 13 (30 March 1802).

12. 19 Stat. 377 (1877).

CITING MULTIPLE PUBLISHERS

The 1789–1873 series of *U.S. Statutes at Large* was published across three decades and had multiple publishers. Rather than cite all, you need only say "various publishers" in square editorial brackets.

13.13 Session Laws: State

See also QuickCheck Model *for* STATUTES: STATE

State-level session laws may have an individual compiler, or the state itself may be the official compiler. In the latter case, you might name the state in the Author Field of your citation or you might simply leave that field blank, as demonstrated below. When no compiler is named, as below, the state is assumed to be the compiler by default.

The "chapter" number referenced in compiled statutes such as this is the "chapter" within a particular law, not a section of the book.

Source List Entry

Laws of the Territory of the United States Northwest of the River Ohio, Passed at the Third Session of the First General Assembly Begun [23 November 1802]. Chillicothe: N. Willis, 1803.

First Reference Note

1. *Laws of the Territory of the United States Northwest of the River Ohio, Passed at the Third Session of the First General Assembly Begun [23 November 1802]* (Chillicothe: N. Willis, 1803), pp. 60–72, chap. 4, "An Act Levying a tax on land."

Subsequent Note

11. *Laws of the Territory of ... Ohio* [1802], pp. 60–72, chap. 4.

SHORTENING OVERLONG TITLES

The above volume spells out the day, month, and year on which the session started. In your Full Reference Note, you may shorten overlong *subtitles* of this ilk by writing the date conventionally and placing that alteration in square editorial brackets, as shown above.

13.14 Statutes: International & Regnal

In regions governed by monarchies (including the colonial U.S.), laws are frequently cited by regnal year. For example:

1 Anne Stat. 8, c. 18, 126–27.

This format would be read as

• Year 1 of the reign of Britain's Queen Anne

- Statutes, vol. 8
- chapter 18, pages 126–27

As an alternative, you might cite bound and published statutes following Book: Basic Format, similar to the Ohio example at 13.13.

Source List Entry
Great Britain. *The Statutes of the Realm.* 11 volumes. London: G. Eyre and A. Strahan, 1810–24.

First Reference Note
1. Great Britain, *The Statutes of the Realm,* 11 vols. (London: G. Eyre and A. Strahan, 1810–24), 8: 126–27, chap. 18, "An Act for the more effectual preventing [of] the Abuses and Frauds of Persons imployed in the working up [of] the Woollen, Linen, Fustian, Cotton, and Iron Manufactures of this Kingdom" (1701).

Subsequent Note
11. Great Britain, *Statutes of the Realm,* 8 (1701): 126–27.

(Slip Laws)

13.15   Slip Laws vs. Session Laws
Slip-law citations are typically used for modern laws. Bound codes or statutes are more often cited for historic laws.

13.16   Slip Laws: Federal
See QuickCheck Model *for* SLIP LAW: FEDERAL

Federal slip laws carry numbers that represent (*a*) the congress, and (*b*) the ordinal number of the passed legislation. In the example below, "94–43" represents the 43rd piece of legislation passed by the 94th Congress and signed into law by the president. The slip-law number does *not* match either the House or Senate bill that proposed that law.

Printed shortly after passage, a slip law is typically a pamphlet, and it remains a historical document in its own right.

Source List Entry
United States. Congress. *National Cemetery Systems Act of 1973.* Public Law 94–43.

First Reference Note
1. *National Cemetery Systems Act of 1973,* Public Law 94–43.

Subsequent Note
11. *National Cemetery Systems Act of 1973,* Public Law 94–43.

13.17   Slip Laws: State

State-level legislative acts and resolutions often include *memorials* to individuals. Like bills and resolutions at the federal level, memorials may be cited as slip law (as in the case below) or from the bound session laws. As a rule, they will not appear in the consolidated codes.

Source List Entry
Alabama. House of Representatives. Bills and Resolutions. 2002.

First Reference Note
1. Alabama House of Representatives, *Resolution Mourning the Death of Dr. Gary B. Mills of Northport, Alabama*, House Resolution 554 (11 April 2002).

Subsequent Note
11. Ala. HR 554 (11 April 2002).

CITING SESSION & CONGRESS (OR LEGISLATURE)
At the state level, House and Senate resolutions may not carry the identification of session and congress (or legislature) that is usually found for federal acts.

DIGESTS & REPORTERS

13.18   Federal Case Reporters
See also QuickCheck Models *for* CASE REPORTERS

The manner in which you cite the published federal cases depends upon several variances:

- The time frame—for cases before 1882 (the year the reporting system was standardized), you will find cases cited under the name of the man who was the official court reporter (i.e., the series editor).

- Whether the case was heard in (*a*) the U.S. Supreme Court; (*b*) a federal circuit court or court of appeal; (*c*) a federal district court; or (*d*) the U.S. Court of Claims. Each has its own reporter system.

- Whether you are using the "official" reporter or one of the two "unofficial" reporters. The three options and the abbreviations used in their legal citations are

  OFFICIAL .... *United States Report* ("U.S.")

  UNOFFICIAL ...... *West's Supreme Court Reporter* ("S.Ct."), 1881–present; issued by West Publishing Co.

UNOFFICIAL ...... *United States Supreme Court Reports, Lawyer's Edition* ("L.Ed." or "L. Ed. 2d"), 1790–present

Source List Entry

(*citing the whole series, using data from title page*)
Peters, Richard. *Reports of Cases Argued and Adjudged in the Supreme Court of the United States.* 17 volumes. New York: Jacob R. Halsted, 1851.
United States. *Supreme Court Reporter: Cases Argued and Determined in the United States Supreme Court, 1882–.* St. Paul, Minnesota: West Publishing Co., 1883–.

First Reference Note

1. Richard Peters, *Reports of Cases Argued and Adjudged in the Supreme Court of the United States,* 17 vols. (New York: Jacob R. Halsted, 1851), 4 (January Term 1830): 287–90 for *Francis Lagrange, alias Isidore, a Man of Colour* v. *Pierre Chouteau, Jun.*; hereinafter cited as *Lagrange* v. *Chouteau,* 4 Peters U.S. 287 (1830).

2. *West's Supreme Court Reporter,* vol. 1, *Cases Argued and Determined in the United States Supreme Court, October Term 1882* (St. Paul, Minnesota: West Publishing Co., 1883), 80–82, *Waples* v. *Hays, Tutrix;* hereinafter *Waples* v. *Hays,* 1 S.Ct. 80 (1882).

Subsequent Note

11. *Lagrange* v. *Chouteau,* 4 Peters U.S. 287 (1830).
12. *Waples* v. *Hays,* 1 S.Ct. 80 (1882).

"HEREINAFTER CITED AS ..."

As a rule, this phrase is rarely needed for short forms that are properly worded. However, legal cases are an exception because the wording of the short form differs so drastically from the bibliographic entry.

13.19 Federal Digests

LexisNexis and West also produce digests, topically arranged abstracts of U.S. Supreme Court cases, and other federal court reporters that serve as indexes. Odds are, you will cite a digest only in your Source List—because it is just an index, a citation to it would normally occur in your Reference Notes only as an interim step in the research process.

Source List Entry

Federal Digest [1754–1939]. St. Paul, Minnesota: West Publishing Co. 1934–39.
United States Supreme Court Digest. Charlottesville, Virginia, and earlier locations: Matthew Bender/LexisNexis (formerly by Lawyers Cooperative Publishing), 1948–.

First Reference Note
1. *Federal Digest* [1754–1939] (St. Paul, Minnesota: West Publishing Co., 1934–39), 113: 33.
2. *United States Supreme Court Digest* (Charlottesville, Virginia, and earlier locations: Matthew Bender/LexisNexis (formerly by Lawyers Cooperative Publishing, 1948–), 21: 159.

Subsequent Note
11. *Federal Digest* 113: 33.
12. *Supreme Court Digest*, 21: 159.

13.20 State-level Case Reporters
See QuickCheck Model *for* CASE REPORTERS: SERIES NAMED FOR EDITOR

Historically, case reporters at the state level have followed the pattern of the early federal courts: initially, they were compiled and published under the name of the man who was the official court reporter. A typical example would be:

Source List Entry
Martin, François X. *Term Reports of Cases Argued and Determined in the Superior Court of the Territory of Orleans, 1809–1823.* 12 volumes. New Orleans: F. X. Martin, 1854.

First Reference Note
1. François X. Martin, *Term Reports of Cases Argued and Determined in the Superior Court of the Territory of Orleans, 1809–1823,* 12 vols. (New Orleans: F. X. Martin, 1854), 1:183, *Adelle v. Beauregard* (1810); hereinafter cited as *Adelle v. Beauregard,* 1 Martin La. 183 (1810).

Subsequent Note
11. *Adelle v. Beauregard,* 1 Martin La. 183 (1810).

13.21 State-level Digests
Typically, the digest published for each state follows a formulaic title, [*Name of State*] *Digest,* although not all are issued by the same publisher. They are cited in the same manner as shown at 13.19 for the *Federal Digest* and *Supreme Court Digest.*

13.22 Sundry Other Reference Works
Several other topical or subject guides to case law (both federal and state) are similar to digests and are cited in the same manner.

- *Annotated case reports* such as *American Law Reports* (originally published by Lawyers Cooperative, now West), in which the selected cases are largely secondary to the annotations that are, themselves, lengthy essays analyzing and comparing other cases on the same issue

- *Restatements* of whole areas of law such as torts, contracts, or agency law

- *Legal encyclopedias* such as West's *Corpus Juris*

PRINTED GOVERNMENT DOCUMENTS

BASIC ISSUES

13.23 Definition, "Printed Government Documents"

Printed government documents (aka published government documents) are a special class of materials, created by a government and ordered to be published by that government. Across time, most nations and states have published the documents they consider critical to their operation and history. This chapter focuses primarily upon U.S. federal documents, but you should be aware that other nations and states have their counterparts.

Traditionally, U.S. printed government documents are distributed free of charge to federal depository libraries nationwide (i.e., libraries officially designated as *depositories* for published copies of all critical government records). Other libraries are government *repositories,* meaning that they maintain collections of published government documents but receive them on a selective basis. Typically, government depositories and repositories are part of large city, college, and university libraries. Many of their rare materials have been reissued by genealogical publishers, and the reprints are widely available in genealogy and history libraries. Many more published government documents are being digitized and are available at the Library of Congress website *A Century of Lawmaking,* as well as the websites of other history-content providers.

This chapter uses the most common printed government documents as examples by which all can be cited.

13.24 Departments or Agencies as "Author"

In citing government publications, the author is typically the name of the agency, bureau, department, etc., prefaced by the jurisdiction:

- U.S. Bureau of the Census
- Connecticut Adjutant General's Office

In shortened citations to government publications, you might choose to omit the department or agency that created it, if it would not otherwise cause ambiguity.

13.25 International Publications

The governments of many countries have published similar volumes. As with American documents, some can be cited simply, using the QuickCheck Models for BOOK: BASIC FORMAT or (chapter 12) BOOK: EDITED. Others are more complicated. This chapter includes several international examples, as a beginning point for researchers. Beyond that, please consult a manual for the country of your choice.

U.S. SERIAL SET

13.26 Background

The 15th Congress of the United States, in its first session (1817), launched a publication series that is still ongoing and now includes more than 14,000 volumes chronicling the activities of both the executive and legislative branches of government. Of these volumes, the most popular among history researchers are referred to as the *U.S. Serial Set*. It carries that name because the volumes are today numbered serially. However, the contents of the *Serial Set* have varied across time. Sections 13.26–13.40 discuss the core volumes and related works that are customarily shelved with the *Serial Set* in government document repositories and depositories. The materials covered herein are also included with the partially digitized *Serial Set* at the Library of Congress website *A Century of Lawmaking*.

Note—In citing Congressional records, you should always cite both congress and session. Almost all congressional materials are labeled and filed by those identifiers.

13.27 1789–1838 (American State Papers)

The first group of documents, covering congressional matters retroactively from 1789, was issued under the title *American State Papers*. Published between 1832 and 1861, the volumes actually span the period 1789–1838. Citations to *American State Papers* are treated at 13.30–13.34.

13.28 1817 to Present

This series presents key congressional records in a formally numbered sequence. Contents have varied across the years, but generally you may expect to find the following:

CONGRESSIONAL DOCUMENTS (13.35–13.40)

The *Congressional Record*
House & Senate Documents
House & Senate Reports
Senate Executive Documents
Senate Executive Reports
Senate Treaty Documents
"Sheep Set" (annual agency reports, reports of special hearings, etc.)

EXECUTIVE BRANCH DOCUMENTS (13.41)

Presidential messages and documents sent to Congress
Annual reports of various federal agencies—usually absorbed into House Documents or Senate Documents.

MISCELLANEOUS DOCUMENTS

Publications from organizations chartered by Congress are usually numbered as part of House Documents or Senate Documents. Among these are six venerable American institutions whose annual reports, etc., are rarely thought of as government publications:

> American Historical Association
> American Legion
> Veterans of Foreign Wars
> Boy Scouts of America
> Girl Scouts of America
> Daughters of the American Revolution

Many of these have been digitized and are available online through the Library of Congress's *American Memory* project known as *A Century of Lawmaking* and commercial enterprises such as LexisNexis.

13.29 *Serial Set Index*

Commercially prepared indexes are available to the *Serial Set*. These are standard publications that can be cited by expanding upon the QuickCheck Model for BOOK: BASIC FORMAT. For example:

Source List Entry

CIS US Serial Set Index. 1789–1969. 58 volumes. Washington, D.C.: Congressional Information Service, 1975–98.

First Reference Note
> 1. *CIS US Serial Set Index,* Part 1, *American State Papers and the 15th–34th Congresses, 1789–1857;* 3 vols., *Subject Index, L–Z* (Washington, D.C.: Congressional Information Service, 1975), 1519.

Subsequent Note
> 11. *CIS US Serial Set Index,* Part 1, *Subject Index, L–Z,* 1519.

(*American State Papers*)

13.30 ASP: Authorized Editions

Between 1832 and 1861, Congress directed the publication of thousands of records deemed critical to documenting the founding and settlement of the United States. Collectively, they are known as *American State Papers.* In using them, be particularly careful to (*a*) copy the details precisely from the title page; and (*b*) identify the edition. Volume and page references in one edition usually do not agree with those in another set.

13.31 ASP: Duff Green Edition

A small, incomplete set of five volumes was published in 1834 by the printer Duff Green. These are found in many government document depositories nationwide. The set can be cited simply by chapter 12's QuickCheck Model for BOOK: EDITED or the present chapter's QuickCheck Model for CONGRESSIONAL RECORDS: CITING FROM TITLE PAGE.

Source List Entry
> United States. Congress. *American State Papers: Documents, Legislative and Executive of the Congress of the United States in Relation to the Public Lands.* 5 vols. Walter Lowrie, editor. Washington, D.C.: Duff Green, 1834.

First Reference Note
> 1. U.S. Congress, *American State Papers: Documents, Legislative and Executive of the Congress of the United States in Relation to the Public Lands,* 5 vols., Walter Lowrie, ed. (Washington, D.C.: Duff Green, 1834), 4: 132.

Subsequent Note
> 11. *American State Papers ... Public Lands,* Duff Green ed., 4:132.

IDENTIFICATION OF EDITOR

The Duff Green edition identifies an editor (Lowrie), in addition to the agency that gets the credit as author (Congress). In such cases, the general editor is named but is relegated to a position after the title of the book. This situation is analogous to the edited work discussed at 12.66 in which there is both a general author and an editor. The Gales and Seaton edition of *American State Papers,* treated below, identifies no editor. The agency (Congress) is credited in the Author Field.

13.32   ASP: Gales & Seaton Edition

The principal edition of *American State Papers* was published by Gales and Seaton between 1832 and 1861. Its thirty-eight volumes are divided into ten classes:

Class 1, *Foreign Relations,* 6 vols.
Class 2, *Indian Affairs,* 2 vols.
Class 3, *Finance,* 5 vols.
Class 4, *Commerce and Navigation,* 2 vols.
Class 5, *Military Affairs,* 7 vols.
Class 6, *Naval Affairs,* 4 vols.
Class 7, *Post Office Department,* 1 vol.
Class 8, *Public Lands,* 8 vols.
Class 9, *Claims,* 1 vol.
Class 10, *Miscellaneous,* 2 vols.

The volumes in each class are individually numbered. Therefore, you need to cite both the *class* and the *volume number within the class*.

Source List Entry

United States. Congress. *American State Papers: Documents Legislative and Executive of the Congress of the United States.* 38 vols. Washington, D.C.: Gales and Seaton, 1832–61.

First Reference Note

1. U.S. Congress, *American State Papers: Documents Legislative and Executive of the Congress of the United States,* 38 vols.; Class 8, *Public Lands,* 8 vols. (Washington, D.C.: Gales and Seaton, 1832–61), 1: 111.

(*or*)

1. U.S. Congress, *American State Papers: Documents Legislative and Executive of the Congress of the United States,* 38 vols. (Washington, D.C.: Gales and Seaton, 1832–61), Class 8, *Public Lands* (8 vols.), 1: 111.

Subsequent Note

11. *American State Papers,* Class 8, *Public Lands,* Gales and Seaton ed., 1:111.

ALTERNATE FORMATS FOR DATA ENTRY
The above example offers two options for the First Reference Notes.

Traditional Format—In the first option, details for both the main title and the class title are cited *before* the publication data.

Software Format—In the second option, only the main title appears in the title field, followed by the total number of volumes. The class title and its data are relegated to the software's free-form "Citation Detail" field, following publication data.

13.33 ASP: Gales & Seaton Reprint Edition
In 1994, a commercial publisher reprinted the eight volumes of Gales & Seaton's *Public Lands* and the one volume of Gales and Seaton's *Claims*—both popular with history researchers. However, the publisher confused the issue by applying the wording from the Duff Green edition to the title of his Gales & Seaton reprint.

> ### Source List Entry
> United States. Congress. *American State Papers: Documents Legislative and Executive of the Congress of the United States in Relation to the Public Lands.* 8 volumes. 1832–63. Retitled reprint, Greenville, South Carolina: Southern Historical Press, 1994.

> ### First Reference Note
> 1. U.S. Congress, *American State Papers: Documents Legislative and Executive of the Congress of the United States in Relation to the Public Lands,* 8 vols. (1832–63; retitled reprint, Greenville, South Carolina: Southern Historical Press, 1994), 5:18.

> ### Subsequent Note
> 11. *American State Papers ... Public Lands,* SHP ed., 5:18.

REPRINT EDITIONS & RETITLED REPRINTS
Other publishers have also reprinted other classes of the Gales and Seaton edition. Usually, these are facsimile reprints, with added materials—although some publishers have issued one-volume sets of abstracts that focus on a particular area.

As with Reprint Editions discussed at 12.75–12.83, you will want to show the years during which the original series was published, as well as the current publisher and current publication date. If the new publication carries an altered title, that fact should also be noted.

13.34 *New American State Papers*: Scholarly Resources Edition
A new and vastly larger series known as *New American State Papers* was

created by Scholarly Resources between 1972 and 1981. Its material is entirely different from that covered by the Gales and Seaton or Duff Green editions. In comparison to the original *ASP* contents listed at 13.32, the *New ASP* offers the following:

> *Agriculture,* 19 vols. (1973)
> *Commerce and Navigation,* 47 vols. (1973)
> *Explorations and Surveys,* 15 vols. (1972)
> *Indian Affairs,* 13 vols. (1972)
> *Labor and Slavery,* 7 vols. (1973)
> *Manufactures,* 9 vols. (1972)
> *Military Affairs,* 19 vols. (1979)
> *Naval Affairs,* 10 vols. (1981)
> *Public Finance,* 32 vols. (1972–73)
> *Public Lands,* 8 vols. (1973)
> *Science and Technology,* 14 vols. (1973)
> *Social Policy,* 5 vols. (1972)
> *Transportation,* 7 vols. (1972)

This Scholarly Resources publication numbers each of its series separately. Unlike the Gales and Seaton and Duff Green editions, there is no overall numbering that spans all 205 volumes—making for a simpler citation. After the main title (*New American State Papers*), you would place a colon, then name the particular series as the subtitle. For total volumes, cite only the number in that particular series.

The examples below demonstrate two types of citations.

Note 1 cites an individual who wrote the introduction to the Public Lands series; the citation covers none of the actual documents.

Note 2 cites a document within the Naval Affairs series. In this citation, the individual who wrote the introduction to the book is not mentioned because he is irrelevant to the material being cited.

Source List Entry
United States. Congress. *New American State Papers: Public Lands.* 8 volumes. Wilmington, Delaware: Scholarly Resources, 1973.
———. *New American State Papers: Naval Affairs.* 10 volumes. Wilmington, Delaware: Scholarly Resources, 1981.

First Reference Note
1. Margaret Beattie Bogue, "Introduction," U.S. Congress, *New American State Papers: Public Lands,* 8 vols. (Wilmington, Delaware: Scholarly Resources, 1973), 1: 11.

2. U.S. Congress, *New American State Papers: Naval Affairs,* 10 vols. (Wilmington, Delaware: Scholarly Resources, 1981), 5: 155.

Subsequent Note
1. Bogue, *New American State Papers: Public Lands*, 1:11.
2. *New American State Papers: Naval Affairs,* 5: 155.

(Congressional Documents)

13.35 *Annals of Congress, Congressional Record, Etc.*

The daily proceedings of Congress, since its first session, are chronicled in a series that has carried four titles:

Annals of Congress, 1789–1824
Congressional Debates, 1824–37
Congressional Globe, 1833 [sic]–73
Congressional Record, 1874—

The first set, *Annals of Congress*, is formally known as *The Debates and Proceedings in the Congress of the United States*. Although that long title is the one you find on each volume's title page, it is generally ignored in legal and academic style citations.

The examples below illustrate citations in two formats:

- a citation to a single volume you might randomly encounter, drawing the identification from the title page following Book: Basic Format;

- the traditional academic style citation that follows this pattern:

VOL. NO. • NAME OF SERIES • YEAR • BEGINNING PAGE NO.

Source List Entry

(Citing individual volumes from title page)
United States. Congress. [*Annals of Congress*] *The Debates and Proceedings in the Congress of the United States ... Ninth Congress ... December 2, 1805 to March 3, 1807*. Washington, D.C:. Gales and Seaton, 1852.
United States. Congress. *Congressional Record, Containing the Proceedings and Debates of the Forty-Third Congress, Second Session*. 3 volumes. Washington, D.C.: Government Printing Office, 1875.

(Academic style, citing whole series rather than individual volumes)
United States. Congress. *Annals of the Congress of the United States, 1789–1824*. 42 volumes. Washington, D.C., 1834–56.

United States. Congress. *Congressional Record, 1874 to date*.

First Reference Note

(*Citing individual volumes from title page*)
    1. U.S. Congress, [*Annals of Congress*] *The Debates and Proceedings in the Congress of the United States ... Ninth Congress ... December 2, 1805 to March 3, 1807* (Washington, D.C.: Gales and Seaton, 1852), 1211–12, Affidavit of Mary Senes [Louise] Brevell.
    2. U.S. Congress, *Congressional Record, Containing the Proceedings and Debates of the Forty-Third Congress, Second Session,* 3 vols. (Washington, D.C.: Government Printing Office, 1875), 3: 40–41, for Affidavit of Rev. Ira M. Condit, San Francisco, 19 October 1874, in Speech of Hon. Horace F. Page on the importation, enslavement, and prostitution of Chinese women.

(*or, academic/legal style*)
    1. *Annals of Congress,* 9th Cong., 1st sess. (1806), 1211–12, Affidavit of Mary Senes [Louise] Brevell.
    2. *Congressional Record,* 43d Cong., 2d sess. (1875), 3: 40.

Subsequent Note
    11. *Annals of Congress,* 9th Cong., 1st sess. (1806), 1211–12
    12. *Cong. Rec.,* 43d Cong., 2d sess. (1875), 3: 40.

CORRECTING MISSPELLINGS IN "PRINTED PRIMARY SOURCES"

Published government documents belong to that class of records academic researchers have traditionally called *printed primary sources,* meaning they are "original" historic records that are now available in printed form. However, they hold significant potential for error in the identification of individuals, given the difficulty that printers in the federal capital would have had in working with penned documents from writers in the hinterlands who were often of a different culture.

When you encounter individuals who are incorrectly identified in published government documents, you may correct the identification in the manner used in note 1 above—that is, place the correct name in square editorial brackets after the printed name.

Annals of Congress / Congressional Record (Online)

Source List Entry
United States. Congress. *Annals of Congress.* 9th Congress, 1st session (1806). Digital images. Library of Congress, *A Century of Lawmaking for a New Nation: U.S. Congressional Documents and Debates, 1774–1875.* http://memory.loc.gov/ammem/amlaw/lawhome.html : 2006.

First Reference Note
　　　1. *Annals of Congress,* 9th Cong., 1st sess. (1806), 1211–12, Affidavit of Mary Senes [Louise] Brevell; digital images, Library of Congress, *A Century of Lawmaking for a New Nation: : U.S. Congressional Documents and Debates, 1774–1875* (http://memory.loc.gov/ammem/ amlaw/lawhome.html : accessed 1 May 2006).

Subsequent Note
　　　11. *Annals of Congress,* 9th Cong., 1st sess. (1806), 1211–12.

13.36　*Annals* or *Congressional Record,* Identifying the Year

The shorter or academic forms for *Congressional Record,* illustrated at note 11 above, call for citing the year that the debate took place, not the year the volume was published.

13.37　*Annals* or *Congressional Record,* Identifying Speakers

The Condit example at 13.35, note 2, introduces another consideration: whether to identify the speaker (congressman or senator) and, perhaps, other details.

Typically, your research notes (and later, your narrative) will be the place to record the details of what the source has to say. However, 13.35 illustrates a more complex situation in which the item of interest is not Congressman Condit's speech but an affidavit he submitted to support that speech. Hence, the affidavit might be cited in the note to assist with subsequent analysis of that source. Whether such detail is needed in a note is a decision you will make on a case-by-case basis.

13.38　House & Senate Documents

See Quick Check Model *for* CONGRESSIONAL RECORDS ... TITLE PAGE

Thousands of reports, memorials, and other documents submitted to congress have been published in at least two or three forms: the original print version that occurred contemporaneously, the microfiche edition of the *Serial Set,* and an electronic edition at the Library of Congress's *American Memory* website. Working from the title page of a typical book-length publication in the series known as *Senate Documents,* you would create a citation such as this:

Source List Entry
United States. Congress. *Memorial of the State of Missouri and Documents in Relation to Indian Depredations upon Citizens of That State.* 19th Congress, 1st Session, Senate Document 55. Washington, DC: Gales & Seaton, 1826.

First Reference Note
> 1. U. S. Congress, *Memorial of the State of Missouri and Documents in Relation to Indian Depredations upon Citizens of That State,* 19th Cong., 1st sess., Senate Document 55 (Washington, D.C.: Gales & Seaton, 1826), 48.

Subsequent Note
> 11. U.S. Congress, *Memorial of the State of Missouri ... Indian Depredations,* 48.

House & Senate Documents (*Bluebook* Style Citation)

Citations to the *CIS Serial Set* fiche edition customarily cite the original, with no reference to the fiche itself. You may use the citation style demonstrated above, working from the title page or the fiche image, or you might use the legal, *Bluebook* Style (see second example at 13.39) that ignores publication details and simply refers to the congress, session, and document numbers.

The example below emphasizes a specific page number, an approach you would typically want to take with a document of this length.

Source List Entry
> United States. Congress. *Senate Documents.* 19th Congress, 1st session. No. 55. 6 March 1826

(or, if you use volumes that span a number of years):
> United States. Congress. *Senate Documents,* 1825–62.

First Reference Note
> 1. *S. Doc. No. 55,* 19th Cong., 1st sess. (1826), 48.

Subsequent Note
> 11. *S. Doc. No. 55,* 19th Cong., 1st sess. (1826), 48.

13.39 House & Senate Journals (Etc.)

Other Congressional records from the *Serial Set* (listed under 13.26–13.28) are cited in similar fashion, as these examples from the House and Senate *Journals* illustrate:

Source List Entry
> United States. *Journal of the House of Representatives of the United States, Being the First Session of the Twenty-Sixth Congress.* Washington, D.C.: Blair and Rives, 1840.

(or, if you use volumes that span a number of years)
> United States. Congress. *House Journals.* 1822–80.

First Reference Note
 1. *Journal of the House of Representatives of the United States, Being the First Session of the Twenty-Sixth Congress* (1839–40) (Washington, D.C.: Blair and Rives, 1840), 332.

Subsequent Note
 11. *Journal of the House of Representatives* (1839–40), 332.

House & Senate Journals (*Bluebook* Style Citation) ■■

Source List Entry

(*To cite multiple volumes in the series*)
United States. Congress. *House Journals.* 1822–80.

(*To cite a specific volume*)
United States. Congress. *House Journals.* 26th Congress., 1st session. 1839–40.

First Reference Note
 1. *H.R. Journal,* 26th Cong., 1st sess. (1839–40), 48.

Subsequent Note
 11. *H.R. Journal,* 26th Cong., 1st sess. (1839–40), 48.

13.40 Other *Serial Set* Models

Models of other kinds of material in the U.S. *Serial Set* are available on the "Citation Guide" page at *A Century of Lawmaking for a New Nation* (http://memory.loc.gov/ammem/amlaw/lawhome.html).

(Departmental & Agency Reports)

13.41 Executive-branch Reports Published by Congress

Many departments and agencies of the Executive Branch of the U.S. government send annual reports to Congress—reports that are subsequently published by Congress. For most publications by government agencies you can follow the QuickCheck Model for BOOK: BASIC FORMAT or (chapter 12) BOOK: EDITED. In either case, you simply take your data from the title page of the book you are using.

Source List Entry
Jefferson, Thomas. *Message from the President of the United States Communicating Discoveries Made in Exploring the Missouri, Red River, and Washita, by Captains Lewis and Clark, Doctor Sibley, and Mr. Dunbar.* New York: A. & G. Way, Printers, 1806.

United States. Census Office. *Statistics of the United States; Including Mortality, Property, &c, in 1860*. Washington, D.C.: Government Printing Office, 1866.

————. Department of State. *Register of Officers and Agents, Civil, Military, and Naval, in the Service of the United States on the 30th of September 1823*. Washington, D.C.: Davis & Force, 1824.

————. Smithsonian Institution. *Eighteenth Annual Report of the Bureau of American Ethnology, 1896–'97*. By J. W. Powell. 2 volumes. Washington, D.C.: Government Printing Office, 1899.

First Reference Note

1. Thomas Jefferson, *Message from the President of the United States Communicating Discoveries Made in Exploring the Missouri, Red River, and Washita, by Captains Lewis and Clark, Doctor Sibley, and Mr. Dunbar* (New York: A. & G. Way, Printers, 1806), 13.

2. U.S. Census Office, *Statistics of the United States; Including Mortality, Property, &c, in 1860* (Washington, D.C.: Government Printing Office, 1866), lxi–lxii, "Table OO, Nativity of Americans Residing in Each State and Territory."

3. U.S. Department of State, *Register of Officers and Agents, Civil, Military, and Naval, in the Service of the United States on the 30th of September 1823* (Washington, D.C.: Davis & Force, 1824), 60; hereinafter cited by its series name *Official Register*.

4. U.S. Smithsonian Institution, *Eighteenth Annual Report of the Bureau of American Ethnology, 1896–'97*, by J. W. Powell, 2 vols. (Washington, D.C.: Government Printing Office, 1899), part 2, plate CXXVIII, "Indian Territory and Oklahoma."

Subsequent Note

11. Jefferson, *Message from the President ... Communicating Discoveries*, 13.

12. *Statistics of the United States ... 1860*, lxii.

13. Dept. of State, *[Official] Register ... 1823*, 60.

14. Smithsonian Institution, *Eighteenth Annual Report of the Bureau of American Ethnology, 1896–'97*, part 2, plate CXXVIII.

NATIONAL ARCHIVES (U.S.) FINDING AIDS

13.42 Background

The U.S. National Archives and Records Administration produces a number of finding aids to assist researchers, some of which you will occasionally need to reference in your citations. The most commonly used types of finding aids are these seven:

- catalogs and guides
- descriptive pamphlets (DPs)

- general information leaflets (GILs)
- inventories (INV)
- nonpublic civilian manuscripts (NCs)
- nonpublic military manuscripts (NMs)
- preliminary inventories (PIs)
- reference information papers (RIPs)
- special lists (SLs)

In order to conduct research in the original records of the National Archives, you will use all these types of finding aids to locate the specific record collections you need. Some are now available online. Many researchers maintain their own reference copies of these guides or consult them at a local library. When you use one of these guides to identify a record of interest and then request a copy of that record, it is best to include in your citation the number of the relevant DP, inventory, NC, NM, PI, or SL.

13.43 Catalogs & Guides

Most guides, leaflets, microfilm catalogs, etc., published by NARA can be cited by BOOK: BASIC FORMAT. The following examples demonstrate citing them by the agency as author or by the names of their editors.

Source List Entry

Eales, Anne Bruner, and Robert M. Kvasnicka, editors. *Guide to Genealogical Research in the National Archives of the United States.* Third edition. Washington, D.C.: National Archives and Records Administration [NARA], 2000.

Matchette, Robert B. et al., editors. *Guide to Federal Records in the National Archives of the United States.* 3 volumes. Washington, D.C.: NARA, 1995.

United States. National Archives. *Guide to Federal Records in the National Archives of the United States.* 3 volumes. Robert B. Matchette et al., editors. Washington, D.C.: NARA, 1995.

————. *Guide to Genealogical Research in the National Archives of the United States.* Third edition. Anne Bruner Eales and Robert M. Kvasnicka, editors. Washington, D.C.: NARA, 2000.

———— . *National Archives Microfilm Resources for Research: A Comprehensive Catalog.* Washington, D.C.: NARA, 2000.

First Reference Note

1. Anne Bruner Eales and Robert M. Kvasnicka, eds., *Guide to Genealogical Research in the National Archives of the United States,* 3d ed. (Washington, D.C.: National Archives and Records Administration [NARA], 2000), 132.

2. Robert B. Matchette et al., eds., *Guide to Federal Records in the National Archives of the United States,* 3 vols. (Washington, D.C.: NARA, 1995), 1: 29.

3. *National Archives Microfilm Resources for Research: A Comprehensive Catalog* (Washington, D.C.: NARA, 2000), 123.

Subsequent Note

11. Eales and Kvasnicka, *Guide to Genealogical Research in the National Archives,* 132.

12. Matchette et al., *Guide to Federal Records in the National Archives,* 1: 29.

13. *National Archives Microfilm Resources for Research,* 123.

Catalogs & Guides (Online)

Source List Entry

Matchette, Robert B., et al., editors. *Guide to Federal Records in the National Archives of the United States.* 3 volumes. Washington, D.C.: National Archives and Records Administration, 1995. Web edition. http://www.archives.gov/research/guide-fed-records/ : 2007.

First Reference Note

1. Robert B. Matchette et al., eds., *Guide to Federal Records in the National Archives of the United States,* web edition (http://www .archives.gov/research/guide-fed-records/ : accessed 15 February 2007), 243.3.1, General Records.

Subsequent Note

11. Matchette et al., *Guide to Federal Records in the National Archives,* web edition, 243.3.1.

CITING BOOK TITLE AS WEBSITE TITLE

NARA's website is an immense offering with many layers through which researchers must drill. When a site of that ilk offers a web edition of a book, and the book's title is presented at the head of it's own "home page," it is simpler to use the book's title as the website title and cite the exact URL for the book itself. Citing the title of NARA's own home page as the website title would be redundant.

13.44 Descriptive Pamphlets (DPs)

When NARA creates a microfilm or microfiche publication whose numbers are preceded by *M*, it also prepares a guide called a *descriptive pamphlet* (DP). This guide appears at the beginning of roll 1 or fiche 1 and is sometimes published as a special booklet. Most DPs are now published online as an accompaniment to the catalog description of the corresponding film or fiche. Models for all these situations follow:

Source List Entry

United States. National Archives. *Registers and Indexes for Passport Applications.* Descriptive Pamphlet M1371. Washington, D.C.: National Archives and Records Administration, 1986.

First Reference Note

    1. U.S. National Archives, *Registers and Indexes for Passport Applications,* Descriptive Pamphlet M1371 (Washington, D.C.: National Archives and Records Administration, 1986), 3.

Subsequent Note

    11. National Archives, *Registers and Indexes for Passport Applications,* DP for M1371, 3.

Descriptive Pamphlet (Filmed)

Source List Entry

United States. National Archives. *Registers and Indexes for Passport Applications.* Descriptive Pamphlet M1371. Washington, D.C.: National Archives and Records Administration, 1986.

First Reference Note

    1. U.S. National Archives, *Registers and Indexes for Passport Applications,* Descriptive Pamphlet M1371 (Washington, D.C.: National Archives and Records Administration, 1986), 3; reproduced on *Registers and Indexes for Passport Applications, 1810–1906,* NARA microfilm publication M1371, roll 1, first item.

Subsequent Note

    11. National Archives, *Registers and Indexes for Passport Applications,* DP M1371, 3.

Descriptive Pamphlet (Online)

See QuickCheck Models *for* NATIONAL ARCHIVES GUIDES: DESCRIPTIVE PAMPHLET

Source List Entry

United States. National Archives. *Registers of Vessels Arriving at the Port of New York from Foreign Ports, 1789–1919.* Descriptive Pamphlet M1066. Web edition. *The National Archives.* http://ww.archives.gov/genealogy/immigration/microfilm/customs-records-1820-1891.html : 2006.

First Reference Note
   1. U.S. National Archives, *Registers of Vessels Arriving at the Port of New York from Foreign Ports, 1789–1919,* Descriptive Pamphlet M1066, Web edition, *The National Archives* (http://www.archives.gov/geneal ogy/immigration/microfilm/customs-records-1820-1891.html : accessed 16 October 2006), 2.

Subsequent Note
   11. National Archives, *Registers of Vessels Arriving at the Port of New York from Foreign Ports, 1789–1919,* DP M1066, 2.

CITING PAGE NUMBERS FOR DESCRIPTIVE PAMPHLETS ONLINE
Web editions of a descriptive pamphlet may not carry page numbers. When you use an unpaginated DP, if you feel someone might have a problem locating the specific information you are referencing, you can cite a specific paragraph or reel number.

CITING BOOK TITLE AS WEBSITE TITLE
See 13.43.

13.45 General Information Leaflets (GILs)
NARA offers various types of leaflets. The simplest are folders such as the item cited at 12.45. A second type of major value to researchers is a formal series of small booklets known as "General Information Leaflets." This GIL series is numbered; each booklet is paginated. Print and digital copies exist.

Source List Entry
United States. National Archives. *Citing Records in the National Archives of the United States.* General Information Leaflet 17. Washington, D. C.: National Archives and Records Administration, 1995.

First Reference Note
   1. U.S. National Archives, *Citing Records in the National Archives of the United States,* General Information Leaflet 17 (Washington, D.C.: National Archives and Records Administration, 1995), 5.

Subsequent Note
   11. National Archives, *Citing Records in the National Archives of the United States,* GIL 17, 5.

General Information Leaflets (Online)

Source List Entry
United States. National Archives. *Citing Records in the National Archives*

of the United States. General Information Leaflet 17. Web edition. http://www.archives.gov/publications/general-info-leaflets/17.html : 2006.

First Reference Note

1. U.S. National Archives, *Citing Records in the National Archives of the United States,* General Information Leaflet 17, Web edition (http://www.archives.gov/publications/general-info-leaflets/17.html : accessed 16 October 2006), "Guidelines for Citing Textual Records," item 3.

Subsequent Note

11. National Archives, *Citing Records in the National Archives,* GIL 17, Web ed., "Guidelines for Citing Textual Records," item 3.

13.46 Inventories & Preliminary Inventories (PIs)

See also QuickCheck Model *for* NATIONAL ARCHIVES (U.S.) GUIDES: PRELIMINARY INVENTORY, MICROFILMED

Hundreds of the record groups at NARA have inventories to help you identify various series of original (textual) holdings within that record group. If the inventory was considered complete and final at the time of preparation, it was labeled *inventory* and published. If the inventory was considered tentative, it was labeled *preliminary inventory* (called a PI). Copies were shelved at NARA and distributed to libraries and individuals upon demand. Both series are numbered separately, with overlapping numbers. Your citations should not only cite the title and other pertinent data, but also the type of finding aid—inventory, preliminary inventory, or special list—and its number.

Printed copies of all these materials are available on site at NARA and (randomly) in government depository and repository libraries across the United States. All those produced between 1936 and 1968 are also microfilmed. Some of the inventories and preliminary inventories are being reproduced commercially. The following examples illustrate citations to all those formats for one particular preliminary inventory.

Source List Entry

(Original edition)
Bethel, Elizabeth. *Preliminary Inventory of the War Department Collection of Confederate Records.* Preliminary Inventory 101. Washington, D.C.: National Archives and Records Service, 1957.

(Reprint, with added material)
Bethel, Elizabeth. *Preliminary Inventory of the War Department Collection of Confederate Records.* Preliminary Inventory 101. 1957. Amplified by Craig Roberts Scott. Athens, Georgia: Iberian Publishing Co., 1994.

First Reference Note
    1. Elizabeth Bethel, *Preliminary Inventory of the War Department Collection of Confederate Records,* Preliminary Inventory 101 (Washington, D.C.: National Archives and Records Service, 1957), p. 125, entry 38.

    2. Elizabeth Bethel, *Preliminary Inventory of the War Department Collection of Confederate Records,* Preliminary Inventory 101, amplified by Craig Roberts Scott (Athens, Georgia: Iberian Publishing Co., 1994), "Appendix A," p. 227.

Subsequent Note
    11. Bethel, *Preliminary Inventory ... Confederate Records,* p. 125, entry 38.

    12. Bethel and Scott, *Preliminary Inventory ... Confederate Records,* p. 227.

CITING PAGE AND ENTRY NUMBERS
See 11.1, for Citing "Entry" or "Section" Numbers from NARA Finding Aids.

Inventories & Preliminary Inventories (Filmed)

Source List Entry
Bethel, Elizabeth. *Preliminary Inventory of the War Department Collection of Confederate Records.* Preliminary Inventory 101. Washington, D.C.: National Archives and Records Service, 1957. Reproduced on *Publications of the National Archives, 1935–1968,* NARA microfilm publication M248, roll 9.

First Reference Note
    1. Elizabeth Bethel, *Preliminary Inventory of the War Department Collection of Confederate Records,* Preliminary Inventory 101 (Washington, D.C.: National Archives and Records Service [subsequently the National Archives and Records Administration], 1957), p. 125, entry 38; reproduced on *Publications of the National Archives, 1935–1968,* NARA microfilm publication M248, roll 9.

Subsequent Note
    11. Bethel, *Preliminary Inventory ... Confederate Records,* PI 101, 123.

NOTING NARA'S NAME CHANGE
When most of the preliminary inventories were published, the agency now known as the National Archives and Records Administration was then the National Archives and Records *Service.* It is not necessary for you to note the fact of the name change in your citations. You may simply cite the agency name as it appears in the publication. If you wish

to add a cross-reference to the agency under its alternate name, you might note the change in square editorial brackets, as shown above.

13.47 Nonpublic Civilian and Military Manuscripts (NCs & NMs)

See also QuickCheck Model *for* NATIONAL ARCHIVES (U.S.) GUIDES: PRELIMINARY INVENTORY

Another significant type of inventory prepared by NARA is a pair of series created for staff use but not formally distributed as National Archives publications. To casual users, there is little visible difference between these NCs and NMs, and the PI manuscripts previously discussed. Because these two series are numbered separately from the other inventories and special lists, and all have overlapping numbers, your citation should clearly identify an NM or NC reference as such.

The "nonpublic" NC and NM inventories are usually cited in the same format as the published preliminary inventories (13.46), except that the series name is usually cited by the initialism rather than the full name of the series. NC and NM inventories that exist in multiple "parts" (volumes) may be cited as follows.

Source List Entry

Johnson, Maizie H. *Preliminary Inventory of the Textual Records of the Office of the Quartermaster General.* NM 81. 2 parts. Washington, D.C.: National Archives and Records Service, 1967.

First Reference Note

1. Maizie H. Johnson, *Preliminary Inventory of the Textual Records of the Office of The Quartermaster General,* NM 81, 2 parts (Washington, D.C.: National Archives and Records Service [NARA], 1967), 1:136, entry 1179.

Subsequent Note

11. Johnson, *Preliminary Inventory ... Textual Records ... Quartermaster General,* 1:136.

13.48 Reference Information Papers (RIPs) & Special Lists (SLs)

These two types of finding aids focus on topics for which materials are found in multiple record groups. As their names imply, the Reference Information Papers commonly provide narrative essays, while special lists are essentially descriptive catalogs. In print form, both can follow the models at 13.43–13.46 for other NARA finding aids.

The models below cover a Reference Information Paper that has a by-lined author and a Special List that is simply credited to NARA itself.

Reference Information Papers (Online)

Source List Entry
Washington, Reginald. *Black Family Research: Using the Records of Post-Civil War Federal Agencies at the National Archives.* Reference Information Paper 108. Web edition. *The National Archives.* http://www.archives.gov/publications/ref-info-papers/108/ : 2007.

First Reference Note
1. Reginald Washington, *Black Family Research: Using the Records of Post-Civil War Federal Agencies at the National Archives,* Reference Information Paper 108, Web edition, *The National Archives* (http://www.archives.gov/publications/ref-info-papers/108/ : accessed 30 January 2007), "Southern Claims Case Files."

Subsequent Note
11. Washington, *Black Family Research: Using the Records of Post-Civil War Federal Agencies at the National Archives,* RIP 108, "Southern Claims Case Files."

Special Lists (Online)

Source List Entry
United States. National Archives. *List of Selected Maps of States and Territories.* Special List 29. Web edition. *The National Archives.* http://www.archives.gov/publications/finding-aids/maps/index.html : 2007.

First Reference Note
1. U.S. National Archives, *List of Selected Maps of States and Territories,* Special List 29, Web edition, *The National Archives* (http://www.archives.gov/publications/finding-aids/maps/index.html : accessed 16 January 2007), key word: Nebraska, item 533.

Subsequent Note
11. National Archives, *List of Selected Maps of States and Territories,* Nebraska, item 533.

CITING "WEB EDITION" VS. DIGITAL IMAGES
If the website provides digital images, you would want to state that fact in the "edition" field of your note. In the two models above, the website does not provide digital images; rather the material is refor-

matted in a Web-based language. Hence, it is identified as a "Web edition."

WORK PROJECTS ADMINISTRATION (WPA)

13.49   Multiple Formats

Volumes issued by the U.S. Work Projects Administration (aka Works Progress Administration) typically exist in two editions: the original typescripts and commercial reprints. While the original typescripts, technically, are manuscripts rather than publications, exceptions exist. Moreover, many have been photocopied and re-bound in ways that obscure the differences between a publication and an unpublished typescript. As a practical measure, both types are generally treated as publications, with only slight differences in language, as illustrated at 13.50–51.

13.50   WPA Works, Original Editions

The original typescripts were typically created in a very limited number of copies—sometimes onionskin carbons. Because they are not widely available, you will want to note the library or archive at which you found the copy you have used.

Source List Entry

United States. Works Progress Administration. *Transcriptions of Manuscript Collections of Louisiana.* 9 volumes. New Orleans: WPA, 1940–42. Typescript. Gorgas Library, University of Alabama, Tuscaloosa.

First Reference Note

1. U.S. Works Progress Administration [WPA], *Transcriptions of Manuscript Collections of Louisiana,* 9 vols. (New Orleans: WPA, 1940–42), 3: 39; typescript, Gorgas Library, University of Alabama, Tuscaloosa.

Subsequent Note

11. WPA, *Transcriptions of Manuscript Collections of Louisiana,* 3: 39.

13.51   WPA Works, Reprints & Revisions

Many WPA transcription and cataloging projects are available commercially—often typeset reprints, rather than images of the original typewritten version. See also 12.75–12.83 for other guidance on the handling of new reprint editions in general.

IDENTIFICATION OF "AUTHOR"

The following example of a new edition also illustrates how to handle the identification of the compiler when the original version provides that identity.

Source List Entry

United States. Work Projects Administration. *Anderson County, Tennessee, Court Minutes, 1801–1809 and 1810–1814.* Annie Roe Mims et al., transcribers. 1936. Sistler edition. Nashville, Tennessee: Byron Sistler & Associates, 1998.

First Reference Note

1. U.S. Work Projects Administration [WPA], *Anderson County, Tennessee, Court Minutes, 1801–1809 and 1810–1814,* Annie Roe Mims et al., transcribers; Sistler edition (1935; reissued Nashville, Tennessee: Byron Sistler & Associates, 1998), 37.

Subsequent Note

11. WPA, *Anderson County, Tennessee, Court Minutes,* Sistler ed., 37.

OTHER GOVERNMENTAL PUBLICATIONS

13.52   State-level Publications (U.S.)

Most of the preceding examples for publications by the U.S. federal government have their state-level counterparts, although few states have consolidated these into a formally numbered *Serial Set* or made them available on microfiche. By and large, as you encounter historical volumes published by state governments, you will find it simpler to cite them using BOOK: BASIC FORMAT. For example:

Source List Entry

Louisiana. Board of Pension Commissioners. *List of Pensioners of the State of Louisiana.* Baton Rouge: Ramires-Jones Printing Co., 1926.

First Reference Note

1. Louisiana Board of Pension Commissioners, *List of Pensioners of the State of Louisiana* (Baton Rouge: Ramires-Jones Printing Co., 1926), 27.

Subsequent Note

11. Louisiana Board of Pension Commissioners, *List of Pensioners* (1926), 27.

House Journal, State Level (Online)

Source List Entry
Alabama. Legislature. *Journal of the House of Representatives of the State of Alabama ... 1821.* Cahawba: William R. Allen, Printer, 1821.

First Reference Note
1. Alabama Legislature, *Journal of the House of Representatives of the State of Alabama ... 1821* (Cahawba: William R. Allen, 'Printer, 1821), 84; online edition, *Alabama Legislative Acts and Journals* (http://www.legislature.state.al.us/misc/history/timeline.html : accessed 16 January 2007), keywords: "Annual Session, 5 Nov–19 Dec 1821," then "Nov 21."

Subsequent Note
11. Alabama Legislature, *Journal of the House of Representatives of the State of Alabama ... 1821*, 84.

13.53   International Publications
If you work extensively in governmental records outside the U.S., you will want to obtain guides to citing their publications. As an interim measure, for the occasional publication issued by other governments, you can usually cite them using the QuickCheck Model for BOOK: BASIC FORMAT, as the following examples illustrate:

Source List Entry
Great Britain. Public Record Office. *Calendar of Inquisitions Post Mortem and Other Analogous Documents Preserved in the Public Record Office.* 18 volumes. London: Various publishers, 1904–1988.
Spain. Oficina General de Información y Estadística de la Iglesia en España. *Guía de la Iglesia en España.* Madrid: Oficina General, 1954.

First Reference Note
1. *Calendar of Inquisitions Post Mortem and Other Analogous Documents Preserved in the Public Record Office,* volume 8, *Edward II* (London: Hereford Times for His Majesty's Stationery Office, ca. 1918), 253–55.
2. *Guía de la Iglesia en España* (Madrid: Oficina General de Información y Estadística de la Iglesia en España, 1954), 22.

Subsequent Note
11. *Calendar of Inquisitions Post Mortem,* 8:253–55.
12. *Guía de la Iglesia en España,* 22.

PUBLICATIONS
Periodicals, Broadcasts & Web Miscellanea

14

QuickCheck Models

Guidelines & Examples (beginning page 791)

QuickCheck Model
JOURNAL ARTICLES
PRINT EDITIONS

Source List Entry

AUTHOR   ARTICLE TITLE
Mills, Gary B.   "Miscegenation and the Free Negro in Antebellum 'Anglo' Alabama:

            ARTICLE SUBTITLE   JOURNAL TITLE   VOL.
A Reexamination of Southern Race Relations." *Journal of American History* 68

ISSUE DATE   PAGES
(June 1981): 16–34.

First (Full) Reference Note

            AUTHOR   ARTICLE TITLE ...
1. Gary B. Mills, "Miscegenation and the Free Negro in Antebellum 'Anglo'

...   ARTICLE SUBTITLE   JOURNAL TITLE
Alabama: A Reexamination of Southern Race Relations," *Journal of American History*

VOL.   ISSUE DATE   PAGES
68 (June 1981): 16–34, specifically 20.

Subsequent (Short) Note

        AUTHOR   SHORT TITLE
11. Mills, "Miscegenation and the Free Negro in Antebellum 'Anglo' Alabama,"

PAGES
33–34.

QuickCheck Model
JOURNAL ARTICLES
ONLINE ARCHIVES OF PRINT JOURNALS

Source List Entry

AUTHOR	ARTICLE TITLE	ARTICLE ...

Rosen, Deborah A. "Women and Property across Colonial America: A Comparison

... SUBTITLE	JOURNAL ...

of Legal Systems in New Mexico and New York." *The William and Mary*

... TITLE	VOL.	ISSUE DATE	EDITION	WEBSITE TITLE	...

Quarterly 91 (April 2003). Online archives. *The History Cooperative*. http://

... URL (DIGITAL ...	ACCESS YEAR

www.historycooperative.org/journals/wm/60.2/rosen.html : 2007.

First (Full) Reference Note

AUTHOR	ARTICLE TITLE	...

1. Deborah A. Rosen, "Women and Property across Colonial America: A Com-

... SUBTITLE	JOURNAL ...

parison of Legal Systems in New Mexico and New York," *The William and Mary*

... TITLE	VOL.	ISSUE DATE	EDITION	WEBSITE TITLE	URL ...

Quarterly 91 (April 2003); online archives, *The History Cooperative* (http://

... (DIGITAL LOCATION)	ACCESS DATE

www.historycooperative.org/journals/wm/60.2/rosen.html : accessed 25 April 2007),

SPECIFIC CONTENT

para. 21.

Subsequent (Short) Note

AUTHOR	SHORT TITLE	SPECIFIC CONTENT

11. Rosen, "Women and Property across Colonial America," para. 21

QuickCheck Model
JOURNAL ARTICLES
ONLINE JOURNALS

Source List Entry

AUTHOR	ARTICLE TITLE	ARTICLE ...

Norton, Mary Beth. "The Refugee's Revenge: The Maine Frontier and Salem

... SUBTITLE	JOURNAL TITLE	VOL.	ISSUE DATE	TYPE or FORMAT	URL (DIGITAL ...

Witchcraft." *Common-Place* 2 (April 2002). E-journal. http://www.com

... LOCATION	YEAR

mon-place.org/vol-02/no-03/norton/ : 2007.

First (Full) Reference Note

AUTHOR	ARTICLE TITLE	ARTICLE SUBTITLE ...

1. Mary Beth Norton, "The Refugee's Revenge: The Maine Frontier and Salem

...	JOURNAL TITLE	VOL.	ISSUE DATE	TYPE or FORMAT	URL (DIGITAL ...

Witchcraft," *Common-Place* 2 (April 2002), e-journal (http://www.common-

... LOCATION	DATE	SPECIFIC CONTENT

place.org/vol-02/no-03/norton/: accessed 8 March 2007), especially part 1, para. 2.

Subsequent (Short) Note

AUTHOR	SHORT TITLE	SPECIFIC CONTENT

11. Norton, "The Refugee's Revenge," part 1, para. 2.

QuickCheck Model
MAGAZINE ARTICLES
PRINT EDITIONS

Source List Entry

AUTHORS	ARTICLE TITLE

Wolkomir, Richard, and Joyce Wolkomir. "When Bandogs Howle & Spirits Walk."

MAGAZINE	ISSUE DATE	PAGES

Smithsonian, January 2001, 39–44.

First (Full) Reference Note

AUTHORS	ARTICLE TITLE

1. Richard Wolkomir and Joyce Wolkomir, "When Bandogs Howle & Spirits

...	MAGAZINE	ISSUE DATE	PAGES

Walk," *Smithsonian,* January 2001, 39–44.

Subsequent (Short) Note

AUTHORS	ARTICLE TITLE	PAGE

11. Wolkomir and Wolkomir, "When Bandogs Howle & Spirits Walk," 42.

QuickCheck Model
MAGAZINE ARTICLES
ONLINE REPRINTS, RANDOM ITEMS

Source List Entry

AUTHOR	ARTICLE TITLE	ORIGINAL PUB'N DATE	ITEM TYPE	WEBSITE ...

Leepson, Marc. "The Levys at Monticello." Undated. Reprint, Thomas Jefferson

CREATOR-OWNER	WEBSITE	URL (DIGITAL LOCATION)	YEAR

Foundation, *Monticello*. http://www.monticello.org/about/levy.html : 2007.

First (Full) Reference Note

AUTHOR	ARTICLE TITLE	WEBSITE CREATOR-OWNER

1. Marc Leepson, "The Levys at Monticello," Thomas Jefferson Foundation,

WEBSITE	URL (DIGITAL LOCATION)	ACCESS DATE

Monticello (http://www.monticello.org/about/levy.html : accessed 10 March 2007),

SPECIFIC CONTENT	CREDIT LINE (SOURCE OF THE SOURCE)

paras. 3–10; reprinted from *Preservation Magazine,* unidentified issue.

Subsequent (Short) Note

AUTHOR	ARTICLE TITLE	SPECIFIC CONTENT

11. Leepson, "The Levys at Monticello," para. 9.

QuickCheck Model
NEWSLETTER ARTICLES
PRINT EDITIONS

Source List Entry

AUTHOR   ARTICLE ...

Engle, Stephen. "Using Obituaries, Primers, Mencken, and Oz to Teach History

... TITLE   NEWSLETTER   VOL.   ISSUE DATE   PAGE

Methods." *OAH Newsletter* 31 (May 2003): 5.

First (Full) Reference Note

AUTHOR   ARTICLE ...

1. Stephen Engle, "Using Obituaries, Primers, Mencken, and Oz to Teach History

... TITLE   NEWSLETTER   VOL.   ISSUE DATE   PAGE

Methods," *OAH Newsletter* 31 (May 2003): 5.

Subsequent (Short) Note

AUTHOR   ARTICLE TITLE   PAGE

11. Engle, "Using Obituaries, Primers, Mencken, and Oz to Teach History," 5.

QuickCheck Model
NEWSPAPER ARTICLES
PRINT EDITIONS

Source List Entries

LOCATION	NEWSPAPER	ISSUES EXAMINED

Louisiana. Alexandria. *Louisiana Herald*, 1820–25. Scattered issues.

First (Full) Reference Note

* ARTICLE	NEWSPAPER	ISSUE DATE

1. "An Order to Suppress Gaming," (*Alexandria*) *Louisiana Herald*, 27 May 1820,

PAGE & COLUMN

p. 3, cols. 2–3.

Subsequent (Short) Note

ARTICLE TITLE	PAGE & COL.

11. "An Order to Suppress Gaming," p. 3, col. 2.

* *Like many articles in older papers, this one has no author.*

QuickCheck Model
NEWSPAPER ARTICLES
ONLINE ARCHIVES

Source List Entry

AUTHOR	ARTICLE TITLE	NEWSPAPER	ISSUE DATE	EDITION

Ringle, Ken. "Up through Slavery." *The Washington Post,* 12 May 2002. Online

...	URL (DIGITAL LOCATION)	ACCESS YEAR

archives. http://www.washingtonpost.com : 2007.

First (Full) Reference Note

AUTHOR	ARTICLE TITLE	NEWSPAPER	ISSUE DATE

1. Ken Ringle, "Up through Slavery," *The Washington Post*, 12 May 2002,

EDITION	URL (DIGITAL ...

online archives (http://www.washingtonpost.com/ac2/wp-dyn?pagename=article

... LOCATION	ACCESS DATE ...

&node=&contentId=A1069-2002May10&notFound=true : accessed 29 January

...	SPECIFIC CONTENT	CREDIT LINE (SOURCE OF THE SOURCE)

2007), para. 4; citing original p. F001.

Subsequent (Short) Notes

AUTHOR	ARTICLE TITLE	SPECIFIC CONTENT

11. Ringle, "Up through Slavery," para. 4.

QuickCheck Model
BROADCASTS & WEB MISCELLANEA
BLOGS

(Source List Entry constructed to cover a single posting)

Source List Entry

AUTHOR	ARTICLE TITLE	CREATOR OF BLOG	BLOG NAME

Davis, David Brion. "The Importance of History." Oxford University Press. *OUPblog,*

POSTING DATE	URL (DIGITAL LOCATION) ...

20 April 2006. http://blog.oup.com/oupblog/2006/04/on_the_importan

...	ACCESS YEAR

.html : 2007.

First (Full) Reference Note

AUTHOR	ARTICLE TITLE	CREATOR OF BLOG

1. David Brion Davis, "The Importance of History," Oxford University Press,

BLOG NAME	POSTING DATE	URL (DIGITAL LOCATION) ...

OUPblog, 20 April 2006 (http://blog.oup.com/oupblog/2006/04/on_the_importan

...	ACCESS DATE	SPECIFIC CONTENT

.html : accessed 25 April 2007), para. 13.

Subsequent (Short) Notes

AUTHOR	ARTICLE TITLE	SPECIFIC CONTENT

11. Davis, "The Importance of History," paras. 13–14.

QuickCheck Model
BROADCASTS & WEB MISCELLANEA
DISCUSSION FORUMS & LISTS
(Source List Entry constructed to cover a number of postings)

Source List Entry

NAME OF FORUM	TYPE OF FORUM	DATE-SPAN READ	URL (DIGITAL LOCATION)

H-Canada, discussion list, 2005–06. http://www.h-net.org/~canada/.

First (Full) Reference Note

AUTHOR	MESSAGE TITLE	NAME OF FORUM	TYPE OF FORUM

1. Jody Perrun, "Conscription in Second World War," *H-Canada*, discussion list,

POSTING DATE	URL (DIGITAL LOCATION)	ACCESS DATE

15 March 2006 (http://www.h-net.org/~canada/ : accessed 25 April 2007).

Subsequent (Short) Note

AUTHOR	MESSAGE TITLE	NAME OF FORUM	POSTING DATE

11. Perrun, "Conscription in Second World War," *H-Canada*, 15 March 2006.

QuickCheck Model
BROADCASTS & WEB MISCELLANEA
PODCASTS

(Source List Entry constructed to cover a single broadcast)

Source List Entry

PRESENTER or GUEST	SUBJECT / TITLE	ITEM TYPE	PODCAST HOST	PODCAST

Reeves, Compton. "Medieval Pastimes." Interview by Brian LeBeau, host. *Talking*

... TITLE	BROADCAST DATE	FORMAT	WEBSITE (WHERE ARCHIVED)	URL ...

History, 16 August 1999. MP3 file. *Organization of American Historians.* http://

... (DIGITAL LOCATION)	ACCESS YEAR

talkinghistory.oah.org/arch1999.html : 2006.

First (Full) Reference Note

PRESENTER or GUEST	SUBJECT / TITLE	ITEM TYPE	PODCAST HOST

1. Compton Reeves, "Medieval Pastimes," interview by Brian LeBeau, host,

PODCAST TITLE	BROADCAST DATE	FORMAT	WEBSITE (WHERE ARCHIVED)

Talking History, 16 August 1999, MP3 file, *Organization of American Historians*

URL (DIGITAL LOCATION)	ACCESS DATE	SPECIFIC CONTENT

(http://talkinghistory.oah.org/arch1999.html : accessed 1 May 2006), minutes 20–25.

Subsequent (Short) Note

PRESENTER	SUBJECT / TITLE	SPECIFIC CONTENT

11. Reeves, "Medieval Pastimes," mins. 20–25.

QuickCheck Model
BROADCASTS & WEB MISCELLANEA
RADIO & TELEVISION CLIPS

Source List Entry

PRESENTERS		CLIP ID	TITLE OF SHOW

Spielberg, Steven, and Diana Fiedotin. "Survivors of the Shoah Foundation." *Ancestors*:

	BROADCAST			
SEGMENT	DATE	FORMAT		NETWORK or ...

Records at Risk, undated. RealVideo format. Brigham Young University Broad-

... PRODUCER	WEBSITE	URL (DIGITAL LOCATION)	ACCESS YEAR

cast Service. *Ancestors.* http://byubroadcasting.org/Ancestors/video/ : 2007.

First (Full) Reference Note

PRESENTERS	CLIP ID

1. Steven Spielberg and Diana Fiedotin, "Survivors of the Shoah Foundation,"

TITLE OF SHOW	SEGMENT	BROADCAST DATE	FORMAT	NETWORK or ...

Ancestors: *Records at Risk,* undated, RealVideo format, Brigham Young University

... PRODUCER	WEBSITE	URL (DIGITAL LOCATION)	...

Broadcast Service, *Ancestors* (http://byubroadcasting.org/Ancestors/video/ : accessed

... DATE

1 February 2007). *

Subsequent (Short) Note

PRESENTERS	CLIP ID

11. Spielberg and Fiedotin, Survivors of the Shoah Foundation."

* *Brief clips do not require citing a specific minute location.*

GUIDELINES
& Examples

BASIC ISSUE

14.1 Distinctions between Types

Periodicals comprise several distinctive types of publications. Over the centuries, writers have adopted certain practices for citing each. The distinctions are more than just technicalities. They help, at a glance, to identify the type of material you are working with—and *type* is not only a factor to weigh when evaluating evidence but also one that affects how and where one goes about finding the material.

The four most common types of traditional periodicals might be defined as follows:

JOURNALS .... Periodicals that emphasize scholarship, targeted to a special interest group, such as economic, family, political, or social history.

MAGAZINES .... Periodicals designed for a "popular" audience.

NEWSPAPERS .... Periodicals issued daily or weekly (usually) with a variety of news, opinions, advertisements, and other features of a general nature.

NEWSLETTERS ...... Periodicals of mixed content like newspapers, but more limited in size and scope.

Periodical innovations that are rooted in the virtual world, rather than the print world, are treated at 14.23–14.30.

CITATION PARTS

14.2 Article Title vs. Periodical Title

You should copy each title *precisely*. The following conventions distinguish article titles from the names of the periodicals in which they appear.

TRADITIONAL MEDIA
The name of the *periodical* is italicized. The name of the *article* within the periodical is placed in quotation marks.

ELECTRONIC MEDIA
Principles vary according to circumstances. Each will be addressed in this chapter as new circumstances are presented. (Also see 2.33–2.37.)

14.3   Author: Anonymous

Author bylines often do not appear in magazines and newspapers. In such cases, the first element of the citation is the article title. It is not necessary to enter "Anonymous" in the Author Field of your citation unless you wish to emphasize that a piece of historical writing was published anonymously.

14.4   Author: Pseudonymous

Journals of the past often published pseudonymous letters to the editor that were signed with a classical or descriptive name. In these cases, you cite the pseudonym in the author field—placing it within quotation marks—as with Aurelius in the example below.

> *Source List Entry*
> *Natchitoches (Louisiana) Courier,* 24 July 1826.

> *First Reference Note*
>   1. "Aurelius," "Communicated," *Natchitoches (Louisiana) Courier,* 24 July 1826, p. 2, cols. 1–2.

> *Subsequent Note*
>   11. "Aurelius," *Natchitoches Courier,* 24 July 1826, p. 2, cols. 1–2.

14.5   Author's Credentials, Degrees, or Honorifics

Many articles of yesteryear and some modern ones include an author's educational or professional credentials in the byline. For source-citation purposes, these may or may not be appropriate. As a general guideline:

Your working files—Record the author's *relevant* degrees or credentials, for evaluation purposes. Relevant means *relevant to the author's expertise on the subject she or he is writing about.*

Your manuscripts for publication—Drop the author's degrees or professional credentials unless you have a special reason for emphasizing their relevance.

Within professional fields where a certain degree is required or expected, the convention is to ignore that degree in citations published within the field.

Exceptions may be appropriate when an author crosses over from his principal profession into a different field, where the nature of his outside expertise is relevant in the new area. (Example: when a toxicologist writes in a history publication on the subject of historical toxicology.) In such cases, your published (edited) bibliography would typically omit the degree or professional credential. However, your First Reference Note would also include it or otherwise note the author's specialized expertise that is relevant to the validity of that article. You would not include it in Subsequent Notes.

14.6   Creator's Role

Chapter 12 (12.6–12.9) discusses situations in which it is advisable to include the author's "role" in your citation. This rule applies whether you are citing books or periodicals. In the Campbell example below, "artist" is added after the name of the creator to indicate the fact that the cited material is artwork, rather than a narrative essay.

Source List Entry
Campbell, Ken, artist. "Barbecue Presbyterian Church." *Argylle Colony Plus,* Journal of the North Carolina Scottish Heritage Society, 6 (April 1992): 59.

First Reference Note
1. Ken Campbell, artist, "Barbecue Presbyterian Church," *Argylle Colony Plus* (Journal of the North Carolina Scottish Heritage Society) 6 (April 1992): 59.

Subsequent Note
11. Campbell, "Barbecue Presbyterian Church," 59.

14.7   Dates, Styles for

Most magazines and newspapers in the United States cite dates using the sequence *month day, year*. Internationally and in family history, the convention for dates is *day month year*. If a date is part of an exact quote within quotation marks, do not alter it.

If your source is a periodical that dates itself in the style of Quaker, regnal, or French Revolutionary calendars, you should preserve the original wording, with quotation marks around it, and place the modern Gregorian style equivalent in square editorial brackets.

14.8   Dates vs. Volume & Issue Numbers

Volume and page numbers may not be enough to relocate material. Many local or privately published periodicals, as well as magazines and newspapers, begin renumbering each issue with "page 1." The result is duplicate sets of page numbers in a volume that contains several issues.

To identify the specific issue, researchers typically use the date of the issue or, sometimes, the issue number.

Evidence Style identifies issues by their dates rather than issue numbers, because unrecognized typing errors are more common with numbers than with words. When an issue number is mistyped and no month or season is specified, it can be difficult to relocate the material—especially when a publication is rare.

14.9   Dates vs. Volume: Variances by Type

Journal citations handle date/volume/issue data differently than citations for most popular magazines and newspapers. The common distinctions are these:

JOURNALS
Identify volume number, then add the month of publication in parentheses:

> 1. Jon Butler, "Magic, Astrology, and the Early American Religious Heritage," *American Historical Review* 84 (April 1979): 317–46.

NEWSPAPERS & "POPULAR" MAGAZINES
Identify by exact date of publication, not by volume and issue numbers. Do not place the date in parentheses. Instead, treat it as another item in the series of items being separated by commas, as with the magazine and newspaper examples below:

> 2. Joyce Wolkomir and Richard Wolkomir, "When Bandogs Howle & Spirits Walk," *Smithsonian,* January 2001, 39–44.
> 3. Dolores Flaherty and Roger Flaherty, "The Struggle to Save Antiquity for Posterity," *Chicago Sun-Times,* 4 May 2003, 14.

14.10   Edition, Page & Column References

Modern citations rarely add *page, p.* or *p. no.* before the actual page reference. However, if you are referencing works that have other numbers to be cited, such as columns, then a citation such as "p. 5, col. 3" will clarify your intent. In your citation, you may spell out those words or abbreviate them.

Regarding whether to cite a specific page or inclusive pages, the convention is usually this:

SOURCE LIST ENTRY ... Cite inclusive page numbers for the full article.

FIRST NOTE .... Cite the exact page or pages used. If you wish to cite inclusive pages also, follow those page numbers with a note such as "specifically p. ___" to call attention to the precise material that supports whatever you have written in your text.

SUBSEQUENT NOTE ... Cite the exact page(s) used.

Theoretically, citing section, page, and column numbers is a helpful practice. However, modern metropolitan papers are often issued in different editions with varying content.

For contemporary or twentieth-century newspapers, you should check the masthead to identify the edition. When one is specified, you would create a citation such as this:

Source List Entry
O'Connor, Anahad. "When the Barn Is the Battlefield." *The New York Times,* national edition, 30 October 2006, page A24.

First Reference Note
1. Anahad O'Connor, "When the Barn Is the Battlefield," *New York Times,* national edition, 30 October 2006, p. A24.

Subsequent Note
11. O'Connor, "When the Barn Is the Battlefield," p. A24.

No column number needs to be cited in this example, because the article occupies a major portion of the page.

14.11   Place of Publication
Whether you will cite a place of publication for a periodical depends upon its type. The general guidelines are as follows:

TRADITIONAL MEDIA

JOURNALS .... Place of publication is not required.

MAGAZINES .... Place of publication is not required, unless the magazine is of such limited circulation that it might not otherwise be locatable.

NEWSPAPERS .... Location is required. When a paper carries either a city or state in its masthead title (but not both), put the missing place name in parentheses within the title. If the title carries no place name, add a place name in parentheses, setting the added material in italics also.

ONLINE ....Physical place of publication is not required. A URL is mandatory.

The following examples illustrate the typically needed additions:

Source List Entry
Louisiana. Alexandria. *Louisiana Herald*. 1820–25.
Markwell, F. S. "A Family Legend." *Midland (England) Ancestor* 7 (December 1985): 364–67.

First Reference Note
    1. "An Ordinance to Suppress Gaming," *(Alexandria) Louisiana Herald*, 27 May 1820, p. 3. cols. 2–3.
    2. F. S. Markwell, "A Family Legend," *Midland (England) Ancestor* 7 (December 1985): 364–67.

Subsequent Note
    11. "An Ordinance to Suppress Gaming," p. 3, col. 2.
    12. Markwell, "A Family Legend," 365.

14.12 Publisher

For major journals and commercial newspapers and magazines, publishers are usually not cited. Some periodicals carry a sponsor's name within their title. For society or agency publications whose formal name gives no hint of its affiliation or focus, you may wish to add the publisher's identity—in regular type, not italics—immediately after the publication's name.

Source List Entry
Prechtel-Kluskens, Claire. "Headstones of Union Civil War Veterans." *The Record*, newsletter of the National Archives and Records Administration, 4 (March 1998): 22–23.

First Reference Note
    1. Claire Prechtel-Kluskens, "Headstones of Union Civil War Veterans," *The Record*, newsletter of the National Archives and Records Administration, 4 (March 1998): 22–23.

Subsequent Note
    11. Prechtel-Kluskens, "Headstones of Union Civil War Veterans," 23.

14.13 Punctuation

In citations to printed material, small differences exist in the conventional punctuation of articles, depending upon the type of periodical.

TRADITIONAL MEDIA

JOURNALS .... Parentheses are placed around the date, followed by a colon, then the page number. Example:

... (May 1890): 12.

MAGAZINES .... A comma goes before and after the date, followed by the page number. Example:

... , May 1890, 12.

NEWSPAPERS .... A comma goes before and after the date, followed by the page number. Example:

... , 15 May 1890, 12.

ELECTRONIC MEDIA

Principles vary according to circumstances. Each will be addressed in this chapter as new circumstances are presented.

14.14 Titles, Shortened

When a title is shortened, it should still include enough words to convey the subject matter and distinguish it from other titles in your source list. In the example below, if your research focuses upon the Swearingens, the first option under Subsequent Note might be sufficient. If your research focuses upon Chief Blue Jacket, his name should remain in the shortened title, as in the second option. Critical identifiers should never be dropped from the shortened titles.

Source List Entry

Johnson, Louise F. "Testing Popular Lore: Marmaduke Swearingen a.k.a. Chief Blue Jacket." *National Genealogical Society Quarterly* 82 (September 1994): 165–78.

First Reference Note

1. Louise F. Johnson, "Testing Popular Lore: Marmaduke Swearingen a.k.a. Chief Blue Jacket," *National Genealogical Society Quarterly* 82 (September 1994): 165–78.

Subsequent Note

11. Johnson, "Testing Popular Lore: Marmaduke Swearingen," 165–78.

(*or*)
   11. Johnson, "Testing Popular Lore: Marmaduke Swearingen a.k.a. Chief Blue Jacket," 165–78.

14.15 Volume & Issue Numbers, Styles for

Modern citations identify volumes with Arabic numbers, even when the original uses roman numerals. In creating shortened citations for articles that appear in only one issue of a periodical, you do not need to repeat the volume and issue—only the author, the article's title, and the page number for the material you are referencing.

——◆——

SPECIFIC EXAMPLES

PERIODICALS

14.16 Basic Format: Journal Articles

See also QuickCheck Model *for* JOURNAL ARTICLES: PRINT EDITIONS

Citations to journal articles traditionally identify the article's author, the article's title, the identity of the journal, and specific detail about the issue in which the material appeared. Journal citations do not include the identity of the journal's editor.

Source List Entry
Rothman, Joshua D. "Notorious in the Neighborhood: An Interracial Family in Early National and Antebellum Virginia." *Journal of Southern History* 67 (February 2001): 73–114.

First Reference Note
   1. Joshua D. Rothman, "Notorious in the Neighborhood: An Interracial Family in Early National and Antebellum Virginia," *Journal of Southern History* 67 (February 2001): 73–114.

Subsequent Note
   11. Rothman, "Notorious in the Neighborhood," 110.

Journal Articles (CD/DVD Reprint Editions)

CD or DVD image editions of journals that originate in the print media will have two formats to address: the original article and the publication details for the new edition. In the shortened Reference Note, however, the citation is the same as if the original had been used.

Source List Entry
Johnson, Linda Bennett. "Name Changes within the Melting Pot: The

Search for 'Frances Vera Gilmore' of Detroit." *National Genealogical Society Quarterly* 85 (June 1997): 85–93. CD-ROM edition. N.p.: Brøderbund, 1998.

First Reference Note

1. Linda Bennett Johnson, "Name Changes within the Melting Pot: The Search for 'Frances Vera Gilmore' of Detroit," *National Genealogical Society Quarterly* 85 (June 1997): 85–93, particularly p. 90; CD-ROM edition (N.p.: Brøderbund, 1998).

Subsequent Note

11. Johnson, "Name Changes within the Melting Pot," 91.

Journal Articles (Online Archives)

See also QuickCheck Model *for* JOURNAL ARTICLES: ONLINE ARCHIVES ...

Online archives for history journals that originate in print are typically accessed through a cooperative or a retrieval service—the result often being a cumbersome URL. Given the evolving nature of the Internet, that may change. In the interim, most style manuals call for citing that URL in full. Your citation to the original print edition should include the date of the issue and its volume number (if that information is available). Unless you are using an image copy of the journal, you do not have to cite inclusive page numbers for the print version you have not used. Instead, you cite a paragraph number.

Source List Entry

Reese, Linda W. "Cherokee Freedwomen in Indian Territory, 1863–1890." *Western Historical Quarterly* 33 (Autumn 2002). Online archives. *The History Cooperative*. http://www.historycooperative.org/journals/whq/33.3/reese.html : 2007.

First Reference Note

1. Linda W. Reese, "Cherokee Freedwomen in Indian Territory, 1863–1890," *Western Historical Quarterly* 33 (Autumn 2002); online archives, *The History Cooperative* (http://www.historycooperative.org/journals/whq/33.3/reese.html : accessed 1 February 2007), para. 7.

Subsequent Note

11. Reese, "Cherokee Freedwomen in Indian Territory, 1863–1890," para. 7.

Journals (Online Images)

Digital images of historic journals may be accessed online through both subscription and free content providers. Because you are viewing an image, you will need to cite both the original and the website that provided access. Typically, you will cite the URL for the provider's page. You may then need to identify a collection or key word that helps to drill down to the exact journal.

Source List Entry
DeBow's Review: Agricultural, Commercial, Industrial Progress and Resources, 1846–69.

First Reference Note
1. "Statistical Bureaus in the States," *DeBow's Review* 8 (May 1850): 422–44; digital images, University of Michigan, *Making of America* (http://www.hti.umich.edu/m/moajrnl/ : 29 January 2007).

Subsequent Note
11. "Statistical Bureaus in the States," 430.

CITING COMMON TITLE *VS.* FULL TITLE
Many periodicals are commonly known by a short version of their name—as with *DeBow's Review* above. In your Source List Entry, you may wish to record the full name, even when you use the common name in your Reference Notes.

14.17 Journal Articles, Serialized
Citations to articles that are serialized across multiple issues of a journal may require an additional element: the identification of the full series. The two examples below demonstrate the handling of (*a*) a long-running series from which you might need to cite many small and random parts, and (*b*) a serialized article in which you and your readers are likely interested in all segments.

Source List Entry
Cruzat, Heloise H., translator. "Records of the Superior Council of Louisiana." *Louisiana Historical Quarterly,* volumes 7 (October 1924) through 22 (April 1940).
Hansen, James L. "The Lootman/Barrois Families of Canada, New York, and Points West." *The American Genealogist* 66 (April 1991): 88–92 and (July 1991): 169–75.

First Reference Note
1. Heloise H. Cruzat, transl., "Records of the Superior Council of Louisiana," *Louisiana Historical Quarterly* 8 (January 1925): 125, petition of Antoine Bruslé.
2. James L. Hansen, "The Lootman/Barrois Families of Canada, New York, and Points West," *The American Genealogist* 66 (April 1991): 88–92 and (July 1991): 169–75, particularly 170.

Subsequent Note
    11. Cruzat, "Records of the Superior Council of Louisiana," *Louisiana Historical Quarterly,* 8: 125.
    12. Hansen, "The Lootman/Barrois Families of Canada, New York, and Points West," 170.

CITING SPECIFIC VOLUME IN SHORTENED NOTES
The shortened citation in note 11 cites both a volume and a page, because the Cruzat series covers many volumes. The shortened citation in note 12 cites only a page number, because all parts of the serialization are within the same volume.

14.18 Journal Reviews

A critical review in a journal will usually have no title. You will cite the author of the review, the title of the work that is being reviewed, and the author of that work, followed by specific publication details for the journal in which the review appears.

Source List Entry
Mason, Matthew. Review of *Toussaint's Clause: The Founding Fathers and the Haitian Revolution.* By Gordon S. Brown. *Southern Quarterly* 43 (Winter 2006): 187–90.

First Reference Note
    1. Matthew Mason, review of *Toussaint's Clause: The Founding Fathers and the Haitian Revolution,* by Gordon S. Brown, *Southern Quarterly* 43 (Winter 2006): 187–90, specifically 188.

Subsequent Note
    11. Mason, review of *Toussaint's Clause,* 188.

Journal Reviews (Online Archives)

Reviews accessed through online archives for print journals follow the basic format for journal reviews, with two modifications: (*a*) the original page numbers do not have to be cited, and (*b*) the electronic details need to be added, as explained in the Reese example at 14.16.

Source List Entry
Paisley, Fiona. Review of *Dancing with Strangers: Europeans and Australians at First Contact* by Inga Clendinnen. *The American Historical Review* 111 (April 2006). Online archives. *The History Cooperative.* http://www.historycooperative.org/journals/ahr/111.2/br_31.html : 2007.

First Reference Note
    1. Fiona Paisley, review of *Dancing with Strangers: Europeans and*

Australians at First Contact by Inga Clendinnen, *The American Historical Review* 111 (April 2006); online archives, *The History Cooperative* (http://www.historycooperative.org/journals/ahr/111.2/br_31.html : accessed 18 January 2007).

Subsequent Note

11. Paisley, review of *Dancing with Strangers: Europeans and Australians at First Contact*, para. 3.

14.19 Journal Review Essays

When critical reviews appear as titled essays, those titles need to be included in the citation. The examples below are all review essays in print journals. Each essay treats a different type of publication: a printed book, a CD or DVD, and a website. Regardless of the type of publication under review, your format for the citation remains essentially the same. Three small differences stem from missing data:

ESSAY TYPE .... In the Richter model, the title gives no clue to the fact that it is a review essay and it does not identify the book. Therefore, a descriptor is added ("Review essay on *American Colonies* by Alan Taylor"). In the Wyatt-Brown example, the title explicitly states that it is a review essay and names the book, but it does not name the book's author. Therefore, the author's identity is added after the closing quotation mark for Wyatt-Brown's title.

MONTH OF ISSUE ...... In the Richter model, the periodical is an annual one; therefore, no month or season is given for it. In the Wyatt-Brown example, the publication is a quarterly; thus, the issue month is identified.

PUBLICATION TYPE .... The title of the website review does not explicitly say that *Valley of the Shadow* is a website rather than some other digital type. Therefore, that descriptor is added.

Source List Entry

(Review of a book)

Richter, Daniel K. "Early America in Process." Review essay on *American Colonies* by Alan Taylor. *Massachusetts Historical Review* 5 (2003): 125–33.

Wyatt-Brown, Bertram. "Going Off Half-Cocked: A Review Essay of *Arming America*" by Michael A. Bellesiles. *Journal of Southern History* 68 (May 2002): 423–28.

(Review of a CD or DVD)

Handran, George B. "Griffith's Valuation—An Essential Irish Source Now Indexed on CD-ROM: A Review Essay." *National Genealogical Society Quarterly* 86 (June 1998): 140–47.

(Review of a historical website)

Kornbligh, Gary J. "Venturing into the Civil War, Virtually: A Review" of the website *The Valley of the Shadow: Two Communities in the American Civil War. Journal of American History* 88 (June 2001): 145–51.

First Reference Note

1. Daniel K. Richter, "Early America in Process," review essay on *American Colonies* by Alan Taylor, *Massachusetts Historical Review* 5 (2003): 125–33, particularly 128.

2. Bertram Wyatt-Brown, "Going Off Half-Cocked: A Review Essay of *Arming America*" by Michael A. Bellesiles, *Journal of Southern History* 68 (May 2002): 423–28.

3. George B. Handran, "Griffith's Valuation—An Essential Irish Source Now Indexed on CD-ROM: A Review Essay," *National Genealogical Society Quarterly* 86 (June 1998): 140–47.

4. Gary J. Kornbligh, "Venturing into the Civil War, Virtually: A Review" of the website *The Valley of the Shadow: Two Communities in the American Civil War, Journal of American History* 88 (June 2001): 145–51.

Subsequent Note

11. Richter, "Early America in Process," review essay on *American Colonies*, 128.

12. Wyatt-Brown, "Going Off Half-Cocked: A Review Essay of *Arming America,"* 423–28.

13. Handran, "Griffith's Valuation ... on CD-ROM: A Review Essay," 143.

14. Kornbligh, "Venturing into the Civil War, Virtually: A Review," 145.

14.20 Magazine Articles

See also QuickCheck Model *for* MAGAZINE ARTICLES: PRINT EDITIONS

Popular magazines are cited a bit more simply than academic journals. Volume numbers are rarely cited for magazines and, in footnotes, the elements are typically linked with just commas. In one other aspect, however, magazine articles can be more complex: journals typically print all of an article on consecutive pages; however magazines frequently put a small portion of an article toward the front of the issue and continue the remainder on back pages. The example below demonstrates the handling of this "broken" pagination.

Source List Entry
Fleming, Thomas. "America 1776." *Reader's Digest,* July 1976.

First Reference Note
    1. Thomas Fleming, "America 1776," *Reader's Digest,* July 1976, 49–56, 197–228.

Subsequent Note
    11. "Fleming, "America 1776," 222.

Magazine Articles (Online Copies)

See QuickCheck Model *for* MAGAZINE ARTICLES: ONLINE REPRINTS, RANDOM

Electronic copies of magazines originating in print may be archived by the publisher (as with Hopley below) or they may have been randomly posted at an outside site (as with Leepson). Slight structural differences may exist in your citations from one situation to the other.

Source List Entry
Hopley, Claire. "North British Migration: From the Irish Sea to the Allegheny Mountains." *British Heritage Magazine*, March 2006. Online archives. *The HistoryNet.com*. http://www.historynet.com/bh/bl-british-migration/ : 2007.
Leepson, Marc. "The Levys at Monticello." *Preservation Magazine*. n.d. Online reprint, Thomas Jefferson Foundation, *Monticello*. http://wwwmonticello.org/about/levy.html : 2007.

First Reference Note
    1. Claire Hopley, "North British Migration: From the Irish Sea to the Allegheny Mountains," *British Heritage Magazine*, March 2006; online archives, *The HistoryNet.com* (www.historynet.com/bh/bl-british-migration/ : accessed 1 February 2007), para. 10.
    2. Marc Leepson, "The Levys at Monticello," Thomas Jefferson Foundation, *Monticello* (http://www.monticello.org/about/levy.html : accessed 10 March 2007), paras. 3–10; online reprint, citing original publication in *Preservation Magazine,* unidentified issue.

Subsequent Note
    11. Hopley, "North British Migration: From the Irish Sea to the Allegheny Mountains," para. 10.
    12. Leepson, "The Levys at Monticello," para. 9.

Magazines (Online Images)

Your citations to image copies of historic magazines will follow the format for original copies, with an added reference to the website that provided access. For more on pseudonymous authors such as Mary F**** below, see 14.4.

Source List Entry
The Lady's Repository, 1841–1876.

First Reference Note
1. Mary F****, "Female Teachers," *The Lady's Repository,* April 1844, 107–8; digital images, University of Michigan, *Making of America* (http://www.hti.umich.edu/m/moajrnl/ : accessed 1 February 2007).

Subsequent Note
11. Mary F****, "Female Teachers," 107.

14.21   Newsletter Articles
See also QuickCheck Model *for* NEWSLETTER ARTICLES: PRINT EDITIONS

Newsletters might be cited as either a magazine or a journal. In history research, publications that bear volume numbers and are archived for their historic value tend to be cited in the manner of journals, even though the content may be less rigorous than that of a scholarly journal.

Many periodicals undergo name changes across time. If you wish to consolidate all citations to a publication under one title in a single Source List Entry, you may combine the titles in the manner below. For handling a single article, see the QuickCheck Model cited above.

Source List Entry
National Odom Assembly Newsletter (variously *N.O.A. News*), 1981–86.

First Reference Note
1. "Documentation," *N.O.A. News: Quarterly Bulletin of the National Odom Assembly* 1 (September 1981): 2.
2. "How About This for a Petrified Man?" *National Odom Assembly Newsletter* 7 (October 1986): 14.

Subsequent Note
11. "Documentation," *N.O.A. News,* 1: 2.
12. "How About This for a Petrified Man?" 14.

CITING THE PERIODICAL IN THE SUBSEQUENT NOTE
As a rule, when citing articles from periodicals, your Subsequent Note will cite only the article title, not the periodical title. That rule is followed in note 12 above. Like most article titles, that one is unique enough to be easily identified. However, when an article title consists

of only one word or is otherwise generic enough that you might be citing several titles that contain the same word or phrase, clarity is served by including the title of the periodical, as in note 11.

PUNCTUATING TITLES WITH QUESTION MARKS, ETC.
When an article title ends in a question mark or exclamation point, you drop the comma that usually appears between the title of the article and the close-quotation mark.

Newsletters (Online Images)
Current and recent newsletters produced by societies and companies are frequently archived online at the sponsor's website. The model below covers a typical issue offered in PDF format.

Source List Entry
New Mexico Jewish Historical Society, newsletter, 19 (December 2005).

First Reference Note
1. Bill Boehm, "The Joseph A. Taichert Company Records and Other Jewish Collections in the Rio Grande Historical Collections," *New Mexico Jewish Historical Society*, newsletter, 19 (December 2005): 8; PDF images (http://www.nmjewishhistory.org), keyword: Publications.

Subsequent Note
11. Boehm, "The Joseph A. Taichert Company Records," 8.

CITING THE VOLUME NUMBER
Newsletters that carry a volume number are typically cited like a journal. Newsletters that do not carry a volume number are typically cited like a newspaper. A comparison of the example above with the one at 7.26 illustrates the difference.

Citing like a newspaper. The online church newsletter at 7.26 carries a date but no volume number. Also, like many local newspapers, the church newsletter's masthead gives no clue to the location of the church. Therefore, at 7.26, the newsletter is cited like a newspaper, with the location added in parentheses, followed by a comma, then the date. No parentheses are placed around the date.

Citing like a journal. With the society newsletter above, no location has to be added in parentheses because the masthead identifies the location as a statewide publication in New Mexico. The newsletter carries both a volume number and a month of publication. If the newsletter were cited like a newspaper, with commas before and after the date, then the volume number 19 would fall immediately before the month, December, creating a question as to whether 19 represents the day of the month. To avoid ambiguity, the newsletter is cited as a journal, with the publication month and year in parentheses after the volume number.

CITING THE WEBSITE'S CREATOR
In this example, nothing is entered in the field for the creator-owner of the website. The name of the society is identified as part of the newsletter's name. Citing it again as the creator of its own website would be redundant.

CLARIFYING THE TITLE
Some society publications carry only the name of the society, without identifying themselves as a publication. You may clarify the situation by adding a descriptive identifier. Do not italicize your addition as though it were part of the title.

14.22 Newspaper Articles
See QuickCheck Model *for* NEWSPAPER ARTICLES: PRINT EDITIONS

Newspaper citations closely resemble those for popular magazines. The key difference is that the structure of newspapers calls for the page citation to include column numbers and (when applicable) section numbers and edition names.

The examples below demonstrate citations to material of various types and length—one of them bylined, the others not. For the addition of place names amid a local newspaper's name, see 14.11. For newspapers that carry the name of major cities, an editorial addition of the state's name is optional. The Ringle example at note 3 below is an exception to the rule that column numbers be cited. In this case, the article consumes most of the two cited pages and covers many columns. A specific column number is not needed for discovery.

Source List Entry
(When citing a newspaper across a span of years)
Kansas. Burlingame. *Burlingame Enterprise.* 1897–1910.
Louisiana. Alexandria. *Red River Republican.* 1847–1853.

(When citing a specific issue)
District of Columbia. *The Washington Post.* 12 May 2002.

First Reference Note
1. "Frank Austin, Sr.," obituary, *Burlingame (Kansas) Enterprise,* 19 May 1898, p. 5, col. 4.

    2. "Land Bounty to Volunteers," *Red River Republican (Alexandria, Louisiana)*, 6 March 1847, p. 2, col. 1.

    3. Ken Ringle, "Up through Slavery," *The Washington Post*, 12 May 2002, sect. F, pp. 1, 3 [OR. SIMPLY F1, F3].

Subsequent Note

    11. "Frank Austin, Sr.," *Burlingame Enterprise,* 19 May 1898.

    12. "Land Bounty to Volunteers," *Red River Republican,* 6 March 1847.

    13. Ringle, "Up through Slavery," *Washington Post,* 12 May 2002.

CREATING SOURCE LIST ENTRIES FOR NEWSPAPERS

Typically in a Source List, newspapers are cited under their geographic locale, as with the Kansas and Louisiana papers above. In citing national and international papers such as the *Washington Post* or the London *Times*, you might choose to list the paper under its name rather than its geographic locale.

Newspaper Articles (Online Archives)

See QuickCheck Model *for* NEWSPAPER ARTICLES: ONLINE ARCHIVES

When print newspapers archive issues online, the section, page, and column details may not be preserved. The following example cites the online archive version of the Ringle article from Notes 3 and 13 above. The page citation given at the website refers only to the first page of the printed article. As with the online newsletter example at 14.21, the example below enters nothing in the field for the creator of the website. The *Washington Post* is cited as the newspaper's name and again in the URL. Citing it a third time as the creator of the website would be pointless. The example below also assumes that you will be citing this newspaper multiple times; therefore, the Source List Entry cites to the newspaper, rather than the specific article.

Source List Entry

The Washington Post, 12 May 2002. Web edition. http://www.washingtonpost.com : 2007.

First Reference Note

    1. Ken Ringle, "Up through Slavery," *The Washington Post*, 12 May 2002, Web edition (http://www.washingtonpost.com/ac2/wp-dyn?pagename=article&node=&contentId=A1069-2002May10&notFound=true : accessed 10 March 2007); citing p. F001.

Subsequent Note

    11. Ringle, "Up through Slavery."

Newspapers (Online Images)   🖥

Digital images of historic newspapers are often accessed through online content providers that are unaffiliated with the newspaper publisher. In those cases, you will need to cite both the original newspaper and the website of the provider. Typically, you will cite only the URL for the provider's home page, then identify the collection or key words needed to access the exact newspaper.

Source List Entry

Pennsylvania. Indiana. *The Indiana Democrat*, 1930–36.

First Reference Note

1. William C. Utley, "Vigilantes War on Rural Crime," *The Indiana (Pennsylvania) Democrat*, 3 June 1936, p. 3, cols. 5–7; digital images, *Ancestry.com* (http://www.ancestry.com : 29 January 2007), Historical Newspaper Collection.

Subsequent Note

11. Utley, "Vigilantes War on Rural Crime."

Newspapers (Online Transcripts)   🖥

When you use an online transcript of a newspaper article, the focus of your citation changes. You are no longer citing the original newspaper, you are citing the transcribed copy someone has made.

Source List Entry

"Callender Replies to His Critics." Transcript by Joshua D. Rothman. Public Broadcasting System. *Frontline*. http://www.pbs.org/wgbh/pages/frontline/shows/jefferson/cron/1802recorder.html : 2007.

First Reference Note

1. "Callender Replies to His Critics," transcript by Joshua D. Rothman, at "Jefferson's Blood," Public Broadcasting System, *Frontline* (http://www.pbs.org/wgbh/pages/frontline/shows/jefferson/cron/1802recorder.html : accessed 29 January 2007); citing original publication in the *Richmond (Virginia) Recorder,* 20 October 1802.

Subsequent Note

11. "Callender Replies to His Critics," at "Jefferson's Blood," PBS *Frontline*.

RADIO & TELEVISION BROADCASTS

14.23 Broadcast Transcripts

Commercial transcripts of radio and television broadcasts typically cover an entire show. If viewed online, the text paragraphs are likely not to be numbered. In that mode, specific statements are typically identified by citing the speaker, whose name will be prominently displayed in each paragraph of the transcript.

When citing a printed download, pagination will depend upon the print settings of your browser and printer. Notes 2 and 12 below demonstrate citing page numbers under those circumstances.

Source List Entry

Beschloss, Michael, and Dan Lynch. Interviews. ABC News, *Good Morning America,* 22 June 2004. Segment transcript by Transcripts.tv. http://www.transcripts.tv/search/do_details .cfm?ShowDetailID+21576 : 2006.

"Shtetl Transcript." For Public Broadcasting Service documentary, *Frontline: Shtetl,* 17 April 1996. Transcript by Journal Graphics. http://www.pbs.org/wgbh/pages/frontline/shtetl/shtetlscript.html : 2006.

First Reference Note

1. Michael Beschloss (presidential history) and Dan Lynch (family history), interviews, ABC News, *Good Morning America,* 22 June 2004; segment transcript by Transcripts.tv (http://www.transcripts.tv/search/ do_details.cfm?ShowDetailID+21576: accessed 15 July 2006).

2. "Shtetl Transcript," for PBS documentary, *Frontline: Shtetl,* 17 April 1996; transcript by Journal Graphics (http://www.pbs.org/wgbh/ pages/frontline/shtetl/shtetlscript.html : accessed 1 May 2006), testimony of Marian Marzynski, p. 33 of 40.

Subsequent Note

11. Beschloss, *Good Morning America,* 22 June 2004.
12. "Shtetl" transcript, testimony of Marzynski, p. 33 of 40.

14.24 Sound Clips

See QuickCheck Model *for* BROADCASTS ... RADIO & TELEVISION CLIPS

Online sound clips of radio and television productions typically require information about the following elements:

- the presenter, host, or guest whose information is being cited
- the title or subject matter
- the name of the broadcast
- the date of the broadcast (if shown)
- the creator of the broadcast
- the digital format of the presentation (length is optional)
- the name of the website at which the clip is accessed or archived

- the URL of the website
- the date you accessed the clip

The order in which some of these elements appear may vary, according to the specific details involved, as illustrated by these examples:

Sound Clips

Source List Entry

(Radio clip, listed under broadcast title)

American Public Media. *Marketplace Morning Report,* 22 August 2003. Archived audioclip. http://marketplace.publicradio.org/morning _report/2003/08/21_mmr.html : 2007.

(Video clip, listed under name of presenters)

Spielberg, Steven, and Diana Fiedotin. "Survivors of the Shoah Foundation." *Ancestors: Records at Risk.* Undated. RealVideo format. Brigham Young University Broadcast Service. *Ancestors.* http:// byubroadcasting.org/Ancestors/video/ : 2007.

First Reference Note

1. Rachel Dornhelm, "The Lucrative Business of Genealogy," American Public Media, *Marketplace Morning Report,* 22 August 2003, 3 minutes 18 seconds, archived audioclip (http://marketplace.public radio.org/morning_report/2003/08/21_mmr.html : 3 January 2007), minute 2: 5.

2. Steven Spielberg and Diana Fiedotin, "Survivors of the Shoah Foundation," *Ancestors: Records at Risk,* undated, RealVideo format, Brigham Young University Broadcast Service, *Ancestors* (http://byu broadcasting.org/Ancestors/video/ : accessed 1 February 2007).

Subsequent Note

11. Dornhelm, "The Lucrative Business of Genealogy."
12. Spielberg and Fiedotin, "Survivors of the Shoah Foundation."

WEB-BASED MISCELLANEA

14.25 Blogs

See also QuickCheck Model *for* BROADCASTS & WEB MISCELLANEA: BLOGS

A *blog* (short for web log) is essentially an online diary in which the blogger periodically posts thoughts, opinions, reviews, and news items. Each item typically has a caption. Reader responses may also be included at the site. A citation to a blog follows the same basic pattern used for most online essays, with minor modifications.

- Your citation will need to include the date the work was posted. Whether you wish to include the time of the posting is a matter of choice.

- If you choose to cite the work in your Source List under the title of a specific article, then you will want to cite the specific URL at which that article appears. If your Source List cites to the blog itself, you need only provide the URL for the home page.

- If you choose to carry the Source List Entry under the name of the blogger, you may either cite the blog generically, with its website root, or you might cite a specific article and its specific URL.

- If the name of the author is part of the Weblog's formal name, that name does not have to be repeated in the Author Field. In that case, however, the name of the Weblog should be included in the Subsequent Note to ensure proper identity and attribution.

- If the blog entry is lengthy (as with the QuickCheck Model), you may wish to cite specific paragraph numbers. For short blog entries such as those below, no paragraph number is needed.

Blog

Source List Entry

(To list under the name of the article)
"Culture Clash and Genetic Similarity." *John Hawks Weblog: Paleoanthropology, Genetics, and Evolution,* 6 January 2006. http://www.johnhawks.net/weblog/topics/race/genetic_ancestry/lemba_visit_cohen_slate_2000.w : 2007.

(To list under the name of the blog for citing multiple articles)
John Hawks Weblog: Paleoanthropology, Genetics, and Evolution, 2006–2007. http://www.johnhawks.net/.

(To list under the name of the blogger)
Meitzler, Leland. "Edmund Reade was Bush and Kerry's Common Ancestor." *Genealogy Blog,* 22 September 2004. http://www.genealogyblog.com : 2007.

First Reference Note

1. "Culture Clash and Genetic Similarity," *John Hawks Weblog: Paleoanthropology, Genetics, and Evolution,* 6 January 2006 (http://www.johnhawks.net/weblog/topics/race/genetic_ancestry/lemba_visit_cohen_slate_2000.w : accessed 25 January 2007).

2. Leland Meitzler, "Edmund Reade was Bush and Kerry's Common Ancestor," *Genealogy Blog,* 22 September 2004 (http://www.genealogyblog.com : accessed 25 April 2007).

Subsequent Note
　　11. "Culture Clash and Genetic Similarity," *John Hawks Weblog.*
　　12. Meitzler, "Edmund Reade was Bush and Kerry's Common Ancestor."

14.26   Chats, Archived Transcripts

Citations to archived transcripts of organized, online "chats" treating specific topics can follow the same basic pattern used for blogs at 14.25. If the date of the chat is included in the title of the archived transcript, you do not have to repeat it in the field for the posting date.

Chats   🖥️

Source List Entry
Roderick, Thomas H. "Genetics and Genealogy: Transcript of Chat, 22 May 2001." *About: Exploring Genealogy.* http://genealogy.about .com/library/blchattrans-roderick.htm : 2007.

First Reference Note
　　1. Thomas H. Roderick, "Genetics and Genealogy: Transcript of Chat, 22 May 2001," *About: Exploring Genealogy* (http://genealogy .about.com/library/blchattrans-roderick.htm : accessed 18 January 2007), paras. 38–42.

Subsequent Note
　　11. Roderick, "Genetics & Genealogy," paras. 38–42.

14.27   Discussion Forums & Lists

See also QuickCheck Model *for* BROADCASTS ... DISCUSSION FORUMS & LISTS

Citations to discussion forums typically cite the home page for the forum, where archived postings are then located by date, topic, and perhaps author. The names of some forums specifically identify them as a forum or a discussion list. Others do not—in which case you may wish to add an identifier to clarify the nature of the material being cited. Because these are not formally published and might be difficult to relocate under their subject line, your shortened citation should include the forum name and the posting date.

The example used for the QuickCheck Model cites the forum itself, not the message, in the Source List Entry. You might follow that model when you have multiple messages from the same forum. The model below cites a specific message in the Source List Entry, a format you would use if this were the only message you are citing from that forum.

Discussion Forums & Lists 🖥

Source List Entry

Proffitt, Merrilee. "New Electronic Resource for Locating Archival Material." *H-Caribbean*, discussion list, 24 April 2006. http://www.h-net.org~carib/ : 2007.

First Reference Note

1. Merrilee Proffitt, "New Electronic Resource for Locating Archival Material," *H-Caribbean*, discussion list, 24 April 2006 (http://www.h-net.org/~carib/ : accessed 25 April 2007).

Subsequent Note

11. Proffitt, "New Electronic Resource for Locating Archival Material," *H-Caribbean*, 24 April 2006.

14.28 E-journals & E-magazines

See also QuickCheck Model *for* JOURNAL ARTICLES: ONLINE JOURNALS

Journals and magazines that exist solely in electronic form are simpler to cite than online copies of print journals, because you have only one format to describe or identify. The following provide models for citing both articles and reviews.

E-Journals 🖥

Source List Entry

Frost, Ginger. Review of *Family Affairs: A History of the Family in 20th Century England*. By Mary Abbott. *H-Albion, H-Net Reviews,* June 2005. http://www.h-net.org/reviews : 2007.

Valeri, Mark, "The Rise of Usury in Early New England," *Common-Place* 6 (April 2006). E-journal. http://www.common-place.org/ : 2007.

First Reference Note

1. Ginger Frost, Review of *Family Affairs: A History of the Family in 20th Century England,* by Mary Abbott, *H-Albion, H-Net Reviews,* June 2005 (http://www.h-net.org/reviews : accessed 2 March 2007), para. 2.

2. Mark Valeri, "The Rise of Usury in Early New England," *Common-Place* 6 (April 2006), e-journal (http://www.common-place.org : accessed 25 April 2007), para. 10.

Subsequent Note

11. Frost, Review of *Family Affairs: A History of the Family in 20th Century England*, para. 2.

12. Valeri, "The Rise of Usury in Early New England," para. 6.

14.29   E-Newsletters

Because electronic newsletters are typically e-mailed to subscribers, you will need to cite the distribution mode, identify the publisher, and provide the URL for subscription or archived issues. If the organization maintains an archive, you should cite the issue date and the date of access in your First Reference Note. If the organization does not maintain an online archive, then you will have no date to cite other than the date of the issue. If, as in Notes 2 and 12 below, the cited article has no author, your Subsequent Note should include the name of the periodical (the institutional author). If the article is not archived, you may want your Subsequent Note to identify both the periodical and the date.

E-Newsletters

Source List Entry

Ancestry's Weekly Journal. 2006. E-mail newsletter from *Ancestry.com.* http://www.ancestry.com.

Chicago History Museum E-News. 2005–06. E-mail newsletter. http://www.chicagohistory.org : 2007.

First Reference Note

1. Juliana Smith, "Preserving Access to Records: What Can You Do?" *Ancestry's Weekly Journal,* 10 April 2006, e-mail newsletter archived at *Ancestry.com* (http://www.ancestry.com).

2. "This Month in History: The Great Chicago Fire," *Chicago History Museum E-News,* 2 October 2006, e-mail newsletter by subscription from *Chicago Historical Society* (http://www.chicagohistory.org).

Subsequent Note

11. Smith, "Preserving Access to Records: What Can You Do?"

12. "This Month in History: The Great Chicago Fire," *Chicago History Museum E-News,* 2 October 2006.

14.30   Podcasts

See QuickCheck Model *for* BROADCASTS ... PODCASTS

Audio or multimedia files of discussions, lectures, and similar matter are analogous to their print-based counterparts. You will need to cite the author, the subject (if more than one is addressed), the podcast (the publication), the format, the date, and the digital location of the file. If possible, you would want to note the "minute"—i.e., the spot at which the cited material appears. The two examples below illustrate these two different situations:

CITING THE WEBSITE

In the Reeves example below, the digital files of the original show are now archived at another website. Thus, both the Source List Entry and the First Reference Note identify the new site. In the Morgan and Smith example below, the name of the podcast and the name of the website are one and the same. The name does not have to be repeated in both citation fields.

CONSTRUCTING THE SOURCE LIST ENTRY

In the Reeves example, the Source List Entry cites a specific date for a single podcast, because the Reeves interview is the only item that has been used from that set of podcast files. The Morgan and Smith example presumes you have listened to all extant files for the cited years and you will be citing several of them. Thus, the Source List Entry cites the podcast to the time span audited.

Podcasts

Source List Entry

Reeves, Compton. "Medieval Pastimes." Interview by Brian LeBeau, host. *Talking History,* 16 August 1999. MP3 file. *Organization of American Historians.* http://talkinghistory.oah.org/arch1999.html : 2006.

Morgan, George G., and Drew Smith, hosts. "PERSI: The Periodical Source Index." *The Genealogy Guys Podcast*, 2005–. MP3. http://www.genealogyguys.com : 2007.

First Reference Note

1. Compton Reeves, "Medieval Pastimes," interview by Brian LeBeau, host, *Talking History,* 16 August 1999, MP3 file, *Organization of American Historians* (http://talkinghistory.oah.org/arch1999.html : accessed 1 May 2006), minutes 20–25.

2. George G. Morgan and Drew Smith, hosts, "PERSI: The Periodical Source Index," *The Genealogy Guys Podcast*, 27 March 2006, MP3 (http://www.genealogyguys.com : accessed 9 May 2006), minutes 21–23.

Subsequent Note

11. Reeves, "Medieval Pastimes," mins. 20–25.

12. Morgan and Smith, "PERSI: The Periodical Source Index," min. 21.

APPENDIXES

Appendix A
Glossary

abstract: (academic context) a brief summary or a précis of principal points in an essay or a thesis.

abstract: (notetaking context) a condensed version of a record, preserving all important detail in original sequence. An abstract may contain verbatim extracts (quotes) of passages from the record, in which case the material that is copied exactly should be placed in quotation marks inside the abstract.

acronym: a "word" coined by combining the initial letter of each word that identifies an institution, a law, etc. Example: NARA, used as a short form for National Archives and Records Administration. Also see *initialism*.

agnatic line: the male line of descent. See also *Y-DNA*.

analysis: the process of examining evidence. For students of history, this typically involves (*a*) studying individual pieces of data for inherent clues, strengths, and weaknesses; (*b*) correlating details from different sources in search of patterns; and (*c*) determining whether the whole body of evidence amounts to more than the sum of the individual parts.

assertion: a claim or statement of "fact."

assumption: a conclusion unsupported by evidence.

attested copy: (legal context) a copy of an original that has been officially compared to the original and attested to be a true copy—aka *examined copy*.

best evidence: an original record or records of the best and highest quality that survives. At law and in history research, a *derivative source* (q.v.) is rarely considered sufficient for documentation when an original or a derivative closer to the original form exists.

beyond reasonable doubt: a legal standard applied in criminal cases, requiring virtual certainty.

bibliography: a list of sources relevant to the subject at hand, citing each source in full. An *annotated* bibliography is one that discusses the sources in addition to providing full citations. A bibliography typically does not cite individual manuscripts or documents; rather, it cites a collection or series in which the manuscript appears. Also see *source list.*

broadside: (historically) a publication that typically consists of a large sheet of paper printed on just one side and intended for wide distribution.

calendar: (archival context) a collection guide that contains brief abstracts of items in that collection, arranged in chronological order.

call name: the name by which a person is or was commonly called. Example: Johann Carl Schmidt might use *Carl* as his call name, rather than the more-common convention of being called by his first name.

circumstantial case: (historical context) a reasonable conclusion reached by assembling, analyzing, and explaining—with thorough documentation—numerous pieces of indirect evidence.

circumstantial evidence: (legal context) testimony based on deductions drawn from various information that can be documented.

citation—the statement in which one identifies the source of an assertion. Common forms of citations are source list entries (bibliographic entries), reference notes (endnotes or footnotes), and document labels.

(to) cite: the act of identifying one's source(s) for statements of fact—not to be confused with the words *site* (as in *website*) or *sight* (as in *eyesight*).

claim: an assertion of "fact" for which no evidence is supplied or else the evidence is insufficient or not yet adjudged.

clear and convincing evidence: a legal standard interchangeable with *beyond reasonable doubt* (q.v.) in some jurisdictions; elsewhere, an intermediate standard between *beyond reasonable doubt* and *preponderance of the evidence* (q.v.).

clerk's copy: a term typically used for the officially recorded copy of a document. See also *record copy.*

conclusion: a decision. To be reliable, it must be based on well-reasoned and thoroughly documented evidence gleaned from sound research.

confirm: to test the accuracy of an assertion or conclusion by (*a*) consulting at least one other source that is both independently created and authoritative; and (*b*) finding agreement between them.

conflicting evidence: relevant pieces of information from disparate sources that contradict each other.

copyright: the exclusive right to copy, distribute, or license a creative work or to exploit it in any other manner. The term should not be rendered as *copywrite*. The issue at law is that of *rights*, not *writing* per se.

cote: a series or major sub-series classification in the archival hierarchy used by major repositories in France. Drawing from this concept, the term *cotation* is used to mean "source citation" when working with material from French archives.

deduction: a conclusion inferred from aggregated clues.

"definitive source": a false concept based on the presumption that a certain source is always reliable or represents the "final word" on an issue.

derivative source: material produced by copying an original document or manipulating its content. Abstracts, compendiums, compilations, databases, extracts, transcripts, and translations are all derivatives—as are authored works such as histories, genealogies, and other monographs that are based on research in a variety of sources.

direct evidence: relevant information that states an answer to a specific research question or appears to solve a research problem all by itself. See also *indirect evidence.*

DNA: the *initialism* (q.v.) for deoxyribonucleic acid, the substance containing the genetic instructions for the development and functioning of organisms; used as an adjunct to conventional historical research to prove identity and kinships. See also *mitochondrial DNA* and *Y-DNA.*

document—noun: (legal context) any piece of writing submitted into evidence; (historical context), a piece of writing, usually official, that has evidentiary merit.

(to) document—verb: to supply reliable evidence in support of a claim.

document label: a *citation* (q.v.) of source placed upon or appended to a document.

dower: the portion of a husband's possessions that the law allots to his wife.

dowry: (historically) the money, goods, etc., brought by a wife to her husband in marriage, usually as a payment by the bride's family; sometimes, a donation made by the husband to the bridal family or to the bride for her separate use.

duplicate original: a copy officially made at the same time as the official "original." *Examples:* The grantor's and grantee's copies of a deed, simultaneously made; or the multiple copies of a census schedule that enumerators were required to make in certain years.

estray book: a register in which a civil official recorded reports of stray animals taken up by citizens.

edition: the version or form in which a publication is presented. It may be identified as an ordinal (e.g., first edition), as a descriptive term (e.g., revised edition, image edition), or a media format (e.g., CD-ROM edition, microfilm edition).

emancipation: the act by which one who is under the power or control of another is set free; typically used with reference to the manumission of slaves or the freeing of minors from the disabilities of minority.

endnote: a *reference note* (q.v.) that is placed at the end of an essay, chapter, book, or other piece of writing.

evidence: information that is relevant to the problem. Common forms used in historical analysis include *best evidence* (q.v.) *direct evidence* (q.v.), *indirect evidence* (q.v.), and *negative evidence* (q.v.). In a legal context, *circumstantial evidence* (q.v.) is also common.

evidence books: record books maintained by some courts in which clerks have transcribed the evidence presented in cases before that court.

examined copy: see *attested copy.*

exhibition copy: (census context) the copy that, in earlier times, was locally posted in public places or made available to the public for examination.

extract: a portion of text quoted verbatim out of a record and enclosed in quotation marks. An extract is more precise than an abstract. Unlike a transcript, it does not represent the complete record.

fact: a presumed reality—an event, circumstance, or other detail that is considered to have happened or to be true. In historical research, it is difficult to establish *actual* truths; therefore, the validity of any stated "fact" rests upon the quality of the evidence presented to support it.

facsimile: an exact copy; a term usually used to describe an image copy.

factoid: a "fact" that is fictitious or unsubstantiated but repeatedly asserted to promote its acceptance.

"fair copy": a term used by the U.S. Bureau of the Census to describe the *duplicate originals* (q.v.) enumerators were asked to submit. Practically speaking, it meant a "reasonably accurate" copy.

family name: a hereditary surname used by successive generations of a family.

footnote: a *reference note* (q.v.) placed at the bottom or foot of the page on which its corresponding "fact" appears.

fair use principle: an adjunct of copyright law, defining conditions under which one may use or reuse portions of copyrighted material.

feme covert: a married woman, whose legal rights are subsumed into those of her husband.

feme sole: historically, a single woman, a widow, an abandoned wife, or a married woman authorized by law to manage her own financial affairs.

FHL: the common initialism used for the Family History Library system centered in Salt Lake City, Utah.

first reference note: the first *citation* (q.v.) for a particular source, at which time the source is cited in full, with any descriptive detail or discussion needed for identification and analysis. See also *subsequent* (or) *short reference note.*

folio: a large sheet of paper folded to make leaves or pages for a book—usually four pages or multiples of four.

fraktur: highly detailed calligraphy and motifs used to illustrate baptism and marriage certificates in Pennsylvania-German culture. The term is also more generally used for the certificates themselves.

free papers: a formal document given to slaves at the time of their manumission, to be carried on their person as proof of their free status; or such a record created at a later date after a free person has provided authorities with oral or other written evidence of that freedom.

genealogy: the study of families in genetic and historical context; the study of communities in which kinship networks weave the fabric of economic, political, and social life; the study of family structures and the changing roles of men, women, and children in diverse cultures; the study of biography, reconstructing individual human lives and placing them into family context across place and time—otherwise, the story of who we are and how we came to be as individuals and societies.*

GEDCOM: an acronym used for the GEnealogy Data COMmunications file format developed by The Church of Jesus Christ of Latter-day Saints to allow the exchange of genealogical databases between various data-management programs.

GROS: an acronym used for the General Register Office for Scotland, the office responsible for the registration of adoptions, births, civil partnerships, deaths, divorces, and marriages.

---

* As defined by the Board for Certification of Genealogy (http://bcgcertification.org : consulted 31 March 2007).

hearsay: typically oral information that is secondhand (secondary), thirdhand (tertiary), or otherwise not original; it may be handed down through the generations or passed around among contemporaries.

hypothesis: a proposition based upon an analysis of evidence at hand; not a conclusion but a premise to focus research more narrowly in an effort to prove or disprove a point.

ibid.: an abbreviation for *ibidem,* meaning "in the same place (source) as the one cited immediately above." Used in reference notes, ibid. applies only when the preceding reference note cites just one source.

image copy: a digital, film, or photo image. In historical research, it is typically treated as an original, so long as no evidence suggests that the image may have been altered.

indirect evidence: relevant information that does not answer the research question all by itself. Rather, it has to be combined with other information to arrive at an answer to the research question.

indirect source: a term used by some writing guides to refer to the source from which our own source obtained its information. Many careful researchers prefer "source of the source" for this concept. Because *source* and *evidence* are terms frequently confused, researchers of the school this manual follows use the term *indirect* only with the word *evidence,* and not with the term *source.*

inference: a "fact" deduced from information that implies something it does not state outright.

information: a statement offered by a source. Information exists in two basic weights, *primary information* (q.v.) and *secondary information* (q.v.).

initialism: a coined "word" created by combining the initial letter or letters of several words that identify a thing, place, or concept. Initialisms are written in all capital letters (or, by the canons of topography, in small capital letters), without periods between the letters. Unlike acronyms, when an initialism is spoken, the individual letters are pronounced. *Example*: FHL for the Family History Library; or OAH for the Organization of American Historians.

LAC: the *initialism* (q.v.) commonly used for the Library and Archives Canada, Ottawa.

legajo: a term used in Spanish archival nomenclature to designate a numbered bundle of records.

letterpress copy book: A volume of correspondence, created by the letterpress process in which a writer would insert a freshly inked letter into a bound volume of blank tissue pages and, after moistening the adjacent tissue, fasten the closed book with its attached screws; when the book was reopened, the transferred ink could then be read through the tissue onto which it had been imposed.

liber: the Latin term for *book*. In various jurisdictions, the term has been used for local civil records. *Example:* a deed register might be referred to as "Deeds, Liber 4."

maiden name: strictly speaking, the surname of a married female's birth family; more generally, the surname used by a female prior to marriage.

manuscript: a piece of writing in its native, unpublished state. Derived from the Latin meaning *written by hand*, the term is also applied in modern times to unpublished *typescripts* (q.v.).

marriage bann: a legal or ecclesiastical announcement of a planned marriage, usually made on three consecutive Sundays or holy days prior to the planned date.

marriage bond: a bond posted by the husband-to-be, with legal security, guaranteeing that the planned union complies with civil laws of the state or colony.

marriage contract: a prenuptial agreement between bride and groom, or (historically) their parents, wherein the parties identify all property and monies being brought into the marriage and stipulate how communal gains should be divided upon the death of one party or legal separation of the couple.

marriage inquisition: an ecclesiastical hearing held to gather evidence (written and/or oral) regarding the legal or moral right of a couple to contract marriage; historically common in some Catholic societies but not others.

Master Source List: a term used by some relational databases to refer to a "pick list" or "master list" of sources.

matrilineage: the female line across generations, with no intervening males; also called *uterine lineage* (q.v.).

minutes: brief notes that describe a proceeding, as in minutes of a court session or a meeting of commissioners. History researchers typically encounter *minutes* as bound volumes maintained by a court or church clerk.

mitochondrial DNA: that which is located in the mitochondria of cells; passed from mother to child across time; a tool for tracking *matrilineage* (q.v.), given that males genetically inherit the mitochondria of their mothers but only females pass their mitochondrial to their children.

monographs: a scholarly piece of writing on a specific (and often narrow) subject, typically book-length.

morganatic marriage: a historic form of marriage between a spouse of noble rank and one of inferior rank, in which it was agreed that neither the "lesser" spouse nor the children of the union would inherit the title or possessions of the spouse of "superior" rank; also a kind of dowry delivered on the morning of a marriage, before or after it.

NARA: the *acronym* (q.v.) used for the U.S. National Archives and Records Administration.

negative evidence: an inference one can draw from the absence of information that should exist under given circumstances.

***op cit.*:** Latin abbreviation for *opere citato*, meaning "in the work [of that name, which has already been] cited."

original source: a source that is still in its first recorded or uttered form. The term is also more loosely applied to image copies of an original record when produced by an authoritative or reliable agency—as with microfilm or digital copies produced to preserve the originals or to provide wider access to them.

patronym: a surname derived from a father's given name. *Example:* Leif Ericson as Leif, the son of Eric.

peer review: the blind or double-blind process by which works of scholarship are appraised or undergo *vetting* (q.v.) by peers within a professional field. In the blind process, the writer is not told the identity of the reviewer; in the double-blind process, neither the writer nor the reviewer know the identity of the other.

plagiarism: the presentation of someone else's words or ideas as one's own, without attribution—whether copied exactly or paraphrased; an ethical issue not to be confused with the legal issue of *copyright* (q.v.), based on the premise that the ideas and words of others cannot be ethically used without attribution.

preponderance of the evidence: a legal standard acceptable in civil cases, whereby evidence on one side of an argument outweighs, at least slightly, evidence on the other side of an argument.

presentments: an accusation made by a court or a grand jury based on its own knowledge or observation without a bill of indictment having been filed by a prosecutor. In pre-Civil War America, presentments commonly involved females who were visibly pregnant or bore a child without a husband to provide support for the child.

presumptive evidence: (legal context) evidence that may not be conclusive but may be reasonably accepted unless demonstrated otherwise.

prima facie **evidence:** (legal context) evidence that appears valid on the surface, without explanation, and—if not contradicted—can be reasonably accepted.

primary information: statements made or details provided by someone with firsthand knowledge of the facts he or she asserted. See also *secondary information.*

primary source: a traditional concept within the humanities that is variously defined as an original record, a contemporary account, or a firsthand account, but not necessarily all three simultaneously. The term is no longer used in sound genealogical analysis because any source (and any statement within a source) can be a combination of both firsthand and secondhand information. For the Research Process Map by which genealogists classify sources, see the endpapers of this book.

printed primary source: a historic record that has been printed, in full or edited form; it may be an *original source* (q.v.) or a *derivative source* (q.v.), and it may be based on either firsthand knowledge or hearsay, so long as it was created by a person contemporaneous with the times discussed or at least peripherally involved in the incident. *Examples*: published congressional records, published presidential papers, etc.

PRO: the *initialism* (q.v.) traditionally used for the Public Record Office, London.

proof: a conclusion backed by thorough research, sound analysis, and reliable evidence.

parenthetical reference: a source citation placed in parentheses within the text of a piece of writing; typically used for scientific-style citations to published works, with the parenthetical reference noting just the surname of the author and the year the work was published, while the text is followed by a *bibliography* (q.v.) or *source list* (q.v.) in which all the referenced sources are fully cited.

proof argument: a well-reasoned, meticulously documented paper in which a researcher describes a research problem, the process by which it was solved, and the evidence that supports the conclusion.

record—noun: an account of an event, circumstance, etc.; a piece of writing created to preserve the memory of certain "facts."

record copy: a legal copy of a document, made by an official charged with the responsibility to create and maintain records. See also *clerk's copy.*

reference note: a *citation* (q.v.) or comment placed at the bottom of a page or at the end of a piece of writing and keyed to a particular statement in the text; its purpose is to identify and/or discuss the source of the specific statement made in the text.

repository: an archive, government office, library, or other facility where research materials are held.

secondary information: Details provided by someone with only secondhand (hearsay) knowledge of the facts. The term *secondary* is also generically used for *tertiary* (thirdhand) and other levels of knowledge even further removed from the original source.

secondary source: a traditional term in the humanities that is variously defined as a copy of a record, an account created long after the fact, or hearsay. The term is no longer used in sound genealogical analysis because any source (and any statement within a source) can be a combination of both firsthand and secondhand information.

separation of bed and board: a legally authorized separation of man and wife that permits them to divide their goods and live separately, while the marriage remained undissolved.

separation of property: a legal division of marital assets that, historically, allowed a female to act as a *feme sole* (q.v.) and protected her *dowry* (q.v.) or other personal assets from creditors of the husband; not a physical separation of man and wife and not a dissolution of the marriage.

sic: a Latin term literally translated as *so* or *thus*. Placed in square editorial brackets after a word or phrase that is copied from another source, it is used to inform readers that the text has been copied exactly even though it may appear to be questionable or erroneous.

site: a location, as in *website*—not to be confused with the words *cite* (as in the act of citing sources) or *sight* (as in *eyesight*).

source: an artifact, book, document, film, person, recording, website, etc., from which information is obtained. Sources are broadly classified as either an *original source* (q.v.) or a *derivative source* (q.v.), depending upon their physical form.

source list: a bibliography or list of sources used for an essay or in a research project.

source list entry: an individual citation within a *source list* (q.v.).

speculation: an opinion unsupported by evidence.

supra: a Latin term meaning *above.* In source citations, the word follows a shortened title and is used to refer generically to the place in which the full particulars have been given; now considered *passé. Previously cited is* commonly used in its stead, today, when a notation of that sort is essential.

subsequent (or short) reference note: an abridged identification of a source that is used to conserve space, once a source has been cited in full in the *first reference note* (q.v.)

surety: (legal context) a person who agrees to serve as a guarantor of a debt or a bond; (genealogical context) a term adopted by developers of some relational database software to place a numerical value upon the level of confidence a researcher may have in a source.

surname: (historically) a name added onto a baptismal name to denote the family to which that person belonged, the place to which that person was attached, an occupation, or some other distinguishing trait. *Example:* Pierre *Le Noir,* meaning Pierre, *the dark one.*

tertiary information: formally, *thirdhand* information; in everyday use, the concept of *tertiary* information is usually incorporated into the term *secondary information* (q.v.).

theory: a tentative conclusion that is drawn after a *hypothesis* (q.v.) has been extensively researched but the evidence still seems short of *proof* (q.v.).

transcript/transcription: an exact copy of a record, word-for-word, preserving original punctuation and spelling.

translation: a copy of a source in which the content has been expressed in a different language.

thesis: a scholarly paper in which one presents findings from his or her investigation of an hypothesis; also used interchangeably with *hypothesis* (q.v.) to represent the concept being researched.

TNG: the common *initialism* (q.v.) for The National Archives of the United Kingdom.

typescript: a *manuscript* (q.v.) presented in typed form; or a typed copy of another published or unpublished work.

uterine lineage: a female line across generations, with no intervening males; also called *matrilineage*.

verify: to test the accuracy of an assertion by consulting other authoritative and independent sources; the term may be applied to the process of searching for that independent evidence or the act of finding that independent evidence. Also see *confirm* (q.v.).

vertical file: a collection of material relating to a narrow subject; typically maintained by libraries in vertical folders within file cabinets, hence the term *vertical file*.

vetting: in the context of historical research: the process of evaluating a scholarly paper to ensure its quality.

vide infra: a Latin phrase which translates as *see below;* once commonly used in scholarly writing, but passé today.

vital records: records of adoption, birth, death, divorce, or marriage.

working source list: a list of sources consulted or to be consulted in a research project. A working source list typically contains descriptive or analytical details that will not be published in a final bibliography, unless the final work presents an *annotated* bibliography. A working source list may also contain references that will not be considered valid or appropriate to the final research product.

Y-DNA: the deoxyribonucleic acid found in Y chromosomes passed from fathers to sons.

Appendix B
Bibliography

GUIDES TO CITATION

ALWD Citation Manual: A Professional System of Citation. Association of Legal Writing Directors and Darby Dickerson, editors. Gaithersburg, Maryland: Aspen Law and Business, 2000.

Berlioz, Jacques. *Identifier sources et citations.* Turnhout, Belgium: Brepols, 1994.

The Bluebook: A Uniform System of Citation. Cambridge, Massachusetts: Harvard Law Review Association, frequently revised.

Canadian Guide to Uniform Legal Citation. McGill Law Journal, editor. 6th edition. Scarborough, Ontario: Carswell, 2006.

The Chicago Manual of Style. 15th edition. Chicago: University of Chicago Press, 2004.

Cheney, Debora Lee, and Diane L. Garner. *The Complete Guide to Citing Government Information Resources: A Manual for Social Science & Business Research.* 3d revised edition. Bethesda, Maryland: LexisNexis and Congressional Information Service, ca. 2002.

Citing Records in the National Archives of the United States. General Information Leaflet no. 17. Washington, D.C.: Government Printing Office [periodically revised]. Online edition. http://www.archives.gov/publications/general-info-leaflets/17.html.

Crouse, Maurice. *Citing Electronic Information in History Papers.* Ongoing updates. http://history.memphis.edu/mcrouse/elcite.html.

Gibaldi, Joseph, editor. *MLA Handbook for Writers of Research Papers.* 6th edition. New York: Modern Language Association of America, 2003.

Harnack, Andrew, and Eugene Kleppinger. *Beyond the MLA Handbook: Documenting Electronic Sources on the Internet.* http://english.ttu.edu/Kairos/1.2/inbox/mla_archive.html.

Lexique des règles typographiques en usage à l'imprimerie nationale. 5th edition. Paris: Imprimerie nationale, 2002.

Library of Congress. "Citation Guide," *A Century of Lawmaking for a New*

Nation: U.S. Congressional Documents and Debates, 1774–1875. http://memory.loc.gov/ammem/amlaw/lawhome.html.

Library of Congress. *How to Cite Electronic Sources.* Ongoing updates. http://memory.loc.gov/ammem/ndlpedu/start/cite/index.html.

Library of Congress Online Catalog. Ongoing updates. http://catalog.loc.gov.

Lipson, Charles. *Cite Right: A Quick Guide to Citation Styles—MLA, APA, Chicago, the Sciences, Professions, and More.* Chicago Guides to Writing, Editing, and Publishing. New edition. Chicago: University of Chicago Press, 2006.

Martin, Peter W. *Introduction to Basic Legal Citation.* Ongoing updates. http://www.law.cornell.edu/citation/front.htm.

Mills, Elizabeth Shown. *Evidence! Citation & Analysis for the Family Historian.* Baltimore: Genealogical Publishing Co., 1997; revised, 16th printing, 2006.

———. *QuickSheet: Citing Online Historical Resources, Evidence! Style.* Revised edition. Baltimore: Genealogical Publishing Co., 2006.

OCLC Online Computer Library Center. *WorldCat [Catalog].* Ongoing updates. http://www.worldcat.org.

Restreto, Irma Isaza. *Citación y descripción de documentos electrónicos.* Medellín, Colombia: Universidad de Antioquia, 2003.

Sola, Rígel Sabater. *Manual de citación en el derecho puertorriqueño.* Rio Piedras: Escuela Graduada de Bibliotecología, 1982.

Turabian, Kate L. *A Manual for Writers of Term Papers, Theses, and Dissertations.* 7th revised edition. Wayne C. Booth, Gregory G. Colomb, and Joseph M. Williams, editors. Chicago: University of Chicago Press, 1996.

United Kingdom. *How to Cite Documents in The National Archives.* Ongoing updates. General Information Leaflet 25. Online edition. http://www.nationalarchives.gov.uk/catalogue/RdLeaflet.asp?sLeafletID=333&j=1.

University of Stirling Information Services. "Guide to Legal Citations," *Doing Research: Writing References.* http://www.is.stir.ac.uk/research/citing/lawrefer.php.

Walker, Janet, and Todd Taylor. *The Columbia Guide to Online Style.* 2d edition. New York: Columbia University Press, 2006. Partial guide online. http://www.columbia.edu/cu/cup/cgos2006/basic.html.

GUIDES TO EVIDENCE ANALYSIS

Best, Arthur. *Evidence: Examples and Explanations.* 6th edition. New York: Aspen Publishers, 2007.

Board for Certification of Genealogists. *The BCG Standards Manual.* Salt Lake City: Ancestry.com, 2000.

Booth, Wayne C.; Joseph M. Williams; and Gregory G. Colomb. *The Craft of Research.* 2d edition. Chicago: University of Chicago Press, 2003.

Drake, Michael, and Ruth Finnegan, editors. *Sources and Methods: A Handbook.* Studying Family and Community History: 19th and 20th Centuries, vol. 4. Cambridge: Cambridge University Press, 1994.

Duranti, Luciana. *Diplomatics.* Lanham, Maryland: Scarecrow Press, 1998.

Henige, David. *Historical Evidence and Argument.* Madison: University of Wisconsin Press, 2005.

MacNeil, Heather. *Trusting Records: Legal, Historical, and Diplomatic Perspectives.* The Archivist's Library, volume 1. Boston, Massachusetts, and Dordrecht, The Netherlands: Kluwer Academic Publishers, ca. 2000.

Kuppuram, G., and K. Kumudamani. *Methods of Historical Research.* New Delhi: Sundeep Prakashan, 2002.

Nickell, Joe. *Detecting Forgery: Forensic Investigation of Documents.* Lexington: University Press of Kentucky, 1996.

———. *Pen, Ink, and Evidence: A Study of Writing and Writing Materials for the Penman, Collector, and Document Detective.* Lexington: University Press of Kentucky, 1991.

Phelan, Peter. *Argument and Evidence: Critical Analysis for the Social Sciences.* London and New York: Routledge, 1996.

Stevenson, Noel C. *Genealogical Evidence: A Guide to the Standard of Proof Relating to Pedigrees, Ancestry, Heirship, and Family History.* Revised edition. Laguna Hills, California: Aegean Park Press, 1989.

Winks, Robin W., editor. *The Historian as Detective: Essays on Evidence.* New York: Harper Colophon Books, 1968.

GUIDES TO STYLE, LEGAL TERMINOLOGY & RELATED MATTERS

Austin, Tim, compiler. *The Times Style and Usage Guide.* New edition. London: Times Books, 2003.

Black's Law Dictionary. Bryan A. Garner, editor. 8th edition. St. Paul, Minnesota: Thompson West, 2004. History researchers may prefer the 4th edition (West Publishing Co., 1968) for its fuller coverage of terms now obsolete.

Bouvier, John, compiler. *A Law Dictionary: Adapted to the Constitution and Laws of the United States of America and of the Several States of the American Union.* Revised 6th edition, 1856. Online edition. *Constitution Society*, http://www.constitution.org/bouv/bouvier.htm.

Federal Civil Judicial Procedure and Rules. 2006 edition. St. Paul, Minnesota: West Group, 2006.

Fishman, Stephen. *The Copyright Handbook: How to Protect & Use Written Works.* Berkeley, California: Nolo, 2005.

Garner, Bryan A. *The Elements of Legal Style.* 2d edition. New York: Oxford University Press, 2002.

Gibaldi, Joseph, editor. *MLA Style Manual and Guide to Scholarly Publishing.* Second edition. New York: Modern Language Association of America, 1998.

Harris, Robert A., and Vic Lockman. *The Plagiarism Handbook: Strategies for Preventing, Detecting, and Dealing with Plagiarism.* Los Angeles: Pyrczak Publishing, 2001.

Merriam Webster's Manual for Writers & Editors. 10th edition. Springfield, Massachusetts: Merriam Webster, 1998.

Ritter, R.M. *The Oxford Style Manual.* New York: Oxford University Press, 2003.

United States Government Printing Office Style Manual. Washington D.C.: Government Printing Office, 2001. Online edition. http://www.gpoaccess.gov/stylemanual/index.html.

Index

A

Index
QuickCheck Models